The Imperative to Write

The Imperative to Write

Destitutions of the Sublime in Kafka, Blanchot, and Beckett

JEFF FORT

FORDHAM UNIVERSITY PRESS   *New York* 2014

Copyright © 2014 Fordham University Press

All rights reserved. No part of this publication may be reproduced, stored in a retrieval system, or transmitted in any form or by any means—electronic, mechanical, photocopy, recording, or any other—except for brief quotations in printed reviews, without the prior permission of the publisher.

Fordham University Press has no responsibility for the persistence or accuracy of URLs for external or third-party Internet websites referred to in this publication and does not guarantee that any content on such websites is, or will remain, accurate or appropriate.

Fordham University Press also publishes its books in a variety of electronic formats. Some content that appears in print may not be available in electronic books.

Library of Congress Cataloging-in-Publication Data
Fort, Jeff (date)
  The imperative to write : destitutions of the sublime in Kafka, Blanchot, and Beckett / Jeff Fort. — First edition.
      pages cm.
  Includes bibliographical references and index.
  ISBN 978-0-8232-5469-9 (cloth : alk. paper)
  1. Sublime, The, in literature. 2. Kafka, Franz, 1883–1924—Criticism and interpretation. 3. Blanchot, Maurice—Criticism and interpretation. 4. Beckett, Samuel, 1906–1989—Criticism and interpretation. I. Title.
  PN56.S7416F68 2014
  809—dc23

                                                    2013030646

Printed in the United States of America

16 15 14   5 4 3 2 1

First edition

CONTENTS

List of Abbreviations — vii

Preface — ix

INTRODUCTION: "Why Do You Write?"—The Fault of Writing — 1

PART ONE / KAFKA

1. Kafka's Teeth: The Literary *Gewissenbiss* — 17
2. The Ecstasy of Judgment — 58
3. Embodied Violence and the Leap from the Law: "In the Penal Colony" and *The Trial* — 101
4. Degradation of the Sublime: "A Hunger Artist" — 144

PART TWO / BLANCHOT

5. Pointed Instants: Blanchot's Exigencies — 163
6. The Shell and the Mask: *L'arrêt de mort* — 213
7. The Dead Look: The Death Mask, the Corpse Image, and the Haunting of Fiction — 248

PART THREE / BECKETT

8. Beckett's Voices and the Paradox of Expression — 293
9. *Company*, But Not Enough — 330

Conclusion: Speech Unredeemed: From the Call of Conscience to the Torture of Language — 347

Notes — 361

Bibliography — 405

Index — 413

ABBREVIATIONS OF FREQUENTLY CITED WORKS

Beckett

C	*Company*
CSPl	*Collected Shorter Plays*
CSPr	*Collected Short Prose*
D	*Disjecta*
End	*Endgame*
HI	*How It Is*
I	*L'innommable*
MaC	*Mercier and Camier*
MD	*Malone Dies*
MeC	*Mercier et Camier*
MM	*Malone Meurt*
MoE	*Molloy* (English)
MoF	*Molloy* (French)
U	*The Unnamable*
WH	*Worstward Ho*

Blanchot

AM	*L'arrêt de mort*
AMV	*Au moment voulu*
CQ	*Celui qui ne m'accompagnait pas*
EI	*L'entretien infini*
EL	*L'espace littéraire*
FJ	*La folie du jour*
IC	*Infinite Conversation*
IM	*L'instant de ma mort*
KK	*De Kafka à Kafka*
LM	*The Last Man*
LV	*Le livre à venir*
MD	*The Madness of the Day*
PF	*La part du feu*
UV	*Une voix venue d'ailleurs*
WTC	*When the Time Comes*

Heidegger

BT	*Being and Time* (Stambaugh translation)
KPM	*Kant and the Problem of Metaphysics*
SZ	*Sein und Zeit*

Kafka

A	*Amerika* (Max Brod edition)
BK	*Beschreibung eines Kampfes* (Max Brod edition)
BM	*Briefe an Milena*
BON	*Blue Octavo Notebooks*
Br	*Briefe 1902–1924* (Max Brod edition)
CS	*Complete Stories*

VII

D	*Diaries* (one-volume Schocken edition)	*Kant*	
E	*Erzählungen* (Max Brod edition)	CJ	*Critique of Judgment* (Cambridge edition)
HL	*Hochzeitsvorbereitungen auf dem Lande* (Max Brod edition)	CPrR	*Critique of Practical Reason* (Cambridge edition)
KA P	*Der Process* (Kritische Ausgabe)	CPuR	*Critique of Pure Reason* (Cambridge edition)
KA TB	*Tagebücher* (Kritische Ausgabe)		
LFe	*Letters to Felice*	Gr	*Groundlaying of the Metaphysics of Morals* (Cambridge edition)
LFr	*Letters to Friends, Family, and Editors*		
LM	*Letters to Milena*	*Nancy*	
Sons	*The Sons*, ed. Mark Anderson	GI	*The Ground of the Image*
T	*The Trial* (Breon Mitchell trans.)		
TB	*Tagebücher* (Max Brod edition)		

Note: Quotations from English translations have in many cases been silently modified; citations of English translations are provided for purposes of reference. Where no references are provided, translations are my own.

PREFACE

The critical approach of this book, which sets out to reveal a number of the problematic aspects discernible in a certain extreme relation to writing, leads me to preface it, by way of counterbalance, with a clear if naive statement of admiration: I consider these writers to be literary heroes. If this study often shows them in a light that is less than flattering, if it is marked at times by a tone of skeptical irony regarding various moves and strategies for exiting what one calls "the real world," strategies that are deeply constitutive of their work, it is not out of a desire to topple these heroes, but rather as a recognition that, in multiple and complex ways, they topple themselves. Kafka, Blanchot, and Beckett are driven in their writing to undermine and undo their own *capabilities*, along with a relation to life and the world that something like capability (and its roots in capture and captation) would secure. Heroes, then, in a drastically scaled back epic of unredeemable shortcoming.

This shortcoming, however, is shadowed by the specter of its own impossible ideals, by temptations of hyperbole and absoluteness, superlative projections, and the compulsive search for an ultimate instance never to be arrived at but without which no beginning can be rigorously thought through: these are the forms of a literary speech driven by the force of its own initiation, pressed on by that which sends it continually in search of its own grounds and conditions, giving writing the shape of a speech compelled to sound its emptiness, and to breach the ground of language's enactment as a making of world. To fail at *this*, however inevitable such failure may be, is to fail at a project dictated by the grandiose dignities and delusions of an entire tradition (which in shorthand can be called *metaphysical*). What is fascinating, and "heroic," in these failures is, ultimately, the confused and stubborn sobriety with which they divest its very ruins. But this treacherous adventure reveals some rather troubling tendencies.

One very attentive and generous reader of the manuscript of this book commented that it berates the writers it discusses; perhaps it would appear so at times. Yet this can also be seen as a recognition that they berate (belittle and lower, degrade and debase) themselves, to the extent that their writing has to do with residual forms of ideality, transcendence, and transgression. Each one knew, in his own way, that a certain "literature" has come to this, that the highest and most dignified literary calling has to (*il faut*) face this ineluctable fact and condition, must acknowledge that high and low no longer hold apart, that what is beyond *is not*, that the only beyond left is one that is rather far down below even the banality of the "real world" it leaves behind, but also that this extreme movement is one of the few chances remaining for *something other*. The world is not enough. And yet leaving it is not so easy. It clings to the voice that would tell of this leaving, it betrays every radical departure, every corrosive disintegration, as incomplete. The stuff clinging to the radically departed voice, its forms, figures, shapes, and texture, are at the heart of this book (which therefore engages very closely with the texts in question), but none of it makes up for the losses and leavings they mark. In any case, this adventure has little to do with the cultural values and virtues usually cited as grounds for such a questionable, even violent, and certainly destructive undertaking, for making more palatable such a sweeping refusal to be satisfied with the fare on offer.

Likewise, if there is an emphasis here on guilt, bad conscience, compromise, cruelty, torture, and even murderous compulsion, it is decidedly not out of a desire to cast accusations, much less to suggest that writing of this sort is beset by some sort of cowardice regarding life in the world and its salutary realities (quite to the contrary: life in language alone is downright *dreadful*, as all three of these writers make painfully clear, though this dread may also be the singularly elusive condition for an ecstasy from which it cannot be separated). If the focus here is placed on a dimension of writing that in fleeing the self tends toward extreme self-exposure, to the point of strange compulsions not devoid of shame, this is not because I believe that that is the end of the story. There is no end to a story that opens on this basis, and that is both the bad news and the good news regarding the lives and afterlives of the literary voice: it will go on.

Put in more conceptual terms, such an emphasis does not mean that I take these modes of linguistic relation to be the essence of literature, or of the works in question; but it does mean that one finds them with striking regularity (even abundance) in the figural language of the writers addressed in this study. These writers court subjection, in every sense; in doing so, they write about *power*, and they find it at work, necessarily, in the language they both mobilize and subject themselves to. They *work through* power (again, in every sense), and find themselves continually speaking at its limits. How could this positioning not give rise to effects of guilt and bad conscience, given that what one inevitably finds at the limits of power is the law—the broken ground and disintegrating force, and face, of the law. And in relation to this limit and this ground, literature is always underneath, is always *outside*, even as its fictive structures are so intimately involved in human speech at large.

The central moment of this book, then, is one that takes many forms; it is the fissure, crack, gap, break, flaw, or fault that separates language from the world it names—the world its speakers necessarily live in, of course, but at an irreducible *remove*, thus establishing the possibility of speech *as* the possibility of fiction—and that also separates the writer from the life out of which one cannot not be writing. But the fault in question is not personal; rather, it inhabits the very structure of language, a broken and ruptured structure that *opens* precisely in the form of an imperative, in a fault that also gives out the form of a wide-ranging error. At times, this imperative berates, not to say punishes, the one to whom it is addressed (or at least appears to punish, if only with the illusory threat of expiation). And in addressing power, it undergoes the temptation not only to elude it, but also to grasp it. On the other side of this temptation is a destitution that is as inevitable as it is open to the incalculable. That incalculable and irreducible dimension of literary speech is what lies on the horizon of this study, which is marked by several mentions of an *enigma* at which it does not quite arrive, though this enigma is figured in various specific ways (milk teeth, death mask, undying voice, and the emptying of all these treasures) in the course of its readings. If anything, this not quite arriving is a shortcoming on my part, a falling short that will have to be made up for elsewhere. "First dirty, then make clean," as Beckett writes. One thing this book would like to show is that "making clean" is a pretty messy affair, inextricable from all the stuff that would be scrubbed; but also that this stuff, the imprints, images, names, and detritus of a life, someone's life, is integral to the precise forms and language in question, for it gives to voice the very shape of time.

The debts owed for a first book necessarily reach a considerable distance into the past, and this book has been long in the making. At each of its successive stages, it was helped along by generous and inspiring people to whom I have long owed many thanks, and I am very happy to have the occasion here to express my gratitude to them. To begin with, and in order of overdueness: I would like to thank Avital Ronell for the intense spark of thinking and reading with which her seminars opened the way to so many texts and adventures therein. Among these were works by Philippe Lacoue-Labarthe, who since long ago left a deep impression, both as a writer and a person, that continues to shape my own modest endeavors. This book is dedicated to his memory—a memory sustained by (among many others) the numerous former students like me who were intensely absorbed by his lectures and charmed by his self-effacing brilliance, both in Berkeley and in Strasbourg.

These toponyms also evoke Claire Nancy, in affection and friendship, whom I thank for all her generosity past and present. My gratitude to Ann Smock goes beyond anything I could say here, not least for helping me to begin to find a way through the texts of Blanchot, just when it was most needed, and for continually demonstrating the kind of nuanced thinking and poetic reading for which I have long admired her. I owe a truly enormous debt to Judith Butler, who provided critical guidance from the beginning of this project, and who despite demands on her time went out of her way to be a generous and supportive adviser and advocate. Michael Lucey also helped in fundamental ways, going very far back, and he has always been extremely clear-sighted and wise in matters both intellectual and academic, and I warmly thank him for his insights and advice over the years. There is little I can say in order sufficiently to thank Helen Tartar for her confidence, perspicacity, and encouragement, beginning with translation projects more than a decade ago and now including a book whose existence owes a great deal to her trust and support. I would also like to thank Leslie Hill, Kevin Hart, and Alain Toumayan for their helpful comments as readers. Since arriving at the University of California, Davis, several years ago, I have been very grateful to have so many wonderful and congenial colleagues, among whom I owe special thanks to Jaimey Fisher and Gerhard Richter, who kept me on my toes, and in my German. Above all I would like to thank my colleagues in French, Julia Simon and Noah Guynn, whose insights have been indispensable in countless ways both large and small; I am extremely grateful to them for many stimulating discussions and, not least, for making the French department such a collegial place in which to work, teach, write, and think. I would also like to thank Dean Jessie Ann Owens of the Division of Humanities, Arts, and Cultural Studies for providing crucial financial assistance in the research and publication of this book.

Many old friends, from graduate school and after, have informed and inhabited the writing of this book; countless thanks and thoughts go out to them. I would like to name a few of them here: Peter Banki, Elliott Colla, David Copenhafer, David Eng, Jason Francisco, Tommaso Giartosio, Ariel Greco, Yuji Oniki, Gerald Posselt, Mark Roberts, and Lincoln Shlensky. Stefan Mattesich helped this project along with astute readings and comments that left their mark on its final form. Pim Higginson went above and beyond.

Finally, it is more than thanks that I must express to Susette Min, without whom this book would never have seen the day, and to Theodora, who helps make the day something to see.

The Imperative to Write

INTRODUCTION

"Why Do You Write?"—The Fault of Writing

How is it that certain writers of the twentieth century were able to experience the literary vocation as an all-consuming task, an exclusive and absolute necessity, a compulsion as demanding as it is ineluctable, and therefore even as a kind of categorical imperative? This study will seek to provide not so much an answer to this question as an analysis of the paradoxes that allow us to pose it, and of the conditions shaping the textual elaborations of such an imperative. One of the most important of these paradoxes, the one from which the readings in this book take their starting point, is that these writers, whose work systematically withdraws the possibility of literature's absolutes, took up such an absolutist position with respect to the necessity of writing itself, as though there could be any grounds for doing so. This introduction will lay out the contours of this impossible position, the unstable forms of the cracked and hollow ground it claims.

The writers discussed in this study expressed themselves repeatedly, and in the strongest terms, on the extreme and exclusive nature of their calling. Indeed, we can say at the outset that a certain hyperbole, a drive to totalize and to exaggerate, a wary tendency to overstep boundaries, is constitutive of the position they appear to share. Kafka: "God does not want me to write, but I, I must."[1] This is one statement among dozens that could be drawn from a corpus of writing that attempted to generate itself from the constraints of an exclusive vocation, which, as is well known, pressed the writer into a brutal struggle with the conditions and circumstances of his own life. In a similar vein, Blanchot the writer refers in the third person to his irrelevant biographical avatar, in order to subsume the latter completely under the silence of a being who is other, and stranger: "Maurice Blanchot, novelist and critic, was born in 1907. His life is entirely devoted to literature and to the silence that is proper to it."[2] The necessity of writing outstrips that of living, as the latter is reduced to the minimal acknowledgment of having been born, sole requirement for all the rest, which is literature. And Beckett, who perhaps more than any other writer integrated such statements into the fabric of his fictional works themselves, large portions of which are spun from their paradoxes: "I must to on, I can't go on, I'll go on" (U 179). Whereas Beckett was not so starkly dualistic as Kafka and Blanchot tended to be regarding the breach, rift, or fault separating writing from life, he did pronounce an unequivocal sentiment on the latter, in a curse that raises many questions about the thing that writing is unable not to do: "Fuck life."[3] Of course this is not the last word on the matter, but that very fact, like the birth that somehow must have happened, is precisely where all the trouble begins.

These programmatic statements may serve as initial emblematic markers for the strangely nonnegotiable imperative one finds articulated, performed, and thwarted in the writings of these authors. We can already see that if this imperative verges toward the "categorical," it does so by severing itself—in a paradoxical attachment—from something called "life," as writing strives to articulate its own irreducibles. And yet there is more than one kind of life, more than one mode of "living," and for each of these writers, writing itself takes the radical chance of seeking a much more strange and uncanny form of existence under this category. In the meantime, what each of them encounters in attempting to strip writing of everything but its own most essential compulsion—in a movement that systematically confounds the difference between elevation and depth, between exaltation and baseness—is an empty necessity that insists all the more brutally for being voided of its contents. In Philippe Lacoue-Labarthe's formulation, it is by means of an "imperative without content [that] 'literature' . . . is given over to its own naked existence as a fact and to a sort of duty without reason."[4] This empty insistence, and the implied devaluation of writing rendered over to compulsion, is certainly not the fault of the writer. If anything, it is the fault of writing: the tiny but irreparable fissure opened as an irritating breach, a hollow kernel in language that cannot be voided, but that opens the space of an imperative that cannot be fulfilled. Such a residue, I will argue, is all that is left of writing's sublimity—in which, despite everything, the writers in question here have a considerable stake. In order to understand this residual investment in the sublime, the faulty position in which it places them must first be delineated.

In responding to the simple but impossible question "Why do you write?" Blanchot sketched out just such a position. In 1984 the newspaper *Libération* sent out a survey to several hundred writers asking this question. Blanchot responded with a surprising degree of substance and seriousness, providing a commentary on the irreducibility of writing's exclusive and compulsive necessity, and on the writer's *position*, literally and in every sense:

> Certes, la question est traditionnelle. Ma réponse ne sera pas originale. Je l'emprunterai au docteur Martin Luther, lorsque, à Worms, il prononça la déclaration de son irréductibilité: *Je me tiens là debout, je ne puis autrement. Dieu me vienne en aide.* Ce que je traduirais modestement: *Dans l'espace de l'écriture, écrivant, n'écrivant pas, je me tiens là courbé, je ne puis autrement et je n'attends nul secours des puissances favorables.*[5]
>
> Certainly the question is traditional. My answer will not be original. I will borrow it from the learned doctor Martin Luther, when, at Worms, he put forth the dec-

laration of its irreducibility: *Here I stand, I cannot do otherwise. May God help me.* Which I would translate modestly: *In the space of writing, writing, not writing, here I sit hunched over, I cannot do otherwise and I expect no help from the beneficent powers.*

Aside from the very interesting (if incidental) gesture of positioning Martin Luther as above all a writer, and thus locating the religious dimension of his "stance" primarily in a kind of literary intransigence, this "modest translation" encapsulates a number of the distinctly downward displacements that will concern us here. From a resolute upright position, in which a categorical necessity is rendered up to divine authority, Blanchot reduces the irreducible fact in question to a strange curving over on itself, a bowed and downward leaning position whose dictated text, as it were, does not have its source in the higher realms. Indeed, there is a hint that if no help is expected from there, it may come nonetheless from lower and more obscure regions (Kafka, for one, will explicitly vindicate such a movement).[6] At the same time, it can be seen as a more sober gesture severing writing from all such powers, high and low, and returning the writer to the earth (to a table . . . a piece of paper). In this sense it puts one in mind of Hölderlin's commentaries on Sophocles, with their Kantian-inspired figure of a "categorical turning away," the *kategorische Umkehr* that severs man from the sacred in a sobriety which alone has any chance of retaining something of the sacred it renounces, but that, most importantly, betokens a law that "compels [*zwinget*] the eternal anti-human course of nature, *on its path toward another world*, more decidedly toward the earth."[7] Blanchot's "modest translation" of this otherworldly trajectory would then contain, perhaps, the entire stakes of his relation to Romanticism, a disjointed relation that was mediated through a reading of Hölderlin (and in particular of the text just quoted)[8]—which, however, does not preclude following a certain path "toward another world," as is the case with Kafka and Beckett as well. But as we will see, this "other world" is not one, for it is purely (or perhaps merely) *literary*, a world of letters and mere images, a worldly way of leaving the world behind in order to enter a space in which the "more modest" task of writing would seek its essentially impoverished conditions. We are in very close proximity as well to Rimbaud's "Adieu" at the end of "A Season in Hell," whose exclamations proclaim the same movement of demotion and return to the earth: "*je suis rendu au sol, avec un devoir à chercher, et la réalité rugueuse à étreindre! Paysan!*" (I am returned to the soil with a duty to seek and a rough reality to embrace! Peasant!) And a few lines later: "*Mais pas une main amie! et où puiser le secours?*" (But no friendly hand! and where to turn for help?).[9] Blanchot's refusal of help is no doubt less "pathetic" (in the strict sense), but it is clearly located on a similarly sobering downward trajectory that is, so to speak, helpless in every sense. Hölderlin's madness, and Rimbaud's abandonment, might well be taken as signs of the difficult impoverishment of the position here vindicated.

The vindication, however, is not only a vindication, and the helplessness I just evoked gives some indication that Blanchot's "translation" is also a neutralization of the *ethical* stance implied in Luther's statement.[10] For not only does it evacuate "the good" implied in the "beneficent powers" visited on the writer (whether from God or Muse); we can also note that this not being able to do otherwise can indeed be heard, at some distance from its residual heroic overtones, in a register of helplessness. If Blanchot's repetition of the phrase continues to make resound a kind of steadfast resoluteness, it nonetheless vacillates according to the very movement of translation to which he submits the rest of the statement. Blanchot's translation of Luther, given as "*je ne puis autrement*," is so to speak left untranslated within the statement (it is the only element that is simply repeated in his restatement), but what does this phrase translate? The famous phrase attributed to Luther is: "*Ich kann nicht anders*." We know it in English in the version I gave above: *I cannot do otherwise*. But surely an equally fitting translation of Blanchot's own use of the phrase would be one that rings quite differently: *I can't help it*. This version touches on a mode of helpless compulsion that necessarily shadows any pretentions to an ethical, much less a sublime, dimension in the task of writing. The resistance to this slippage in certain of Blanchot's narratives (despite their clear and constant suggestions in this direction) will be a prominent feature of the readings of his texts in the section devoted to his work below. The important point to begin with, which applies as well to Kafka and to Beckett, is that the irreducibility of writing's imperative is itself subject to disturbing vacillations that remove it from the sphere of ethics, and that reduce its echoes of sublimity to the varied and empty figures of its failure—figures of a law in default. For in literature writing *takes on the law*, in every sense, for it not only inhabits and assumes the law (with certain effects of guilt and bad conscience, as we will see), but in doing so it also touches on the essence of law, leaving it in ruins that necessarily fail to embody it; literature thus both wields and undoes the *force of law in speech*.[11] At the same time, if the search for the "irreducible" remains a constant, what is found to be irreducible takes many questionable, and singular, *forms*. In a certain sense, then, it is with the various and telling shapes, figures and figurations of these irreducible forms, the insistent remains and leftovers of a sublime vocation now curved down onto the poor space of letters, that the present study takes as its specific material. We should recall as well that Kafka's hunger artist proffers yet another version of the "*ich kann nicht anders*," as he sinks at last into the straw—de facto shroud of his unceremonious burial, his disappearance into mere hunger.

By way of elaborating the peculiar nature of that material, its ambiguous vacillation between poverty and riches, I would like to quote Beckett's rather different, and yet really quite similar response to the very same survey, which also carries out a steep downgrade, but much more succinctly. Unlike Blanchot's relatively elaborate reflection, Beckett's answer sits like a little lapidary lump on the page. To the question, "Why do you write?" Beckett shrugs: "*Bon qu'à ça*."[12] But even this little hiccup gives much to be read (and that is perhaps the very form of the curse that Beckett always attached to "meaning"). First, of course, by way of translation: the phrase means, "it's all (I'm) good for," as though in self-deprecating response to the Hölderlinian "*Wozu?*" implied by the survey's question.[13] Why do I write? Because I'm good for nothing (else). The phrase thus speaks of exclusivity (*bon* qu'*à ça*), but precisely in the mode of abjection and default, a reduction not so much to the irreducible as to a last shred of something still left over, luckily (or not), at the end of a near-total process of elimination. This reduction almost to nothing also happens to be the regular course of Beckett's fictional world in general, a homology which suggests that the extreme stripping away carried out "within" the writing is also the very form of the writing vocation itself, as it dwindles into the recesses of a life reduced to little else. In Beckett's fiction, especially in a work like *The Unnamable*, this remainder is the very thing that, ravenous for silence, obstructs the dissolution of speech and keeps the torture going. In this respect, the sheer painful abjection of the writer's "position" is most deliberately and explicitly staged in Beckett's work (although Kafka is certainly a forerunner in intimately linking writing with torture, not only in "In the Penal Colony" but also in many statements in his letters and diaries).[14] Indeed, Beckett's work poses, more sharply and urgently than either Kafka's or Blanchot's, the question of a troubling limit between literary language, as a cultural and ethical value, and a kind of speech that in its compulsive brutality crosses into an experience that must in some sense be considered "nonliterary." "When one listens to oneself," said Beckett in an interview, "it's not literature that one hears."[15] The "vocation" of writing thus verges toward a harassing "vocalization" that bears its compulsions openly, risking an exposure that might exceed—that is, fall far short of—the categories that would dress it in more redemptive terms.[16] There is more than a hint of shame to be read in some of Beckett's hilarities and melancholies, and the residues of so much elimination and stripping away have affective tonalities, even (I will argue) an unexpected sentimentality, that it will be important to register in the bare but intensely charged figures that Beckett obsessively stages.

 I have stressed what might be considered the more "embarrassing" side of the writer's position, as translated, revised and minimized in Blanchot's and Beckett's public statements. But just as Blanchot does, after all, assert a kind of steadfast propensity, a constant holding and maintaining ("*je me tiens là*"), however unsteady ("*écrivant, n'écrivant pas*"), and therefore a persistence that is and must be affirmed, so does Beckett's "*bon qu'à ça*" imply some slim margin of "good" that still attaches itself to *that*. We are very much within the joke-logic of Kafka's hunger artist, who devotes himself so fanatically to fasting only because (here's the punch line) *he couldn't find the food he liked*, leaving only this poor starving performance to live on. Is Beckett likewise suggesting that if only he had found something better he would have plunged in without hesitation? Yes, certainly, but like that of the hunger artist, his downgrading gesture is comic precisely because we know what extraordinarily high stakes have been invested in the thing called literature (art), and in particular what Beckett himself invested in it, which was virtually everything he had (though here again he was a bit less absolutist, if one can put it thus, than Kafka or Blanchot). If he is "good for nothing but" writing, it may also be that nothing is quite so good as writing, that writing is the last holdout against the good's corrosion and dispersion, the one thing that has managed, after all, to resist elimination in the all-devouring process of rejecting everything on offer (and in that sense it is analogous with the very hunger of the hunger artist, the last thing left of all, and the most irreducible, as we will see in a reading of that story in Chapter 4).[17] In other words, the minimal and minimized vindication of writing actually harbors an extreme and hyperbolic affirmation, or even a receding and residual version of transcendence, that holds out the hope (and the persistent demand) of unparalleled satisfactions, not to say ecstasy, even in the midst of the extreme attenuations already noted. We can think of this as the rather more exalted side of the impoverished remainder in question here, for it does seem to remain, and insistently so—indeed, all the more insistently in that the satisfactions in question have become radically *impossible*, deeply incompatible with the experience of a subject, and this is perhaps what gives the search for them its sharpest ethical edge. In this vein, Kafka wrote in his diary: "Nothing else will ever satisfy me" (D 302). Blanchot, for his part, would write of "the call of [an] all-powerful affirmation" (AM 126). It is this sort of language that justifies speaking here in terms of the sublime.

As is already evident, the notion of the sublime can be introduced into this context only with the recognition that it is definitively subject to translation—and indeed, the specific inevitability of such an attenuating translation is one of the central concerns of this book. The Kantian version of the sublime (and of the moral law to which it would give access), whose residual movements and structures are of crucial importance in the chapters that follow, still does clearly resonate in these authors' works, but only across a number of irreversible displacements. Blanchot's "modest translation" of Luther already illustrates this, in a way that is not as anachronistic as it might seem. For if we grant that Kant (the Pietist) has in some sense already "translated" Luther, primarily by dislodging divine authority from the moral law that governs the categorical ethical subject and replacing it with pure reason as a self-grounding and universalizing structure—and as the ultimate treasure revealed in the sublime's violently downgrading uplift—then Blanchot's version of the imperative merely takes this *reconfiguration of the law* a step further. This is a step withdrawn from the beyond, both in its divine and in its empty and purely rational form, and a step down, one that may well open another more problematic "beyond" that is not beyond (an other world called *fiction*, in its essential relation to the ancient schema of the Odyssean *nekuia*—but for the moment this is a digression).[18] The important point is that this downward arching inflection of the writer's task specifically translates the sublime insofar as it reconfigures the writer's relation to a law that would command, authorize and "help" this activity—or, in Kantian terms, that would "drive" it, with an "incentive" (a "*Triebfeder*") making it possible for transcendence to touch the flesh, and to move it.[19] Whatever "powers" may intervene, or not, they have little to do with pure reason, or if they do, it is only insofar as the latter is itself driven by forces that cannot be extricated from sensibility (and so is no longer "pure").[20] And yet somehow the task itself remains categorical, "irreducible," and strangely singular, without any grounding instance or structure that could be *cited*, invoked or called upon, whether as an authority or as a founding text—as Luther cites God, as Kant cites pure reason. Thus it appears that we have to do with something like a "categorical" movement *of sensibility* at work in the writer's task. But the name of such a movement is precisely *compulsion*—only a compulsion stripped of its objects and ends.

Indeed, Kant already spoke of a paradoxical "drive of reason," a cruel compulsion moving beyond all that is given in mere sensibility, a drive toward totality and the ideal that would outstrip the senses and all their objects. This drive has an important role to play in the experience of the sublime, for it is what torments the imagination, faculty of images and representation, to strain beyond its limits and to strive, in impossibility and failure, toward the totality that reason necessarily demands. The ruination of imagination, and by implication of the entirety of experience, of the very world itself as the field of all sensible objects, is thus the triumph of reason and of the "moral law in its power" that is thus revealed to the rational ethical subject.[21] This is the only true object of the sublime experience, as Kant repeatedly emphasizes, and its confusion with the very large or very powerful thing in the world that provides the overwhelming occasion for this experience occurs only by way of a "subreption"—the illegitimate substitution of an image for what necessarily outstrips all images.[22] Thus, at the end of the painful trajectory in which the subject is stripped of its world and is cast into the objectless void opened by sublimity, this subject, as a rational being, is granted an extraordinary compensation for all these losses, an incommensurable and inexhaustible treasure that Kant calls, using a term that speaks directly to our concerns, a "vocation." This *Bestimmung* (a word that can also be translated as "determination") is the ultimate reward and destination waiting at the far end of what would otherwise be an extremely melancholy affair—or even a kind of hell.

Kant does not speak much, in the *Critique of Judgment*, of the melancholic aspect of the sublime's hyperbolic losses; he is too energized by the task of conveying its boundless and eternal returns.[23] But such a melancholy is the most important link between the aesthetics of the sublime—and by extension the transcendentalizing tendencies of romanticism found well into the nineteenth century and beyond—and a more skeptical literary modernity that is nonetheless also driven, as a matter of aesthetic principle, to leave the world behind, but whose returns (in every sense) are much more equivocal.[24] In other words, we have to do with a "vocation" (as calling: *Beruf*) that has been stripped of its "vocation" (as destination: *Bestimmung*)—and no doubt even of its "call" (*Ruf*)—and that, in leaving behind all objects and occasions—in becoming "categorical"—finds itself bereft of the sort of treasure promised by critical metaphysics and *its* translation (by Kant and all that followed him) into the sphere of sensibility, into the dwindling chances of art. It is in this sense that I speak of a *destitution of the sublime* in the radical leave-taking that constitutes literary space: if writing has persisted in a movement that would strip bare or strip away—that would despoil and disfigure—

the worldly conditions of its production, and if there is after all something of a sublime law, a "categorical imperative," haunting this movement, it is a sublime that has been destituted of its treasure, and that threatens a loss *without return*.

Kafka, Blanchot, and Beckett are exemplary figures in this respect, not only for the insistent imperative I have already indicated, emblematically, in their hyperbolic rhetoric, but also because the drive behind the imperative is one that leads, strangely, into spaces that explicitly constitute an *other world*. Let me summarize this major point with three more emblematic image-phrases (among a number of possible ones): Kafka's "wooden bridge," which leaves behind the past *almost entirely* and leads into the uncanny world of the castle village; Beckett's "timeless void," the infernal Dante-inspired spaces toward (and in) which every possible figure endlessly dwindles; and of course Blanchot's "literary space," a notion that was derived in part from "surveying," as it were, Kafka's landscapes of "error" and wandering, and whose otherness to the world is a point so insistently made as to raise questions concerning the urgency, and completeness, of this supposedly absolute departure (questions that will be addressed in some detail in Part II). The term I use for this strange literary alterworld is *radical fiction*. This is a fiction that in a sense would root out the world, extricate all past experience, and sever literary language from lived reality, leaving only a barren but powerfully fascinating landscape of images (including language's image of itself, as Blanchot puts it [EL 31–32]), a place with laws of its own, laws that unfold only as it does. What is "real" in this radically fictive space has nothing to do with representational realism, but emerges rather from the sort of insistent and irreducible drive that I have been attempting to locate, and that stubbornly inhabits literary speech, one might say, as the leftover of a voice: a voice still left and leaving still as it speaks. The ambiguity of such a voice's "leavings"—its departures, farewells ("Adieu"), residues and remnants—opens the space for the interrogations pursued here.

Is this voice a treasure of its own? In other words, does the reduction and destitution of language's insistent drive render up its own rewards? This question threads throughout the studies that follow, and there are many occasions when one might well suspect such a recuperative compensation, particularly when the rhetoric and staging of extreme destitution reaches a hyperbolic pitch (however deep the tones of irony may be at times). Blanchot's "all-powerful affirmation" at the end of *Death Sentence*, an indestructible affirmation emanating from the recesses of a living death to the world, stands out as one such moment; likewise the very beauty of Beckett's lyricism, undercut with irony and yet indulged all the same, strikes one as the richness of a lost world and life returned in the passions of a dying voice. A similar ambiguity can be read (as we will see in Chapter 8) in the sarcastic-ecstatic "exit weeping" from the evocation of life's and art's redolent riches, in "Three Dialogues with Georges Duthuit." But this is also the text in which Beckett warns against taking art's destitution as simply another occasion for a more or less jubilant renewal. This is a warning that ought to be heeded, difficult as that may be, and it is unclear to what extent any of the writers discussed here is really able to do so, even if their lucidity is what makes us aware of this dilemma. For that very reason, I propose to take this fake weeping "seriously" and to wonder whether the passionate and lyrical tones that so often sound in these works, in the wake of the extreme reductions and absolute departures that constitute their most intimate imperative, do not in fact belie a disavowed affective attachment, perhaps an attachment to loss itself—a condition otherwise known as melancholy. The question will be, in part, whether that attachment seeks underhandedly (subreptitiously) to restore a properly sublime (supersensible) dimension to what *is left*, to what returns as having been left (behind), or whether these remnants can bear their emptinesses, if one can put it thus, into the texts that open them. When Kafka, in an early letter, narrates a parable in which a man clings ostentatiously to a locked box—patent allegory of a young writer holding onto his "inner" treasure—whose precious contents turn out to be nothing but "two milk teeth," we might be tempted to gauge his entire accomplishment by the systematic sobriety with which, over many years of writing, he *empties that box*, giving it over from even this meager sign to a nothingness which, however, may still never completely efface every sign of the stuff that used to be there. Likewise—to mention another emblem that will be of great importance in Part II, on Blanchot—at the beginning of *Death Sentence*, when Blanchot's narrator evokes the necessity of telling a retrospective story of which virtually nothing remains *but* this necessity, he writes of "the shell of an enigma," an empty castoff thing that both calls for, and is, the work it will have "contained," *en creux*. This hard and hollow core is also a crux, a complex knot or buckle in which the destituted sublime vacillates between a newly projected promise to stay eternally there ("éternellement, elle est là," as Blanchot lyrically writes), and a groundless drive to nothing that bears its emptiness openly, having only that and nothing more to give.

But this nothing, as I will emphasize more than once, is never simply and entirely nothing. It continually takes the form of the thing that gives it a contour and makes it "visible." In the context of what I have called radical fiction, this means that it continually wends its way, in tiny fissures or massive cavernous voids, through the figural material that populates the space of fiction. Even Blanchot's extremely attenuated *récits*, even Beckett's abstracted algebras and impersonal geometries, are populated by such figures. All the more clearly is this the case with Kafka, whose closer proximity to (and strong identification with) the great novelistic traditions of the preceding century meant that his fiction, particularly in the signal works of his first maturity, became a struggle with the weight of a certain programmatic figural density, a striving for gapless continuity that would overwhelm, not to say overcome, the schematic fault in which it originated (the name of that weight and struggle, as we will see throughout that section, is *judgment*). All this is to suggest that the figural moment, in these subtly allegorical fictive worlds, is precisely the moment of subreption and treachery, an inevitable "translation" in which both the void and its biographical impossibility are betrayed. In other words, the demand of figuration (as compulsion or imperative), a demand that is never fully repudiated by these writers, draws these extreme fictions back around from their absolutely other worlds into the autobiographical dimension from which they work so fiercely to sever themselves. Radical fiction is thus, at the same time, radical autobiography, a writing so intimate that it cannot help but mark the "self" whose possibility it scatters into the alienating forms that constitute it. Breaking down the word *autobiography*, one could say that the "auto" continually haunts any "graphism" carried out in the midst of a "life" that finds itself driven panicked into language, compelled into speech—life as narrative's compulsive return—and so a life placed at stake in the severance thus opened within it. And one must add, conversely, that any "self" placed at stake in the gap between language and life is necessarily haunted and disrupted by the dispersion of writing's formal and machine-like processes (in that sense, the ghost *is* the machine). Following Heidegger's paradoxical notion of *Ent-fernung*—an extreme distancing that cancels and collapses distance, a suffocating intimacy that opens a gaping and unclosable space—Philippe Lacoue-Labarthe calls this logic a "hyperbologic," which he defines in these simple terms: the farther it is, the closer it is; the more "proper" it is, the more inappropriable it must be (and with this "must" the formula introduces an element of necessity that is also an ambiguous and exigent demand). It is in this sense as well that the hyperbolic rhetoric I have mentioned marks the extremity, but also the intimate and singular scale, of the destituted space continually at issue in the readings of the texts that play out this paradox.[25]

The problem of reluctant self-exposure mentioned before—in close connection with guilt, shame, bad conscience and other self-looping auto-affective structures—inserts itself precisely here, in the fault that opens this space *in its compulsive figurative attachments*, and in the repetitions of its "primal scenes." I should stress that there will be no attempt here to "traumatize" these writers, in the sense of locating the pressing origin of their writing in a biographical trauma attached to an autobiographical scene striving dully to be recounted through all this fiction—no biographical or autobiographical readings in that sense. The autobiographical moment that obtrudes into these texts does so in a way that, in its extremity and ungraspability, *demands* fiction, that finds itself forced and torqued into scenes and figures, despite the impossibility of such a narrative localization. Blanchot's own use of the phrase "a primal scene" in *The Writing of the Disaster* is perhaps the best indication of this (as we will see in Chapter 5)—a use that is hedged with parentheses and a question mark (he writes: "(A primal scene?)"), but that nonetheless compulsively turns and tropes through the contours of a scene cast simultaneously as an eternal and irresistible autobiographical return and as mere fictive "supposition" (ED 117; WD 72). Fictive figuration, then, as a necessary compromise formation, under duress of extreme strangeness and radical depersonalization. However, this strangeness, as an uncanny haunting and *revenance* (a mode that is especially prominent in Blanchot), also delineates the material that in each case *gives the writer away*, so to speak, as being in part the remaindered voice of a singular time that has not been fully dissolved in the corrosions of fictive language. Time as *temps*, but also as one time, *une fois*—a time whose structure (to move very quickly) can be condensed into something like a logic of having-been, which also means having once been born. "Born into language," one might say, if this did not ring as the oxymoron Beckett shows it to be when he writes: "Birth was the death of him."[26] Or as he writes in the very autobiographical text *Company*, in which the day of the protagonist's birth is also described as the moment when "it was over at last. Over!" (C 14). In speaking of "life," then, and in showing its odd material and figural intrusions into fictions that strain to sever themselves from any previous existence on earth, I mean nothing more than that: a narrative structure dogged and haunted by the unfortunate fact of having once been singularized as someone's. If anywhere, the "trauma" of these texts is located in the tiny tunneling hole of that "once," and thus the painful passage from infancy to language, and conversely (but not symmetrically) from language as a pregiven formal structure (*langue*) to the speech that is its singularly appropriated and assumed mobilization (*parole*).[27] Such a life will never have been anything but the residue of language, but to emphasize the odd singularity of this residue *in each case*—the peculiar shape of its compulsive figures—will involve tracing a movement that struggles first to lose them, whether by casting them off or, one might say, by devouring them unto eternity. And it is in the struggle to transform, escape, throw off, or surreptitiously keep the leavings of an abrupt and impoverishing entry into literary space that much of the tension is generated in these texts.[28] If this resembles a traumatic structure, it is not because there is a barred or repressed narrative, but because the breach or fault to which telling returns, eternally and again, continually defies the figural compulsion that commands it. As such, it is a mere disappearing *point*, and a necessarily empty one—but this is the very structure of the imperative in its defaulting force.

The situation can thus be summarized in the following terms: the only story that can be told is one that has been invented, but every invented story—and the more radically invented, the more abyssally will this be demonstrated—betrays the contingency, the temporal, topographical and idiomatic embeddedness, of its imperative's *imprint*, the initial impact of its unaccountable preinscription. (Such an imprint could also be considered in terms of style—another term for autobiography as displaced remnant.)

The complexity of this figural material and of its intertwined patterns requires an attention to textual detail that is borne out in the textured readings I endeavor to present in each case. But the overall shape of these readings can be indicated here in a schematic and preliminary fashion. With respect to Kafka, the figural schema that traverses all of his first mature fiction is played out in what can be called a *scenography of judgment*, the staging of an interiority's obstructed externalization and of a failed self-defense in language that (as I show in Chapter 1) already found its first elaborations in letters and diaries that precede the "judgment stories" in which it culminates (from "The Judgment," "The Metamorphosis" and "The Stoker" and on through *The Trial* and "In the Penal Colony"). But this is a problematic "culmination" that mitigates the telic and progressive narrative of the writer's emergence to which Kafka himself often had recourse, for from the beginning these stories also seek to undo the constraining conditions of a burdensome courtroom paradigm, and, in the end, to exit the theater of the Law—as we see Josef K. doing, at least partially, in *The Trial*. Blanchot too finds himself facing an instantiation of the law, in the feminine figures that serve both to open the path out of the world—in strange allegorical steps—but that, especially in *Death Sentence*, leave behind a troubling specter, projective and concrete remainders, ghostly corpse-images, and above all an enigmatic death mask that takes on an unexpected transcendental force. This death mask will be crucial in the reading of Blanchot presented here (in Chapters 6 and 7), not only because it may well be the shell of a treasure the writer clings to despite everything; for it also allows us to interrogate (by way of Jean-Luc Nancy's comments on Heidegger's strange references to a death mask in *Kant and the Problem of Metaphysics*) the basis of the image and its "look" in the ground of which Blanchot appears to situate the fundamental paradox of his fiction: a relation that ruptures all relation.[29] It is surely no coincidence that the figure through which this operation takes place is a feminine figure, and even at some level that of a beloved woman, and these chapters will be centrally concerned with her place in the rather dubious movement that turns back to efface her, *as such and in her time*, from the encounter she makes possible.

In Beckett we find a similarly passionate turn to time past, to a life now reduced to dust and numbers, for the sake of a voided present trafficking in sheer absence and dispersion. But with Beckett's expelled and expulsive moribunds and tramps we also find a much more overt, if constantly ironized, attachment to the world left behind, and a greater willingness to play explicitly on nostalgia and sentimentality—in order to corrode them, certainly, but also with a view to the strange rights they seem to claim in the infernal and totalizing losses that call them up. Even the unnamable voice of *The Unnamable* will be unable not to mark, express, or expectorate the signs of *a* past on which its very existence structurally depends, however indeterminate, unspeakable, and inappropriable this past has become. All the more, then, will the inevitability of the return of a past in a flattened narrative voice be demonstrated in a text like *Company*, which loops around on itself ("lapped as it were in its meaninglessness" [C 61]) as though this were the very structure of the fictive flight into a formalization that is both grammatical and, even, algebraic and mathematical. In that light one can say that *Company* shows the formal inevitability of a material return—the return of narrative material charged with an affect generated no less by the torture of grammar than by the "heavy" (C 38) or "sick heart" (C 26) bent on breaking, which in that text thumps toward its last countable thump. The fact that this return does nothing to reduce the alienating otherness of its enabling conditions, or to make it more assimilable as "mine," is nothing but the fundamental poetic and vocal given of Beckett's afterlife fiction. But I read Beckett's overt melancholy as the sign of an at least partial nonabsorption into this hell, a strange resistance that cannot be resolved into the kind of affirmative eternities one finds voiced, no less lyrically, in the Blanchot who proclaims: "To her I say 'come,' and eternally she is there" (AM 127). Beckett's affirming angels are less ubiquitous, more intermittent (as in the late television play *Nacht und Träume*, where she or he arrives for the passing moment of a consoling gesture; or in . . . *but the clouds* . . . where she appears only long enough to whisper the words of the title and the final phrases of "The Tower," a poem by Beckett's fellow Irishman, William Butler Yeats). On another related level, in all three of these writers, one of the strict conditions of entry into the destituted sublimity of literary space is a turn from—if not a repudiation of—love, and of women, a move that is completely explicit and fundamental in each case. Blanchot's Orphic schema is the most paradigmatic version of this turn—a turn that begins by turning back toward . . . but that ends with fleeting and receding phantoms, taking us once again into an underworld of mere images. The apparent necessity of a woman's appearance/disappearance—a necessity required precisely for disappearance to appear, as Blanchot puts it[30]—is a troubling element in the melancholy economies that govern writing's destituted but insistent figural extortions.

In sum, then, we will see that fiction *in extremis* is intimately bound up with an autobiographical dimension of writing that pursues the writer into the far reaches of radical depersonalization: writing's curved trajectory leads back, eternally and again, to the obtrusive stuff of a life that, in the logic of these leavings, really ought to have been left behind. *Faute de quoi*—failing this—and in default of such a permanent and absolute leave-taking, what is left is in fact a dense residue that bears witness to a compulsion arising from the breach that writing opens in a life, which it *leaves there*. The vacillation of this fault between abjectifying failure and imperious command makes up all the ambiguity of the mundane but untenable positions taken up by these writers.

This vacillation was indicated by Philippe Lacoue-Labarthe in the essay mentioned above, whose title succinctly names its unsteady movement: "*Il faut*" (one must; it is necessary) is the expression used in French for an imperative that, while simply stating a necessity, also expresses an empty, impersonal and categorical obligation.[31] The pertinence of this idiomatic phrase and its forceful but faltering rhetoric to the writers addressed in this study is also indicated in the first words of Lacoue-Labarthe's essay, which quote Blanchot: "*Ecrire, l'exigence d'écrire*" ("To write, the exigency to write"), a phrase that can be seen, once again, as a translation of the essay's title phrase. It is also no coincidence that Lacoue-Labarthe ends the opening paragraph by recalling Beckett's "*Bon qu'à ça*," which he places "in a register quite close" to that of Blanchot's exigency. This register is one that finds itself doubled in the phrase's etymological ambiguity: *falloir* (to be necessary), as Lacoue-Labarthe points out, derives from the same Latin verb as *faillir*, which means rather to fall short, to fail, to have almost done something (often accidentally) that did not in fact occur. Thus the most forceful expression of an imperative is also, and already, a marker of the command's breach and failure, a default, deficiency, and collapse that are both presupposed and demanded by the imperative, as though its very force depended on its weakness, as though failure were the essence of necessity—and particularly the necessity to write (which is the central concern of Lacoue-Labarthe's essay, devoted to Hölderlin and the task of poetry). In this sense, the imperative "*il faut*" also says, simultaneously and necessarily, as the very form of its command: *it faults*, or *it fails* (or perhaps: it falls (short)). Lacoue-Labarthe could also have quoted Beckett's strange injunction in *Worstward Ho* to: "Fail again. Fail better"—a gesture linking failure with a "good" whose slim and singular chances lie, here too, only in the tiny irreducible margin between the least bad and nothing at all. It is in this sense that the readings presented in this study attempt to locate an insistent imperative in a *fault of writing* that fissures a life and renders it over, across greater and lesser distances, to language's faltering but imperious demands. If this fault seems to implicate the writer in an ethical lapse that would call up all the dubious powers of guilt, bad conscience, diabolical trickery, even violence and graver trespasses, we would do well to recall once again the writer whose "Adieu" Lacoue-Labarthe also mentions in his essay's opening paragraph—namely Rimbaud, the young poet who recognized his vocation with an apt and straightforward personal disclaimer: "I have discovered that I'm a poet," writes the poet, and adds, disarmingly: "It's really not my fault."[32] I underscore this statement, lest the critical remarks offered in this study appear at times to be aimed at the person of the writer, whereas their aim is rather to delineate the treacherous conditions of the task in question, and to point to the slim margin of freedom it may open.

PART ONE

Kafka

CHAPTER I

Kafka's Teeth
The Literary *Gewissensbiss*

OVERVIEW: FROM THE COURT TO THE REPORT

"God does not want me to write, but I, I must." Thus writes a twenty-year-old Franz Kafka in a letter to a friend. This is one of many astonishing pronouncements threaded through the Kafkan corpus, and it provides a striking formulation of the imperative to write, in the image of the overpowered writer struggling with the forces arrayed against him. It is well known that Kafka frequently evoked the extremity of his calling, in numerous emphatic statements whose terms are unmistakable, not to say strident and melodramatic. The letters and diaries are punctuated with extraordinary proclamations on his task as a writer and on his devotion to an exclusive and all-absorbing literary vocation, proclamations that have done their work well, if the frequency of their isolated repetition is any indication. I have just bowed to the weight of this critical tradition, by citing (again) one of the first and most astonishing, from an early letter that Kafka wrote to a schoolmate. Years later, he proclaimed the following, in a letter to his fiancée Felice Bauer: "I am made of literature, I am nothing else and cannot be anything else" (LFe 304)—this by way of indicating, not to say dismissing, his suitability to be something called a husband. Such statements read like the lapidary gnomes of a man in the throes of an impossible mission, forced to strike home his uncompromising point for the dull and uncomprehending ears around him. At times, this insistence places the writing within (even if also against) a dubious transcendental dimension, as when he claims that his writing is "the earthly reflection of a higher necessity" (LFe 313). But more often than not, they place him *at fault*, whether in relation to the demands of the social world (marriage, etc.), with which writing is considered to be incompatible, or under the weight of the absolute demands of the tremendous task of writing, a task that must be coextensive with life itself. But the gap between life and writing, between writing and the law, will mark out a fault, a generative breach, out of which Kafka will work out the terms of a singular imperative to write, elaborating from it the very shape of his first mature fiction.

When Kafka writes, with apparent thunder in his voice, "This is how it is with me: God does not want me to write, but I, I must," he is addressing his gymnasium and university friend Oskar Pollak in a letter dated November 9, 1903.[1] Bracketing this important context for the moment, we can ask what this statement says, in the form of the gnomic self-assertion that it clearly strives to take. It brings us immediately into the sphere of guilt and prohibition, in the mode of a stubborn and persistent defiance. Already prone to extreme and hyperbolic rhetoric when speaking of his writing, Kafka claims a necessity to write as a kind of counter-absolute, a categorical necessity borne by a doubly affirmed "I, I . . ." posited in conflict with the Absolute itself, and caught up in a transgression of the most powerful Law there is, the very will of God, personally directed at him and his pernicious writing. Against this incontrovertible force, the young writer asserts another lesser but still more imperious law, driven by its own irrevocable "I must." The complex guilt already projected by such a scheme will take many forms in Kafka's writing, becoming not only a fundamental matrix of his first decisive fictions, but also a primary notion through which the entire corpus and figure of Kafka continue to be understood. Indeed, one of my tasks here will be to follow the elaboration of this scheme of guilt and transgression as the young writer works his way into the anxious fictional worlds of judgment and punishment for which he is well known. But I will also suggest that in the later fictions he leaves behind the schema of guilt and punishment and develops other forms of presentation, in a shift from a more familiar Oedipal structure into a different and more diffuse anxiety centered in the *voice* and, in the novels, scattered into rumor.

My focus, however, will not be these gnomic proclamations as such, in all their metaphysical, theological, and cosmic drama, however compelling these may be. And they certainly are compelling. At the very least they convey the fact that, to put it very simply, something tremendous is at stake in the writer's vocation—indeed, nothing less than everything. Such is the tenor and scale of their hyperbolic rhetoric, here as elsewhere. But I am not sure that these dramatic proclamations are the most fruitful place to look for a substantive rendering of the imperative to write driving and structuring Kafka's work. More relevant to my purposes is a much broader structural-figural accretion that is to be read in the relationship between such proclamations and their larger context, both in the texts where they appear, and in Kafka's project as a whole: a project that involves an explicit effort at self-fashioning and transformation into a writer, a strange being that maintains a vexed and impossible relationship with the empirical existence of the author. This "being-a-writer" or "writer-being" (*Schriftstellersein*), of which so much has been made, serves here as the cipher for Kafka's self-conscious striving for a certain literary transcendence—but it will also be a signpost on the way to the failure of these strivings, about which Kafka had a perfectly sober awareness, expressed very clearly in later writings. This striving follows a trajectory that passes through the consolidation of the writer-being who ecstatically wrote "The Judgment" and the texts that quickly followed, and then, further and "downward," into a mode of writing at pains to burrow into its own earthbound conditions, closely tied to the conditions of a speaking voice. It is the trajectory of this movement that I will begin to trace in this first chapter. As in subsequent chapters, it will be a question of tracking the destitution of a sublime *vocation*—that is, its most "authentic" self-recognition in impoverishment, anxiety, and diminishment, along with the stubborn assertion of an inextinguishable *insistence*.

I can illustrate this trajectory more concretely by returning to the quote from the 1903 letter—which already contains *in nuce* its entire movement, and its comically lopsided structure—but this time placing it within the grain of its context, a figurally rich (if somewhat mixed and arbitrary) metaphorical context that wraps the gnomic utterance in various layers of figural and rhetorical complexity. Here is the entire paragraph in which it appears:

> By the way, no writing's been done for some time. It's this way with me: God does not want me to write, but I, I must. So there's an everlasting up and down; after all God is the stronger, and there's more anguish in it than you can imagine. So many powers [*Kräfte*] within me are tied [*gebunden*] to a stake, which might possibly grow into a green tree. Released [*freigemacht*], they could be useful to me and the country. But nobody ever shook a millstone from around his neck by complaining, especially when he was fond of it [*wenn man sie Lieb hat*]. (LFr 10; Br, 21)[2]

It is important to foreground the fact that Kafka is addressing a peer with whom he has discussed the ongoing travails of writing and literary ambition, as well as the heroes they both share (more concrete avatars of the forbidding "God" evoked here), in relation to whom they of course fall woefully short. In this paragraph, taken as a whole, the gnomic utterance suddenly becomes much less thunderous; it even takes on a playful and self-belittling irony that renders derisive its "theological" pretentions: the obstacles preventing me from writing are so tremendous they may as well be likened to God Himself—hence the futile but endless "up and down" struggle. This sort of wishful grandiosity, defensively ironized, pervades these letters. Further, what looks like a cosmically defiant gesture appears also as mere self-beratement: the lament over not writing (whereas "I must," categorically and despite all obstacles), a lament that will resound especially in the early diaries, gives a clear sense of the *disciplinary* nature of the guilt mentioned above, the fact of not measuring up or adhering to something like a regular schedule. I will here precipitously state a gnome of my own, which may serve as a rough principle of reading (and which will be drastically complicated when we return to it later): guilt in Kafka is derived—only in part but at a fundamental level—from a faulty and faltering relation to the banal everyday discipline required by writing in its "highest" aspirations. No less than the Law of God, it is the mundane law of writing as (a) practice that has been violated ("no writing for some time"), and in being violated, *gives rise to this hyperbolic figure of divine struggle in the first place*, a figure that then proliferates into a rapid series of disjointed images evoking up and down movement, bound captivity, release, and punishment (even a "liking" for punishment)—terms which, not incidentally, name the fundamental topographic and dramatic categories of Kafka's first mature fiction. Thus from a breach in the counter-law of writing—I must!—emerges a dramatic fictive *figure* which, in distorted and exaggerated form, stages the assertion of this counter-law as inviolable (endless struggle with God). Put another way: I have broken the law ("my" law, that of writing's *must*), but in fictively projecting this breach in writing, I may thereby remedy it. It is surely not indifferent to this dynamic that the figure itself (a struggle) suggests both punishment and defiance, and I will return to this important question below. For the moment, the essential point is this: Kafka's fiction is generated *in part* from the elaboration of an autobiographically registered conflict concerning the necessity of writing itself.[3] This conflict, with its "eternal ups and downs," will put into play in Kafka's work a powerful motif of elevation and descent, in close proximity with a guilt that has to do directly with "forces within" as they demand to be bodied forth, liberated (*freigemacht*) and externalized. As here, the imperative to write for Kafka will long be understood in terms of being bound (to a stake, by a millstone), and of finding release. In this welter of images, a strange ambiguity appears between the bonds of discipline, which make possible the writing that defies God, and the bonds (and burdens) of captivity, which is already figured as a kind of punishment, *but also as the very condition for the work that is required*.[4] This dilemma will be crucial to Kafka: writing demands liberation, but of what and from what? Does the liberation of writing exonerate or inculpate? Does guilt arise from not writing (disciplinary breach) or rather from a writing that releases forces waged against the might and will of the Righteous Powers?[5] Finally: is writing itself a crime or a punishment? A tightening of binds or a dangerous loosening? Or is it somehow simultaneously all of these together, the barely habitable place where they merge? One might note that elsewhere in the letters to Pollak, the space of writing is also figured instrumentally as a desk that physically tortures the writer as he writes, and depending on his writing.[6] The disciplinary demands of writing are inflected with a juridical dimension that is already and immediately a form of punishment. And the sublime law of writing's striving is directly inscribed on the suffering body without which it cannot be practiced.

This single example, then, has already sent us a considerable way down the interpretive path I would like to follow through Kafka's work: by bringing the transcendent statement (*God doesn't want it, but I must*) down into its textured elaboration, and by linking this statement with the precise figures through which it is further articulated, we can see Kafka performing the very operation that will open the way to his first mature fiction: a figural world born of an intensely anxious thinking about the extreme demands of writing, about not writing enough or well enough. By the same token, we see taking shape the schematic figures that will give graphic form to this fiction, especially with regard to the well-known structural features of judgment, guilt, punishment, and the perverse scenes of their enactment, which largely shape the theatrical narratives of the stories I will focus on.

The first major aim of the present chapter will be to demonstrate the ways in which Kafka undertook in his "personal" writings, especially these letters to Pollak and the early *Diaries*, to elaborate the metaphorical and narrative structures that would issue into his first mature "successful" fictions, beginning with "The Judgment" and including "The Stoker," "The Metamorphosis," "In the Penal Colony," and *The Trial*, all written in succession within roughly a two-year period.[7] Put another way, I will show how Kafka explicitly and deliberately undertook the former "biographical" writings in such a way as to derive and elaborate from them the narrative motifs, configurations, and even the driving impetus, of a fictional writing that did strive, after all, for a standalone perfection (and thus, at least in that sense, a kind of "absoluteness"). The first of these fictions, "The Judgment," bears in its title the name of their central matrix and dominant mode. This story, which was written in the pages of notebooks that we now read under the title *Diaries*, culminates a movement that is already roughly sketched in the above example—with its emphasis on guilt and shortcoming, the externalization of intense but invisible inner forces, and a losing but determined "up and down" struggle with sublime powers—but with a crucial addition that is common to all of the stories Kafka wrote in the subsequent highly productive period (1912 to 1914), namely, a *judgment scene*. All of the major narratives written during this "decisive" period[8] hinge around a parajudicial judgment in which the protagonist fails to defend himself because he is unable to manifest an inner conviction or reality, an a priori or "categorical" innocence, that is overwhelmed by the powerful social theatricality before and within which it must appear, and thus by the narrative's absorption into "outward" appearances as such. The protagonists of these stories must plead a case for innocence before a hostile, aggressive, or at the very least highly skeptical judge; and the failure of their self-defense casts into doubt the very medium in which Kafka himself struggled to conjure them: language as the persuasive presentation of an otherwise occluded interiority. It also ends invariably in their condemnation and punishment, if not outright destruction; the inevitability of such a fate in these stories will be interrogated in its proper place.[9] It is one of the major axes around which this phase of Kafka's fiction is constructed.

I will thus be arguing for a certain "autobiographical" derivation of Kafka's first major narratives, but it is important to emphasize that, in this phase, the stress should be placed on the "graphic" element of the term *autobiographical*. If Kafka writes (his way) out of his "own life," it is because he already seeks to enter the medium of writing as a site in which to forge another radically different life and world constituted in and by fictive language. In *L'espace littéraire*, Blanchot emphasized that literary language is an image of language—not a "*langage imagé*" (EL 32) that uses more and better metaphors, but a language that is itself an image of language. It is precisely in this sense that Kafka's language is "literary," and is so *already* in his letters and diaries. In that regard, one need not impose a "biographical reading" on Kafka's judgment narratives in order then to claim that they are *drawn from* autobiographical material (just as the writing of fiction invades "real" life at its very core), for Kafka very clearly did this himself. He read, and wrote, his life into texts (letters, diaries) that, as texts, clearly show his concerted efforts to cast this life into fiction—as one casts a stone into a river.

Of course, I am hardly the first to point out this derivation of Kafka's judgment stories from his "personal" writings. The specific aim of my demonstration, however, will be to show that the derivation in question is grounded in an elaboration of, and a complex (figural and conceptual) reflection on, the very structure of an imperative to write, a structure that demands precisely the movement I have been suggesting: an uncanny passage from autobiographical material into radically fictional narratives that strive to break free of personal experience. That is, a passage from life to art, or, better yet, from the written elaboration of "personal" experience (in the mode of its depersonalization) into the life that is life-as-text. But already "within" the first of these two terms (life, as written), Kafka works to *literarize*—to render in densely literary form—the life in question. Indeed, he explicitly states this as a goal for his self-referential writing, when he speaks of a descriptive language that would enter "into freedom [*in das Freie*]" and "release one's foot from lived experience" (D 80, TB 77; October 20, 1911).[10] At another level, how else are we to understand the fact that Kafka's corpus integrally and legitimately includes his letters and diaries? For these latter are not treated as auxiliary documents, neither by editors nor by scholars, but rather are rightly seen as constitutive elements of Kafka's writing as he left it. Whence this imperative, in Kafka's case, to include everything, not to mention the ongoing search for lost notebooks? Among other things, it confirms that the strange and problematic sense that these "personal" documents will have always been "literature"—a point that is clearly borne out by any attentive reading of these texts within the perspective of the corpus as a whole.[11] To be sure, at some level these "personal" documents have attained this status retroactively, on the basis of the fictional narratives they led to and helped to forge (likewise on the basis of the fiction's subsequent canonical status, which it achieved despite its "failure" even to constitute a work, as Walter Benjamin claimed[12]); but the peculiar work of literary elaboration carried out in all of Kafka's notebooks, and even his letters—their effort to "literarize" their material—is immanent to the very drive that engenders them, and to the figural texture that results.

By stressing the "graphic" aspect of "autobiography," I also mean to invoke the visual projection that characterizes the earlier stories, in distinction from many of the later stories, which rely more heavily on ruminating first-person voices. The judgment stories are highly visual artifacts that unfold in dreamlike scenarios often plotted out in precisely structured scenographies. As mentioned, they revolve around judgment *scenes*, and their visual, dreamlike quality has everything to do with the problems of guilt and obstructed self-presentation at their core. Consider Kafka's well-known diary entry in which he projects his task as a writer, indeed his very reason for being "here" on this earth, as that of a dangerous but liberating externalization:

> The tremendous [or monstrous: *ungeheure*] world I have in my head. But how free myself and free it without being torn to pieces. And a thousand times rather be torn to pieces than retain it in me or bury it. That, indeed, is why I am here [*Dazu bin ich ja hier*], that is quite clear to me. (D 222; TB 224; 21 June 1913)

Freeing the uncanny inner world—this baldly stated *fact*—is a kind of duty multiplied by desire ("a thousand times rather . . ."), whose dangers, however, will require the discipline we have seen emerging as indispensible to these efforts. Discipline is one answer to this question as to "how" to bring out such a sharp-edged "world," and in this strangely physical process writing itself is staged as a kind of bodily performance—one which, not surprisingly, gives rise to narratives organized around the mise-en-scène of a speaking body placed in danger as such.

A little over a year later, Kafka specifies the nature of this troubling world in the head, and of the drive associated with it, when he speaks of his "fate as a writer" in terms of externalizing an inner life that is like a *dream*, in a diary entry from around the time when he began work on *The Trial* (August 6, 1914); not incidentally, he describes it as a process that requires all of his exclusive care and attention:

> What will be my fate as a writer is very simple. My talent for portraying [my sense for presenting: *der Sinn für die Darstellung*] my dreamlike inner life has thrust all other matters into the background; my life has dwindled dreadfully, nor will it cease to dwindle. *Nothing else will ever satisfy me*. (D 302; TB 306; August 6, 1914; my emphasis)

This statement too has been quoted many times; it signals, once again, Kafka's "sense" of the exclusive devotion he owes to his task as a writer, and the withering of life's poor remainder as a result. It thus sketches a kind of economy, whose positive element is a "satisfaction" that is the specific locus of the hyperbole in this case: *Nothing else* will *ever* satisfy. There is no doubt less melodramatic thunder in this statement than in the God-defying assertion discussed above, but its absolutist tendency is clear. Moving quickly, and in anticipation of later arguments, one can say that such a description points toward a sacrificial economy that would yield a kind of *ecstasy* in return for a truncated outward—or perhaps merely organic—life, for surely the unremitting drive toward this exclusive satisfaction aims at something beyond an ordinary livable or life-sustaining satisfaction. Kafka, who was somewhat perversely preoccupied throughout his life with questions of food, nourishment, and physical debility, and who wove these motifs into his narratives in highly significant ways, at times seems to conflate, in the necessity to write, a kind of metaorganic drive with a quasi-spiritual calling; this is clearly the case here, where "satisfaction" is somehow both a bodily condition and something that outstrips the body (but in a way one would hesitate to call "spiritual").[13] Hence the importance in this passage of the word *Sinn*, or sense, posited here as a kind of organ or even an instinct with its own proper aim or telos. This strange metaorganic drive is one of the modalities in which Kafka cast the imperative to write in its impersonal necessity, and the invocation of a highly, even exclusively satisfying and pleasurable telos indicates, at one end of the process, another dimension of the guilt in question. Kafka refers to the operation it demands as "the presentation of my dreamlike inner life," the externalization and display of a life that contravenes (mere) life—and that, as we will see, may well require a completely unknown kind of nourishment capable of feeding this other very dubious kind of life. But here it is important to delineate a determinative parallelism, for with this formula, which on one hand describes the process of writing, Kafka also in fact projects a basic schema for all of the judgment stories that will result from it, not only in terms of their dreamlike scenography, but also in direct parallel with the compulsion under which each of their protagonists invariably find themselves, namely to *externalize a hidden inner condition* that alone will absolve them, to "present" their unmanifest innocence, invisible as it is to the social world that condemns them. That they must do this by speaking before a judge is thus the point (or the disjointed line) where Kafka's task as a writer, at least at one level, parallels that of his characters, in displaced and often untraceable forms, but in a way that is discernible both structurally and thematically. That they fail to do so precisely where Kafka "succeeds"—that their guilt is established, and their punishment enacted, in the absolving literary language of Kafka's guilt-producing writing—constitutes a paradox, and a literary-biographical knot, well worth examining.

In sum, then, one can say that in the first "successful" phase of Kafka's writing, beginning with "The Judgment," guilt becomes the name for a kind of linguistic ontology at the core of the writer's being (the being of the writer "I must" be, must become . . .), and is related to the necessity of bodying forth an inner life and world; the scene of judgment is its immanently dictated narrative form, the look and shape of its most intimate imperative.

After the judgment stories, however, beginning around 1915 to 1917, Kafka's fictions begin to take other quite different forms. One could well say that Kafka's stories change dramatically over time—and commentators have not failed to point this out—from the visually oriented scenographies of justice and guilt (all written in the third person, and in thrall to classical figures such as Goethe and Flaubert) to a more ruminative open-ended type of text proffered in the first person and much less focused on the narration of inscenated events.[14] These later stories, which foreground the speaking voice itself as the site and medium of the story's anxious, conflicted energies, also have a different mood or *Stimmung* in comparison to the earlier stories, a strange tonality marked by the singularity of a *Stimme* (voice), and they draw on a much less dramatic or scenic impetus, unfolding a very different, less visual and more "vocal" logic.

In carrying out the analyses of texts dominated by judgment scenarios in what follows, we will also be moving toward this other, and stranger, horizon that passes through Kafka's work (if I can thus describe a border that is both out beyond and yet also internal to the texts in question). For the stylistic and thematic shifts that emerge in Kafka's later narratives signal a change in Kafka's thinking, indeed, a shift toward *thinking speech* as the form of art's relation to the law and, therefore, to the imperative that structures it. In negative terms, the law, in Kafka, will cease to be sublime, at least in the (visual) sense of a towering, overwhelming, and punishing power toward which art itself ought to strive. If Kafka works to "destitute" the sublime in his judgment stories, it is in part as a way to exit the juridical regime installed as the founding schema of this phase of his work. The obsessive and even repetitive treatment of certain aspects of the judgment schema, the continually reelaborated patterns that we encounter in these stories, serve to indicate just how deeply embedded they are in the initial impetus of Kafka's writing, and how much ingenious and unsettling work was required to open them onto another kind of freedom, into different modalities of *das Freie*. While the chapters that follow present the main strands of these densely textured patterns, it is important to keep in view the scenically emptier and more destitute horizon toward which, in the end, they steadily but circuitously move—along with what I take to be the terminal figure of this movement, the emptied out and starving hunger artist, whose melancholy tale is related in the first person by an unknown witness. The emblematic formula I propose for this movement is that of a passage from the visual schema of the court to the vocal logic of the report, from the *Gericht* to the *Bericht*. In what does this passage consist? A brief sketch of its trajectory will allow us to see more clearly how Kafka negotiates the conditions that tightly structure the very cohesive set of judgment narratives, these "successful" narratives that threaten to trap, and to kill, even as they vibrate with an unknown freedom. As a shift of emphasis from the visual to the vocal, this movement might also be described, in parallel and summary fashion, as a shift from "theory" to thought, a displacement from the "contemplation" (*Betrachtung*) with which Kafka began toward an unaccountable dimension of the voice on which his final story ("Josefine the Singer") ruminates.

It is worth stressing, then, that Kafka's later more vocal narratives—including especially "A Report to an Academy," "Investigations of a Dog," "The Burrow" and "Josefine the Singer" and, to some extent, *The Castle*[15]—are not ruminative, "meditative," "reflective" or "cogitative" in only a superficial stylistic sense; indeed, they set out to articulate a fundamental thinking of language, truth, and freedom that one might well regard as a properly philosophical—or perhaps one could say postphilosophical —"ontology." This specific but very broad claim will have to be justified elsewhere; but in pointing toward the vocal structures of these stories, as they puzzle through questions of knowledge, art, sensation, memory and time, and as they undertake their reports and "researches" on the conditions of their own linguistic possibility, it is not difficult to discern the philosophical and aesthetic questions these texts clearly invoke and through which they suggest a different form of the imperative to write. Put most succinctly, what changes between the two phases is this: from an imperative to *present something* (a powerful inner world, vision, or life, a conviction of innocence, a notion of justice or of Justice, a dear and identifiable inner treasure), Kafka's narratives come to be driven by an imperative to *present nothing*, and a markedly external nothing at that (or rather one that defies this distinction). The voices that speak in these later stories do not have a determinate (internal) object that demands to be persuasively projected and rendered as socially operative; rather, like the narrator of "Josefine the Singer," they are confronted with a *nichts*, a nothing or nothingness that demands precisely an interminable thinking speech. Josefine is described as a "nothing in voice," a "nothing in accomplishment" (*"dieses nichts an Stimme, dieses nichts an Leistung . . ."*). And this same narrator provides another term for the ungraspable phenomenon in question: it is *ein Rätsel*, an enigma. He speaks of "the enigma of her great effect" (*"das Rätsel ihrer grossen Wirkung . . ."*). The word (or a close variation) appears in every one of these stories (as does the word *nichts*), always in highly significant formulations. It is the name of a new mode of thinking legible in Kafka's later work, one that has very little to do with Oedipal dramas of guilt and punishment, and everything to do with a radical elaboration of the very possibility of speech in its conjunctions with sensibility and presentation *as such*.[16]

In the "reports," then, we have to do with an eminently philosophical mode of "investigation" which, no longer foregrounding the metaphorics of the law, has rather emptied the latter of any sublime power in speech, an emptying-out that, in the judgment stories, is systematically pursued from within the domain of an overbearing law whose visible structure contravenes it. This conflict necessarily gives rise to a certain violence, and as mentioned above, the protagonists of these stories invariably succumb to the power they confront, even as their tales scramble the relations that allow it to be wielded. The abject, weak, and wounded artist figures that populate the later stories drastically reconfigure this process, and thus bear witness to a more radicalized destitution, one that leaves art not only stripped of its "higher" pretentions to power and grandeur, but evacuated of all its treasures, all the rich interiority and compensatory returns promised by the sublime (even in its residual, parodic, or "diabolical" forms). Borrowing a term from Freud's book on jokes and the comic, I will refer (in Chapter 4) to a *Herabsetzung des Erhabenen*, which Freud calls (using the English phrase in a note) the "degradation of the sublime," but which I will translate also as a "put-down," in every sense.[17] The joke-structure of "A Hunger Artist," in particular, will reveal the kind of deflation and destitution undergone by art's sublime strivings, along with the entire presentative schema of the earlier narratives, to which Kafka turns in that story in a highly critical, ironic mode—in order, precisely, to put them down, or to gently lay them aside, in a reconfiguration of art's relation to failure and shortfall. In tracing a movement from the scene of (autobiographical) writing to the scenography of judgment and the court, and from there toward the "vocal" modality of the report, these readings of Kafka will stop just at the threshold marked by the "joke logic" embodied by the hunger artist. Beyond this ironic figure of desublimed and empty presentation, one would have to look for something like an *enigmatics of the unpresentable* structured by an anxiety more radical than any image of judgment.

THE HOLY OF HOLIES AND THE PARABLE OF THE LOCKED BOX

I would like to begin a discussion of some motifs in Kafka's letters to Oskar Pollak by first quoting the brief text that precedes them in the *Letters*, although it was not written to Pollak but to a girl named Selma Kohn.[18] In 1900, a seventeen-year-old Kafka signed the guest book of her family's country house, and the text has been preserved. The very first in the letters, and the first in all of Kafka writings that we possess, it sets the tone and, in a strange combination of sublimity and industry, lays out the essential "terrain" of the discussion I would like to pursue, for it also points to the "treasures" that will be at issue throughout. Kafka writes:

> How many words in this book.
> They are meant for remembrance. As though words could carry memories.
> For words are clumsy mountaineers [*Bergsteiger*] and clumsy miners [*Bergmänner*]. Not for them to bring down *treasures* from the mountains' *heights*, or up from the mountains' *depths*.
> But there is a living thoughtfulness that has passed gently, like a stroking hand, over everything memorable. And when the *raging flame* shoots up out of these ashes, hot and glowing, strong and mighty, and you stare into it as though spellbound by its magic, then—
> But no one can write himself into this kind of pure mindfulness with unskillful hand and crude tools [*Handwerkszeug*]; one can write only in such white, undemanding pages [*anspruchslosen Blätter*] as these. I did so on September 4, 1900. Franz Kafka (Br 9; LFr 1; my emphasis)

Aside from the precious mood of these lines (in which one might hear certain "Heideggerian" tones), with their incantatory evocations of "remembrance" and "living thoughtfulness," this inscription presents a number of motifs that will continually reemerge in the first phases of Kafka's writing. First of all, we see Kafka doing exactly what he will do in the quotation from the early letters I have already cited (on the struggle with God to write): generating figural motifs from out of a reflection on the immediate conditions and necessity of writing. So many words! What are they for? From this question about writing, Kafka draws out numerous figures *for* the writing process, namely: ascent and descent in search of treasures buried within; a deep interior which threatens or promises to deliver a mighty fire that will exert an irresistible occult force on its immobilized and staring spectator; and finally "inscription" itself (*hineinschreiben*), a penetrating with tool and pen into a "chaste" interior, which in this case at least is not as demanding as the true treasure, since here it is merely the empty pages of a blank book. All this should also be seen in the light of a seduction that permeates the relationship framing the writing: clearly Kafka is trying to impress his addressee with his delicate poetic sensibilities and talents, even as he renounces penetration for the sake of a caress.

The rich imbrication of writing and reading with the flaming, roiling libidinal energies of an overpowering but frustrated seduction will be no less evident in the letters to Pollak that immediately follow this inscription (after an eighteen-month gap) in the *Letters*.

In the letters to Oskar Pollak, we see a young Kafka engaged in this work in the context of an ambivalent and highly charged friendship. These passionate letters are not without their own erotic overtones, as commentators have pointed out, and their drama hinges at almost every point on a tense play between self-exposure and evasion, approach and withdrawal, emotional vulnerability and sarcastic dismissiveness. The risks and attractions of self-exposure reveal these letters to be complex, rhetorically wrought documents that hold out in offering what they simultaneous retract. This ambivalence operates both at the level of what Kafka writes in the letters—the obvious passion for and identification with his addressee, the demand for an emotional reciprocity—and with regard to the all-important question of sharing writing, giving his literary efforts over to a judging gaze, in a relationship clearly fueled by literary aspirations and rivalrous competition. What is remarkable is that it is precisely in the evasions and retreats that the "more literary" passages emerge in the letters—which is to say (aside from the many fanciful images and metaphorical constructions), the interpolated narratives featuring characters, in more or less legible displacements and projections of "personal" issues into fable-like stories. Indeed, as we will see, Kafka seems to end the correspondence, and the friendship, with an idealizing parable that makes it clear that the real addressee of his writing *must be sublime*.[19] Real literature, as practiced by real, and not merely virtual, writers (like Goethe and Hebbel, who will play important roles here), demands nothing less.

"Traffic" and the Two Aestheticisms

Before looking more closely at the texts of these letters, it is important to lay out briefly some elements of the larger social and cultural context as well, for this context directly informs the process of literary self-fashioning that Kafka in his early writing is explicitly engaged in, especially as it bears on the relationship between outward appearance and a rich and authentic (but "chaste" and inaccessible) interiority. We owe a debt to Mark Anderson for his incisive discussion of this early writing which helps to clarify what might otherwise appear to be merely fanciful and arbitrary aspects of these texts, particularly with regard to Kafka's early interest in the aestheticist discourses of his day and the complex ways in which these discourses are taken up within an ambivalent relation to the urban *Verkehr* (traffic or circulation) of the paternal sphere, embodied primarily in the family business and in the superficial "accessories" associated with it, namely clothes.[20] One might most succinctly summarize this ambivalence by saying that Kafka confronted and cultivated *two distinct forms* of aestheticism which at first seem mutually exclusive, but which ultimately prove to be tightly interwoven (as it were) in Kafka's developing sense of his textual art. On the one hand, there is the superficial and alienating "aesthetic" realm embodied by Hermann Kafka's fancy goods shop, which sold clothing accessories and various "inessentials" meant to create a symbolically invested surface impression according to the social codes of a modern city; by extension, urban life itself is seen as alienating and unhealthy, in all its incessant depropriating circulation, its unclean air and unwholesome stress on mere outward *appearance*, in every sense of this word. On the other hand, and as a salutary response to the dangers of this first realm, there is a more properly "aestheticist" view, what one might call an "essentialist" aesthetics, associated with the journal *Der Kunstwart*, a socially conservative *Jugendstil* arts periodical to which both Pollak and Kafka subscribed, which touted the benefits of a more simplified and stripped down aesthetic that would merge art and life into a harmonious whole, supposedly in order to manifest and release a more authentic and essential self.[21]

These competing aestheticisms, and the stakes of their apparent opposition, imply a certain traditional religious metaphorics that is highly relevant to the letters to Pollak, and to Kafka's earliest fiction, in which the body is cast as the alienating clothing of the soul; by extension, clothes themselves—and all they represent by way of mere outward appearance, deceptive surfaces and the sullying and distorting commerce with the world of the senses—must be refashioned and reconceived.[22] One can see how, for an artist with a vexed but pronounced religious sensibility, this would pose a peculiar problem: how to manipulate appearance (as an artist must do) while cultivating and remaining faithful to a more essential and authentic self that does not readily lend itself to visible manifestation? In other words: how to *essentialize mere appearance*? This problem converges as well with a project of literary self-fashioning through which Kafka would not only become-a-writer, but would *become writing*, in order to "be literature" (as he put it later), to be absorbed without remainder into language and text—and into an exclusive vocation. In the letters to Pollak, Kafka puts it thus (after praising Marcus Aurelius, whose self-admonitions and self-directed imperatives, as paraphrased by Kafka—"be calm, be indifferent, cast passion to the wind, be steadfast"—provoke his skepticism): "It's fine if we can use words to cover ourselves up from ourselves, but even better if we can adorn and drape ourselves with words until we have become the kind of person that in our hearts we wish to be" (LFr 14; Br 26).[23] Literature is language as it fashions the writer into a being in harmony with a true (and more spiritual) interior, while still remaining a question of semblance and "appearance." Such a conception remained central to Kafka's thinking on the exigencies of writing for many years to come, though it would also have to come to terms with the ever-shifting diabolical (and residually paternal) element of false appearances implied by artistic practice, and in particular by the medium of fictive language in its endless, and ultimately ungrounded, displacements—a conception given a celebratory emblem in the "downright endless traffic" that concludes "The Judgment." Beyond that, these endless displacements come to define, formally and thematically, the linguistic and spatial movements of the novels, as well as some of the later stories. The remainderless absorption into literature would thus throw off the outer shell of a false self, but insofar as literature remains in the realm of the visible, of mere appearance and image, it will continually cast up its stripped away leavings as essential to the movement of its own construction: in writing, the outward image is *of the essence*, or in other terms, the outward visible shell *is* the kernel of the literary thing. Kafka will have to come to grips with the elusive groundlessness of this very strange sort of essence.

Finally, it should be remarked in this light that the movement into the literary element as though into a more authentic realm—and (supposedly) out of the threatening, depropriating and alienating realm of clothes, social appearance and "intercourse" (*Verkehr* as business, urban traffic, and sex)—represents for Kafka in these early writings, at least to some degree, a form of escape from and evasion of his own social, cultural and religious identity (within the urban, bourgeois and Jewish milieus of Prague). If Kafka strives to become a "self-made" man, it is in a sense quite different from that of his businessman father, Hermann Kafka, from whose shadow he spent most of his life trying to escape, as he claimed in yet another dubious hyperbole.[24] But Kafka's goal is more radical: to escape into art as an escape from the self as such.[25] Stanley Corngold, who places great stress on this aspect of Kafka, speaks rather in terms of a destruction of the self, in all its empirical determinations.[26] It seems undeniable that Kafka conceived and articulated his task as a writer, at least at some level and in certain phases, in these terms. And the ambivalent figure of clothes, as that which must be stripped away, down to an inner ground or core that would constitute the true "thing" at stake in artistic endeavor, gives an early image of this conception. What I would like to stress, however, is that if this is the case, there is always at the same time a certain *residue* that lingers in the work, *giving away* (for it is simultaneously a kind of gift, the irritating grit of an unfulfilled *Aufgabe*, and a betrayal) an empirical and singular temporal moment in the construction of the literary world, which in other respects would constitute something like an absolute, a world apart, a space radically separated from the (empirical, social, bodily and psychical) world purportedly left behind. It is in this sense too that Kafka's writing is radically autobiographical, precisely in its most extremely fictive spaces, consisting of an always incomplete passage from life to art. And it is in the gap of this incompletion that a fault opens in Kafka's writing, out of which writing will compulsively form its specific material, in the stubborn persistence of a singular imperative.

Tiny Bites

In the letters that Kafka wrote to Oskar Pollak, it is clear that he is working to open a path for this passage, while also continually elaborating the terms and figures of its specific conditions. The fact that the attempt involves an actual addressee, about whose opinions and judgments in literary matters Kafka seems to passionately care, complicates matters enormously. What it means, among other things, is that the project of forging a more true and authentic being by way of literary writing is from the start determined by the very depropriating social relation from which this project would escape: the perceiving and judging gaze of another, which in these letters is sought with the urgency of a badly needed confirmation, while also being dreaded in its powers of negation and destruction—as though this gaze were the true seat and source of the writer's being, *conferring* it no less than confirming it. Such an "eccentric" structure proves unworkable, for Kafka, at the level of the friendship in question. Without dwelling on the details of the interpersonal dramas that these letters evoke (for the most part rather obliquely), I would like to show the precise path by which, after much vacillation, Kafka moves toward a certain literary solitude, first of all with respect to his addressee, whom he idealizes to the point of disappearance, in order to replace him with a greater, more distant and more sublime judge, thus disburdening himself of a more concretely proximate one (his friend). In the end, as we will see, only the sublime gaze of literary greatness is capable of penetrating into the true essence of the upward striving soul, as it seeks its manifestation in the treacherous sphere of writing. That this penetration is also a painful wound, a kind of debasement and destitution, is an insight that coincides with the textual instantiation of the gaze that inflicts it.

From the beginning, then, the problem is how to figure the rich and authentic interiority that must be brought before such a judge. In mise-en-abyme fashion, the first attempt to do this involves the interiority precisely of one of the stand-ins for such a judgment: Goethe. *His* interiority becomes a matter of some debate after Pollak has sent Kafka a postcard from Weimar, where he has visited Goethe's home, maintained as a literary shrine and a "National Museum." Apparently, Pollak has harshly criticized this "nationalist" exploitation of Goethe, and especially of what he calls an *Allerheiligste*, a "holy of holies": the master's study. Pollak's letters are not extant, but we can infer these points from Kafka's response (dated August 24, 1902), which comes a few paragraphs after the torture-desk mentioned above (an auspicious opening to this aggressive letter), in which Kafka mocks Pollak for the "conceits and schoolboy ideas" that have led him to criticize the museum in a way that "seems to me totally twisted and wrong" (LFr 3). There follows an outburst so sarcastic it is difficult to say exactly how Kafka is trying to position himself, but the stakes of the exchange become clearer in the next paragraph, when Kafka offers—half tongue-in-cheek, half heart-pounding sincerity—another more *subtle* version of Goethe's *Allerheiligste*. In a way that is surely not coincidental, this passage will also introduce the motifs of tasting, eating, biting, and conscience that will take on greater importance as we proceed:

> But do you know what really is the most holy [*das Allerheiligste*] we could have of Goethe's as a memento [*als Andenken*]—the footprints of his solitary walks through the country—they would be it. And here comes a joke, a marvelous one, that makes God in His heaven weep bitterly and sends hell into hellish convulsions of laughter. It's this: We can never have another person's holy of holies, only our own [*nur das eigene*]—that's a joke, a marvelous one. Once before I gave you the chance to nibble

at [*angebissen*] tiny bits and pieces of it—in the Chotek gardens. You neither wept nor laughed. That's how it is—you're neither God in heaven nor the wicked devil. (LFr, 4; Br, 12)

The true "holy of holies" would thus be located not in a study with its desk and writing tools (torture instruments all, no doubt, even for the great and holy Goethe), but in the fugitive traces of the writer's rural solitude, a kind of "writing" destined to disappear unread, the inaccessible remnants lying outside the work left behind and not subject to display, but that fleetingly mark the "ground" of its authenticity, in the Nietzschean crucible of thought in walking. The "joke" that follows, with its anxious mock-levity projected (once again) into cosmic and theological dimensions, manifestly is not one; rather it expresses an insight so tragic that it requires this sharpened irony to deflate the painful truth it conveys: one can never have another person's *Allerheiligste*, only one's own—*nur das eigene*. If there is a sacred inner space associated with writing, it cannot be shared or shared out, but only metonymically evoked in its ungraspable disappearance. Pollak's response to Kafka's own samples, which he nibbled in little "bites" as though having a picnic in the park, only proves the point: neither God nor Devil, Pollak could only show a restricted and all-too-human sense of "taste" when offered this invaluable (but perhaps not fully ripe) fare, that is (one surmises), when Kafka read him some of his writing. No doubt, the weeping of gods and the laughing of demons signal the beguiling temptation to share this inaccessible treasure called "one's own," along with the devilish victory over any such attempt, in the corrupt realm of fragments and mere appearances here below. But the image of these morsels, and the scene of judgment in which they are implicated, will soon enough give way to a more all-consuming remorse and a correspondingly violent chewing over of things, as we will see in a moment. The *bite* that is risked and courted in the exposure of an otherwise inaccessible interiority will soon take on its full dramatic and narrative dimensions. At stake in this bite is the mode of appearance, the making-sensible, of a thing whose religious and metaphysical transcendence Kafka here both mocks and maintains.

The Allerheiligste *and the Remnants of Art*

Mark Anderson cites this passage on Goethe's *Allerheiligste*,[27] but only in passing and with a different purpose, and without pointing to its constitutive place in Kafka's laboriously elaborated *schema* of writing: the externalization of an "ownmost" interior that must simultaneously be reduced to its ungraspable stripped-down "naked" core, resistant to presentation, *and* be outwardly visible, be *seen* in the guise of a work of art. It is important to stress that the "religion of art" ideology into which Kafka self-consciously attempts to inscribe himself in these early writings is one that invests appearance and sensibility themselves with the chance of touching on a transcendence residing precisely there, in sensibility—that is, in a dimension of sensation that exceeds and ruins its conceptual and narrative mapping. This is the paradoxical fissure that runs, for example, through all of Proust's "philosophical" ruminations on art and the writer's vocation in his massive novel. In Kafka's case, the demands of presentation trump the more purist versions of transcendence with which they flirt, and which, for their part, become more and more minimal in their pretensions (eventually coming to be placed under the name of "nothing"). This "minimalism" is the sobriety that counter-poses Kafka's more ecstatic moods with a sense that even the greatest triumphs have their element in the realm of art, not religion. In other words, Kafka holds fast to the obtrusive residues of his strivings, however "pure, true and immutable" these may appear to be at certain moments of exultation.[28]

In this perspective, it is worth noting that in a later diary entry from the *Blue Octavo Notebooks* (January 1918), Kafka has recourse once again to the image-verging-toward-invisibility that is the *Allerheiligste*:

> Before setting foot in the Holy of Holies, you must take off your shoes, yet not only your shoes, but everything; you must take off your travelling garments and lay down your luggage; and under that you must shed your nakedness and everything that hides beneath that, and then the core [or the kernel: *den Kern*] and the core of the core, then the remainder [*das übrige*] and then the residue [*den Rest*] and then even the glimmer [*den Schein*] of the undying fire. Only the fire itself is absorbed [*aufgesogen*] by the Holy of Holies and lets itself be absorbed by it; neither can resist the other.[29] (BON, 39; HL 77)

This paragraph is followed by another one-line entry, separated by a space: "Not shaking off the self, but consuming the self [*Selbstaufzehrung*]." These remarks too were written around the time of "A Country Doctor," during a period when Kafka was struggling, both personally and as an artist, to negotiate, in rather ponderous theological terms, the boundaries between life and its other (Deleuze and Guattari state simply that he was "sad, tired . . . incapable of writing"[30]). Here Kafka indulges in an image of remainderless "absorption" and "consumption." But insofar as it is an image for the process of writing, it does not do justice to the artistic and textual by-product (so to speak) in which such reflections sit quite uncomfortably, for if it expresses a certain ideal of disappearance for Kafka, it also implies this ideal's ruination when it comes to the *work* that would be the inevitable remainder of this process. The very existence of the fragment itself attests to the way in which this ideal falls into the ruins of its own visible figurations. And Kafka knows that there is no escaping from the irreducible remnant of a *Schein* that adheres even to the radical projection of pure and total disappearance and "self-consumption." Indeed, the use of these concrete terms to describe this impossible process—in which clothes, shell, kernel, remainder, residue, fire, and merest semblance itself is either stripped away or invisibly dissolved (or slurped up, *aufgesogen*) leaving only the leftover of speech itself—provides something like a figural key to Kafka's paradigm of spiritual failure. It is this, too, that he shares with Blanchot and Beckett—in precisely the same terms and through the same figures. Another name for this remnant failure is also the name of the written work that it secures, namely *fiction*. This fragment bears witness to the inevitability of this failure-in-fiction precisely there where all figuration would be abjured, dissolved, and swallowed whole.[31]

The Teeth in the Box

If we return to the letters to Pollak, in which the specter of appearance is experienced as the hyperbolic anxiety of a possible failure *to appear* (rather than in the calm cryptic mode of parabolic pronunciation), it is clear that a different kind of "consumption" is at stake: piecemeal bites that leave a bad taste, a distinct residue of doubt as to the very existence of a *Schein*, much less of a fire to project or absorb it. The concern, at this point, is less with the pure flame itself than with the little bits of it that manage to find their way out as ingestible solids. It is this externalizing process that Kafka wants to bring into the rigors of discipline and outwardly sharable work; his complaints of "not writing for some time" attest to this, as do the many figures of such an upbringing, updigging, or uphauling movement that would render the inner treasure. That is again how he speaks of it, for example, in a letter (dated "September 6 [1903?]" [*sic*]), when he writes to Pollak of the "high hopes" he had for the summer, which he blurts out in a kind of confession: "I'll say it: to bring out at one stroke what I believe I have in me (I don't always believe it)" (LFr 7; Br 17). The key phrase is this: to bring out at one stroke, *in einem Zug zu heben*. A very literal translation would be "to bring *up*" in one draw or draft, one tug or pull, what I have inside. I especially underscore the expression, *in einem Zug*, in that it remarkably anticipates the terms in which, some ten years later, Kafka will celebrate the ecstatic composition of his first truly successful haul, to be titled "The Judgment." He wrote this story, he says in this well known diary entry, "*in einem Zug*," lifting it out of himself "like a birth," during a long night of extraordinary and continuous "effort" and "joy" (D 212; TB 214). The repetition of this relatively common German phrase (which will occur elsewhere as well) might not be so significant if the expression did not succinctly encapsulate the ideal of continuity and cohesiveness that powerfully and explicitly governs Kafka's writing throughout its first long phase (as the early *Diaries* make clear). This image thus adds an important element to the peculiar imperative that Kafka is formulating in this early writing: not only to "bring out" an as yet unverified inner richness, but to do so in an uninterrupted and continuous whole, a totality which, in a forceful persuasion, would thereby confirm the existence of what it manifests. This is the formal and "generic" model that will govern Kafka's strivings for many years—and one reason why he turns so decisively toward the short story as its most fitting realization.

Of course, at one level the imagery of writing as "expression" (excavation or expectoration, mined treasure or secreted substance—Beckett will call it "oozing"), as the "outing" of an inner richness, is utterly banal. It is the bedrock myth of a certain rough and general "romanticism" which Kafka worked hard to inherit and to rearticulate. What is curious, and highly determining, in Kafka's case are the particular corporeal, and more specifically the oral, gustatory and even *dental* forms this mythic metaphor takes. It is very much a question of physical exposure and bodily mutilation, of a biting into the "stuff" (*Sache*, but also *Stoff*) that Kafka has to offer to his addressee—this in close association with the dilemma of whether to share at all or whether, instead, to keep it to oneself and hold fast to isolation. Following just after the passage quoted above, Kafka plays fancifully on the image of a nameless tight-lipped companion who for that reason makes him "uncomfortable," and then he writes, suddenly inserting an odd, unlocatable narrative:

> Now, however, there's something that's tearing my lips wide apart, or is it a gentler feeling, no, tearing is right—and someone who is standing behind the tree says softly to me: "You won't do anything without others." But I am now writing solemnly and with choice sentence structure: "Isolation is repulsive; honestly lay your eggs out before all the world and the sun will hatch them; better to bite into life than bite your tongue; honor the mole and its ilk but don't make it into one of your saints." (LFr 8; Br 17–18)

Kafka will indeed have to bite his tongue over these resolutions, which demand the exact opposite of what he ended up doing, at least with respect to—and even within—his writing; for while he did not make the mole a saint, he did make it, first, a miraculously outsized object of rumor, in "The Giant Mole," then later, in "The Burrow," into the very figure of the deeply solitary anxious artist (or "*Baumeister*") seeking to defend his hidden treasures from all external enemies, that is, from all externality, period. (And of course most of Kafka's "eggs" hatched only posthumously, thanks to the light beamed at them by his impresario, Max Brod.) Now what is the relationship between "biting into life" and biting into text—or giving it out to be bitten? This entire discourse is the prologue to an announcement that he will be sending Pollak a "bundle" that "will contain everything I have written up to now," or almost: for, he says, there are "things I cannot show even to you, for we shudder to stand naked and be fingered by others, even if we have begged on our knees for that very thing" (LFr 8; Br 18). Despite the ambivalence over this troubling encounter—part clinical checkup, part erotic stimulation—when it comes to all this "merely cool" stuff, he says, "I know that another pair of eyes will make everything warmer and livelier when they look at it" (LFr 9; Br 19). The "life" in question thus seems to be represented by a trusted but (therefore) dangerous recipient of these treasures, whose gaze has the power to give their possibly dead matter a life they did not have before, and may not have at all—but that also, by implication, brings the risk of a destructive, deadly violence. Lest Pollak miss the vulnerability involved in this textual-bodily exposure and dissection, Kafka concludes by saying, "I am taking a piece [*Stück*] (for I can do more than what I am giving you, and I shall—yes), a piece of my heart, packing it in a few sheets of inscribed paper, and I'm giving it to you" (LFr 9; Br 19). In a gesture of love that merges writing and affection in this unmistakable metaphor, Kafka, strange butcher of his own palpitating inwardness, extracts the dearest piece of himself and sends it wrapped in writing to its "indifferent" or "reluctant" addressee (words he uses in imagining Pollak reading what he is sending)—with the mitigating promise that there is so much more, that I know I can do better!

Clearly Kafka is worried about the reception that may await this inwardly held "stuff," now cast out through the mail, and he has invested a great deal in the judgment and taste of its recipient. The letters give no indication of Pollak's response. The correspondence continues for another five months, during which time it appears that the two visited each other at least twice (November 9, 1903: "Perhaps I am glad you have left"; December 21, 1903: "I'll soon be able to talk with you"), but the last two letters follow soon after, in January 1904. These extraordinary final letters are crucial to the schema and the trajectory I am tracing; they clearly show Kafka taking his distance, retreating into the inaccessible uniqueness of his "own," far from even the closest friends, and disengaging the "inner" treasure of writing from the judgment of any specific addressee. After this leavetaking, most of Kafka's letters in this volume are addressed to Max Brod, with whom he had an entirely different kind of relationship. Indeed, Brod reports his surprise, and evident jealousy, on finding these effusive offers on Kafka's part to share his writing, whereas later with Brod it was rather like pulling teeth.[32] With Pollak, Kafka pulled them himself. Indeed, he presents these teeth as such, enigmatically and quite literally, in the penultimate letter of their correspondence.

This letter contains one of Kafka's first parables, which I will refer to as the *parable of the locked box*. Its "literariness," its figural and narrative density as a stand-alone fiction, is an index of the distance it is meant to open (one almost has the impression that Kafka wrote it first on its own, then found a way to incorporate it into the letter). This distance is also indicated by Kafka's remarks as he leads up to the story, where he describes how "embarrassing and incomprehensible" it is when someone "takes my arm" (the German, *sich einhängt*, also evokes the linked interdependence of "hanging onto" someone); but the tale itself hinges entirely around the major problem I have been exploring, namely the meager or null possibility of revealing one's enclosed interiority—or rather, conversely, the strange spectacle of emphatically, ostentatiously refusing to do so, the problematic pretense of even possessing such a precious hidden thing, as well as the equivocal position of any spectators who might witness such a negative performance. The story thus provides yet another version of the *Allerheiligste*, one complicated by its own enigmatic demystification. The passage comes just after the reference to Marcus Aurelius, and the wish to drape oneself with words, quoted above. I give it here in its entirety:

> Do you know what is special about some people? They are nothing, but they cannot show it, cannot even show it to their own eyes, that is what is special about them. All these people are the brothers of the man who went about the city, knew nothing [understood nothing: *sich auf nichts verstand*], could not bring out a sensible [reasonable, rational: *vernünftiges*] word, could not dance, could not laugh, but con-

stantly carried about, clutched tightly in both hands, a locked box [*eine verschlossene Schachtel*]. If some sympathetic person [someone taking part: *ein Teilnehmender*] asked, "What are you carrying in the box so carefully?" the man drooped [*senkte*] his head and said uncertainly: "I know nothing, that's true, and I can't bring out a sensible word, I can't dance either and I can't laugh, but what is in this locked box, that I cannot tell [*sagen*], no, no, that I will not tell." After an answer like that all the sympathetic people naturally drifted away, but a certain curiosity, a certain suspense, lingered in many of them and they went on asking, "What is in the locked box?" And for the sake of the box they came back to see the man every so often, but he revealed nothing [betrayed nothing: *nichts verriet*]. Well, curiosity, that kind of curiosity, doesn't last, and suspense dissipates; and in the end no one can stop himself [*niemand hält es aus*] from smiling when an insignificant-looking locked box is everlastingly guarded with inexplicable anxiousness. Then again, we've given the poor man a halfway decent sense of taste [*Geschmack*], maybe he'll come round to smiling himself, though somewhat crookedly. —Now instead of curiosity there is indifferent, distant pity, worse than indifference and distance. The sympathizers, fewer in number than in the past, now ask: "Whatever are you carrying around in the box so cautiously? Maybe a *treasure*, eh, or a proclamation [an annunciation: *eine Verkündigung*]? Anyhow, open it up; we need both; oh well, leave it closed, we believe you anyhow." Whereupon suddenly there was an especially shrill scream; the man looks around startled; it was himself. After his death, the box was found to contain *two milk teeth*. (LFr 14–15; Br 26–27; my emphasis)

In light of the previous remarks, one might well translate *Schachtel* here as "packet," in order to evoke the "bundle" of writing on which Kafka has staked his own self-exposure. The difference is that this packet remains locked unto death. Kafka closes the letter at the end of this story, simply signing "Franz" (rather like a painter signing his canvas than a friend signing a letter), as though this portrait had given away (*verriet*) enough. But if the tale is a self-portrait, it gives (itself) away also by turning away, by averting into literature, by turning (troping) into the density and impersonality of a relatively autonomous narrative. This turn, a peculiar hybrid of self-exposure and extreme evasion, is one of the major modes of Kafka's writerly compulsion in the "personal" documents we have from his pen. That it takes the form of a riddle *and* a demystification—a puzzling over the redolent and opaque remainder *of* a demystification—says a great deal about the nature of this turn and its animating force, as it hinges around the unstable border between "inside" and "outside."

I find it impossible not to read this tale retrospectively, in the light of a later one for which it is practically a first draft: "A Hunger Artist," written some twenty years later, shares its basic structure, its central dilemma, and even the arc of its plot, not to mention some of its precise language. The spectacle of a man emphatically *presenting* himself as *refraining* from something at first draws a crowd, but interest wanes, indifference sets in, and the entire abject affair ends with a kind of punch line, a final revelation of the true banality at the heart and kernel of it all. The linguistic repetition involves the significant and parallel use of the verb *aushalten* (to hold out or endure): just as the spectators in the locked box parable cannot "hold out" in their increasingly frustrated effort not to smile (*niemand hält es aus, nicht endlich zu lächeln*), so does the hunger artist wonder why his spectators are so impatient that they cannot "hold out" longer than forty days: "If he endured [*aushielt*] fasting for longer, why wouldn't they endure [*aushalten*] it?" (CS 271; E 194). The limit marked in both cases is that of a public no longer willing to "take seriously" the far-fetched demands of such a ridiculous and childlike performance, which is undercut in the end by the mundane banality of the "object" at issue. These objects are closely associated and yet each is of a different order: milk teeth versus mere hunger. But in both cases, this banality presents the further enigma of an irresolvable residue: "I had to fast, I couldn't help it . . . I couldn't find the food I liked," says the hunger artist, as in his dying breath he poses an even more recalcitrant riddle than his pseudo-sublimely pretentious fasting: why was no food good enough? (Here's a hint: don't bother asking a panther.)

Surely it is no accident that the image in question in the locked box parable also evokes eating, nourishment, loss, and death. These milk teeth are a kind of tombstone to hunger fulfilled. In one sense, their revelation does not justify all the fuss the man makes to draw attention to the intriguing fact that he *cannot say* what is in the box. They are no "treasure," they announce nothing—or rather, they are this and do this not for the audience their occlusion fails to hold, but only for him, as part of a miniature and private *Allerheiligste*. Mere leftovers of a life, intimate ciphers of a henceforth illegible past, they are the metonymic figures for a passion and pathos that, however, they do not and cannot effectively communicate, but can only stand for. The milk teeth are a treasure, then, a very telling one, but as such they are equivocal and opaque. Strictly speaking, we do not even know whether the teeth are his own or whether (to push the pathos further) they belonged to a lost beloved being; but this is not decisive. For what they mark, ultimately, and precisely as a mute metonymic embodiment, are the vulnerability of bodily and affective exposure, the breach between past and present, and a kind of wound constitutive of time itself, of a "life time," so to speak. The milk teeth, as residues of a singular life, are the obtrusive kernel at the empty "core" of an irritating drive to *manifest*. The man's stripping down (he cannot speak, cannot laugh, cannot dance . . .) leaves them as the sole remainder of a radical despoliation, a *dépouillement* (to use a term I will return to in discussing Blanchot) that cannot resolve into a mere nothing of nothing. The leftover milk teeth give an image of *what must be told*. Hence the conversion of the tale's initial "nothing," which cannot be shown, into these banal things, this speechless but determinate *something*, performs the inevitable "betrayal" always risked by radical fiction in its hyperbologic mode. The displaced sentimental and autobiographical kernel of a fictional work that would be absolute thus issues in a residue that demands narration by both defying it and hollowing it out, leaving the shell it cannot cast off.

In this parable of the locked box, then, an outward surface *seems* to harbor something extraordinary, but the remainderless stripping down required by the *Allerheiligste* reveals not the impossible disappearing core of the core of the true inner self's flame-like spiritual essence (etc.), but rather a little resistant piece of singular time (actually, two little pieces, but why two?), the multiple concrete residue of *a* past, and by extension the woundlike opening of that strange breach in being called "hunger." I will broach the question later, in a further discussion of "A Hunger Artist," as to whether this breach ought to be considered, in some problematic sense, as a form of transcendence, and what the point of that would be. It would have to be a point touching directly on this wound and its mordant insistence in the formation of a problematic economy of writing.

THE WOUND OF CONSCIENCE: SUBLIME EXAMPLES

That is exactly the point, a sharp and biting one, that Kafka touches on in his last extraordinary letter to Pollak, to which I now turn. It is a letter on the sublime nature of the linguistic experience required by and for "great literature" (the phrase is never used, but it is everywhere implied). It is also a mystifying and mythologizing gesture that puts an end to a friendship and fixes the fundamental schema of Kafka's relation to the act of writing—and of the narratives that it unfolds—for the dozen or so crucial years to follow.

To approach this letter, it is necessary to take a brief step back into the preceding letters, in order to delineate one essential aspect of the relationship that is in play throughout, but that is violently refigured in the end: Kafka's intense *identification* with his addressee, that is, with the one to whom he exposes himself (his writing), and before whose friendly but powerful and dangerous gaze he places himself in part to be judged. At one level, this gaze is projected as an intimate, domesticated and orienting view that provides Kafka with a way to see outside, that is, as a clarifying "window" on the confusing welter of the external world. In one of the letters' most breathless declarations, Kafka writes:

> I have really spoken with you alone, among all the young people, and when I did talk to others it was only incidental or for your sake or through you or in reference to you. For me, you were, along with much else, also something like a window through which I could see the streets. (November 9, 1903; LFr 9; Br, 20)

To speak here of "identification" also means—I think this is clear—to speak of love, a stabilizing (if narcissistic) attachment that gives some sense to the world of "traffic" in the streets outside. Such feelings tend to elevate their "object," of course, and therefore the gaze they project and situate. This is clearly the case in the paragraph just quoted, which continues and concludes with one further sentence: "Alone, I could not do that, for tall though I am, I do not yet reach to the windowsill" (ibid.). In the dialectic between solitude and the sharing (out) of life (of writing), the writer is manifestly undergoing a certain uplift. But it is precisely this elevating and idealizing movement that leads past Pollak, the concrete addressee, toward the sublime projections of the final letter. Already at the beginning of the letter just quoted, the extreme elevation in question, and its dependence on a projected judging gaze, is humorously cast in terms that are no longer theological but rather *astronomical*. The letter begins:

> Dear Oskar, Perhaps I am glad you left, as glad as people would have to be if someone climbed to the moon to look at them from there, for this sense of being observed from such height and distance would give people some small assurance that their movements and words and wishes are not altogether comical and foolish, as long as astronomers in their observatories hear no laughter from the moon. (LFr 9; Br 19)

Pollak has not gone to the moon, but rather to a castle near Pilsen (Plzen), where he has been hired as a tutor. For Kafka the prospect of being regarded from on high, and from a great distance, is consoling, but it contains the potential for mockery and humiliation—as though this height and distance also revealed a kind of transparency, a gaze not only down but also through and within, somehow confirmed by strange telescopes that could hear the lunar laughter. I will have occasion to comment further on the optico-astronomical metaphors introduced here and occurring, with a strange structuring significance that reaches deep into the fiction, in the early *Diaries* as well.[33] For the moment, I would like to interject two brief remarks that look toward later fictions and help to clarify the fundamental shift that will take place in Kafka's itinerary after the judgment stories. While Pollak in his castle elicits this image of celestial spectatorship, with its all-observant meaning-giving gaze, Kafka's later image of ubiquitous observation, which occurs precisely in a work called *The Castle*, is pointedly lacking in this unifying cohesion: if K. is supervised, it is haphazardly, partially, and downright inaccurately (as is evident from Klamm's second letter, which congratulates K. for work he has not done); the principle of cohesion in *The Castle* cannot be attributed to such an elevated gaze, but rather resides in the discursive interweavings of the various serially encountered characters—this despite the "vertical" and unifying illusions created by this weave itself, for which there is no better name than *rumor*. Likewise, the powerful (Oedipal) judging gaze that not only looks down but also "sees through" into a defaulting interior is the structuring moment of the "The Judgment," as we will see. In that story, Georg's father speaks of "seeing through" (*durchschauen*) (E 51) his son, and it is precisely his ability to grasp and reconfigure the totality of the fictive situation, inside and out, that makes him the terrifying instance of destructive judgment he turns out to be. In the letters to Pollak, the consoling cosmic gaze is thus also the germ of a dangerous panoptic threat, a menacing eye of judgment—and the form of judgment is laughter. Keeping in mind that this is the same letter which ends with Kafka's proclamation that "God doesn't want me to write, but I, I must," together with the devilish laughter evoked in the letter on the *Allerheiligste*, we can see that a vast stage is set for an *agōn* not only between the writer and his God, but also between the real reading judge to whom Kafka addresses himself in these letters (Pollak), and another much mightier or, one might even say, *hungrier* one looming beyond them. For here too, in this sadistic and devouring gaze, it turns out to be a question of biting, eating, chewing, and being dangerously enveloped and "absorbed."

It is with just such images that Kafka begins the final "tale" of his correspondence with Pollak, in a complex of figures this time addressed directly to him (its goal being an unequivocal dismissal), and presented as a *parable of literary conscience* based on a striking scene of sublime exemplarity. Fittingly, it begins with an apology, and an assertion of the high stakes in play in the letter itself. I have not responded in weeks to your "dear letter," writes Kafka, partly because my answer would be "more important than any other previous letter I have written to you," and partly because:

> I read Hebbel's diaries (some 1800 pages) all at once [*in einem Zuge*], whereas previously I had always just bitten out [*herausgebissen*] small pieces that struck me as insipid [*geschmacklos*]. All the same I started to read consecutively [*im Zusammenhange*]. At first it was just a game, but eventually I came to feel like a caveman who rolls a block in front of the entrance to his cave, initially as a joke and out of boredom, but then, when the block makes the cave dark and shuts off the air, feels dully alarmed and with remarkable energy tries to push the rock away. But by then it has become ten times heavier and the man has to wrestle with it with all his might before light and air return. I simply could not take a pen in hand during these days. Because when you're surveying [*überblickt*] a life like that, which *towers higher and higher without a gap* [*ohne Lücke wieder und wieder höher türmt*], so high you can scarcely reach it with your field glasses [*Fernrohren*], your conscience cannot settle down. But it's good when your conscience receives big wounds, because that makes it more sensitive to every bite [*Biss*]. (LFr 15; Br 27; my emphasis)

Once again Kafka brings to bear the profusion of a figural and hyperbolic imagination in a maneuver designed both as evasive self-defense and as the exposure of extreme vulnerability (and as before, the figural elaboration emerges from the gap between the two). Everything here depends on the consolidation of an elevated and idealized exemplar who is set off against the poor dumb caveman creature haplessly burdened with an impossible task, on which his survival suddenly depends. Consolidation, as solidification, is given as petrifaction, and the "everlasting up and down" with God is rendered here as a mere heaving against the downpressing force of a "block"—that of a caveman-reader, but also by extension, as Kafka explains, a writer's block, preventing him from taking up his pen (I will return to this ticklish plume or *Feder* in a moment). If it is a question in this scene of constraint and compulsion, then, it is that of a reader who finds himself overwhelmed, overshadowed, and "blocked" in. But the block is quickly transformed into a more properly awe-inspiring "tower," the massive structure of a life looming beyond the reach even of a telescopic view, gaplessly filling and exceeding the field of vision. Unlike the mock hyperbole that places Pollak on the moon, this image beyond image, as an example of plenitude and immensity, is sublime in the most classic, literal and *painful* sense possible; it is the sublime of elevation, grandeur, and power, but likewise of a crushing immensity that communicates the force of the law it instantiates by rendering sensible an ideal. In terms of tone, the humor of the not-even-Sisyphean (premythic) caveman gives way to a deadly earnest gravity stripped of the manic irony that marks the fanciful exaggerations of earlier letters in the correspondence.

Before resorting to these images of massive weight and size, however, Kafka begins by mobilizing the familiar metaphorics of eating, biting, and ingesting, all modes of reading's cumulative incorporations. Here he takes his revenge on the summary judgments of taste—or tastelessness—based on mere piecemeal bites (as occurred with Pollak in the Chotek garden), but it is he himself who suffers this revenge. Here the tentative biter himself becomes engrossed, engulfed, and engorged by what he is attempting to assimilate.[34] The sacred interiority of an *Allerheiligste* and its subtle essences has become a gloomy and imprisoning inner space that can best be likened to a tomb: the reader is buried alive (or, in another register: it is he himself that is locked in the box). He is eaten and bitten where it hurts most of all, in what he calls his *conscience*. This bitten conscience—the mordant sensitivity of a *Gewissensbiss* (the common German term for the "bite" or pangs of conscience)—arises from the attempt to ingest a totality, to take in a text *and* the exemplary life it relates, in one continuous movement, *in einem Zuge*, and in its cohesive unity, *im Zusammenhange*. We encountered the former phrase above, where it was a question of "bringing up what I have inside me"; here the train is turned, and Kafka takes down in a single draft something that by this sustained effort is rendered in its properly sublime aspect. The phrase and its companion together designate a textual and artistic ideal that is itself both the product and the cause of an abyssal sensitivity, the massive gnawing, gnawed, and twitching wound of a literary bad conscience.

A Kantian Scene?

Regardless of any question of direct influence, the classical topos of the Kantian sublime—in its problematic intersection with a moral law accessed through a painful, negatively felt exemplification—could not be more evident here (though it is also inflected with distinctly Freudian tones that would have to be considered as well: one could say that what is at issue is a form of castration that projects its own compensatory assumption of authority). The name that Kant gives this problematic intersection is *respect* (*Achtung*), that feeling which is not one, the incentive or *Triebfeder* by which the moral law in all its binding but merely formal power is capable of moving us pathological creatures, who are bound for the most part rather to our affects and inclinations. To formulate this motif as it appears in Kafka, one could use a revealing play on words: if the young writer is blocked and crushed by the sublime example, and is incapable of taking up his pen, his *Feder*, he nonetheless finds in the open wound inflicted by this overwhelming example the "incentive" of an extreme writing ethos, the *Triebfeder* as a *drive of writing* spurred by an affective tonality (*Stimmung*) unmistakably similar to the negative affects of Kant's sublime violence and the moral vocation (*Bestimmung*) to which it attests, whose "positive" side is respect. For Kant, this respect is the *only* legitimate *Triebfeder*, the only nonpathological "feeling" in which true moral actions can rightly find their motivating ground; but it does its work through a number of necessarily painful affects, variously enumerated by Kant in terms of an infringement (*Abbruch*) or thwarting (*Eintrag*) of inclination and self-love, a weakening, humiliating and striking down (*Niederschlag*) of self-conceit, harsh resistance to sensible incentives, intimidation, casting of reproach, and finally a submission or subjection (*Unterwerfung*) to the absolute commands of the moral law.[35] Indeed, many of these affects/effects—whose names evoke breaking, forcefully inserting, battering and hurling down—are vehiculated by the powerful example of a person who imposes respect, not for himself *as* a person, but for the moral law which speaks through him (Kant refers later to a "voice" of practical reason [CPrR 204]), and thus "either casts a reproach [*Vorwürfe*] on us or imposes on us the following of such an example in the way suitable to us" (CPrR 203). Kant touches closely (though in the converse direction) on the matter at hand for Kafka, when in one passage he points to the effort made to "find fault" with these exemplary figures, in order "to compensate us for the humiliation that comes upon us through such an example" and to try to "lighten the burden of it for us." "Even the dead," writes Kant, "are not always safe from this critical examination, especially if their example appears *inimitable*" (CPrR 202; my emphasis). He concludes the paragraph with the following, which describes a defensive impulse that Kafka will forgo, for the sake of a complete and ecstatic submission:

> This respect, then, which we show to such a person (strictly speaking to the law that his example holds before us) is not mere admiration [*Bewunderung*], as is also confirmed by this: that when the common run of admirers believes it has somehow learned the badness of character of such a man (such as Voltaire) it gives up respect for him, whereas the true scholar still feels it at least with regard to his talents, because he is himself engaged in a business and a calling [*Berufe*] that make imitation of such a man to some extent a law for him. (CPrR 203)

For his part, Kafka does not attempt to lighten this burden by finding faults or gaps; on the contrary he exults in the magnificent but painful spectacle of an imposing and unending faultlessness ("higher and higher without a gap"). He wants to take on the Law, to take it in, to appropriate it; and he senses that in order to do so he must, impossibly, imitate this example, or rather: that it is imperative to strive toward this (inimitable) exemplarity in a way that is radically singular. But how to cultivate one's own inimitability? A preposterous and unattainable goal, it nonetheless bears down on the young writer precisely as a "calling," a vocation, and "to some extent a law." But only to some extent. For what is the real, effective law that is called and evoked by such an example? If we turn to a closely related text by Kant, we find a surprisingly relevant and even banal answer. In a long footnote from Section I of the *Groundwork*, Kant poses the problem of exemplarity and respect in terms nearly identical to those in the *Critique of Practical Reason*, but this time he stresses the *cultivation of talent by practice*. "Because we regard enlarging our talents as a duty, we represent a person of talents also as, so to speak, *an example of the law* (to become like him in this by practice), and this is what constitutes our respect" (Gr 56; Kant's emphasis). It is precisely in this manner, and to this extent, that the sublime exemplary figure dictates a burdensome law—a command not to figurally imitate by copying, but to laboriously cultivate what is given as "my own." The sublime law as it impinges on the young Kafka's literary conscience, is thus primarily a law of *disciplinary practice*, an injunction derived from the idealizing (and toweringly phallic) projection of a mighty plenitude, apparently achievable in turn only by these pitiful and inadequate means. Hence the pain and pang of the wound. It is not difficult to see that an intensive regime of (self-)punishment must be an intimate part of this process. The towering heights are structurally conditioned by a very low ground of debasement, but one that seems, after all, to hold out the possibility of redemptive elevation, as implied by the "good" that Kafka claims a bad conscience can do. But the fault, if there is one, thus lies with the one who merits this punishment, which is to say: this chance of elevation in turn.

In something of an inverted anticipation of the debasement in question, which will return in a decisive manner in Kafka's late fiction (especially in "A Hunger Artist"), I will leave Kant for now by quoting an ultimate, incredulous complaint, in which he takes to its extreme the criticism of those who *find fault* with the source of an unbearable moral burden, which they attempt to lighten by diminishing the "terrifying" (*abschreckenden*) and humiliating force of respect: "Even the moral law itself in its *solemn majesty* is exposed to this striving to resist respect for it." Why else, he asks, would we be so ready "to demean [*herabwürdigen*] it to our familiar inclination?" (CPrR 202; Kant's emphasis). Such a "demeaning" movement—from powerful sublimity and the subjection/subjectification it demands to a lowly compulsive sensibility harboring abjection—is precisely the one at stake in the larger trajectory we are tracing. For if the young Kafka discovers an exemplar without faults ("*ohne Lücke*"), he also dramatizes its violence as the wounding force of a bitten bad conscience that would henceforth serve as its affective site and drive—and these in turn stand to lose their own transcendental urgencies. The sublime, in the palpable *force* of its elevation and grandeur, is necessarily contaminated by the mundane banality of sensibility, such that these two registers enter a zone of indistinction, making it possible to "bring down" the uncompromising ethical imperative by the very sensibility it must solicit. If Kant is scandalized by the downward movement of a *Herabwürdigung*, Freud, for his part, will find it rather a matter for joking, in the *Herabsetzung des Erhabenen* that constitutes one mode of the comic.[36] This parallel in language between Kant and Freud (*Herabwürdigung, Herabsetzung*), one that bears precisely on a displacement in the aesthetic and moral vocation of the sublime, indicates a crucial realignment of the relation between law and affect, in which a strict separation between feeling and the categorical Law becomes, rather, a gnarled and obscured entanglement. For when Freud rereads the sublimity of the moral law, he also thinks in terms of "pathology," not as a paradoxical breach of its pure grounding, but as that which *constitutes* it, specifically in the psychic instantiation of a superego, with its basis in melancholia and the castration complex. And in the "categorical imperative" he hears quite distinctly (as Nietzsche did before him) the sadistic beratement of a complex drive structure converging in the cruel vocal phenomenon known as *conscience*. Indeed, the *bite* of this conscience receives a further elaboration when Freud links it directly to "incorporation," cannibalism, and sadistic orality.[37] The sublime, in its relation to the voice of the moral law, thus enters the register of a ravenous hunger—so that, with regard to Kafka, we should not be surprised to see the emaciated figure of the hunger artist on the horizon of this scene. It is in this light that the irresistible downward draw into a complexly determined *embodiment* of moral life, inextricable from all "higher" striving, links the sublime to Kafka's wound in the more problematic modes of punishment, discipline, self-surveillance, and the pathological (and painful) subjection to bad conscience itself.

Bite, Stab, Fist, Ax

Kafka's language enters this register even more vividly and unequivocally in the sentences immediately following the invocation of conscience quoted above, in the penultimate paragraph of the final letter to Pollak. The bodily penetration wrought by an invasive hacking is here elaborated in all its violence. At the same time, the transition from the sublime *figure* to the powerful wounding force of his *corpus*, that is, from a massive and faultless life to the downpressing text that has issued from it, is made by locating the bite of conscience in a strange bookish materiality, and in images of what they *should do* to us:

> I believe we ought to read only the kind of books that bite and stab us [*beissen und stechen*]. If the book we're reading doesn't wake us up with a blow of the fist [*Faustschlag*] on the skull, what are we reading it for? So that it will make us happy [*glücklich*], as you write? My God, we would be happy precisely if we had no books, and the kind of books that make us happy are the kind we could write ourselves if we had to. But we need the books that affect us like a misfortune that causes us pain [*wie ein Unglück, das uns schmerzt*], like the death of someone we loved more than

46   KAFKA

>   ourselves, like being banished into forests far from everyone, like a suicide. A book
>   must be the axe for the frozen sea inside us. That is my belief [*Das glaube ich*].
>   (LFr 16; Br 27–28)

This passage is well known. It is often cited without reference to its place in these letters, no doubt precisely because of its general manifesto-like quality, its (quite literal) status as a "credo" ("This I believe"). As with other similar statements, it too stands to benefit, in its hyperbole and "absolutism," from a clearer sense of its context, if only by measuring the distance it marks from the precious stylized turns that wind through the rest of the correspondence with Pollak—which this letter abruptly brings to an end. The passage is hyperbolic, high-flown, heavily emphatic and "extremist," but it is all these things in a distinctly different tonality, and by way of a very different set of images, in comparison to what has come before. To put the point in an image: we are no longer strolling in the bucolic countryside where Goethe left his fugitive footprints, but are rather wandering in a wasted landscape of exile and totalizing loss, in a specific figural shift from ephemeral *Fußspuren* to an indelible (and yet no less Goethean) *Faustschlag*.[38] In other words—and in distinction from the merely frustrated enjoyment of an otherwise secure inner treasure—we are in a space of infinite and irrevocable punishment and expropriation, not merely anxious alienation but an utterly devastating expulsion. Likewise, the intimacy of the *Allerheiligste* has been turned out, as it were, into a radical and open exterior, located out there, in the woods, in banishment, in one's own death, in the *Unglück* of acute melancholic pain, the destitution of "one's own," and the tragic assumption of infinite mourning. Oedipus as the castrated (blinded) exile, not as the pompous ass unwittingly in search of himself (that is, Oedipus as imagined by Hölderlin, destined to "wander under the unthinkable"): does this not give the true abject image of Kant's uplifting *Niederschlag*, here rendered as the result of an awakening *Faustschlag*? (We are speaking of a Kant who understood nothing about tragedy, including the tragic implications of his own thought, its terrible wound to philosophy and to *speculation*, and its banishment of the absolute—a wound acutely lived by Hölderlin.)[39]

It is as though, with this unmitigated melancholic *Stimmung*, the young and somewhat manic Kafka of these letters, the Jugendstil-inspired aesthete engaged in a radical self-fashioning, has rather "found his voice" in the evocation of literary conscience as a sublime punishment. The images for this experience come forth in grave and measured profusion, and in an authoritative tone that signals the assumption of the very Law whose breach the images would figure. But they also collect to form a vector pointing toward the distant origin of authority and punishment itself, the true sublime moment in these proliferating emblems: for the violent blows delivered in this catastrophe of bad conscience would have to be imposed by a judging instance outstripping even the towering figure of Hebbel. There is implied here a lawlike power by which the dull (untasting) reader evoked at the beginning is permanently stricken, liquidating all "proper" interiority, leaving only a wound, strange site of an endless unsavory parasitic gnawing, which is also a more purely violent *stabbing* (an image that anticipates the permanent letdown staged in "In the Penal Colony"). Only thus does the sublime bad conscience come, paradoxically, into "its own," in a tragic depropriation giving voice to a totalizing loss. But if this wound opens a "vocation" and establishes a kind of duty ("we ought to . . ." "a book must be . . .") in its "incentivizing" function as commandment and law, it does not dictate a specific task or the content of an act that would exonerate, restore, or redeem; it does not provide a rule derived from or legible in the sublime example. In this it still resembles, on one side, the Kantian moral law, and this empty indeterminacy will structure all of Kafka's judgment fictions (especially *The Trial*). But, in its aspect as a painful outward drive, the wound marks the site of a compulsive and ambivalently cathected source of speech and language: the imperative as gnawing pain and seeping "ooze" (to repeat Beckett's image), as implied also by the image of a frozen sea hacked open, a bleeding and release of the stuff locked away "in us."[40]

The fate of this inner treasure is thus bound up with the pain-inflicting voice, not of "pure reason" (the law in its pure formality) but of a materially and affectively brutal conscience, a punitive and destituting *Stimmung* that for Kafka *is literary*, insofar as it opens (reopens) the space of language's originary fault, its being driven by the pressure of a painful but exhilarating *il faut*. This "vocalization" of conscience might well be likened to a "call" that would plot the distant space of a vocation,[41] warping it upward in the direction of its exemplary source in a grand and masterful model. Does this voice, and the figures through whom or which it is heard, constitute something of a return on losses and a treasure to be recuperated from the ruins (or *as* the ruins)? There can be no doubt that the exile, wandering and suicide evoked by Kafka have as their counterpart, and indeed as the very tone and style of their proffering, the potentiality of a treasure to be had somewhere beyond the horizon of debased self-regard. The wound is mortal, but it will have been salutary. And yet the chances of this rescue having dwindled, right along with the restriction of resources, down to the exposed and vulnerable body, the grounds of any such return are extremely precarious, so that the literary movement called for here risks being deprived, too, of the sublime's supersensible compensations. The "treasure" that is left can be no more than a strange form of affect tied to language, at risk of being reduced, perhaps, to a mere residual emblem, an empty schematic "core," a hard and opaque remnant: a couple of mute milk teeth gnawing at nothing.

It is striking to note that, in embracing such a totalizing melancholic loss, Kafka is also in the very same gesture effectively ending a friendship (much as, years later with Felice Bauer, the ax of writing would be raised over the frayed knot of engagement and marriage). The letter concludes, rather tartly: "I feel as if I have wronged you [*Dir ein Unrecht getan*] and must ask your forgiveness. But I know of no wrong" (LFr 16). This indeterminate pang of conscience, no sooner asserted than disavowed, marks the ambivalence of the scenario we have been reading. One result of which is that, in the shadow of a grander and more powerful ideal, the friend—the singular, namable judge and addressee—must be renounced, to be replaced by an unappeasable Other, through whom self-reading is rendered as a scene of merciless self-judgment—a mercilessness that in the fiction will translate almost invariably into murder. In such a scenario, "guilt is never to be doubted" (as Kafka will write in "In the Penal Colony"), and the result of punishment—the hacked-open sea as the prelude to, and the material form of, writing's externalization—can always only confirm and feed the grounds of punishment. In this schema, the debt of literary guilt is infinite, self-replicating, and self-transmitting.[42]

This is precisely the dynamic structure of guilt and renunciation described by Freud, as he confronts the vast and torturous legacy called "civilization."[43] What is essential for our purposes is the way in which Kafka seeks to instantiate the superegoic *Instanz* or "critical agency" of a harsh and unrelenting judgment as a fundamental condition of the literary vocation, *and* as the figural schema out of which this vocation will realize, at least initially, its outward, visible, artistic form, its figural contours and narrative topography—particularly in a repeated staging and scenography of judgment. The structural form of the imperative to write thus *draws out*, if only schematically, the shape of what must be written, and how: in the image of the wholeness and continuity of the sublime example to whom, as stand-in and short-circuit, writing will be submitted, as though to its own imperious law of origination. The sublime conscience thus sketches its own inevitable subreption, in the exilic space of figuration and fiction. Kafka's striving for this ideal, its simultaneous consolidation *and undoing* in the fictions that would seek it, can be read with remarkable clarity in the writing intended, more than any other, to bring about the brilliant appearance of the writer as such, the site of discipline and practice now published as the *Diaries*.

THE INVISIBLE COURT: SETTING FIRE

Let us continue to trace the elaboration of Kafka's fiction from out of his "personal" and "autobiographical" writings by pursuing a number of figural threads through the early diaries, begun in the summer of 1910, up to the composition of "The Judgment" in the pages of the diary itself, in September 1912. For it is there that the "juridical" shape of Kafka's first mature stories is more and more densely consolidated, and in closer proximity than ever to the courtroom and judgment schema through which he continues to elaborate his own relation to the task and discipline of writing. It is striking to see that as Kafka begins the *Diaries*, more than six years after breaking off the correspondence with Pollak, he continues to draw on the same figures, even the very same phrases, that he used there to graphically articulate a relation to writing as a process of defaulting appearance before a condemning judge—but also, at the level of the textual body itself, as an attempt to approximate more and more closely the ideal of unity, wholeness and cohesiveness projected there. In the *Diaries* this ideal is explicitly and self-consciously applied to the writer as such, who must be *made to appear*, right there in that writing, which, as disciplined practice, will bring this being into existence in and as the flaming (but brittle) core of his perfected story. This ideal was in fact achieved, in Kafka's own judgment, with the story "The Judgment," whose composition he famously celebrated as having occurred "*in einem Zug*"—at one sitting, or in one *draft*, in a single powerful pull that was, by the same token, a full and complete success on the first attempt. Moreover, given Kafka's desire to achieve completion or even "perfection" in a first draft, rather than through laborious planning and revising, it could be said that writing for Kafka was always in some sense a one-time performance.[44] In the diary entry following "The Judgment," he goes on to say that "the story developed before me, as if I were gliding through water [*in einem Gewässer*]," and, in a shift of metaphorical register, exclaims:

> How everything can be said, how for everything, for the strangest fancies, there waits a great fire in which they perish and rise up again. . . . *Only in this way* can writing be done, only with such coherence [*Zusammenhang*], with such a complete opening [*Öffnung*] of body and soul. (D 212-213; TB 214; Kafka's emphasis)

Here the "opening" is not a violent hacking on a frozen sea, but an ecstatic availability, a rendering up that presents a smooth and unresisting aquatic surface, in a movement that is also likened to a powerful flaming forth. This unmistakable appearance and flawless performance of the textual body as a swiftly moving unified whole is the reward for the disciplined workout for which the *Diaries* are the designated space and stage, as indicated by the many fragments in its first pages that work over and repeat elements of the same story. As Blanchot remarks of Kafka in reference to the *Diaries*, "*il s'exerce, il fait son apprentissage*" ("he is practicing, he is carrying out his apprenticeship") (PF 22). This function of practice and apprenticeship must always be kept in mind in reading Kafka's early diaries, which are less concerned with recording daily events (though they also do that) than with the imperative to "cultivate one's talents," to "open" and visibly manifest them. It is in the lapses of this self-forming process that the topoi of guilt, judgment, condemnation, and punishment emerge and crystalize as a figural and scenographic nucleus for the fiction to which they open the way. In the distance between what does appear and what *must* appear, an imperative continually operates, commanding, however faultily, that the gaps be filled. To take one example, Kafka complains (on November 5, 1911) about being unable to "draw up out of me [*aus mir zu heben*] all the possibilities of my talent" and expresses a frustrated wish to "write something large and whole, well shaped from beginning to end" (D 105; TB 105). Paradoxically, he will have done this only by drawing, in part, on the endless guilt and punishing judgment inherent in the very effort to attain this ideal.

One figure of this paradox—as a self-cancelling, self-consuming appearance fueled by its own internal contradictions—is the fulgurating fire evoked above. It already flashes out in the opening entries of the diary, in the very first warm-up session. Following a few fragmentary practice sentences, Kafka writes in a more discursive, self-referential vein (although we could also hear it, as is the case with the *Diaries* in general, as contaminated by the fictional notes that surround it, and by the status of literature that all this writing seeks to confer upon itself: thus as a fictive fragment in the first-person, the beginning of a story):

> Finally, after five months of my life during which I could write nothing that would have satisfied me, and for which no power will compensate me, though all were under obligation to do so, it occurs to me to talk to myself again. Whenever I really questioned myself, there was always a response forthcoming, there was always something in me to catch fire [*herauszuschlagen*], in this heap of straw that I have been for five months and whose fate, it seems, is to be set afire during the summer and consumed more swiftly than the onlooker [*Zuschauer*] can blink his eyes. If only that would happen with me! (D 12; TB 11)

At the liminal stage of his diary, Kafka does not evoke the Muse, he prays for the anonymous flames. While these flames once again bring to mind a certain sacrificial *Allerheiligste*—along with the entire religious and metaphysical symbolics of fire as naked spirit stripped of its surfaces—what is decisive here is that this fire appears in response to a questioning voice and *before a spectator*, who would see not the substance of spirit but the sheer flashing forth of an instant barely visible, engulfing a mere hollow tuft of matter. "Not a throwing off of the self, but a consumption of the self" (BON, 39; HL 77), as Kafka wrote later. The diary's purpose is thus to strike the spark that will ignite this consuming flame, which will then leave all this tentative writing behind, remains of ash and dust.[45] But at the same time, it will also form, display, and track the poor flimsy body on which this process nonetheless depends. A few lines later, Kafka projects this flaming body in a more high-flown image (once again using an astronomical figure): "But every day at least one line should be trained [*gerichtet*] on me, as they now train telescopes [*Fernrohre*] on comets. And if I should appear before that sentence once, drawn [*hergelockt*] by that sentence . . ." (D 12; TB 11). Kafka thus gives the classical trope "*Nulla dies sine linea*" a strange modern turn—the very turn by which this line is "trained" like an optical instrument back upon the writer himself, an emergent being who, through disciplinary repetition, would thus be brought to visibility in the first place. The *Fernrohr* that could not encompass Hebbel's sublimity makes an appearance now as an instrument of "training" in every sense, both corporally subjecting and visually supervising the writer of this sentence, but also aiming and projecting him into the elevated position of a flaming comet. As in the letters to Pollak, the cosmic projection of telescopic observation, in being *gerichtet* or directed at the writer in training, strangely merges into the judgment of a *Gericht*, a court of judgment that is taking shape here precisely in the *Bildung* of image formation and writerly cultivation.[46] This training is thus a body-*Bildung* designed to prepare the more spiritual appearance of the writer as flaming figural corpus, its powerful emergence before the spectator-judges, whose commanding perspective he himself has assumed and internalized; further, he now wields the very instrument of this elevated perspective in his train of words—a drawing out that is also the *Zug* of a dense and continuous language in its strange action at a distance, exerting the specific gravity of the *sentence*.[47] For it is there and there alone that the writer has a chance of making his awaited but elusive appearance *in flagrante*.

The *Gericht* obliquely implied in this process is indeed on its way and will soon be convoked in the name of Goethe and the fiery celestial figure that appears in *his* diary. This occurs a few months later when Kafka's conscience flares up as a result of breaking his promise and lapsing in his regime: "I did not adhere to my new time schedule, to be at my desk from 8 to 11 p.m." The very next day he intones: "Read a little in Goethe's diaries. Distance already holds this life firm in its tranquility, these diaries set fire to it" (D 31; TB 24). Goethe enters the breach of Kafka's promise to write and installs there the fulgurating example of someone whose diaries have done to his life exactly what Kafka hopes his own will do to his: "set fire to it." Apparently in an attempt to make up for neglected duties, and to shine in his own right, Kafka goes on to write a rather forced, metaphorical sentence commenting on Goethe's diaries, a sentence which must not have "drawn" him, for the following day he writes disparagingly: "How do I excuse [*entschuldige*] yesterday's remarks about Goethe. . . ? In no way [*Mit nichts*]. How do I excuse my not yet having written anything today? In no way." Conducting his own cross-examination in the court of literary conscience, Kafka can offer "nothing" in his own defense, whether the accusation is writing badly or not writing at all. But once again, an anxious writing about the necessity of writing, and of writing well, a confrontation with the conditions in which writing *must* take place and yet fails to do so, becomes a generative moment in the elaboration of a far-reaching fictive schema. For it is at this point that the metaphorics of judgment and the courtroom, latent in all the images of visual observation (and even in the word by which its instrument would be *gerichtet*), suddenly becomes explicit in the most striking manner, as Kafka exclaims just afterward: "I have continually an invocation [*Anrufung*] in my ear: 'Were you to come, invisible court of justice! [*Kämest du, unsichtbares Gericht*!]'" (D 31; TB 25). This precipitous passage to what might be called a supersensible figure, an invisible court that is somehow sensed, constitutes a crucial moment in the trajectory I am tracing; indeed it gives the precise juridico-sublime schema that will determine its subsequent course. Let us lay out its logic within the elaboration of a writerly vocation and the fictive world that it will generate.

The Coming Court

Starting from a small guilty scene of self-interrogation, in which Kafka berates himself in the name of the sublime example he fails to emulate, we quickly find ourselves projected into the domain of a "higher" and more ideal court of justice capable, presumably, of the most definitive and irrevocable judgment. What would happen if this court were to come? The fact of having "nothing" to say in one's own defense, of an accusation without response, would meet with its ultimate consequences, whose unfaltering and all-too-seeing justice would outstrip any punishment inflicted by a given *figure*, including the sublime example in whose name he initially condemns himself (in this case Goethe). Already identified with this figure, the self-judging writer passes even "higher" toward an "invisible" court in which the superegoic cross-examination ("How do I excuse . . .") surpasses even the sublime instance who will have represented its source and standard merely "by subreption." In this way the lowly judged and guilty party raises himself into an intimate "vocal" proximity (a kind of silent whisper "continually in my ear") to the very ideal realm that threatens to annihilate him. Does this operation not precisely mimic that of the sublime vocation, by which the crushed and overwhelmed finite being is raised into the supersensible? The vocation staged here is simultaneously "legal" (structured as law) *and literary*, a *Beruf* that takes the form of a summons, an *Anrufung*, invoking a strange invisible figure for the writer's ultimate and always defaulted responsibility, in the movement from a nonresponse to an infinite response, from a "*nichts*" to a voice "always in my ear." For we must notice another crucial aspect of this "invocation": it does not summon the writer; rather it is the writer who, *adopting* the voice of the call, summons an invisible court that will never come: "*Du . . . Gericht!*" It is the writer whose voice incessantly calls for the ultimate instance of his own judgment, and gives a schematic figure to his "vocation." *The writer calls for his own conscience*, as the seat, and the very form (vocal address), of his own infinite task.

However, it should also be noticed that the movement of idealization by which the invisible court is summoned (summons itself) out of a self-accusation, occurs only through the illusion of an acoustic projection, an illusion that has its own specifically literary structure. This structure can be described as a complex rhetorical gesture: a hyperbolizing apostrophe proffered in the mode of prosopopoeia. Already in interrogating himself ("How do I excuse . . ."), the writer assumes the voice of conscience in order then to "hyperbolize" this voice as an invocation that he himself addresses to its absent, and ultimate, instantiation. The illusion in question is thus a "transcendental illusion" very close to the Kantian sense, in that it engenders the apparent reality of an ideal (metaphysical) object on the basis of a set of finite conditions for which "the voice of reason" demands a single, unified, unconditioned ground.[48] The avowedly vocal and literary dimensions of this illusion are crucial to the numerous fictions by Kafka that put into play a pseudo-transcendental structure, a point I will return to in a moment. For now I would like to stress an essential aspect of Kafka's call for an ultimate judgment, or for a powerful instance that would carry it out, if it ever came: not only does this "invocation" vacillate in tone between thunderous admonition and wishful longing, it also vacillates affectively between (to put the point somewhat crudely) masochism and sadism. In other words, while at one level it seems to express a desire to be punished by an ultimate power, with total justice and without mercy, it also evinces, precisely in the assumption of a voice that speaks simultaneously in apostrophe and prosopopoeia, a presumption to speak in the mighty tones *of* that sublimely higher instance of power. Whispered in tremulous dread, the invocation quakes no less with the sublimity it longingly evokes: "*Kämest du, unsichtbares Gericht!*" The sentence itself could serve as a prime example of sublime enunciation, though it is made by the very one on whom the power it calls down would be visited. Put another way, the literary invocation of an impossible ideal judgment that would *subject* the writer to its power is also, paradoxically, a statement in which the writer takes the side of this sublime power and appropriates its voice, in a strange play of power and powerlessness, and in a simulacrum of both. We should note as well that the space of this play is opened by the decisive distance of a "you," an address that both comes from, and is aimed at, the writer—and in a subjunctive mode that seals its power into a pure and unending imminence.[49]

In this remarkable exclamation, then, Kafka apostrophizes the sublime power of judgment as the ultimate and illusory limit-scene of his own writing, and he thus lays out the productive schema of the fiction that, in another paradox, will constitute his first "successful" response to the juridico-literary call enacted here. Can there be anything at all surprising in the fact that the first of these fictions would be called "The Judgment"? In that story and those written in its wake, Kafka will figure this ideal invisible court through a series of treacherous but powerful "instances" of judgment (various fathers and their proxies). With the "invisible court," in its demand to be visibly figured in writing, Kafka gives name and shape to a basic projective schema of his fictive world, in a schematizing crux that directly articulates the faulty structure of the imperative to write with the thematic content through which it will find a first "satisfying" enactment. The conjuring of the invisible court thus implicates the demands of writing in a kind of graphic layout, a strange schematic law marking the outline of an imperative that must unfold *as fiction*. Grasping itself crucially as a kind of self-administered tribunal, Kafka's writing is drawn forth into figures that, in a highly complex fashion, would translate the exigency of its own production. *One* of the central animating moments of this exigency is the compelling danger of writing's appearance before a judge. To put the point in the form of a chiasmus, which also describes the arc traced by this analysis: the judgment of writing, having (sublimely) outstripped its own provisional instantiations, becomes in turn the writing of a singular inscenated judgment. The following section will clarify this movement further, and even more "literally," as we read a diary entry in which the young writer is judged, and cursorily dismissed, by a family member—not a father but an uncle. If Kafka finds himself drawn to stage compellingly written scenes of judgment, it is at some level in order to prove himself—that is, to prove himself "innocent."[50] These "personal" stakes may well be displaced, inverted, forgotten, permanently scrambled, or ecstatically transformed in the writing of fiction (and certainly they undergo—are continually undergoing—these processes); they remain no less legible in the graphic impression they leave on the path leading away from them—like so many footprints shuffling indelibly toward a receding horizon.

THE USUAL STUFF / THE COLD SPACE OF OUR WORLD

As a final transition between the early diary entries and the narrative works I have referred to as "judgment stories," there is one more scene, also narrated in the *Diaries*, that demands attention. It will serve here as a last relay, still just barely on this side of the blurry border between the autobiographical and the impersonal-literary, in the passage from the former to the "absolute" fictions that open a radically other space. The scene hovers on this border in a dizzying play of mise-en-abyme structures, both spatial and referential, in which the imbrication of life and writing becomes all the more vertiginous for being put in the service of separating them definitively. Put another way, it shows fiction engulfing life—specifically the familiar life of the family in its relation to writing—precisely by breaking the writer away from this life and affirming a definitive and resolute imperative to secure suitable conditions for *living elsewhere*.

The scene I am referring to is, quite overtly, a scene of judgment, a family scene in which Kafka depicts himself as writing a page of fiction that is summarily evaluated and dismissed by an uncle "who liked to make fun of people." The diary entry in which it occurs, written one month after the invocations of Goethe and the invisible court cited earlier, begins as a retrospective glance at past writing. Kafka claims, with a passion for new beginnings and celestial spaces that we have already seen, "I shall either have to wish myself off the earth or else . . . start afresh like a baby," and says that

> externally, this will be easier for me than before. For in those days I still strove with hardly a suspicion after a description in which every word would be linked to my life, which I would draw to my heart, and which would transport me out of myself [*von meinem Platz hinreissen*]. With what misery . . . I began! What a chill [*Kälte*] pursued me all day long out of what I had written! (D 36-37; TB 31)

I would interject here, as before, that one can already hear in this voice an uncanny air of fiction, one that surrounds many of the first-person passages in the *Diaries*, even when they plausibly and concretely refer to Kafka's lived experience. This margin of referential uncertainty, an ineradicable structural feature of all first-person narrative, is exploited by Kafka as the gap through which autobiography births (itself as) a fictive voice. At stake here, however, is the chilling separation between words written and the blazing other world they strive to open, the true site of this merger of life and language. This chill evokes the dead matter of language falling short of its vocation—which is meant to transport (*hinreissen*) the writer, rocketlike, out of his "place" (or one might say, from his "seat" at the family table). Failing that, familiarity itself threatens with its own deathly chill. In the scene that follows, everything hinges on the ponderous air of that familiarity and the slim chances of setting it alight with an entirely different kind of warmth. I cite this crucial passage in its entirety:

> Once I projected a novel in which two brothers fought each other, one of whom went to America while the other remained in a European prison. I only now and then began to write a few lines, for it tired me at once. So once I wrote down something about my prison on a Sunday afternoon when we were visiting my grandparents and had eaten an especially soft kind of bread, spread with butter, that was customary [*übliches*] there. It is of course possible that I did it mostly out of vanity, and by shifting the paper about on the tablecloth, tapping with my pencil, looking around under the lamp, wanted to tempt [*verlocken*] someone to take what I had written from me, look at it, and admire me [*mich zu bewundern*]. It was chiefly the corridor of the prison that was described in the few lines, above all its silence and coldness [*Kälte*]; a sympathetic word was also said about the brother who was left behind, because he was the good brother. Perhaps I had a momentary feeling of the worthlessness of my description, but before that afternoon I *never paid much attention to such feelings* when among relatives to whom I was accustomed [*gewöhnt*] (my timidity [*Ängstlichkeit*] was so great that it made me half-way happy in the midst of the accustomed [*im Gewohnten*]), I sat at the round table in the familiar room and could not forget that I was young and *called to great things* [*zu grossem berufen*] out of this present tranquility [*Ungestörtheit*]. An uncle who liked to make fun of people finally took the page that I was holding only weakly, looked at it briefly, handed it back to me, even without laughing, and only said to the others who were following him with their eyes, "The usual stuff [*das gewöhnliche Zeug*]," to me he said nothing. To be sure, I remained seated as before over the now useless page of mine, but with one thrust I had in fact been banished [*vertrieben*] from society, the *judgment of my uncle repeated itself in me* with what amounted almost to real significance, and even within the feeling of belonging to a family I got an insight *into the cold space of our world which I had to warm with a fire that first I wanted to seek out*. (D 37; TB 31–32; my emphasis)

This is a story about conflicting topographies, interconnected spaces twisted open internally by the framed projection of a fiction. For within the frame of this family scene, the scene of a writer writing among nonwriting onlookers, Kafka embeds another, in the space of his written page, a novelistic space that is both a prison and a far-away land. But unlike the family scene, with its single writer protagonist, that internal frame encloses a duality of "two brothers," one of whom ("the good brother") is unjustly condemned to prison in Europe, while the other (presumably the bad one) has fled to the New World, a fictional freedom also called Amerika. Meanwhile, the avatar of their progenesis sits in his own prison of comfort and familiarity (otherwise known as a boring Sunday afternoon with the family), writing them and their alternate spaces into existence—spaces whose separation is defined by struggle (they "fought each other") and guilt, condemnation and punishment, expulsion and exile. But this writing is itself staged as a performance meant to draw the admiring gaze of an audience quickly transformed into a tribunal, an assembly of spectators who, awaiting a pronouncement on the evidence, "were following . . . with their eyes." This audience thus becomes a silent but complicit jury, once the uncle hands down his verdict: *the usual stuff*. So ordinary it is not even worth making fun of. In other words, the banality, mediocrity and boredom of this page turns out to be completely homogeneous with the flat familiar/familial world from which its production was meant to transport its writer, who is secure to the point of complacency in his knowledge of being "called to greatness." The index of the future writer's elevation above this scene, a page of fiction, is abruptly transformed into the dead weight marking, rather, his de facto inferiority. In these sudden torques and reversals, a complex Borgesian vertigo, both threatening and generative, opens through the scene's multiple levels and performative effects: the warmth of bread and butter, familiar people, and a large round table is inverted in the displaced fiction of a cold and silent prison, which, as now worthless writing, pursues the writer into his regular world, freezing him out *even from there*. Like the good brother, he is internally banished, driven out of the social space in the most degrading way possible, both trapped in it and excluded from it. One aspect of this exclusion is that if this writer is working toward a vocation of greatness, he is the only one to know it. To everyone else, he looks like the "usual" sort of young man, perhaps just a bit more vain and conceited than most. Kafka goes out of his way to play up this impression, and his purpose is not to defend the erstwhile efforts so brutally judged here. But it is precisely in response to that judgment that the crucial moment occurs, the transformation of these spatial displacements into a temporal projection, in the form of a task, not to say a Promethean quest: *set this cold place on fire*. In a more modest register, it is a question of being able to survive under the conditions reflected by this harsh, inhospitable, and culpabilizing written environment defined by prison and banishment, to provide warmth enough (and innocence) to be able to stay there, and to carry out a "search" for its fire.

But where is this *there*? At one level, it may be called "Amerika," for at issue here is indeed an early draft of the novel that will be set in that fabulous, distant and exilic place. And yet, conversely, the anecdote reveals something else more surprising: the other place or "world" in question is not simply beyond or exclusive of the family, for the internal exile "in the familiar" that Kafka narrates here, along with the judgment that seals it, are formative elements in the fictions soon to come, as the banalities of family life follow the writing/written self into this other world, to reveal their own violent and unlivable machinery. It suffices to note that all of the shorter "judgment stories" are family stories (including, one could argue, "In the Penal Colony," with its ghostly paternal Ur-Commandant, and its filial Officer "defendant"), and all of them stage a scene at least analogous to this one, though the object of presentation differs.[51] To approach the point from another direction, one could ask: What does Kafka mean when he writes "the cold space of *our* world"? This plural is the anecdote's most enigmatic moment. For it locates the "world" in question in an uncannily hovering space that encompasses the family and *its* judgment *within* the opening alter-world of writing, while populating that world with a "we" whose "family feeling" (*Familiengefühl*) fuels the drive that would lead to a radical elsewhere, in which (in turn) those familial structures and forces will be essentially operative (etc.). But the first person plural also projects a strange community of virtual comrades whose ranks extend, no doubt, from battling brothers to the grand fraternal order of the classical German tradition (Goethe et al.).[52] Finally, it should be remarked that the performative force of the uncle's judgment, whose meaning in being pronounced is "almost" fully realized (*mit schon fast wirklicher Bedeutung*), anticipates the father's judgment in "The Judgment," and, one could say by extension, the sort of real-fictive speech Kafka is striving for in general during this period. This is a speech that, as outlined above, *mimics power*, but here it does so by creating effects of reality and truth, by virtue of the uncanny and immediate persuasive force it wields, regardless of any referential truth it may or may not have. Recall Kafka's remark (from the very next diary entry after the uncle anecdote, dated exactly one month later), in which he exults: "The special nature of my inspiration is that . . . I can do everything, and not only what is directed to a definite piece of work. When I arbitrarily write a single sentence, for instance, 'He looked out of the window,' it already has perfection" (D 38; TB 33; February 19, 1911). The gaze trained by this sentence rather scopes the vanity of its pretentions, in the perfection of an entire world conjured from nothing but an ordinary sentence and still awaiting its unfolding. That it is manifest only to a single gaze is deemed irrelevant for the moment; for this self-contained micro-exaltation extends uncannily into all possible writing henceforth: pronounced into existence, this perfection therefore really does exist. In sum, then, if the uncle's judgment effectively repeats itself, it will have done so *as literature*, that is, once again, as the instantiation of a literary conscience, a schematic tribunal, within the hollow and resonating core of the writing imperative. The echo of a judgment voiced (and assumed as one's own) thus gives an image for the structure of the drive that installs it. It is clear that the diary entry staging its pronouncement already seeps into that other space, as the blank diaries await further pages, further fictions.

CHAPTER 2

The Ecstasy of Judgment

> Le monde du jugement s'installe comme dans un rêve.
> —Gilles Deleuze, *Critique et clinique*

UNGRASPING JUSTICE

The judgment scene from the early *Diaries*, which in the last chapter I called the "uncle anecdote," provides a remarkable relay point through which the scenic and metaphoric configurations elaborated in the letters and diaries are cast into Kafka's first mature fictions, beginning with "The Judgment." I will begin this chapter with a brief recapitulation of the former as a way to introduce a discussion of the latter, and to bring into relief, however schematically, the features by which they communicate.

In his early letters, Kafka figures the task of writing as bringing up an inner richness, and manifesting a singular interiority, a "holy of holies" (later figured as a "tremendous world in the head" and a "dreamlike inner life") which demands externalization in part in order to display and confirm its very existence. This is a paradoxical task in that this inner core of authenticity cannot be shared, as Kafka writes to Oskar Pollak, because one has access "only [to] one's own" (LFr 4; Br 12). But the demand remains, and it requires the exteriority not only of the written word, but of that word's appearance before the reading eyes of another, who thus becomes a judge, and a spectator (and who may find only the banal remnants of something precious, nothing but a couple of "milk teeth," as related in the "parable of the locked box" included in one letter). For the young Kafka, Oskar Pollak occupied this powerful position of reader and judging spectator, at least for a time. The friend, the addressee of letters and writings that risked this exposure, is thus elevated, but he remains within reach, which also means that he can be *removed*. Indeed, he is soon displaced by a much more remote and powerful judge, the sublime and crushing exemplar of a literary ideal, a stand-in named "Hebbel," who appears to represent the Law (as its "faultless" figural projection), and whose shadow thus measures out the infinite distance of the striving writer's faulty shortcoming. Judgment becomes absolute and unappeasable, this infinite distance being also the separation of exile and the opening of a painful biting and stabbing wound called *conscience*. Painful, but salutary: for what Kafka calls "the axe on the frozen sea inside us" not only punishes but also hacks into the inert inner material that is thus liberated for its own distant chances of attaining sublimity, and thus for the externalization required by such striving. The tightly contained inside must come out; the inner wealth must be made to appear, which also means that the writer as such must come into visible existence, through a process that becomes both utterly urgent and utterly futile, in the face of an unforgiving judgment conjured hyperbolically as an "invisible court." From these projected heights of ideality, populated by Hebbel, Goethe, and other fiery figures, writing *descends* into the scope of the sentence, and the impossibly distant judgment of sublimity in turn descends into the delineated forms of a tribunal, one that is projected not into the heavens but into a theater, in the form of a precise fictive elaboration: Judgment is rendered as a *scene*, and that scene takes place, in the first instance, as a scene of writing. Enter the Uncle, transitional autobiographical avatar of Kafka's many fictive judges, both terrifically powerful and banally familial/familiar. In the anecdote related in the *Diaries*, the uncle's dismissive judgment of a page of writing, with its categorical pronouncement (no appeal) and its immediately effective performative force, reduces the writer (the defendant) to silence, banishing him to an internal exile within the sphere of mere social appearances, which is henceforth incompatible with the young writer's pure inner conviction of "being called to greatness" (D 37; TB 31–32), and *a fortiori* with the rich inner world whose products seem *so far* to be nothing extraordinary. Guilty here means (still means) something like: inadequate to "what I believe I have in me" (LFr 7; Br 17) and therefore appearing to all the world as unjustified in this belief. Thus the sublimely striving (vain, conceited, over-reaching, self-aggrandizing . . .) writer stands accused, and the only defense left is not so much to directly counter this accusation as to respond to its demand for self-justifying speech by finding, and wielding, a fire whose force will outstrip that of the judgment itself: the fire of a fictive performance. The imperative to write, then, comes to be staged as an imperative to speak in oblique self-defense by taking hold of the socially performative force of the very judgment that threatens it with nullity. That is, *to take hold of power in speech*, in such a way as both to appropriate and undo that power in the very grounds of its possibility. This is the essentially literary paradox of Kafka's writing imperative, insofar as it is structured, during this phase of his writing, as a relation to law and an inscenation of judgment. At the same time, this imperative continues to be an imperative to *manifest*, to *present something* like an inner reality the nature of whose existence, however, is incompatible with the sphere of mere (social) appearance on which, and *as which*, it must impose itself: mere images trafficking in mere images. In such a paradoxical situation, the writer is inevitably *at fault*, whether in the crushing shortfall of failure, or in the diabolical dissimulations of success. Put another way, guilt—a bad conscience shadowed by the ideal—is (re)produced in the very ambition of overcoming it. For the movement of overcoming is itself spurred by a shattering penetration, a wounding bite, whose first movement is to turn back on the structures, and sublime stand-ins, that inflicted it—whose stinging blows, however, have long since sunk in. The task thus becomes, however surreptitiously, to write one's way *out* of the clenched circle of authority that seems to call for sublime overcoming in the first place. But this will require a long and dogged undermining, a persistent and perhaps repetitious reinscription of animating motives and motifs, and an emptying of the treasures of failure *and* of success. That is one reason, no doubt, why the circle of these stories is relatively restricted, and why their themes are so consistent—not to say compulsively repetitive.

The Judgment Stories: Coughing Up Corpses

I have tried to give this summary in a way that would remain true to the "personal" texts we have read so far while also corresponding (again, if only schematically) to the dramatic and figural structures running through *all* of the judgment stories. When we turn to these stories, what do we find? In every case, the main character is faced with a judgment that has been, soon comes to be, or is always about to be pronounced, requiring a defense in speech—according to the capacities of speech and gesture available in each case—that would present an inner or otherwise socially unmanifest innocence, or that (as in "In the Penal Colony") would attest to a transcendent Justice that has lost its social legibility and is on the verge of oblivion. In every case, the necessity of speech in self-defense is staged before a judge/audience that draws language and its objects into the unsteady element of socially and linguistically manipulable appearances, in a diabolical theater of speech that overwhelms any possibility of "authentic" self-presentation. The judges themselves—fathers, military or quasi-military officers, a traveling diplomat—all represent, and actively wield, power through speech, which is of course an essential part of what constitutes a judge. And they do this through performative speech acts inaugurated by the most startling among them, the death sentence pronounced by Georg Bendemann's raving father in "The Judgment" and immediately, compulsively, even acrobatically carried out by the condemned party. The ideal of a fully and immediately effective performative speech, a speech that would directly issue in the reality it names and evokes, haunts these stories at several levels: that of their literary ambitions (to "already have perfection," to be "indubitable"), that of the authorities in them who pronounce judgment, and that of the protagonists who fail disastrously to live up to it, and who as a result are subjected to it in the form of social, psychical, and physical violence. For it also happens in each case that the character enjoined to defend himself invariably fails to do so, whether because his speech is unpersuasive ("In the Penal Colony"), ridiculously infantile ("The Judgment"), or totally incoherent ("The Stoker"), or because he cannot speak at all ("The Metamorphosis").[1] This latter variation shows Kafka systematically pursuing a narrative strategy that *depends on* the breakdown of speech in order to trace all the more clearly the contours of what remains unspoken, unpresented, and even at some level *ungraspable*. I emphasize this last term because of the frequency of its appearance (across variations) at crucial moments in which the stakes of these stories take on a residually transcendental dimension, in the resistant remainder that does not lend itself to speech, or to any kind of appearance, that lies outside and continually eludes the grasp of language in its social and historical effectivity. Perhaps the clearest example of this is the transcendent justice at issue in "In the Penal Colony," but it applies no less to the innocence of the stoker (whose case is referred in passing to a "higher tribunal"), and to that of the other "defendants" in these stories as well. I will be concerned in what follows to identify this remnant something—passionate inner conviction or conceptual beyond (or both at once)—which constitutes, more or less explicitly in each story, a site of ruined transcendence that must in each case be relinquished. *That* it is a something, a positive transcendence which remains tragically out of reach—*ungreifbar*, not *handgreiflich* enough, insufficiently palpable or otherwise foreclosed from sensible presentation—is a feature connecting all of these stories, through a haunting ideal of sublime instantiation. This is also what gives them the quite classic (Freudian) form of melancholy that fundamentally structures their narratives: the formation of a degraded ideal, visible only as a critical and sadistic judge, from out of the ruins of a more genuine one that can only appear as lost.

The staging of these failures, their ruination and emptying out of the ideal and its power, are thus a no less programmatic aspect of the judgment stories, in the sense that their *writing*, the often perplexing singularities of their executions, seem to thrive on the basis of their protagonists' delirious, stammering, stymied or completely foreclosed speech, and to do so in a way that strangely twists the positions of subjection in relation to the law that orchestrates their demise. In bringing his protagonists to failure, Kafka has them destroyed at the hands of various representatives of the law, or of a Law that remains difficult to discern in its singular application (and this blurring of the law's generality is essential to the specifically literary process in question); but he also reveals the very workings of their power in the guilt-producing speech that they wield, *and* in the fantasmatic projections of socially embedded protagonists on whose bodies the theater of bad conscience is played out. In mounting this complex theater, Kafka attempts to take hold of the very knot of language that ties literature to the law as an ultimately ungrounded manipulation of power in speech. In a strange and astonishing rivalry with the figures of power in the judgment stories—unsteady images of a wavering, indeterminate and always undermined authority—Kafka the writer works to liquidate, again and again, the subjected bodies who *literally* suffer the force of speech that makes them. For this is, in some sense, the same speech that both conjures forth their existence and dispenses with them, with one implicit or explicit word: guilty. Guilty, and therefore fit to be killed. By sketching out this logic, which threads through all of the judgment stories, we too will search for the knot that binds a sublimely striving literary speech to the structures of effective law that it *breaks down*, in every sense. As we will see, this is a knot bound in violence—and tied into the "master's whip" that Kafka invokes in a note on the masochistic fantasies inherent to the desire for mastery.[2]

In speaking, then, of a ruined and henceforth ungraspable transcendence, we will necessarily encounter the specific figures of these ruins, most pointedly in the series of corpses and abjected bodies that are expelled in turn by each of the judgment stories. To move quickly, and to speak in the emblematic mode proper to these corpse images, we can say that as Kafka's judgment narratives work over their Oedipal obsessions, and as they reconfigure the basis of writing's imperative, they will also have to finish coughing up corpses—the lifeless and abjected bodies that flesh out, so to speak, the "milk teeth" discovered in the letters to Pollock as the secret interior, the banal but terrifying treasure of writing exposed. Is the expulsion of these corpses a way for Kafka's writing to empty itself of the beguiling treasures promised by its sublimely wounding initiation? Is that what in the end "must" come out of the frozen sea hacked open? In the philosophical terms implied by these questions: is the vocation of "pure reason" (as generator of the ideal) and the transcendental destination of language actually . . . a cadaver? We recall Blanchot's striking formulation: "idealism has, in the end, no other guarantee than a corpse" (EL 347). This indeed appears to be the emblematic figure for what is necessarily left over in a process that can reach its end only in the devouring of a body (though we will also see that it points in the other direction, toward a childhood that emerges, somewhat surprisingly, as another constitutive limit in these stories). The connection I would like to make here between these corpses and the "milk teeth" treasure of Kafka's early fable is a complex one that, for the moment, can be anticipated by pointing out that hunger and nourishment, and indeed images (and sounds) of teeth and toothless mouths, regularly obtrude into these stories in perplexing ways whose meaning can be glimpsed, I think, by tracking the process of evacuation and destitution carried out by the *Gewissensbiss*, the biting conscience impelling and structuring them. The spitting out of corpses, and the coughing up of the machinery of justice—both presented so graphically in "In the Penal Colony"—can also be seen as a voiding and emptying of writing's own dear treasures, the stripping away of all objects and aims from a gnawing need ravenous for its own peculiar but ungraspable nourishment: what Gregor Samsa believes he hears in his sister's music, or what Karl Rossmann must mourn in the stoker, that innocent victim who is also "a treasure one must renounce." What will be left at the end of this trajectory is *nothing*—but hunger itself. In the shifting modalities of this strange and mounting hunger, outstripping any possible material satisfaction but likewise finding nothing "spiritual" or otherwise to grasp instead, we may be able to discern a very different form of the imperative to write that will come to haunt Kafka's fictions with a less murderous melancholy, and with a voice less bound to the law of self-defense. In the later stories, this imperative will be associated rather with a strange "freedom" inflected by rumor—a turn that can be seen already in *The Trial*, where Josef K. learns of the law only through gossip, and has a "foretaste of freedom" as he exits the suffocating law courts.[3] In the following discussions of the shorter judgment narratives, we will attend both to the obsessive schemata of judgment and to the indications of what exactly emerges from their shattered machinery.

"THE JUDGMENT": DIABOLICAL SPEECH

In approaching "The Judgment," let us recall the background provided above by referring to one precise point from the uncle anecdote: the writer sits at a table on a Sunday afternoon and sees this writing harshly judged. Likewise, let us recall once more the sentence just after this anecdote in the diaries: "I can do everything . . . When I arbitrarily write a single sentence, for instance, 'He looked out of the window,' it already has perfection." Now, is it a coincidence that Kafka's first "successful" story begins with its protagonist "looking out the window" (Sons 3; E 43) as he sits at a writing desk on a peaceful Sunday afternoon? Or that this is in fact a scene of writing *accomplished*? Moreover, when we learn what is in the folds of the letter Georg Bendemann has just finished writing, it becomes clear that something of this attitude is in play for him as well: *I can do everything*. The sense of capacity and power suggested by this sentence also haunts Georg's writing, as we learn from his reflections on the letter that he seals, at the beginning—a capacity further echoed by Kafka in the diary entry immediately following the composition of the story, in which he exults in its ecstatic composition: "How everything can be said, how for everything, for the strangest fancies, there waits a great fire in which they perish and rise up again" (D 213). We will return to this well-known page of the *Diaries*, but for now it is clear not only that Kafka has found the fire he wanted to seek out, but also that its strange power is shared, across complex ambivalences and hesitations, by this object of familial judgment whose fate is decided in "The Judgment." In tracing out certain contours of Georg Bendemann's relationship to writing and to power, we will also keep in view a number of such parallelisms with his author's writing project, as it enfolds and generates the performance of this story. As elsewhere, the strange success of a work of fiction here depends crucially on the failure of its protagonist to wield power in speech, with the result that speech itself is converted into the immediate and effortless production of a corpse—that is, the production of a fiction aimed at the ideal *and* at its demise. Georg's initial assumption of power in letter writing is destined to be reversed, in a grotesque confrontation with the father, so that the writer of it all—in the end neither father nor son, neither powerful nor powerless—can emerge from the stream of images, including, precisely, that of a corpse in the making. Georg's suicide, carried out under the unexpected sign of a "hunger" that his sacrifice can only sharpen, provides the fuel for a machine that manifests in this story its fundamental schema of operation, in which a body must be devoured and ejected by the immediately actualized speech of the law. In the reflections on such effectivity that traverse this story and its protagonist, one thus finds an intense concern for what language *can do* to its addressee, and a strange, ecstatic anxiety that in certain conditions what it does above all, at its constitutive limit, is kill the one it grips. We will see as well that in this schema the production of a theater of guilt and (failed) self-defense converges with the production of fiction tout court, in a generalized fictioning of social relations, a revelation of their grounding fantasms.

It is not incidental to this schema, then, that "The Judgment" begins with a sealed piece of writing whose author seems to be satisfied with it and believes it is ready to be displayed. It is as though Kafka had marked the beginning of his story, proleptically, with an image of its own effectiveness and completion, but placed it in the hands of a writer unaware of the gaping holes in his argument, which will allow the power he seeks to be turned directly against him. Georg Bendemann's writing gives him away—especially when seen in the light of his own disingenuous reflections on the social relations woven into it, which are related in indirect discourse in the first third of the story and serve as the prologue and foundation for the father's later incriminations. We do not have the space here to detail the many subtle strands linking these two moments of the story—Georg's ruminations, tinged with bad conscience, and the court of paternal judgment that terminates the tale—but we can begin by pointing out a crude but often overlooked component of this letter writing, indeed its most pointed reason for existing. What is the imperative to write this letter to his friend, and how is this imperative knotted into Georg's condemnation? In a word, and to move quickly, we can say that Georg writes the letter for the purposes of seduction and sex. The compulsive hesitations and ambivalence that mark its composition stem from his enjoyment in satisfying this exigency and displaying this fact, and from a guilt that is explicitly associated with it. These assertions require some explanation, which can be presented against the background of the power relations implicit in the letter's composition.

Many are the ways in which Georg indulges in, but also attempts to conceal, his sense of power and superiority in relation to this abject failure of a friend to whom he must write. The exilic "Russian friend," a figure notorious in discussions of Kafka if only for the force with which it has drawn interpretations to itself, can plausibly be associated with the "cold space" for which Kafka here seeks and finds the fire required to make it livable. But for Georg, the cold space inhabited by this bachelor friend emerges in a perspective of degradation, pity, and disavowal. "What could one write to such a man, who had obviously gone badly astray [*verrannt*], a man one could be sorry for but not help" (Sons, 3; E 43). This attitude of superiority is elaborated in terms of wayward and diminished traffic, in every sense. Both Georg and the friend are businessmen, and the former's condescension is first expressed in a comparison of the "scope" and size of their respective business ventures: Georg's is expanding, ever since he has managed to displace the moribund father who had hindered him, whereas the friend's numbers are rapidly shrinking (or "disappearing": *verschwindend*). But soon this aspect of Georg's swelling potency is overshadowed by another more explicitly erotic one: he is to be married, an apparently dangerous piece of information that in his "peculiar epistolary relationship [*besondere Korrespondenzverhältnis*]" he has concealed for fear of *inflicting harm*, and rendering an implicit judgment—indeed, at the limit of this logic, a condemnation to permanent bachelorhood. Thus does Georg's feeling of his writing's power balloon from the banal ability to put down, debase, or insult its addressee into a hyperbolic force capable of permanent destruction, much as this complex written treatment of the friend will be enlarged, and reversed, in the more delirious and phantasmagoric paternal condemnation it contains in germ. Now it is precisely here, at the node of linguistic power and social success, that Georg's enjoyment of his higher stature is crossed with a guilt marked as erotic, as the story reveals the most immediate motive for writing the letter in the first place. Why must Georg Bendemann compose this dangerous and guilt-provoking letter to a friend who will be dwarfed and crushed (he believes) by the magnificence of the news it will impart, and by the tremendous figure it projects—that is, a man on the verge of actually marrying a woman who has consented to his intimacies? We learn the answer to this question, as Georg's reveries drift through the weave of his letter's logic, in a flashback to those very intimacies, and in particular to a scene of frustrated eroticism. Georg and his fiancée, Frieda Brandenfeld, have "often spoken of this friend and of the strange epistolary relationship" that has made it difficult for Georg to confess his engagement, because it would be too cruel to invite this lonely exiled bachelor, dwindling away in a foreign land, to a wedding that would appear to seal his fate in all these directions—again, as though it were a condemnation. "If you have such friends, Georg, then you shouldn't have gotten engaged at all," complains Frieda, drawing a stark conclusion whose grounds are difficult to discern. Georg's response, and the scene that follows, provide us with the answer to our question as to what has driven Georg to write the letter:

> "Well, we're both to blame for that [*Ja, das ist uns beider Schuld*]; but I wouldn't have it any other way now [*nicht anders haben*]." And when, breathing heavily under his kisses, she still added, "All the same, it does upset me," he thought it would really *not do any harm* if he were to *write everything* [*alles zu schreiben*] to his friend. (Sons 6; E 46; my emphasis)

Exactly what Frieda means by "such friends" must remain a matter of speculation.[4] But this much is clear: Georg agrees to write the letter to his friend because Frieda, hurt by the secrecy required by this "peculiar relationship," rebuffs his amorous advances—which are clearly not being made for the first time—thus compelling him to "tell all" *in order to overcome this obstacle*. Suddenly, Georg finds his resolve, as the passage continues (I translate very literally): "'That's how I am and he'll just have to accept me or not,' he said to himself. 'I can't cut out some person from out of myself [*aus mir einen Menschen herausschneiden*] that would be more fitting [*geeigneter*] for our friendship than I am'" (Sons 6; E 46). Now exactly "how is" Georg, and what does this have to do with a "guilt" shared by the two lovers? As always in Kafka, there are many strands to unravel here, but for our purposes we can say that Georg is, first, the kind of person who has been able to seduce a woman and convince her to marry him—perhaps in a marriage whose necessity follows from this very seduction. Why else would their engagement be immediately understood as a decision for which they share the "guilt"? And, second, he is someone who turns to writing in order to achieve erotic satisfaction. What appears to be an indirect connection becomes, for the author of the story, perfectly direct and explicit, if we can credit Max Brod's report of a statement by Kafka likening the last line of "The Judgment"—with its "unending stream of traffic" going over the bridge after Georg's suicidal fall—to a "gigantic orgasm."[5] Is this the reward for "writing everything"? It could certainly be seen as a conversion of the story's menacing gigantism, embodied by the father who is "still a giant" (Sons 8; E 47) and who reads an "enormous newspaper," even before he rises to tower over a cringing Georg, whom he accuses of writing "false little letters," diminutive *Briefchen* (Sons, 12; E 51)—a conversion, then, of the story's grotesque grandeurs, potencies, and belittlements into the ecstatic ascension and release of writing.[6] The point I would like to make, by way of Georg's specific (erotic) imperative to "write everything" and the strange guilt located at the very basis of this imperative, is that the story stages within it an analogous relation to, and use of, writing *for which the writer will be judged and punished as such*. Georg's ascent, expansion and dominance will be "put down" by a judge who is able "to see through" him (as the father puts it), and who, essentially, makes a negative judgment about his writing. We should note that this transparency is in crucial contrast to the inveterate obscurity, opacity, and ambiguity of the story itself, and therefore of the (ecstatic, orgasmic) subject of its writing. We readers cannot play Herr Bendemann to Kafka's little text, no matter how full of lies it may be.

Perhaps this is one essential difference, then, between Kafka the writer and his written creature, a vulnerable figure who writes his way into a court that is able to expose his guilt by making it visible and transparent—and by doing so in the very medium of persuasive speech at issue. Later in the story, during the judgment scene proper, when the father demotes Georg's letters to the friend, he does so precisely in terms of transparency and domination, while also weaving the letters into the main strands of guilt and betrayal for which the son is about to be condemned.

> "And . . . you've had to lock yourself up in the office—the boss is busy, mustn't be disturbed—just so you can write your lying little letters [*falsche Briefchen*] to Russia. But fortunately a father doesn't need to be taught how *to see through his son* [*den Sohn zu durchschauen*]. And now that you thought you'd pinned him down [*untergekriegt*], so far down that you could plant your rear end on him so he couldn't move, then my fine son [*mein Herr Sohn*] decides to up and get married!" Georg looked up at the terror-image [*Schreckbild*] of his father . . . "But can he move, or can't he?" He stood up unsupported and kicked his legs about. He radiated insight. (Sons, 12–13; E 50–51; my emphasis)

We might well hear in this an echo of Kafka's letter to Oskar Pollak, the "everlasting up and down" struggle between a God who "does not want me to write" and the poor writer who must nonetheless—an echo which confirms our sense that this dynamic of dominance and reversal *in* writing is deeply constitutive of *what* Kafka writes, which is here given its condensed and primitive form in a kind of brute Oedipal wrestling match. This moment itself comes just in the wake of the reversal it recounts: following the many indications that the father has been reduced (implicitly: by Georg) to a state of ill health, childishness, and filth (dirty underwear), this abject figure has now leapt upright on his bed with a mighty "No!" thus transforming himself into the *Schreckbild* he remains for the rest of the "trial"—in which he dishes out his accusations from above, as Georg mostly cowers in a corner. The superior and potent letter writer thus suffers a reversal that is then graphically explicated to him by the father in precisely the terms he has put into play in his writing: dominance, subjection, and seduction. In other words, this *Schreckbild* and its harangue are implicit in the fantasmatic fabric from which Georg cuts his letter in the first place; it externalizes the implicit fantasy structure on which it is built and thus, strangely, aligns him with the father. And this is precisely what the father can "see through" to, *for he himself is the figure and embodiment* of this fantasy structure, including, obviously, its moment of vindictive retribution for disavowed wrongs. It is as though the creature and form of Georg's bad conscience were here projected, inversely, as his progenitor and *author*—as a father whose "radiant insight" gives him direct access to Georg's interiority, which he is now capable of manipulating *and even creating* with mere words. And indeed, from here on out, in a scene that plays like a delirious theater of speech in which words physically "collide" (Sons 12; E 50), ricochet, and "hiss" (Sons 14; E 52), the father is fully in charge of the script, and in immediate diabolical control of the power wielded by speech. Meanwhile, Georg, for his part, is reduced to nonsensical stammering, and each of his retorts only feeds into the father's gripping power.

Now while the motif of an avenging Oedipus turning on the presumptuous death-wishing son is very familiar—and surely not unwarranted—in interpretations of this story, it is nonetheless revealing to pull out the single strand of a *rivalry over writing*, a vying for power in speech, that deeply structures the proceedings, including at the level of the story's composition. That the judgment is in a crucial sense a judgment of writing is made even clearer when the father figures himself as the author of more compelling texts, a more potent writer whose victory consists in literally crushing Georg's diminutive efforts.

> "How you amused me today, coming in here to ask if you should tell your friend about your engagement. He knows all about it already, you stupid boy, he knows it all [*er weiss doch alles*]! I've been writing to him, for you forgot to take my writing things [*Schreibzeug*] from me . . . he knows everything a hundred times better than you do yourself, with his left hand he crumples up your letters unopened while with his right he holds mine up to read!" (Sons 14–15; E 52)

In this harsh treatment of a page of writing, and in the usurpation of the writer's position by the father, who in his powerless abjection *has been deprived of all other recourse*, we have not just any form of struggle among others, but the very nerve center of this story, the point where its stakes are revealed *en toutes lettres*. For writing is figured here not only as the form and medium of the father's victory, but also as the means for converting isolation, weakness, and decline into a self-amplifying force that outstrips all others. It is through writing that the father figures his overcoming of internal exile and its degradations. More than that, in casting himself as the true purveyor of effective writing, as the one whose missives unfailingly command the attention of their addressee, the father takes hold of the lever by which an entire social reality is constructed by speech alone—that of this enigmatic friend and his relation to Georg, and by extension the latter's entire social and familial world as it relates to the father. In other words, he has grasped the mechanism by which intimate fantasms are projected, and invested fictions are rendered into effective realities, through the masterful use of a "radiant," "insightful," and persuasive language. That lever is the *Schreibzeug* he claims still to hold, whose operation takes on greater and greater dimensions as this exchange proceeds. Indeed, it is here that this story calls up the specter of the sublime, in a manic bout of one-upmanship, a rivalrous *surenchère* aiming derisively at infinity. The passage continues:

> In his exhilaration [*Begeisterung*] he waved his arm over his head. "He knows everything a thousand times better!"
> "Ten thousand times!" said Georg, to make fun of [*verlachen*] his father, but in his very mouth the words took on a deadly earnest tone [*einen toternsten Klang*]. (Sons 15; E 52–53)

The delirious ranting father, carried away by his "enthusiasm," might well cut a ridiculous figure worthy of mockery; but by now Georg is so fully absorbed into the father's fantasmatic construction that his very speech is merely an extension of the father's logic, which it is unable to reverse or undo. Georg is incapable of any comic *Herabsetzung*, any Freudian put-down of the father, whose totalizing power, instead, absorbs even ridicule and thereby *actually expands* geometrically. Thus we see Georg miserably losing what is essentially a war of words, in this first sign that the father's speech has full dominion over his person, and (in a prologue to suicide) that the deadly logic of this speech is being assumed *in force* by its addressee. Put another way, Georg is no less subject to the father's speech—and to the entire fantasmatic mise-en-scène that it mounts—than a fictional character is to the author writing him into existence. These are the precise conditions in which the father's final judgment will be pronounced in all its immediate and mortal effectivity. This is also the point of tightest convergence between the story's writer and the diabolical figure through which it circuits the power of language to self-actualize as an independent existence, that is, the power to produce fictions in the mode of effective realities. What is revealed at bottom in these exchanges of power, image and speech performance is that speech itself is the very element of the diabolical force projected by, but thereby visited upon, the creature to be judged in this story.

Indeed, as Georg Bendemann is stripped of all interiority, and of virtually all capacity to speak, as the *Schreckbild* of the father takes absolute hold of appearances in order to manipulate them as forcefully gripping realities, we can see that the "sublime" instance of this tale is distinctly marked by a certain *diabolism*. The father's speech is both "sublime" (pseudodivine) and diabolical precisely insofar as it has entered the sphere of its own total self-actualization, in a perfect equivalence between simulacrum and reality—and in the laying out of these as a trap—and by introducing a strife that verges toward a limit inherent to such absolute speech, that is, a sadistic putting to death.[7] Such is the grotesque form of the destituting sublime as it is staged in this story (a point we will return to in a moment).

The Judgment and the "Innocent Child"

It is all the more striking, then, as we consider the various rivalries structuring this text, to recall that the father condemns Georg for a devilishness of his own, in contrast to an innocence that emerges here for the first time, but only at the moment of its irreversible foreclosure.

> "So now you know what there was outside of yourself [*was es ausser dir gab*], up to now you have known only about yourself! An innocent child [*ein unschuldiges Kind*] you truly were, but even more truly were you a devilish human being [*ein teuflischer Mensch*]! — Therefore know this: I sentence you now to death by drowning!"
> (Sons 15; E 53)

That so much of this judgment hinges on a difference between an "outside"—represented by the father and all the betrayed parties and interests with which he aligns himself, mere images all—and an interior known as "yourself," which has been the sole object of knowledge up to now: this structure reinforces a crucial aspect of the movement operated by the scene unfolding up to this point, namely that this scene is itself the staging of an externalization into which Georg himself is now fully absorbed, image among images. In that sense, there is nothing left, no internal resistance, no kernel of true subjectivity that could lend itself to an indignant or inert countermovement out of the traffic of mere images (and of words as mere images) and against the father's force of law; there is only Georg and the father in the diabolical element of this reality-producing speech. In other words, Georg is finally, in a sense, "nothing but literature," and as such he precisely embodies one aspect of the hyperbolic ideal that Kafka will soon claim for himself—in that regard he too inhabits the position of "father" in this judgment and in this text. In his diabolical adulthood, Georg has always been on the side of the father's pure power of speech and image, but without acceding to a full knowledge of its grounds and implications. Could it be that his guilt, in *this* respect— not the guilt of a disavowed ambivalent narcissism for which he will have to be punished, but the deeper guilt of a knowledge that "true" speech traffics in power—is that he has clung to the innocence of a childhood which is hereby dispensed with? Georg's ridiculous stammering failure to defend himself before the accusations of the *Schreckbild* father can be seen as an index of his being emptied, like a shell, of a last remainder of deep interiority—that is, precisely, of childhood, and of the innocence it would harbor. This process, which has its own limits, nonetheless constitutes a severing from the past as a controlling and generative limitation on language. If "I can do anything," it is on condition that this "I" be torn away from the established parameters of its doing, and from the inhibiting residues of a sedimented past, however "innocent" it might be. That is, it has entered radical fiction.

What I would like to suggest, then, is this: if there is in this story an "authentic" and innocent interiority whose presentation and externalization is required as a defense in the theater of judgment, doomed to failure though it may be, it is here given the surprising name of "childhood." That is the name of the residue that, as infancy, cannot be rendered over into the element of speech, and which is thus destroyed insofar as the effective reality of that element is concerned. But I would also like to suggest that this residue of the "innocent child" has perhaps not in fact been entirely dissolved into the medium of pure-speech-as-immediately-actualized-image-reality. Something of it persists into the very heart of the punishment that ensues, for it is precisely as a son emptied of childhood that Georg submits to the judgment in virtuosic style. And in a rather perplexing fashion, this childhood performance is reduced to a bodily automatism and is strikingly linked with *hunger*, an unexpected element that cannot help but draw our attention.

I am referring to the climax of the story, following immediately after the father pronounces his judgment, which Georg executes with a gymnastic skill acquired in his youth, "to his parents' pride," but that here serves to fulfill the deadly logic of performative mastery that has overdetermined the story's scenography. Only here this mastery, following the apogee of its manifestation in speech on the part of the father, has now transferred entirely into the realm of bodily movement. "The Judgment" quickly rushes with this body to its conclusion.

> Georg felt himself chased [*gejagt*] from the room, the crash [*Schlag*] with which the father collapsed [*stürzte*] onto the bed rang in his ears as he fled. On the staircase, which he rushed down as if its steps were an inclined plane, he ran into the cleaning woman [*Bedienerin*] on her way up to do the morning cleaning of the room. "Jesus!" she cried and covered her face with her apron, but he was already gone. Out the front door he leapt [*sprang*], across the roadway to the water he was driven [*zum Wasser trieb es ihn*]. Already he was holding tight to the railing *as a hungry man holds tight to his food* [*schon hielt er das Geländer fest, wie ein Hungriger die Nahrung*]. He swung himself over, like the distinguished gymnast he had been in his youth, to his parents' pride. He still held on with ever weaker hands, spied between the bars of the railing [*Geländerstangen*] a bus that would easily cover the sound of his fall, called out quietly: "Dear Parents, I have always loved you, all the same," and let himself fall [*liess sich hinabfallen.*]
>
> At that moment a downright endless stream of traffic went over the bridge.
> (Sons 15–16; E 53; my emphasis)

It is impossible not to see this *ballet mécanique* of complete and utter subjection to the father's judgment as, at the same time, a kind of liberation: stymied and stuttering during the judgment scene itself, upon pronouncement of the "sentence" Georg suddenly finds an astonishing capacity for resolutely directed movement, complete with bounding leaps and acrobatic flourishes (indeed, this is the first in a series of such leaps and *Sprünge*, provisional exits from the space of the law, that regularly punctuate each of the judgment narratives, as we will see in Chapter 3). At the same time, an impersonal "it" drives Georg compulsively onward, and this drive demonstrates a mastery of bodily movement in inverse proportion to the loss of speech in the scene that precedes it. One could put it thus: if the father's tirade has divested Georg of speech—the medium in which the judgment, and the guilt it is based on, are actualized—his powerful climactic performative utterance nonetheless releases and impels Georg's *body* into another mode of mastery which, however, is fully subordinated to the regime that must destroy it. Freedom and masterful bodily movement are rendered in the disciplinary telic logic that releases them, like a trigger, unto death alone, as though this transfer could obfuscate the speech power that it relays. At the same time, it is precisely here that performance is explicitly linked both with childhood and with the exoneration that speech has failed to secure: this gymnast's turn also recalls Georg's childhood innocence, indexing what he "truly" has been, in a way that his now devilish words (or writing) cannot. This point is brought home with Georg's farewell, which amounts to a kind of miniature oral suicide letter, a final statement of self-defense (after all) that is undermined by an ambiguity leading directly back to the diabolical multiplicity of language: "Dear Parents, I have always loved you, all the same"—"*ich habe euch* doch *immer geliebt*"—says Georg to no one. The ambiguity (a translator's anguish) revolves around the adversative *doch*—for what does it counter, what (slanderous) presumption does it protest? The sentence could mean: Dear parents, I have always loved you, *despite what you say*, or: *despite appearances*, or perhaps even: *despite also having hated you*, and therefore, by implication—an implication vividly elaborated in the father's accusations—having wished for your removal and destruction (a wish that in the first two thirds of the story seems to have been realized). Or, finally, it could mean *despite your having hated me*, even as I perform the mastery of your dictates unto death. This speech is no defense. Whatever it is that Georg would have had to *present* in order to exonerate himself in the court of Oedipal bad conscience, has been condensed into a performing body that is already condemned and can now only sink into a stream of pure images, "drowned out" as it were by the "ceaseless traffic" that will henceforth absorb the remainder of total judgment, the released and sinking child-body. It is this impersonal onrushing flow that finally dominates, bringing the fiction into the element of its final frozen mobility, that of an unending circulation of images. Exulting in the permanent movement of *pure circulation*, the story declares the terms of its own survival in the transformation of scenography, the speech and movement of judge and judged, into sheer serial displacement, the impersonal realm of empty time—the pure space of fiction. Put formally, this coincides, in the last sentence, with the speech of an omniscient narrator finally released from the perspective (and from the knotted, looping conscience) of its primary fictive avatar. We note once again that this occurs on the condition that a corpse be produced (and absconded), that a son be judged, and killed.

Grasping Hunger: The Toothless Father

In this perspective, what do we make of the odd invocation of hunger, as Georg is "driven" toward the water and grasps the railing, as though reaching out for the object of his compulsion? The metaphorical knot that Kafka tightens here is very dense: in reaching for the railing as an object of need and/or desire, Georg reaches not only for the parental pride revived, in absentia, by this gymnastic feat, but also for the death dictated by its logic, a death he appears to crave. The drive for mastery within the sphere of visible performance converges quite literally with a death drive. But this "nourishment" (*Nahrung*) is not there to satisfy. It is important to look closely at Kafka's very precise language: he does not write (as some translations seem to suggest) that Georg grabbed the railing the way a starving man reaches out for food that he will thereby eat. Instead he writes of Georg: "Schon hielt er das Geländer fest," he already held fast to the railing, where the verb *festhalten* implies holding on to something *so as not to let go*; but if Georg holds the railing thus, "wie ein Hungriger die Nahrung," like a starving man holding fast to his food, this means that he holds *rather than eating it*. It is here that a resolutely unsatisfied (and childish) hunger crosses, disjunctively, with a scenography programmed by bad conscience and its pseudosublime "bite." And what we notice in this disjuncture is that the truly excessive remnant of this economy's consumption/consummation, the moment where its logic is both sealed and systematically eluded, is to be located *in hunger itself*. Within the narrative of "The Judgment," however, this is a structural moment made visible only within the frame of a drive toward death programmed by the elements we have laid out here (rivalrous exchanges of power, fantasmatic projections, disavowed guilt, the depropriations of diabolical speech). For Georg does let go, of course, only not in order to ingest what hunger demands, but rather to feed himself into the diabolical machinery that has made him. It is in that sense that the hunger he grasps, somewhere on the other side of judgment, itself remains unassimilated as such. It is the "inward" pocket of resistance that, in its insistent and recalcitrant emptiness, will eventually undo the entire schema of operation of the judgment stories.

Keeping this prospect in mind, we can also point back to suggest that with this strange counter-economy of holding-onto-but-not-using—and of letting go only at the moment of death—we enter once again into the fabulistic sphere of the man with the locked box. That man from the letter to Pollak "can do nothing," but he holds fast to a treasure—remnants of past nourishment—that cannot be displayed, or consumed: two milk teeth. That man's element too is hunger, and his secret has to do with childhood—a childhood impossibly indexed in an emblematic *thing* that will not lend itself to presentation, except by way of its occluding container. The analogue of that treasure for Georg Bendemann is, in a very complex fashion, something like the occluded love voiced by an emptied out child who must then be given over to the deathly element of guilt, in the form of a no less occluded cadaver—sole guarantor of the higher powers affirmed in this climax.

These higher powers are not represented as such in the story, but rather only "by subreption" in a father who is suddenly gripped by the force of self-actualizing speech. Indeed, it is important to stress that if the father has represented these powers, he does not fully embody them; this triumph of judgment is not his apotheosis, for he too "falls," even crashes or collapses (*stürzte*) in the end, thus renewing on its downslide a homology that has been marked elsewhere in the story between Georg and this paternal figure who in many respects is himself quite childish and abject. Aside from details such as his dirty underwear and Georg's undressing him and carrying him like a child to his bed, we note one significant point that is particularly relevant here: the father is described as being "toothless."[8] This occurs precisely at the moment when the father demands to be heard, very much in the manner of a berating bad conscience: "'Georg,' said the father stretching his toothless mouth wide open, 'listen to me! [*hör einmal!*]'" (Sons 9; E 48) He goes on to demand that Georg "tell me the whole truth," threatening to "stir up matters" that probably ought to be left alone, and insisting that his son not deceive him, before asking a question that draws the entire scene into its native element of fictive speech: "Do you really have this friend in St. Petersburg?" In other words, at the very moment when the father is shown to lack any "bite," he rises to haunt Georg like a bad conscience, and *accuses him of writing fiction*. The father's toothless mouth, "drawn wide apart"—a hideous detail that passes almost unnoticed—is thus the chasm through which Georg's "reality" comes to be engulfed in its own implicit diabolism, but in a way that he cannot acknowledge and that does not yet take hold of him. For he disregards the father's question ("Never mind my friends!"), and begins instead to *accuse the father* of unhealthy living—that is, to *accuse himself* of neglecting the father, thereby confirming this decisive turn in the proceedings. Most pointedly, he complains, somewhat oddly, that the father only "takes little sips from" his breakfast ("*du nippst vom Frühstück*"; Sons 10, E 48), a phrase that both reinforces the father's lack of bite and adds an element of starvation to the image of the melancholic old child wasting from neglect.[9] One might suspect that he is only waiting for the son he calls "*mein Früchtchen*"—his "little fruit"—to ripen in this element of radiant "insight." But the father does not eat the son, who, as this expression also implies, is "spoiled rotten."[10] Instead, he takes hold of and ejects the son by means of a force that "drops" him as well, once the scenography of judgment has run its course. If the starving, toothless father rises to the height and power of a sublime judge, the story makes it clear that this occurs through a mechanism that depends on his collapse in the end, and that in delivering the blow of judgment, this mere stand-in must also suffer the *Schlag* that dissolves the story's specific figures into the schematic image of their sheer circulation—their unending traffic—as the fundamental condition of their production. But even this impersonal infinite traffic requires a kind of "combustion," and it points, structurally and logically, to a strange and problematic "subject," if only in the "it" of a compulsive movement: *zum Schreiben trieb es ihn*?

The Author's Ecstasy: The Consummating Fire

If the climax of this work comes when its protagonist disappears into the watery element that will swallow him whole, Kafka, for his part, will celebrate the effulgent appearance of the writer who has birthed it, and he does so in terms of the destructive-generative element of fire he has long been seeking. I would like to return for a moment to the diary entry immediately following the composition of "The Judgment," which clearly manifests the strange and disjointed continuity between fiction and autobiography (autobiography radically transformed into fiction) in the different modes of Kafka's writing: composed in the pages of the diary, the story is followed by a space and a line drawn across it, after which Kafka continues, writing the narrative of the writing: "This story, 'The Judgment,' I wrote at one sitting. . . ." The description of this ecstatic success also mobilizes virtually all of the figural language through which Kafka has developed an ideal of writing that has been long and laboriously pursued, and is here finally accomplished. What he celebrates is nothing less than having attained something of the sublimity of his heretofore crushing and suffocating models. The elated sense of triumph is palpable:

> This story, 'The Judgment,' I wrote at one sitting [*in einem Zug*] during the night of 22nd–23rd September . . . how the story developed before me, as if I were gliding over water. . . . How everything can be said, how for everything, for the strangest fancies, there waits a great fire in which they perish and rise up again [*vergehn und auferstehn*]. . . . Only in this way can writing be done [*nur so kann geschrieben werden*], only with such coherence [*Zusammenhang*], with such a complete opening of body and soul. (D 212–213; TB 214)

We recognize here not only the specific figural language from Kafka's last letter to Pollak—where in a long single draft ("in einem Zug") of reading, the gapless continuity (*Zusammenhang*) of Hebbel's life is ingested, to be then upwardly projected in all its immense and towering cohesiveness; and we find not only the "opening" of body and soul that is first painfully inflicted as an ax on the frozen sea, which also figures the expressive, expulsive, externalizing movement traversing much of Kafka's writing (on writing); we also confront once again an image of the holy fire that miraculously produces more and greater than it consumes. The significance of this diary entry, in the terms I have used to frame the current interrogation, amounts to this: here Kafka looks upon his own writing and judges it worthy, its substance subject to a sublime transformation, insofar as it is animated by a fire that is both deeply inward and to be found only in the extreme reaches of a vast other world that has here been made visible.

This fire, then, this great force and capacity to *say everything*, remains the secret treasure of this otherwise violent and destituting experience. And it too is understood by Kafka entirely in terms of performance and spectatorship, a persuasive appearance subject to a judgment that must be won through these means. This becomes clear in the most literal way possible when, in an enigmatic and isolated sentence that comes immediately after the celebratory diary entry, Kafka writes: "I, only I, am the spectator in the orchestra [*ich, nur ich bin der Beobachter des Parterres*]" (D 213; KA TB 461[11]). How strangely this phrase ("ich, nur ich . . .") echoes with the "ich aber, ich muss" pronounced earlier in a letter to Pollak—as though the forbidding God who struggles against writing were replaced here by a single judging spectator, lonely in his triumph. But the spectatorship soon expands, and the necessity of a performance and appearance of the text before an audience is given its due, as Kafka writes a few days later of reading the story to a group of friends and family (his sisters). At the end, he says, "There were tears in my eyes. The indubitability of the story was confirmed" (D 214; TB 216; September 25, 1912).

One cannot help thinking that, at some level, these ecstatic tears have something essential to do with the ecstasy of Georg Bendemann's speech-driven demise, as though the fate of both character and writer converged in the complex logic of performance. But whereas Georg's masterful performance must in its total subjection produce a corpse, as I have stressed, Kafka's performance, which cannot be reduced to the phantoms that populate it, leaves behind, rather, a text, which does not merely fulfill but necessarily confounds and exceeds the law of its production. The paradoxical name I have proposed for the moment of that excess, following the story's own hint, is *hunger*: an empty point of contact between language as power and language as a disruptive failure no longer able to dictate death. The problem, for Kafka—a problem seen in hindsight, to be sure—will be to empty that hunger to the point of releasing all its precious objects, including the body ecstatically consumed by its "sublime" logic and, especially, the "radiant" if terrifying image of its dictating instance: the galvanizing paternal *Schreckbild* and its deadly subreption of the Law.

If "The Judgment" establishes the basic motto of the judgment stories as something like "A son is being killed," it also thereby reveals something fundamental about *what language can do*. That is, it shows that at one extremity of inscenated speech, language *kills through mastery*. One troubling implication of the indubitable success in writing this particular story, insofar as it is aligned with the kind of power wielded by the father's speech staged within it, is this: to become a writer means to grasp hold of a force of speech that, at the far end of its unhinged manipulations, harbors a power to kill as its always virtual destiny. In brushing past a hunger that must remain radically unsatisfied, "The Judgment" hurls itself across a chasm not containable in its consuming ecstasies (though it will reappear soon enough in other texts).

Georg's grasping of the railing is programmed, rather, as a grasping for nourishment in the mode of a hunger for death performed—but the hunger in question is not satisfied by death, which gives nothing more to grasp but a body to be eliminated.

The Fall: Hinab-, Herab-

Everything, in the end, is thus a matter of rising and falling, springing up and sinking down, until the story resolves finally into an endless movement of horizontal circulation. I would only point out, to conclude this analysis of "The Judgment," that when Kafka composed the story in his diary notebook, the verb he used to describe Georg's fall was not *hinabfallen*—as it stands in the published version ("*Georg . . . liess sich hinabfallen*")—which implies a perspective from above, watching Georg fall away . . . but *herabfallen* (KA TB 460), which orients the perspective rather at Georg's level, and thus in the end even farther down below, in the lower parts, in the waiting water, bringing us all down with it. This tiny change betrays something essential at stake in the shifting layout of Kafka's judgment stories. In composing the penultimate sentence of his first indubitable triumph—the sentence that "physically" realizes the death penalty in question all along—Kafka places the writer, the narrator, and the reader in that low place toward which Georg plummets, and not at the higher vantage from which we would watch him disappear, *hinabwärts*, and he thus acknowledges a position he felt it necessary to displace in handing the story over to the public: in the theater of power, the triumphant writer, too, is also at risk of merely sinking into sublimity. From there the task will be to rupture this opposition between *hinab-* and *herab-*, to dissolve (in the filmic sense) not only Georg's dreamy recalcitrant narcissism but also the tyrannically structuring force of the father's *Blick* and image, his unique *Schreckbild*, to disenchant the Oedipal circle (which in a striking expression from the *Diaries* Kafka refers to as the *Blutkreis*, the circle of blood encompassing father and son), and to *fall otherwise*—out of enthrallment to the image *and* out of sublimity.[12] That is, to dissolve the blood bond that ties together the violent ends of speech. Put yet another way, and as a question: how to make the Law lose its univocal voice (its capital, its *caput*), so that the sublime imperative is dispersed into the multiple singularities of circulating speech? Or perhaps, finally: how to *do justice* to the endlessness of language's traffic?

In the judgment stories that followed "The Judgment," this movement and its obstacles can be read in the rapid inversions of power and powerlessness that inflect their shifting relations: each of these stories stages numerous reversals, substitutions, and cyclical turns that both reinforce and perversely scramble their established hierarchies of power and prestige. At the same time, these reversals pass through similar crossed trajectories of stymied speech and bodily mastery or abjection (or both). My focus in schematically laying out these elements will be, once again, the nature of what *must be presented* within the tribunal set up in each story, what each speaker/defendant must persuasively give forth in self-defense in his respective theater of speech, and how in every instance this exigency meets with ruin, such that the "inner" or transcendent truth in question (innocence, Justice) is lost in the treacherous "external" element of speech performed. But also to ask what remains in and from this ruination—what insistent leftover clogs the change of regime enacted in every case, lodged within the machinery of appearance that Kafka must, at the same time, vindicate as the "proper" element of his art. Is there some unassimilable residue that blocks or slows the "unending traffic" into which Kafka would fully absorb the diabolical economy of writing as pure appearance? One indication may be found in the mute and monstrous body of Gregor Samsa as it, too, is slowly transformed into a corpse.

"THE METAMORPHOSIS": THAT THING . . . THROWN AWAY

Kafka's most famous story, begun not long after the completion of "The Judgment," extends, echoes, and transposes numerous aspects of the earlier text. It, too, is essentially a family drama taking place almost entirely in an urban domestic space in which a son is exiled (internally this time), cut off from the rest of his family, and punished with death. Gregor Samsa, too, undergoes a judgment dramatized in not one but three separate judgment scenes, corresponding to his "appearance" at the dramatic high point of each of the story's three sections. I will not be able to examine each of these appearances and judgment scenes in detail, but the judgments pronounced or enacted on Gregor, while less formal and explicit than that of "The Judgment," revolve all the more clearly around the same disjunction at work there—between an "interior," a subjectivity posited as innocent but dispossessed by (and of) speech, and an external theater that performatively generates the guilt it sets out to condemn, and the death thereby required. In both cases, it is the father who imposes capital punishment (although in "The Metamorphosis" we see that there is an even graver punishment cutting closer to home, this time pronounced by the sister); and in both cases a son is unable to speak in his own defense. But whereas Georg Bendemann manages to stammer a few senseless retorts, here Kafka locks his character into a complete social mutism that corresponds, on the other end, to the extremes of terror (for others) and bliss (his own) occasioned by his extraordinary and monstrous body. The fact that the magnificent insect body is reduced in the end to a starving shell of itself—literally something that must be thrown away (*weggeschafft*)—points us in the direction of the remnant that this story must spit out of its harsh economy in order to reach its conclusion in the horrifying banality of renewal.[13]

Compulsive Appearance

The story is structured entirely around this rupture between the "inner" world of Gregor's consciousness, to which the reader is given direct access, and the "external" sphere of social speech from which the former is utterly sealed away. Indeed, such an absolute break is so indispensible to the story that Kafka goes to great lengths to foreclose the slightest possibility that Gregor would be understood by the family. If it did not seem so misplaced, given that this is a tale about a man who turns into a giant vermin, one could even say that the story stretches credulity on this point: why would Gregor, who seems quite resourceful in other respects, not think (for example) to spell out some desperate message with the food scraps left by his sister for him to taste—an otherwise successful, if minimal, experiment in communication—or even more obviously with the "traces of the sticky stuff" ("*Spuren seines Klebstoffes*") that Gregor's insect feet leave behind on the walls— a fact mentioned in the very same sentence as the possible removal from his room of his *writing desk* (Sons, 83; E 83)? It is clear that Gregor *must not speak*, or write, for only thus can his ultimate rejection and abjection be prepared, his apparently remainderless expulsion from the family. In the meantime, what he must do, rather, is *appear*. That is the specific imperative bearing on the entire first segment of the story, constituting it as a judgment scene. This scene too is conditioned by a presumption of guilt, to which this appearance would be a necessary response. The dilemma of Gregor's guilt in the opening sequence is that it consists in the fact that he is still around to defend himself against it; and yet this still being around is of course conditioned by his transformation, which has rendered speech impossible, at least for the tribunal of spectators waiting to hear what he has to say for himself. These constraints, which Kafka has carefully imposed on the theater of "The Metamorphosis," mean that Gregor's entire social being is concentrated in his body and in the web of dramatic responses and associations elicited by this body's mere appearance. And it turns out that this appearance is extremely *powerful*, at least at first.

The most substantial and specific structural parallel that I would draw between "The Judgment" and "The Metamorphosis" is between the judgment scene proper in the former—beginning with the father's transformation and his explosive "No!"—and the first appearance of Gregor Samsa, which is equally explosive and gives rise to strikingly similar effects, and even to similar phrasing, as Gregor exerts an impelling and compulsive force quite comparable in its irresistible automatism to that undergone by Georg Bendemann. After speaking at length behind the door, only to learn that his interlocutors hear nothing but a buzzing "animal voice," and after straining to turn the key in the lock with his toothless jaws (a detail that will take on greater resonance later), Gregor finally maneuvers into view for the assembled spectators, first of all the Prokurist or Chief Clerk who has promptly arrived—as a comically literal voice of bad conscience—to berate the tardy and negligent subordinate under his supervision. This petty overbearing figure of authority and endless futile labor (in essence a displaced stand-in for the father, for whose debts or "*Schulden*" Gregor must use his earnings) is the first to react. Gregor

> heard the chief clerk utter a loud "Oh!"—it sounded like a gust of wind—and now he could see the man, standing as he was nearest the door, clapping one hand over his open mouth and slowly backing away as if he were being *driven out* by some unseen but continuous and unwavering force [*als* vertriebe *ihn eine unsichtbare, gleichmässig fortwirkende Kraft*]. (Sons 65–66; E 68; my emphasis)

The father, for his part, clenches a fist with a hostile expression, before sinking into tears, such that "his powerful chest shook." This sinking and loss of power on the part of the parents will soon enough be reversed, especially for the father; but for now, it is Gregor who has the power. Indeed, to continue the comparison with "The Judgment," structurally speaking Gregor is in a position precisely analogous to that of the Bendemann father—hallucinatory locus of toothless but irresistible force—whereas the Prokurist, like Georg Bendemann, is compulsively driven out the door and down the stairs. In this case, it is the purveyor of guilt who is the guilty one in need of redemption, and the narrator says this explicitly. After a long speech by Gregor, which of course no one understands (and to which we will return in a moment: it is nothing if not a defense speech), the narrator switches back to the other axis of this dual perspective in order to describe the Prokurist's reaction in all its pressing automatism:

> But at Gregor's very first words the chief clerk had already backed away and only stared at him with parted lips over one twitching shoulder. And while Gregor was speaking he did not stand still one moment but inched toward the door, yet *without taking his eyes off Gregor*, as if obeying some mysterious command not [*als bestehe ein geheimes Verbot*] to leave the room. He was already in the hall, and to judge from the suddenness with which he took his last step out of the living room one could easily have thought he had burned the sole of his foot. Once in the hall he stretched his right arm before him toward the staircase, as if some supernatural power were waiting there to deliver him [*als warte dort auf ihn eine geradezu überirdische Erlösung*] (Sons 67–68; E 70; my emphasis)

The interplay of law and force in this description is much more complex than that found at the end of "The Judgment," where they correspond in a one-way push toward exit and extinction. Here there are opposing trajectories, as though the "force" exerted by Gregor's powerfully apotropaic body were countered by another Law, also somehow emanating from this body, a "secret interdiction" (*geheimes Verbot*) against leaving the room—a complexity compounded by the form, status and position of the players in question, in which the relatively simple father-son relation in "The Judgment" is transposed into a more symbolically ramifying (and indeed quite puzzling) employee/insect-supervisor/family relation. The important point for my purposes is this: Gregor's sudden usurpation of social power, short-circuited and "muted" as it is in his shocking insect form, has effected an inversion in which his superior is now subject to a literally electrifying expulsive force, to which he submits with the automatism of a body's involuntary motion (his bizarre "twitching" only serves to confirm this). Driven down the stairs, the Prokurist gestures toward a "*gerade überirdische Erlösung*," literally a "virtually supra-earthly redemption" which strangely recalls, in its precise syntax (and even in its sense), the "*gerade unendlicher Verkehr*," the virtually infinite traffic that figures Georg Bendemann's absolution, or dissolution—but now in terms that emphasize the dimension of height, elevation, and celestial sublimity that such a moment of extreme horror seems to call for. Indeed, Gregor, too, is a *Schreckbild*, and is in fact later referred to as a *Schreckgestalt* (Sons 99; E 101). As such, his terrorizing force galvanizes the gaze of the Prokurist onto himself as its sole possible object, and it is precisely in this compulsively aimed gaze that the secret interdiction is registered ("without taking his eyes off Gregor, as if obeying").[14] If, as began to appear in "The Judgment," the realm of the law in its effectivity is in part the realm of the powerful *image*, Gregor now stands at the burning and radiant center of that sphere; and yet the text leaves a margin precisely here, specifying that the force exerted by this overwhelming appearance is "invisible," that redemption from it is "supra-mundane" (while also hedging the implication of a transcendent dimension with a careful "as if"). This margin, which would be the space in which speech would supplement the power of the image, opening the possibility, at least, of a defense, closes instead on the consciousness of Gregor sealed into an animal carapace. That consciousness is the initial inaccessible remainder of this story, a hidden (if not "authentic") interiority locked out of the sphere of social appearance; but it is there that the law remains in force in all its banal familiarity (that is, in Gregor's highly conventional subjectivity). The extinction of this awareness in the end will only confirm the order that has been temporarily disrupted; but it will also displace the unruly remainder into another obtrusive but disposable form, as we will see.

Speech Embodied: Gossip and Judgment

Despite the startling and complex inversion enacted in the beginning of the story, whereby the lowly Gregor becomes magnificently powerful by transforming into the most vile creature imaginable, Gregor's own awareness continues to follow the ruts laid out in his former life. As has been pointed out (by Deleuze and Guattari, for example), Gregor's failure consists partly in the fact that he does not fully assume for himself the magnitude and consequences of his own semi-successful escape attempt, and this does overdetermine his adventure. But in a certain formal sense, it is missing an important point: as with Kafka's decision to close Gregor off from comprehensible speech, his intact preservation of Gregor's all too human subjectivity within the monstrous body now visible to the rest of the world is clearly a deliberate and unwavering structural feature of the story. It allows Kafka not so much to play out the possibility of a change in desire that might result from his newly invented body, but, much more predominantly, to bring out the latent aggression and unsteady hierarchical structures of the social milieu—as internalized by one of its most faithful sons—which is the story's most constant critical target. Somewhat paradoxically, perhaps, Gregor's unmitigated submission to the reigning order of this milieu gives the precise measure of that critique, and a proper gauge of its strategic exaggerations and foreclosures.

This point reaches to the very heart of Kafka's social and political thinking, which can be read most incisively, perhaps, in what I would call Gregor's "defense speech," given during the scene I have been describing, at the beginning of the Prokurist's horrified flight. For this speech shows exactly what Gregor perceives himself—however dimly—to be repressed by, what he is the victim of, the nature and structure of the wrong and the wound that draws from him, at the precise moment of his first appearance before the assembled tribunal-audience, a compulsive speech that no one can hear, for two very good reasons: because he is an animal, and because all anyone can do in any case is stare in shock at his monstrous appearance. Immediately after he emerges from behind the door and even after the first horror is registered in the Prokurist's windy "Oh!" Gregor persists in addressing the authority the Prokurist no longer is for him, in a speech that uncannily reflects the origin of Gregor's unexpected problem that morning. This origin itself is to be found in the bodily effects of social speech:

> "And you know very well that a traveling salesman, who is almost never seen in the office all year long, can so easily fall victim [*Opfer*] to gossip [*Klatschereien*] and to bad luck [*Zufälligkeiten*: chance occurrences, contingencies] and groundless accusations [*grundlosen Beschwerden*] he *can't defend himself* against because he generally *knows nothing about them* and only finds out when he comes back exhausted from one of his trips and then *has to suffer on his very body* the bad consequences whose causes he can no longer even see into [*die schlimmen, auf ihre Ursachen hin nicht mehr zu durchschauenden Folgen* am eigenen Leibe zu spüren bekommt]. Sir, sir, don't go away without saying a word to me that shows that you think me at least partly in the right [*recht geben*]!" (Sons 67; E 69–70; my emphasis)

This is what Gregor is compelled to say in his own defense, as he articulates the wrong done to him and accounts, in an oblique third person displacement, for his present condition. In language that anticipates the central trope of "In the Penal Colony," as well as that of *The Trial*, Kafka places Gregor's dilemma within the register of legal defense, while also clearly implying that Gregor's transformation is the result of a *graphic bodily inscription of slanderous speech*. For that is what Gregor says here: against groundless accusations, made in his absence and without his knowledge, there is no defense, only a confused perception of their effects as they "come to be felt directly on his body" ("*am eigenen Leibe zu spüren bekommt*").[15] The use of the verb *spüren* also evokes the *spuren* or traces thus inscribed into this body, such that what Gregor is "feeling" now is the vermin form that this speech has carved out for him. While the legal sense of the term used for these "accusations" (*Beschwerden*) gives them, potentially, the formal status of slander, the name given to this speech here is that of a more diffuse "idle gossip," *Klatschereien*, as though this were the very "ground" of the legal proceedings that are in fact taking place, in the distorted form of Gregor's "appearance" before the law. I cannot show here what a careful reading of this moment, alongside similar developments in *The Trial* and especially *The Castle* (among other texts) would reveal, namely that for Kafka gossip and rumor, both pointed accusations and diffuse public speech, constitute the essential ground and effective field of law and politics. In the present context, the important point is that, in crooked parallel (as it were) to the compelling Law and its redemption projected beyond or above the horizon of Gregor's visible world (into the *überirdische*), there is another law that, by force of speech, pushes gradually down, with such constant and imperceptible pressure as to be indistinguishable from one's very own body and voice. This is the banal law, and the unaccountable guilt, in which Gregor's own silent voice is hermetically sealed, and its formative pressure renders up the figure of the unspeakable vermin body. But this law also provides the conditions for the turns of fortune inflecting the Samsa family drama.

I am referring especially to the imminent "rise" of the father and the concomitant re-descent of Gregor, culminating in a final judgment scene that leaves the insect son literally and bodily wounded, dying, and *punished*. The dramatic high point of the entire story arguably occurs in Part II, when Gregor, having discovered a new and blissful occupation in crawling on and hanging from the walls and ceiling of his room, nonetheless reacts with intense aggression to the sister's plan to empty his room of its human accoutrements, especially the writing desk or *Schreibtisch*, whose potential removal induces a defensive threatening posture (he sticks himself against the picture of the woman with a fur muff and waits angrily and visibly on the wall). Gregor escapes from his room, sending the mother and sister into a panic. When the father returns home from his new job as something resembling a security guard in a bank, we are given the measure of his own transformation—from the feckless lazy old man he is described as being earlier in the story, to the stiff-backed fascistic functionary he figures at this point.

This scene also provides an important inflection of the observation made earlier, namely the aspect of "gossip" that establishes guilt through unfounded prejudgment based solely on hastily interpreted appearances. For is essentially on this basis that Gregor is judged and condemned by the father in the story's second judgment scene, as tendentious description verges into slander. "Mother fainted, but she's better now. Gregor has broken loose [*ausgebrochen*]," says Gregor's sister, underscoring his status as caged beast and recalcitrant prisoner. "'Just what I expected,' said his father. . . . It was clear to Gregor that his father had taken the worst interpretation of Grete's all too brief statement and was assuming that Gregor had been guilty of some violent act" (Sons 88; E 88). This assumption of guilt by the father plays directly on the disjunction of private consciousness and public appearance on which the story is based, insofar as Gregor has not committed a violent act but is now in no position to defend himself, that is, to state his case in response to the sister's summary prosecution. "Gregor must now try to calm his father, since he had neither the time nor means [*Möglichkeit*] for an explanation." The scene repeats the appearance before the Prokurist, but in this case the spectator in question, the father, is not driven away but is rather coming at him. Gregor has already lost his prestige and his power, and his imminent condemnation is prefigured in the imposing image of the father he now sees towering above him. "Truly, this was not the father he had imagined to himself." Much like Georg Bendemann, Gregor had imagined rather an abject father "wearily sunk in bed," and who could sink only lower. But now, corseted into his bank uniform, emblem of the subordinate authority as which he is now officially invested, "he was standing there straight as a stick." The description of this clean cut and well-ordered figure continues along these lines, culminating in a banal but excruciating detail that seems literally to impart something fundamental about his transformation, however opaquely: "his formerly tangled white hair had been combed flat on either side of a shining and painfully exact parting [*zu einer peinlich genauen, leuchtenden Scheitelfrisur niedergekämmt*]" (Sons 89; E 89). This "*Scheitel*" or parting strikes one as a startling and horrific figure, inscribed as bodily hygiene and social appearance, for the division or "*Urteil*" the father has already starkly drawn. The pains taken, and the disciplinary regime expressed in, this rigorously divided part surely have something to do, uncannily and dreadfully, with the splitting pain and punishment the father is about to inflict on Gregor's animal body.

But as if that were not enough, Kafka trumps this small but stark image with another that stretches the precise objective detail of the scene to the point of expressionistic distortion, precisely in terms of scale, perspective and height (a narrative strategy he often uses to great effect). He describes the father's approach: "his hands in his trouser pockets, [he] advanced with grim visage [*mit verbissenem Gesicht*] toward Gregor . . . he lifted his feet unusually high off the floor, and Gregor was dumbfounded at the enormous size [*Riesengrösse*] of his boot soles. But Gregor could not risk standing up to him" (Sons, 89–90; E 89). What else would a panicked insect see if not the outsized threat of a looming boot sole? Despite Gregor's own dimensions, much larger than any human shoe, he now knows that he can be squashed like any other bug. This demotion in power and prestige, and the distortion of perspective that displays it, give the measure of Gregor's reduction to lowliness and vulnerability, whereas his father has become "a giant of a man" powerfully towering over him, *about to inflict a wound*. It does not seem too great a leap to associate the metaphorics of the sublime axe of bad conscience raised in the final letter to Oskar Pollak with the penetrating wound that Gregor is about to receive here, once the father starts hurling food at this insect on the floor. We are very much within the complex knot of bad conscience and biting penetrations that winds through all of the judgment stories. Further, these apples, their use as weapons, and the festering wound one of them causes—which leads to further degradation and precisely to starvation—constitute the peculiar core of this decisive judgment scene, and indeed perhaps of the story as a whole. For not only does the apple/wound/punishment consummate the tensions of law, transgression, and authority that have played out up to this moment, it also points beyond these to a dimension that, as I suggested above, has already been opened by the question of food and hunger in "The Judgment." As a first index, I would point to Gregor's toothless jaws (along with the wound caused by their grip on the key that frees him in part I), which find an odd counterpoint in this judgment scene, as the father sets upon him "*mit verbissenem Gesicht*," with a clenched and bitten face, a face biting back its urges even as they are about to be aggressively unleashed.

This bitten father—a submissive subordinate in his own right, and never more so than when he is inserted into the hierarchy of authority at one of its lowest points—also has a bite, which he exerts, again, by hurling *a piece of food*. And this food is ingested by

Gregor not as such, but as an inassimilable externality that "nails him fast." In a strange reversal of Georg Bendemann's starving *festhalten*, Gregor Samsa, in being *festgenagelt* by the apple in his back, is himself held fast by the food he cannot eat but that rather bites its way into him. In a further enigmatic touch, Kafka imputes to these apples the very sort of impersonal force exerted by Gregor's image on, and against, the departing Prokurist (in part I): "These small apples rolled around on the floor knocking against one another *as if electrified* [*wie elektrisiert*]" (Sons 90; E 90; my emphasis)—casting them as so many atom apples ricocheting through a newly reconfigured field of force. It is as though the father had wrested this galvanizing power back from Gregor's image, which he thereby reduces to a defeated, abject, and unthreatening version of itself, no longer the commanding source of an irresistible interdiction. At most he evokes a law and a memory no longer binding the family: the first paragraph of part III refers to the wound being fixed in place "as a visible memorial in the flesh [*als sichtbares Andenken im Fleische*]," and, in an uncharacteristically moralizing commentary, meant no doubt to reflect some aspect of Gregor's wounded brooding, the narrator speaks of a now irrelevant "commandment of family duty" ("*Gebot der Familenpflicht*"), a commandment "to *swallow down* one's repulsion and to have patience, nothing but patience" ("*den Widerwillen hinunterzuschlucken und zu dulden, nichts als zu dulden*").

Such a "memorial in the flesh" marks, among other things, the father's transgression of that family duty, his refusal to ingest rather than to discharge his disgust. Instead, it is Gregor who has to eat what the father suffers and dishes out in turn. Finally, this painful "memorial" wound inflicted from above recalls Nietzsche, who in his *Genealogy of Morals* dramatically emphasized the importance of physical punishment in the formation of a memory in the human animal; Kafka emblematizes, but also derails, this process in a gruesome *Andenken im Fleische*, a festering hollow of hunger and rotting food that ruptures the defensive shell of the unspeaking animal surface. If Kafka engages here the founding image of a literary vocation struck from a schematic bite of conscience, he links this schema all the more closely to the question of *what* is bitten, and by implication what evades or exceeds any such grasping compulsion.

Unknown Nourishment

To take these associations further, we must look briefly at the troubling juxtaposition, in Part III, of dinner, music, and sisterly eroticism. Gregor's irreversible downward slide is indexed in various ways, notably in the filth that surrounds and begins to cling to him, but especially in an ongoing process of starvation. "Gregor was now eating hardly anything. Only when he happened to pass the food laid out for him did he take a bite of something in his mouth as a kind of game [*nahm er zum Spiel einen Bissen in den Mund*], kept it there for hours at a time, and usually spat it out again" (Sons 97; E 95). While Gregor himself voids all nourishment, his room becomes a kind of storeroom for the overflow of the house, and even a waste room, the place for the ash can and the garbage bin, by implication turning Gregor himself into something between superfluous furniture (like the items surrounding him which are "not worth trying to sell but not ready to be thrown out either") and extraneous waste product. From this room, Gregor spies on the dinners enjoyed by three comically pompous boarders, who with their identical beards evoke (anachronistically) nothing so much as the Marx Brothers in *A Night at the Opera*, and whose hunger is met with all the massive steaming food it needs, promptly and dutifully served by the doting family. The sounds of their eating create an initial link between toothlessness, starvation, and another kind of nourishment.

> When they were alone again they ate their food in almost complete silence. It seemed remarkable to Gregor that among the various noises coming from the table he could always distinguish the *sound of their chewing teeth*, as if this were a sign to Gregor that *one needed teeth in order to eat*, and that even with the finest of toothless jaws one could do nothing [*nicht ausrichten könne*]. "I'm certainly hungry [*ich habe ja Appetit*]," said Gregor sadly [*sorgenvoll*] to himself, "but not for this kind of food [*nicht auf diese Dinge*: not for these things]. How these boarders are stuffing themselves [*sich nähren*], and here am I dying of starvation [*und ich komme um*]!" (Sons 98–99; E 97; my emphasis).

I have not modified the translation in this case in the hopes that showing how it distorts the substance of this crucial moment will serve to illuminate it. First, the tone of Gregor's remark is not "sad," but rather anxious and panicked; full of care and concern (*sorgenvoll*), he affirms his appetite, but worries that it does not have a *proper object*. For this object is not food in any sense; he *is* hungry, but for other *Dinge*, for other things than those that satisfy the boarders in their chewing silence (*Stillschweigen*). He is not indignant that they are "stuffing themselves" plentifully, as though it were a matter of quantity, but simply that they have found suitable nourishment: "*Wie diese Zimmerherrn sich nähren*," literally "how these boarders are nourishing themselves"—"*aber ich komme um!*" He does not even say here that he is starving; the verb *umkommen* means to perish, in every sense, for it can also imply going bad, to turn in the sense of to rot. And while it certainly engages the plot element of Gregor's physical starvation, Kafka's language draws the gravity of this concern away from the register of food and starvation properly speaking. Gregor's worries, then, not about starving from lack of food, but perishing from a lack of proper nourishment, where the latter is precisely being wedged away from "things" as edible *objects*, and toward some Thing that would nourish otherwise. This Thing, his access to it and capacity to grasp it, are indexed in his missing teeth. The sound *they* make, precisely in their absence, is quite different from the chewing of these (self-) satisfied boarders. In this text, as elsewhere, Kafka calls it *music*.

In the sentence immediately following the passage just quoted, Kafka introduces the scene of the sister's violin playing: "Precisely this evening" ("*Gerade an diesem Abend*"). What follows turns out to be the evening of Gregor's death, as though with the failure of this last recourse there is nothing left but to expire—or as though this last recourse itself, figure here as a path beyond bodily nourishment, necessarily touches on death. The sister begins playing in the kitchen, but is invited into the dining room, exclusive purview of the masticating boarders, and so the performance begins. The audience of three, however, quickly loses interest, implicitly pronouncing a judgment that is no doubt in line with their all too literal tastes (indeed, after Gregor appears, they "apparently found [him] more entertaining than the violin playing" [Sons 101; E 99]). Gregor, for his part, is irresistibly drawn by her playing ("*von dem Spiele angezogen*" [E 98]) to exit his room, dragging filth, dust, hair and pieces of leftover food (*Speiseüberreste*) along with him. To him her playing is "so beautiful." In its thrall, he "crawled a little farther forward and lowered his head to the ground so that it might be possible for his eyes to meet hers [*ihren Blicken zu begegnen zu können*]." This last description does not make much spatial or pictorial sense, but it does convey Gregor's position as lowest of the low, right down on the floor, at the very moment when he would seek a gaze on high that is quite different from those we have seen up to now: feminine, musical and generous, rather than masculine, visual and punishing. Of course, these associations will soon change, when the sister turns on him, but at this point Gregor sees only a nearly redeeming sweetness; it is here that Kafka writes these well-known sentences: "Was he an animal, since music gripped him so [*da ihn Musik so ergriff*]? It seemed to him as if the way to the unknown nourishment he longed for was showing itself to him" (Sons 100; E 98). I render these sentences very literally, because once again Kafka's precise language is very important: Gregor is "gripped" by this language, he is compelled and drawn on by it, to the point of showing himself in all his filth; he is pressed toward (but not yet down) a path (*Weg*) that seems to "show itself" (*sich zeigen*) in a medium that surpasses "showing" and points toward an object that is no object, a nourishment designated as "longed-for unknown": *zu der ersehnten unbekannten Nahrung*. Whatever it is that this music "grips," it places in question the animality of Gregor's visible form, and therefore, perhaps—to make rather too quickly an observation that would require more elaboration—beyond the *object of discipline and punishment* as which he has suffered the wounding law of Authority, derisory stand-in for the sublime power that is at stake throughout the story. If music's grip displaces Gregor from his brute and guilty animal form, it is not in order to install him securely in the human, but rather to point him in the direction of another quite different transhuman regime, in which nourishment, for its part, would not be subject to any objective grasp.[16]

This is the direction toward which Kafka's judgment stories continually veer—as though toward their own empty centers—along the outer edges of their highly visual object-oriented dreamlike dramas. Indeed, we immediately return to this theatrical stage after the brief excursion into an unaccountable moment of music and invisibility, first in the mode of Gregor's own fantasy, in which he would "press forward" (*vorzudringen*) all way to his sister, pull on her skirt, take her into his room, and never let her out again for as long as he lives (Sons 101; E 98–99). The imponderable treasure of music is thus quickly displaced by another sort of compensation altogether, one that engages his visible form to the point of making it instrumental: "his frightful appearance [*Schreckgestalt*] would become, for the first time, useful to him; he would watch over all the doors of his room at once and hiss back at any attackers" (Sons 101; E 99). But of course the sister, the object of these precautions, would stay voluntarily, especially after he has seduced her with money for music lessons. "His sister would be so touched that she would burst [*ausbrechen*] into tears, and Gregor would then raise himself [*sich erheben*] to her shoulder and kiss her on the neck, which, now that she was working in business [*ins Geschäft ging*], she kept free of any ribbon or collar." A transgressive incestuous desire pointing toward a potentiality of liberated desire? Or merely a compensatory Oedipal fantasy retooled by the desperate brother-bug on his last weakening legs? Everything here indicates the latter, from the *Schreckgestalt*, which seems to aspire to the power akin to that of the raving father's *Schreckbild* in "The Judgment," to the desire to "*sich erheben*," to potently "rise up" in a way that indeed sounds almost sublime (*erhaben*), to the "*Geschäft*," the "shop," site of work and commerce, with its heavily ambivalent charge of social tyranny. Indeed, this term, the sister's place in the "traffic" it invokes, turns her into a kind of commodity, no less in Gregor's fantasy than in that of the parents, when they watch their daughter stretch her young, vibrant (and marriageable) body at the story's most horrifying conclusion. Much like the father in his uniform, the insertion of the sister into an economy of labor and exchange gives rise for Gregor to outsized fantasies of paternalistic beneficence, only here, in rather classic fashion, her position as subordinate locates her within a phantasm that strips her bare, and in which Gregor's status, erotic and otherwise, would be on the rise again.[17]

Instead, this scene is the beginning of the end for Gregor, yet again as a result of his mere (mute) appearance in the social sphere. His reveries are of course rudely interrupted when his presence is noticed, and from there it is a short path through ultimate rejection ("*Weg muss es!*"—"It must go!" cries the sister, denying that this creature could possibly be Gregor), to solitary death, to elimination as a mere piece of garbage, thrown out by the servant woman. This time the morning appearance of a *Bedienerin*, rather than evoking a savior (as in "The Judgment": "Jesus!"), merely facilitates a tidy effacement, the conditions for oblivion: that thing in the next room ("*das Zeug von nebenan*"), she says, has already been "thrown out" ("*weggeschafft*"). "You don't need to worry about anything. It's been taken care of"[18] (Sons 109; E 106) . It is then that they decide to get rid of her—to efface the effacer? But this absconded shell of a body cannot help but haunt the all-devouring economy of this story (which the living insect brother had burst open from within) as it tries to close without remainder like a wound without a scar—a body that one might well associate, *a contrario*, with the strange image of the butcher's boy (the *Fleischergeselle* or "meat boy") uprightly climbing the stairs ("*in stolzer Haltung heraufstieg*") with a tray of meat on his head, as the expelled borders descend (*hinunterstiegen*) and disappear, all under the gaze of the family leaning on the rail out on the landing. This surrogate expulsion of the boarders, and the infusion of proud edible flesh back into the domestic sphere, leaves the family "lightened" ("*erleichtert*"), as though the hidden and desiccated insect body had been ritually replaced with a much more digestible substance, proudly held aloft and steadily ascending. One finds a similar disappearance and replacement—an incommensurable exchange between starving body and meat-eating joy—many years later, with the panther at the end of "A Hunger Artist." But already in "The Metamorphosis," in a very different context, Kafka is posing a similar question, namely: What does the incommensurability of these regimes leave behind in the gap between them, precisely there where this gap appears to be effaced by the triumph of a closed economy that attempts merely to devour its excesses? This leftover appears to take the form of an effaced memory of unsatisfiable hunger, and of the ejected shell that once "contained" this supreme and abject emptiness. In this sense, even "The Metamorphosis," this perfect circle of "mortuary perfection" (as Deleuze and Guattari put it [*Kafka*, 39]) that begins again even after the end, already plants the enigma that will be foregrounded in later texts with a much less perfect architecture, and that we will return to especially in reference to "A Hunger Artist." In that light, the investigating dog, like the underground animal in his burrow, will pass through their hunger as well, but in much less geometrically legible patterns.

In Gregor's case, this enigma has to do with an innocence that remains invisible and unpresentable, overwhelmed by the dreamlike logic of judgment. By foreclosing the speech demanded by the theater of judgment, Kafka programs the destruction of the insect body, which itself has not been able effectively to go beyond mere visibility; but at the same time, by keeping open for the reader the "inner" space of Gregor's awareness—however conventional this largely remains—he maintains a margin of ungraspability that is the obverse side of unpresentable innocence. As we saw in reference to Gregor's experience of music, the ungraspable is lodged somewhere between the animal and the human, and beyond what speech might secure, but also beyond all possible satisfaction. If *guilt* continues to be its name (in default), and if the structure of its driving imperative continues to be grounded in a demand for absolution, over and against an assaulting power raining down from on high, we see that there is also something else at stake, however muffled and fleeting its manifestation may be, something that can only have the form of a question: what is gripped when music grips? What is gripped is nothing that can be held—perhaps relinquishment itself? Or at any rate, at the limit of this story's configurations, a letting go of the Law. In which case the imperative, too, would be in the process of losing its objects.

But such a statement is premature. The remaining judgment narratives by and large do not go very far in this direction; they have a great deal more hollowing out to do in the direction, rather, of an unattainable ideal, and through the violent ground of the law's ingrown force, before emerging somewhere on the other side of Kafka's "dreamlike inner life" (like rose-red worms peeking out of a wound?). In these stories, the imperative continues to operate within the regime dictated by this violence. With "The Stoker," Kafka's critique of this violence enters more fully into the register of a militaristic discipline, while the supplementary remainder—still what is at stake in the intense scenography of these stories—begins to take on the allure of a transcendent ideal called *justice*, but an ideal threatened with conversion into sheer bodily abjection.

"THE STOKER": "A TREASURE ONE MUST RENOUNCE"

It is perhaps no surprise that in his search for a fire that would heat "the cold space of our world," and in his ongoing efforts to write as though "gliding through water," Kafka would encounter a maritime figure called *the stoker*. The story that bears this name hearkens back to some of Kafka's earliest fiction—indeed, to the very story of exile in the new world referred to in the diary entry (the "uncle anecdote" of January 1911) in which the writer vows to find the fire his first fictions need. Karl Rossmann is clearly an avatar of one of those two brothers who fought each other, and one of whom was sent away to America. In "The Stoker," and in the rambling novel the story introduces, we thus have to do with a long preserved remnant of the narrative schema, and the particular narrative figures, crystallized in the judgment stories: an unfounded but socially effective judgment allowing of no defense and resulting in a son's permanent expulsion. If Karl Rossmann is congenitally innocent, he is nonetheless socially and structurally guilty, having been ejected by his family for seducing the maid, an accusation that in the course of the narrative is revealed to be a grave and unjust distortion. What Karl finds in the stoker, whom he happens across on board a shipped docked in New York harbor beneath the surreal allegory of a sword-wielding Statue of Liberty, is a potential comrade in the defense of lost causes, and cases. For the stoker has his own false accusations to counter, his own grievances to air, and Karl is there just in time to help him do so, in a heady atmosphere of indubitable innocence and in the hopes of convincing the authorities in power of the injustices suffered. But the stoker, like every other accused in the judgment stories, will fail to defend himself, and just as in those other narratives, this failure is a structural precondition for the increased movement and circulation that results from it—in this case, Karl's movement through the social (narrative) space he is entering at the threshold of this very ambulatory novel. In the trial scene that constitutes the largest part of the story, the stoker's descent into speechlessness and corporeal abjection, all tinged with a distinct hint of violence (shouts and flailing fists), is the inverse of Karl's sudden upward move, as he finds himself captured by the social order in the guise of another uncle figure, here given the symbolic status of "senator," who claims and adopts him in an unexpected act of legitimation. This legitimacy will not last; Karl will soon enough be kicked out and sent on his itinerant way.

But the appearance and disappearance of the stoker (which gives another resonance to Kafka's title *Der Verschollene*, "the one who disappeared") played out in this opening judgment scene, the emergence and collapse of the prospect of Innocence vindicated—for Karl has "no doubt whatever" (Sons 30; A 18) about the justice of the stoker's cause—this projection and destruction of an ideal Justice appears to open the way to the strange diabolism of a speech that deeply determines the tense shapes of Kafka's judgment fictions. "The Stoker" stages the triumphant force of fictive social speech as diabolical appearance (and as "slander"), over the innocence initially posited by its protagonist, and attributed to a representative whom he barely knows. And this triumph is deeply tinged with melancholy and abjection. Stripped of his title and function within the disciplinary regime in which he has begun to appear as an outmoded remnant, the stoker attempts a self-defense that not only fails to secure justice for his a priori innocence as *a non-manifest given*, it also reduces him to an abject shell of shattered speech, and at the same time will be seen by Karl as "a treasure one must renounce [*einen Schatz, auf den man verzichten muss*"] (Sons 48; A 34). What is lost in this renunciation, signaled more than once by the childish tears of a young man beside himself with grief? And what remains in the melancholic ruins of this loss?

Theater of Slander, Scene of Writing

The highly theatrical judgment scene in "The Stoker," which takes place in the captain's office after Karl and the stoker make their entrance, thus hinges around the question as to whether the justice demanded by the title character, and the innocence presupposed by Karl, can be inscribed into the medium of social speech through which it must pass *in order to exist*. But of course this is also the very medium in which the stoker finds himself robbed of his status and prestige, for it is his semi-powerful superior, a certain Schubal, whose insults and complaints regarding the stoker's work, along with the rumors surrounding this treatment and the stoker's response to it, lay the ground for the wrongs in question. The key term here, as elsewhere in Kafka, is slander (*Verleumdung*).[19] This word quickly rolls off Karl's own tongue: after a bizarre and chaotic ingress into the captain's cabin, during which Karl is lunged at by an attendant "swooping with arms spread wide as if chasing an insect [*als jage er ein Ungeziefer*]" (the hint of a perceived equivalence with another vermin couldn't be clearer), Karl manages to grab onto a nearby desk, to which he holds fast ("*festhielt*") so as not to be dragged away, at which point he gives a rousing extemporaneous speech, based on nothing but the previous half-hour's acquaintance with the stoker, in which he declares that an injustice has been done, that Schubal is to blame, and that it is all based on "sheer slander" (Sons 30; A 18). This strange and disruptive intervention, which itself introduces the strangeness of fiction and false speech into the tight order of power and authority, will be effective; the stoker will be invited to speak. But he will have a much greater linguistic and social distance to traverse than Karl, who in effectively opening the space of power to the stoker's voice, also introduces this voice into an element of theatrical performance and groundless speech in which it will be unable to perform.

Already in the descriptions leading up to this decisive point in the narrative, the "trial" scene in the captain's office is set in precise detail, like a stage on which all the actors are rigorously positioned, and the narrator will continually cast the focal perspective around the room in order to register, above all, the various states of attention and distraction, and thus the interest in the stoker's case and the effectiveness of his attempt to plead it (as these steadily decline). Along with this highly orchestrated scenography, it is worth noting that the initial description of this scene sets it up as a scene of *writing*, and an uncannily threatening one. The ship's quasi-military personnel are seen scribbling briskly with a "*Feder*" driven by the exigencies of a quasi-military bureaucratic order, among "piles of various papers" and long rows of thick notebooks ("ledgers," *Folianten*)—and that at one point the narrator refers to an officer who, while voicing dictations, "was constantly making an odd little noise with his teeth." In light of our previous commentary, this conjunction of toothy noises, authoritative language (dictation), bureaucracy, and writing seems designed to mark a decisive generative nexus of Kafka's writing, all the more so in that it is followed by a kind of treasure box, open wide and containing nothing. Next to a man working at a writing table "stood an open safe which, at first glance at least, seemed to be empty" (Sons 28; A 16)—apparently because the important documents it contains have been removed. This constellation of images is no doubt too schematic to be linked in a substantive way with the "locked box" and "milk teeth" parable previously discussed. And yet the odd reference to teeth, this peculiar but constant feature punctuating the judgment stories, does evoke the sense of an uncanny danger that might well be associated, here too, with an imminent bodily wound, a gnawing bite that threatens to destroy the body inserted into its symbolic structure. In any case, it is precisely through these images that the scene is set for the abject dispossession of body and speech that follows, as the stoker prepares to address this theater-court mounted by accusations and slander.

Following Karl's initial gambit, however, and as though in a necessary ratification of the stoker's tenuous standing, it is the captain who formally opens the proceedings, pronouncing a summons in a voice whose description reveals its immediate performative force and underscores the extreme importance of the speaking voice itself, while also being coupled with an explicit gesture of inauguration: "He stretched out a hand and called to the stoker: 'Come here!' in a voice so firm as to strike it with a hammer [*mit einer Stimme, fest, um mit einem Hammer darauf zu schlagen*]" (Sons 30; A 18). This very literal translation renders the physicality of Kafka's striking image.[20] The captain's voice is formative and productive; its solidity is capable of *making* what it says, and also of making it resound; moreover, it turns the judge's gavel into something akin to a philosopher's hammer, a manufacturer of ideals and values (to use the Nietzschean terms this image evokes). Clearly, such speech is what builds and forms the world in which the stoker is about to speak in turn. It is in this light that the narrator clarifies the high stakes at play in what follows: "Everything now depended on the stoker's behavior, for about the justice of his case [*die Gerechtigkeit seiner Sache*] Karl had no doubt whatever" (Sons 30; A 18). Will this indubitable but as yet invisible justice, sheer projection and presupposition, stand any chance in the realm of masterful and authoritative speech hammered out by power and discipline? Or will it rather be stammered into something unrecognizable, the distorted remains of an a priori innocence pulped into oblivion? And in the latter case, what does this say about the speech that frames the entire adventure, the narrative speech hereby sent on its way through a fictive space *that it alone opens*, a world made of words that can only *appear*?

To pose the question from a different angle, we can ask what exactly is at stake in Karl's alliance with the stoker, and thus in the stoker's performance at his "trial," a prelude that will decisively condition Karl's entrance into the fiction of Amerika. As the scene progresses, it becomes clear that what is being played out is, once again, the ruptured relation between a body and the speech that in self-defense it must but cannot master, a rupture that, in this case, brings with it the ruination of a certain ideality. For the severing of a more and more abject body from its capacity to speak is doubled by an irreparable split between the Justice of the stoker's case and the effective power determined by the captain's hammer voice. And, once again, this process is marked as a problematic relation between writing and the sublime, in which the former falls away from the latter, is emptied out by it, and rendered useless. The references to writing and written documents mentioned earlier, embedded as they are in the structure of bureaucratic authority, are countered (potentially at least) by another set of writings, those of the stoker himself, and indeed these are soon rendered useless. Responding to the captain's summons, his thunder-like demand for speech, the stoker first opens a locked trunk which he has brought from his cabin and pulls out the treasure of his writings, his "*Bündelchen*," the little bundles he takes hold of *mit dem ersten Griff*, literally, with a first grab or grip, a small sign that so far the possibility of grasping, and grasping (through) writing in particular, has not yet been ruined. Like a well-prepared lawyer, the stoker exposes his pages to the onlookers, laying them on the windowsill (for some reason), and he begins to speak, at first calmly and respectfully. At this point Kafka introduces a strange but telling image that provides another sign of writing's emptiness or vacancy, linking it indirectly with the question of sublimity. Having secured the stoker's standing and now hearing the voice called on to speak in self-defense, Karl stands beside the "vacant desk" which he had previously latched onto, and feels "so pleased that in his delight he kept pressing the letter-scales down with his finger" (Sons 31; A 19). This odd moment, so characteristic of Kafka in its opaque but multiply signifying logic, shifts the image into an allegorical register that calls for interpretation, or at least for a careful associative elaboration. One thinks, of course, of the "scales of justice," with which Karl seems to be playing, as though he is able tip these scales at will; the "sheer pleasure" (*vor lauter Vergnügen*) of this play is suggestive (is it a displaced eroticism? a satisfying sense that the machinery of justice is in operation? an enjoyment of arbitrary mastery?), but its empty mechanism seems to annul the process that has just begun.

The allegorical circuit is enlarged when one recalls that in *The Trial* Justice with her scales is refigured by the painter Titorelli as a winged and mobile "Goddess of Victory" (*Siegesgöttin*) (T 145; KA P 196), a figure surely not far removed from the dreadful Freedom Goddess (*Freiheitsgöttin*) presiding with her sword over the traffic of New York harbor (the traffic of ships and goods about which Karl, staring out the window, soon begins to daydream [Sons 32–33; A 20–21]). I would suggest that it is somewhere in the intersection of these allegorical figures that we can hear in the story the resonance of a tenuous sublimity—that of a sublime power reduced to the subjecting violence that would guarantee it (soon to be rendered in terms of military discipline, as we will see). And it is precisely as a failure to make *writing* register in the scales of justice, as it were, to convert written evidence into the force and weight required by authority, that the story will reveal the irreparable breach between its projected transcendences and the sphere of speech and social traffic. It is into this breach, the chasm between speech and the Ideal it would inscribe, that the stoker will fall, and along with him Karl's own "idealism" and innocence.

A Higher Tribunal

This fall is traced in precise and vivid detail, as the stoker's voice fades, as he loses the audience's attention, and as his speech disintegrates into an "awkward" and "pathetic hodgepodge," "rigmarole," "babble," "insufferable rantings," and even finally into "nothing" and "silence"—beyond which it becomes inarticulate screaming and weeping. At the same time, as the stoker is more and more "out of control," his body takes the relay of this inarticulate but "boundless indignation" over his case and begins to act out in a disordered automatism that includes profuse sweat, trembling hands, flailing tightly balled fists, and pounding on the table.[21] Karl, who intervenes at certain moments with rhetorical and literary advice (e.g., to "narrate more simply and clearly" [Sons 33; A 21]), soon realizes that "everything is lost, everything," that he has reached "the end of all hope" (Sons 34; A 22). But just as total loss begins to dawn, there enters into this melancholy situation a final glimmer of victory, ironically in the guise of the stoker's "enemy" and accuser. Schubal's sudden and highly theatrical appearance signals, *a contrario*, the possibility of a Justice that would be rendered through the manifestation of the ills and evils making its defense necessary in the first place. It is here that the scene's dimension of transcendence and ideality is most explicitly evoked, at the moment of its greatest theatrical intensity and in the shadow of its imminent and definitive failure. It is entirely a question of the figure of the courtroom, of which kind of tribunal will be effective here and now.

> One now might still be able to assume that, in the confrontation between Schubal and the stoker, the result due to them before a *higher tribunal* [*die ihr vor einem höheren Forum zukommende Wirkung*] would not fail to be achieved [*nicht verfehlen*] also in this human one, since even if Schubal was good at playing his part [*sich gut verstellen konnte*], he would not be able to hold out to the end. A brief flare-up of his baseness [*Aufblitzen seiner Schlechtigkeit*] would suffice to make it visible to these gentlemen, and Karl would take care of that. (Sons 36; A 23–24; my emphasis)

We are closer than ever to the "invisible court" summoned and dreaded by Kafka in the early diaries. This passage reveals that what is at stake in the stoker's case is the *assumption* of a fragile a priori—or in simpler language, a kind of naïveté—that would ascribe to a higher and truer world the power to inscribe itself into ours here below. But this assumption must be tested in a "confrontation," this time not with a judge, but with an adversary who has just entered into his native element, the theatrical sphere of authority secured solely through effectively performed speech, a sphere determined by the capacity for dissimulation (*gut verstellen*), and into which Karl himself will soon be fully integrated *once the stoker has been renounced* and eliminated. We will return to this question in a moment. What becomes clear at this point, when Schubal enters and speaks in defense of himself, is the strange complicity that aligns him with Karl, who has already demonstrated his own skills of persuasive speech based on nothing but appearance and hearsay. Karl's hope, at this point, is that Schubal's underlying baseness or evil will "flash out" for everyone to see (here too in an image that recalls Kafka's first diaries, where he wishes for a spark of language that will set fire to his life [D 12; TB 11]), but ironically, it is precisely Schubal's clear and persuasive human speech that constitutes this evil's most diabolical manifestation. For no one can see through it but Karl, who immediately detects in Schubal's "fine speech" the holes and gaps of a "bad conscience" (*Schuldbewusstsein*) at work (Sons 38; A 25). Only Karl's fine-tuned sense of guilt is able to register this, as attested by the astonishing and elaborate critical exegesis reported through the narrator's indirect discourse. For everyone else, this speech is a return to intelligible human language: "Thus spoke Schubal. It was the clear speech of a man [*die klare Rede eines Mannes*]," says the narrator, "and from the altered looks of the listeners one might have thought they were hearing a human voice for the first time after a long interval" (Sons 37; A 24–25).

It is worth noting that in Schubal's brief speech this new defendant refers to the evidence he claims to have on hand "in my writings" (*Schriften*), which, although nowhere to be seen, are thus posed against the stoker's now completely useless pages, just as Schubal's diabolically human aspect in general is contrasted with the stoker's subhuman or even nonhuman abjection, which reaches its extreme point precisely at the moment of his enemy's appearance on the scene. "Was the stoker even capable of speaking [*reden*]. . . . There he stood, his legs asprawl, weak in the knees, his head slightly raised, and the air flowing in and out of [*verkehrte durch*] his open mouth as if there were no more lungs inside to work it through [*als gäbe es innen keine Lungen mehr, die sie verarbeiteten*]" (Sons 37; A 24).[22] Once again, Kafka's precise language is critical: the air is not exactly "flowing in and out" of the stoker's mouth, like breath, but is rather "coursing through," as though it were mere wind passing through an inert hole unattached to any lungs. This image presents the complete and utter evacuation of the stoker's "interior," even down to his bodily organs, not to mention anything like a conscious, linguistic interiority. Thus the previously assumed innocence, the cause of a more just and higher court, is not passing through the conduit of the stoker's speech, but has rather sunk *below* the human, and the human tribunal itself is completely given over to the likes of Schubal—and to Karl, who understands his task in terms that will give the precise figure of his failure. Once again, it is a matter of grasping and presenting, in the theatrical order of social speech, a still invisible reality that must be brought into appearance:

> Everything was clear [*Alles war klar*] and had even been clearly presented [or performed, *dargeboten*] by Schubal against his will, but it *had to be shown* to these gentleman by other yet *more palpable* means [*noch handgreiflicher zeigen*]. They must be shaken up. Now then, Karl, quick, at least make use of the time before the witnesses enter the scene [*auftreten*] and overwhelm everything [*alles überschwemmen*]! (Sons 38; A 25; my emphasis)

The witnesses in question are Schubal's accomplices awaiting his word just outside the door; their overflowing proliferation threatens to convert the scene into pure theater (or perhaps filmic farce, as the slapstick that eventually ensues would suggest), to the detriment of any juridical purpose. This purpose slips away as its most urgent imperative is most clearly articulated: to show more concretely, more palpably, *handgreiflicher*, a justice on the point of being drowned out by a welter of fictive appearances. But there turns out to be nothing to grasp, as prefigured in the stoker's balled fists, in Karl's empty scales. For the time remaining to Karl to carry out this task ends precisely here, as the captain waves the litigants away and asks the uncle, who has made motions to interrupt, what he would like to say, thus initiating the recognition scene that will literally take hold of Karl and carry him away. If Karl's resolve in the passage above is to speak into social being his unproven insight into Schubal's diabolical nature, he is suddenly silenced by this transfer of speech into the register of pure power stamped as symbolic status: the senator will now claim, by name, his errant but worthy nephew. This displacement turns the focus of the story, if not of Karl's emotional attention, away from any directly staged judgment of the stoker, whose fate becomes clear when the "mob" outside does in fact flood through the door, ready to bear witness against the stoker and to decide the already lost case.

Justice and Discipline

Graspability, then, or one might say *manipulability*, would be the form of the ideal's manifestation within the visible, the precise link between the higher and the human tribunal—that is, to put the point in the register of the metaphysical language I am drawing on, between the idea, as concept (*Begriff*), and its concrete instantiation. The definitive failure of this grasp can rightly be seen as a kind of relinquishing, but also as an abandonment. First, after Karl recognizes his uncle, and is recognized in turn, through a highly ritualized performative gesture that involves not grasping but kissing a hand (we will return to this in a moment), his newly elevated social status decouples him from the stoker and abandons the latter to the captain's autocratic disciplinary *Beurteilung*: judgment as assessment and evaluation. "What will happen to the stoker now?" asks Karl, insisting on the "question of justice" he thinks must still have a chance; but the uncle admonishes him: "The stoker will get what he deserves.... Don't misinterpret the situation . . . this is perhaps a matter of justice [*Sache der Gerechtigkeit*], but at the same time it is a matter of discipline [*Sache der Disziplin*]. On this ship both of these, and most especially the latter, are subject to the judgment [*unterliegt hier die Beurteilung*] of the Captain" (Sons 46–47; A 32).[23] The stoker is abandoned to the machinery of discipline, which is subject to (*unterliegt*) the judgment soon to be hammered out by the captain's voice. The story thus splits subjection in two directions: the stoker's submission to a crushing discipline, in a drive toward abjection and, ultimately, in his sacrificial expulsion from Karl's wayward symbolic economies, and on the other hand Karl's subject-formation, by which he is reinserted into the system of authority as newly legitimate, as having a recognizable status that invests him with a voice capable of speech, *as long as he no longer insists on speaking for the stoker*. This foreclosure, the renunciation of speech as a means to secure an innocence incompatible with the theater of power, is the condition for the two forms of subjection just mentioned. At this point in Kafka's fiction there does not seem to be a third alternative. One could anticipate the turns this fiction will take, however, by noting the similarity between the stoker's abjection and the recalcitrant and obtrusive figures who will soon emerge and refuse to disappear entirely (Odradek, the hunter Gracchus, Josefine). In that sense, the stoker opens a troubling in-between space that has the potential of eluding the double law of subjection, but the plot of the story requires that he be absconded—not, however, without an odd scene of heartbreaking sacrifice.

The moment I am referring to takes place when Karl says his final farewell to the stoker. One could say that this moment is experienced by Karl as a renunciation not only of the stoker, but also of the inert, unpresentable inwardness around which the story has revolved up to this point, along with the transcendent ideal that has been invested in it. Like Georg Bendemann's fall into the river, and into the endless circulation it indexes, Karl Rossmann's exit down into the waves signals, despite his tears, a certain liberation—watched over by a sword though these waters may be. But it also preserves, in melancholic fashion, something of that interiority's determinate and precious contents. Indeed, in the scene I am referring to, it is explicitly a question of an impossible *treasure*. The affective (and not only conceptual) register of this treasure is marked in this scene by yet another kiss on the hand, less as a performative seal than as a passionate farewell. Thinking that he can "do nothing [*nichts*] without offending everyone," and realizing that the stoker no longer has any allies among the spectators, Karl

> slowly went over to the stoker, pulled the man's right hand out of his belt and held it playfully in his.
>
> "Why do you [*du*] say nothing [*nichts*]?" he asked . . . An injustice has happened to you [*Dir ist ja unrecht geschehen*] . . . this I know." And as Karl drew his fingers back and forth between the stoker's, the stoker gazed around with shining [*glänzenden*] eyes, as if blessed by a great happiness [*als widerfahre ihm eine Wonne*] that no one could begrudge [*verübeln*] him.

"Now you must get ready to defend yourself . . . or else these people won't have any idea of the truth. . . . I won't be able to help you anymore." And then Karl burst out crying and kissed the stoker's hand, taking that rough and almost lifeless hand [*die rissige, fast leblose Hand*] and pressing it to his cheek like a treasure that one must renounce. (Sons 48; A 33–34)

At this point, the uncle "led him away if only with the slightest force [*Zwang*]"—not unlike the executioners who arrive at Josef K.'s door in the last chapter of *The Trial*, or the policeman who arrests the murderer in "A Fratricide"—and admonishes him again, saying, "Don't take this . . . too far [*treibe . . . nicht zu weit*] and learn to comprehend your position [*deine Stellung begreifen*]" (Sons 47; A 34).[24] The imperative to make more graspable what is as yet invisible has elided into an imposed compulsion to renounce, to take up an enforced social "position" that requires a relinquishment of the stoker and of the treasure he "holds." Oddly, this treasure is emblematized by his rough and inert hand. In its dry and cracked (*rissig*) lifelessness, it resembles that of a corpse, or a plaster cast, a mere thing that has to be pulled from his belt like a toy—something grasped but not grasping. What is the treasure of this hand if not the lost capacity to grasp "more handily," *handgreiflicher*, the inner truth that has just failed to enter into the sphere of presentation, thus destroying the categorical presumption of that inner truth and the rights due to it in the social world? In this strange paradoxical moment, Karl is grasping (with a kiss) the necessity of a relinquishment—a relinquishment of grasping itself, insofar as it would take hold of a determinate inward object. Note that this necessity is generalized by the text, which does not say that he, Karl, must renounce this treasure, but that it a treasure "one must" renounce: *man muss*. Within the sphere of disciplinary subjection, there is no keeping this treasure, which is constituted by the necessity of its renunciation, where this "must" has the generality of a law, one that bears on Karl at this juncture like the price to be paid for rising into the sphere of masterful speech and social legitimacy, precisely in a shift of alliance from the stoker to the uncle-senator. But this rise is already belied by the abject emblem that marks its symbolic precondition, the obtrusive bodily remnant of an ideal in default—in this case, not a corpse per se, but a hand that likens death. Like the mystery of an ostentatiously guarded locked box whose treasure is withheld from view, the promise of the stoker's case—its cause, *cosa*, *chose*, and thing—is reduced to nothing but a desiccated hand, the very one that fed the fire we've been seeking, but that, in feeding it, must be consumed.

Assuming Guilt

And yet there is something even more peculiar about this moment, for it is not only Karl who finds himself in the presence of a treasure bearing an intense affective charge issuing in a stream of tears. In a description that seems to oddly isolate the figures in question, we see the stoker's shining face gazing off at no one as he is overcome with ecstasy, a bliss (*Wonne*) that has come to him from Karl, and that *no one can ruin* (*verübeln*) for him. What is this unbreachably blissful blessing? It lies somewhere between this lover's gesture, as Karl draws his fingers back and forth through the stoker's, and the no less freighted certainty that Karl has just expressed, in a subjectless syntax that is irreplaceable: "*Dir ist ja unrecht geschehen.*" Very literally: to you has unjustly happened. The uncapitalized *unrecht* functions not as a substantive/subject, but as an adverb. What has happened, and by whom it has been made to happen, here become fully indeterminate and unlocalizable (just as the social scene surrounding them has for a moment receded to a hazy margin).[25] What is essential is that the stoker be positioned as one who merely *suffers and undergoes unjust events*—and this is the treasure that Karl imparts to him in his bliss. It comes upon him in a syntax that repeats and maintains this passive stance: "*als widerfahre ihm eine Wonne,*" as if a bliss came upon him.

This "position" is the very same categorical position of passively culpabilized innocence that Karl must renounce in the stoker, and for himself. As though consigning this extraordinary good fortune to him, Karl is led away into the sphere of power, commerce and, not least, "fine speech," to which he has just acceded. "Well spoken!" exclaims the uncle, in response to a speech by Karl following immediately upon the ceremonious kissing of *another* hand, the uncle's, in a performative gesture that seals his new position ("'You are my uncle' said Karl, kissing his hand and receiving a kiss on the brow" [Sons 44; A 30]). With this kiss of recognition, Karl is taken up into the sphere of a guilt that does not merely supervene upon a categorical innocence, but that touches on the very ground of his social and linguistic existence. This guilt is constituted by an absorption into social power and by the capacity for speech whose "evil" is demonstrated and embodied by Schubal; it is structured in its ungrounded legitimacy by the uncle-senator, and guaranteed by the captain (by the violence of the hammer and the sword), whose next task will be to liquidate the stoker by means of an impending judgment that will relegate him to a dissociated ecstasy. Hence the necessity for his abjectification into the mere bodiliness of a quasi-cadaver, a thing that can be "*weggeschafft.*" Rising into legitimate speech thus means, for Karl, *assuming* this guilt, in every sense, and leaving behind the assumption of innocence—leaving behind the stoker—that has served as something like a regulative ideal, and a potential compensation for his losses. But it is here that the stoker's throw-away body, marked with an indescribable affective charge, is converted into an overflowing affect, into tears, which are now the form of the remnant Karl will carry off the boat, the throbbing hollow of that lost treasure, a beloved but now empty *Schatz* that must be left behind. Karl's tears attest to a sorrow over the knowledge not only that the Ideal, and its grounding in an authentic interiority, cannot enter unscathed into our cold world, but that it *must not*, that it must be relinquished as a condition and price for entry into the endlessly circulating space of exchange and substitution, represented, at this juncture, by the pompous and self-satisfied uncle.

That space of circulation is one major aspect of the space of writing, and its specific form is here that of a long narrative fiction that will set off to navigate the field of established but foreign and opaque social codes. Its initial and fundamental condition, however, is a *guilt that cannot be expiated* insofar as it has been absorbed into a speech burdened through and through with the task of enunciating (from the position of) the law. Karl has entered into the sphere of language deployed as disciplinary effectivity and finds himself ranged, however uncomfortably and provisionally, on the side of authority. Faced with this prospect, and on the threshold of the watery world that will mediate it, Karl weeps again. In the story's dense final paragraph, after Karl bursts for a second time into "violent sobs" as he and the uncle are about to descend from the ship into a boat that will carry them ashore, Karl reflects on the exchange and substitution at hand. The passage describes a descent (*Hinuntersteigen*), a downward movement by which Kafka yet again approaches the end of a story, in this case punctuated, not incidentally, by more than one uncanny hand gesture, and by another agile leap, a single downward bound. I will cite this passage at some length, in order to convey its strange and precise choreography and its uncanny details:

> Their conductor [*Führer*] leapt down into the boat with a single bound [*mit einem einzigen Satz hinuntersprang*], and the sailors in the boat rose [*erhoben sich*] and saluted. The Senator was just warning Karl to be careful how he came down [*Hinuntersteigen*], when Karl, as he stood on the top rung, burst into violent sobs. The Senator put his right hand under Karl's chin, held him tightly [*hielt ihn fest an sich gepresst*] and caressed him with his left hand. In this way they slowly descended step by step and, tightly bound together [*engverbunden*], entered the boat . . . the sailors pushed off . . . rowing at full speed . . . and one of the sailors made the artful gesture [*machte das Kunststück*] of flinging a kiss up [*eine Kusshand hinaufzuschicken*] to the ship without interrupting the regular rhythm of his rowing. It was now as if there were really no stoker at all. Karl looked [*fasste*] more carefully at his uncle . . . and doubts came into his mind whether this man would ever be able to take the stoker's place. And his uncle evaded his gaze [*Blick*] and stared at the waves on which their boat was tossing [*umschwankt*]. (Sons 50; A 35–36)

The uncle, who guides Karl in a "tightly binding" grip that is both a caress and an arresting pressure, must somehow replace the stoker, a substitution that clearly will not hold. But there is another substitution here as well: how not to see this *Kusshand*, so artfully cast up to the spectators watching the boat row away, as an uncanny response to the rough and lifeless hand-thing so treasured by Karl, but now voided by an earlier kiss on the uncle's hand. The sailor's theatrical gesture affirms the performative order of things precisely, also, as the order of art and semblance, but his *Kunststück* has a disquietingly mechanical air about it: it is carried out with the well timed precision of a highly disciplined body, exactly the sort of body the stoker has shown himself not to possess. Unlike Georg Bendemann, whose subjection to the law is momentarily compensated by the disciplined acrobatic body that it renders back to him (allowing him in turn to render himself fully unto this law), the stoker is not redeemed by any such mastery. If anything, his sheer abjection could be read as a sign of resistance to the disciplinary regime that is about to devour and abscond him, a disappearance supplemented by Karl's mourning, his very accusatory tears. Invisibility gives way to effacement and nonexistence: "It was really as if there were no longer any stoker." And indeed, there is not; despite the fact that the text bears his name, or rather his title (the name of the function of which the story strips him), there is no place for him in the law-bound narrative structures laid out by Kafka, from which the stoker must fall away like so much inert detritus. But if the *Kusshand* is a definitive farewell to the mute, obtrusive, and resistant remainder embodied by the stoker, his type will nonetheless resurface elsewhere in Kafka's fiction, in greyer zones less fully overdetermined by a closed system of judgment and discipline—that is, a system guaranteed by disciplinary violence—especially in the figures already mentioned such as Odradek, the hunter Gracchus, and Josefine, who also merely disappears into oblivion (redeemed only, if at all, by the conflicted text that reports her enigma). But as long as Kafka's stories compulsively stage confrontations between, on the one hand, judging representatives of the law—more or less sublime, more or less degraded—and, on the other, faltering defendants whose only possible fate is to be fully assimilated into that law or else expunged from it in corpse-like abjection, there will be no possibility of avoiding a supposedly purifying sacrificial violence, nor of freeing language from the cycle of justification and retribution that impels it.

CHAPTER 3

Embodied Violence and the Leap from the Law
"In the Penal Colony" and *The Trial*

> Rien ne (se) tient devant la loi.
> —Jacques Derrida, "Préjugés"

In the preceding chapters, I have argued that the complex scenographies and economies of judgment mounted in Kafka's "judgment stories" were derived in part from early and ongoing articulations of an imperative to write, in which exoneration and guilt exchange places in a tight circle of near-equivalence, centered on the demands of a disciplinary regime striving faultily for a sublime *appearance*. In Kafka's final judgment narratives, "In the Penal Colony" and *The Trial*, the unviable contradictions of this regime are taken to, and beyond, the extremes of its logic, in ways that dismantle and distend its machinery, starkly revealing, but also sequestering away, the violence that grounds it. This is the violence of an absolute subjection to language insofar as its social enactment, in the form of a "court," projects a transcendental dimension that would positively guarantee and enforce it. In one case ("In the Penal Colony"), this is presented quite concisely, in a short-circuit of judgment and in the graphic dismantling of a machine, and in the other (*The Trial*), in an infinite postponement that allows for the textual/narrative unfolding of fantasmatic structures leading, nonetheless, to the same end: a highly theatricalized death by stabbing. We will have occasion to mark the incongruity between this execution, as the "End" of both book and trial, and the uncloseable processes of law and speech that otherwise structure the novel—which thus appears to continue the schema of the judgment stories, whereas in fact it drastically reconfigures this schema. But insofar as both narratives incorporate physical violence directly into the substance of law as speech, the bodies they expel as by-products of this regime of justice (that is, of language tuned to murder) take their places alongside the other corpses and lifeless abject creatures conjured away at the end of the earlier stories.[1] This gallery of bodily remains ought to tell us something, if only that Kafka is working very hard to kill off some persistent *figure* that continues to bug him. That figure has deeply embedded autobiographical origins, which can be understood partly in terms of a highly cultivated identification with the (literary) law's sublime instantiations, sources of ecstasy and of deep-cutting pain, agents of elevation and crushing descent. I have focused on the central dramatic element of judgment, but the further Kafka proceeds into the ground of these scenarios, the more the act of judgment merges with the violent murder that immediately expresses and consummates it. Language, as law, becomes overt violence; and speech, suffused with a guilt that both wounds and drives it, issues more or less directly into putting-to-death.

At the same time, it can be seen that the sacrificial economy that would sanction such violence is gradually neutralized, initially in the mode of a collapse (from the father's "crash" at the end of "The Judgment" to the self-destruction of the machine of "In the Penal Colony"). Through this neutralization, devoid of return or recuperation, we begin to see another less sharply circumscribed horizon for Kafka's first mature writing, in a "critique of violence" that shifts the ground of the law just enough to empty a space for a different form of speech and voice, and to destitute the sublime treasure it would secure. The most telling emblems for such an empty space in these two stories are the stripped and naked body of the condemned prisoner set free ("In the Penal Colony"), and the blank piece of paper that (in *The Trial*) Josef K. holds aloft on the palm of his hand (as though to present his confessions). These blank surfaces will *not* be filled in with the writing that would both produce and absolve the guilt demanded by the voracious machinery of justice to which they are initially offered up (the prisoner is freed, Josef K. will not write the autobiographical "petition" he imagines will fully exonerate him), and this not-being-written signals an emergent shift in the very form of writing in question. For indeed, these blank surfaces are already fully subordinated to the machine in question, which does, in the end, find the fodder it needs. The hacked and stabbed bodies rendered up by these narratives continue to give a clear indication of the kind of recalcitrant remainder that obtrudes at the far end of judgment's violence; but it will also be necessary to ask how things stand with the literary ideal that has arrived, within the sphere of the fiction, at this extreme of total subjection—and whether Kafka has not reached an impasse requiring another trope than that of the court, a turn or twist different from Georg's suicidal *Turnen* over the rail, or from those given to the knife in Josef K.'s heart. In lieu of radical culpability and impossible expiation, perhaps the loss of a grasp on the treasure of the law, of a sublime and ideal guarantee, can turn rather toward a loss *of that loss* (that is, once again: the locked box can be voided of its precious contents). By staging a definitive relinquishment, "In the Penal Colony" and *The Trial* begin, more clearly and deliberately than any previous stories, to turn in that direction. At the very least, they carry out an erosion, and an extreme distension, of the metaphorics of law and the court, attenuating it to such pointedly hyperbolic extremes that nothing remains but a murdered body that can no longer suffer the inscription that has produced it. Its emptiness will haunt what follows, as will the peculiar hunger that it opens.

"IN THE PENAL COLONY": JUSTICE IS HAPPENING NOW

"In the Penal Colony" is a crucial text in Kafka's corpus, not only in the sense that its bizarreness, violence, and perversity, its stark but enigmatic configurations, have long posed to its readers pressing questions that seem to encapsulate Kafka's work as a whole, but also in the specific sense that it constitutes an unresolvable crux, a kind of internal limit within the corpus, running along one of its major axes. If Kafka's "judgment stories" dramatize at some level the *figuration* of the writer's vocation out of bad conscience and sublime punishment, they do so for the most part through an elaborate scenography that touches on the question of writing at a more or less oblique angle. "In the Penal Colony" places writing, as an act of inscription, in immediate and thoroughgoing contact with embodied guilt and justice, as though these were coextensive. The contact in question is staged as the law's direct inscription on a body, and the justice it carries out actually bypasses judgment, short-circuiting it in a fantasm of pure presence. "Everyone knew: Justice is happening now" ("*Alle wussten: jetzt geschieht Gerechtigkeit*"; CS 154, E 164). So says the officer, in his nostalgic past-tense evocation of the procedure he must now defend, in which a broken commandment is reestablished by being incised into the body that trespassed it. I will return to this important sentence, which places justice in the register of a shared knowledge presumed as given ("Everyone knew"), rather than in the effectuation of a judgment, and introduces into the proceedings the dimension of a lost *a priori*.

"In the Penal Colony" can be called a judgment story, then, not because of the justice once achieved by the inscription machine, but rather because the text consists almost entirely of the officer's verbal defense of that machine, whose mechanical demonstration *ought to*, but no longer does, speak for itself. The entire question is whether it can still "speak" at all, now that it has been socially divested of the performative power of its previous operation. This problem requires the verbal intercession of the officer, who, in the absence of a community's established *conferral* of this power (and thus in the apparent collapse of its unstated presupposition), must not only explain the mechanics of the procedure, but must also state a case before a supposedly impartial judge. The judge he addresses is the foreign traveler, whose presence is explicitly accounted for in terms of the task of judgment, and to whom the officer appeals directly for support in his case. It will be noted that this judge does not have, or at least does not appear to exercise, the sublime and destructive power wielded by his predecessors; but this apparent difference is one of the sharpest questions raised by the story. As a representative of (broadly speaking) the liberal bourgeois order of the rule of law, the traveler also represents "us," Kafka's readers, and by extension something like "civilization" in the sense that Freud gives to this term in diagnosing its inherent discontents. Surely these discontents, including our sense that violence is not external to but rather *inherent in* "civilization" and the law, are part of our uneasy response to this story, which, far from seeking to resolve them, strives to render them more acute than ever. The scale of the stakes put into play in this very pointed but ambiguous narrative also helps to explain its privileged status as Kafka's most *incisive* story.

For my purposes, what is essential is the way in which "In the Penal Colony" implicates writing in its ambivalent relationship to guilt, law, and the transcendence of a "Justice . . . happening now," thus opening as well the literary (and autobiographical) dimension in which Kafka's imperative to write most squarely confronts its own structural, historical, and aesthetic conditions. The story's "critique" of these conditions reveals the violent ground of a projected transcendent justice as being, at the same time, *the grounding violence of the sublime drive to write*—or of the drive to write sublimely. This is a troubling discovery that, within the story, must survive its disavowal by the new regime which seems to have surpassed it, while nonetheless maintaining a certain sublimity in its structure, as expressed in the meta-commandment enunciated in the uncanny overlap between old and new: "Be just!" If justice functions as a devouring disciplinary machine, the judgment by which this machine itself arrives at its end—the traveler's "no" in response to the officer's defense—is nonetheless met by an even more naked violence, when the officer places himself in the machine and is simply hacked to death, a violence which, as I will suggest, is also more *ravenous* in its disjointed, unhinging failure to make "justice happen now." In a sense, what happens in this story is that justice *starves*, as evidenced by the corpse it can no longer assimilate into its faultless functioning. The faultline permanently opened by this failure, here too an allegorical cleft in which a connecting grasp comes undone, may well be the narrow passage through which writing wrenches itself toward another horizon—not entirely devoid of violence, but freed, perhaps, from the violence of *legality*. For now, however, what we see most prominently is a writing that punishes itself for seeking a positive transcendence that would manifest as *pure radiant power*.[2]

What Times Those Were

"How different was an execution in the old days!" (CS 153; E 164) exclaims the officer, apologizing for the sorry state of the spectacle "today." Back then, he says, it was a two-day festival attended by everyone, who came "only to see." While such a description calls to mind Nietzsche's comment that at public scenes of punishment there has always been "so much that is *festive*!" and while it might recall any number of gruesome events evoked by Foucault in his work on penality, in Kafka's story there is very little of that grim terror mixed with anxious relief ("it's him, not me") that one tends to associate with such spectacles.[3] On the contrary, as the officer tells it, it is pure lightness and music—indeed, there are even fanfares and finely dressed ladies, and overall a kind of public, civic-minded cheerfulness unclouded by any sacred horror. The similarities between this scene and the one that greets the tortured hunger artist when he is forced to break his fast, might well indicate the kind of hunger being fulfilled by this feasting of eyes, as the body is placed in the machine "before hundreds of eyes (*vor hunderten*

Augen)"—an image refashioned later as "hundreds like flies swarming around" the freshly laid corpse (E 165). The machine itself serves as a gleaming transcendental point ordering society as a whole in its hierarchical structure: "All of society—and no high official was allowed to miss it—ordered itself around the machine." Ultimate ground and culminating point of the social order that it structures, the machine and its operation bear a precise signification, a knowledge of which precedes any single operation, having been established before and beyond any particular manifestation. This is so true that, though all have come only to see, one need not even look in order to do so: "And now the execution began. No discordant noise [no false note: *kein Misston*] spoiled the work of the machine. Many no longer even watched but lay with closed eyes in the sand. Everyone knew: Justice is happening now [*alle wussten: Jetzt geschieht Gerechtigkeit*]" (CS 154; E 164). Are these closed eyes the sign of a rich and radiant inwardly turning "vision," or the mere complacency of ideological subjects resting in their dogmatic presuppositions? This question, which cuts through the text as one of its deepest ambiguities, must remain open, but it indicates the axis around which the question of transcendence must turn in this story. An intensely visual narrative, its high stakes are nonetheless not fully contained within the visuality that it foregrounds. Indeed, much will depend on what one hears and hearkens to, as sound and listening open a further and "higher" dimension in the proceedings. In the quotation just given, the musical or at least acoustic aspect of the spectacle is strangely underscored by the exclusion of any "false note," as it is in the sentence that follows: "In the silence one heard nothing but the condemned man's sighs," moaning sounds that used to be intensified, explains the officer, by a "*beizende Flüssigkeit*" (E 164), a caustic fluid that dripped from the biting needles, but that he is no longer allowed to use.[4] It is no doubt this acoustic element that for some in the audience makes it unnecessary to watch the spectacle unfold in order to "know" that it presents a full and immediate instantiation of Justice, as it "happens now."

Such, in any case, is the precise form of transcendence projected by the scene, a transcendence which one could describe, in philosophical terms, as having achieved concrete appearance through the phenomenal presentation of an ideal conceptual abstraction: Justice instantiated. Or, to put the point even more schematically: Kantian reflection has been short-circuited into Hegelian speculation fulfilled. The Idea is inscribed directly into the order of events, and Justice thus passes (*geschehen*) into history (*Geschichte*). It is now *actualized* in the present. This is the startling speculative claim made by Kafka's penal colony officer, in the name of a procedure of "Justice" and the social order of spectators assembled around it, like sunbathers lying prone in the sand. This image too calls up philosophical references, not least Plato's intelligible sun, here rendered palpable to the masses through a martyrological mise-en-scène and a luminous transmission in the victim's beatific face. In a central image of his evocation of "the old days," the officer exults over the radiance of this face, which reaches a high point at the "sixth hour" (out of twelve), and reveals the important pedagogical function it served: at that crucial moment, it is the children who are given priority among the thronging spectators. With his arm around a child on either side of him, the officer bathes in the radiance of the dying man's face:

> "How we all absorbed the look [*wie nahmen wir alle den Ausdruck*] of transfiguration on the face of the sufferer [*gemarterten Gesicht*], how we held our cheeks in the radiance [*Schein*] of that justice, achieved at last and fading so quickly [*schon vergehenden*]! What times these were, my comrade!" (CS 154; E 164)

The officer's language for the decisive moment is peculiar; literally translated it reads: we all *take from the martyred face its expression* of transfiguration, we *hold our cheeks* in the *Schein*—the radiance and/or semblance—of this Justice finally achieved and already passing away. This "taking" and "holding" of expressions and faces evokes a strange manipulation, like so many masks giving and receiving imprints and impressions.[5] One might well see here a kind of death mask that would emblematize the true point of contact and exchange in the procedure's social, pedagogical, and historical imaging of a beyond of vision.[6] The closed eyes of those lying in the sand counter the radiant death-face with a semblance of its own imminent trespass.

The much-quoted lines I have been commenting on thus contain an essential ambiguity: Justice manifests as the visibility of a *Schein*, a powerful supraworldly radiance that, however, is also merely semblance, *Schein* in the sense of illusion. But what is remarkable is that for the officer and the scene he describes, this distinction is rendered inoperative. As the officer gives his impassioned testimony—his own *martyros*—it can only be a matter of complete indifference whether this *Schein* is an overwhelming ultimate reality or merely an illusion (the *Schein* of an *Erscheinung*), categories of experience that are irrelevant here. Just as it is irrelevant whether the guilt of the accused has been verified (the officer's only juridical "principle" being: "Guilt is always indubitable"). In a regime of order and Law in which language and perception have the power to *posit* their objects, the strictures of verification have no meaning, and we are thus in the realm of a kind of *performative dogmatism* (otherwise known as authoritarianism). If guilt is indubitable, this is in part because the word of authority is immediately binding.[7] But this can only occur in very specific circumstances, which the story sets out to interrogate in the mode of a retroactive narration.

This is why the true import of "In the Penal Colony" in no way hinges on whether the officer is a delirious and deluded maniac conjuring projected fantasms or whether his testimony of times past harks back to some true but bygone historical reality, for his testimony strives in any case to *make that reality true*, but in the only mode possible, as an appearance that is always already lost ("in the *Schein* of this Justice reached at last and already passing away"). In other words, it is a *legend*, and it is only as such that it can function in the present of the officer's discourse. What the story does hinge on, then, is the ability or inability to reproduce that merely passing appearance *of* transcendence, given the social disinvestment of the form of justice at issue—destitution as deinstitution —and therefore, even more to the point: the decision as to whether it can or ought to be recuperated. As the officer remarks, in a statement that delineates the precise rhetorical dilemma of his speech: "I still possess some of the old Commandant's persuasive force (*Überzeugungskraft*), but his power (*seine Macht*) is completely lacking to me" (CS 153; E 163). Persuasive force without power, linguistic *Kraft* stripped of paternal and Oedipal *Macht*: this is the position at stake in the officer's demonstration and appeal, and in the visiting traveler's "judgment."

For the reasons just given, it is important in referring to the Justice of former times to say "recuperated" and not "maintained." Despite the apparent ongoing nature of the old commandant's justice system, the story very carefully refrains from any precise scenographic reference to more recent executions, and it is clear that the officer's defense speech derives all its urgent passion from an evocation of "earlier times," *früherer Zeit* (or "those times," *jene Zeiten*") in distinction from "today" or "nowadays," *heute* (E 164, 165). It is in the historical gap between these two "times" that the officer's rhetoric, both visual and verbal, must do its work. In a sense, he must reproduce the surprising "seduction" exerted in former times, he claims, by the sight of the ecstatic martyr's face, on which Understanding, even for the dullest among them, dawns in the end and always: "Understanding dawns even on the stupidest [*Verstand geht dem Blödesten auf*]. It begins around the eyes. From there it spreads. It is a sight [*Anblick*] that might seduce one to lie oneself down beneath the harrow" (CS 150; E 160). But the officer, for his part, must seduce through language, in a persuasive speech performance, and not by way of a radiant image. His inability to do this reveals a gap not only between "times," but also between forms of "speech" that are more or less capable of taking hold of a subject's interiority—and of implanting there an Understanding that would shine forth in the very moment of its intense and violent implantation.

But in another register, this temporal gap must be bridged in a mode that resonates with remarks made above on the allegorical split in "The Stoker," and more generally with the entire dimension of conceptual and other forms of "grasping" indicated by the verb *begreifen* and related terms. Indeed, this is exactly what the officer says, after exclaiming: "What times those were, Comrade [*Was für Zeiten, mein Kamarad*]!" Quite carried away, he embraces the traveler, to whose keen embarrassment he "laid his head on his shoulder," revealing that the gap between times is also a rhetorical and fantasmatic gap between a haunting and conjured passion and a more sober interlocutor who does not recognize his projected status as a "comrade." Instead we see him gazing around uncomfortably at the dull present stripped of any richness, seeing in it only "the wastes of the valley [*die Öde des Tales*]" (E 165). The officer's uncommunicated passion is thus something like his own dear treasure, here embarrassingly revealed; but he quickly gets hold of himself ("*fasste sich schnell*"). Now it is precisely at this moment, when an unshared and incommensurate vision is affectively registered, that the historical breach of "times" becomes a question of the ungraspable: "I didn't want to upset you . . . I know it is impossible to make those days *graspable* now [*jene Zeiten heute begreiflich zu machen*]" (CS, 154; E 165; my emphasis). He knows it is impossible, but this is precisely the task of his defense, to make graspable, comprehensible, or palpable a passionate experience that cannot be conveyed by concepts—that requires the presentation of what is a stubbornly ungraspable truth now stripped of its social conditions and existing only "within" the officer, or, possibly, by way of his speech. If there was a "now" when justice was happening, that now is now no more. If it subsists, it must depend on his language to be conveyed, for the image-spectacle itself no longer *works* on the social body. Thus the officer's performance already operates within the sphere of the ungraspable, but he will *insist* on his task, the impossible one of displaying the *Schein* of this no longer shining treasure that continues to obsess, haunt, and inhabit him in the mode of an unshared "persuasion" or "conviction" (*Überzeugung*)—but also, as mentioned, in the image of a radiant mask-like face of death. He goes on in this same paragraph to concede, with an edge of bitterness, the conditions of this impossibility, projecting a self-contradictory image of the autotelic machine unloading its own precious leftover, and localizing the *unbegreiflich*, once again, in a corpse:

> Anyhow, the machine still works [*arbeitet*] for itself. It is still effective in itself [*sie wirkt für sich*], even though it stands alone in this valley. And the corpse still falls at the last into the pit with an incomprehensibly gentle wafting motion [*in dem unbegreiflich sanften Flug*] even though hundreds do not swarm around like flies [*wie Fliegen*] as formerly. (E 165)

Here the story does refer to the present conditions in which the executions are now carried out, but it does so only to concede its withdrawal from all spectatorship, all social staging, and in order to assert its self-contained "effectivity." But let us clearly note the specter this calls up: a machine working by and for itself, tossing the bodies of its victims in an incomprehensibly gentle flight (*Flug*), a term echoed in the description of the hundreds of spectators who used to surround it like flies (*wie Fliegen*), insect-like creatures that would both be parasites on and presumably also *supply* the bodies devoured by this automatically functioning machine. To describe this flight into the grave as *unbegreiflich sanft* (and to do so almost immediately after lamenting the impossibility of making *begreiflich* what was once so radiantly manifest), seems to reinforce a limit of graspability that passes through the corpse, last vestige of the old order in its historical public effectivity. If the incomprehensible did have a chance of being visually displayed in the present judgment scene, it would be precisely there, and we know that the machine must now produce a corpse for the traveler, as its last line of defense against his predictable judgment. But the image of the used-up cadaver tossed aside like a carcass or a piece of fruit squeezed dry gives an indication as to the naked exploitation and serial consumption at issue in this machine's operation "for itself," as it continues in the wasteland of the present. In these conditions, the machine's withdrawal from the gaze of the community—from the scene of a galvanizing spectacle—can only turn it over to the sheer automatism of isolated mechanical repetition, a kind of pointless insatiable hunger.

Have we thus arrived at an image of the violent drive lodged within the ground of this story's fantasms, both "old" and "new"? And if so, does the officer's fantasy of a self-contained effectivity, hard at work even in the absence of all social investment, merely underestimate the annihilating power of historical oblivion, or is it the story's most trenchant remark concerning the persistence of the juridical machine-schema in the shadow of its official disavowal? To approach the question of continuity or rupture between the two regimes, it would be necessary to delineate more precisely the modes of violence in question, as these manifest in the machinic treatment of the body and the production of a corpse, especially of the actual corpse that appears on the scene at the end of the story (and not those "ungraspably gentle" ones related as legend by the officer). At one level, it seems clear that the corpse as leftover constitutes the decisive remainder of the procedure at hand. What is perhaps more surprising is that this corpse is in fact presented in various ways as a piece of chewed-on food that resists assimilation no less than it seems to guarantee the ideals at stake. In that light, I would like to introduce some of the motifs associated with biting and eating that will continue to take on importance, as the destituting processes we are tracing verge toward a more and more radicalized hunger that would elude the fulfillment, if not the violence, of its drives. The interplay of these motifs in relation to the penal colony apparatus constitutes a significant phase in the terminal emptying out of the Law's transcendent treasures.

IN THE ORAL COLONY

Images of food and eating, along with a number of clearly associated terms, appear in surprising ways throughout the story, whose vivid scenography is traversed by an intense and forceful *orality*. Not only is there almost non-stop talking (at least until the officer places himself, like so much fresh (guilty) meat, in the jaws of the machine), the scene itself is set in the depression of a mouthlike valley studded with toothy rocks, "a deep hollow enclosed on all sides by stark naked crags [*von kahlen Abhängen ringsum abgeschlossenen*]" (CS 140; E 151). One could say that the motif of food and eating is introduced, obliquely and proleptically, as early as the story's first paragraph, in the description of the condemned prisoner's animal-like appearance and behavior, in accordance with which he has been beaten with his superior's riding whip (as we learn soon enough); it is his response to this treatment that has earned him his punishment (referred to throughout as an "*Urteil*"): "Throw the whip away or I'll eat you up [*ich fresse dich*]" (E 157). The threat of gobbling up (*fressen*) his superior officer like a hungry animal defending itself from abuse by a whip also brings the story into the crude element of disciplinary subjection against which this threat would be an overt, if merely reflexive, rebellion. Clearly the discipline administered by the whip is at best merely able to reduce its subject to a more or less submissive animal, but one who necessarily maintains a margin of nonsubmission, an untouched drive that may still lash out in turn; but such discipline is not quite sufficient to guarantee the remainderless spiritual-corporeal absorption this law requires, which must kill the body it fully penetrates. As the story articulates the aggressive authoritarian fantasy of reaching into the spirit through painful subjection of the body, animalistic impulse and devouring are thus posed, as sporadic resistance, against the consummation/consumption of a disciplinary wounding. But it is unclear, in the end, which of these has the ascendency, or even whether there is ultimately any significant difference between the two—indeed, the machine itself is rather like an animal in the story's final pièce de résistance, to which we will return. As a further and quite horrific form of orality, this machine is equipped with a "felt gag" meant to deaden the victim's screams and prevent him from biting his tongue (at least for the first two hours, after which it is removed, since at that point he no longer has the strength to scream). Its name in German, *Filzstumpf*, actually echoes the initial bestializing description of the prisoner as a dull-witted "*stumpfsinniger Mensch.*" But this rhyme becomes dissonant when the *stumpfsinnig* prisoner is forced to take the disgustingly dirty and reused *Stumpf* into his mouth; apparently more sensitive than he seems, he vomits ("*sich erbrach*") all over the machine. This disgusting "outbreak" of visceral innards gives rise to a rant on the part of the officer who faults the new commandant for this sorry state of affairs ("*Alles Schuld des Kommandanten!*"), in which the leader's ladies ply the prisoner with sweets before the execution, and no one provides the officer with a change of felt for the gag.

> "Have I not tried for hours at a time to get the Commandant to grasp [*begreiflich zu machen*] that the prisoner must fast for a whole day before the execution. But our new, mild direction [*Richtung*] thinks otherwise . . . He has lived on stinking fish his whole life long and now he has to eat sugar candy! . . . How should a man not feel sick when he takes a felt gag into his mouth which more than a hundred men have already sucked and gnawed [*gesaugt und gebissen*] in their dying moments [*im Sterben*]?" [CS 152; E 163]

It turns out that the tortured prisoner must also be something of a hunger artist, if only the officer could make himself understood by the dull-witted administrator who fails to grasp the urgency of this prescription. The passage from stinking fish to candy, however, provides a concrete image for the merely incremental difference that actually separates the old regime from the new, at least as far as edible nourishment is concerned. For is it not largely a question of how easily it all goes down? But the "sucking and biting" to which the dying prisoners are reduced has as its object something for which ingestible nourishment is an inferior stand-in, as the story's figures of orality veer definitively away from the food that provides its occasions.

It is in that light that we can regard perhaps the most perverse item of all—a perversity deriving from the horrific banality it pictures—namely the heated tub of rice pap at which the victim "grabs with his tongue" (CS 150; E 160) during his torture. This part of the punishment appears to be designed to defang the violent threat for which he has been laid there, for it is indeed a kind of domesticated *fressen*. The tub of pap also provides Kafka with many opportunities for the slapstick gestures that punctuate the story, as its preparation, placement, and handling by the soldier assistant—a figure closely aligned with the prisoner, in terms of both rank and sensibility—constantly edges into puerility (at one point there is practically a food fight), especially during one long segment in the middle of the story, when the prisoner, strapped into the machine, shares a meal of it with the soldier throughout the officer's explanations and appeals. However, in the latter's glassy-eyed recollections of past executions, this gruel-like food substance marks an important turn in the ascent toward enlightened Understanding. No one, he says, foregoes the opportunity to enjoy the stuff, but at the decisive moment the eating stops, and hunger too is transformed:

> "Only about the sixth hour does the man lose all pleasure in eating. I usually kneel down here at that moment and observe this phenomenon [*diese Erscheinung*]. The man rarely swallows his last bites [*den letzten Bissen*], he only rolls it around in his mouth and spits it into the pit. I have to duck just then or he would spit it into my face [*sonst fährt er mir ins Gesicht*]." (CS 150; E 160)

Let us grant to the officer the notion that, instead of deliberately spitting in his face in a rage over their torment, the torture victims eject their food for the same reason that makes him bend down at this crucial moment: the transfiguration is nigh. And so, says the officer, he stoops to absorb the transcendence of its *Erscheinung*, as the prisoner stops eating, as though the heightened reception that occurs at the sixth hour left no room for any other assimilating functions. There is only "hearkening," which is also a kind of reading: "the man begins to decipher the script, he purses his mouth, as if hearkening [*er spitzt den Mund, als horche er*]." The mouth no longer chews or spits, it "*spitzt*," it puckers in a deterritorializing gesture welcoming an intake of an entirely different order than mere eating or nourishment, which is excluded at this most "spiritual" moment. Once again, the acoustic register of this very visual narrative becomes decisive at the point of its highest pretension to transcendence: at one level, it projects a call that is structurally homologous to the "invocation in my ear" of Kafka's invisible court (at least in its passive and receptive moment); at the same time, and more strangely, by opening a split between different orders of listening—mere hearing versus a sublimely attuned hearkening of the Law—this acoustic dimension also opens a split between heterogeneous types of "nourishment," in a movement similar to the one we saw in "The Metamorphosis," where music points the way to an unknown-longed-for nourishment that appears to outstrip any graspable object. This split will be restaged in a much more ironic mode with the hunger artist—who upon dying puckers his lips as well, but in his case in order to speak the puncturing letdown of his final deflating words.[8] The man taken captive in the penal colony machine can express or expel only the undifferentiated pap of his "last bites," as he himself is gnawed by the machine, and consumed by its avid onlookers, especially those inwardly turned eye-closers, who have apparently already eaten him up—that is, have already internalized the justice he himself is finally and definitively assimilating, through neither mouth nor even ear, but rather directly on the "understanding" (E 160).

The most decisive turning point in the story, however, comes with the traveler's judgment in speech, in response to which the officer frees the prisoner from the machine in order to place himself in it, in a scene that continues to develop the motif of eating and chewing, but this time in an even more unsavory fashion (as we will see in a moment). In order to understand the simultaneously legal and oral (even dental) violence of the story's culminating letdown, it will be necessary to lay out the logic of the defense-judgment-punishment scenario that leads to it, aligning it with similar scenes in the other judgment stories, whose fundamentally violent schema it articulates as an unsurpassable limit—that is, as a dead end in which the procedure's logic is tangled into an inescapable knot, but also (therefore) as an impasse that will force a displacement of its basic presuppositions, toward another form of writing.

The Judgment: "No"

The precise nature of the traveler's judgment and its consequences can be clarified only by setting it against the observation the latter makes during the officer's appeal, namely that if everything appears to depend on the traveler, then an effective judgment has already been tacitly passed by the new commandant (CS 156; E 167). At this point the narrator asks: "Did the officer *grasp* [*begriff*] this? No, he did not yet grasp it" (CS 156–7; E 167; my emphasis). The officer does not grasp the fact that the grasp of the machine no longer holds, as he shakes his head and glances stupidly over at the stupidly eating soldier and prisoner—who, noticing his gaze, "flinched away from the rice" for a moment, startled by this renewed surveillance. It is here that the officer begins explicitly to plead his case with the traveler, and to lay out his "plan": "And now I make this plea to you: help me oppose the Commandant!" (CS 157; E 167). This plea for help against a powerful superior who has *already* judged him places the pair in a position precisely analogous to that of the stoker and Karl Rossmann (even if the latter is a traveler more amenable to the categorical assumptions of the case confronting him). Indeed, when the traveler begs off, the officer becomes more and more like the stoker, balling his fists and striking fear into the traveler ("The traveler saw with some fright that the officer was clenching his hands into fists [*die Fäuste ballte*]") (CS 157; E 167). A sense of desperate indignation grows as the officer lays out his final defense against the maleficent powers pitted against him. And here, with this structure in place, Kafka installs at this precise point in the narrative the basic schema of all the judgment narratives: a defense speech presented in the urgency of an imminent pronouncement of judgment, but a speech that is programmed to fail.

Now what is remarkable about the officer's final delirious speech, with its fantastical "plan," is that it too consists of a vividly imagined trial scene, which Kafka thus embeds within the larger judgment scene of the story as a whole. The officer himself refers to this embedded scene as a "*Schaustellung*," a theatrical spectacle, engineered, he claims, by the new commandant, but as such also subject to the officer's machinations. In fact, what he narrates at this point is not so much a plan as a highly elaborate fantasy in which the traveler would intervene at a large official meeting ("*eine grosse Sitzung*"; CS 158, E 168) in order to pronounce the favorable judgment the officer "must" have from him. This fantasy has all the surreal scenographic precision of Kafka's most compellingly rendered and "dreamlike" scenes, and even includes variations in the possible scenarios (for example, the traveler should stand "against the balustrade [*an die Brüstung*]," as though in the witness stand, and bellow out his judgment for all to hear; no, no, he should whisper almost inaudibly to a lady beside him . . .). The fantasy scenario ends with the officer taking over the proceedings, delivering his own speech with thunderous indignation, "and, believe me, if my speech [*Rede*] does not drive him out of the hall [*aus dem Saale jagt*], then it will force him to his knees, so that he must make the acknowledgment: Old Commandant, I bow before you" (CS 159; E 169). The officer concludes by shifting this "must" to the traveler: "That is my plan; will you help me execute it? But of course you are willing; what's more, you must." At this point, as the narrator tells us, the officer is screaming so loudly that the soldier and the prisoner, who understand nothing (they do not speak French), interrupt their eating and stare dumbly over at the traveler, slowly chewing their pap (CS 159; E 169). With this parody of the legendary moments when beatific prisoners interrupted their eating and "only hearkened," the officer, unheeded and reduced to screaming, must rest his case. After this, only the machine awaits him.

I have underscored some elements that clearly call to mind earlier judgment stories, including, once again, some repetitions of precise images and phrases from "The Judgment" (especially a speech that chases and drives out, *jagt*); and one could say that this desperate speech sharpens their most essential characteristics into a single formulaic alternative: *by force of speech, I compel you to bow down or to flee*.[9] Note that the speaker of the "defense" ending with this image has passed over, in the officer's fantasmatic projection, to the position of the sublime judge occupied in previous stories by figures such as the family fathers and the stoker's captain. Indeed, despite its imminent failure, it falls along a continuum plotted by the performative force attributed to the voices of these figures, including that of the traveler, who is about to pronounce, in his more quiet but no less authoritative manner, a "no" that echoes down along the chain to the father's abrupt explosion in "The Judgment."

Now it is also by way of the voice that the new commandant is implicated in the "old" form of judgment. Indeed, the thunder of the officer's fantasized judgment, far from being superseded, has in fact merely been stolen from the new commandant, a fact made clear in a passing reference that places him, too, on the side of the sublimely higher powers. This occurs when the officer reports that the ladies call the new commandant's voice a "*Donnerstimme*," a thunder-voice (CS 156; E 166), a description that places the legislative locus of the new regime in close proximity to the hammer-voice of the stoker's captain, as though both of these figures were descended from some long forgotten hammer-wielding Thor god. Such an allusion is not merely associative play; moving quickly, we may allow it to stand in for the pagan or mythic forces that persist through every form of authoritarian power mounted and enacted in these stories. The officer's screaming aspires to this as well, but of course this cry is, for the reader, a written one born from its own imminent deflation, and we cannot fail to note that the fantasmatic slippage from beleaguered defendant to sublime performative power enacts the effort we have seen in Kafka to locate writing's movement in a striving (and always failing) to grasp the knot of power as an irresistible force of speech. That is, to attain, in writing, a position that will outstrip any judgment bearing on it, to become a hyperbolic instance of the law's most immediate effectivity—and at the same time to reveal the limits, unstable contours, and internal tensions of this force *pressing through language*.

The officer's failure is thus the most clearly articulated refusal on Kafka's part to grant these efforts their rights, on the very terrain of the legalistic fantasy that transcribes and stages their initial conception in the tribunal of bad conscience. The hint of a *Donnerstimme* sounding still in the current commandant's "new" order of the law indicates the depth and extent of the barrier thus erected, for it necessarily crosses the two regimes that otherwise seem to divide the story's change of epoch into a strictly separated "before" and "after." It is important to stress once again that, at every point in this story, we are already in the after. And it is precisely in the regime of that *after* that the officer submits to the (as it turns out) murderous commandment, "Be just." His break with the old regime—in response to the traveler's simple judgment: "No"—turns him over to this more conceptual (and less figural) meta-commandment that nonetheless has the same "author," namely the old commandant, and relies on the very same machinery for its enforcement.[10] In the zone of overlap between the two epochs, writing, as programmed machinic dictation and spiritually invested automatism, breaks down; it becomes, as I will show in a moment, mere stabbing and *chewing*. What this might say about the writing vocation for Kafka is quite difficult to decipher at this point, but it seems clear that we are in the tightening space of an impasse. The important point to stress is that the shift I want to delineate in Kafka's writing ethos, in the modulating imperative that haunts and structures his fictions, in no way corresponds to the change of legal regime reflected in "In the Penal Colony," which as a whole remains *within* the schema of judgment. At most it merely exposes the extreme and unsurpassable horizon determined by this schema.

Machine Animation: Cog Bites

If the writing of the law—writing grounded in law as discourse and bodily submission, writing as sublime dictation—breaks down in the officer's submission to it, it is not entirely accurate to say, as any reader of this story would be inclined to do, that the machine itself breaks down. On the contrary, once it has taken hold of the officer, it appears finally to have come into its own, as indicated by the peculiar descriptions of its apparently self-determined "actions," which transform the machine from a merely functional mechanism into a kind of sentient organism. This transformation begins at the precise moment when the officer is strapped into his machine, but cannot reach the crank that would set it going: no need, says the narrator, for it begins to work all by itself (CS 164; E 174).[11] The machine's "behavior" at this point is one of the story's recalcitrant enigmas. Why would it suddenly cease to work as it had before, now that its "master" is the one to be punished/enlightened? Is there something inherently unfulfillable in the abstract meta-commandment it has been assigned to inscribe, as though "Be just!" could not be transposed from the old commandant's "*Schriften*" into the medium of a merely living body? Is it that the failure of ecstatic transcendence implied by the traveler's negative judgment necessarily leads to a collapse of the new law's (conceptual) transcendence as well? Has its instruction of the body fed to it been reduced to mere destruction and to simple revenge (as the released prisoner thinks)? Certainly there is a contradiction in the officer's placing himself in the very machine that has administered a judgment now judged unjust, and to do so in order to expiate that injustice. But by what logic, exactly, does this contradiction lead to the machine's quasi-Frankensteinian animation and to the sheer (extra-legal) murder of its maker (in the guise of his living representative), and, finally, the expectoration of its own innards? What does it mean that the deligitimized machine of justice becomes a kind of wrathful and ravenous animal, as Kafka's descriptions make very clear?

The story does not allow us to answer these questions with anything but speculation. I would like to approach them, at least, by way of the last one, which requires that we look closely at the language in which this machine-animal is driven, but fails, to eat the object/subject of the Law.

It is clear that this machine too has passed through a change of regime and, far from breaking down, is doing exactly what it "wants" and not what it has been commanded or preprogrammed to do. Its automatism thus takes on a very different aspect that seems to have surpassed its status as technical machinery, a fact indicated by the inexplicable silence of the previously squeaking, worn-out cogwheel that had disturbed the officer's demonstration—as though the material grinding of metal parts is no longer its mode of operation, or perhaps as though it has returned to its previous functioning "with no false note," but in a now heightened and more focused intensity, in a different mood, as it were. Its treatment of the officer thus appears to be impelled by something akin, rather, to *affect*, an aggressive destructive drive, or a kind of hunger. . . . Thus we return to the orality discussed above, and, further, to the sort of hacking and biting we have been tracking all along, in the basso continuo, the deeply "mordant" action of the legal-literary *Gewissensbiss*. This association is justified in part by the way in which the officer's body, instead of being written on, is rather bitten and chewed by the machine, spitted but not spit out: at the end, the traveler has to force the soldier and the condemned man to help him remove the body from the harrow that has impaled him. Thus chewing takes over from a writing previously invested with a more spiritual vocation, the implication being that we have returned to the realm of stinking fish and mealy pap (and candy), which is also the one in which a sacrificed body can only hang suspended and bleeding like a piece of meat.

The notion that the machine in some sense tries, unsuccessfully, *to eat* this indigestible body finds further justification in a peculiar detail that links the machine's internal organs with the mechanics of ingestion, and gives a strange significance to the "expression" of its insides. When the "designer" slowly, uncannily opens its lid and begins to squeeze out it parts, "as though some *great power* were squeezing the designer together" (my emphasis), the "cogs" that are spit out in this operation are called *Zahnräder*, literally *teeth-wheels*, and just like the harrow with its piercing points, these spiky wheels are described as having *Zacken*, a term often translated as "teeth" (CS 164; E 174). Thus we might say that the hungry machine of the Law has broken its teeth on a recalcitrant body it can no longer properly ingest; and rather than spit out the body, as it has done at the end of previous executions (with a gentleness that is downright *unbegreiflich*, etc.), it *holds onto* its "food"—the obtrusive leftover of a now inassimilable nourishment—and spits out its own "teeth." The internal secret of its previously flawless effectivity is now rendered up merely as detached material remainders. *Lex edentata*: the law as such loses its teeth at the very moment when writing, as visible and socially performed incision, comes uncoupled from the theatrical instantiation of Justice. Such a formula is not contradicted by the "biting" teeth of the machine, the needles that penetrate the body, for this penetration is no longer carried out as part of the law's application but rather in the *dissolution* of its bodily link with transcendence—that is, as sheer compulsive drive, and yet not as mere mechanism. The specter of sentience endows the machine with an imponderable interiority, even as its inner treasure is exposed as so many defective gears (one might be tempted to call them "blood teeth").[12] When the "designer" opens the lid of its locked box and begins to expel its contents, one might well see in this externalizing display the logic of Kafka's milk teeth fable, but now crossed with a specific reconfiguration—a stripping bare and evisceration—of the sublime law in its violent penetrating force. Only the dimwitted former prisoner is there to chase these fascinating treasures around in the sand, trying but failing to grab hold of (*fassen*) them.

The Body Ungrasped

Is it possible that this fascinated subject is gripped by something that no one else is able to perceive?

I wonder whether this figure of undeserved punishment and unearned liberation might not point, however dimly and incompletely, in the direction of a different relation to the law, in the context of a story otherwise completely determined by a logic of the violent sublime. Or whether, despite his "doglike submission," he nonetheless represents in his very stupidity and *Stumpsinnigkeit* a persistent and ineradicable form of insubordination. What we notice in any case is that the law of the machine does not touch him, or just *barely*: stripped naked and placed in the machine, he nevertheless escapes with nothing but "a few small lacerations," "*einige kleine Risswunden*" (E 171)—a term that evokes not only the cuts in his skin, but also, more obliquely, the very "design" (*Riss*) he has escaped having inscribed on him by the "designer" (*Zeichner*) (and this design itself is the most secret and schematic treasure of this story, as the officer's protective treatment of the old commandant's drawings (or writings: *Schriften*) clearly shows), and even, I would suggest, the "*rissige Hand*" of the stoker—which, it will be recalled, is the explicitly named treasure that must there be renounced. It is as though the inscription of language, and the higher rewards associated with it, were disarticulated on his mostly blank, naked skin, leaving him free for a strange anarchic playfulness in relation to the machine and its now disjointed gears. Its teeth do not bite into him. He is in a sense a figure withdrawn from conscience, whose impulsive and fascinated stupidity places him, in a muted but perhaps salutary way, on the hither side of the law's sublime subjection, its tortures and promises. His release, which is not even exactly a pardon, and his redemption, which is no redemption, thus mark out a kind of flattened zone of liberation, but one no wider than the margin of his mostly unspeaking resistance, and really no different than it was at the beginning of the story. To be sure, he remains in the end confined within the sphere of penality, in its absolutist colonial form—in which he himself is forced to function as a cog. The condemned man is freed from the inscriptive apparatus of execution, but the underlying structure of his confinement remains constant. Ultimately, he must stay on the penal island.

That underlying structure is emblematized most directly by the obtrusive residue it has produced in the officer's corpse, through a process of progressive destitution that remains unresolved. The divestiture, in every sense, of the officer's body, the stripping away of its prestige (his uniform and his sword) and the unredeemed violation of its nakedness, leaves only an image of what it was in life, a dead face resting in its ruined and destituted conviction. The "eyes were open, they had the same expression as in life [or "had the expression of life": *hatten den Ausdruck des Lebens*], the look [*Blick*] was calm and convinced [*überzeugt*], through the forehead went the point [*Spitze*] of the great iron spike" (CS 166; E 176). It is perhaps in this death mask remnant that the story most clearly displays its critical thrust, in an emblem of violent living death that refuses to fall into sublimity but rather remains in a suspended and horrific abjection. If "In the Penal Colony" is the text in which Kafka most starkly uncovers the grounding violence of the law as such, in its specific convergence with the sublimely striving imperative to write—a convergence I have given the emblematic name of *Gewissensbiss*, placing it in close proximity to the disciplinary spectacle of judgment and punishment—then it is no doubt with the peaceful expression of conviction on this corpse's face that the writer locates the impasse he deliberately erected at the far end of judgment's dream, in the unredeemable remnant of its ecstasy, the impassibly staring death mask of the law.[13] The sublimely hacked and bitten body, once the inward reservoir of a "frozen sea," now renders up no more than this opaque emblem.

FROM "IN THE PENAL COLONY" TO *THE TRIAL*

However ambiguous "In the Penal Colony" may be in terms of its ultimate implications, the very precise, fixed, and self-contained contours of the tableau it presents—with its localized machinery of justice, explicit judgments, and vivid, cadaverous by-product—stand in stark contrast to the extreme indeterminacy of the juridical apparatus set in motion in Kafka's second novel. But this indeterminacy is also what allows *The Trial* both to radicalize and to surpass the figural schema of the judgment stories, and thus to elude the impasse pictured in "In the Penal Colony." That story mounts a scene of judgment, in which speech continues to be determined as disciplinary violence and performative effectivity, in a process leading inevitably to the mute and static image of a corpse. With this corpse and its living-dead "expression," the series of figures that would embody the Law as an image—whether as its sublime author or subjected representative—curls to a self-devouring close around its furthest and deadliest extremity, in a tight terminal knot that is also, as it were, an irreducible kernel blocking any further passage.

Many readers have commented in productive ways on the fact that Kafka wrote "In the Penal Colony" during a moment when work on *The Trial* was stalled (late summer and early fall of 1914).[14] Whatever the precise reasons for this blockage, the difference in form between the two narratives points to a stark incompatibility: it is as though it were necessary to excise this jaggedly precise figural irritant from the generative schema of a novel that is structured, by contrast, as a wide-ranging movement of endless displacement.[15] The need for such a removal and isolation of the penal colony's overtly murderous dead-end writing machinery is no doubt one reason why the story must be contained on an island, which the traveler will then leave behind—as he brandishes a knotted rope, a threatening barrier to the island dwellers who want to follow. But that traveler, who *as a judge and by force of speech* remains deeply implicated in the violent juridical spectacle of the penal colony island and its disciplinary apparatus, will surely return home to a place very much like the urban metropole depicted in *The Trial*, where such determinate visions of justice/punishment are indeed tightly contained, displaced, or absconded (in one case literally hidden in a closet).[16] By asking how the novel registers the traveler's violent disciplinary visions and knotted (t)ropes, we may be able to discover how the trial as a "process" of movement begins to turn away from writing as self-defense, and to exit the scenographic space of the courtroom, even as "the court" and the guilt it produces become inescapable universal conditions projected beyond the grasp of any scenic presentation. Nowhere in the novel do we find any judges who appear as such (except in a painting), or any judgment scenes that actually take place. Such a radical removal of any authoritative *instance* of judgment, its projected deferral into inaccessible indeterminacy, hyperbolically inflates the sphere of guilt; but it also opens the space for a profoundly ironic stance before any possible scenic or figurable grasp of Justice (this is true regardless of whether Josef K. is able to take up that stance;

it nonetheless defines his position). Such an irony may well take some of the bite out of bad conscience, but this only amplifies the intimate and unsettling music that haunts it. In Kafka's novels, beginning especially with *The Trial*, this music is that of an anxious dialogue tuned to rumor; and it is announced by the "foretaste of freedom" that Josef K. has when he leaves the stifling offices of the court for the very last time (a scene I will return to). One result of this breaching of the confines of the court, as we will see, is that the speech of self-defense is disjoined from its accusatory addressee, unmoored from its punishing/exonerating Other, such that this mode of speech, too, reaches an impasse, as indicated in the blank piece of paper that Josef K. bizarrely holds aloft to no one (in the section titled "The Manufacturer"), as though presenting his impossibly exhaustive confessions. I will attempt to read this unwritten blankness and the impossibility it expresses as the index of a differently configured imperative to write, one that is determined by exigencies other than those of exoneration—and entering, instead, into the mode, mood or *Stimmung* of a much more diffuse anxiety completely at a loss to grasp its objects.

Josef K., Traveler

Let us return for a moment to the penal colony and to the traveler who, in the end, must travel home. If the overtly gruesome scenery of that story had to be literally isolated (set apart as an island, and distanced as an outlying colony), the returning traveler, who has just pronounced a judgment that fixes its newly reigning law, thus consolidating its regime, would nonetheless relay certain of its elements back to the metropole he represents, that is, precisely to the sort of modern European city in which *The Trial* takes place. This is a space inhabited as well by the protagonists of the other judgment stories, and by Kafka himself, who clearly drew on his native city, and on the general professional milieu of office work familiar to him, in laying out the territory of his novel. There are a number of specific indices that link the penal colony traveler to this space as it appears in other fictions. First of all, as a traveler (*Reisende*), he already occupies a continuum shared by the city-dwelling Gregor Samsa, whose former life as a traveling salesman (Kafka calls him a *Reisender*) makes uneasy (nominal) twins of these two figures. And whom do we meet on the first page of the novel but a man who has come to arrest Josef K. dressed in something that looks "like a traveler's outfit [*ähnlich den Reiseanzügen*] . . . provided with a variety of pleats, pockets, buckles, buttons and a belt."[17] The whole thing appears to be "eminently practical," but to what end it is hard to say (T 3; KA P 7). Josef K.'s adventure is thus placed, however opaquely, within the sphere of travel, to which he is being subjected by this strange proxy of the law, whose name, it turns out, is Franz. The fact that Franz, while projecting the appearance of a *Reisende*, is in no way a judge, and that one can discern neither the law he represents—as a penal apparatus in force—nor the destination of the journey he vaguely evokes, indicates precisely the sort of transfer deposit made by the figure of the penal colony traveler into this novelistic narrative stripped of its authorizing instances. It may also provide a discreet clue regarding the shift in the schema of writing that I have been tracing, precisely one from judgment to a kind of endless, indeterminate displacement or "travel." In *The Trial*, the machinery of judgment continues to be projected and mobilized, and the law continues to be exerted, eminently so; but its more dispersed movement will never arrive at the endpoint it projects. As commentators have pointed out, Josef K.'s movement, as such, is potentially endless. Continually threatened with judgment, he will nonetheless never *face it*.[18] By retaining the schema of judgment, and indeed expanding it indefinitely, while withdrawing the figuration of a fully invested judging authority, the novel maintains a continuity with the judgment stories, but also opens the endless movement that distinguishes it from them (a movement that Blanchot will call *erring* and *error*). It should be noted that the new potentialities thus opened in the novel depend on the necessary relinquishment of the ideal of continuity and wholeness (*in einem Zug, im Zusammenhang*) that has weighed on the writing of Kafka's shorter stories, and it could be argued that "In the Penal Colony" carries out at some level precisely the relinquishment of such a comprehensively condensed form, making possible the novel's continuation—in a kind of circulation that one might well call "*geradezu unendlich*" (virtually infinite, to use Corngold's translation). The novel thus concretely engages the endlessness that is only schematically indicated, and immediately interrupted, in the short story. But this will also require a revision of the relations between guilt, the law, and the body on which these are registered.

The Law and the Body

Throughout the judgment stories (and well before), the crucial relation of a "defendant" to the law and judgment is played out in the latter's contact with the body of the former—the commanding, captation, and incising of a body, its grasping and ungrasping, that we have seen staged in various more or less dramatic forms. In this respect, as well, *The Trial* opens up the narrative form, and the "legal" structures implicated in it, by introducing a crucial equivocation at precisely this point, where the law would grasp a body and make itself sensed. On the one hand, there is a clear continuity between Josef K.'s execution and the other judgment stories: the guilty party is executed, and a corpse is produced, inevitably, as "The End" (as that chapter is called) or goal of the juridical "process." On the other hand, *The Trial* introduces from the very beginning a mode of "grasping" and "feeling" that cannot be reduced to direct bodily seizure: in formulas that point toward both earlier and later narratives (notably "A Hunger Artist"), the novel appears to unfasten the law's direct grip on the body and to indicate something more closely resembling the later text's relinquishment of any inward *object*. Further, this decoupling can be traced through a number of precise phrases that Kafka uses to invoke these points of contact, in a series that clearly plots the shift in question. In *The Trial*, this occurs in the first few pages, in the exchange between K. and the guards who have come to arrest him. K. does not understand, of course; there must have been a mistake. One of the guards replies,

"There's been no mistake. After all, our department, as far as I know, and I know only the lowest level, doesn't seek out guilt among the general population, but, as the Law states, is *attracted by guilt* and has to send us guards out. That's the law. What mistake could there be?" "I don't know that law," said K. "All the worse for you," said the guard. "It probably exists only in your heads," said K.; he wanted to slip into his guards' thoughts somehow and turn them to his own advantage or accustom himself [*sich dort einbürgern*] to them. But the guard merely said dismissively: "You'll feel it eventually [*Sie werden es zu fühlen bekommen*]." Franz broke in and said: "You see, Willem, he admits that he doesn't know the Law and yet he claims he's innocent." "You're right there, but you can't make him understand anything [*ihm kann man nichts begreiflich machen*]," said the other. K. said nothing more. (T 8–9; KA P 14–15; my emphasis)

In a first inversion, one that marks the entire logic of *The Trial*, it is not the law that patrols in search of hidden guilt; rather it is the latter that sets the law into motion, in a kind of magnetic "attraction" that will soon be given its aesthetic and even erotic dimension (it is said that the accused are more beautiful [T 185; KA P 251]). This strange process is even identified with the law ("That's the law"), establishing the locus of the latter not in a text or a code but rather in the indeterminate element, and the attractive force, of guilt itself. But K. thinks he can read the law by reading the minds of those who mediate it—in the mistaken belief that if he could only slither (*sich einschleichen*) into their thoughts, indeed even set up home there (as "*sich einbürgern*" implies), he would then grasp it in its very seat, that is, "in your heads." But that is not the seat of the law, as the guard succinctly explains: K. may not *know* the law, but he will *get to feel it* (*zu fühlen bekommen*). In this complex play of inaccessible thoughts and fanciful but obstructed intersubjective exchanges, the law is locatable first and foremost as an indeterminate *feeling* drawn by the attractive pull of guilt—a phenomenon that itself hovers between affect and discourse—and *not* as the direct conjoining of speech (the language of the law) with the subjected body.

In this perspective, let us recall the formulations from other judgment narratives that secure this conjunction in strikingly similar language. We find this most vividly, of course, in the penal colony officer's explanation that the condemned prisoner "will experience [the judgment] on his body [*er erfährt es ja auf seinem Leib*]"; even more than that, he says, "our man deciphers [the script] . . . with his wounds" (CS 145, 150; E 155, 160). Such is the short-circuited paradigm posited in that story: inscription of the law as self-deciphering wound. In the sphere of the penal colony, "that's the law," and at this remainderless point of its application there is no margin between the speech of judgment and the legal body that it constitutes (and kills). In "The Metamorphosis" there is a more subtle and diffuse mode of inscription, described in terms almost identical to those in the above passage from *The Trial*. In his incomprehensible "defense speech," Gregor Samsa complains that "gossip" and "groundless accusations," even when one does not hear them, have palpable effects on the body they are aimed at; but it is only after returning home from an exhausting trip, he says, that "one" learns of these effects, "when he comes to feel the consequences on his own body [*wenn er . . . die . . . Folgen . . . am eigenen Leibe zu spüren bekommt*]" (Sons 67; E 69). Dispersed but pointed social speech thus inscribes itself on the body of its unsuspecting referent, and the law of this speech is realized in stark and unsettling physical transformations. Interestingly, this subtle hint regarding Gregor's metamorphosis gestures toward the dispersal of speech (in rumor) that will determine the form of Kafka's novels in their fundamental difference from the judgment stories, even as it posits the direct contact between speech and body—between law and sensibility—which *The Trial* will open and distend, in the mode of a more diffuse "feeling." Finally: when in *The Trial* the guard named Franz complains that it is *impossible to make anything graspable* (*begreiflich*) to this stubborn fellow Josef K., he not only places the ungraspable fully within the register of an imminent "feeling," he also anticipates an almost identical statement in "A Hunger Artist" that seals this convergence, but, in that case, in the name of "art." In an unusual aside, and as a comment on the public's indifference to the previously renowned hunger artist, the narrator exclaims: "Try to explain to someone the art of fasting! If he does not feel it, you cannot make it graspable to him [*Wer es nicht fühlt, dem kann man es nicht begreiflich machen*]" (CS 276; E 198). We will return to this moment in "A Hunger Artist"; for now we can say that it is no longer a question there of grasping or being grasped by the law, whether through direct inscription or the indirect conversions of social speech; instead, the ungraspability at issue involves, as it does in *The Trial*, a "feeling" that is not subject to dramatic externalization or persuasive presentation, but that must rely on other modes of transmission, a disclosive sense that must precede any grasping comprehension. We saw above that a similar impossibility haunts "In the Penal Colony," where "those times" can no longer be made "*begreiflich*," but where the Officer believes he still has a chance of closing the gap in which he must speak.

In the light of these persistent repetitions and variations, I would argue that it is by shifting the terrain from the wound of law's inscription to the indeterminate feeling of its elusive and unending imminence that *The Trial* opens the possibility of exiting the very schema of the "court" it seems to totalize, along with the entire set of configurations that subtend it. When Franz evokes the impossibility of making the law "*begreiflich*" to K., it is clear that the ungraspability of the law does not follow from its locked-away interiority (it does not exist "only in your heads"), from its foreclosed transcendence, or from any namable but unreachable *thing*—for in *The Trial*, the law is not a thing, but a discourse, and one that, in this case, does "justice," as it were, to the indiscernibility of its limits, ends and "literal" embodiments. The law is wide open. In that very same light, then, this narrative will not require the monstrous distortion or evisceration of the body in question: it will not, in fact, require the closure of a corpse. For Josef K. the law's ungraspability follows rather from a refusal to read guilt as a feeling grounded in an inability to name its object. This inability is called *anxiety*; and in

The Trial, this unnamable, ungraspable feeling displaces Oedipalized terror (projected as *Schreckbild* or *Schreckgestalt*) and henceforth establishes the peculiar objectless mood, but also the unlikely prospect of freedom, in which the novel will unfold.

The Martyred Instrument

But let us turn for another brief moment to the overtly penal, or at least corporally punishing, aspects of *The Trial*. For in the end, or at least in the chapter labeled "The End," K. does get to feel the law directly on his body, in the form of a knife, and this might well be interpreted as the "feeling" invoked by the guard. One can certainly say that the execution scene returns the narrative, albeit quite jarringly, to a corporeally applied penal regime that it has otherwise displaced; and in fact, it appears that the scene was written around the same time as the beginning of the novel (and therefore before "In the Penal Colony").[19] There is no indication in any of the chapters in which K.'s fate is most explicitly discussed (especially with the painter Titorelli) that a guilty verdict necessarily means a death sentence. At most we might say that it is perhaps because of K.'s refusal to accede to the law of indeterminate anxiety that he must suffer the other, penal law with its more *punctual* application—which, in the event, is manifestly structured as spectacle and theater. At the same time, the execution scene does stand in a certain continuity with the penal colony machine (especially when set to "stab"), and is even given a similarly isolated and barren setting (an abandoned quarry), features which mark the scene as heterogeneous to the rest of the narrative in *The Trial*. Indeed, there is only one other punishment scene in the novel, and it irrupts into the story as an eternally staged punishment-torture scenario tightly sequestered in the limbo of a junk closet.

It is in that strange space of physical punishment that we arrive in tracing the remnants of the penal colony island that seem to have stowed away with the traveler and insinuated themselves into *The Trial*. And as K. opens the door to this closet in the bank where he works, attracted by "the sound of groans" (T 80; KA P 108), one cannot help being struck by a number of similarities and echoes. For one, the guard wearing a *Reiseanzug*, who announces that K. will get to feel the law, is here seen getting to feel the blows inflicted by a half-naked leather-clad flogger who beats him senseless with a rod (*Rute*), a close relative of the riding whip (*Reitpeitsche*) that initiates the penal festivities in the short story (and not far removed from the knife just discussed). The rod is described at one point, rather strangely, as having a point or "*Spitze*," moving mechanically up and down, as though by its own power and volition: "The rod found him on the floor as well . . . its point swung up and down in a regular rhythm [*die Rute fand ihn auch auf der Erde . . . schwang sich ihre Spitze regelmässig auf und ab*]" (T 84; KA P 113)—almost as though it were stabbing him. The guards subjected to the beating are forced to strip naked, and at one point K. thinks that "it would almost have been simpler . . . to strip and offer himself to the flogger in place of the guards" (T 85; KA P 115), as though he wished to place himself in the machine he has set into motion. For his part, the flogger is described as having something of a tropical maritime air about him; "sunburnt like a sailor" with a "savage ruddy face," he too is apparently an experienced tropical traveler (T 82; KA P 111). He is inflexible ("Their punishment is as just as it is inevitable" [T 82; KA P 110]), and cannot be swayed by bribery. At least not before K. quickly slams the door, for fear of being found in this compromising position by someone attracted by Franz's strangely mechanical scream; rising "steady and unchanging [*ungeteilt und unveränderlich*], it seemed to come not from a human being but from some tortured instrument [*von einem gemarterte Instrument*]" (T 84; KA P 113). Before slamming the door, however, K., who has essentially if unwittingly ordered this punishment by complaining about the guards, gives Franz a good solid push, reducing him to a writing abject body, having shoved him "hard enough that the witless man fell down and clawed convulsively at the floor with both hands" (T 84; KA P 113). It is at this point that the clockwork of the rod finds him, repeatedly, on the floor. And it is also precisely here that the critique and foreclosure of writing as a machine-borne process of transcendence (as articulated in "In the Penal Colony") becomes most clearly analogous to a similar critique carried out, less literally, in *The Trial*: when K. hears *Franz* screaming like a *martyred instrument*, pushes him ever deeper into the isolated scenery and machinery of punishment, and slams the door on him so that this torture music will stop sounding.

This moment takes on even greater resonance when we recall what Kafka had written to Felice Bauer (on November 1, 1912) regarding his *instrumental* function as a writer in the hands of a "higher power":

> My life consists, and basically always has consisted, of attempts at writing, mostly unsuccessful. But when I didn't write, I was at once *flat on the floor*, fit for the dustbin [*wert hinausgekehrt zu werden*].... If there is a higher power that wishes to use me, or does use me, then I am at its mercy [literally, I am in its hand: *dann liege ich . . . in ihrer Hand*], if no more than as a well-prepared instrument [*deutlich ausgearbeitetes Instrument*]. If not, I am nothing, and will suddenly be abandoned [*übrig bleiben*] in a dreadful void. (LFe 20–21; BFe 65–66; my emphasis)

Is this not the version of writing that both "In the Penal Colony" and, more implicitly, the flogging scene in *The Trial* attempt both to expose and to disown, disavow, or repudiate—to banish to an island or to lock away in the junk room? By transposing the "higher power" into a leather-bound flogger subordinated to the machine-like automatism of dictated Law, and by figuring the well-prepared instrument, whose existence is justified by its lofty service, as a martyred one that merely registers abject pain, Kafka signals the disturbing collapse of fine-tuned sublimity into the crushed submission of a noise-making thing. The power that "plays" this instrument (or wields it "in his hand") is implicated in a sadistic violence that can be quelled only by muting its moans. In a certain sense, Kafka (K.—or "Herr K." as he calls himself in the letter just quoted) does place Kafka (Franz) in the punishment machine *in place of himself*, only to leave the by-product permanently lodged as a residue (*übrig bleiben*) within the occluded topography of a novel whose protagonist cannot bear the sight of his own constitutive fantasms. There can be no doubt that the violence of these fantasms will continue to resound in the space that would enclose them. Indeed, the fact that this sequestered violence is an ongoing structural condition of K.'s guilt—the endlessly played scene of his bad conscience—is made comically clear when he passes the same door the very next day, opens it "as if by habit [*wie aus Gewohnheit*]," and finds the exact same scene as before. "Herr!" shout the guards to the master. "K. slammed the door shut at once and pounded his fists against it, as if that would close it more tightly" (T 87; KA P 117). Is this eternally repeating scene not the tightly encased "motor" of the narrative, *insofar as* it is driven by the force of Law in its violent sublimity, determined by the unilateral force of speech as command? At one level, the flogger scene reveals the conditions for the "mastery" that K. continually clings to and attempts to safeguard, which is after all a mastery of speech, and the ability to effectuate realities (such as the warders' punishment) merely by speaking. And yet, is it possible also to see in K.'s distress at the sight of this painfully repetitive scenography something more or other than a desperate disavowal? Could it not suggest a limit, or a new turn, with respect to the intolerable and unsavory scenario in question? What if the sadistic (and by turns masochistic) punishment fantasy were in the process of exhausting its capacity to serve as the condition and guarantee of masterful speech? That is, at another level, what if this condensed reinscription, within the novel, of the judgment stories' paradigmatic impasse signaled a decisive turn in the literary "vocation" and its basic "vocalization"—an inflection of the voice and *Stimmung* that, in moans, screams and thunder, has up to now been striving for greatness, in a struggle with a legitimizing but dictatorial and murderous law which, in being answered, must also be appropriated (if only as derisive parody)? What if K.'s trial must become a search not for exoneration and exculpation, but above all for a way out of the suffocating sphere of power's persuasive *manifestation*?

WHIP, ROD, AND ROPE: THE LEAP FROM THE LAW

I have spoken of the impasse of "In the Penal Colony," a characterization justified not only by its starkly contoured self-containment, but also by the final image that actually closes (off) the story: the menacing rope that blocks its exit, and that lies along the series of disciplinary instruments beginning with the riding whip, passing through the penal inscription machine and on to the flogger's rod and the knife in K.'s heart. This object literally knots together the closed-circuit loop formed by these things. In the final paragraph of "In the Penal Colony," the soldier and the prisoner race down a long stairway leading to the rowboat that is about to ferry the traveler to the steamer that will convey him from the penal colony island back to the metropole. "They probably wanted to force [*zwingen*] the traveler to take them with him at the last moment." The boat is unmoored from the bank just as they arrive at the bottom of the stairway. The story ends thus: "They could have jumped [*springen*] into the boat, but the traveler picked up a heavy knotted rope from the floor, threatened them with it and held them back from making the leap [*hielt sie dadurch von dem Sprunge ab*]" (CS 167; E 177). Perhaps more than anything else in the story, this threatening gesture reveals the traveler's ongoing functional role in the sequestered fantasy structure whose confines he, at least, is able to exit. But we have seen that after setting up and reaffirming this limit, he brings the rope back with him, as it were, insofar as this figure establishes a link with the "civilized" world he represents. Further, the continuity of this rope with an entire series of disciplinary fantasms is reinforced by the many invocations of such instruments throughout Kafka's writings—especially the whip, which appears numerous times as a threatening and inciting force of training, discipline and punishment (a prominent one is found in "A Report to an Academy"), most pointedly in the telling aphorism from the notebooks cited above: "The animal wrests the whip from its master and whips itself *in order to become master*, not knowing that this is only a fantasy produced by a new knot in the master's whiplash" (BON 24; my emphasis). This complex and abyssal statement would require much patient scrutiny if one wanted to undo its many knots, especially those binding together the real and the fantasmatic, mastery and submission, oneself as disciplining master and oneself as untamed animal, oneself as oneself and oneself as other—each distributed and circulating through these various positions. As it stands, the aphorism provides a remarkable image of the looping circuit of disciplinary subjection whose limits are forcibly sealed at the end of "In the Penal Colony," for it shows that the "ascent" from flogged to flogger is programmed by an ineluctable "descent" into a fantasmatic field that marks out the conditions of violence and aggression which make it possible. This being said, it is important to point out that at the end of "In the Penal Colony," the animal-like former prisoner and the soldier do not wrest the knotted rope from the traveling master, who calmly departs. But that leaves the question: from whom has the latter wrested the whipping rope he holds?

Kafka was unhappy with the ending of the story, which he tried to rework several times, before finally publishing it in 1919, several years after it was written. But it may be that the impulse to rework the ending, and thus perhaps to open up the stifling, unbreachable "pessimism" of the story, was better served in the end by such an explicit and overt sealing away of the untenable conditions it lays out. To see the precise shape and outline of a place where there is *only discipline*, newly ratified by a more refined and oblique form of judgment, could be one important tactic in the reconfiguration of literary space, such that in it might be found a heretofore unknown exit from writing's ponderous but "invisible court."

Der Sprung: *Exit from the Court of Judgment?*

In order to discern something of this exit in Kafka's fiction, and in *The Trial* in particular, I would like to develop here an observation of a topographical order that bears on all the narratives we have been examining. It is a striking and curious feature of the judgment stories that, without exception, each of them features a very similar spatial movement, a climactic moment of flight and departure that involves *descending a stairway and exiting an enclosed space*—or, in the decisive variation just mentioned, failing to exit. A brief look at these moments reveals a number of striking regularities, the crucial one being a liberating leap or *Sprung* by which the character in question (which is not always the main character) exits the theatrical space of judgment carefully mounted in the story. The first occurs in "The Judgment" with Georg Bendemann's spectacular rush down the stairs ("over whose steps he rushed as though down an inclined plane") and leap out the door across the road toward the bridge's railing and, beyond it, the river ("aus dem Tor sprang er, zum Wasser trieb es ihn"). Here the precipitous leap is tightly bound with a compulsion dictated by judgment, as is the case in "The Metamorphosis" as well, where the scene from "The Judgment" is precisely repeated, but with important variations. There the Prokurist flees in terror from Gregor; much like Georg Bendemann, "he leapt down several steps at once and vanished [*er machte einen Sprung über mehrere Stufen und verschwand*]," this after "ridiculously holding fast to [*festhielt*]" to the rail of the landing as Gregor lunges toward him, trying to explain. . . . This dramatic moment is echoed in a more measured fashion at the end of the story, with the exit of the boarders ("the three boarders slowly but steadily descended [*hinunterstiegen*] the long stairs" [Sons 109; E 105]), whose expulsion is a displaced removal of the last living vestiges of Gregor Samsa's presence in the house. At the end of "The Stoker," when Karl and the uncle make their "careful descent [*Hinuntersteigen*]" from the ship, exit and capture are conjoined in their uneasy embrace as they step "closely bound [*engverbunden*]" into the boat that (moving in a direction contrary to that of the penal colony traveler) will take them to shore. Karl's tears during this scene testify to his knowledge that in leaving his treasure behind, he is disembarking into the hellish but open-ended world to which he appears to be destined. In this case, the descent is disjoined from the leap, which is carried out rather by their "Führer" who has led them off the boat and who is greeted by rising, saluting sailors when he "leapt down [*hinuntersprang*] into the boat in a single bound." Finally, there is the concluding scene of "In the Penal Colony": there, as noted before, the soldier and the prisoner race down the stairs ("*rasten die zwei die Treppe hinab*"), but the desired exit does not take place; they are "held back" from their *Sprung* by the departing traveler and his knotted rope.

With such a consistent repetition of these scenes, and even of their specific verbal and spatial markers—with their *Treppen*, *Stufen*, and *Geländer*, their stairs, steps and rails, their downward-moving *hinuntersteigen*, *hinabfallen*, *hinabrasen*, and various *Sprünge* toward or into watery or maritime environments—it seems clear that, knowingly or not, Kafka had found in the architecture of exit, and in the choreography of hasty departure, a decisive structural element for these stories. It is as though Kafka were obsessively staging the release and exit from judgment and the "court" which the writing of these law-bound stories ought in the end to provide. We can recall in this light an often quoted diary entry written many years later (in January 1922), and in a rather exalted mood, in which Kafka speaks of "the strange, mysterious, perhaps dangerous, perhaps redeeming [*erlösender*] comfort that there is in writing: it is a leap [*ein Hinausspringen*] out of murderers' row, an observation-act [*Tat-Beobachtung*]." He goes on to evoke the height and freedom that is clearly at stake in this action that would remove the writer from the threat of the law: "It is an observation-act in that it is a higher type of observation, a higher, not a keener type, and the higher it is and the less within reach of the 'row' [of the series: *von der Reihe*], the more independent it becomes, the more obedient to its own laws of motion, the more incalculable, the more joyful, the more ascendant in its course" (D 406–407; TB 413). This high-flown ideal reads like a belated reversal and conversion of the "leaps" staged within the early judgment narratives, for there the leap is always *downward*, always a descent, and it does not in fact liberate from "death row," that is, from the series of corpse-producing text-machines we have been examining. One could say that the very "row" or "series" *from* which this leap would liberate the writer is indicated precisely in the repetition, from story to story, of this action—and of many other elements, as we have seen—as though in a clear attestation of its failure, despite the highly inventive revisions and displacements to which it is subjected. Indeed, the repetition of this limit-scene, the constant return to its topography and the redistribution and replaying of its forces, seems to indicate that when pursued *in this way*—that is, through a flight from judgment *as a disciplinary absorption* into appropriated Law and mastery—the exit in question is not quite yet releasing the spring of the mechanism at work; obsessively reprogrammed, it merely continues to turn and to return. The blocked *Sprung* at the end of "In the Penal Colony" seems to acknowledge this trap, tightening it into a knot shaped by discipline (and by the exigency of providing it with a sequestered alibi), a knot looped back on itself like a noose. Its psychic form is the fantasy of becoming-master—of making-oneself-master—indulged by an animal still and always being whipped by an Other, including the stand-in of the Other it would strive to become by taking hold of the disciplinary tool—that is, when that Other, in a fictive/fantasmatic subreption, is played by oneself.

I have already suggested that *The Trial* effects at least a partial shift in this structure. It is all the more significant, then, to observe that the novel, too, engages this obsessive repetition by staging *yet another* scene involving an urgent exit and an ambiguous leap down a flight of steps. The scene occurs not at the end, but relatively early (at the end of the chapter designated "In the Empty Courtroom/The Student/The Offices"), when K. has a fit of vertigo (*Schwindel*) (KA P 99, 101) in the bad air of the court's attic offices, and has to be escorted out by a man and a woman who carry him to the door like an inert clump of matter—where he suddenly recovers "all his strength" in the outside air and bounds down the steps in great leaps that astonish even himself. While this moment does not conclude the narrative, it does mark the end of all direct and voluntarily sought contact with the courts.[20] In that sense, at least, it does constitute something of an exit, though certainly not a complete extrication, for the court's representatives return to haunt (the flogger), to rebuke (the prison chaplain) and finally to punish K.

in the end (the executioners). Not definitive freedom, then, but at least a "foretaste of freedom" (KA P 106) that K. enjoys in a liberating gulp of fresh air. What are the nature and effects of the bad air from which K. suffers, and how exactly does he escape from it?

Following an absurd series of encounters that (one could show) invoke in multiple ways Kafka's own previous fiction (for example, there is a reference to a "great transformation," "*eine grosse Verwandlung*" [T 73; KA P 98] that K. is about to undergo, *but does not*), the suffocating atmosphere of the attic law offices makes K. so nauseous and dizzy that he must be carried like an inert body by a young woman and a joking fellow referred to as "the information officer." We sense that, in a deeper way than any execution, it is thus that K. is finally "getting to feel" the law in its unviable native element. "Up with you now, you feeble fellow," says the information officer in a sort of "heave-ho" that leads to a distinctly maritime moment, one of the most disorienting of the entire novel:

> He felt seasick. He thought he was on a ship, rolling in heavy seas. It seemed to him that the waters were pounding against the wooden walls, there was a roar from the depths of the hallway like the sound of breaking waves, the hallway seemed to pitch and roll, lifting and lowering the waiting clients on both sides. That made the calm demeanor of the young woman and the man who led him all the more incomprehensible [*desto unbegreiflicher*]. He was at their mercy; if they let go of him, he would fall [*hinfallen*] like a plank. [T 78; KA P 105–106]

Such "seasickness on dry land" is an "experience" (as he calls it) that reaches back into the earliest period of Kafka's literary efforts, and is here brought to such a point of crisis that it can only be resolved by taking leave of this nauseating territory.[21] The crisis is even signaled by "a steady high-pitched sound like a siren" that seems to ring through the entire place—a description that anticipates the "steady and unchanging" scream let out by Franz in the flogger scene, and beyond that to the sirens who, for their part, will present rather an enigmatic silence, across less turbulent seas.[22] For now it suffices to make contact with "a draft of fresh air [*ein frischer Luftzug*]" (T 78–79; KA P 106) which, when it comes, feels as though it has torn through the wall ("*als wäre die Wand von ihm durchrissen*" [T 78; KA P 106]). It is here, finally, at the exit of this impossible, uninhabitable world, that K. has his first "foretaste of freedom" in a more breathable atmosphere. As though to underscore the difference of worlds, as between two planets with different atmospheres, K.'s companions cannot stand the fresh air and almost fall into a swoon, "the young woman might have collapsed [*abgestürzt*] had K. not shut the door as quickly as possible" (T 79; KA P 107). K. slams the door on these people much as he does on the more brutal scene of the guards and the flogger—another scene into which he fails to absorb himself, despite his inclination to insinuate himself further into its machinations. Not to absorb the law through the body, whether that law is (supposedly) perfectly legible in its textual existence—in its letter—or so opaque and inaccessible that the submission it demands devours space and time as well (in the endless waiting of an ignored petitioner), but rather to be expelled into another order of movement, another less oppressive or deadly relation to the law: such is the experience suggested by this scene. Is the pocket mirror that K. takes out at this point, stroking his hair into place, the sign of an egoic reestablishment, or is it perhaps merely a tiny zone of specularity and reflexivity in which Kafka has already embedded (as this review of the passage suggests) a number of elements previously introduced into his fiction, in order to dispel their now stifling bewitchment? In any case, he repeats, precisely here, the leap that has so far only bounced back to where it began, but this time he adds a further twist or turn (*Umschwung*),[23] going so far as to associate it with a possible "revolutionizing" that strikes a note quite different from those of previous failed transformations: "K. . . . raced down the steps [*lief dann die Treppe hinunter*] with such long, energetic leaps [*Sprüngen*] that he was almost frightened [*fast Angst bekam*] by the sudden change [*Umschwung*]. . . . Was his body going to revolutionize [*revolutionieren*] and prepare a new trial for him, since he bore the old one so effortlessly?" (T 79; KA P 107). Such a surprising turn is all the more reason to consider consulting a doctor and to resolve to put the free time of his Sundays to better use in the future, as K. does in the final words of the chapter. But how can K. possibly think that his "old" trial has been so "effortless," and what sort of difficulties would a "new" one present? K. does not begin a new trial, but he does enter into a different modality of negotiating the current one. This difference is determined, in part, spatially, in that he will never return to the precincts, the direct embodiment or *instance*, of the law courts. Henceforth his adventure will take place elsewhere, through other mediations. What has taken a turn here is perhaps the very configuration of Kafka's literary space in general.

Modes of Literary Space

Throughout this discussion of Kafka, in posing the question of the imperative to write, we have been dealing with a certain spatialization of writing, in part through the projected figures whose towering or even astronomical presence calls up the specter of judgment and opens the specific scenography of the courtroom (as was shown in Chapter 1). But these figurations are particular modalities of a more general problem, one that reaches back to Kafka's earliest writing, namely the vexed and difficult "entry" into literary space from the more familiar, given, everyday world of personal experience. Such a formulation might seem naive, but it is precisely in these terms that the young Kafka tracks the passage into fiction in his early text "Description of a Struggle," in which the protagonist takes an abrupt journey into a strange and radically other place (sharply distinguished from the social world of Prague depicted up to that point in the story), a schematic realm consisting of "a vast but as yet unfinished region" that can be instantly formed and manipulated through speech alone—and whose melancholy landscape resonates with "frightful sighs" and "terrified sobbing" (CS 21, 24; BK 19, 23). It is as though this early writing clearly registered a still new and dreadful rift between the world and its literary other, along with the loss, anguish and tears entailed by a definitive move into the latter. Later, in a similar but slightly more exalted movement, Kafka will evoke "the cold space of our world" in need of a fire that will infuse it with its own peculiar (and more persuasive) forces. Later still, around the time leading up to *The Trial* (in May of 1914), he will evoke an even more intense dread of this space insofar as it *has not yet taken shape*, when, in a remarkable one-line diary entry, he evokes simply: "The horror in the merely schematic" ("*Das Grauenhafte des bloss Schematischen*"; D 269; TB 273). Such horror, dread and melancholy mark the painful "entry" into fictional space, a stripping away that reveals a strange and demanding schematism in an unsteady movement of world-making that is not quite yet another world of its own.

Josef K.'s sudden leaping escape in *The Trial* thus harks back to the inaugural problem of the viability, or survivability, of literary space as an alternate world both obtruding into and breaking off from the ordinary familiar one. Indeed, this is the overall structure of *The Trial*, in which Josef K.'s heretofore undisturbed life is disrupted by the intrusion of an alternate and contiguous reality that draws him into its precincts and makes greater and greater demands on him. The entire plot hinges on the problem of what he can know about these demands and how he manages, or not, to take them on (in every sense). In this light, the urgent and precipitous exit from the law court offices might be seen as a retreat from that other world, for reasons of fatigue and incapacitation, as though it were the defeat of a "weak man" who is finding it more and more difficult to tolerate the rigors of this demanding and very *other* place. In other words, the alien atmosphere of the law courts could be seen as an allegory for, or a dramatic staging of, the rigors of literary space in its suffocating strangeness.[24] There is certainly something to be said for this interpretation, given K.'s obduracy and his categorical refusal even to entertain the possibility of his guilt—that is, at one level, to understand that this guilt exceeds the legalistic terms with which he approaches it. And yet, even if he does not grasp this, his subsequent path, and even his own anxious experience, reflect it very clearly, in the ever starker divide between his previous everyday life and the obsessive and compelling world of the trial, which no longer has anything directly to do with the law courts or their offices.[25] In addition to this general splitting off, the scene's localization inside the space of the court allows us to see it in more precise terms, as though K.'s exhausted exit confirmed the closure of the by now old and familiar space of the *Gericht*, the space of a trial that, after long intercourse or *Verkehr* (now both dissipated and blocked) has become "effortless" in its almost formulaic repetitions. If the "*alte Process*" has become "*mühelos*," this is perhaps because it continues to unfold *the same type of scene over and over*, with astonishing variations, to be sure, and yet with machinelike regularity. It is as though the particular fire that finally did manage to warm the cold space of that world—deployed always as the space of a court staging a judgment, of a law suffusing a body—now gives rise to an unbreathable atmosphere, and to the muggy vertigo of well worn repetition.[26]

I propose, then, to see something of that "new" mode of the trial in the "*Angst*" that K. "almost" gets to feel when he flees the law court offices. There is certainly a sense in which the escape scene allows K. to return to his old life, work, and self, but this is merely a reprieve, for that life has been irreversibly disrupted, pried apart from itself along the faultline of an indeterminate guilt. In that sense, upon leaving the court offices, K. is in a position analogous to that of Gregor Samsa if he had somehow managed to get out of bed, catch the train, and go back to work, as though nothing had happened.... The nontransformation of K.'s body has this significance too, in that he can return to the familiar space of his existence in the belief that he is still the one he used to be, as a quick glance in the mirror seems to confirm. And yet this other world has completely taken hold of him. Not only do other people notice some kind of transformation (as when his uncle exclaims: "You have been transformed [*Du bist verwandelt*] ..." (T 94; KA P 126), he is in fact completely absorbed in his trial, regardless of where he is: "The thought of his trial never left him now" (T 111; KA P 149). As it turns out, it is precisely at this moment that thinking compulsively about the trial is linked directly with thinking about writing; the next sentence reads: "He had often considered whether it might not be good to work out a written defense [*eine Verteidigungsschrift auszuarbeiten*] and submit it to the court" (T 111; KA P 149). This sentence reads like a précis of Kafka's writing life up to and during the period of the judgment stories, except that, unlike K., he did not limit himself to mere contemplation. I have argued that at a certain level—involving precisely their elaboration from out of a number of autobiographically registered exigencies—the judgment stories constitute a defense-writing (*Verteidigungsschrift*) cast into the form of staged defense speeches addressed to a *Gericht*; here the necessity of a defense speech has circled back to an imperative to write directly embedded within the narrative space and explicitly delimited as the exigency of a court procedure, but one that exceeds that procedure and *begins to merge entirely with the very life* of the "writer" concerned. Surely we can locate here a highly charged reflection on a certain form of the imperative to write that has inflected Kafka's literary elaborations, as the specific juridical shape of this imperative opens onto a generalized fictive space that absorbs life as such, in its non-juridical aspects as well. In Kafka's novels, literary space, as a fundamental structure of experience, is universalized. Kafka's implicit critique of the juridical determination of writing within the ever-expanding literary space of *The Trial* is borne out in the stubbornly narrow focus of his character, whom he shows struggling against the constricting and exhausted futilities it defines, that is, against a guilt that must be disproved. If Josef K. decides to "play along" (T 7; KA P 12) with the initial premise of the novel as laid out in its opening chapter (you're under arrest, you must answer to the court, etc.), he will nonetheless attempt to evade the space of guilt (the courtroom schema) that engenders him, for he believes that he can master and defeat it. But this bad faith is ironically what opens the novel to an outside of the legal crypt, a beyond of judgment, in a leap from the law court into the generalized conditions of fictive speech, and into the "world order" of "the lie" (as Kafka writes in the "Cathedral" chapter [T 223; KA P 303]).

In terms of K.'s self-defense in language, the shift from speech to writing occurs partly in the wake of a speech he makes early in the novel, during his first visit to the law court, in the chapter entitled "Initial Inquiry." But unlike in the other judgment stories, this defense speech does not so much fail, in the sense of issuing into his judgment and condemnation, as refuse to be a defense speech at all, becoming instead a self-righteous harangue and an upstanding attack on the legitimacy of the court—an approach whose value is attested by the howls of laughter with which its audience receives it. So much for masterful speech. The next time K. returns to the court, it is empty. That is when his real adventure begins.

DEFENSE WRITING UNWRITTEN

In reading the scene of K.'s dramatic gesture of "presentation," with its emblematic image of a blank piece of paper standing in for his entire life justified in writing, I will argue that the voiding of defense in its parodic culmination can be seen as an allegory of a more general turn away from "defense writing" for Kafka, its evacuation and dispersal into, among other things, the scattered forms of rumor.

K.'s fantasies about writing come in the context of a dilemma as to whether he should fully undertake his own defense, which means, in part, taking over from his lawyer the task of writing an initial "petition" (*Eingabe*) that does not seem to be getting written—and that in any case risks becoming a pile of "worthless scraps of paper" (T 121; KA P 163) if left to the lawyer. K.'s initial notion of the kind of writing he would have to do reveals very clearly the bad conscience that structures it (regardless of whether he feels it as such). In the *Eingabe*,

> he would offer a brief overview of his life [*Lebensbeschreibung*], and for each event of any particular importance, explain why he had acted as he did, whether in his present judgment [*Urteil*] this course of action deserved approval or censure, and what reasons he could advance for the one or the other. (T 111–112; KA P 149)

Such an approach could only be entertained by an awkward and earnest amateur of self-exoneration whose *Gewissensbiss* could indeed use some sharpening and refinement. But the essential structure is there, in the exigency of an autobiographical account under the pressure of a judgment taken onto himself, a judgment that will soon broaden hyperbolically beyond this narcissistic faith in his own. But in finding its Other, this judgment will become both infinite and impossible, and writing, as interminable *Verteidigungsschrift*, will be radically emptied of its content.

This brings us to K.'s blank piece of paper, his uncanny offer to no one. The scene occurs later in the same chapter, after a long digression consisting of an indirect report of one of his lawyer's "inexhaustible" (T 122; KA P 164) monologues, which ends with the image of a "clean wound" waiting to heal. (This is the lawyer's own hopeful metaphor for the unexpected but not fatal setbacks of a case.) But K.'s wound is not clean, as his trial continues to seep into the ordinary life he can no longer keep separate from it (whether through gossip, his own indiscretions, or the obtrusive presence of its players in his home and office): "in short, he no longer had a choice of accepting or rejecting [*anzunehmen oder abzulehnen*] the trial, he was in the midst of it [*stand mitten darin*] and had to defend himself" (T 125; KA P 167). The extent to which K.'s notion of his defense and its effectiveness is fully submerged in a deluded and voluntaristic image of the law is revealed in his fantasy of how his defense, once written, would be made effective: "He, or the women, or some other messengers, would have to besiege the officials day after day and force [*zwingen*] them to sit down at their desks and study [*studieren*] K.'s petition, instead of staring through the grille into the hall. These efforts must be continuous, with everything organized and supervised [*überwacht*]; for once the court was going to run into a defendant who knew how to stand up for his rights" (T 126; KA P 168–169). K. tries to reduce his addressees to distracted schoolchildren who have to be disciplined and "watched over." In this perspective, far from exiting the regime in which he is caught, he is so absorbed into it that in his impotence he can merely caricature its baseline function of disciplinary oversight. This fantasm fully conditions the writing project he conceives, but it also leads to its hyperbolic arrest, its blocked blanking out. At first this is registered in K.'s sense that the task would be "overwhelming," along with a feeling of "shame" (T 126; KA P 169), not because of any guilt or bad conscience, but rather because he would have to do the writing himself rather than hand it over to a representative paid to do the work for him. But the passage that interests us begins in earnest with a repudiation of this shame, under the undeniable pressure of the task: "Today K. no longer thought of shame; the petition had to be written." The sentences that follow create a vertiginous vortex in which the description of the character's unwritten autobiographical writing project *becomes autobiographical* in that it so clearly evokes the dilemma of Kafka's own writing life (especially in his numerous complaints about work, the office, etc.). The passage continues: "If he couldn't find the time for it at the office, which was quite likely, he would have to do it nights at home. And if the nights weren't sufficient, he would have to take a leave of absence. Anything but stop halfway, that was the most senseless course of all" (T 126–127; KA P 170). The autobiographical resonance of these sentences is all the more uncanny in that the repeated cycle of office work/leave of absence/writing /office work did not really begin for Kafka until several years later, after the diagnosis of his illness; but it is hardly surprising that the wish for an *Urlaub* for the sake of a long-term writing project would have occurred to Kafka at this juncture of his story.[27] In any case, this doubly autobiographical context invites us, I think, to give some weight to what is said about the specific role of writing in the rest of the scene, especially since it takes place in K.'s office. In its entirety, and on multiple levels, this scene opens the question of the relation between office work and writing—and more generally, between everyday affairs and the abysses that both inhabit and exceed them—in a way that aggravates the incompatibility of these realms and introduces an anxious and uncanny separation between the everyday world of work and the more compelling world of the trial (or of *The Trial*). It is within the latter that the force of attraction is squarely situated by the end, when K. completely ignores his work, including the businessmen or the "parties" who have waited for hours to see him (petitioners in this other sphere, where K. is supposedly in charge), and "left the bank, almost happy [*fast glücklich*] to be able to devote himself totally to his case for a while" (T 139; KA P 188). This "almost happy" collides with K.'s "almost *Angst*" in a strange space of activity that can no longer be carried out exclusively in the form of defensive writing. He must enter wandering into the unpredictable spaces opened by its less clearly defined exigencies, in the form of a search and through an adventure of unforeseeable alliances.

But if we remain for a moment with the "defense-writing," as the "autobiographical" passage cited above continues, we are given the fuller version of the self-narrating task it seems to set:

> Admittedly, the petition meant an almost endless task. One needn't be particularly faint of heart [or full of *Angst*: *man musste keinen sehr ängstlichen Charakter haben*] to be easily persuaded of the impossibility of ever finishing the petition . . . because without knowing the nature of the charge and all its possible ramifications, his entire life, down to the smallest actions and events, would have to be called to mind, described [*dargestellt*], and examined from all sides. And what a sad job [*traurige Arbeit*] that was. Perhaps, someday after retirement, it might provide a suitable occupation for a mind turned childish [*den kindisch gewordenen Geist*], and help to while away the lengthening days. (T 127; KA P 170)

How sad indeed it would be to write one's life in exhaustive detail only in order to present it for scrutiny to a judgment in search of grounds for condemnation. While this is a pretty fair description of the workings of an ordinary bad conscience, watched over by the disciplinary instance of the superego, the task of transposing this "process" into a totalizing project of writing-as-exoneration brings K.'s trial into the hyperbolic dimension of a bad infinity. But because K. insists on nothing other than complete exoneration, this is the form of his future, structured as an infinite debt owed to a court whose accusation has been proffered in the withdrawing of its content. In that sense, K. is *just guilty*. But his refusal of guilt does not prevent the onus he is beginning to (almost) feel from fissuring his everyday world: "There was no guilt," he insists. "The trial was nothing other than a large business deal like any other that he had concluded advantageously for the bank" (T 125; KA P 168). But this equivalence is belied by the utter perplexity in which K. finds himself as his business day wears on.

Enter the Manufacturer (*der Fabrikant*), there to discuss one of those business deals. But looking down at the Manufacturer's figures and tables, K. soon stops listening completely "and limited himself to staring at the bald head bent over the papers" (T 128; KA P 172). K. seems to expect the man to read his mind and surmise that he hasn't the slightest interest in any of this; instead, his visitor actually expects a response. K. does his best to fake it, but we see him losing his grip. "'It's complicated,' K. said, pursing his lips, and since the papers, the only thing he could grasp [*das einzig Fassbare*], were covered, he sank against the arm of the chair." At this point K. is saved by his rival, the bank's vice president, who suddenly enters "somewhat blurred, as if behind a gauzy veil" (T 129). Completely indifferent to his own role in the business deal, K. wants nothing but for the two of them to leave. Instead, they begin an animated conversation bent over the desk at which K. still sits slumped over. The manufacturer complains that K. has shown "so little inclination for the business project [or simply, for business: *für das Geschäft*]" (T; KA P 173). Indeed, we have seen that he has other things on his mind, as this scene begins to take on the guise of another project incompatible with this "business." In a moment that combines expressionist distortion with the gestures of absurdist theater, K. finally takes an incomprehensible stand:

> it seemed to K. as if the two men, whose size he mentally exaggerated [*deren Grösse er sich übertrieben vorstellte*], were negotiating with each other about him [*über ihn selbst verhandelt*]. Slowly he tried to ascertain with cautiously upturned eyes what was happening *above* him, took one of the sheets of paper from the desk without looking at it, placed it on the palm of his hand, and lifted it at last to the men as he himself stood up. He had *nothing in particular* in mind as he did so, but simply acted in the belief that he would have to behave thus when he finally prepared the grand petition [*grosse Eingabe*] that would totally exonerate [*gänzlich entlasten*] him. (T 129–130; KA P 174; my emphasis)

This moment parodies, with great economy, the entire sublime juridical schema that we have traced throughout Kafka's writing up to this point, going as far back as the letters to Pollak. But it is curious to note the effort that K. must make actively to project a distorted and exaggerated height or "greatness" (*Grösse*) onto these two figures, who, far from the towering embodiments of sublime grandeur negotiating over the fate of a shortfalling aspirant, are just standing there discussing a business deal. K.'s "*grosse Eingabe*" means nothing to them. But K.'s fantasmatically shaped perception is constitutive of the world (the theater) he now inhabits, and his gesture, which also parodies the solemn and self-righteous judgment fantasy that opens Rousseau's *Confessions*, reaches up toward a mighty judge who would be capable of granting "total exoneration" based on a grand piece of writing.[28] This piece of paper is in fact met with a judgment, one that immediately deflates K.'s fantasy, at least in its social existence, in a manner that will also be familiar (especially considering that we are once again in close proximity to an uncle figure very much concerned with K.'s case).

> The vice president, who had followed the conversation with the closest attention, simply glanced at the sheet, not even bothering to read over what was on it, since whatever was important to the financial officer [*dem Prokuristen*] was of no importance to him, took it from K.'s hand, said: "Thanks, I already know everything [*Danke, ich weiss schon alles*]," and laid it back calmly on the desk. K. gave him a bitter sidelong glance. But the vice president didn't notice at all, or if he did, it only amused him; he laughed aloud several times. (T 130; KA P 174)

If this parody of a powerful judge dismisses K.'s imagined defense, he does so with an ironic but no less belittling omniscience: "I know everything." With this rewriting of the "uncle anecdote" from the *Diaries*—in which an uncle "who liked to make fun of people [*der gern auslachte*]" summarily judges a page of Kafka's writing ("the usual stuff")—the sublime pretentions of writing as redemptive, exonerating *Verteidigungsschrift*, here receive a final blow. But this blow does not so much wake one with a fist on the head, or hack open the frozen sea inside, as it pierces a little point of bitterness whose outward echo is best met with a hearty laugh. And yet, this point or puncture is powerful in its way; indeed, it actually divides the world in two, placing K. on the nether side of a partition between a place where the smug actors in charge "already know everything," and another space populated by the "accused" like K., whose grandiose fantasies of exoneration (*entlasten*) are a product of being "overburdened" (*überlastet*) and of feeling this burden in such a way as to undergo a strange and estranging *collapse*. As much as readers of *The Trial* may remark on K.'s own smugness and obstinacy, this scene clearly dislodges him from the world where these attitudes reign and effectively *operate*—the world of power as functional business being accomplished—a world which continues to blur and sink away, "as if behind a gauzy veil" (T 129).

K., however, does not understand this burden: after the manufacturer and the vice president finally leave his office, he sits on the windowsill staring out. "He sat like that for a long time, without knowing what was actually troubling him [*was ihm eigentlich Sorge machte*]" (T 131; KA P 176). He manifestly does not "already know everything" (at least not anymore), and while his understanding of what is required of him is limited to a self-defense with the force of a counter-compulsion, this is sufficient to accomplish the essential, which is to "expose himself" to a "greater danger" (T 131; KA P 176) that requires him to be dislodged from his everyday reality and the position that has secured him in it. Regardless of the form he assumes it must take (defense), K. realizes that a full engagement in the world that is calling him out of his world will require complete absorption in the former, and a break from the latter. Again, this registers as a panic at having to work in the office, at the bank: "didn't a painstaking [*sorgfältige*] defense simultaneously imply the necessity of cutting himself off [*sich abzuschliessen*] as far as possible from everything else? Would he successfully survive [*glücklich überstehn*] that? And how was he supposed to do that here at the bank?" Working at the bank, while his case churns on somewhere up there, in unknown attics, handled by unknown officials distractedly going over documents (*Schriften*), who no doubt need watching over—insofar as this bank work keeps him from his trial, it suddenly appears to K. as a "torture" (*Folter*) that is yet somehow also a part of the trial, he thinks, a torture compounded by the fact that no one at the bank would ever take the "special situation" of the trial into account in judging his work (*bei der Beurteilung seiner Arbeit*). And just as Gregor Samsa frets over the gossip (*Klatschereien*) and groundless accusations that buzz through his workplace, K. too worries about rumor (*Gerücht*), which is beginning to emerge as this court's true and effective field of discourse. The *Gericht* reveals itself to be founded in *Gerücht* as its essential condition.[29]

In absorbing himself in his trial, K. enters into the sphere of rumor (which includes slander, legend, and every form of hearsay), where he more or less remains as he proceeds from conversation to conversation. The shift from the *Gericht* to the *Gerücht* (T 132; KA P 178) that actually founds it and determines its unfolding, marks the turn that K.'s trial takes at this juncture, as he severs direct ties with the representatives of the court: he will not return to its offices; he will fire the lawyer; he will go to see Titorelli—who is also known to be a gossip (*geschwätzig*), and moreover, a liar ("Titorelli gossips a lot," says the manufacturer, who first sends K. to see the artist; "he certainly also lies" [T 135; KA P 181]).

Now it is precisely in this way that the fantasy of a definitive exculpation won by a forceful self-defense addressed once and for all to a sublime and powerful judge has reached its limit in the hypertrophy of an all-consuming autobiographical *Verteidigungsschrift*; but it is also here that this fantasy begins to *disaggregate* into the shifting micrological movement of rumor, articulated in Kafka's novels in the specific form of an intimate hermeneutical dialogue—and (in the case of Titorelli) under the perverse surveillance of a lewd pack of girls. This is the path that K. follows into what might be called *radical fiction*, considered in the perspective of its dispersed social effects; that is, as a fictive discourse that, cut off and occluded by everyday social practices, actually founds and structures the social order. Kafka's exploration and uncovering of this terrain is taken very far in *The Trial*; it later finds its purest and most elaborate articulation in *The Castle*, which can be read as a rigorous demonstration of this principle. The limitations of such an elaboration in *The Trial* correspond to K.'s limitations in his understanding of the law, namely his refusal to accept the effectively ordering force of a fictive discourse that no one can fully master or control; instead he seeks to counter it with his own *grasp* of justice, a grasp he interprets, at the outer limit of its intelligibility, as the imperative to present an effective defense *in writing* to the proper and sufficiently powerful authorities. He expresses this limitation most pointedly in his dismissive but extremely insightful remark at the conclusion of the exegesis of the parable "Before the Law" (another tightly argued dialogue): "*Die Lüge wird zur Weltordnung gemacht*" (KA P 303). Literally: the lie is made into the order of the world. K.'s gravest fault is no doubt his belief in the truth of the language of his trial, which of course is also the fictive language of *The Trial* as it scatters into rumor. One could put this another way:

Whereas K.'s relation to the law has in fact been radically ironized, in the sense that the direct and definitive appearance of the law as a fully embodied authority becomes more and more impossible and distant, exposed more and more clearly as a transcendental projection, K. himself remains deadly earnest. Surely it is for this reason, more than any other, that his trial would verge toward an execution; for this is implicitly desired in his continued impatience for a definitive judgment. Indeed, as mentioned, in the scene where it arrives, he is waiting for it, almost as if he had summoned his executioners.

As an instructive contrast, we can point to K. in *The Castle*, who embraces, at a certain level at least, the ironic relation that the unbridgeable distance to the castle establishes between him and his "purpose"—which is not to find justice, or anything resembling exculpation, nor is it even a "position" as land surveyor, a plot element that is little more than a carefully chosen MacGuffin.[30] In *The Castle*, Kafka returns to the form of the obsessive hermeneutic dialogue, often driven by a wound of indignation and injustice (as in Amalia's tale, and in numerous conversations between K. and Frieda), but he has left behind the apparatus of the court and its essential articulation in the defense speech. *The Castle* contains a great deal of compulsive speech, and ricochets with many competing interpretations that often ring with legalistic and lawyerly overtones, but *there is no judge*, not even a projected one. There is *only authority*, both "upwardly" projected and revealed as immanent to social speech, again largely in the form of rumor. The disaggregated language of rumor, no matter how often it evokes the higher unitary powers, can only scatter in a flurry of accumulating narrations, proffered by voices that fully inhabit the singular perspective each one manages to open (interestingly, in *The Castle* there is a predominance of feminine voices). And from the very first page, the castle, the sublime instance and destination to which all aspirations would be directed and addressed, is given the ambiguous status of a *scheinbare Leere*, a merely apparent emptiness that is also, in an equally plausible translation, an *emptiness that appears as such*. This emptiness and its appearance are generated by the structure of a narrative voice in the loosening grip of its own imperative conditions of speech—conditions that are not completely free of the transcendental illusions they continually project, but that nonetheless wander wide of the disciplinary and penal apparatus that so strictly and regularly sets the scene in the judgment stories. Put another way: in *The Castle*, the whip is wielded by a barmaid, not to discipline or punish anyone, but to empty the bar.

THE HUMAN TRIBUNAL?

In Kafka's novels, the defense speech gives way to rumor and exegetic dialogue as the constitutive forms of linguistic address. In the later stories, however, Kafka goes on to develop rather a type of monologue that he calls, in one of the first such instances, a "report" ("A Report to an Academy"). In both cases the rhetoric and scenography of the courtroom recede and fade, and the "law" of writing's imperative unfolds from out of a different ground—in different terms and through different figures—determined by the structure of the narrating and "reporting" voice itself. The autobiographical dimension of this process—in which a voice gives an account of the conditions that generate the possibility and pressing necessity of its own speech—not to mention its embeddedness in the empirical chronology of Kafka's life, justifies a very simple but difficult question: What happened? In posing this question, one can even specify the dates: What happened between 1914, when Kafka wrote "In the Penal Colony" and *The Trial*, and 1917, when he wrote not only "A Report to an Academy" but also the last of the narratives that can be considered "judgment stories"?[31] As it turns out, Kafka's biography does shed some light on the nature and direction of this shift, particularly with regard to the tight hold of the courtroom schema. To draw on this biographical material does not amount to providing an "explanation" for the changes in question; but it does mean engaging with Kafka's own written interpretation of two major events in his life.

These events coincide, since one is the cause of (or perhaps the long-awaited pretext for) the second: 1917 is the year when Kafka was diagnosed with tuberculosis. In the wake of this news, which positioned him as socially unviable, as a dying man, he definitively broke off his second engagement with Felice Bauer, almost exactly five years after his first letter to her. Aside from the fantasmatic and linguistic connections linking Felice to "The Judgment" (as we saw above), it is well known that Kafka had already placed this relationship under the sign of criminality and the "courtroom," not only in an extended metaphoric sense involving his unsuitability as a husband (and everything this entailed), but also in the concrete terms he used to depict two important scenes from these inauspicious *fiançailles*. In a diary entry dated June 6, 1914, Kafka writes: "Back from Berlin. Was tied hand and foot like a criminal. Had they sat me down in a corner bound in real chains, placed policemen in front of me, and let me look on simply like that, it could not have been worse." This does not describe some terrible scene of accusation and recrimination (that comes later). Rather, as Kafka puts it in the next sentence: "And that was my engagement" (D 275; TB 275). This happy occasion was followed less than two months later with a truly unpleasant scene, which Kafka explicitly refers to as a tribunal. This is the famous "trial" that took place in the Askanischer Hof hotel in Berlin, during which Felice and her friend Grete Bloch accused Kafka of mendacity, treachery, and disloyalty (he had been secretly writing some rather passionate letters to Miss Bloch, who was supposed to be mediating the couple's difficult relationship).[32] He noted the event in his diary:

> 23 July. The tribunal in the hotel [*Der Gerichtshof im Hotel*]. . . . Suddenly [Felice] gathered herself together and said very studied, hostile things she had been saving up. . . . At her parents'. Her mother's occasional tears. Her father understood it from every side. . . . They agreed that I was right, there was nothing, or not much, that could be said against me. *Devilish in all innocence* [*Teuflisch in aller Unschuld*]. Miss Bl.'s apparent guilt [*scheinbare Schuld*]. [D 293; TB 297; my emphasis]

In this scene of accusation and interrogation, obvious guilt (Kafka's) is countered by a mere appearance of innocence, which is all the more diabolical for that, especially when the guilt appears to shift elsewhere (to Bloch). No one knows how Kafka defended himself, but there is little doubt that this experience at least inflected the writing of "In the Penal Colony" and especially *The Trial* (in which Kafka once again features a sexually charged female character who shares Felice's initials, K.'s neighbor Fräulein Bürstner). Three years later, when the once-broken-off and once-renewed engagement with Felice is broken off again, this time definitively and in the shadow of a life-threatening illness, it is difficult not to see the end of this "trial" as concomitant with the exit, in the fiction, from the courtroom paradigm and a shift toward a "style" much less restricted by its peculiar imperatives—and in that sense, as a kind of liberation. For Kafka, during this period, one of the imperatives that weighed on writing, insinuating its pressure into the very cells of his rhetoric, was the imperative to marry. Tuberculosis released him from this imperative, though it placed him vividly and acutely before the law of mortality.

Now what is striking is that, in speaking *to Felice* of this mortality, as he does at the end of their correspondence, Kafka almost seems to embrace it, or at least (to use his own terms) to take hold of it like a weapon. That is exactly what he calls his illness: *eine Waffe*. In the penultimate letter to Felice, Kafka spins out for his soon to be former fiancée an astonishing allegorical interpretation of his own illness that will clarify in no uncertain terms not only the impossibility of their relationship, but, more cruelly, his intended use of the illness as an incontrovertible excuse that will finally put the whole unfortunate affair to rest. Two opponents fight "within me," he explains to Felice, one on her side, and one on another much more equivocal, even "evil" side (though he also says that they have at times reversed their roles . . .). The party to this other side of the fight is never stated outright, but he clearly associates it with the thing he has worked to protect all along: his writing. Tuberculosis has brought an end to this struggle. "I had thought it could last longer, but it can't. The blood issues not from the lung, but from a decisive stab delivered by one of the combatants [*aus einem entscheidenden Stich eines Kämpfers*]." This is mystifying enough, but soon Kafka makes his point clearer—for the real weapon is not the knife that drew this real or allegorical blood, but the wound itself. He imparts this to Felice as a "secret," an admission that must seal their separation, and almost as a threat: "And now I'm going to tell you a secret . . . which is bound to be true: I will never be well again. Simply because it is not the kind of tuberculosis that can be laid in a deckchair and nursed back to health, but a weapon that continues to be of utmost necessity as long as I remain alive. And both cannot remain alive" (LFe 546; BF 757). The frank perversity of this gesture is breathtaking: eager already at this stage to proclaim the illness incurable and fatal, he almost seems to desire this fatality and the threat of death it announces, in the knowledge that in the meantime it can therefore serve to ward off all accusations, all demands, all encroachments on the precious thing that must be protected, which is not his life, but his writing—and he goes so far as to explain this strategy to the person whose complete and final rejection it will now mercifully secure. He even admits to her that this ultimate weapon is only the last and most powerful one in the series he has long wielded against her: "It is a weapon compared to which the countless others used earlier . . . look expedient and primitive." Indeed, who can argue against a dying man? Neither a jilted fiancé, nor an insurance institute, nor a grumbling father. Diabolical in all innocence . . .

Canetti calls this letter "the most painful letter of Kafka's we have."[33] Its callousness as human communication must be set against the extreme frankness of its message, which admits, and analytically dramatizes, the very system of aggressivity it thereby sets into operation; in other words, the letter becomes the weapon it sets out to display, and brutally dispenses with Felice. The fact that Kafka's interpretation is a highly wrought mythologization and a self-serving confection does not speak against its authenticity as a statement of purpose, nor, especially, against that statement's *literary* validity. On the contrary, the specifically literary intrigue of this letter is that it proclaims, through a figural reading of a bodily illness (and its conversion into a "sign"[34]), the actual supremacy of the literary argument—that is, of the lie.

It does this especially in another passage from this letter that returns us to the image of the court, and to another leap into mere appearance, in an even more radical and uncanny reversal that drastically reconfigures the courtroom scene itself. This is also the moment when Kafka becomes most mendaciously honest, that is, deceptively honest about his invincible mendacity. "I am a mendacious human being," he says, "*ein lügnerischer Mensch*," but rather than leading to the dead end of the liar's paradox, this well known statement opens onto a peculiarly Kafkan leap of logic, in which the diabolism of deceptive appearance becomes so universal, and so persuasive, that it can no longer be considered deception.

> When I examine my ultimate aim [*Endziel*] it shows that I do not actually strive to be a good person [*ein guter Mensch*], to answer to a supreme tribunal [*einem höchsten Gericht*]. Very much the opposite. I strive to know the entire human and animal community, to recognize their fundamental preferences, desires, and moral ideals, to reduce them to simple rules [prescriptions: *Vorschriften*], and as quickly as possible to adopt these rules so as to be pleasing to everyone, indeed (*here comes the leap* [*hier kommt der Sprung*]) to become so pleasing that in the end I might openly act out my inherent baseness before the eyes of the world [*vor aller Augen*] without losing its love—the only sinner not to be roasted. Taken in its entirety [*zusammengefasst*], my only concern is the human tribunal [*das Menschengericht*], and I would like to deceive even this, and what's more without actual deception. [LFe 545; BFe 755–756; my emphasis]

Far from the manifestation of a radiant inner authenticity, far even from the persuasive and forceful presentation of a conviction of innocence deserving full justice, what is at stake here is the possibility of acting out (*ausführen*) an indwelling "baseness" or vileness (*Gemeinheiten*) *without being judged*, that is, in escaping the judgment otherwise universally applied. Through such a paradoxical process the entire machinery of justice would be eluded on the basis of a favorable and pleasing *appearance*. Kafka was at any rate pleased with the appearance of this extraordinary piece of writing: he not only copied it into his diary (D 387) but also sent it in a letter to Brod (LFr 152), confirming the spirit of its composition and multiple address as inherently literary. In that sense as well, it performs the very paradox it explains. Its address—patently not singular and personal—exceeds the nominal addressee, and enters into the very sphere of a universal human tribunal that it projects *onto Felice*. "You are my human tribunal," he says, essentially admitting that what he has done all along is seduce her for the sake of this seduction itself.

In this perspective, if we take seriously Kafka's characterization of himself as a "mendacious human being," and all the "baseness" that follows from this, it goes without saying that this is not in order to disparage or to judge, but rather to agree with the unflinching insight, and in all consciousness of its dangers, that the equivocal movement of *truly false appearances* is constitutive of literary experience, and moreover to propose that it is this insofar as such experience is *the very abyssal ground of social reality*. If this movement still appears to put something like grandeur and sublimity into play, especially when it comes to our thinking of literature as a value and a cultural good, that is perhaps only because we have not yet taken the writer's self-debasement seriously enough.

CHAPTER 4

Degradation of the Sublime
"A Hunger Artist"

"A Hunger Artist" was written in 1922, well after the transitional period (around 1917) mentioned in the previous chapter, and in many respects it clearly belongs among the later stories that can be described as "reports." Narrated by an unidentified observer of the phenomenon in question, it sets out to comment on an important change in public tastes (or in the "mood of the times," the *Zeitstimmung* [CS 274; E 197]), and on the ever-declining fate of one hunger artist in particular.[1] One researcher has pointed out that Kafka likely drew on newspaper reports of historical hunger artists and derived from these reports the particular tone of the story's narrative voice.[2] While such a "collective" or representative voice differs from the singular first person voice in "A Report to an Academy," it remains a first person voice, much like that in "Josefine the Singer," and as such is quite distinct from the impersonal third person narrators of the judgment stories. The narrators of the "reports" speak explicitly from within the situation being reported on, even when they take a certain ironic or temporal distance from it, as is the case in "A Hunger Artist." Most important for my purposes, however, there is nothing like a courtroom or penal apparatus in this story, and while there is something of a judgment, as we will see, this judgment is not pronounced by an embodiment of the Law, but rather comes down in the form of negligence and disregard on the part of the public at large (that is, precisely as a result of rumor made concretely manifest). And the consequences of this judgment are not a punishment, but consist rather in mere oblivion—that is, if it weren't for the report itself . . . My aim here will be to show that the fate of the hunger artist consists, very pointedly, in a destitution of the sublime "vocation"—*and* of the failures that are thoroughly structured by it—that overdetermines all of the judgment stories. The ironic tone with which this destitution is shown to be irrevocably accomplished, and indeed to have always already been so, is one sign that with this ever diminishing artist figure we have left behind the territory in which other much grander ambitions remained operative.

At the same time, the connections with the judgment stories, and with their sources in Kafka's early project of literary self-formation, are yet deeper and more extensive. For the parody of the sublime topos in "A Hunger Artist" appears to be a retrospective commentary on the artistic/literary striving that found figural and dramatic expression in the courtroom schema determining those stories, a schema that reaches back into much earlier figural elaborations in the letters and diaries. No doubt its clearest link with the judgment stories passes by way of "In the Penal Colony," to which it has been fruitfully compared, precisely as a staging of transcendental pretentions played out directly on the body as an object of discipline and as the site of a supposedly spiritualizing suffering; and in both cases there is a change of epoch, an *Umschwung*, that turns the formerly celebrated practice into something presently "incomprehensible," *unbegreiflich*.[3] The later story, however, leaves no doubt as to the nature of the practice, its fundamental banality and nonsublimity, even before any such evolution occurs.

"A Hunger Artist" is a wry and ironic (and eminently autobiographical) *putdown* of these initial pretentions, and even, I would argue, an open farewell to them, this time articulated explicitly on the terrain of artistic activity. This putdown has the structure of a joke, in which sublime strivings are brought down to the level of mere helpless compulsion. As the hunger artist says: *Ich kann nicht anders* (I can't help it). In order to understand both of these, the putdown and the compulsion, we will turn to what Freud in his book on jokes calls "*die Herabsetzung des Erhabenen*"—literally the "putdown" of the sublime, though Freud uses the word *degradation*, from an English text he cites in a footnote.[4] For Freud, this "putdown" is one of the effects of humor, and in this story Kafka's humor clearly has a similar aim. But the fact that this humor is at the expense of the very one who delivers the joke's punch line (and who is not without some similarities to his author) opens the story to a more melancholic affective dimension. This melancholy, with its basis in a radically unsatisfiable hunger, is the much-reduced remainder of the sublime that will concern us.

In a similar vein, the resemblances between this story and the much earlier "parable of the locked box," from the letters to Oskar Pollak—with its dramatic withholding followed by a final banal revelation, as well as the motifs of eating, nourishment and nostalgia—will allow us to bring this long thread of judgment full circle to one of its earliest generative moments, and simultaneously to suggest that Kafka has indeed entered into a new mode of thinking with regard to the presentative task of art. From the fulgurating flash of a rich interiority (or, to use another image: from a monstrous birth or bodying forth of a thing that is living, whole and complete), Kafka's writing passes through a destitution (of the grand judge who demands such an appearance *and* of the powerful "defendant" who attempts, however unviably, to live up to it) that renders it over into a much more problematic, and more ungraspably enigmatic, emptiness. In this late retrospective tale, that emptiness continues to be called *hunger*. Despite the story's sharp irony, it shows that this hunger, stripped of all possible objects, continues to *insist* and that it will survive in the very oblivion that threatens, in attempting to bury it, paradoxically to fill the breach that it must leave open. The necessity of "reporting" on this fragile persistence gives some idea of how for Kafka the imperative to write has been reconfigured, precisely in the absence of any graspable treasure to be revealed—which for the hunger artist converges with the banal impossibility of "finding the food I like." Despite their empty banality, however, the impossibility and dissatisfaction attested by this story continue to harbor their enigmas.

INTERIORITY AND DISTANCE

Like any good joke, "A Hunger Artist" saves the punch line for the end, at which point it effects a sudden fall or *chute* (as a punch line is aptly called in French). But up to then, everything in the story leads us to believe that the hunger artist is earnestly, even "fanatically" (CS 273; E 196), striving for the heights. Even so, it is immediately apparent that the kind of heights in question are already a let-down of sorts: if the hunger artist's art consists of fasting, there is never any indication that this activity is meant to lead him to the sort of ecstatic, mystical, or purifying supra-subjective experience often associated with ascetic deprivation. The relationship between the act of fasting and the hunger artist's subjective states is hardly even mentioned in the story (until the end), except to say that it weakens him for the ongoing battle with the entertainment industry, which must cater to the short attention span of the public. On the terrain of this battle, however, we do learn what the hunger artist wants, which is not limited to the public's mere attention. What he desires is an extreme and highly focused admiration and astonishment; he wants fame and glory (*Ruhm*). This is the form of the "court" now in force, the much more diffuse "court of public opinion" (or of the market) before which he appears.[5] But for what does he want to receive this glory? Not for reaching deep into inwardness or (thereby) into the beyond of the spiritual realm but, simply put, for doing something that *appears* to ordinary spectators to be *extremely difficult* and beyond their grasp. It is entirely in terms of such apparent difficulty that the story opens onto a subjective or "internal" dimension it cannot entirely bypass. We should first note that it is of course a difficulty that can be described in terms of training and discipline, the willful control and mastery of bodily impulses and a restraint imposed on the need to eat—sublime or "spiritual" topoi par excellence. The hunger artist displays this discipline in the form of his emaciated body, the site of its inscription, but he supplements this display with a visible attitude of subjective self-absorption. Between moments of engagement with the crowd, answering questions and even sticking his arm through the bars to make his emaciation more palpable to the spectators reaching out to feel it (*befühlen*) (CS 268; E 191), he spends most of his time "sunk in himself, concerned with no one," staring before him "with almost closed eyes." This is the outward image of his inward effort, but also of his separation from the public, on which he keeps his eyes cracked open after all, since these spectators must remain in view, if only vaguely in the distance. For, despite the occasional palpation, what he presents to the public is precisely his *distance* from them, even his superiority over them, which is expressed in terms of a *capacity* that sets him apart. The entire spectacle, including all the precautions against an unlikely recourse to cheating, is staged as a demonstration meant "to show . . . that he was fasting as not one of them could" (CS 269; E 192). It is at this assertion of will to power that the story aims its most pointed irony, partly in the Nietzschean mode of a critique of asceticism, and partly as a commentary on the status of art as a commodity subject to a market and the artist as a cultural laborer. Indeed, it is precisely for the sake of this critique that the story holds on to the node or knot of interiority it sets out to reconfigure.

In itself, then, the freakish body that results from the art of starving might earn the hunger artist some of the shocked attention just mentioned, but there is still a more essential element in this performance, which lies in the projected *agent* of its difficult discipline. It is in the circuit or loop of discipliner and disciplined, and thus in the remnant of autonomous subjectivity haunting this story, that something other than sheer bodily performance and visual presentation enters into its structure, even as everything seems to be reduced to mere image and spectacle. In the hunger artist's self-presentation, as the showing of a negative act of restraint and refrain, the surface elements of his appearance fold back onto themselves to form an implicit interiority. It should not be surprising that this turning back comes to be figured as the gnawing of a bad conscience, or that it should be described in relation to an ungraspability, an *Unbegreifliche*, that remains so even in the end. (I will return to this in a moment.) The crucial point is that the story undermines its pretentions to an internal, unreachable subjective space, but without foreclosing the latter entirely. It is the downgraded and destitute nature of this inevitable remnant, revealed in the waning shadow of an insatiable bad conscience, that is of essential concern to us here.

NEVER SATISFIED: THE EASIEST THING IN THE WORLD

If the hunger artist embodies and displays, *en creux*, an ability and mastery that far surpasses the public, we also learn that the negative space of interiority is accompanied by a knowledge that would seem to empty it of its force as an act, namely that the difficult accomplishment of fasting is in fact "the easiest thing in the world" (CS 270; E 193). So the narrator tells us, reporting the hunger artist's thoughts—and it is this unsettling knowledge that gives rise to the gnawing dissatisfaction at the center of this tale. After a vivid descriptive introduction to the circumstances and staging of the hunger artist's performances, regarding especially the problem of whether the continuity of his fast can ever be fully verified by the butchers (!) who keep watch over him, the story abruptly narrows its focus to the solitary sphere of the hunger artist himself, a sphere that congeals around this knowledge: just as he alone can know that he has not cheated, "he alone knows" how easy it is to fast. It is because of this that he is "never satisfied" (*niemals befriedigt*):

> It was not perhaps mere fasting that had made him so extremely thin [*abgemagert*] that many people had regretfully to keep away from his exhibitions, because they

could not bear the look of him [*seinen Anblick nicht ertrugen*], perhaps it was only dissatisfaction with himself [*aus Unzufriedenheit mit sich selbst*] that had so worn him away [*abgemagert*]. For he alone knew, what no other initiate knew, how easy it was to fast. It was the easiest thing in the world. He made no secret of this, yet people did not believe him . . . He had to put up with all that, and in the course of time had got used to it, but always this *dissatisfaction inwardly gnawed away* [*innerlich nagte diese Unbefriedigtheit*] at him. (CS 270; E 193; my emphasis)

Not unlike Gregor Samsa, whose repressed and pressurized bad conscience transforms him into a creature impossible to look at, the hunger artist presents such an aspect (*Anblick*) of skeletal reduction, has become so monstrously thin (*abgemagert*), because he is being eaten away by the "inward gnawing" of a complex discontent. Now what is this discontent and why would it thin him so? What exactly is the logic of this strange self-devouring hunger, and what is the "end" toward which its restless dissatisfaction reaches?

First, it is important to note that the bad conscience described here has nothing to do *at this point* with any deception that might be implied in the hunger artist's demand to be admired for something that is easy (though his final words will complicate this impression). On the contrary, he admits it openly, and it soon becomes clear that the admission of easiness is meant, at least at first, merely to radicalize the separateness and superiority of the hunger artist with respect to his foodbound public. The point is rather that fasting is so easy, he is capable of showing himself to be so far beyond them, that he should be allowed to fast as long as he can, and not merely the symbolic forty days—when he is forced from his cage before large crowds and much fanfare (garlands on the bars, military music, and so on). He must be compelled to stop fasting because he is *able* to continue and therefore prefers not to stop. But taken only that far, his art remains merely on the plane of the feasible (to use a phrase from Beckett), and within the sphere of what can, after all, be grasped. The public's enthusiastic interest in the fortieth-day festivities is precisely proof of this relative graspability. The remarkable and dramatic description of this scene, when the skeletal hunger artist is drawn from his cage before a thrilling crowd, includes a number of details that recall the festive gathering evoked in "In the Penal Colony." Carried forth by two ladies (*Damen*), described as a martyr (*Märtyrer*) and displayed to the public as the "work of heaven" (CS 271; E 194) the hunger artist's body provides the galvanizing focus for a dramatic "happening" that consists essentially in the reassimilation of a dying body into the emphatic spectacle of life, sustenance, and satisfaction. What "is happening" here is neither Justice nor any other ideal made palpable and legible; it is not the decipherable inscription of the text of transcendence. It is merely the public vision of a body being compelled back into the order of nourishment—and so perhaps into a more implicit ideal occluded by its very banality, namely that of the normal, the average, the everyday, the given. Unlike the penal colony prisoner, who continues to eat until just before the moment of ecstasy, and whose body is externally punctured ever more deeply, this hungering body has simply been "hollowed out" ("*der Leib war ausgehöhlt*" [CS 271; E 194]) and is thus manipulated like a puppet. That is what the hunger artist in his fasting presents to his admiring public, not the instantiation of anything beyond, but rather an unsettling *hole* in the world, which now must be filled once again. This coerced replenishment is the "outward" source of his discontent. What is eating him, then, is not hunger, but nourishment, which abrasively stuffs the hole that he would only like to widen, incomprehensibly, to its farthest extremity. That is why, after these spectacles, only he is unsatisfied with the show: "*mit dem Gesehenen unzufrieden*," as the narrator cannily puts it: "unsatisfied with what was seen" (CS 272; E 195), or one might say, with "the Seen" as such.

It is with respect to the public's demand to be satisfied with what gives itself to be seen—what one might call a subreptive demand for vision as fulfillment—that the language of the sublime enters most explicitly into the text, when the narrator presents, in a kind of indirect rant, the hunger artist's resentment of his disloyal public and their meager attention span. It is in the lexicon of the sublime that this resentment is articulated:

> Why stop fasting at this particular moment, after forty days of it? He had held out for a long time, an *illimitably* [*unbeschränkt*] long time; why stop now, when he was in his best fasting form, or rather, not quite yet in his best fasting form [*im besten Hungern*]? Why should they deprive him of the fame [*des Ruhmes berauben*] he would get for fasting longer, for being not only the *greatest* hunger artist of all time, which presumably he was already, but also to outdo himself, *to surpass himself unto the ungraspable* [*aber auch noch sich selbst zu übertreffen bis ins Unbegreifliche*], since he felt *no limits* [*keine Grenzen*] to his capacity for fasting [*Fähigkeit zu hungern*]? His public pretended to *admire* [*bewundern*] him so much, why should it have so little patience with him; if he could endure fasting longer, why shouldn't the public endure [*aushalten*] it? (CS 271; E 194; my emphasis)

Before drawing out the topos of the sublime that is so clearly engaged here, we can now answer more precisely the question regarding the hunger artist's gnawing bad conscience and self-dissatisfaction (*Unzufriedenheit mit sich selbst*), at least according to his own logic. He is "thinned down" from his discontent because it is generated from the limits imposed on his "greatness." As was the case in earlier writings that directly evoke the sublime (especially the letters to Oskar Pollak and the diaries), it is an as yet unachieved or unrecognized greatness that bites into the Kafkan conscience; here this bite is self-administered, and the gnawing conscience, rather than the result of a wound inflicted, is a mere hollowing out from within. To pose the problem in a somewhat Beckettian manner: What does gnawing gnaw after? Gnawing gnaws after itself. The gnawing conscience wants only more empty gnawing. In other words, it gnaws after something it cannot get its hands on. It strives for the utmost extreme of its own dissatisfaction. That is why, to put the point in the hunger artist's terms, it is not sufficient to be recognized as the world's greatest hunger artist, and so merely to have surpassed all other hunger artists; it is imperative to surpass oneself, farther and farther, to become incomparable and inimitable, to enter into a beyond of absolute incomprehensibility. It is here that the story engages (albeit in parodic form) what might be called the transgressive movement of metaphysics: an interminable movement outstripping all mediation, stepping beyond every stopping point, and outstripping all measure, on its way to the absolute.[6] In Kafka's already deflated and ironized version, such a movement, driven by a gnawing after more hunger, amounts to this: Only an absolute of hunger could still the gnawing. But an absolute of hunger, as the destination of a concrete temporal movement, would manifestly amount to death—and would, once again, leave but a corpse. For the moment, however, let us call it "the sublime" (which in this sense is coterminous with metaphysics), and place it in the vicinity of a Kafkan "critique of pure hunger." It will also be necessary to ask after its equivocal compensations. How do these revise or "translate" the classical schema of the sublime?

INCOMPREHENSIBLE HUNGER

The passage quoted earlier uses language that unmistakably evokes the sublime in its metaphysical, Kantian version: limitlessness, unboundedness, greatness, a self-surpassing "into the ungraspable," together with the "admiration" that accompanies and propels it. Even more specifically, the type of sublimity that the hunger artist strives for, in a measurement that would reach numerically into the immeasurable, is what Kant calls the mathematical sublime. Now when we turn to Kant, we see that this movement, while it passes through sight and vision, is in the end a radical leaving behind of the senses.

Let us briefly recall the analysis, for the sake of clarity. In the section of the *Critique of Judgment* that treats the mathematical sublime, Kant describes the latter as an experience in which the senses are confronted with an object so large that its magnitude exceeds any possible estimate of measure; no *aesthetic* apprehension of the object can represent it in its totality; but the imagination, the faculty of representation, Kant says, must at the behest of a *demand of reason*, strive toward this ungraspable totality. In doing so it painfully encounters its own limits and, beyond these limits, a "supersensible vocation" dictated by reason, a vocation precisely toward totality and toward that which is beyond the grasp of, and superior to, all forms of sensibility. Thus the painful limits of the imagination—of sensibility—reveal the powerful limitlessness of reason.[7]

Despite its obvious structural similarities, the hunger artist's trajectory cannot have the same shape, and his compensations, if they came, would necessarily be of a different order. First, the grandeur he seeks is not attached to that of a visible object, but consists rather in the conjunction of a diminishing (visible) body, and a hyperbolically increasing (invisible) renunciation. If the grandeur in question is related to an object, it is that of an object renounced, which is beginning to approach the scale of the entire world and even all possible (assimilable, "edible") phenomena. In other words, hunger itself—and not a mastery of the inclination to eat (remember: fasting is the easiest thing in the world)—has replaced reason as the drive, *and the reward*, of sublime striving, which nonetheless continues to be structured as an ascent beyond measure—even as it evokes the kitschy notion of a "world record hunger artist of all time" and rests ultimately on the kind of fame this implies. The hunger artist's problem (one of many) is that in surpassing even this measure, he wants to take his public with him. But they do not appear to be interested in the ungraspable, being content rather *"mit dem Gesehenen,"* with what is seen. It should be stressed, however, that Kafka's irony bears much less on this "worldly" attitude on the part of the public than on the hunger artist's delusion that his spectators ought to follow his abject performance into some other higher place devoid of objects (except maybe numbers, units of measured time, counted days). If anything, the story's irony is generated in large part through the narrator's adoption of this more pragmatic point of view, precisely as a way to index his progress toward a goal that is rather "elevated" beyond measure, not amenable to direct perception, and ultimately a matter of complete incomprehensibility.[8] In that sense, the hunger artist respects the imperative to give a sensible form to his task—which is what makes him an artist, after all. The problem, the paradox that gives his story its fundamental tension, is that in this task he clings, passionately and essentially, to a remnant of the supersensible, even as the latter is reduced to a refusal of the sensible, the corrosive power of a sensation called hunger. But in the end, this paradox complicates, to the point of neutralizing, the sacrificial economy that it seems to rely on.

Melancholy Reason

Returning to Kant for a moment, we see that the necessity—or the "vocation"—to renounce or sacrifice all objects of the senses is completely explicit in his treatment of the sublime. If in Kant there is no sense of abjection or melancholy in this renunciation, it is because that is precisely what the sublime is designed (or destined) to hold at bay with the extraordinary reward it provides, at the end of its painful process of stripping away, its long destructive drive into the supersensible. Kant repeatedly emphasizes that sublimity is not contained in the object itself but in the subject as a rational being, in reason (whose power and grandeur are identified with an object only "by subreption"); thus the truly sublime "object" of admiration, in which all aesthetic experiences of the sublime invisibly converge, is not an object at all but "the moral law in its power [*Macht*]," and—Kant goes on to say—"this power actually makes itself aesthetically knowable only through sacrifices [*Aufopferungen*] . . . a deprivation [*Beraubung*] . . . in return for which it reveals in us an unfathomable depth of this supersensible faculty" (CJ 153). Sacrifice both reveals and delivers (because in principle it was carried out *by*) the purely intellectual power of the moral law, which holds sway over us sensible creatures "only through the dominance [*Gewalt*] that reason inflicts on [*antut*] sensibility"

(CJ 154). The sublime compensation for sacrifice, for "setting aside our needs [*Überhebung von Bedürfnissen*]" (CJ 157), consists in a limitless and unfathomable supersensible power exercised over us, but also "in us," by reason. That is the sublime's unsurpassable reward, the inexhaustible treasure of reason's power. Kant stresses that the power of the moral law "remains" precisely "where the senses no longer see anything before them" (CJ 156), in other words, only when the phenomenal world as such has disappeared. What is at stake in the sublime compensation, then, is nothing less than *the ability to forego the entire world as an object of the senses*; the surpassing of the sensible world thus implies an unacknowledged *loss* of the world, such that the sublime experience, in relation to the world that is left behind, and by virtue of the idealization that replaces it, is profoundly melancholic.

Now because the loss entailed by the Kantian sublime is inherently totalizing, it must remain melancholic even if it receives the unlimited and unfathomable recompense it reveals, for this is not a recompense in kind. It is not another object. To drown out the melancholy tonality of this experience with the mighty "voice of reason," as Kant does, is part of a strategy to disavow the destitution and abjection that lurks even here, in its most classical and triumphant form. This aspect of the experience becomes all the starker when no return is forthcoming, leaving it stranded somewhere beyond sensibility, and yet somehow not beyond mere images; that is, in the still imagined ruins of the imagination itself ("Imagination Dead Imagine"), or, finally: in something like "literary space." Structurally analogous in this sense to Kant's supersensible realm, the world of fiction, of writing, becomes for Kafka the mode in which the world is lost, for the sake not of its overcoming by reason but of its groundless and multiplicitous imaging in and as language.[9] As I will show in a moment, a number of statements from the diaries bear witness to this, while also anticipating "A Hunger Artist" by approaching this loss, first of all, as a loss of weight—before radicalizing it in this story as a loss of this loss's compensation. This will also mean, in another remarkable analogy, *a contrario*, with the Kantian trajectory, the loss of the Law "in its power," and therefore of its mighty or tiny theater of sacrifice and punishment.

As we saw in the letters to Oskar Pollak, the sublime trajectory of writing passes first by way of its conscience-inflicting exemplars, and the painful instantiation of the Law through a wound. In a sense, then, Kafka begins the journey where Kant ends it (in the Law), but in the mode of being separated from it, belittled by it, falling far short of it. And as we have seen throughout, gaining access to it is a matter of *discipline*—it is the narrow gate of discipline that demands, and engenders, the starving/writing body with which Kafka will long be preoccupied. The topos of the sublime evoked so explicitly in "A Hunger Artist" thus engages a movement that Kafka had long associated with the demands of writing, namely the sacrifice of the senses (of the world) for the sake of a higher compensation, and articulated from early on in terms of a thinning down, starving, and atrophying of the body. In an often-quoted programmatic statement from the *Diaries* (from January 3, 1912), Kafka wrote:

> It is easy to recognize a concentration in me of all my forces on writing. When it became clear in my organism that writing was the most productive direction for my being to take, everything rushed in that direction and left empty all those abilities [*Fähigkeiten*] which were directed toward the joys of sex, eating, drinking, philosophical reflection, and above all music. I atrophied [*magerte . . . ab*] in all these directions. . . . Naturally, I did not find this purpose [*Zweck*] independently and consciously, it found itself. . . . The compensation [*Ausgleich*] for all this is clear as day. My development is now complete and, so far as I can see, there is nothing left to sacrifice [*aufzuopfern*]. (D 163; TB 167–168)

The curious inclusion of "philosophical reflection" in this list is telling, as is that of music, the implication being perhaps that while these "directions" follow the high road toward their lofty rewards, those of writing are of another "lower" order, determined by a kind of devouring automatism. This amounts to saying as well that the alterworldly vocation in question, here figured as a kind of organic telos, far from being determined by something like "the supersensible," must be organized, as it were, *from below*. If writing sacrifices (most of) the sensible world, it still depends directly on "the organism," and, in that sense, its compensations do not quit the senses. (This acknowledgment is continuous with Kafka's later assertion of the diabolism and sensuality of writing.)[10] In this respect we can recall the diary entry quoted earlier (from August 6, 1914), which makes a very similar point precisely in reference to a strange "sense":

> What will be my fate as a writer is very simple. My sense for presenting [*der Sinn für die Darstellung*] my dreamlike inner life has thrust all other matters into the background; my life has dwindled [atrophied: *verkümmert*] dreadfully, nor will it cease to dwindle. Nothing else will ever satisfy me [*zufriedenstellen*]. (D 302; TB 306)

The exclusive satisfaction to be gotten on the basis of a demanding presentative "sense" that starves all the others, would be a great deal more than what the hunger artist receives for his trouble. A creature of insatiably gnawing *Unzufriedenheit*, this artist is stripped by his author even of the slim gratification professed by the latter, at least according to the regime he had set in place during that phase of his writing. This quote from the diaries is from the period of the "judgment stories" and it expresses what we have seen to be one of the basic structural schemes of their engenderment: the ecstatic externalization of an internal image world as such (chiasmatically projected into the fiction as a failure to present a defense, and as punishment). By contrast, however, the hunger artist, *at the very height of his art*, is already "hollowed out," and the object of his presentation passes—in the logic of endless surpassing that he would like to follow—beyond the body/artwork he gives to be seen, and on "into the ungraspable," *bis ins Unbegreifliche*. But in this there is no satisfaction.

The removal of this satisfaction surely also means a removal from the regime of judgment, as the gaze watching over the hunger artist's accomplishment gradually drifts away. To be sure, as the story tells it, the turning away of the public's gaze does constitute a kind of judgment, though not a juridical one. It is rather the end result of a historical *Umschwung* that renders his entire art form incomprehensible. After losing his audience, and therefore the financial base available at the "high point" (*Höchstzeit*) of his great performances, the hunger artist has no option but to join the circus, where he becomes a freak show outright. But the crowds mostly walk past him on their way to the animals, especially the loud meat-eating predators (*Raubtiere*), and so people get used to his strange and out of place claim on their attention; that is, they no longer even notice it, "and with this familiarity [*Gewöhnung*], the judgment [*Urteil*] over him was pronounced [*gesprochen*]" (CS 276; E 198). This judgment speaks by not speaking, dismisses him quite literally as "the usual stuff," *das gewöhnliche Zeug*, not worthy of comment. It cannot be staged as a theater of condemnation and punishment, nor answered in self-defense. In a sense, the hunger artist merely fades from sight and becomes irretrievably banal, incomprehensible in the sense of historically illegible. The narrator explains this as a disjunction in affect, an ungraspable sense, as we approach the melancholy heart of this story:

> He might fast as much as only he could, and he did so; but nothing could save him now, people passed him by. Try to explain the art of fasting to someone! If he does not feel it [*nicht fühlt*], you cannot make it comprehensible to him [*nicht begreiflich machen*]. . . . And so the hunger artist hungered on, as he had once dreamed [*erträumt*] of doing before [*früher*] . . . but no one, not even the hunger artist himself knew how great his achievement was, and his heart grew heavy [*sein Herz wurde schwer*]. (CS 276; E 199)

The fate sealed by the public's "judgment," mere oblivion and negligence, is arguably much worse than the punishment inflicted by any representative of the Law's sublimely powerful speech, in which the judged party at least remains directly an object of authority's attention, and thus a locus of transcendental persecution. But that speech has been displaced, once again, into something resembling rumor, the swarming but decisive verdict of the masses. If the position of the judge has been evacuated and dispersed, then so has the very space of exile into which it would cast the condemned, a space which has been turned inside out: there is nowhere that is not exile, and the internal confinement of the law's painful point of application, the place where it might manifest in its power, has been completely "hollowed out." Nothing can come from it, or come (pouring) out of it; it has no point of contact with, and no effect on, social reality. And so literally nothing remains for the hunger artist now, except a feeling that cannot be transmitted comprehensibly, and which forecloses the very question at issue: How is it possible to make graspable the ungraspable *as such*? The feeling of the ungraspable has become, constitutively, that of melancholy, the affect that grasps only its own destitution, and refuses to relinquish it. Likewise, the "dream" of a boundless achievement in unlimited emptiness is dissolved in its banal and unremarked realization.

Hence the hunger artist's "heavy heart" (which almost literally names the *Schwermut* that is melancholy in German). This figure introduces an element of persistence installing itself as a feeling that tends rather downward. But its heaviness is no sign of plenitude. On the contrary, it involves a supplemental loss added to that of the sensible world, namely the loss of what the text calls "his compensation" or "reward": *sein Lohn*, a word that can also simply mean his payment. Having wondered why, despite his high striving (*hohe Streben*), he should be "deprived of fame and glory [*des Ruhmes berauben*]" (E 194), the hunger artist now hungers on without end, "working honorably [*ehrlich*]" but definitively "cheated" by the world from which he has removed himself: "*Die Welt betrog ihn um seinen Lohn*"—"The world cheated him of his reward" (CS 276; E 199). Reaching (into) the ungraspable is apparently not its own reward. But when the world stops watching, or more specifically, stops marking the number of days and displaying this "cipher," *Ziffer* or figure as the index of a hunger that knows no bounds, the social voiding of the hunger artist's task is complete. In these conditions, the hunger artist is not performing; he is merely a body dwindling, disappearing, and dying. The drive to self-surpass is thus revealed quite simply as a drive toward extinction. In a circuit that we have been tracing throughout these readings of Kafka, the sublime vocation curves back onto its own historical and psychic conditions in a drive that must end in death, and in the quickly absconded image of a corpse.

KANN NICHT ANDERS

This brings us back, finally, to the question of compulsion as it relates to the hunger artist's hunger.

What is left to him once he is deprived of the compensation of historical inscription? The last resort of all: the compulsion to confess. And what is more: the compulsion to confess a compulsion. It turns out that the "easiness" of fasting has, as its obverse, the extreme difficulty, not to say the impossibility, of *not* fasting, of being able not to fast, so that the endless capacity to fast is only the visible or outward aspect of the true imperative at work in all this supposed striving: *not to eat the given*. Kafka articulates this totalizing principle in a negative and derisory fashion, as a merely contingent lack. And so, at the end of the hunger artist's story, we get to the punch line of the joke it has slowly become. Having sunk completely into the straw of his apparently now empty cage, the hunger artist is finally remembered by the overseer of the circus, who prods him out with a pole, and with whom he has the following exchange, in which one can hear the comedy of vaudeville banter mixed with a bitter drop of melancholy that Kafka's humor does not dissolve:

> "Are you still fasting?" asked the overseer, "when on earth do you mean to stop?"
> "Forgive me, everybody," whispered the hunger artist; only the overseer, who had his ear to the bars, understood him. "Of course," said the overseer, and tapped his

forehead with a finger to let the attendants know what state the man was in, "we forgive you." "I always wanted you to admire [*bewundert*] my fasting," said the hunger artist. "We do admire it," said the overseer, obligingly. "But you shouldn't admire it," said the hunger artist. "Well then we don't admire it," said the overseer, "but why shouldn't we admire it?" "Because I have to fast, I can't help it [*Weil ich hungern muss, ich kann nicht anders*]," said the hunger artist. "Well anybody can see that," said the overseer, "and why can't you help it?" "Because," said the hunger artist, lifting his tiny head a little and speaking, with his lips pursed as if for a kiss, right into the overseer's ear, so that nothing would be lost [*damit nichts verloren ging*], "because I couldn't find the food I like [*die mir schmeckt*]. If I had found it, believe me, I should have made no fuss [*kein Aufsehen gemacht*] and stuffed myself [*mich vollgegessen*] like you and everyone else [*wie du und alle*]." These were his last words, but in his shattered [*gebrochenen*] eyes remained the firm though no longer proud conviction [*Überzeugung*] that he was fasting on [*dass er weiterhungre*]. (CS 276–277; E 199–200)

After all the fuss that the hunger artist did in fact make—demanding to be watched over and admired, striving for the beyond of the beyond, wasting away from the loss of his deserts—it turns out to be a banal affair indeed. He has demanded hyperbolic admiration for something he "cannot help" doing anyway—or rather, and more precisely, for not doing something he cannot help not doing. It will be important to ask in a moment whether the food he could not find really is just food, something that could be grasped with the hand and bitten by teeth, and so whether not finding it really is a merely contingent accident, as he seems to say (and it is this deflating implication that turns the story into a joke); the answer to this question will greatly inflect our understanding of the compulsion confessed here, and of the type of artistic thing it might indicate beyond its apparently negative form.

Freud and Comic Unmasking

For the moment, however, let us remain with the surface of the text and with the logic of the joke. It is the kind of joke that could easily find a place in Freud's book on the *Witz*, particularly in the section that deals with what he calls, using the phrase I have already referred to: *die Herabsetzung des Erhabenen*, the "degradation of the sublime."[11] Freud gives the term *Herabsetzung* as a translation of *degradation*, but the former has a distinct sense not only of symbolic demotion but also of a spatial lowering, a bringing or setting down, and by extension (as mentioned above), a putdown. Of the different comic modes of the putdown that Freud discusses, the story belongs most clearly among what he calls unmasking, *Entlarvung* (he also mentions caricature, parody, and travesty). The common ground between the story's punch line and Freud's description is in fact quite striking (despite obvious differences). "Unmasking," he says, involves the method of degrading [*herabsetzen*] the dignity of individuals by directing attention to the frailties [*Gebrechlichkeit*] which they share with all humanity, but in particular the dependence of their mental functions [*seiner seelischen Leistungen*] on bodily needs. The unmasking is equivalent here to an admonition: such and such a person, who is admired [*Bewunderte*] as a demigod, is after all only human like you and me [*wie ich und du*]. (*Jokes* 202; *Witz* 188)

The hunger artist, while clearly not such an exalted personage, has nonetheless aspired in his way to be something of the sort, and is fully brought down to earth, precisely with respect to the universality of bodily needs. "*Wie du und alle . . .* ," says the hunger artist in similar fashion: like you and everyone else I would have eaten my fill. His "broken eyes" (*gebrochenen Augen*) even reflect the "frailty" (*Gebrechlichkeit*) invoked here, emerging from beneath the mask of impassivity. But Freud specifies further what exactly is unmasked. He continues: "Here, too, are placed the efforts at laying bare the *monotonous psychical automatism* that lies behind the *wealth* [*Reichtum*] and *apparent freedom* of psychical functions" (*Jokes* 202, my emphasis). It is to this ground of psychic and bodily automatism that the hunger artist's final confession brings him down from his pretentions to freedom, the rich treasures of inwardness and the bad infinity of a purely numerical sublimity. For as slim and spare as these pretentions are, they nonetheless depend at some level on the presumption of an inner "wealth" and "freedom" belied by his admission of mere compulsion. It is in this sense too that he is "hollowed out," as the last possible vestige of a praiseworthy interiority is dissolved, along with his claim on the public, completing the process of his destitution. The unmasking reveals an empty shell fit to be thrown away—a shell of mere hunger unsatisfied. This shell does not contain any wealth or treasure; its empty space does not bespeak freedom but rather the banality of a compulsion: *Ich kann nicht anders*. It is subject to a mordant melancholy, but it has no bite.[12]

And yet, a slim and empty margin of difference persists between the hunger artist and those he leaves behind—between his "like you and everyone else" and Freud's "like you and me"—from whose banal universality he remains excluded, after all. If the hunger artist does not break from the automatism his fasting would appear to transcend, he does nonetheless introduce a tiny rupture into the economy of plenitude that demands he "eat his fill," but in which, instead, he remains lodged as an obtrusive *hole*, one which somehow must now be absconded or covered over. In that sense, his degradation lowers him *even further* than "you and me" and our universal bodily needs, into the abyssal and hollow ground of a radical hunger *for nothing* (for surely, it is worth adding, no amount of glory and fame could resolve the dissatisfaction that no food could still). When taken in its multiple ambivalent registers, in its simultaneously comic and melancholic aspects, the unmasking of the hunger artist not only shows the mask itself to be a death mask, manifest emblem of a drive beyond nourished life and into extinction; it also reveals the gnawing hollow, recalcitrant to all it would be fed, that is opened in a body haunted by a compulsion *without end*. The hunger artist's automatism is thus also *without reason*, and the sublimity for which he strives, degraded to the point of overt destitution, is definitively stripped of any returns, and reduced, once again, to a corpse. Other than that, it has, as it were, nothing to show for itself. In that regard, this strange automatism—this derisive sublimity—just lies open, a nagging unresolve in the text that reports not its closure but merely its passing from view. This passing we see very clearly in the story's remarkable coda, a final paragraph that turns the melancholy joke into a deceptively "affirmative" allegory.

Lack of Nothing

The preceding description stands as the exact opposite of the magnificent panther who, at the story's end, replaces the hunger artist "in the cage that had been desolate [*öde*] for so long" (CS 277; E 200). This creature of strength and plenitude is characterized above all else by his powerful jaws and teeth, his *Gebiss*, which he gladly sinks into the fresh meat brought by the circus attendants who watch over him (*die Wächter*). Kafka's rendering of the spectacle presented by this *faultless* body rings with the tones of an exaltation, but there is a menacing undercurrent that one might well read as a warning folded into the story's conclusion (which follows immediately after the hunger artist's death in the passage previously quoted):

> "Well, clear this out now! [*Nun macht aber Ordnung!*]" said the overseer, and they buried the hunger artist, straw and all. Into the cage they put a young panther. Even for the dullest senses [*selbst dem stumpfsten Sinn*] a feeling of recuperation [*eine . . . fühlbare Erholung*] came from seeing this wild creature leaping around the cage that had so long been dreary [*in dem so lange öden Käfig*]. The panther lacked nothing [*Ihm fehlte nichts*]. The food he liked was brought him without long reflection [*ohne langes Nachdenken*] by the attendants; he seemed not even to miss his freedom; his noble body, equipped almost to the point of bursting with all that it needed, seemed to carry freedom around with it too; somewhere in his teeth [*Gebiss*] it seemed to be lodged [*stecken*]; and the joy of life streamed with such ardent passion from his throat [*kam mit derart starker Glut aus seinem Rachen*] that for the spectators [*Zuschauer*] it was not easy to withstand it [*ihr standzuhalten*]. But they overcame themselves [*sie überwanden sich*], pressed around [*umdrängten*] the cage, and did not want ever to move away. (CS 277; E 200)

This panther is the anti–hunger artist. Point for point, his qualities stand in opposition to the dwindling creature whose disappearance he seals, not least in that his radiant force manages to penetrate even the dullest wits, the *Stumpfsinn* of the spectators, whose resistance he overcomes, not to say overwhelms, compelling their vision, galvanizing their very bodies. They come to feel it. And in return, they *overcome themselves*, in a movement that strangely mimics the desired self-overcoming of the hunger artist in that its result is actually an unmoving stasis. But here is the difference: their self-overcoming leaves no room, as it were, for the kind of opening and spacing that the hunger artist insistently poses and exposes, after all, though he may fail to impose it. The panther, for his part, succeeds all too well—*at least in the perception reported here*—in closing down the gnawing fault that the hunger artists cracks into the order of the given. Kafka says this difference very succinctly, in three words: *Ihm fehlte nichts*, literally: *nothing* was lacking to him. No fault or default fissures the spectacle of his presence and power. In this sense, since all along we have been speaking of a kind of taste, one could say that with regard to the fascinated spectators gripped in its field of force, this perfectly formed bodily plenitude smacks of fascism—as does the overseer's initial call to order, which is also a call to forget and "to bury" the little problem of the hunger artist, so easily cast into oblivion. Is the "nothing" that the panther lacks not precisely what the hunger artist has tried, and failed, to grasp and hold, like a world record? Such a comical misreading of what is at stake in his performance—a misreading of sublimity's destitute remainder, as dictated by dominant forms of social and historical reckoning—does not close the twisting breach that the hunger artist actively opens in his inability not to not eat, an inability that Kafka renders over to some strange unknown eternity, as the "broken" hunger artist in expiring is nonetheless "fasting on" in a haunting survival. The hunger artist's inability is therefore also something of a categorical refusal, not in the form of a heroic act of will (the entire story speaks unambiguously against this), but, again, as the experience of a gnawing craving that has *essentially* no possible object. Seen in this perspective, the hunger artist's joke itself relies on a sly subreption, the replacement of an object-image, a metaphor, for an experience that is incommensurate with its phenomenal occasion. For it seems clear that the hunger artist's search is not for a food he "never found," but rather for the *nothing* that he cannot grasp or make graspable. In that light, food is not the literal matter in question, but a metaphor for the stuff of total refusal, an all-inclusive passing over, and the cipher for a critique of taste as such.[13] This kind of hunger, far from seeking satisfaction, *merely insists*, and thus opens a minimal transcendence, a pointless demanding movement that no object can stop, that no gaze can capture, and that no teeth can get hold of. At the same time, the story acknowledges that, for the hungry, there is nothing other than food—leaving only hunger itself as the poor remainder of anything beyond. This craving insistence on nonfulfillment is the hole that the hunger artist breaches in the plenitude of the world. But it is also something that can be effaced, buried and forgotten. Hence the necessity of something like a "report" that attempts to bear witness to its slim chances of communication.

This report approaches the presentation of a voided, obtrusive, and insistent "interior" not within the sphere of guilt and exoneration, but by means of a narrating, commenting, and interpreting *voice* inhabited by a receding enigma it cannot shake. By showing the *Gewissensbiss* reduced in the final paragraph to a mere clenched *Gebiss*, Kafka reaches once again the hard internal limit of a literature mounted, machinelike, as the devouring spectacle of conscience, and (unlike the spectators for whom freedom has its seat in a kind of bite-power) he turns away, ceasing to struggle with a writing cast in those terms. Other terms were always visible within the subcorpus of "judgment stories" and their prehistory, on which I have focused here, but "A Hunger Artist" turns back to these stories in order, I would maintain, to affirm the relinquishment of their restrictive and repetitive schemata. In this way, Kafka's "vocation" destitutes artistic striving unto mere compulsion, but in doing so vindicates the insistent demand underlying the dramatic lures of grandeur and the treasures of its abjection: to leave open the tiny puncture that passes through everything and renders it ungraspable, not as a beyond but as an enigma elusively within reach. In this, it turns toward a speech that is not so much compelled by a looming Other, as it is driven unaccountably to echo the empty breach that opened it.

JOSEFINE'S ENIGMA

"A Hunger Artist" was first published in a volume of stories bearing the same title, the last of his life that Kafka himself prepared for publication. The story immediately following it in that edition is "Josefine the Singer." Just as the book's title story ends by proclaiming, equivocally, the irresistible power of a feline creature who "lacked nothing," the next story begins, on the very next page, by evoking "the power of song" as practiced by the mouse Josefine, only to insist soon after that her song "presents nothing out of the ordinary [*nichts Ausserordentliches darstellt*]" (CS 360; E 200–201). In this nothingness and its enigma, art, as music, risks oblivion, but it does not entirely fail to make itself felt. If in the end Josefine must disappear nonetheless, it is surely not her fault. The writing, the ruminating voice that names her, can only bear her forth as the thing it will have lost, but that it keeps lodged in the ground of a voice haunted by her time.

PART TWO

Blanchot

CHAPTER 5

Pointed Instants

Blanchot's Exigencies

. . . il comprit qu'on ne s'évadait pas du Temps . . .
—Chris Marker, *La jetée*

THE OTHER OF EVERY WORLD

What is the relation between writing and life? In what sense does a writer have, or not have, a past? And this past, which the writer may or may not have: what does writing *have to do* with it? Finally: is it possible to locate in it a problematic point where writing is impelled to begin?

These questions are doubtless naive, particularly with regard to a writer such as Maurice Blanchot, who continually engages them but in terms so radical and extreme as to render them nearly unrecognizable, or impossible. Blanchot's work seems to deny writing a past (in every sense of this phrase) even as it speaks of nothing so much as the writer's experience—and in this experience all is paradox. Not least when it comes to the fact that, for Blanchot, in order to write, as he puts it in *L'espace littéraire*, one must already be writing: "*Pour écrire, il faut déjà écrire*"[1] ("in order to write, one must already be writing"). This is one way of saying that in order to "enter" literary space, in its radical separation from the ordinary course of the world, one must already have entered it—one must already *be writing*, in all of the strange and vacillating senses indicated by this expression. To be writing (already): surely this names a fundamental condition of being in language (and thus of any writing undertaken in view of a work), an obscure but pervasive precondition that the writer—like everyone else—must already inhabit, a precondition one could describe as *the separation of language*, the abyssal fault by which "the world" and "life" are always already removed, remote, distanced, in the very ground of any language that would appropriate them, that would make them be in being told. And yet, with regard to this strange space as a *literary* space, and without reducing the distance it both requires and opens, I want to ask, naively: How do you get there? And more specifically, what in Blanchot's literary writing marks such a singular entry? Are there residues, leftovers, or remnants of a past time that bear witness to this necessary passage? Is the "transformation" (as Blanchot often puts it) of experience in (into) writing in any way incomplete? One of the guiding intuitions in what follows is that, despite the extreme strangeness and otherness of the fictive world or nonworld that Blanchot calls "literary space," despite its utter foreignness to the time left behind, this movement will nonetheless bear the marks, cuts, punctures or faults that have been left in leaving it. One tactic to be pursued here, in part through a number of such deliberately naive questions and formulations, will be to cut into (I do not say "through") the complexity of these issues so as to explore not so much the truth or falsity of Blanchot's assertions, as the conditions that form some of his work's most cherished movements and figures.

These conditions are to be read, of course, almost entirely within the fabric of Blanchot's fictional and essayistic texts themselves, especially as these attempt to establish themselves as a space *apart*.[2] This is especially true of the writing that Blanchot published in the late 1940s and throughout the 1950s, in which the question of literature and the peculiar space and movement of writing are given near exclusive priority, in a textual and personal withdrawal from every engagement that would distract from this absolute task. "*Maurice Blanchot, romancier et critique, est né en 1907. Sa vie est entièrement vouée à la littérature et au silence qui lui est propre.*" ("Maurice Blanchot, novelist and critique, was born in 1907. His life is entirely devoted to literature and to the silence that is proper to it.") Thus reads the terse biographical note on the flyleaf of *L'espace littéraire*. In responding to the demand for the author to appear "in person," born at a given time and still living a life, this note both acknowledges a link between life and writing and severs, mutes, or reduces that link to an exclusive devotion to an unpresentable silence. A silence, that is, with regard to something resembling life, whereby life thus comes to be contained entirely in the speech called literary, which therefore seems to require the absolute barring of the one who has lived it. One of the primary aims in what follows will be to scrutinize this attenuated or ruptured link between life and writing, the paradoxes and evasions it gives rise to, the hyperbolic rhetoric it evokes in Blanchot's literary reflections, and, in particular, certain of the haunting remnants which obtrude, as the generative residue of a highly deliberate procedure, into that part of his writing that can be called narrative fiction. These remnants involve especially the haunting presence/absence of dying or dead feminine figures constitutively lodged within the "literary space" that they thus also *open*. For it is these figures that have accompanied the writer into a space that cannot entirely sever itself from the time of a life that *comes to be* disrupted, even ruined, by the eventual violence of an imperative to write. In the liminal narrative of *L'arrêt de mort*, especially, we will see how it is the *leaving of a woman*, in every sense—both the stripping away of a relation from a life that must depart the order of such relations, and the remnants left behind in her wake (particularly in the form of an emblematic death mask)—that seals in the end a triumphant affirmation, which for its part is cast, somewhat dubiously, as indestructible. But on the way to this affirmation, the feminine figure who has occasioned the decisive and disruptive encounter comes to be effaced as inessential. *She*, it turns out, is lost beyond telling—though she *must* also *have been told*, her figure inscenated and encountered, in order for the work that leaves her to come to be.[3] We will therefore ask, doubtless naively, what has happened to her—for it is clear that something of her lives on in the haunted heart, core, or kernel of Blanchot's writing, even as this haunting is attested by nothing but the empty "shell" the writer evokes as the token of its enigma.[4]

In the preceding chapters on Kafka, I referred to the relation between Kafka's early autobiographical writing and the fiction that emerged in its wake, in terms of derivation and elaboration. In writing about himself, in his letters and diaries, Kafka worked out, partly on the basis of material from his "personal" experience (though not only on that basis) the fundamental figural, thematic, and structural features of his first mature fiction, much of which unfolds as a scenography of judgment. In this respect, one can follow certain threads in Kafka's fictional texts "back" to earlier and in some sense more personal and experiential material through and out of which the writer found himself wending his way into fiction as such—though of course it must also be stressed again that that earlier writing also *is writing*, that there too Kafka is "already writing" (even if perhaps in a way that is still "not yet" writing in Blanchot's severe and rigorous sense), and that the entire process occurs as a textual elaboration providing no privileged access to the material in question as lived experience. Indeed, at another level, these "personal" writings are indisputably a part of Kafka's corpus, in accordance with the imbrication of life and writing to which Kafka's "experience" bears witness in so many ways. But when we turn to Blanchot, we see that this complex situation is drastically simplified, for us readers, at least in the sense that there are no such "personal" writings to be had—that is (to focus on the question of concern to us here), no letters or diaries that would chart the movement *through writing life*, and into literature, as we are able to do, to some extent, for Kafka. The "biographical" statement quoted above is emblematic of the larger and very deliberate exclusion by Blanchot, in principle if not in fact, of anything approaching literary space from that of mere life, or even just hovering around its edges.[5]

It is precisely these terms of an approach to forbidding edges (*abords*) that one finds in an essay on "Le journal intime et le récit," where the practice of diary writing is dismissed with a scorn and sarcasm not usually found in Blanchot. "*Comme s'il y avait le moindre intérêt à penser à soi, à se tourner vers soi*" ("as though there were the least interest in thinking of oneself, turning toward oneself"), he writes, condemning this unsavory mixture of introspection and confession (LV 256). The manifest aversion and even disgust expressed in this essay are telling, but it is precisely on the subject of Kafka's diaries that the question becomes more complicated, and perhaps even more revealing. Pointing out that these diaries are full of sketches and stories, literary beginnings that have been abandoned, Blanchot admits: "*Nous sentons bien cependant que ces fragments 's'articulent,' comme le dit Marthe Robert, 'entre les faits vécus et l'art,' entre Kafka qui vit et Kafka qui écrit*" ("We sense however that these fragments 'articulate,' as Marthe Robert says, 'lived facts and art,' the Kafka who lives and the Kafka who writes"). But no sooner has he conceded this "articulation" than he quickly moves to dissolve it: "*Nous présentons aussi que ces fragments constituent les traces anonymes, obscures, du livre qui cherche à se réaliser, mais seulement dans la mesure où ils n'ont* pas de parenté visible avec l'existence dont ils semblent issus, *ni avec l'oeuvre dont ils forment l'approche.*" ("We also have a presentiment that these fragments constitute the anonymous, obscure traces of the book that seeks to be realized, but only to the extent that they have *no visible kinship* with the existence *from which they seem to be derived*, nor with the work to which they form an approach"; LV 258, my emphasis). It is difficult to know how such a "visible kinship" could be gauged, or deemed absent, or whether it could even be subjected to such a logic of complete rupture and effacement; but it is striking to see how insistent Blanchot is in asserting this logic, this on the part of a thinker for whom no opposition is immune to its own founding ambiguities. Is Blanchot himself "naive," then, when it comes to *this* opposition, between the personal and the impersonal, or (likewise) between writing and the life from which writing would only "seem" to be derived? One senses a strange muted panic in this essay, something akin, in fact, to the urgent self-avoidance staged in many of Beckett's texts, as when the narrator of *Company* repeats, at certain dangerous and abyssal junctures of potential self-confrontation: "Quick leave him." Perhaps this is what leads Blanchot in this essay to close down the very possibility of reading a writer's diary for what it might reveal, as though to render such a prospect harmless, when he concludes his observations on Kafka's diaries (in the two sentences that follow the preceding quotation): "*Si, donc, nous avons ici un pressentiment de ce que pourrait être le journal de l'expérience créatrice, nous avons en même temps la preuve que ce journal serait aussi fermé, et plus séparé, que l'oeuvre accomplie. Car* les abords d'un secret *sont plus secrets que lui-même.*" ("If, therefore, we have here a presentiment of what the journal of the creative experience might be, at the same time we have the proof that this journal would be just as closed, and more separated, than the finished work. For the *outer edges of a secret* are more secret than the secret"; LV 258–259, my emphasis). What Blanchot elides here, by enclosing the leftovers of a writer's efforts in the atomized containers of their scattered secrets, is that their kinship "articulates" them not only to the singular work that it fails to become, but also to other work, and other writing, past and to come, sketchy and complete, and even to the strange being of an author who is continually *coming into being*, along a textual spectrum that itself constitutes one mode, among many, by which one might trace the life—and the disjointed time—of writing. Kafka himself frequently asserted this kinship, no doubt reifying the desired relation to the point of mystification (a son writing of sons and wishing, thereby, for a true (literary) son at last), but nonetheless acknowledging a complex link he knew to be not only inevitable but also essential to the very fabric of the work he strove to engender. At the same time, Blanchot's denials are belied, in his fiction and in his essays, by a knowledge that he too could not avoid engaging, and articulating—a knowledge that something of a singular past necessarily remains "visible" and palpable (legible) in the impersonal work. But the effort to make these denials, and to establish an absolute separation between life and literary space, leaves deep traces in his writing, unstable faultlines that are worth reading for what they say about how an imperative to write comes to be instantiated, violently or gradually, within the time of a life. It will also allow us to perceive the form that such an imperative takes in the complex looping structures of Blanchot's fiction, especially the *récits* that "realize" it—ever failingly—within the temporalized field of narratives haunted by figures, punctuated by events, and engaged by a time-troubled voice.[6]

In and Out of the World: Blanchot and Heidegger

When Blanchot writes, as he frequently does—especially in *L'espace littéraire*, where such formulas proliferate—that the writer is someone who has been "thrown out of the world," he is both echoing Kafka and responding to Heidegger.[7] In general, *L'espace littéraire* ought to be read in many respects as a critical response to Heidegger's thinking on space, death, possibility, and authenticity, particularly in terms of a "world" into or out of which one finds oneself thrown, knocked or jolted, by way of certain extremely strange experiences. Whereas in Heidegger the unsettling disruptions of anxiety and uncanniness separate one from the world only to make heard a "call of conscience" that prepares a more resolute habitation of worldliness—a turning back to world in the mode of "being toward death" projected as one's "ownmost possibility"—in Blanchot's writerly adventure, the direction of thrownness is decidedly centrifugal.[8] Literary space, far from all authenticity, does not promise a more resolute return, and the version of Dasein that Blanchot calls "the writer" is, as such, in a permanent state of unworldliness. We could think of these as different vectors of *Unheimlichkeit* with respect to the world or nonworld that is revealed or opened (reopened) in estrangement. For Blanchot, who carefully surveys Kafka's uncanny exit from life into the "desert" of writing, the world in question is radically *other*—it is even, as he puts it more than once, "*l'autre de tout monde*" ("the other of every world") (EL 89–90, 303). Or as he writes in the final sentence of that essay: "*le 'poète' est celui pour qui il n'existe pas même un seul monde, car il n'existe pour lui que le dehors*" ("the 'poet' is one for whom there exists not even a single world, for there exists for him only the outside") (EL 101). These hyperbolic and exclusive formulations place us once again before the naive question of transport, or "entry," "into" the space in question. Heidegger, who is not specifically concerned with the being of the writer, begins with "being-in-the-world" and gives a schematic account of how absorption in the everyday is disrupted, unsettled, and altered: the familiar world *becomes* strange, it resounds differently in an anxious *Stimmung*, a term that could be thought of (or translated) as a kind of "vocalization," so that one is thus "called" out of everydayness by the unsounding voice of an anxious conscience drawing one singularly into nothing, into the nothingness that opens in the ground of finitude. Thus does Heidegger introduce into the thick of the world the crack or space of a fault that resounds, indeed, with a "guilt" stripped of its objects, a "*Schuld*" voiced without ground, "striking" one from out of separation itself.[9] In Blanchot, for whom such an account of estrangement remained constitutive, the stripping away and "deobjectification" of the world is, however, much more abrupt and definitive. He does not (at least not in *L'espace littéraire*) give an account of how it happens, how it arrives "within" or "comes over" ordinary experience; the "transformation" of which he speaks so often in *L'espace littéraire* and *Le livre à venir* has indeed, in this essayistic discourse, always already taken place—since we are always following "the writer" as such in his or her errant movements; and there is little indication of how one might "return" from this strange and altogether other space that is literary, except to say that it depends on an abrupt kind of blindness and negligence—the rash turn, and the voided return, of Orpheus. (At the same time, we learn of the multiple dangers of this space, one of which is that one may never return.) Blanchot is simply not interested in "articulating" this passage, from lived facts to exigent art, insisting on the contrary and at (virtually) every step on the absolute separation of these realms—a separation he refers to at one point, in the extreme formulation of a perfectly hyperbolic redundancy, as "*absolument absolue*" (EL, 93). The "world" for Blanchot is something that *must have been left*. But it is worth noting that this formula too ("the absolutely absolute") is derived, in fact, from a reading of Kafka, and most especially of *The Castle*, in which Blanchot finds the absolutely separated wanderer/surveyor (a figure closely analogized with the writer) also engaged with nothing but sheer images, and thus caught up in an "exigency of figuration" (EL 97) that is all the more rigorous and demanding for being severed from the real. And yet it must be admitted that this realm of sheer visibility is precisely what threatens to betray its "kinship" with—its stubborn derivation from—the world from which it has been stripped away. Indeed, Blanchot gives the "impatience" of this stripping, surpassing, and superseding of images in the errant space of writing a significant name, when he calls it "*la faute essentielle*" (EL 94–95)—the essential *fault of writing* whereby sheer separation becomes the very movement of fiction. But I would add (for Blanchot does not say this) that this is also where writing is threatened with the persistent visible and material remainders of a world that, if its images have been stripped away, has also been *lost*, albeit, as we will see, in the mode of an affirmed renunciation. But for Blanchot this loss/renunciation is always cast as something already accomplished, and is always approached from the perspective of its having been overcome, in the space of a poor and endless return that we will nonetheless have grounds once again (as in the case of Kafka) to see as a kind of treasure.[10]

One could argue, based on an attentive reading of *L'espace littéraire*, that however incisive Blanchot's response to Heidegger is, the notion of a world and its absolute other is too starkly dualistic, no doubt in part because of a problematic conflation, occurring precisely in the concept "world," of Heidegger and Hegel. For where Blanchot thinks "world," he also thinks "work," in the sense of the negative's productive labor (*travail*) and the dialectic movement of time as history.[11] And for Blanchot this is a logic that it is urgent to contest, to undo, and to escape, a task for which only the sheer dissimulation and inoperative neutrality of literary language has any chance. But one result of this precipitous conflation is that the "non-Hegelian" elements of Heidegger's "world," or at least those that might problematize Hegel's thought—including precisely the limit-experiences of uncanniness and suspended, objectless anxiety that Blanchot folds into his own reflections (one could also mention boredom, another route to Heidegger's peculiar determination of transcendence[12])—that these elements are deprived of their ambiguity with respect to the strange border between the world in which we "factically" find ourselves, and the world in its originary constitutive structure, the opening that, in the midst of what covers it over, can always only be *re*opened. Simply put (too simply no doubt), Blanchot's ontologization of literary experience ironically deontologizes Heidegger's analysis of "world"—so as to place this latter concept squarely on the side of mere given reality (indistinguishable from its dialectical negation), and thus, from the perspective of literary space, to foreclose it.[13] I will not develop this argument further here but will instead begin with Blanchot's clear and repeated presumption of foreclosure, and with the stark and absolute separation it establishes, in order to show that the world marked as void by the voided images of literary space cannot help but bear witness to the *leaving of these images* (in every sense), such that the equivocal figuration of their remnants as ghosts, specters, corpses, and revenants—or rather, for the most part, *revenantes*—renders them over to a melancholic temporality continually voicing, and muting, its stubborn residuals. Indeed, in Blanchot's *récits* the world left behind, *is not*. Its face, and its look, speak still in the distant guise of a telling disfiguration—and at some level Blanchot recognizes this inevitability. But for the most part, the losses and returns seem to pass unreckoned into a would-be oblivion.

Melancholy Economies

To invoke melancholy in reference to Blanchot is at once to indicate something that is overwhelmingly obvious and to touch on a deep disavowal traversing the work in ways it is often difficult to register. In one sense, melancholy is the very element of Blanchot's work, its founding condition, to the extent at least that literary experience itself is constituted by the exit from the world just discussed, and insofar as this exit is also a "loss of the world" (a formula one finds in *L'espace littéraire* [EL 61]).[14] Blanchot rarely speaks in terms of loss, and the word *melancholy* is very infrequent in his texts, its use never rising from the level of an incidental descriptor to that of a concept. And yet the absolute break from life and world demanded by the literary work, together with the haunting return of its beloved figures within the space of the *récits*—an "eternal return" that places them out of reach of the time of mere events—is an extreme mode of loss verging into what I have referred to in earlier chapters as a *destitution of the sublime*. Exit from world as totalizing loss of world, what Kafka likens to "exile" and "suicide," both originates in and reveals a sublimity that in turn, having promised a Law beyond all figures (including the figure of the one who dealt the terrible blow of this loss), nonetheless renders only its sinking and hollow absence *in an endless proliferation of fictional figures*. Such a knotted intersection of loss, melancholy, sublimity, and law's haunting figurations occurs, term by term, in Blanchot as well—where, however, the figures in question are never paternal proxies, and almost always ghostly feminine apparitions. What kind of difference does such a sexual difference make? At this point it is very difficult to say, but aside from introducing elements of passionate erotic attachment directly into the (fictive) text of imperatively unfolding writing, we see already one major difference in Blanchot: whereas Kafka's engagement with sublimity and law engendered an intense commerce with the complex topos of bad conscience, such a thing is strikingly absent, or at least deeply muted, in Blanchot. And yet we will see, in a reading of Blanchot's *L'instant de ma mort* (in the present chapter), a text that touches very closely on the sublime, that the *instance*, the instantiated and "insisting" authority of this death, resounds unmistakably with the "*kritische Instanz*," the "critical agency" of which Freud speaks in establishing the conjunction between the idealizing introjections of melancholy and the projected exigencies of the superego.[15] We might say that Blanchot's "instant" renders up rather a kind of parody of Freud's bad conscience—much as the feminine figure of "the Law" in *La folie du jour* projects a parody, tremendously serious, of a sublime authority whose vulnerable sovereignty eludes all contact. Similarly, the brief and shattering autobiographical text "Une scene primitive?" from *L'écriture du désastre* (also discussed in this chapter) can be seen as recasting, and destituting, the sublime by staging a melancholic relation to "what there is" (ED 117), a totalizing loss figured in a "black sky" that for its part also parodies, and voids, Kant's sublime and star-marked space. What is unclear, however, and extremely equivocal, is the question as to whether these melancholic destitutions of the sublime do not also parody the retrieval of a supreme and permanent return and compensation for all that is lost—not Reason, and not Authority, of course, but something strangely inseparable and indestructible nonetheless, something prized and precious. Something that, moreover, seems to have an essential place in the retrospective casting of a vocation to write.

In what follows, then, there will be grounds for wondering whether Blanchot's fiction does not in fact engage a complex melancholic economy, a relation to time's elusive figures and their ghostly returns, determined by a certain compensatory logic: all has been lost, but in the wake of this complete stripping away emerges something that *cannot be lost*, an unloseable something that is not a thing, is not a possession, but that "can never go away again" (AM 117), that "is incapable of disappearing," and that, most magnificently and hyperbolically: "eternally . . . is there" (AM 127). To be hyperbolic in turn, one must concede that for Blanchot this "being there" is infinitely problematic; surely it is not univocal, as presence is imbricated with an absence not merely its opposite; but its repeated assertion, often in close conjunction with the explicit disavowal of specific losses ("*Qu'importe*," Blanchot serenely writes on many such occasions, "What does it matter"), raises many questions regarding the figural economy of the narrative passage out of the world, and of exactly *what it leaves*.

Versions of the Image, Necessity of the Récit

In *L'espace littéraire*, Blanchot evokes a *"résidu inéliminable, irréductible"* that emerges in the *"fiction absolue"* of poetic language, the total realization of an all-consuming irreality that "says being" only when it has *"'usé,' 'rongé' toutes les choses existantes, suspendu tous les êtres possibles"* ("worn away, gnawed away all existing things, suspended all possible beings"; EL 47). This process of reduction and "gnawing away," elimination and suspension, is constitutive of Blanchot's thinking of existence in its relation to literary space, but also to the unfolding of the narratives that precisely thereby seek their hardest empty kernel and core. In the context of the quote just given, Blanchot refers to this residue in an ontological register in terms of "being" (or as *"le mot même: c'est"* ["the very word: it is"]; EL 48). And the *image*, he says in another essay that repeats the same formulation (*"le résidu inéliminable de l'être"*), might have the function of humanizing this residue, rendering it palpable and appropriable (EL 342)—much as he says in another essay that in the essential strangeness of the night a ghost is there *"pour dérober, pour apaiser le fantôme de la nuit"* ("to hide, to calm the phantom of the night"; EL 214). But these versions of the image, and of the ghost, are not the most essential to Blanchot, who pushes them beyond such taming and pacifying operations into the very abyssal ground that they might otherwise seem to mitigate. Rather, in their most unsettling *aspects*, the image and the ghost put into play the very constitution of visibility from out of the ground of its own limit and undoing—which is also an unreal proliferation, a proliferating *of* unreality. In "Les deux versions de l'imaginaire" (EL 341–355) (a text to which we will turn in Chapter 7), Blanchot analyzes this process with respect to the *corpse* in all its errant and unsettling features, and as a privileged image *of image*, an image that makes manifest the fundamental structure of images. The ghosts in Blanchot's *récits*, especially the feminine specters that haunt the writing of *L'arrêt de mort*, are precisely such privileged images, invested with the prestige of *figures* in the most charged and enigmatic sense of this term: images that make seeing visible by opening a gap—a fault or *faille*—within it, out of which they seep as though from the very possibility of beginning a story. For all of Blanchot's *récits* emanate from what he casts as an *encounter with an image*.[16] Such figures are likewise the fascinating masks of a troubling and "ineliminable" residue which they do more than merely mediate or cover over— for in a sense they *are* also *its* residue, necessitated by the inevitability of their figural projection within the space of recitical narration, and no less impossible to eliminate from the field of this narration's engagement *at some point*, however indefinite, with the time of the world. In an analysis of this paradox in Blanchot, we will see that what has been stripped away (*dépouillé*), the singular leavings and remainders (*dépouillements*) of an unstoppable movement of elimination and severance, merge uncannily with the image of corpsely remains (*la dépouille*) that Blanchot places in the empty ground of the image.[17] In the search for an "essence" of literature, the errant movement that strips world away also reveals that what has been stripped, the discarded remains (and the lost ghostly beings that they project), are also constitutive of this empty essence. And indeed, as mentioned before, Blanchot calls it—this brittle core that is a mere leftover— "the shell of an enigma" (AM 9). It too is unloseable, indelible—whether consoling or harassing—but the narrator's insistence on leaving it is what gives him away. For in its opaque insistence, it never ceases to *look back*, in every sense. We might thus call it (in anticipation): the gaze of Eurydice. Despite the slope, vector, or cadence of his favored scenes, Blanchot does not fail to institute the law of this gaze, no less than that of the male figure of Orpheus with which he identifies (perhaps in a deep misrecognition) the displaced "center" of his literary thought.[18] Literature's loss of the world is also necessarily that of Eurydice's look *returned*.

With regard to Blanchot's narrative work, the shell or remnant that is left in the space of the *récit*—as if deposited or embedded there by events and figures in the process of dissolving their own categories—takes the concrete figural form of the death mask mentioned above, along with the cast moulds of a woman's hands which are uncannily implicated in the story's writing, its *manu-scripting*, one might say. In the commentary presented in Chapter 7, I will consider the death mask as a schematic emblem of literary experience, in close proximity to Blanchot's reflections on the corpse, but also in relation to an essay by Jean-Luc Nancy, entitled "Masked Imagination," in which the death mask takes on a peculiar significance in Heidegger's reworking of the Kantian schematism and the "transcendental imagination."[19] These references will allow us to elaborate the complex relationship between the image as a "look" (*Anblick*) bound to the schema of time (which Heidegger calls "the schema-image"), and the deathly gaze that seems to remove the look from the world which it nonetheless forms. Blanchot's melancholic temporality thus takes on a specific *outline*, drawing out what I take to be the contours of an intimate drive to speak, which is also an imperative to write that, if it is "categorical," is also imprinted with the events and figures that initially hollowed out its insatiably gnawing impulse (*"ayant 'usé,' 'rongé' toute les les choses"* [EL 47]). For beyond or before the death mask we find projected the ever-receding figures of the women who occupy the space of this story in its passionate attachment to a singular time. These women, whose death and effacement the unworldly movement of the *récit* seems to require, will preoccupy us at some length (in Chapter 6), in a reading of *L'arrêt de mort* that attempts to trace the path from a love for an embodied (if *unheimlich*) woman to the triumphant affirmation, in the final lyrical lines of the text, of a feminine "*pensée*" that appears to dissolve the flesh it has gnawed away—a path haunted by ghosts and strewn with several female corpses, and thus leading out of this world into a strangely temporal and linguistic eternity: "*à elle je dis éternellement: 'viens,' et éternellement, elle est là*" ("and to her I say eternally: 'come,' and eternally, she is there"; AM 127). This conclusion, this closure of narrative in the eternal shadow of its originary opening (and to the ecstatic benefit of the male voice that speaks (from) it), leaves us worrying over the fate of a woman whose name means birth (Nathalie), but whose story encrusts her finally, near-invisibly, in the gaze of death alone—even as she is survived by the eternal *thought* that "she" has engendered *within the order of a narrative* without which this thought would never be textually encountered. The point is not to demand that *this woman* be rendered up living to the daylight of a previously disclaimed existence, but rather to insist that her passage be marked also, and *essentially*, in the singular imprints it leaves on something like a life, a life this passing might indeed have ruined. If she is sublimed out of life, "volatilized" into an unstable figure of the Law (the law of writing as seconded vocation), she is also the remnant of a love that once (*une fois*) opened a passion striving beyond all objects; and this "opening" is after all another name for ruination, though perhaps not in the permanently salutary sense that can be read in Blanchot's temporally ecstatic affirmations.

It should be stressed once again that I am not contesting the truth of what Blanchot says about literary space, a question I would prefer to leave suspended, indeed permanently unsettled, as is proper to it. Rather I am trying to bring out some of the linguistic and graphic contours that remain visible, after all, in Blanchot's haunted, melancholy version of it. This "version" is not peculiar to Blanchot (though he does give it a singular turn), and it does I think say the truth of a certain relation to writing that has a discernible historical generality—one might indeed suspect that the renunciations in question lie densely embedded in the ground of what is called "modernism," insofar as this is a name for the sounding and unfolding of depth and interiority, its radical *externalization*: inwardness *as* boundless exteriority. But as open as Blanchot is, after all, about the haunted melancholy constitutive of his work, it nonetheless seems to me to involve an insistent disavowal, its panic rendered into taut serenity, along with a movement of retention and compensation that is repeatedly affirmed in the wake of the extreme loss and destitution that set the tone, the very minor *Stimmung*, of Blanchot's *récits*, and of his reflections on literary experience. These reflections will be our starting point in the next section, first in terms of the *exigency* by which writing's demands outstrip the sphere of ethics by being emptied of all objects, and then with respect to the *point* that structures, and destructures—that threatens to destroy—literary space in its compelling fascinations. Such a "punctual" and punctured narration will be analyzed in turn in the two much later autobiographical texts whose central instants, while they defy mere plotting, appear to open a point of contact between a lived past and the initiating *coup* of an exigent vocation (also its retrospective seal). These riven and faulty attempts at narration will turn us, in an irreducibly paradoxical fashion, not only toward the figureless void, but also and no less compulsively toward a time, a single time, that continually imprints its instants and slips away, thus leaving an insistent and volatile residue sticking to language—much as salt sticks to the sea one hears in a shell.

THE EXIGENCY: THE AIR WE MUST BREATHE

Blanchot's literary essays in *L'espace littéraire* and *Le livre à venir* articulate a set of concepts and figures that attempt to expound literary experience as it were from a certain distance. The writing in these essays is not "engaged in the depths of the *récit*" (a phrase Blanchot uses to describe Kafka's narrative notes and drafts); rather it seeks to lay out, if not exactly to survey, an otherwise unlocatable experience in terms of the temporal, spatial and figural paradoxes that constitute these "depths."[20] This is in contrast to the *récits* themselves, which one can describe as, indeed, already absorbed into this space. One could thus say, if somewhat abusively, that the difference between Blanchot's critical essays on literary space and the literary works in which he and his narrator are "engaged" in this space is itself a spatial difference, in the sense that it can be described, in terms of tonality, rhetoric, and figurative and narrative strategies, as an allegory of inner and outer distances. Blanchot's turn to mythical figures in the critical essays (Orpheus and Eurydice, the Sirens), together with a focus on the generic "experience" of the writer, indicate clearly enough that in these essays we are approaching literary space from somewhere along its edges, according to traditional figural schemas (and on the terrain of a certain cultural inheritance), but also, in most cases, with reference to individual authors and works that often serve as the pretext for broader reflections. It is striking to see Blanchot, so insistent on the impersonality and the loss of the "I," preoccupied with something he calls "Kafka's experience"—and despite his disparagement of diaries, he does not hesitate to quote those of this important predecessor. It is no less striking to see the strange continuity that is maintained between different levels, modes, or avatars of literary experience: as when Ahab must become Melville, or Odysseus Homer, in order to relate their tales (LV 13).

Now the fact that it is quite emphatically a question of experience authorizes us to broach the complex question of autobiography in relation to Blanchot's fictions, if obliquely and with many precautions. Since one of the questions I would like to raise here has to do with the strange relations between the time of a life and the time of writing, over and against Blanchot's absolute foreclosures, it will be all the more important not to reduce that strangeness or to flatten its sinuous paradoxes, much less simply to replace one prioritized mode with another (though there is little risk of reducing Blanchot's fiction to the empirical data of his biography). It is important to stress from the beginning that Blanchot's writing makes demands that, I believe, ought to be heeded in all their complexity, even or especially when the secrets they harbor may be otherwise troubling. If in approaching the question of literary space in Blanchot I insist on some very naive questions—How did he get there? How did that space open for the writer, for Blanchot?—it is not only because Blanchot's own literary essays continually place this question before us, in a logic of the "always already" mentioned above, but also because Blanchot himself later returned to scenes in his own life which he manifestly presented as inaugural moments, violent and disruptive *points* that locate, however problematically, the initiation, confirmation, or affirmation of a vocation, and the decisive inflection of a trajectory located somewhere within a life. One could call each of these a *point de vocation*: the punctuation, puncturing, and decisive rupturing of lived time by a point that abyssally shatters and opens it. Is that where writing begins? With this question in mind, I will first discuss the thematization of the "point" and its exigent fascination in Blanchot's literary essays from the 1950s (especially in *L'espace littéraire* and *Le livre à venir*), before distending this fleeting point in the direction of the later autobiographical texts already mentioned ("(Une scène primitive?)" and *L'instant de ma mort*), in which writing is impelled by past time and by the unworldly instants that continue to resonate through it. What these instants resonate *with*, Blanchot calls an *exigency*, and it is with this term that we can most directly approach the question of the imperative to write in its time-bound origination.

Written as a form of literary journalism, and often tenuously linked to the circumstance of a recent publication, Blanchot's critical essays—not unlike the narratives whose secret structures they strive to articulate—soon leave their occasions behind, in an effort to lay out the most essential features and exigencies of literary experience. Amid the specific questions and issues that arise in relation to the author or topic at hand, Blanchot inevitably returns to a few key terms that together convey, in a kind of schema, the temporal and spatial structure of the literary movement whose unfolding is continually projected in these essays. Indeed, reading Blanchot's essays we are repeatedly reliving the same discoveries, it seems, and yet the obsessive elaboration of this schema somehow manages not to become unnecessarily redundant (insofar as such fascinated repetition is not exhausted by its "content"), for it is dictated by the essentially enigmatic quality of the point that Blanchot persistently strives to approach. And that is precisely the basic form of this schematic movement: the impossible approach to an impossible point that is never fully encountered in its presence and thereby presses with an unaccountable force. The schema thus related, very roughly reduced, can be described roughly in the following terms: the writer, someone who has somehow been knocked, thrown or otherwise impelled out of the bounds of the familiar world, finds himself or herself[21] drawn from the time of the ordinary day (the time of effective work, productive agency, and projects) into an uncanny and anonymous space of writing, cast into an endless movement of sheer image and fascination; in this movement, language itself becomes its own image, goes vainly in search of an extreme and ultimate *point* which, in its tremendous force and ungraspable irreality, threatens to ruin the possibility of the work (*l'oeuvre*) to which at the same time it gives rise—while also transforming the writer into a strange impersonal being, mere shadow and image, who must continually *turn away* from this essential and dangerous point in order to reemerge into the space and time of history with a real artifact, a written work: "*hélas un livre, rien qu'un livre*" ("alas a book, no more than a book"; LV 16).[22] In his literary essays, Blanchot figures this "point" in various ways, or rather he gestures toward it, dramatizes it, and outlines it with figures that can never quite render it—particularly with mythological figures of Odysseus and the singing sirens, Orpheus and Eurydice, Ahab and the whale. The compulsive element of this movement (as reflected in Odysseus' desire to hear, Orpheus' impulse to turn around, Ahab's obsession) is given the name of *fascination*—and I will return to this notion and to the element of imaginary visuality that it calls up. More often, however, and more consistently across his work, Blanchot uses a term that hovers between compulsion and resoluteness, also between passivity and activity, and that places its moving force as much in the thing approached as in the one approaching (for it bears on both, to the point of indistinction): he calls it an *exigency*, a word that punctuates the essays from the 1950s perhaps more than any other major term in Blanchot's critical lexicon. This term designates an essential dimension of writing in its most extreme and denuded, but also its most galvanized movement, a harsh demand that is also a pressing but impersonal need, an imperious force—an *imperative*, in every sense.

If there is something like an "ethics of writing" in Blanchot, it must begin—before beginning—somewhere in the vicinity of this exigency, which itself, however, lies beyond or before any ethics. Blanchot is very clear, even emphatic, about this point, stating that the exigency has no content, is an "*exigence qui n'en est pas une, car elle n'exige rien, elle est sans contenu, elle n'oblige pas, elle est seulement l'air qu'il faut respirer*" ("[an] exigency that is not one, for it demands nothing, it is without content, it does not oblige, it is simply the air one must breathe"; EL 61–62)—a somewhat surprising way to describe it, given that Blanchot usually evokes the suffocating atmosphere of this space, born from an event "*si abrupt qu'il vous coupe le souffle*" ("so abrupt that it takes your breath away"; LV 18). Or when he asks, almost breathlessly:

> Quelle sorte d'exigence s'annonce là [dans l'oeuvre d'art], telle qu'elle ne puisse être captée par aucune des formes morales en cours, qu'elle ne rende pas coupable celui qui la manque, ni innocent celui qui croit l'accomplir, qu'elle nous délivre de toutes les injonctions du "Je dois," de toutes les prétentions du "Je veux" et de toutes les ressources du "Je peux": pour nous laisser libres? mais cependant non pas libres, ni privés de liberté, comme si elle nous attirait en un point où, *épuisé l'air du possible*, s'offre le rapport nu qui n'est pas un pouvoir, qui précède même toute possibilité de relation. (LV 43; my emphasis)

> What sort of exigency is announced there [in the work of art], such that it cannot be captured by any of the moral forms in circulation, does not make guilty the one who has not fulfilled it, or innocent the one who believes he has, such that it delivers us from every injunction of an "I must," every pretention of an "I will" and from all the resources of an "I can": in order to leave us free? and yet neither free nor deprived of freedom, as if it drew us to a point where, *the air of the possible having been exhausted*, there is offered the naked relation that is not a power, that even precedes all possibility of relation.

This "obscure exigency" (the title of the section of the essay from which these quotations are taken) leads us into a region where "*la morale se tait*" (LV 42), where morality falls silent, where the "I" and its speech are denuded of the desire, power, or obligation that would allow us to see this imperious necessity as in some way an ethical duty, but that is stripped of content and even, paradoxically, of any binding, determinate exigency.[23] Blanchot continues: "*Comment ressaisir cette exigence, mot que l'on introduit parce qu'il est incertain et que l'exigence est ici sans exigence?*" ("How to grasp this exigency, a word introduced here because it is uncertain and because here the exigency is without exigency"; LV 43). This exigency maintains strange, forbidding, and playful relations with the law (as we will see below with reference to *La folie du jour*), but it is not the source of any law, nor is it essentially subject to any law, whether it be the absolute (sublime) moral law or the violent law of tyrants and states. "*L'oeuvre d'art ne craint rien de la loi*" ("the work of art fears nothing from the law"; LV 43), writes Blanchot. But as the preceding quotation makes clear, neither is it a matter of freedom. Rather we have to do with an "attraction," a demanding draw or an insistent push toward a point that promises nothing, neither guilty pleasure nor an absolution unto innocence—but that does somehow hold out the prospect of a passionate ecstasy. Again, we will return to this point, for it is the true matter at hand. Its imperious but empty enigma places us in close proximity to an "*il faut*" that it makes resonate as though it were a constraint, an absolute need, a mandate, or a vocation not to be denied. After quoting one of Rilke's letters to a young poet exhorting the latter to ask himself, "Must I write?" Blanchot continues: "*La réponse 'il le faut' peut bien, en effet, être entendue, elle s'entend même constamment, mais ce qu' 'il faut' ne s'entend pas, est réponse à une question qui ne se découvre pas, dont l'approche suspend la réponse et lui ôte la nécessité*" ("The response, 'It is necessary' can indeed be heard, it is even constantly heard, but what 'is necessary' is not heard, is rather a response to a question that is not revealed, the approach to which suspends the response and removes its necessity"; LV 44).[24] The denuded imperative, constantly sounding, is thus emptied of its "what," of any objective or object, and is stripped even of the necessity apparently inscribed within the "*il faut*" that one hears, and that *one continues to hear constantly nonetheless*. The paradoxical result is that a necessity presses all the more categorically in falling short of its own status as necessity. What is left, then, if not merely a voice, one which, even (to paraphrase Blanchot) as that of a "demon" imposing shame, guilt and bad conscience for the frivolity of such a *démarche* (at least in the eyes of the world), invites one ever farther up the imperceptible slope—or down it, it is impossible to say which—into an "other solitude" where none of these categories are operative (LV 47–48).[25] Indeed, we have to do precisely with a voice structured as an imperative on the basis of its own incapacity to dictate a law, an action, anything at all *except its own insistent resonance as a voice*.[26] In that light, Blanchot arrives at the extreme point of paradox prepared by this logic, a point where there is "*plus de faute, mais pas d'innocence*" ("no longer any fault, and yet no innocence"), and where the possibility of ethics itself has been neutralized: for what could possibly be demanded in this exigency, emptied to the point of sheer pressing nullity and disposing of all possibility? "*Rien—sauf ceci qui est l'exigence la plus étrange: qu'à travers lui parle ce qui est sans pouvoir, qu'à partir de là la parole s'annonce elle-même comme l'absence de pouvoir, cette nudité, l'impuissance, mais aussi l'impossibilité, qui est le premier mouvement de la communication*" ("Nothing—except this, which is the strangest exigency: that through it speaks what is without power, that from there speech announces itself as the absence of power, this nakedness that is powerlessness, but also impossibility, which is the first movement of communication"; LV 48). "What" one "must do" is, impossibly, to speak in such a way that speech be denuded of the very power that makes it possible to address anyone at all (in a movement that continually erodes and eludes the performative grasping of power that we saw enacted in Kafka's judgment narratives). Literature is the privileged site or "space" for this inconceivable movement, dictated by a voice without authority, in relation to which neither failure nor attainment has any hold.

Such language—such thinking—calls to mind later texts by Blanchot which more heavily foreground the question of speech's powerlessness, its originary rupturing of every relation, as the very ground of any relation that this same speech would make possible, texts including certain essays in *L'entretien infini*, but especially *Le pas au-delà* and *L'écriture du désastre*. These texts have largely left behind the directly literary preoccupations that preponderate in the period we are considering here. But this evocation of an ethics of speech that precedes, exceeds (falls short of) and undoes all ethics, in the context of a discourse on literature, crucially shows that Blanchot's later thought on the neuter, the relation without relation, "*le rapport du troisième genre*,"[27] were formed by way of the experience of literary language as an impossible response to a voice demanding nothing but the transmission of its own empty and powerless insistence. The specifically literary context, however, which Blanchot later attenuated to the point of becoming almost apologetic in raising it again,[28] leaves intact an element of figuration that deeply and intensely haunts the fiction that he wrote during this period. Before moving on in his later works to eliminate virtually all scenographic and figural presentation in his writing, given over more and more to reflection, dialogue, and the fragment, Blanchot formulates the paradoxical exigency of writing in a register that implies a working through of figuration and narrative. In general, one can ask about the significance of this shift, which entailed the disappearance of fictive figures, including the feminine figures who populate so many of his narratives, together with the disappearance of the motifs of passionate attachment and eroticism, which play such a crucial, if elusive, role in the *récits*. Moving quickly, we can ask (crudely, doubtless naively): Could it be that Blanchot had in some way "exhausted" certain passionate obsessions embedded in the specifically literary (narrative, figural) adventure? Did they somehow fade or lose their draw, their edge, their pointed urgency? It is intriguing to speculate that a certain passion—pressing, mad and yet measured, striving blandly for eternity—somehow attenuated over the course of Blanchot's writing, and that this attenuation is also that of literature itself, insofar as literature, for Blanchot, is founded on the haunting of a fascinating image. It is of course difficult to answer such a question. But it is worth noting, on the way to a discussion of the feminine figures in the *récits*, that the incandescent matters of desire, love, and women which electrify the literary work also virtually disappear—with one important exception, in the essay "Une voix venue d'ailleurs" (1992), which strikes a late and uncharacteristic note of melancholic nostalgia that one could even call *sentimental*. The "*rapport du troisième genre*" will have elided, perhaps, the tremendous force of the feminine and the erotic relation. And it is clearly the case that, within the Blanchotian corpus, this is also to some extent an elision of the literary work in its involvement with inscenated figures, and in its absorption into "*la profondeur du récit.*"

To return to the exigency, then, as voiced in a literary space determined as narrative fiction, we see that it insistently places denuded speech in relation to an image, a relation that remains nonrelation but within the ecstatic medium of time, that is, in the form of a narrative unfolding in the direction of its own originary consummation. This structure, which gives the schema of Blanchot's first and most passionate articulation of writing's necessity, places this necessity within the field of force that he calls *fascination*, and gives it the form of a temporal adventure that constantly begs, and withdraws, the question of its initiation *in a singular time*, and *in the order of events*. In other words, the necessity of writing, as an unaccountable demand *to relate* (in every sense) *without relation*, constantly brushes against the "linear" contours—figural, temporal and narrative—which it thereby also twists, convolutes, diffuses, blurs, and fades. That is, finally, language's rupture of relation, modulated through literary fiction, thus entails a confrontation, in all obliquity, with the problems of chronology, reference, and representation. Fiction becomes its own mode of reality, bracketing not only the events related, but also the one relating them, while also threatening this strange narrating being with a kind of existence more complex, and more dangerous, than mere unreality; likewise, the question of this being's origination and trajectory, its very strange "life," becomes more impossible to track than ever. Let us look at this difficult negotiation as Blanchot articulates it in the crucial opening sections of *Le livre à venir*.

LITERARY SPACE AND THE VIOLENCE OF BEGINNING

Le livre à venir presents, in its first two chapters, a striking juxtaposition: on one hand, in "La rencontre de l'imaginaire," the fabulous song of the sirens, sounding deeply and distantly within a space severed from the past, and on the other (in the chapter that follows), Proust's *Recherche*, the great novel of time lost and found, whose heavily circumstantial turn toward the time of a life renders that life's remnant tales—and especially its loves and past suffering—unto literature.[29] This juxtaposition aligns these stories, and the "experience" to which they bear witness (the second chapter is called "L'expérience de Proust") in such a way as to suggest an imaginary point of convergence lying somewhere on the horizon surrounding the figures and narrative/narrated circumstances projected in each one. At one level, the implication is clear enough: even Proust's "lost time," the grand edifice of the past that the novel mounts, is no less "absolutely separate" from real time than the fabulous and elusive music of the Sirens. And certainly this is true insofar as Proust's tale, too, is a fiction born of fascination, albeit a heavily autobiographical one (and we will return in a moment to the question of an irresistible conflation that haunts the reading of this work). But what does this convergence say about the paradoxical irruption of writing's beginning into the texture or *trame* of a life, especially given that Proust's narrative is that of a "vocation" whose punctual revelations pierce the plot of a single life otherwise at risk of oblivion? Let us briefly situate this point as Blanchot elucidates it in the opening essay of *Le livre à venir*, before asking whether the treatment of Proust, in all its complexity, might not strain too tautly toward the sirenic erasure of someone's (written) life.

The Secret Law of the Récit

In Blanchot's version of literary experience, what essentially drives the writer can be described, schematically, as the attraction and fascination of a *point*. Both the goal and the origin of the alluring oeuvre it seems to promise, this point and its twisting force are what give the space of the *récit* its paradoxical temporality: a "past" point of origination as the beckoning distance of an encounter *to come*, at once inflecting past and future through the indefinite present of the recitical space, in what Blanchot describes (once again in a Heideggerian mode) as a coincidence and imaginary simultaneity of the "temporal ecstasies" (LV 18). But the force of this point is such that it gives rise to the unfolding of a narrative and to a movement described as an encounter. I will cite a well-known passage from "La rencontre de l'imaginaire" that condenses the essential features of this paradoxical spatial-temporal structure.

> Le caractère du récit n'est nullement pressenti, quand on voit en lui la relation vraie d'un événement exceptionnel, qui a eu lieu et qu'on essaierait de rapporter. Le récit n'est pas la relation de l'événement, mais cet événement même, le lieu où celui-ci est appelé à se produire, événement encore à venir et par la puissance attirante duquel le récit peut espérer, lui aussi, se réaliser.

> [T]he character of the *récit* is in no way understood when one sees in it the true relation of an exceptional event that took place and that one attempts to report. The *récit* is not the relation of the event, but the event itself, the approach to the event, the place in which the event is called upon to occur, an event still to come and by whose attractive power the *récit* too can hope to be realized.

The event to be recounted is not located inertly in the past, a parcel of reality awaiting its representation and conveyance in the medium of narrative speech; rather the event, the encounter—such as that between Odysseus and the sirens, Ahab and the whale—

which narrative speech situates in the past tense, is in fact, for the writer under its sway, still something yet to come, an imminence whose lack of reality awaits its realization in the *récit* itself, and *as* the realization of that *récit*, which nonetheless depends on it as a generative moment of beginning, as a force impelling the voice that speaks it, so that it might be. In the next paragraph, this paradox is condensed into the point we are seeking:

> C'est là un rapport très délicat, sans doute une sorte d'extravagance, mais elle est la loi secrète du récit. Le récit est mouvement vers un point, non seulement inconnu, ignoré, étranger, mais tel qu'il ne semble avoir, par avance et en dehors de ce mouvement, *aucune sorte de réalité*, si *impérieux* cependant que c'est de lui seul que le récit tire son attrait, de telle manière qu'il ne peut même "commencer" avant de l'avoir atteint, mais cependant c'est seulement le récit et le mouvement imprévisible du récit qui fournissent l'espace où le point devient réel, puissant et attirant. (LV 14; my emphasis)

> This is a very delicate relation, no doubt a kind of extravagance, but it is the secret law of the *récit*. The *récit* is the movement toward a point, not only unknown, unheard-of and strange, but also such that it seems to have, in advance and outside of this movement, *no reality of any kind*, and yet which is so *imperious* that it is from this point alone that the *récit* draws its attraction, in such a way that it cannot even "begin" before having reached this point; but at the same time it is only the *récit* and the unpredictable movement of the *récit* that provides the space in which the point becomes real, powerful and attractive.

A point of beginning that must already have been reached, an "imperious" point which alone draws the *récit* imperatively into being, yet also an obscure, unattainable, radically unreal point that cannot even first come to be without the space opened *for it* by the movement of narration that has, however, been initiated only *by it* and its imaginary force: such is the multiply looping circuit of what Blanchot calls "the outside" insofar as it is structured by the extreme and singular point of an encounter-event, impossible encounter with the sheer promise of a worldless absolute, the threat of "*cet espace sans monde*" ("this space without world"; LV 16). Blanchot also calls it "*la voix du gouffre*" ("the voice of the abyss"; LV 15), the song of the sirens falling silent in dangerous proximity to the one who would hear it, in "*la région-mère de la musique*" ("the mother-region of music"; LV 10) that is also the only place that is completely devoid of music. This extra-vagance, this wandering out and away, is a "relation" and a secret law: it must have preceded its own beginning in language, otherwise speech would not begin; and yet it must take place uniquely in the language that relates it, and is it.

With these circuitous formulations I am trying to say, to reiterate, the "*il faut*" that fissures and opens Blanchot's recitical space as a *faille*, a fault and an *écart*, an irreducible distance across which a narrative voice must reach toward its own compelling point of origination, in a time that also opens every "now" to its self-divided spacing.[30] What is remarkable is that, as mentioned, for Blanchot during this period, this division opens a space inhabited by the strange present of an *image*, in relation to which (a distant, untraversable relation) literary speech is compelled to begin, but in the time of its already having begun.

Proust and Past Time: A Fascinating Confusion

Now it is significant that in stripping this "already" and its image-encounter of any determinate past, Blanchot turns in this context—that of a rereading of the mythic tale of the sirens—to none other than Proust, for whom the sirenic encounter, in its promise of a work to come, "semble *aussi le renvoyer vers la profondeur du passé*" ("*seems* also to direct him back toward the depth of the past"; LV 17, my emphasis). Blanchot will attempt to attenuate even this semblance, thus aiming at the very structure and matter of Proust's work and thought, particularly with regard to the narration of a "vocation" concretely visited upon a man who is not yet a writer but who *must become one* on the basis of a charged but intermittent relation to the past. Since Blanchot is preoccupied here precisely with the obscure and twisting passage from life to writing and back again, it is worth examining for a moment the complexities of his extremely equivocal treatment of "Proust" and the "experience" that makes him write.

Of course, it is true that the "past" recounted in Proust's *Recherche* is only a "seeming" past, a fiction; but Blanchot means something more radical than this merely generic observation, of which he is of course aware, yet which he also seems continually to disregard, precisely when referring to the relation between Proust's writing and the life it "seems" to write. Conflating author with narrator (as many critics have done), Blanchot then, quite strangely, treats this novelistic life as the real life whose derealization he must assert in the name of literature's total unreality—this in order to void the biographical past from which the fiction was *drawn* (in every sense: recall Proust's metaphor of multiple models sitting for a single written portrait). This complex approach is all the more striking, and confusing, in connection with the revelatory experiences of sensation-memory that punctuate the novel, and the "life" of its character/narrator, analogues to the disruptive and promising encounter, the fascinating point, that Blanchot poses as its secret law. Whatever the complexities of Proust's novelistic elaboration of biographical material, it is quite jarring to read the naive "objection" that Blanchot projects as a response to the irreducible futurity of the sirenic encounter he has just described, in a formulation that brackets (in quotes) the past "life" it seems to vindicate, but that, on many levels, never was:

> On objectera: mais à la "vie" de Melville, de Nerval, de Proust appartient d'abord cet événement dont ils parlent. C'est parce qu'ils ont déjà rencontré Aurélia, parce qu'ils ont heurté les pavés inégaux, vu les trois clochers qu'ils peuvent se mettre à écrire. Ils déploient beaucoup d'art pour nous communiquer leurs impressions

réelles, et ils sont artistes en cela qu'ils trouvent un équivalent—de forme, d'image, d'histoire ou de mots—pour nous faire participer à une vision proche de la leur.

One will object: but the event of which Melville, Nerval, or Proust speaks belongs first to their "life." It is because they have already encountered Aurélia, because they have stumbled on the uneven paving stones, have seen the three steeples, that they are able to begin writing. They deploy a great deal of art to communicate their real impressions to us, and they are artists in that they find an equivalent—of form, image, story or words—to make us participate in a vision that approximates their own.

"*Les choses*," adds Blanchot in admonition, "*ne sont malheureusement pas aussi simples*" ("things are unfortunately not so simple"; LV 17). Indeed, they are not, and with this supposedly commonsense objection, they are becoming more and more complicated. First of all, we might point out that such a statement could be made only by someone who has collapsed Proust into his novel, that is, by someone like Blanchot, for whom such fictional encounters, in a genuine enigma, take on the status of experiences no less real than any other (as they do earlier in this essay with reference to Odysseus becoming Homer, and Ahab becoming Melville . . .). And everywhere it is clear that when Blanchot refers to "Proust," he means virtually anything but the biographical personage who answered to this name (a being he refers to more than once as "*le fils d'Adrien Proust*" ("the son of Adrien Proust"; LV 24, 29)—as though the status of *son* were a less ambiguous sign of extraliterary existence). This need not pose a significant problem, in the end, if it were not that in speaking of "Proust" as the man who has lived through the events narrated in the *Recherche*, Blanchot also wants to say something decisive regarding the relation between that past life and the exigency of writing that appears to issue from it—indeed he *wants to deny such a relation* as having any essential role in the formation of the writer. This vertiginous gesture cannot be equated with the notion, for example, that the narrator of the *Recherche* did not actually write the book he has finally resolved to write at the end (indeed, Blanchot does not appear to believe this, speaking instead of the "circular," or even spherical, structure of the work, which, he says, recounts the formation of the one who wrote it; LV 26). The past life that gave rise to this story is, for Blanchot, never anything other than the one that it itself recounts, so that it is precisely the *fictional* rendering of that life and its "marvelous shocks" (LV 35) that Blanchot must, more paradoxically than ever, strip away from the time and space of literature.[31] Matters become all the more vexed when we note that, in the opening lines of the essay on Proust, Blanchot speaks of *Proust's* confusion—"*une confusion fascinante*"—between "*la navigation imaginaire*," in the manner of Odysseus, and "*sa vie réelle*," a "real life" immediately transposed into the decisive terms we have already encountered: "*celle qui l'a amené, à travers les embûches du monde et par le travail du temps destructeur, jusqu'au point fabuleux où il rencontre l'événement qui rend possible tout récit*" ("the one that led him through the traps of the world and by the destructive work of time, to the fabulous point where he encounters the event that makes possible every story"; LV 19). These accumulated confusions lead Blanchot to pose the very question begged by his paradoxical articulations of life and writing, but also to give it a no less confusing answer: For if "real" life, for Proust, somehow leads into the unreality of the sirens' singing, "*alors comment peut-il jamais 'en venir là,' s'il lui faut précisément être déjà là, pour que la stérile migration antérieure devienne le mouvement réel et vrai capable d'y conduire?*" ("then how can he ever 'get there,' if he must precisely already be there, so that the preceding sterile migration may become the real and true movement capable of guiding him there"; LV 19). The reader will recognize here the problem we have been exploring all along. Blanchot's answer is really quite disorienting.

> C'est que Proust, par une confusion fascinante, tire des singularités du temps propre au récit, singularités qui pénètrent sa vie, les ressources qui lui permettent aussi de sauver le temps réel. (LV 19–20)
>
> It is because Proust, through a fascinating confusion, draws from the singularities of the time proper to the story—singularities that penetrate his life—the resources that also allow him to save real time.

I will not venture to fully parse the dense intrications and reversals that characterize this "confusion" as formulated here—in which "real time" seems to mean the radically *unreal* time of literature's scrambled and spatialized temporal ecstasies insofar as they have been projected from out of the work, while the "time of the *récit*" seems to refer to "real" time as lived . . . in a story (precisely the fictional, autobiographically structured story *that Proust has written*, that constitutes his work). I would simply like to remark that if we are attempting to trace a movement "into" literary space, this strange formulation does not breach that border, for according to its terms we are still, and always, "already there." This is the case even as Blanchot invokes the singularities that, in penetrating the life of a writer, would allow him to *draw from it* the resources, the figural shapes, of an uncanny adventure. Is it not possible that such a "drawing" (which I have also called a derivation) does not also reach, if ungraspingly, toward a sphere in which an ambiguously identifiable *fils de famille* has navigated through a landscape marked by a history of affective attachments and detachments, that is, marked by history as figural and fantasmatic investments, losses, and unaccountable transformations? This, too, is an essential dimension of Proust's narrative, and of the experience that casts its originating impulse as a past-haunted vocation. Perhaps this is precisely what is so fascinating about the confusion that Blanchot indicates, where literary and real time are deeply enmeshed and interpenetrating, where each serves as a "resource" for the other, in a zone of indistinction that both precedes and seals their difference.

Now, in speaking of "resources," one risks slipping into a certain mystification—as the novel in question certainly invites one to do—regarding the "richness" of experience projected and safeguarded, not to say exploited or extracted, by a massive and monumental work such as Proust's; likewise with regard to the notion of "saving" time, or finding it again. And yet one cannot help but sense that a too great violence is done to Proust when Blanchot reduces the essential matter of the *Recherche* to a purely void sirenic tale stripped of all its decisive links to a past and its painfully, or gradually, imprinted figures (however fungible these may be).[32] In an attempt to straddle the two modes of "formative" time at work in "Proust's" vocation, to articulate its long cumulative duration with its sudden and intermittent revelations, Blanchot speaks of a transformation that occurs "*aussitôt quoique peu à peu*" ("immediately yet little by little"; LV 26)—a phrase that has already appeared twice before in the converse order ("*peu à peu quoique aussitôt*"; LV 16, 22), but that is here reversed, as though to facilitate the abrupt and pointed emphasis that Blanchot clearly wants to give it. One might encapsulate the point by saying that despite the insistence on this remarkable formula, Blanchot really does not do justice to the *peu à peu*, the indefinite extension of a "*longtemps*" without which, after all, nothing could begin, but with which, in Proust, everything literally does begin. Indeed, it is in order to lay such a long duration aside that Blanchot introduces the expression here, after a quotation from *Le temps retrouvé* that bears precisely on the *material* with which a life "nourishes" the vocation that springs from it; it is worth giving this quotation at length, as Blanchot does:

> Ainsi toute ma vie jusqu'à ce jour aurait pu et n'aurait pas pu être résumée sous ce titre: Une vocation. Elle ne l'aurait pas pu en ce sens que la littérature n'avait joué aucun rôle dans ma vie. Elle l'aurait pu en ce que cette vie, les souvenirs des ses tristesses, de ses joies formaient une réserve pareille à cet albumen qui est logé dans l'ovule des plantes et dans lequel celui-ci puise sa nourriture pour se transformer en graine . . . (*Recherche* 3:899)

> Thus my entire life up to that day could have and could not have been summed up under this title: A vocation. It could not have been, in the sense that literature had played no role in my life. It could have been, in that this life, the memories of its sadnesses and its joys, formed a reserve similar to that albumen lodged in the ovule of plants and from which the ovule draws its nourishment in order to transform itself into a seed . . .

This is from the same passage in which the narrator states, as a preface to the preceding quotation: "*je compris que tous les matériaux de l'oeuvre littéraire, c'était ma vie passée*" ("I understood that all the material for the literary work lay in my past life"). Once again, one might well be wary of such totalizing gestures (toute *ma vie* . . . tous *les matériaux* . . .), which operate the work's crucial, and generative, mystification, precisely that of a life's capacity to be synthesized into a whole; no less than the problematic organic metaphor of nourishment and of the forming and developing seed that would lead to a heretofore unconscious "maturation" ("*Ainsi ma vie était-elle en rapport avec ce qu'amènerait sa maturation*" ["Thus my life was related to what its maturation would bring"]).[33] But the image of a life's "material" deposited, sedimented, or imprinted like a residue is one that Blanchot himself has found indispensable, as we will see with regard especially to *L'arrêt de mort*. The fact that he evokes there the image of an essential but enigmatic "shell" left behind by events suggests that the reconfiguration he proposes—in voiding the remainder of its living center—is played out on the same terrain, as yet another mode of time's residual insistence. The convergence of these concerns, that is, of Blanchot's own "experience" and the one he finds in Proust, occurs in the last sentences of the section I have been quoting. Referring to the "slippage," through scrambled time and space, of a transformation that separates the writer from himself, drawing him out of himself toward that part of him that has become imaginary ("*et d'abord cette main qui écrit*" ["and first of all this hand that writes"]), Blanchot writes:

> Glissement dont Proust, par une décision énergique, a essayé de faire un mouvement de *résurrection* du passé. Mais qu'a-t-il reconstitué? qu'a-t-il sauvé? Le passé imaginaire d'un être *déjà* tout imaginaire et séparé de lui-même par toute une suite vacillante et fugitive de "Je" qui peu à peu l'ont *dépouillé de soi*, délivré aussi du passé et, par ce sacrifice héroïque, l'ont mis à la disposition de l'imaginaire dont il a pu alors disposer. (LV 28; my emphasis)

> A slippage that Proust, in a forceful decision, tried to make into a movement of *resurrecting* the past. But what did he reconstruct? what did he save? The imaginary past of a being *already* entirely imaginary and separated from himself by an entire series, vacillating and fleeting, of I's which little by little *stripped him of his self*, also delivered him from the past and, through this heroic sacrifice, placed him at the disposition of the imaginary, which he was then able to make use of.

Proust, *mon semblable, mon frère*: Blanchot too will write, in *L'arrêt de mort*, of resurrection, of self-separation, of being stripped of oneself to the point of becoming something of a wandering corpse, and (thus) of being liberated from the past in such a way as to inaugurate the reign of an affirmation no longer in need of the material whose fading shapes were required to arrive at it. In a sense, what Blanchot says here is incontestable: the "past" and selves "resurrected" in Proust, and in any other fiction, *indeed in any narrative at all*, cannot exit the realm of the imaginary and are thus forever consigned to the distance and separation inherent to it, no matter how real they have seemed. I would simply like to point down the other slope of this inevitability, toward an equally inevitable aspect that forms the paradox at issue, according to which a resurrected past and self, all imaginary and ungraspable, nonetheless has a history that cannot help but obtrude in the shapes that give it a face, as it were, in a way that cannot help but problematize the I's total sacrifice. The sacrifice in question would be "heroic" partly because it remains sublime, as does the tremendous return projected here as a now destitute world henceforth eternally available (strongly inflected in Blanchot's case by the fact that this sacrifice will also be that of a woman). For now, the doubtless naive question still remains as to how one passes "into" the space of a literary vocation that must always already be underway. Is there a point at which this movement can be said to begin?

Before looking at the complex structure of this movement in the *récits*, however, I would like to jump to a later moment in Blanchot's corpus in which this animating feminine figure has in fact long disappeared, but where the question of a life's disruption by an evocative puncture is directly staged. Blanchot spent decades emphatically *not* writing about himself, at times disparaging the "temptation" to do so (as in "Le journal intime et le récit"). And yet in two of his most important late texts, Blanchot turns toward himself as a young man, and as a child—indeed as another who used to be these but is no more, but in "scenes" which imply that this having-been is far from indifferent to the project of writing that would have delivered from them someone who was, or who became, a writer. Both of these apparently autobiographical texts, the brief section entitled "(Une scène primitive?)" in *L'écriture du désastre* and the very late narrative *L'instant de ma mort*, have received a great deal of commentary, to which I do not pretend to add more than one small point here. But it is a troubling point that sharply calls into question the absolute separation from a life's "singularities," while also giving us some vivid hints regarding what I have called the *point de vocation*, its structure and force, the persistence of its figural, material and "vocal" instantiation. The very fact that Blanchot would "turn toward himself," however distantly and obliquely, should arouse our interest and alert us to the singular force exerted by these instants insisting on a past.

THE INSISTING INSTANT: *L'INSTANT DE MA MORT*

L'instant de ma mort was Blanchot's last major text. He was in his eighties when he published it in 1994, clearly offering it as something of a testamentary writing, a final *récit* that, unlike those written decades earlier, locates itself, however problematically and disjointedly, as much in historical as in literary time and space—or perhaps one could say, in a space that renders these categories difficult to distinguish. The story refers to events during World War II, to geographically locatable places, and to the author, albeit across the distance of a grammatical third person and in the impossible guise of "my death." Its narrative tone and movement do not sit altogether comfortably with the extreme and hyperbolic rhetoric of the great literary essays of the 1950s—whose insistence on withdrawal and exit, on the absoluteness of literary space, can, however, be biographically related to the violent and ecstatic borderline experience related in this wartime story. Blanchot's postwar withdrawal into literary space here finds itself converging with the historical and (dare I say) personal exigency of a testimony.[34] This is a story that must cite its dates; but, as we will see, it is also compelled to wrench them out of the calendar of historical events. The *déchirure* of this wrenching locates, strangely and problematically, a rupture or puncture of the writer's life, the empty hole of a persistent and originary instant. This hole, it turns out, is a feeling, the remains of a pointed ecstasy distended through time.

The story takes place in 1944, at a time when Blanchot had already ceased for several years the "worldly" political journalism that had dominated the previous decade. In that regard, the "young man" he tells of here is already in a certain state of withdrawal. The brutal facts of France's defeat and the German occupation, along with the compromises that led up to these national failures, played a major role in this rupture (*L'arrêt de mort* will give, in 1948, some important indications regarding this break in its own historical references to the period leading up to the war, beginning in 1938). In 1944, Blanchot recounts, "*les Allemands, déjà vaincus, luttaient en vain avec une inutile férocité*" ("the Germans, already beaten, were fighting in vain with a useless ferocity"; IM 7). They knock on the door of the house inhabited by the "young man" (Blanchot's family house in Burgundy, though the text does not directly identify it as such). A Nazi lieutenant calls him and his family outside, brandishes weapons and ammunition, and then "*mit en rang ses hommes pour atteindre, selon les règles, la cible humaine*" ("placed his men in a row in order to strike, according to the rules, the human target"). What the text leaves unstated, and must be inferred by the reader, is that "*les douilles, les balles, une grenade*" ("the cartridges, the bullets, a grenade"; IM 9) that the lieutenant accusingly places before the young man are simultaneously the evidence, the verdict, the sentence and (synecdochally) the means of execution in a *trial* pronouncing Blanchot guilty of collaborating with the *maquis*—who in fact show up later in the text to "*porter secours à celui qu'ils savaient en danger*" ("to bring help to the one they knew was in danger"; IM 11). If there has been a literary withdrawal, then, it has taken place at the level of writing, while another sort of engagement pursues its worldly course, attested here in Blanchot's style of extreme indirection. If this text is a kind of testimony, it is partly to this that Blanchot wants to testify: he worked, and perhaps fought, on the side of the *maquis*. He broke with the right-wing politics that he had espoused in the 1930s and that led others to collaborate with the collaborators. Now, it is not my concern here to investigate the rich but equivocal gesture this text thus carries out—a political and historically charged gesture that seeks, precisely, to link the story to the past of the one who wrote it, possibly for very pragmatic purposes—but rather, for the moment, to place this gesture in tension with another dimension of the story to which Blanchot's text bears witness, and to which it gives a strange and perhaps troubling priority.

For if this political gesture constitutes one level of the testimony in question, there is another that is presented as more ecstatic, enigmatic, and "transcendental," more "essential" (a word that is used in this text as well; IM 15). Like the earlier "purely" fictional *récits* (which however are closely subsequent to the experience narrated here), it attempts to approach an encounter that both has and has not happened, this time an encounter with what Blanchot calls "death itself" (IM 20), in an event/experience that disrupts the order of narratable events which have placed him in this extreme position—against the wall, facing death, waiting for the guns to fire. It also produces an equivocating *glissement* in the limpid language of this text. Reverting to the first person, Blanchot writes:

Je sais—le sais-je—que celui que visaient déjà les allemands, n'attendant plus que l'ordre final, éprouva alors un sentiment de légèreté extraordinaire, une sorte de béatitude (rien d'heureux cependant), —allégresse souveraine? La rencontre de la mort et de la mort?

A sa place, je ne chercherai pas à analyser ce sentiment de légèreté. Il était peut-être tout à coup invincible. Mort—immortel. Peut-être l'extase. Plutôt le sentiment de compassion pour l'humanité souffrante, le bonheur de n'être pas immortel ni éternel. Désormais, il fut lié à la mort, par une amitié subreptice.

I know—do I know it—that the one at whom the Germans were already aiming, waiting only for the final order, experienced then an extraordinary feeling of lightness, a sort of beatitude (and yet nothing happy)—sovereign elation? The encounter of death and death?

In his place, I will not seek to analyze this feeling of lightness. He was perhaps suddenly invincible. Dead—immortal. Ecstasy perhaps. Rather the feeling of compassion for humanity in its suffering, the good fortune of being neither immortal nor eternal. From now on, he was bound to death, by a surreptitious friendship.

As though to underscore the unworldly space of this double encounter with death and with death, as it slips inevitably toward a kind of allegory of itself, Blanchot adds: "*A cet instant, brusque retour au monde, éclata le bruit considérable d'une proche bataille*" ("at this instant, an abrupt return to the world, there burst forth the considerable noise of a nearby battle"). Enter the maquis, who provide the occasion for Blanchot's real life escape. Is it pressing too hard on the word *considérable* to glimpse in it, through an etymological link, the sidereal space that will later be voided of its astral order (by the dis/aster evoked in *L'écriture du désastre*), but that here, in this worldly instant is rather an abrupt return *to* that order (and to the time of datable events)? For there is clearly more than one kind of instant—though it is tempting to say that they pass or flow through the same tiny hole in experience, articulating two sides of time, as it were. On one side, the suspension of passing time, the "instancing" (if one can put it thus), of a feeling of lightness, an opening of the extraordinary, and with it, the unbinding bond of a strange, secret, and surreptitious friendship with death, in a literal "subreption" of what is otherwise *unfigurable*, a gesture in the direction of the residually sublime (whose most proper rhetorical name is *allegory*). Further, one might well hear in this affirmation of a friendship with an impossible Other an echo—placed retroactively prior to what it echoes—of the declaration of love addressed to *une pensée* at the end of the first postwar *récit*, *L'arrêt de mort*. As though it were always, with this *thought*, a question of death and perhaps even of this death, encountering itself and itself, in 1944. This instant thus draws us into an extremely complicated temporal structure with many levels of implicit consequence. Let us follow its logic for a moment along the border that is supposed to separate "the empirical and the essential," as Blanchot puts it in a later passage. It may be that these are not so easy to distinguish; indeed, it can be argued that their indistinction, their porous, hazy, and unfixable border, is crucial to this tale.

Blanchot relates that when the considerable noise of a nearby battle erupted, the Nazi lieutenant left the scene to see what was happening, and in his absence one of the soldiers—who in an extraordinary twist turn out to be not Germans but rather Russians of the Vlassov army—"*lui fit signe de disparaître*" ("signaled to him to disappear"), which he does.[35] He runs off to hide and wait in the woods. In the meantime, the Nazis/Russians wreak havoc in the area, burning all the farms, and killing three farmers' sons, apparently in place of the young *châtelain*, the castle-dweller who has escaped, and whose "castle" remains intact.

> Les seigneurs avaient été épargnés . . . Alors commença sans doute pour le jeune homme le tourment de l'injustice. Plus d'extase; le sentiment qu'il n'était vivant que parce que, même aux yeux des Russes, il appartenait à une classe noble.
>
> The lords of the land had been spared. . . . Then began for the young man, no doubt, the torment of injustice. No more ecstasy; the feeling that he was alive only because, even in the eyes of the Russians, he belonged to a noble class.

A different, no longer ecstatic feeling, and a first irrecoverable loss emerge in the text: a loss of justice and, more concretely, of innocent lives perceived to be lower and more disposable. The three dead farmers' sons are described as "*bien étrangers à tout combat, et qui n'avaient pour tort que leur jeunesse*" ("strangers to all combat, whose only wrong was their youth")—in other words, they had *not* been involved with the *maquis*, but had died in place of someone who had been. The young man's very survival is thus based on an injustice that is both intensively localized and of tremendous historical resonance.

In an amplification of both of these dimensions, the sparing of the castle-dwelling writer, and of "the castle" itself, occasions an excursus on the cultural and historical inscriptions of this dwelling: Was the Nazi lieutenant sufficiently cultivated (like the officer in Vercors's *Le silence de la mer*?) to know his historical dates, such as the one over the door of the house: 1807? This was the year, Blanchot writes, when Napoleon, Hegel's "world soul," entered Jena on his small gray horse. But Hegel, who in these grave matters "knew how to distinguish the empirical and the essential," surely also knew how to read a calendar, which that year would have borne the date 1806, not 1807. In a further and surely just as deliberate twisting of calendar time, Blanchot has also added two years to the life of his family's "Castle," which according to his biographer, Christophe Bident, says very clearly over the door: 1809 (an inversion of Napoleon's 6?). Bident also reports that Blanchot was fascinated by numerology, particularly with reference to dates, and a similarly playful manipulation of dates in *L'arrêt de mort*, together with various references there to chiromancy and alchemy, give some support to this claim.[36] I would only signal the fact that the preferred but fictive year of 1807 is exactly one hundred years before Blanchot's own birth, thus uncannily aligning, in a strange sidereal resonance, these disparate events.[37] I will resist the temptation to elaborate on this displaced date of birth—for example with reference to Blanchot's treatment of "*maisons*" and dwellings, their uncanny transformational exchanges with high-placed characters (*Aminadab*) and the role of a certain well known literary castle in the birth of Blanchot the writer—in order to point out simply that these manipulations puncture yet another hole, in the historical appurtenance of the experience in question in this text, thus complicating yet further the location of this experience and the generic principles of the text that would convey it—a tiny but decisive grain of fiction that unhinges it from its (autobiographical, historical) facts, dissolving (or ab-solving) its bond with the history that frames it. These facts, while necessarily embedded in the very stuff of the story—surely, they are part of the point (as one says)—are as though already lost, fugitive, passing, and effaced, in comparison with what more essentially remains, the *demeure* not so much of a dwelling as of an enduring and elusive feeling.[38] It is to this feeling that Blanchot wants, "essentially," to bear witness. After relating the injustice of arbitrary vengeful death and class privilege, the text returns to the *demeure* in its more permanent, more ungraspable remainder: the feeling of lightness. Blanchot writes:

> Demeurait cependant, au moment où la fusillade n'était plus qu'en attente, le sentiment de légèreté que je ne saurais traduire: libéré de la vie? l'infini qui s'ouvre? Ni bonheur, ni malheur. Ni l'absence de crainte et peut-être déjà le pas au-delà. Je sais, j'imagine que ce sentiment inanalysable changea ce qui lui restait d'existence. Comme si la mort hors de lui ne pouvait désormais que se heurter à la mort en lui. "Je suis vivant. Non, tu es mort."

> There remained, however, at the moment when the rifles were suspended in waiting, the feeling of lightness that I could never translate: liberated from life? infinity opening? Neither happiness nor misfortune. Nor the absence of fear and perhaps the step/not beyond. I know, I imagine that this unanalyzable feeling changed what existence remained to him. As if the death outside of him could from now on only collide with the death in him. "I am alive. No, you are dead."

What remains, what abides and dwells in the punctuated but distended time of the *désormais*, is a *feeling* that resists translation and analysis, that in demanding name and witness gives rise only to the slippage of tentative formulations and the quasi-figural compromise of a *comme si* ("*Comme si la mort . . .*"): as though the essential point of this feeling-instant were a strange allegorical conversation between death and death. "I am alive. No, you are dead." An encounter and a shock that takes place along a border between two deaths: an "already" and a "to-come," an inside and an outside, which continually change places—"externalizing" the death that has happened, "internalizing" the death that is coming. It is there, in the mobile, unlocatable, untranslatable *now* of the *from now on*—the *or* of *désormais*—that the insistent *pressure* of the event continues to exert itself, to be felt, to dwell, haunt, and obsess, pressing forth above all *into speech*, a necessarily fictive testimonial speech that would convey not a set of facts and deeds but an untranslatable sentiment, sealing a death-bound speech that may also be a liberation from life.

Now we also encounter here a precise point where this text intersects with the question of life, writing and vocation, even more particularly, and unexpectedly, with their rendering in the essay on Proust from four decades earlier. Proust, who famously likened the writer's task to that of a translator,[39] also structured the narrative of the writer's vocation as a series of instants with the puncturing force of a *désormais* (drawn out, in his case, in the intermittent drama of illumination and relapse). And just as Proust stages these moments as the irruption into a life of experiences that would instantiate an insistent imperative to write, here too Blanchot locates in historical time, and in his own life, albeit in an extremely problematic and ambiguous way, a point that divides this life in two (at least two), infusing it with a sharp feeling that might indeed be considered transcendental, both constituting and separated from life, and that, as he writes in a pointed use of the simple past, "*changea ce qui lui restait d'existence*" ("changed whatever existence remained to him"). It is true that so far in this text Blanchot has said nothing explicitly concerning the relation of this violent experience to the exigency or imperative to write—though he does mention a manuscript taken from the house by the pillaging soldiers, another irrecoverable loss, to which I will return in a moment. But it is arguably the case that the fundamental subtext of the entire piece is the establishment—the retrospective (re)casting—of an in-dwelling death-bound drive to write, and there is a clear indication of this in the line just quoted, which I give here again in its complete form: "*Je sais—j'imagine—que ce sentiment inanalysable changea* ce qui lui restait d'existence" ("I know—I imagine—that this unanalyzable feeling changed *whatever existence remained to him*"; my emphasis). Blanchot knows, imagines, that the fictive share of this testimonial text is in part what opens its narrative dimension to the staging and figuration of a life-changing event, an imagined rupture and sudden transformation of a life that puts the imagination and fiction themselves directly into play, that demands a fictive articulation of life, death, and writing, and that retrospectively makes of this life one that has been jolted in the direction of a nonworldly affirmation—indeed, an affirmation that can, at some level, dispense with the world it has obsessively returned to. In other words, even though Blanchot does not mention writing here, everything is in place for the implicit assertion and sealing, or at the very least a decisive inflection, of the writer's literary vocation.

In this perspective, it is striking to note that in "L'expérience de Proust," written some ten years after the events of *L'instant de ma mort*, Blanchot uses a very similar phrase in a reflection on the death-bound "conditions" for an experience capable of forming a "vocation" pursued by a man who is "*rassemblé sur cette plume à laquelle* tout ce qu'il a encore de vie*, et d'enfance préservée, se communique*" ("condensed into this pen to which *all the life that still remains to him*, all its preserved childhood, is communicated"; LV 24–25 [my emphasis]). But in this context, as we continue to read the passage, we see that Blanchot refers to this remainder of life in order to *deny* that such a living writing man is at issue at all: "*nullement,*" says Blanchot, is he the one concerned (no more than is the child who has fathered him). Rather we have to do entirely with his shadow. I mention this strange echo of a *life that remains* in order to bring out both the continuity in Blanchot's thinking and the difference that obtrudes in *L'instant de ma mort,* where the biographical elements that are folded into a vocation narrative, while they are similarly bracketed and suspended, cannot so easily be rendered inessential.

Of course, Blanchot works very deliberately to depersonalize and distance this autobiographical material, through the third person and through a narrative voice that is as exquisite in its indirection as it is limpid and smooth in its calm and careful *démarche*. Surely such procedures are justified, with respect to the tremendous distance—in time, space, scene, and voice, in the vicissitudes of memory, and in sheer ungraspability—that separates the writer from the experience in question. But indeed, unlike in earlier *récits* such as *L'arrêt de mort*, he does not and cannot simply dismiss the factual dimension of the narrative as sheer nullity and nonsense. Those facts too are integral to its necessity as a story, its very conditions and origin, at least along one of its sides or "slopes." Blanchot himself cannot help but be *in it*. This factual, referential side, and the author's biographical appearance, thus intertwine but also compete with the other more ecstatic side to create a tension that Blanchot attempts to resolve by asserting quite openly the preeminence of one over the other. It is the feeling of lightness and its complex temporal articulations, its mortal paradoxes of mortality, and its perdurance despite all else, that in the end are privileged over the historical dimension of the tale. This latter, however, has its own pointed wounds which have obviously insisted on their voice as well, if only to be rendered secondary, no doubt as the price of their obtrusions. The first of these was mentioned above under the name of *injustice*, and the guilt (a word not pronounced by Blanchot in this text) of being saved by illegitimate privilege and knowing that innocent lives were taken in place of his. "*Demeurait cependant . . . le sentiment*" ("there remained however . . . the feeling"). But there was also another loss, which was if not more grave then surely no less poignant for Blanchot personally, namely that of a "thick manuscript" taken by the ransacking soldiers—again, from a house left standing. The loss of this manuscript gives rise to the remarkable brief coda to the text, in which both Malraux and Paulhan are enlisted in "*des recherches qui ne pouvaient que rester vaines*" ("searches that could only come up empty"). A second irrecoverable loss—of what, exactly? a novel? Blanchot does not tell us. But clearly it was not something easily abandoned, quite to the contrary. And yet here, on the last page of the textual space that has been verging through the debris of history toward a moment that would ultimately be lifted free of it, Blanchot dissolves this loss, and all loss, in a lapidary phrase that introduces the culmination and endpoint of *L'instant de ma mort,* its brief and dense final sentence.

> *Qu'importe*. Seul demeure le sentiment de légèreté qui est la mort même ou, pour le dire plus précisément, l'instant de ma mort désormais toujours en instance. (IM 20; my emphasis)
>
> *What does it matter*. There remains only the feeling of lightness that is death itself, or, to say it more precisely, the instant of my death insisting always from now on.

What matters what has been lost, what matters if all has been lost, one thing alone remains: the feeling of lightness, which is death itself, which is . . . a formulation that begins with the title of the very text we are reading: *l'instant de ma mort désormais toujours en instance*. It is a formulation that comes at the end of a chain of translations and that itself demands further translation, while making impossible demands on translation. I would note first of all that here the necessity of translation gives rise, within the text's own formulations, not to a schematic fictive-allegorical scene populated by death and death, in conversation with itself (themselves), but rather, more "conceptually," to the complex temporal structure analyzed above, centered on the impossible "now" of a death that would be, always imminently, "my death." But in addition to this, Blanchot's use of the difficult to translate phrase *en instance* hints at a further intriguing juridical dimension in a text that begins with injustice but only glancingly situates the implied guilt within its surface texture—indeed, a guilt, and a loss, that this final gesture all but elides in favor of *another* instant. The expression *en instance* applies to certain official processes whose resolutions and results are imminent and pending, particularly a trial; and while it applies to other contexts besides the legal proceedings of a court, it is difficult not to see such a judging instance implicitly installed here in the instant that would be "death itself . . . my death" (a juridical register that Blanchot plays on in his *Death Sentence* as well). The bad conscience that is not named in this text nonetheless sounds throughout its language.[40] It is as though this death both has already passed and has yet to pass judgment on the one whose death this is, and whose life it draws into its gaping space, together with a past that is also indelibly "mine"—in a *Schuldigsein* that does after all resonate with the singularizing call that can be considered "of conscience."[41] These associations are reinforced not only by the instantaneous trial and judgment *within* the text, to which I have already referred (conducted by the Nazi lieutenant), but also by the entire context of the war, the Germans and collaboration, allegiances to the left or the right, and the nature and grounds of a withdrawal from politics, all very charged historical points around which a number of accusations have been aimed at Blanchot, with differing degrees of justification, pertinence and tact. But even if we limit ourselves to the one crucial disjuncture clearly visible in the story, between an "empirical" set of circumstances disrupted and marked by violent events and their attendant losses, and an "essential" experience whose pressing and insistent remnants persist beyond these contingencies, there is a strange infection or haunting of the latter by the former, a sense, *un sentiment*, that what remains are also the remnants of these *losses as such*. I am pointing here to a sense of melancholy that would resist the liquidation apparently effected by the resolute *Qu'importe*, a dismissive gesture that seems to dissolve the material traces of a singular past, or that, after being driven by the imperative of a testimony to inscribe them within a narrative, would then neutralize their specific imperative force, *their* exigency, as obtrusive figures and demanding points of return. And surely the force of this melancholy is not without a touch of guilt that would exert itself along with, as part of, internally to, and *constitutively within* the more transcendental version of the instant's insistence and the feeling's ongoing pressure—an ambiguous contamination that would problematize the very notion of the transcendental, if only because it occurs not as a purified beyond, but as a paradoxical "*pas au-delà*." But if there is anything of which experience is purified in this story, it is loss itself, even as it verges on the total loss of world, of all phenomenality, that characterizes the sublime's fundamental destitution.

At one level, then, my question is whether the *Qu'importe* and the abiding feeling it shelters are an attempt to claim a compensation for sublime loss analogous to the treasure of reason's *Bestimmung* (and the moral law it offers up) in the Kantian scenario. Does Blanchot in this text enter into the landscape of historical time in order, in the end, to affirm a strange and perduring treasure in the not-beyond of death's ecstatic time? And if so, what does this treasure have to do with the enigma of writing, which it seems to confirm and bear forth, from now on? What is striking is that if this moment enacts, or parodies, a sublime destruction of the image and of imagination—a loss of every figurable object for the sake of an indestructible "vocation"—it also leads back, necessarily, into the register of figuration and image, the subreption of a scenography as irresistible as it is inadequate: a mise-en-scène of death's disaster as the compulsive restaging of a *given* rupture, the abrupt introduction of a fault that remains "mine," both ruining and seconding a vocation, in a voice that still must bear witness, after so many years, to that time when it happened. Is it that, in this happening, the "insisting" force of a death *en instance* (a "literal" translation that names the exigency permanently instantiated *in feeling*) simultaneously strips the life it befalls of any visible and graspable returns, while at the same time securing a voided *thing*, empty and denuded but unloseable, safeguarded from the dull erosions of intermittence?

A PRIMAL SCENE?

Having leapt to the end of Blanchot's work, and having found there a conflict between autobiography (as datable history) and ecstasy (as mitigant of historical loss), between running away with your feet and escape from the time of the world, or finally, between sheer painful loss with its historically imaged ruins and the perdurance of a strange, destitute and yet generous *feeling*, a certain tonal undercurrent draws us back into an earlier moment of sublimity reconfigured. A short text in *L'écriture du désastre* that bears the heading "(Une scène primitive?)," has much in common with *L'instant de ma mort*. In various figural and rhetorical aspects that will become apparent, it can serve as a relay point for a subsequent movement yet further back toward the *récits*.

I would also like to place the following remarks on this much commented text under the sign of Cixous's admiring but highly skeptical commentaries on Blanchot (written before *L'instant de ma mort* had appeared), which have influenced my own approach throughout.[42] Her reading stresses the text's engagement in and rewriting of the Kantian sublime, but also suspects this "posthumous" text of wanting to guard its secret *like a treasure*. "Nothing moves [Blanchot]," she writes,

> except a desire *to keep his treasure*. In order for his treasure not to disappear entirely—because whether he writes to God, to himself, or to a madman, he nevertheless writes—he hid it in the brief scene of *Writing of the Disaster*, in the primal scene of the child who saw but will not tell. Blanchot writes: I will not tell you. He draws something the way he would write in sand. For those who understand the sign, it is good, and otherwise *it is of no importance*. (*Readings*, 100; my emphasis)

Thus Cixous registers the dismissive *Qu'importe* of a text that has not yet been written, but that is everywhere implicit (the phrase does show up, with some variations, on many other occasions in Blanchot). But most important, I want to share to some extent in Cixous's recognition of the melancholic retention at work in Blanchot, a reserve and a *retenue* that often passes under the name of *discretion*, but that when seen in a certain light bears the scars of a fierce defensive effort. I say "to some extent," because it is also important to acknowledge, with Blanchot, that the disastrous temporality problematically figured in terms of an instant and a point ultimately cannot be tethered to a single locatable event or experience. There is no question of seeking to reduce or to flatten this *excess*—which is, in a sense, the very kernel of Blanchot's thought. And although Cixous is right to point out that, when it comes to the sorts of accidents that knock someone out of life into writing, "We do not know what happened to Blanchot. But he did have an accident" (98), it must also be said that even after *L'instant de ma mort* we still "do not know what happened" to Blanchot, for the event recounted in the later text does not finally resolve the question. But we do know more, and can see more clearly the sharpening outlines of loss alongside the self-effacing affirmation of a treasure that cannot be taken away. I believe that Cixous approaches an important aspect of Blanchot's strategies when she bluntly states: "The meaning is clear: there is no loss" (108). And surely she is not without some justification in placing Blanchot's ecstatic but retentive engagement with the sublime on the side of a "masculine libido" (100) that resists pleasure and disavows loss for the sake of an absolute (dis)possession which, in turn, might risk leaving the structure of law and of authority strangely, singularly intact. *Seul demeure* . . . I evoke for now these critical elements of Cixous's discussion, leaving aside what is problematic in her approach. It is enough that she allows us to open here the dimension of a strange foreclosure, and a guarded occlusion—a point of libidinal obscurity that bears the marks of a discursive strategy—in Blanchot's passionate affirmations. And therefore also in the construction of an imperative to write and of an exclusive lifelong devotion to writing: a Vocation. As we will see in *L'arrêt de mort*, these questions are clearly haunted by gender, sexual difference, and the passionate distance of eros.

The Black Sky, a Voided Sublime

"(Une scène primitive?)" is staged under the sign of "the disaster." A scene that resists scenographic anchoring—first of all by suspending it in parentheses and adding to it a question mark that did not appear when it was first published separately[43]—it nonetheless attempts to figure an initial and initiatory moment strictly analogous to the rupturing instant in *L'instant de ma mort*. Its autobiographical status is more a matter of inference than of evidence, an inference based in part on its tone, the distant intimacy of its mood, and the decisive manner in which it inhabits the point of view of its child protagonist. How else to put it but thus: it would be extremely, jarringly uncharacteristic of Blanchot to project such a scene, especially in the midst of the devastating figurative destructions that dominate the overall discourse of *L'écriture du désastre*, unless it were somehow cast not in the guise of pure fiction—the dreary pretense of an arbitrarily invented character—but with the tenuous authority of a past experience reconstructed, however distant or suspended it might be, and despite its being displaced into the third person and into the attenuations of fictive supposition (all of which apply as well to *L'instant de ma mort*). In addition to this, the scene of this scene, its characteristic setting—the view out a window at an enclosed space outside—had appeared many years before in *Celui qui ne m'accompagnait pas*, where the narrator evokes it as part of that text's shifting space, but also as giving him "*le sentiment de toucher le fond d'un souvenir*" ("the feeling of touching the ground of a memory"; CQ 84).[44] The scene's repetition is a clear sign of its persistence, and I see little reason not to think of the memory in question, at least in part and with appropriate caution, as one of Blanchot's childhood house (perhaps the same house as in *L'instant de ma mort*). In *L'écriture du désastre* the emphasis falls on a shattering moment presented in terms that clearly resonate with the extraordinary instant in *L'instant de ma mort*. As mentioned, this short text has received a great deal of commentary. I provide the fragment here in its entirety, for memory, to be followed by an analysis that will bring out the paradoxes most relevant to the present discussion.

> (Une scène primitive?) Vous qui vivez plus tard, proches d'un coeur qui ne bat plus, supposez, supposez-le: l'enfant—a-t-il sept ans, huit ans peut-être?—debout, écartant le rideau et, à travers la vitre, regardant. Ce qu'il voit, le jardin, les arbres d'hiver, le mur d'une maison: tandis qu'il voit, sans doute à la manière d'un enfant, son espace de jeu, il se lasse et lentement regarde en haut vers le ciel ordinaire, avec les nuages, la lumière grise, le jour terne et sans lointain.

> Ce qui se passe ensuite: le ciel, le *même* ciel, soudain ouvert, noir absolument et vide absolument, révélant (comme par la vitre brisée) une telle absence que tout s'y est depuis toujours et à jamais perdu, au point que s'y affirme et s'y dissipe le savoir vertigineux que rien est ce qu'il y a, et d'abord rien au-delà. L'inattendu de cette scène (son trait interminable), c'est le sentiment de bonheur qui aussitôt submerge l'enfant, la joie ravageante dont il ne pourra témoigner que par les larmes, un ruissellement sans fin de larmes. On croit à un chagrin d'enfant, on cherche à le consoler. Il ne dit rien. Il vivra désormais dans le secret. Il ne pleurera plus. (ED 117)

> (A primal scene?) You who live later, close to a heart that beats no more, suppose, suppose this: the child—is he seven years old, or eight perhaps?—standing by the window, drawing the curtain and, through the pane, looking. What he sees: the garden, the wintry trees, the wall of a house. Though he sees, no doubt in a child's way, his play space, he grows weary and slowly looks up toward the ordinary sky, with clouds, grey light, the flat day without distance.
>
> What happens next: the sky, the *same* sky, suddenly open, absolutely black and absolutely empty, revealing (as though through the broken pane) such an absence that everything has since always and forever been lost in it, to the point that in it is affirmed and dissolved the vertiginous knowledge that nothing is what there is, and first of all nothing beyond. The unexpected aspect of this scene (its interminable trait) is the feeling of happiness that straightaway submerges the child, the ravaging joy to which he can bear witness only by tears, an endless flow of tears. They believe it's a child's grief, they try to console him. He says nothing. He will live from now on in the secret. He will weep no more.

Addressed to future survivors who remain close to one whose heart has ceased,[45] this scene is projected into a time beyond the grave (one that would then be projected back, again (for its first retrojection occurs precisely here)), and like *L'instant de ma mort*, it, too, is a testament, a last one, addressed to the writer's survivors as a kind of legacy: I leave you this; when I am no more, you shall have this. It is thus a scene that also sets a task, a strange demand to suppose, to posit, and to *project*.[46] The scene opens onto a gray day pressed flat, condensed into a space that is *extremely ordinary*, if one can put it thus, pressing into fatigue, boredom and the dull anxiety of a world that is all too familiar (and familial, as it turns out). An unspoken question bears down on the first paragraph with all its leaden force: *Is this all? Is this all there is?*[47] No, it is not, for in these extremes of ordinary a pressure is exerted that shatters the frame, blackens the sky, and submerges the scene, surprisingly, with joy. *Stimmungswende*: a turn in tonality or a "mood swing" with transcendental implications. The Heideggerian resonance is confirmed by the manifestation of a *Nichts*, a nothing that reveals not a beyond but merely itself as the ungrounding *Ab-grund* of what is there. Feeling of happiness, feeling of lightness, irrupting into a closed but total space and opening the leaden lid of the sky (surely akin to Baudelaire's splenetic *couvercle*, as seen through a child's bored eyes) not onto a vast cosmic order but onto its own impenetrable but endless ground of black. Is this all there is? No: nothing is what there is. Whereas *all this*—this scene and the totality it figures—is not quite nothing. Rather it both gives and is rendered unto nothing, and thus unto itself, "intact," in the *same* sky now pseudo-allegorically black, as seen through a pane of glass shattered by a strange "as if" incapable of breaking anything, a turn or figure that points, for the reader and in the time of reading/writing, toward an unseen *secret*: the sky turned black, the nothing that there is, the unspeakable joy of being cast into an "everything" of absence. Truly, how could such a "scene," and the point or puncture it makes, find a stable, locatable place in the course of a life, and in an autobiographical narrative? From this perspective, it necessarily falls *outside*, exceeding the coordinates of time and space, and is thus engaged in the fictional dimension we saw in *L'instant de ma mort* as well.

Blanchot makes further efforts to separate the scene from experience and historical time, in the commentary on it that one finds in a long fragment occurring later in *L'écriture du désastre*, staged as a conversation between two unnamed interlocutors. The word "scene," says one of the speakers, contrary to what one might think, here has the advantage of *not* designating something that happened at a specific moment; rather, the word is used *"simplement pour ne pas en parler ainsi que d'un événement ayant eu lieu à un moment du temps"* ("simply in order not to speak of it as an event that has taken place at a moment in time"; ED 176). It is a "scene" suspended out of time, *"une ombre, une faible lueur, un 'presque' avec les traits du 'trop'"* ("a shadow, a feeble glimmer, an 'almost' with the features of a 'too much'"), and therefore *out of joint* with respect to any actual event. So it is with any specter or *revenant* (this time a dead child—ancient *in-fans* of the currently writing self—in lieu of a dead father? the child as the father of the writer . . .). Blanchot widens the disjunction further, drawing the scene out of any possible coordinates, as his speakers' exchanges become more and more pithy, more lapidary, and approach the kernel of the matter:

> Revenant vers l'interpellation initiale qui invite à la supposition fictive sans laquelle parler de l'enfant qui n'a jamais parlé, serait faire passer dans l'histoire, dans l'expérience ou le réel encore, à titre d'épisode ou à nouveau de scène immobile, ce qui les a ruinés (histoire, expérience, réel) en les laissant intacts. — L'effet généreux du désastre. — La sénescence du visage sans rides. — L'insulte majeure de la poésie et de la philosophie indistinctes. (ED 178–179)

> Returning to the initial interpellation that invites one to the fictive supposition without which speaking of the child who has never spoken would bring into history, into experience or again into the real, as an episode or as another immobile scene, what has ruined them (history, experience, reality) by leaving them intact. — The generous effect of the disaster. — The senescence of the face unmarked by age. — The major insult of poetry and philosophy in their indistinction.

The call to fiction that opens the scene ("*supposez, supposez-le*") is a call to resist drawing the scene into history, experience and the real, and thus to resist reducing its excess to the parameters of a mere scene, an experience that a person happens to have had in the past, reproduced in its visible, describable aspects. I have stressed that we must give this ungraspable excess its due place in Blanchot's thought, otherwise this thought itself would risk being resolved into the effects of biographical accidents; and although I want to lay great stress on the autobiographical aspect of this fragment, it is imperative to avoid such a reduction. But to place a counter-emphasis on this other *scenic* slope of the fragment's narrative structure would mean recognizing the *inevitable* autobiographical effects it relies on to produce its uncanny rupture, precisely as the rupture of a scene with its place in a life (however indeterminate and fictively cast). It is thus also necessary to recognize that *the scene as such* insists—its memorious evocation in *Celui qui ne m'accompagnait pas*, noted above, attests to this—and that it too, if it is ruined by what it tries to tell, is "left intact," returning in Blanchot's texts as a point to which his writing returns, as though to a persistent and haunting residue, a point remaining *en revenance*. In that sense, the conjugation of the eccentric recital point with autobiographical material is "not accidental," in that, however contingent the link may be, this point and its poetic-philosophical remainder (black sky, vertiginous knowledge of nothing beyond) is *given* in the staged time of the scene *and nowhere else*. In other words, the scene is presented, after all, as an experience that someone had at a certain (indeterminate) time, and that, in shattering that time, left enduring effects, and obtrusive images, on the life it punctured: "*Il vivra désormais dans le secret. Il ne pleurera plus.*" ("he will live from now on in the secret. He will weep no more"). Blanchot's "primal scene" (if it is one) thus relies as much on a presumption that it is, at some level, historical, experienced, and real as on the fictive register that allows it to twist itself away from these and to approach the strange quasi-transcendental point of the *récit*'s enigma. In this sense, the figural compulsion to which the "primal" or originary scene gives rise *is also* an autobiographical compulsion that cannot dispense with the historical side of the "point" it makes, and that thus constitutes precisely the initial articulation of a life's vocation. "*Insulte majeure de la poésie et de la philosophie indistinctes*": this is the trauma or "attack" (according to the etymology of *insult*) that opens the co-possibility of poetry and philosophy in a violent and singular point irreducible to the thoughts and images that it gives. For that too is what the disaster does in this scene, it *gives an image*, indeed even imposes one, schematically but with a certain specificity, in the singular "mineness" of autobiographical time, even as this image exceeds itself in the direction of its originating force. Do we have to do here with a "transcendental imagination" bearing some relation, at least, to the one deployed by Kant and reread by Heidegger? That is indeed the direction we are moving in, and must continue to do so, while also making drastic translations where necessary (for example, with regard to the imagination as a "productive faculty" responsible for a certain unifying operation; I will return to this)—and while recognizing that this is an imagination already preceded, constituted, and haunted by its sublime ruination. For the image in question is not only the scene itself, of course, but also that of the impossible "black sky," what one might call (keeping the abovementioned etymology in mind) the "inconsiderate" starless void which pays no heed, refuses to signify, addresses no one, and is named only outside the experience into which it inserts itself, like a tiny point that can be conjured but not conveyed.

Blanchot's revision of the Kantian narrative of the sublime—which is likewise, it will be recalled, the narrative of being jolted into a vocation, a *Bestimmung*—thus turns the void of the image's beyond into the voiding also of the "starry sky," once the visible counterpart to "the moral law within."[48] Blanchot's response: *point d'étoile*. The disastrous extinction of the stars is an elimination of the universal and cosmic dimension of the sublime narrative, which is thus singularized in a "vocation" bearing on the inhabitant not of a cosmos but of a language (an uncanny habitation that originally separates from home and familiars—as does the logos of reason, already). It is also the singularization of the law insofar as the law bears on a voice bound to (and for) a point that dissolves every imperative, but that demands a return, and that does, after all, give something unspeakably generous. Not reason, exactly, but rather something Blanchot enigmatically refers to as the enigma of "the secret." It is there that the child will live *désormais*. He says nothing, will weep no more, but the implication—read through the successive frames one finds around this scene: book, oeuvre, writing career as *curriculum vitae* (in the strict sense)—is that he *will write instead*, replacing tears with written words which, in fact, lie firmly here on the page (and on thousands more that have preceded this one, in Blanchot's name), a replacement that is definitively set on its way at this instant, and to which this text retrospectively bears witness across the decades. Surely such a vocation is here *evoked*, voiced out into a strange textual time. To weep no more, to leave the *infans* of childhood behind, means living henceforth in the secret as in the open enigma of language. Language itself is the black sky—reduced to a point that is also a voice—but it is also the secret to which the voice speaking now, punctured out of quotidian time, must attest, not childishly, with "an endless stream of tears," but in the *Unheimlichkeit* of an endless written oeuvre.

It could be said, however, that in distinction from the blank figure of the black sky and its concomitant vertiginous knowledge which exceeds historical time, these tears, *which must appear in order to be desiccated and evaporated*, are precisely what place this scene irresistibly within historical time (if only because the other people there could themselves bear witness to them). They are the arresting autobiographical residue of this scene, bearing witness to a ravaging joy, but also to an element of loss and mourning that is quickly dismissed, and not only by the adults in the scene—as childish chagrin. Indeed, this dismissal is the crux and burden of the fragment, its explicit task. To be sure, the text does say its loss, but it does so hyperbolically, as nothing less than *total*: in the black sky is revealed "*une telle absence que* tout *s'y est depuis toujours et à jamais perdu*" ("such an absence that *everything* has since always and forever been lost in it"; ED 117, my emphasis). As I have suggested, it is a sublime loss of world as such, leaving as image only the pseudo-image of the black sky, *along with the scene itself*, its imposing figural *hantise*, and especially these tears, which, far from the transparent manifestation of a childish distress, are rather the opaque sign of a more messy transcendental residue, touched no less by libidinal, cathectic, economic, and circumstantial elements. Blanchot moves quickly to transform them in this initiatory moment into a more resolved and resolute last time, a "nevermore" of weeping (more resolved and, I would venture to add, manifestly implausible, a fiction whose resolute rigidity indicates something other than temporal excess: rather a self-protecting carapace?[49]). The categorical *jamais . . . plus* (never . . . more) sublimates these tears straightaway, in the sense of immediately vaporizing them, and this process, which disposes of the material and affective forms of the fragment's "testimony," even as it compulsively narrates the haunting effects of their insistent remainder, is the one that delivers to Blanchot the unloseable treasure one can discern in this scene. Cixous again: "Nothing moves him, except a desire to keep his treasure. . . . The meaning is clear, there is no loss" (*Readings*, 100, 108). The profound complication here is that this treasure is a treasure *of absence*, such that loss, of a kind, is its very form and condition. Once again, the word for this condition is *melancholy*. To put it no doubt too simply: Blanchot loses the world but keeps its forever absence as his resource and treasure, his reserve of nothing—a reserve from which writing, a life's vocation, "*vouée au silence*," will henceforth be drawn: *puisée, épuisée . . .*

In this sense, Cixous's statement should be modified to read: there is loss, even total loss, but there is no mourning. In Blanchot's primal scene, the sublime undergoes a characteristic transformation into a melancholy that attempts to purify itself of its residues—or of what Freud called a *Niederschlag*, the cumulative precipitate of our libidinal losses and leavings. (The term strikingly suggests the beating down of a material sediment, as well as the downward movement of a *Herabsetzung* that subjects the sublime to degradation and ridicule. But unlike Kafka's degraded sublimity, pulp and remainder of starved aspirations, Blanchot's—at least in this case—is devoid of humor, and of the *Stimmung* of a *Witz*'s lightning flash able to crack open, perhaps, even the faultless vault of darkness.[50]) Once again, if the sublime vocation and its transformations are revealed or effected "*peu à peu quoique aussitôt*," as Blanchot claims they are in Proust (LV 22, 26), it is clearer than ever that Blanchot does not give the "*peu à peu*" its due. Indeed, this fragment instead reduces loss and absence to "everything," all at once, rendering the entirety of life, too, over to "the secret."

Does this *secret* give the "proper" name of the treasure incorporated here? In what does it consist? The secret is of course not merely a hidden content, hereby revealed on page 117 of a book called *L'écriture du désastre*; it does not correspond with what is problematically "revealed" in the story's images and enunciations. It is rather what Blanchot calls, in an essay written around the same time as *L'écriture du désastre*, the open reserve of "*le Dire inqualifiable*" ("the unqualifiable Saying"), which he directly associates with a voice. This purely open and unconditional saying is, he writes (in a text contemporary with *L'écriture du désastre*),

> ... la gloire d'une 'voix narrative' qui donne à entendre clairement, sans jamais pouvoir être obscurcie par l'opacité ou l'énigme ou l'horreur terrible de ce qui se communique. (*Après coup*, 98)
>
> ... the glory of a "narrative voice" that clearly makes itself heard, without its ever being able to be obscured by the opacity or the enigma or the terrible horror of what is communicated.

It is the clear resounding of the voice as such that constitutes the secret, making heard the empty but indispensable condition of any communication. In the same essay, Blanchot also refers to this open emptiness as "*la loi du récit*"—a formulation that places it in close proximity to "*la loi secrète du récit*" in "Le chant des sirènes"—the fact that the *récit*'s secret is nothing other than its own inexhaustible "vocal" manifestation, its "Saying" in a voice that before all else says its own manifest clarity, its very opening.

But as we draw back toward the voices of the *récits*, it is important to ask: is there necessarily a violence, a puncturing and painful irruption, in the suddenness of this opening, and thus in the origination of any such voice, along with the story that compels it?

VIOLENCE OF THE EVENT: *THE RÉCITS*

If every *récit* moves toward a point where an encounter that has already occurred must also be summoned into being for the first time, but by a language that can never draw it from its radical unreality (i.e., that can never "truly" arrive at the encounter)—then what is the "point" of Blanchot's *récits*?[51] As elusive as this point must remain, does it tend to take a certain shape or form in the *récits* that approach it? What is the *look* taken on by the encounter that entices these *récits* and their narrators back into an enigmatic past and, simultaneously, forward into the indefinite future of narration? In other words, what is the status of the event in the *récits*, and how does its exigency relate to the "autobiographical" narrative structures we have been analyzing?

It may seem strange to emphasize the "events" in Blanchot's *récits*. What stories could be more uneventful! And yet, despite their rarefied atmosphere, these texts are full of remarkable moments whose agitation, tumult, and even violence stand out all the more for being placed within such an otherwise uneventful and largely meditative medium. Scenes of sickness and fevered shivering; strange physical fights "*à bras-le-corps*" (AMV 124; also AM 67) that seem to arise without provocation; moments of extreme shock in which a character makes a "*mouvement brusque ... un bond presque sauvage*" ("an abrupt movement ... an almost savage leap") (AMV 84, 86) or shouts unexpectedly;[52] unprovoked acts of aggression, such as in *La folie du jour*, where the narrator recounts almost losing his sight because someone had "*écrasé du verre sur mes yeux*" ("crushed glass in my eyes") and tells elsewhere of "*un étrange fou ... [qui] m'a pris la main et y a planté son couteau. Que de sang*" ("a strange madman ... [who] took my hand and planted his knife in it. Blood everywhere"; FJ 21, 15–16). Often these moments occur as though from out of nowhere and seem merely to reinforce the atmosphere of strangeness and tense volatility dominating the *récits*. But at other times they are invested with a great deal more significance, as though the mysterious force of their violence structured the entire narrative, driving the very need to speak, or fixing, in some way, the basic scenographic and figural features of the *récit* (location, "characters," situations).

One such event occurs near the beginning of *Au moment voulu*. Like many of these events, it takes the form of a "*coup*," a blow that leaves a permanent imprint. The narrator has come to the apartment of a woman named Claudia, but when he knocks, the door is opened by another woman, Judith, whom he recognizes from somewhere out of his near or distant past: "Time had passed," he says, "and yet it was not past." This had-passed-but-was-not-past designates the knotted temporal structure, the permanent superimposition, in which the *récit* continually unfolds. We never learn much about the past shared by these figures, but the narrator tells us that

> il y avait manifestement entre nous une telle accumulation d'événements, de réalités démesurées, de tourment, de pensées incroyables et aussi une telle profondeur d'oubli heureux qu'elle n'avait aucune peine à ne pas s'étonner de moi. Je la trouvai étonnamment peu changée. (AMV 8)

> there was clearly such an accumulation of events between us, excessive things, torments, incredible thoughts and also such a depth of happy forgetfulness that it was not at all hard for her not to be surprised by me. I found her surprisingly little changed. (WTC, 1)

Here there is a sense of accumulation, instantly or even *already* felt, as the narrator is welcomed by this woman with whom he has an immediate and profound but indefinite complicity, and enters the apartment as though he were stepping into the element of the *récit*'s dense and unspoken familiarity—for it is here, in this apartment, that the story of this *récit* will have occurred, the life shared there, for a while, by the narrator and these two women. But not long after this liminal moment, there is another "false step" which, within the self-contained logic of the text, appears to seal his relation to this space as the unique site of an inevitable return (of an "instant") around which the *récit* will develop. A few moments after entering, having gone in search of the kitchen and a glass of water (an odd motif in this text), the narrator gropes through the dark apartment, which, indeed, he appears to know from times past; but in a disjunction of mind and space, he says that "*tout était clair dans mon esprit, mais pas au dehors. Diable de couleur, pensai-je, était-il donc si long?*" ("everything was clear in my mind, but not outside. Devil of a hallway, I thought, was it really so long?"). This devilish hallway seems in fact to lead into a painful, eternal, hellish space. The narrator recounts this never-ending passage:

Je ne suis pas sûr d'avoir même éprouvé une sensation désagréable jusqu'au point où, à la suite d'un faux mouvement (m'étant peut-être heurté au mur), je ressentais une douleur abominable, la plus vive qui fût,—elle me fendait la tête—mais peut-être plus vive que vivante; il est difficile d'exprimer ce qu'elle avait à la fois de cruel et d'insignifiant: une violence horrible, une abomination, d'autant plus intolérable qu'elle semblait m'atteindre à travers une couche fabuleuse de durée qui brûlait tout entière en moi, immense et unique douleur, comme si je n'avais pas été touché à ce moment, mais il y a des siècles et depuis des siècles, et ce qu'elle avait de révolu, de tout à fait mort, pouvait bien la rendre plus facile mais aussi plus difficile à supporter, en faisant d'elle une persévérence absolument froide, impersonelle, que n'arrêtait ni la vie, ni la fin de la vie. Assurément, je ne pénétrai pas tout cela aussitôt. Je fus seulement traversé par un sentiment d'épouvante, et par ces mots, en qui tient ma bonne foi: "Mais est-ce que cela recommence? A nouveau! à nouveau!" Je fus en tout cas stoppé net. D'où qu'il vînt, le choc m'avait si vigoureusement rattrapé que, dans l'instant présent ouvert par lui, j'étais assez au large pour oublier éternellement d'en sortir. Marcher, avancer, je le pouvais sans doute, et je dus le faire, mais plutôt comme un boeuf assomé: c'étaient les pas de l'immobilité. Ces moments furent les plus pénibles. Et il est bien vrai qu'ils valent encore pour maintenant; à travers tout, je dois me retourner vers eux et me dire: J'y suis encore, j'en suis resté là. (AMV 13–15)

I'm not sure I even felt anything unpleasant until the point when, after an awkward movement (having perhaps knocked against a wall), I experienced an atrocious pain, the most lively pain possible—it split my head open—but perhaps more lively than alive; it is hard to express how it was at once cruel and insignificant: a horrible violence, an atrocity, all the more intolerable because it seemed to come to me across a fantastic layer of time, burning in its entirety inside me, an immense and unique pain, as though I had not been touched at this moment but centuries ago and for centuries past, and the quality it had of being something finished, something completely dead, could certainly make it easier to bear but also harder, by turning it into a perseverance that was absolutely cold, impersonal, that would not be stopped either by life or by the end of life. Of course I did not fathom all that right away. I was simply penetrated by a feeling of horror, and by these words, which I still believe: "Oh no, is this beginning again? Again! Again!" I was stopped short, in any case. Wherever it came from, the shock had overtaken me so vigorously that, in the present instant opened by it, I was so far out in the open as to forget eternally to emerge from it. Walk, go forward—I could certainly do that, and I must have done so, but rather like an ox that has been hit over the head: my steps were the steps of immobility. These were the most difficult moments. And it is really true that they still endure; through everything, I must turn back to them, and say to myself: I'm still there, I stayed there. (WTC 3–4)

Such an instant has a great deal in common with that recounted in *L'instant de ma mort*, especially in its fabulistic distension and twisting of time (from across a "*couche fabuleuse de durée*" [a fantastic layer of time]) and the fixing of a point that insists—"*à travers tout*" ("through everything")—on a constant recognition. This moment marks the point, internal to the *récit*, through which the narrator would have entered an infernal and fabulous space, and time, opened by the violence of a shock, a space in which it would be possible to "*oublier éternellement d'en sortir*" ("to forget eternally to leave it"), and which will in some sense fix the "setting" for the *récit* to follow. But while this passage provides an elaborate articulation of such an entry, and while at the same time it links this entry to an event within the *récit*, it does not do so in the same way as *L'instant de ma mort*, for not only is this event merely surmised ("*m'étant peut-être heurté au mur*," "having perhaps knocked against the wall"), the shock it evokes has no determinate origin ("*D'où qu'il vînt, le choc*" ["wherever it came from, the shock"]) and seems related to the subsequent *récit* only by way of its site, and not in terms of the much more charged element in which it occurs: the narrator's relation to the two women with whom he will have lived there. If the encounter is one that passes between them, this "shock" only very obliquely—contiguously, metonymically—locates the "point" from which the *récit* draws its compulsive force.

This point is indicated more directly, perhaps, toward the end of the *récit*, where the narrator ruminates at length on another feminine figure. In one of the many delicate, discreet, and utterly noneventful relations depicted in the *récits*, the narrator describes how, once while "*habitant seul dans le Sud*" ("living alone in the south"), at the end of the day he would open his door and see a woman "*un peu en contre-bas, le corps à demi ployé, la tête inclinée vers les genoux . . . assise . . . en bas de l'escalier, sur la large marche du tournant . . .*" ("slightly lower than I was, her body half inclined, her head bent toward her knees . . . sitting down at the bottom of a stairway, on the large step where the stairs turn"; AMV 138/WTC 61); he also describes her as "*cette femme assise près du mur, la tête penchée vers ses mains*" ("this woman sitting near the wall, her head leaning slightly toward her hands"). He would simply open the door and look at her, though she would not look at him and may not have even known he was there. Her melancholy indifference seems to seal the magnificence of this simple moment for the narrator—a moment he dares not disturb by turning it into a manifest or reciprocal relation—such that he proclaims finally (evoking the title of the *récit*) that "*pour l'un et pour l'autre cet instant était bien le moment voulu*" ("for each one of us this instant was indeed the perfect moment"; AMV 139). This instant would seem in some way to constitute the dislocated center of *Au moment voulu*, and the enigmatic point from which it would emanate. The fact that it involves a distant non-relation with a woman will take on a clearer significance as we proceed to a commentary of *L'arrêt de mort*, with its ghostly feminine figures and eerily haunted atmosphere.[53]

Au moment voulu thus gives a clue as to the essential place of feminine figures in the *récits*, as well as of the relation of this place to the more violent blows and cutting or puncturing moments that seem to instantiate their telling as an insistent imperative. Here already we see that the violent pain of these moments is displaced away from the central feminine figures and onto a kind of bodily accident. Much as the occasion and its violence give way in *L'instant de ma mort* to an allegorical formulation of the encounter ("*Rencontre de la mort et de la mort*") marked less by pain than by "a feeling of lightness," in *Au moment voulu*, the blow on the head absorbs into itself a pain which seems to be altogether absent from the melancholy but unbinding nonrelation to the distant woman who invokes the title phrase and seems to instantiate, as it were, the unapproachable "point" of the *récit*. In this sense, the "event" does not quite coincide with the "encounter," and as a result the plot, such as it is, is separated from the essential relation (and all its unspeakable complicities) that is the *récit*'s truly enticing "point"— the presence/absence of a distant, inaccessible, and haunting woman.

A similar structure is discernible elsewhere in the *récits*, where strange and suffusing complicities assert themselves across unbridgeable distances, and are punctuated by rupturing events which seem only to hark back to some unmentionable disaster that has long since been imposing its aftereffects. Much as in *L'instant de ma mort* and "(Une scène primitive?)," in the *récits* Blanchot is fascinated with decisive ruptures and momentous events after which nothing is any longer what it was before. But these moments are only alluded to in the most oblique and sentencious manner, and are never the subject of any direct narration. For example, again in *Au moment voulu*, the narrator writes: "*Je voudrais dire ceci: quand l'homme a vécu l'inoubliable, il s'enferme avec lui pour le regretter, ou il se met à errer pour le retrouver; ainsi, il devient le fantôme de l'événement*" ("I would like to say this: when a man has lived through something unforgettable, he shuts himself up with it to grieve over it, or he sets off to find it again; he thus becomes the ghost of the event"; AMV 135/WTC 59). In this case, however, the narrator makes this remark only to point out that the "scene" he has just narrated is *not* such an unforgettable and spectralizing moment.[54] In *Le dernier homme*, the fascination exerted by the last man radiates precisely from the traces of such a disaster; speaking of the "*vide*" that seems to allow the last man to "*supporter tout*," the narrator writes:

> C'est sans doute pourquoi il nous invitait à penser que sa vie avait été sans événements, sauf un seul, quelque chose de monumental et d'abject qui l'avait poussé où il était, ou bien ni grandiose ni démesuré, peut-être ce qui nous eût paru le plus insignifiant et qui exerçait cependant sur lui cette pression telle que tous les autres événements s'en trouvait volatilisés. (DH 30)

> This was no doubt why he invited us to believe that there had been no events in his life except for one, something abject, monumental, that had driven him to the point where he was, or something neither grandiose nor excessive, maybe something that would have seemed to us quite insignificant but had brought such pressure to bear on him that all other events were volatilized by it. (LM 15)

Such a volatilizing pressure seems to be the very atmosphere into which the *récits* constantly drift. But there is never any question in *Le Dernier homme* of such an event having happened to the narrator himself, and we know nothing about why he is in the sanatorium in the first place or what lies behind him such that he must enter into the space of narration. Curiously, though, the narrator does interrupt his narrative at one point with another gnomic aside, in terms that clearly resonate with the experience related in *L'instant de ma mort*. Remarking that, after emerging from a "*mauvaise passe*," the last man looks terribly weak, he adds:

> et pourtant, pas seulement faible. C'était comme si une puissance démesurée, en s'abattant sur lui, lui avait communiqué, par cet écrasement démesuré, une puissance, pour lui donner ce nom, supérieure à tout, une impuissance sur laquelle maintenant nulle supériorité n'avait de prise.

> and yet, not only weaker. It was as though an inordinate power had swept down on him and by crushing him so excessively had endowed him in turn with a power—to give it that name—superior to everything, a powerlessness over which, now, no superiority had any hold.

And here he adds a parenthesis:

> (Qu'arriverait-il à un homme qui aurait affaire à une mort trop forte pour lui? Tout homme qui échappe à la mort violente porte *un instant* le reflet de cette dimension nouvelle.) (DH 84; my emphasis)

> (What would happen to a man who came up against a death too strong for him? Every man who escapes from a violent death wears, *for an instant*, the glimmer of that new dimension.) (LM 49)

In addition to this mention of an "instant," the hesitation over what name to use for this strange "power" given by a crushing "*écrasement*"—together with the chopped syntax—points forward to the later text and the "*dimension nouvelle*" to which it attests. There, as here, that new dimension is one in which something remains that can never be taken away, something that is inviolable and indestructible ("sur laquelle maintenant nulle supériorité n'avait de prise" ["over which, now, no superiority had any hold"]), the strangely powerful powerlessness of an abject sovereignty, which, under the force of a "volatilizing" event, slips out of the circuit of power and domination. Blanchot's oblique self-reference in this passage—confirmed retrospectively by *L'instant de ma mort*—gestures toward the autobiographical point that may be driving this *récit*, but that is not anywhere figured within it.

A similar and even more telling instance of such a narrative structure can be found in *La folie du jour*. There Blanchot makes what appears to be a direct reference to the episode of *L'instant de ma mort*, though it is still very allusive:

> Peu après, la folie du monde se déchaîna. Je fus mis au mur comme beaucoup d'autres. Pourquoi? Pour rien. Les fusils ne partirent pas. Je me dis: Dieu, que fais-tu? Je cessai alors d'être insensé. Le monde hésita, puis reprit son équilibre. (FJ 11)
>
> Shortly afterward, the madness of the world broke out. I was made to stand against the wall like many others. Why? For no reason. The guns did not go off. I said to myself, God, what are you doing? At that point I stopped being insane. The world hesitated, then regained its equilibrium. (MD 6)

The "*peu après*" with which the quotation begins refers back to an earlier mention of having lost "*des êtres*" whom he has loved, which would place the loss roughly around the time of the events in *L'arrêt de mort*. No other reference is made in *La Folie du jour* to the near-execution in *L'instant de ma mort*, and it is certainly not presented as the decisive event behind the present narration. Rather it is placed alongside other equally decontextualized events, some of which are indeed rather violent (the broken glass and knife in the hand mentioned earlier). One of these, however, would seem to have the status of an "instant" in its insisting force.

While most of the text of *La folie du jour* appears to be proffered as though for no reason, it eventually becomes clear that it has been requested of the narrator by institutional authorities investigating the incident in which glass was crushed in his eyes. "*On m'avait demandé: Racontez-nous comment les choses se sont passées 'au juste.'—Un récit? Je commençai: Je ne suis ni savant ni ignorant . . .*" (FJ 31) ("I had been asked: Tell us 'just exactly' what happened. A story? I began: I am not learned; I am not ignorant . . ."; MD 18). The beginning of this *récit* within the *récit* reprises the beginning of *La Folie du jour*, as though the entire text were elicited by this institutional demand *en instance*—and *en abyme*—in search of a resolution of legal proceedings. "*Portez-vous plainte?*" ("Will you press charges?"), they ask him repeatedly, insisting that he tell them who crushed the glass in his eyes; but this is not his question. The true impetus behind the narration does not lie in this legalistic scenography, or even in the violence of the crushed glass. The text rather seems to situate it in the experience following this incident (after the glass has been removed), on the path back from darkness to a vision of "the day" which can hardly be contained in the empirical notion of that phenomenon. Concerning the period when his wounds have been dressed and are healing, the narrator exclaims,

> J'avais à tenir tête à la lumière de sept jours: un bel embrasement! Oui, sept jours ensemble, les sept clartés capitales devenues la vivacité d'un seul instant me demandaient des comptes. Qui aurait imaginé cela? Parfois, je me disais: "C'est la mort; malgré tout, cela en vaut la peine, c'est impressionnant." Mais souvent je mourais sans rien dire. A la longue, je fus convaincu que je voyais face à face la folie du jour;

telle était la vérité: la lumière devenait folle, la clarté avait perdu tout bon sens; elle m'assaillait déraisonnablement, sans règle, sans but. Cette dècouverte *fut un coup de dent à travers ma vie*. (FJ 22–23; my emphasis)

I had to hold my own against the light of seven days—a fine conflagration! Yes, seven days at once, the seven deadly lights, become the spark of a single instant, were calling me to account. Who would have imagined that? At times I said to myself, "This is death. In spite of everything, it's really worth it, it's impressive." But often I lay dying without saying anything. In the end, I grew convinced that I was face to face with the madness of the day. That was the truth: the light was going mad, the brightness had lost all reason; it assailed me irrationally, without control, without purpose. That discovery *bit straight through my life*. (MD 11–12)

The light and "the day" with which he claims in these moments to "*avoir affaire directement*" ("to have direct dealings"), and in which the seven days of calendar time are condensed into "*la vivacité d'un seul instant*" ("the vivacity of a single instant")—this day is not the one that shines for all to see, but the "mad" one that illuminates the space of thought, a space suffused with death and lacking all order. "*Qui aurait imaginé cela?*"— who would have imagined that the imaginary, reduced to its own resources, would begin to "*demander des comptes*" ("call me to account"), as though it were asking after its own punctual origin, which is also its death? Where does this light come from after all, and what strange and chaotic worlds does it give to be known? The narrator raises this experience to the status of a "discovery," evoking again the image of a blow, this time a curious "*coup de dent*," a violent bite cutting its way through the center of his life.

It is precisely here, at the point where a biting wound is linked directly with the experience of an "assailing" light that overwhelms and threatens madness, that we can glimpse the shadow cast upon this text by something like the sublime. In terms that cannot help but recall the wounding bite of conscience in Kafka, and the strange tooth that is implicated in its hidden treasures, Blanchot here situates a painful opening that cracks open the ordinary and familiar world of "the day" and reveals something akin to a conscience, the exigency of an "accounting" for oneself, and even, in a way that becomes almost comically explicit and concrete in what follows, the figure of the law as an elusive but overbearing figure. One major difference from Kafka, however, is that in Blanchot this figure is decidedly feminine.

Indeed, not long after this passage, the narrator begins his bizarre conversations with a female figure he refers to as "*la loi*," the law whose silhouette he first perceives behind the backs of his medico-legal interrogators. Born in some obscure way from the narrator's "direct affairs" with the day, this allegorical figure serves as the voice of a conscience, "*insatiable de ma gloire*," speaking within the space of a terribly lucid madness. "*La loi critiquait vivement ma conduite*" (FJ 32) ("The law was sharply critical of my behavior"; MD 16). Like a troubled conscience, a *kritische Instanz* literalized as a feminine instantiation, she is an intimate but alien presence: "*Elle en venait à des paroles futiles: 'La vérité, c'est que nous ne pouvons plus nous séparer. Je te suivrai partout, je vivrais sout ton toit, nous aurons le même sommeil'*" ("She was reduced to saying futile things: 'The truth is that we can never be separated again. I will follow you everywhere. I will live under your roof; we will share the same sleep'"; FJ 31). But despite her extreme proximity, she is distant and unattainable, asking imperiously: "*Qui ose penser jusqu'à moi?*" ("Who dares to think unto me?")—and although "*elle m'avait une fois fait toucher son genou*" ("Once she made me touch her knee"), her response to the narrator's declaration that he is not one to be satisfied with a knee, is a categorical refusal: "*Ce serait dégoutant!*" ("That would be disgusting!") Such jokes, and the entire atmosphere of hallucination and madness permeating the text, make of this strange relation a lighthearted game, a fictional encounter lightened by the artifice of allegorical play. Just as the narrator sees the blazing day behind the day, he sees the Law behind the machinery of legality, and it is these encounters that occupy the center of *La folie du jour*. But the feminine figure of the Law remains pure allegory, untouchable and unloseable. (Indeed, we may suspect that she arises from an economy of "remains" and a search for the unloseable, an attempt to stabilize a feminine other.) Thus in *La folie du jour* Blanchot locates within the narrative a number of encounters which in various but inadequate ways constitute an "instant" impelling narration.

The most suggestive of all, however, is one that, once again, is only alluded to without being narrated, but which seems to lie at the vanishing point toward which they all appear to be aligned. It is mentioned in the first pages, which are concerned with loss and the instability of fortune, and where the narrator makes statements very similar to those found at key moments in *L'instant de ma mort* and "(Une scène primitive?)." For example: "*Mon enfance a disparu, ma jeunesse est sur les routes. Il n'importe: ce qui a été, j'en suis heureux, ce qui est me plaît, ce qui vient me convient*" (FJ; my emphasis) ("My childhood has disappeared, my youth is behind me. *It doesn't matter*: I am happy about what has been, I am pleased by what is, and what is to come suits me well enough"). And just after that: "*je vois le monde, bonheur extraordinaire. Je le vois, ce jour hors duquel il n'est rien. Qui pourrait m'enlever cela*" ("I see the world—what extraordinary happiness! I see this day, and outside it there is nothing. Who could take that away from me?"; FJ 10; my emphasis/MD 6). It is in these terms that the narrator establishes, at the threshold of his narrative (and on the far side of a now ancient childhood), an inalienable affirmation and a "*bonheur*" that cannot ever be taken away. But immediately after this comes the most poignant, and yet still blunted, statement of the entire text, in which an irretrievable loss is alluded to, never to be mentioned again:

> J'ai aimé des êtres, je les ai perdus. Je suis devenu fou quand ce coup m'a frappé, car c'est un enfer. Mais ma folie est restée sans témoin, mon égarement n'apparaissait pas, mon intimité seule était folle. (FJ 11)

> I have loved people, I have lost them. I went mad when that blow struck me, because it is hell. But there was no witness to my madness, my frenzy was not evident; only my innermost being was mad. (MD 6)

This madness remains without a witness, without testimony, and strikes a blow that has opened a "hell" of which the present text seems to expose only the calm and well-lighted exit. The narrator does not say here that these "beings" are women, nor even that their loss came about through death (though this latter seems clear enough). But later he establishes a link between women and death.

> J'ai pourtant rencontré des êtres qui n'ont jamais dit à la vie, tais-toi, et jamais à la mort, va-t'en. Presque toujours des femmes, de belles créatures. (FJ 13)
>
> Yet I have met people who have never said to life "Quiet!", who have never said to death, "Go away!" Almost always women, beautiful creatures.

These sentences have often been quoted (including by Cixous) as a beautiful, affirmative statement on the powerful affirmation of such "beautiful" creatures. I find it rather extremely equivocal; but the point I would like to make has less to do with particular characteristics attributed to women and men in Blanchot than with the intimate complicity, not to say identification, between women and death, and the way in which this complicity constitutes literary space on the basis of a displaced encounter that does not reckon with the losses it requires. The following chapter will take up this question in more detail in a reading of the *récit* that brings it most clearly into relief, *L'arrêt de mort*.

CHAPTER 6

The Shell and the Mask
L'arrêt de mort

The overview presented in the preceding chapter, on the "punctual" and "puncturing" events that structure the *récits*, indicates that somewhere beyond or before the more dramatically violent points figured within these narratives lies a point of another order, one that puts loss and mourning more directly into play. This *other* point moves in a direction that I would like to follow here, on the way into a reading of *L'arrêt de mort*. Elusive and obliquely approached, this is a *point de fuite*—a vanishing point that "flees" when approached—in at least two senses: the point in question continually recedes into the distant horizon of these narratives, all of which however seem to align in its direction; but it is also perhaps the point *from* which the narratives themselves seem to flee, as from a *coup* too painful to assimilate, and as such it is strictly *interdit*, barred from being drawn into the figural and referential texture of the narratives. As pointed out before, these narratives begin already in "la profondeur du *récit*," with a "monumental" event far behind them, and the voices that proffer them are in the grips of this "far behind" even as they introduce elements that play on its return and re-engagement, its *revenance* in other guises ("*Mon Dieu! encore une figure de connaissance... A nouveau! à nouveau!*" [AMV 7, 14]). But it could be that some events are "farther behind" than others, and more radically transformed upon return, their singular features drastically reshaped by their immemorial inaccessibility. (Indeed, what the nature of such an "event" could be, and its relation to "thought" is central to Blanchot's late reflections, especially in *L'écriture du désastre*.) In that sense, the *récits*, for their part, largely avoid directly addressing the question I have been asking: How is a life in the world "pointedly" transformed into a search for the point that drew it, as a voice, into the "already other" space of the *récit*? Or rather, the *récits* make gestures in the direction of such initial openings, but only to occlude, blur, mute, deaden or even dismiss them ("*n'importe...*"). The barely emerging figures of lost "beings," in conjunction with the charged and haunting feminine presences that populate the *récits*, give, I believe, the most compelling clue as to the direction in which this *point de fuite* should take us. I have already suggested that in the convergent crux of this point, in the out-of-joint

213

hinge of its horizon, there hovers a dead woman's face—death mask and emblem of writing's enigmatic origins.

ARÊTES DE VIE: DESPOLIATIONS

In the overview of the *récits* presented in the preceding chapter, little mention was made of *L'arrêt de mort*. This is partly because of its exceptional status, on at least two accounts: it is both a transition narrative, a kind of border-crossing, relating the narrator's passage out of the world and into recitical space, "the other of every world"; at the same time, it clearly and directly marks this passage as one that requires the encounter with, and the disappearance or "evaporation" of, feminine figures whose loss marks and opens the way to be followed (as in *Le dernier homme*, *L'arrêt de mort* refers to the "subliming" process of a "volatilization"—though perhaps in a sense that is rather alchemical than chemical). One way to describe the difference between *L'arrêt de mort* and the other *récits* would be to say that in the former, while the narrator is "already" in the grips of a compelling and enigmatic past, while he tells his story "from there"— from the alter-worldly space that the experience to be recounted has brought him to (though at first he does not seem to be clearly aware of this)—the "events" he turns to in order to relate this enigma are themselves legibly located in the time of the world and of the calendar, as indicated first of all by the date given in its opening sentence ("*Ces événements me sont arrivés en 1938*"; "These events happened to me in 1938"). Likewise, *L'arrêt de mort* is by far the most circumstantially elaborate of the *récits*, providing in relatively dense detail the worldly (historical and social) material that will be sloughed off in the end. The entire book, in both of its two parts, is thus structured as the halting movement from the historical time of "the world" into another time and space, and toward the infinite, categorical affirmation proper to that realm. *L'arrêt de mort* is the story in Blanchot's oeuvre that brings stories into their true recitical dimension, that traces out a passage from "the world" into its absolutely other, and that thereby draws or drags the storyteller into the unhinged—unbound and unbounded—space of a more radical literary experience. At the same time, it clearly bears the scars of this ecstatic but unhappy transformation, a lacerating point that does, after all, cling to the *récit* as the ineliminable dross of the world that has been left. Christopher Fynsk is right to lay great stress on the *malheur* of this passage, a painful dimension of loss and impersonality, but it is important to acknowledge as well that in the logic of the *récit* this loss is also the enforced renunciation and "volatilization" of a woman, for the sake of a transcending "thought."[1] Strangely, since in *L'arrêt de mort* thought is a woman (*une pensée*), it is precisely the feminine allegory that demands the elision of the woman she appears *to have been*. But at the same time, this passage leaves a trail of abandoned remnants, including the corpses and remains of several women, cast off residues that are no less *dépouillements* than *dépouilles*, leavings that are also perhaps—as this language surreptitiously suggests—the despoliations that will be deeply deposited into a melancholic treasure henceforth to be guarded, but likewise impossible to be rid of.

In approaching the enigma of *L'arrêt de mort*, I would thus like to shift the rhetorical or figural emphasis from the unreachable *point* "itself" to its discardable outer guises, the scars and residues produced by its lacerating puncture, slice or bite. Not that the structural figure of the point is irrelevant to *L'arrêt de mort* (indeed, it will continue to be the central question pressing upon the narrative); but it manifests differently in this tale, with more figural and material density. As mentioned before, Blanchot's narrator speaks early on of "the shell of an enigma," a phrase that I will explicate in its context in a moment, but that indicates precisely the aspect of leavings, residues, peelings away and *dépouillements* that the adventure of *L'arrêt de mort* both presents *as* the story/text (in its figural and linguistic surface texture), and attempts to discard as inessential on the way to a central paradoxical affirmation, articulated in its final pages. That, too, is the "secret law of the *récit*"—the necessity of simultaneously casting up and casting off the story's constitutive figures. But the enigma, the shifting and fleeing point of the voice's haunting compulsion, subsists in its strange emptiness. In other words, the kernel *is* the shell, in the sense that it has no proper subsistence and must be exorbitantly *manifested*, and yet it is also always elsewhere, is never "contained" or fully coincident with what gives it to be seen, such that the visible figures through which it must pass always invite the violence of a *dépouillement*, a transcendentalizing violence that seems to promise the pure core but nonetheless remains stuck with the figures and phenomena it could not help but conjure.[2] The ineliminable nature of these sticky figures can be summed up in the obvious fact that they are what make up the story itself, such that, in the case of *L'arrêt de mort*, if the story leads out of the world it projects, one look back from the volatilized endpoint necessarily recalls all the stuff it took to get there (and this look back is structurally inscribed in the *récit*'s enigmatic demand to be reread, always and again). Put yet another way, this look back must show once again the dread face of Eurydice, who in the end appears to have vanished for good. She is still with us, and with the narrator—not only as "thought" but also as figure—as the *récit* itself more or less openly admits when it presents her spectral image in the present space of its writing ("she is here, in front of me," states the narrator in reference to his writing space). One measure of the complexity and difficulty of Blanchot's *récits*, as stories that strive toward their own originary "point," is that their narrator both fights against (attempts to flee) and embraces this constitutive paradox in the actual texture of the works: their inaugural self-refusal in the first *récit*, *La folie du jour* ("*Un récit? Non, pas de récit, plus jamais . . .*"), is continually, even compulsively belied.[3] Christopher Fynsk speaks of a "delirium" in the elision of figures and "facts" carried out by Blanchot's narrator.[4] While giving such a delirium its ecstatic and passionate due, I would like to look as soberly as possible at certain singularities of the narrative published under the title *L'arrêt de mort*. These singularities mark out a tortuous and complex transit between fictive figures and something like the transcendental condition of haunted narration.

In *L'arrêt de mort*, if the kernel is the shell, the shell, as outward image and figure of narration, largely takes the form of a man's relation with dead and dying women. The story's *dépouillements* are thus also *dépouilles*: leavings as corpses. The proximity between these words indicates the tight but ruptured link between the figure and its transcendental emblem, the emblem of the origin of figures as such. It is well known that the corpse plays an essential part in Blanchot's thinking of the image, especially as articulated in "Les deux versions de l'imaginaire" in *L'espace littéraire*. If the corpse, *la dépouille*, is a mere leaving, it is also, in that analysis, the very image of image—the *thing* that is left when nothing is left, the residual and irreducible "phenomenon" that collapses the world and gives, uncannily, an experience of its scrambled origination. I will address these issues in more detail in the next chapter; at this point I would like to locate in the central figure of *L'arrêt de mort*—the cast of a face in its deathly implications—the broken hinge, as it were, between the image and the transcendental as a near-coincidence of kernel and shell, of *dépouille* and *dépouillements*. But also, as we will see, as a ghost that binds death to the animation of a necessity pressing into narrative speech. Shell as kernel, *dépouille* as transcendental origin, ghost as being's residue and as pressing imperative: these are the figures of Blanchot's cryptography, which is also an "*hantologie*" in the sense that Derrida has outlined,[5] and they are the fundamental figural coordinates of *L'arrêt de mort*.

It is remarkable to note that Derrida has indicated in very similar terms the privileged status of both the shell/kernel figure *and* the figure of the ghost, in two very different texts separated by many years but linked by a striking continuity in the topology, or tropology, of Derrida's thought (in the contours of its figural elaborations). In both cases it is a question of a figure that figures the structure of figuration itself, a figure that shows something of how figures come to appear, and in gesturing toward this crux, the statements resemble each other very closely, down to their very grammar. First, in an essay from 1979 on Abraham Torok's psychoanalytic work *L'écorce et le noyau*, Derrida speaks of "*la figure écorce-noyau qui, à l'origine de toute traduction figurative, de toute symbolisation et de toute figuration, ne serait pas un dispositif tropique ou topique parmi d'autres*" ("the shell-kernel figure which, being at the origin of every symbolic and figurative act, is not merely one tropic or topical mechanism among many").[6] Originary figure of figural origination, the shell-kernel schema is at the generative core of all figures (and is thus at least analogous to a transcendental schema).

Later, in *Specters of Marx*—where Derrida finds it necessary to invoke the Kantian schematism more than once in relation to the structure and phenomena of spectrality and time's disjointedness (not to mention death masks and glass coffins)—he says something strikingly similar, but in reference to a different figure, a different figure of figures, suggesting that "*la figure du fantôme n'y est pas une figure parmi d'autres. C'est peut-être la figure cachée de toutes les figures*" ("the figure of the ghost is not just one figure among others. It is perhaps the hidden figure of all figures").[7] The specific reference here is to the "fantastic panoply" mobilized in Marx's rhetoric; but as part of a passage aiming at "certain invariables," the statement is programmatic: the phantom lies hidden (like Kant's "art hidden in the human soul") at the origin of figures, both rhetorical and phenomenal. Like the "shell/kernel figure," the specter is not "one . . . among others," but the one that figures the origin of figuration.

In *L'arrêt de mort* it is precisely these two versions of the figure of figures that converge in the narrative's central animating *thing*: the set of casts, "of my head and of my hands" (AM 119), left behind by the ghostly woman who haunts the space of writing even *now*, as the narrator writes, reminding us more than once that "this same person" (AM 66) is there with him in his writing space . . . In other words, a feminine ghost who is somehow also the molded and morcellated hands and face of a dead-living woman: her leavings are what generate the narrative and provide its figural texture, even as, in the end, she commands a radical leaving of the world. In the figural residues that remain, however, one can see not only an *arrêt de mort*, but also the jutting *arêtes de vie*, the sharp edges and contours of a life that the usury of the narrative voice can never manage to wear down to nothing.[8] Indeed, it is difficult not see him literally embracing them as he moves, painfully and fitfully, almost desperately, toward the affirmation of a transcendental something that cannot ever be taken away, eternally safeguarded by "her" and her peculiar truth, absent of all facts.

Put another way, *L'arrêt de mort* deals very *graphically* with the *point de fuite* and its material aftermath that I have been tracing. Is it possible to approach the enigma of Blanchot's *récit* while also translating some of its figures into the very legible terms of a melancholy economy determining some rather suspect operations over a woman's dead body, even if such an approach risks merely displacing the text's empty shells in a game that Blanchot has laid out for us in the first place? It is difficult to see how this text's mystifications can be dispelled, or at any rate brought into clear relief (and these are not necessarily the same), without entering into the densely constructed logic of its crypt. This text announces itself in multiple ways as a *trap* (as we will see), both for the women it casts off, and for us readers.[9] But to read it without working one's way into the fascination it seeks to evoke would surely be to bypass what is most urgent in its equivocal tensions—which is not to rescue a living woman from its clutches (this would be to succumb to another mystification, the very one the text attempts to counter), but to separate the desire for eternity *in time* from the spectacle of a feminine corpse. And thus to leave this image, finally, in the unsuppressed oblivion it craves. Would this be the condition for a return that would not lord it over writing like a Law bound to its murderer? And finally, to conclude these rather cryptic remarks (for which I beg indulgence for the moment), and before discussing *L'arrêt de mort* in more detail: is it possible to separate the imperative to write from the mournful movement of sublime separation itself? We may not learn this in any definitive way from *L'arrêt de mort*, but this question will haunt our reading of it.

L'ARRÊT DE MORT

The plot of *L'arrêt de mort*, which a brief description can only caricature, involves the apparent death and resuscitation by the narrator of a woman he calls J., and then, in a second part, an extremely uncanny relationship between the narrator and another woman he calls N. (for Nathalie; J.'s name is never given).[10] In the course of the second part, N. strangely merges with something the narrator calls his "thought," a feminine *pensée* that is both external to the narrator and yet more intimate than intimate (in her undecidable presence, she is what Lacan would call *extimate*). One is tempted to deduce, on the basis of certain very ambiguous indices, that N. is somehow a reembodiment of J., or at least another *version* of her, and of the force that she communicates—Blanchot's narrator *all but* says this, and yet the omission and its reserve are crucial in maintaining the undecidability of several borders, across which the tale pursues its transformations. It can be said that the book's "aim," extraordinarily obscure at first, but clearer by the end, will have been to affirm the bond or alliance with this strange being, a death-woman-thought amalgamation or confluence who/which, as we will see, governs from a deeply intimate distance the space in which writing *must* take place—not least the writing of the narrative of this very being's emergence as such, and of her leaving-behind. After much equivocation and vacillation, the apotheosis or "volatilization" of a woman into such a being occurs, rhetorically speaking, in the last long paragraph of the book, which I will look at in some detail (it "occurs" there, or is rather asserted as having been effected since long ago . . .). The "hinge" of this conversion, as I have suggested, consists of the casts of N.'s head and hands, or the "project" of having them made, which is also revealed in the very last pages, and these references provide a direct link to an earlier mention, in the first part, of a cast made of J.'s hands (for the purposes of a palm reading). Finally, these cast hands are in turn associated with the narrator's own act of writing, in that he suggests not only that he has the casts there with him as he writes, but even more uncannily that they are the ones writing. . . . These suggestions are echoed in numerous references to hands throughout the narrative. A full exposition of the intricate *enchevêtrements* or entanglements of these hands would require a great deal of space; I will attempt to evoke above all their uncanny *manoeuvres*, their disquieting operations at the heart of the work.

Like the other *récits*, *L'arrêt de mort* is proffered by a voice speaking in the intimate urgency of a pressing enigma, in the grip of an experience that far exceeds it but that, for some reason, demands impossibly to be told. This is the primary and most directly manifest form of the imperative bearing on Blanchot's recitical narrators, and this pressure is made explicit here. Something *must be* told: "*il faut que je parle*" ("I must speak"; AM 57) says the narrator, attributing this necessity to the solitude that engulfs him in the space of writing, which however is located "*dans une chambre . . . dans la maison*" ("in a room . . . in the house") and so still in a *place* somewhere within the architecture of the world (haunted and estranged as it may be). Similarly, but unlike in the other *récits*, the pressing enigma of *L'arrêt de mort* is, at first, directly associated with events located in calendar time. The text opens with the line I have already quoted: "*Ces événements me sont arrivés en 1938*" ("These events happened to me in 1938"; AM 7). The testimonial dimension of the story is thus established from the beginning—although it should be stressed again that as the story progresses, this dimension has less and less to do with calendar time and more with the upheaval of an exit from it.[11] The imperative pressing the voice is conjoined directly with an elementary form of haunting, in that the narrative is a return to and of the past, on the basis of an urgency that is felt *in the present of writing* but that is clearly a remnant of that past's enigmatic and irreducible persistence. The complex torsion of this looping temporality is already a clue that the narrative's testimony will not long remain within the confines of calendar time before drifting into another territory, thus unmooring the narrative voice from whatever facts may have surrounded the events in question. What haunts the narrator does require a turn to specific events, but is not contained within them. At the same time, there is an intimate, even confessional quality to the tone of *L'arrêt de mort*, as though a man were writing about some extremely important thing that happened to him and that he feels the urgent need to tell about. In that sense, the book is overtly structured as a kind of autobiographical document. But this, too, is a ruse designed to reshift, and to blur, the focus. If *L'arrêt de mort* is structured as an autobiography, the tale it strives both to tell and to be released from telling—by finally being able to *en finir*, as the narrator puts it on the first page—is itself to be radically released from the conditions of a life in the world and to "enter" the "outside" of writing, whose conditions are entirely other. The "autobiographical" voice of *L'arrêt de mort* thus sets out to strip itself of its "life," to be "*dépouillé de soi, délivré . . . du passé*" ("stripped of oneself, delivered . . . from the past"), as Blanchot says elsewhere of Proust (LV 28). And the story provides many direct indications that its essential drama is the protagonist-narrator's reluctant but inevitable movement out of time and the world, out of his life, toward what he calls "*l'autre côté d'une vie*," the other side of a life. This is the Rilkean phrase that Blanchot uses in *L'arrêt de mort* for the life that is separated from life by a kind of death to life, and thus for the task of taking this other life into hand by writing.

How does the narrator "get there"? How does he suggest that he has done this, and through what exactly has he passed? *L'arrêt de mort* is a love story, but it is, at the same time, and almost in precisely the same narrative events, a ghost story. The story of a love for a ghost, then, and yet not entirely, for there is a persistent noncoincidence between a loved *woman* and the ghost that appears, most clearly as such, in the narrator's references to the *now* of his writing: *maintenant*. It is in these strange references to a spectral presence in the writer's room, and as he writes, that the ghostly form of the imperative, and of the entire experience (and all the "events") in question, becomes visible. As indicated earlier, these presences take two forms which, bluntly put, can be described as: full sized ghosts standing (and gliding about) in his room, and the strange plaster hands that seem to be doing all the writing (along with a death mask that we will return to later). I will foreground these moments, beginning with the second, since that is what the narrative begins with, albeit very obliquely.

The narrator begins by laying out an entire field of remnants and remains that appear to link the present back to the "events" that draw him into this narration, but he appears to do this primarily in order to discount and even liquidate them, in order to clear the way for *this* beginning—as though he were purifying the narrative space of so much detritus, so many failures and false approaches. First, he refers to an earlier attempt to write down "these events"—"*mais . . . je détruisis le manuscrit*" ("but I destroyed the manuscript"). Ashes, or paper shreds. Next he claims that "*de ces événements il y a plusieurs témoins*" ("of these events there are several witnesses"), but he dismisses them, mentioning instead the apartment where the events happened, and wondering about the sister of "the young woman" (this latter turns out to be J., of whom this is the first mention): "*Qu'est-elle devenue? . . . Je la suppose morte*" ("What became of her? . . . I suppose she is dead"). A supposed corpse. This sister is the first of the dead women strewn throughout the pages of the tale, emerging and disappearing here at its threshold in close proximity to the leavings mentioned next. After some sketchy information about the young woman's family (her father was killed in 1916, her mother remarried and squandered the family fortune), he returns to the question of the more mysterious events at hand:

> De ces événements, je garde une preuve "vivante." Mais cette preuve, sans moi, ne peut rien prouver, et j'espère que de ma vie personne ne s'en approchera. Moi mort, elle ne représente que *l'écorce d'une énigme*. (AM 9; my emphasis)
>
> Of these events I have a "living" proof. But without me, this proof can prove nothing, and I hope that while I am alive no one will approach it. With my death, it can represent only *the shell of an enigma*.

Unique witness to a barely "living" proof, the narrator wants to place himself at the center of a complex of signs that *require his life* in order to speak from out of their own. The shell, at this point, obtrudes as mere dead matter which, with his death, must be abandoned, thrown away, as he insists in the Kafka-like injunction that follows, asking that those close to him destroy everything he leaves behind (letters, photographs, everything: "and above all do not open what is closed"; AM 10). This first dismissive evocation of the "shell," however, is made before the writing we are reading has become the book that still awaits its unfolding. To open such a shell would be to find only emptiness—but it is precisely this emptiness that is on its way to being transformed into something more intimately attached to the very existence of this shell: a *récit* that has been written and left to read.

Now what is this "*preuve 'vivante,'*" this "living" shell without fruit or core? The narrator does not say here, nor does he explain the strange scare quotes, which in bracketing life evoke rather its deathly semblance. But a later passage gives a clue. As the narrator's description of J.'s mortal illness begins to unfold more circumstantially (her ailments, proposed treatments, the surrounding personages, etc.), he mentions "*un incident curieux*" that arose in part out of anxiety and uncertainty over her fate:

> A un garçon qui s'occupait—professionnellement—de chirologie et d'astrologie, j'avais remis un très beau moulage des mains de J. et je lui avais demandé d'établir les grandes coordinées de ce destin.
>
> I had sent a very beautiful mold of J.'s hands to a young man who was involved—professionally—with chirology and astrology, and I had asked him to establish the broad coordinates of this destiny.

He describes her hands as being marked by "*lignes . . . tout à fait singulières, hachées, enchevêtrées, sans la moindre unité apparente*" ("completely singular lines, cross-hatched, intertwined, without the slightest apparent unity"), and says that he wouldn't know how to describe them, before adding the following: "*bien qu'*en ce moment même je les aie sous les yeux et qu'elles vivent" ("even though *at this moment I have them before my eyes and they are alive*"; AM 21, my emphasis). This casual statement is then dropped, as he moves on to further describe, in the past tense, J.'s hands and their "*profond coup de hache*," her violently hacked line of fate.[12] This time, in this scandalous and completely fantastical statement, there are no quotes around the life of these remnants: Her hands are there, now, *maintenant*—a word that is beginning to take on an unexpected and eerie literality—as I write, I can see them and they are alive. Surely this is the "living" proof referred to earlier (leaving aside for now the question of what sort of life this may be)—or at least part of it, for a set of casts that play a pivotal role in the second part of the book have their place here as well. It is also the first direct indication of the kind of haunting that animates the text and its spaces: a spooky animation of the unliving, and one of the classic examples of the uncanny in fantastic literature: the severed hand as revenant.[13] For Blanchot, who discreetly and with no apparent irony introduces into the narrative the themes of chirology and astrology, this "occult" dimension of the tale opens the *récit* to a set of generic associations to which, however, the true enigma at hand will not be limited. The schematic and "generic" (or generative) importance of this uncanny intrusion will become clearer later; for now it introduces in a rich and textured figure the essential dimension of a figural haunting out of which the tale will be proffered, while also evoking the spectral and compulsive hand writing the story *maintenant*, as though it were the hand of another, pressed on by what Blanchot elsewhere refers to as the "*préhension persécutrice*"—the "imperious exigency" of a "sick" hand driven in a fit of automatism to grasp a pencil, and to write without cease, despite the will or desire of the writer.[14]

This passage should suffice, then, to indicate that the haunting staged in *L'arrêt de mort* is perfectly "literal" (at least as "literal" as it is "alive"), but there is more—and this brings me to the other form of spectral presence already mentioned. If this haunting accretes at first in the text around the casts of a woman's hands, another troubling figure is projected into this space as well. This time the reference to the present haunted scene of writing is inserted into the description (in the second part of the *récit*) of a scene involving a woman who turns out to be N(athalie): one night she enters the narrator's room unannounced and stands before him motionless and spectral. At this point in the narrative, we, like the narrator, do not know who she is, and so we also do not yet know that she is thus initiating their relation, essentially by chance, as was the case with J.[15] It is very unclear what sort of creature she is: dead, living, fact or figment, statue or phantasm. . . . But if she has the immobility of a statue, her element, rather than stone, is pure feeling.

> Je voulais écrire qu'elle ressemblait à une statue, parce que, tournée vers la fenêtre et immobile, elle avait en effet un air de statue; mais la pierre n'était pas son élément, c'était plutôt la peur qui était sa nature, non pas une peur folle ou monumentale, mais quelque chose qu'expriment ces mots: pour elle l'irrémédiable était arrivé. (AM 65)

> I was going to write that she was like a statue, because she was motionless and turned toward the window, and she really did have the look of a statue; but stone was not her element, her nature was rather made of fear, not a mad or monumental fear, but something that is expressed by these words: for her, the irremediable had happened.

At this point the narrator compares her, bizarrely, to a squirrel that has entered a cage "*avec dedans un petit tas de coquilles*" ("with a little pile of shells inside") only to realize that the trap door has shut. This image can serve as a clear enough indication, again through an accretion of associations, that the space of writing is a trap, even a prison, into which a few shells can lure its prey (and everyone concerned is in danger—the woman, the writer, the reader, even the poor squirrel who must live on a metaphor). The narrator goes on to evoke her weak, meager, vibratory presence, as though she barely exists: "*il lui restait tout juste assez de force pour demeurer, debout, dans cette chambre, sans se volatiliser*" ("she had just enough strength left to remain standing in this room, without dissolving into thin air"). It is here that he refers again to the haunted space of writing *maintenant*:

> Je pourrais dire beaucoup de choses sur l'impression que j'avais, mais cette impression est celle que j'ai *maintenant* en regardant *cette même personne*, de dos, arrêtée à quelques pas de la fenêtre et juste devant la table; c'est à peu près la même heure, elle est entrée et elle avance (la pièce est différente). (AM, 66; my emphasis)

> I could say many things about the impression I had, but this impression is the one I have *now* as I look at *that same person*, with her back to me, stopping there a few steps from the window and just in front of the table; it is about the same hour, she entered and is moving forward (the room is different).

This "scene" is clear enough, but very strange: she is there, that same person who entered his room one night, but now he sees her entering and "advancing"—a movement one can easily see as the almost motionless drifting of a ghost, calmly observed. But this calm is not without a violent, passionate and vertiginous undertow, an *entraînement* that leads into an anxious compulsion directly bearing on the writing happening now:

> A la voir ainsi, aujourd'hui où elle n'est plus une surprise, j'éprouve un saisissement bien plus grand, un sentiment de vertige et d'égarement que je n'ai jamais eu alors, mais aussi quelque chose de froid, un étrange serrement de coeur, au point que je voudrais la supplier de revenir en arrière et de rester derrière la porte, pour que, moi aussi, je puisse sortir. Mais la règle le veut et l'on ne saurait s'en affranchir: dès que la pensée s'est levée, *il faut la suivre jusqu'au bout*. (AM 66–67; my emphasis)[16]

> Seeing her thus today, when she is no longer a surprise, I am gripped by a much greater feeling, a feeling of vertigo and confusion that I never had then, but also something cold, a strange pang, to the point that I would like to beg her to turn back and to remain behind the door so that I too might be able to leave. But there is a rule from which one cannot be released: when a thought has arisen, *it is necessary to follow it to the end*.

This gesture toward the fantastic is so casual that one feels the need to restate what is already so clearly said: as the narrator writes, he sees before him "the same person," the phantom of a woman who is "dead," to whom the "irremediable" has happened, and who in the initial scene had "*déjà glissé hors de l'ordre des choses*" ("already slipped out of the order of things"; AM 67). His room, and by extension his writing itself (with which the room is, rigorously speaking, coextensive) is haunted by her, in every sense. She inhabits the space of writing as the figuration of its "rule" and as the "thought" that writing must follow: *il faut*. Note that here the Orphic roles have been reversed: he must follow her. It is worth noting too that earlier in the text the narrator has emphatically stressed his solitude in the present. Clearly this solitude is far from unpopulated. But who is this "she" that he must follow? We soon learn that, if she is a specter haunting the writer's *now*, she has also *been* a woman, and her name is Nathalie. It is the figure of Nathalie—figure of birth through death, even of resurrection—that the *récit*, and its narrator, must follow to their final paradoxical affirmation.

Who is Nathalie? In a sense, the crux of the text's many ambiguities lies in this question, which puts into play a set of very unstable (and always already scrambled) oppositions: is she a woman represented, or an allegory of the unpresentable (of the sublime)? A lover touched and held or an inaccessible ghost? An outwardly existing person or a "thought"? A figure who lives in the world, or a figure of world's unfigurable other—of a space that is "the other of every world"? The narrative presents her in all these aspects, and Blanchot is careful to modulate its rhetoric such that, true to the radical ambiguity of literary space, we need not, indeed cannot decide. But as the text advances, it emerges that the drama in which the narrator finds himself embroiled, the set of "events" (which uncannily enfold the event of writing itself, along with the "encounter" it stages and surpasses), while it involves various oscillations between these poles, tends in the end in the direction of figural effacement. The specific effacement undergone by N. (and, less directly, by J.), is mediated by the ghost who precedes her, generically and anonymously, in the text. Within the first paragraphs of the second part, the narrative prepares us for their eventual assimilation.

> Mais, une pensée n'est pas tout à fait une personne, même si elle agit et vit comme elle. Une pensée exige une loyauté qui rend difficile toute ruse. Elle-même est parfois fausse, mais derrière ce mensonge je reconnais encore quelque chose de vrai que, moi, je ne puis tromper.
>
> But a thought is not quite a person, even if she [*elle*] acts and lives like one. A thought demands a loyalty that renders difficult any ruse. She is herself sometimes false, but behind this lie I still recognize something true which I myself cannot deceive.

This demanding thought which is "not quite" a person comes to resemble one more and more, as if pulled by figural language into this fictive element. The narrator continues to speak of his strange thought-companion:

> A la vérité, c'est sa droiture qui me fascine. Quand elle se lève, cette pensée, il n'y a plus ni souvenir ni crainte, ni lassitude ni pressentiment, ni rappel d'hier ni projet pour demain. Elle se lève et peut-être s'est-elle levé mille fois, dix mille fois. Qui donc m'est plus familier? Mais la familiarité, voilà ce qui entre nous s'est à jamais perdu. Je la regarde. Elle vit avec moi. Elle est dans ma maison. Parfois, elle se met à manger; parfois, quoique rarement, elle dort près de moi. Et moi, insensé, je me croise les mains et je la laisse manger sa propre chair. (AM 55–56)
>
> In truth, it is her uprightness that fascinates me. When she rises, this thought, there is neither memory nor fear, neither weariness nor presentiment, neither recollection of yesterday nor project for tomorrow. She rises, and perhaps she has risen a thousand, ten thousand times. Who then is more familiar to me? But familiarity is something between us that has been lost forever. I look at her. She lives with me. She is in my house. Sometimes, she begins to eat; sometimes, although rarely, she sleeps next to me. And I, out of my senses, I cross my hands and let her eat her own flesh.

This passage occurs before the introduction of the figure of N. into the narrative, and has the status of a somewhat awkward allegorical figuration, the forcing of a feminine figure and the abstraction of "thought," mediated by the arbitrariness of grammatical gender (*la pensée, elle* . . .), a slippage that is even more evident in English, which requires a choice between "she" and "it." Much will follow from this arbitrary marker, for these meanings are in fact simultaneous: this thought is both "she" and "it," a palpable presence embodied enough to have flesh that can be chewed on, while also eluding a familiarity that can only be "lost forever." This grammatically motivated vacillation or merger is manifest in a more theatrical or phenomenal register as well, when in a later scene the narrator sees N. and says outright: she was my thought (AM 98). This uncanny vision of N. walking through the space of the world *as his thought* occurs one evening when, after an argument, he unexpectedly sees her at the theater accompanied by "*un garçon inconnu*" (AM 97):

> elle était là. Elle me parut extrêmement belle. Je la voyais passer devant moi, aller et venir dans un lieu tout proche et infiniment séparé et comme derrière une vitre. Je fus frappé par cette idée. J'aurais sans doute pu lui parler, mais je ne le désirais pas et peut-être, en effet, ne le pouvais-je pas. Elle se tenait en ma présence avec la liberté d'une pensée; elle était dans ce monde, mais dans ce monde je ne la rencontrais encore que parce qu'*elle était ma pensée*; et quelle connivence s'établissait donc entre elles, quelle complicité pleine d'horreur. (AM 97–98; my emphasis)

> she was there. She seemed very beautiful to me. I saw her passing in front of me, walking back and forth in a place that was very near and infinitely separate and as though behind a pane of glass. I was struck by this idea. No doubt I could have talked to her, but I did not want to and perhaps indeed I was not able to. She remained in my presence with the freedom of a thought; she was in this world, but in this world I was encountering her again only because *she was my thought*; and what tacit understanding was therefore being established between them, what complicity full of horror.

The horror of this moment is that of an intimate complicity between "thought" and "being," the abyssal terror of a "vision" in which the intimacy of thought is rendered as the exteriority of an other—particularly of this other who is becoming a more and more beloved woman. It is thus the horror of an irreducibly double origin for both "sides" of this divide (interior, exterior), such that the overwhelming proximity and familiarity of this figure is also at a glassy remove, an experience Blanchot's narrator refers to elsewhere as "*le phénomène de la vitre*" (the phenomenon of the pane of glass). From behind this pane of glass stare back all possible phenomena, but it is of course the gaze of this woman-thought, as she walks at an infinite distance through a public social space, that is most unsettling.

> J'ajoute qu'elle me regardait comme quelqu'un qui me reconnaissait très bien et même amicalement, mais c'était une reconnaissance de derrière les yeux, sans regard et sans signe, une reconnaissance de la pensée, amicale, froide et morte.
>
> Cette impression fut-elle sans lendemain? Il me semble qu'elle déchira ma vie, qu'à partir de cet instant, je n'eus presque plus rien à apprendre, et cependant, si je regarde ce que je faisais et comment je vivais, rien encore n'était changé . . . Il faut toutefois se rappeler les événements . . . (AM 97–98)

I will add that she looked at me like someone who recognized me very well and even in a friendly way, but it was a recognition from behind the eyes, without a look and without a sign, a recognition of thought, friendly, cold, and dead.

Was this a passing impression? It seems to me that it tore my life apart, that from that instant I had almost nothing left to learn, and yet, if I look at what I did and how I lived, nothing had yet changed. . . . Yet I must recall the events.

This is the closest we come in *L'arrêt de mort* to the sort of puncturing (or tearing) instant discussed earlier. It is a moment when the narrator's "place" in the world, his participation in real events, vacillates, when the bonds that attach him to this world are "torn apart," or at least now "seem" to have been (we are in the theater, after all, space of dissimulation and manipulated appearance). For, as he says, nothing really changed, the events of the day (the crisis of an approaching war) continued to assert their dominance over his actions. But the damage has been done, the rupture has been opened, and will continue its ineluctable course. In this case, however (as compared with the other *récits* discussed in the previous chapter), there is a more legible connection between this *déchirement* and the infinite distance, the presence-absence, of a woman, and with the possibility of loss, a terrible foretaste of *malheur* and mourning. The dread of such a loss is less evident here, but it will soon come to the fore. At this instant, the overwhelming feature of the experience, what introduces the rupture of an infinite distance—and the strange sensation of looking at the world from behind glass—is N.'s mortal gaze, "friendly, cold, and dead."[17] The gaze is the thing: it is through its irruption into this theatrical space that the narrator "learns" definitively that he is on his way out of the world, and out of this worldly, erotic relationship—or rather that he is already outside of it, placed there by a distant (distancing) and imperious look that confronts him as an ineluctable confirmation—but it will take some time for him to absorb (into) this.

This dead gaze has its place in an entire series of gazes that punctuate the narrative of *L'arrêt de mort* (in tandem with the motif of hands) as it proceeds toward the image of the death mask and the final disfiguration that the mask appears to operate. It is interesting in this regard to note Derrida's association in *Parages* (207, 215), echoed as well in *Specters of Marx*, of this glass covering with a glass coffin. In "Survivre," speaking of the relation between the narrator of *L'arrêt de mort* and the two main women in the tale, Derrida writes:

Or *il* les aime. Il les aime mortes. Il aime les voir. Il aime *à* les voir. Il aime les voir mortes. Il aime *à* les voir mortes. Mais elles sont mortes dès qu'il les voit. Dès que de ce regard terrible elles le voient, comme leur mort. Elles sont mortes dès lors qu'il les aime. Il ne peut d'ailleurs aimer ou désirer que sous vitre, dit-il ailleurs. On imagine un cercueil vitré, c'est un thématique de ce *récit*—et d'autres, que je réserve ici. Mais chacune figure aussi le double, masque mortuaire, moulage, fantôme, corps à la fois vivant et mort de l'autre. Séparées par une vitre infranchissable d'une

> histoire à l'autre. Séparées: réunies. Elles restent deux, absolument autres, infiniment séparées par l'arrêt de mort entre deux récits hétérogènes. (*Parages* 206–207)
>
> But he loves them. He loves them dead. He loves seeing them. He loves *just by* seeing them. He loves seeing them dead. He loves *just by* seeing them dead. But they are dead as soon as he sees them. As soon as with this terrible look they see him, as their death. They are dead as soon as he loves them. Anyway, he can love or desire only behind glass, he says. One imagines a glass coffin, this is a theme of the *récit*—and of others which I refrain from mentioning here. But each one of the two is also figured by the double, a death mask, a mold, a ghost, body of the other at once living and dead. Separated by an unbreakable glass from one story to the other. Separated: joined. They remain two, absolutely other, infinitely separated by the *arrêt de mort*, the death sentence and the suspension of death, between two heterogeneous *récits*.

Derrida gestures here toward the narrator's dead love, the intrication of love in its very possibility with the deathly vision of the women whose infinite distance lays its groundless ground. Death is the condition of this strange love, but a death that *appears*—directed, as it were, at dead women who "phantomize" and who do so by both giving and receiving the mortal looks of a dead gaze and a gaze of death. Both giving and receiving: for the narrator too is an allegorical figure of "death," which becomes clear in the first part of the *récit* when J. asks, "*Avez-vous déjà vu la mort?*" and later points to the narrator, with her "living" hand, and says as much: "*Maintenant . . . voyez donc la mort*" (AM 48; "Have you ever seen death? . . . Now then, look at death"). Love in *L'arrêt de mort* thus falls under a theatrical regime of looking, gazes and faces all suffused with—and radiating—death, as imminent threat or fait accompli.

The imbrication of death and the gaze becomes most dramatically evident at the moment of J.'s death and revivification in the first part of *L'arrêt de mort*. Here is the narrator's evocation (it's not really a description) of the "*regard terrible*" evoked by Derrida; it occurs at the decisive moment of J.'s return to life, in response to the narrator calling her name "*à haute voix, d'une voix forte*" ("out loud, in a strong voice"):

> A ce moment, les paupières étaient encore tout à fait closes. Mais, une seconde après, peut-être deux, brusquement elle s'ouvrirent, et elles s'ouvrirent sur quelque chose de terrible dont je ne parlerai pas, sur le regard le plus terrible qu'un être vivant puisse recevoir. (AM 36)
>
> At that moment, her eyelids were still completely closed. But one or perhaps two seconds later, suddenly they opened, and they opened onto something terrible of which I will not speak, on the most terrible gaze that a living being can receive.

This is a "scene" of the gaze and of its "reception," but in a receptivity complicated by an opening that is a "*s'ouvrir sur*," an opening-itself-onto . . . This ambiguous locution would seem to indicate what the opening eyelids reveal behind them when they open, her terrible gaze; but it could also indicate what the gaze opens *to see*, what its opening gives access to that is outside itself (like a window opening on . . .), what becomes visible to the one that opens "from the inside," that is, the look or face *of the narrator*—certainly terrible, if he is death himself. The circuit of looks implied by this ambiguity is deeply intriguing: how could the narrator describe his own gaze at that moment? How could he see his look and how he looked? And relate it with such a clear vision of the terror it embodied and conveyed? The narrator seems to see himself seeing and being seen; one could say: he sees himself see(m)ing. Indeed, only death itself could occupy such a position "*au fond du regard*," in the ground of the gaze (to anticipate Nancy's terms).[18] Only death could see out of and see himself seen as the face/gaze/mask that he would be wearing/showing at this moment of death's overcoming. And this is her gaze as well, "onto" which her eyelids open, as a mask that he sees but "holds in reserve" here. This exchange, merger, or identity-in-difference of the dead gaze of death-coming-alive constitutes one of the central abyssal vortices of this tale and its figural nexus. In his essay on Kant, Heidegger, and the death mask, entitled "Masked Imagination," Nancy speculates that in the figure of the dead, withdrawn gaze, one might after all have a sort of access to the other's dying; indeed, Blanchot appears to be staging just such a moment in this "scene." Christopher Fynsk also points out that in this moment "the narrator has effectively violated the solitude of her dying" ("On Death Sentence," 248).[19] Indeed, in a sense, he comes to haunt it—and vice versa.

I will not comment further on this peculiar moment, but we can say that the gaze in question is one that *breaches* the narrative, opening the possibility of a shared death, a death *partagée*, divided out into looks that render its vertiginous ground of invisibility. The abysmal vortex of dead see(m)ing looks, will be taken up later, through a series of gazes punctuating the text, into the projected death mask that precipitates the story's final affirmation—and the beloved woman's disappearance.

UNHEIMLICHE MANOEUVRES: THE GAZE AND THE HAND

The second part of *L'arrêt de mort* is largely the tale of an *alliance*—the giving of a pledge and the forming of a bond, a complicity, between two beings who are both infinitely distant and bound in extremest intimacy.[20] The dénouement of the tale is constituted by the sealing of this pledge, bond, alliance, fidelity—*loyauté*, insofar as it is at bottom a question of the law (*la loi*), and therefore of an imperative that must be "followed to the end." This situation is deeply equivocal, even impossible, since there is no way to determine who these two beings are. In such a context, the cultural and legal institution of marriage could only be a distant analogue, or rather precisely the cultural and legal effect, of a more originary alliance. This is no doubt why the specter of marriage haunts *L'arrêt de mort*, especially when it makes a very "fictive" appearance in the story, when the narrator and N. are trapped by a crowd ("*une foule pressante et pesante*") in the metro during an air raid, and the narrator playfully asks her to marry him "in her language," a language foreign to him:

> Je lui offris au moins deux fois de l'épouser, ce qui prouve le caractère fictif de mes propos, étant donné mon éloignement pour cet état (et mon peu d'estime), mais je l'épousais dans sa langue. (AM 100)
>
> I offered to marry her at least twice, which proves the fictive character of what I was saying, given the distance (and lack of esteem) I have for that state, but I married her in her language.

In a sense, then, he asks for her hand. And in the end, *au fond*, he gets it, as we have seen. But not in marriage, a condition for which, as he says here, he has "*peu d'estime.*" The contract or bond sealed between the narrator and N./J. is of another order—and is in fact not with either of these figures, but rather with an unfigurable "*pensée*" that, up until the last pages, has borne their names and faces.

Let us move, then, toward this dénouement. Everything in the final scenes revolves around the gaze—dead and immortal—and that hand which the narrator will have received and kept. These scenes also bring to its culmination, if not to its resolution, the torment of a radical (radial) turn from the world and from the life of this world to the other side of world and life, "*au lointain.*" Once again, as we will see, the hinge of this turn, and the empty shell of figuration in which it *can* be told, is fixed in a schematic image of death: casting of hands, withdrawal of gaze, projection of death in its blind empty mask.

The pivotal scene takes place in a hotel room, which it is important to situate briefly. After being separated from N. by the crowd in the metro, the narrator spends a tormented evening trying to find her:

> j'étais moi-même perdu. Ma folie ne venait plus de mon inquiétude ni de mon intérêt pour Nathalie, mais d'une impatience, chaque minute plus grande, qui dépassait tous les buts, et faisait de moi un errant à la recherche de rien. (AM 104–105)
>
> I myself was lost. My madness did not come from my anxiety or from my interest in Nathalie, but from an impatience, growing greater by the minute, which surpassed every goal, and made of me a wanderer in search of nothing.

This language clearly recalls (or rather, anticipates) the terms Blanchot will use in *L'espace littéraire* to speak of the writer's wandering/erring, and of Orpheus's impatience, which impulsively "passes beyond every goal." But finally a certain clarity and sobriety return, "*du moins un sentiment assez froid et clairvoyant qui me dit: il est temps, il faut maintenant faire ce qu'il faut*" ("at least a quite cold and clear-sighted vision that said to me: it is time, now I must do what must be done"). This enigmatic and opaque imperative, dictated by a cold and clear feeling, is never specified. But the resolve that it induces involves returning to the hotel room in question—the narrator's second room, where he says he has only some books, where he never goes anymore unless he absolutely must, and from which he has capriciously banished N., asking her never to go there. It is to this room that he now returns:

> l'ascenseur ne marchant pas, dans l'escalier, à partir du quatrième, une sorte de relent étrange descendait vers moi, une odeur froide de terre et de pierre que je connaissais à merveille parce que dans la chambre elle était ma vie même. (AM 106)
>
> Since the elevator was not working, in the stairway, beginning on the fifth floor, a sort of strange odor descended on me, a cold smell of earth and stone that I knew extremely well because in my room it was my very life.

The cold smell of earth and stone is the smell of a tomb he inhabits in what is clearly figured as a space of writing. He begins to speak of this room in all its living-dead force; it is one of the most uncanny haunts of this story, as it begins to take on the status and dimensions of the narrator's beloved death-women.

> De cette chambre, plongée dans la plus grande nuit, je connaissais tout, je l'avais pénétrée, je la portais en moi, je la faisais vivre, d'une vie qui n'est pas la vie, mais qui est plus forte qu'elle et *que nulle force au monde ne pourrait vaincre*. Cette chambre *ne respire pas*, il n'y a en elle ni ombre ni souvenir, ni rêve ni profondeur; je l'écoute et personne ne parle; je la regarde et personne ne l'habite. Et pourtant, la vie la plus grande est là, une vie que je touche et qui me touche, absolument pareille aux autres, qui, avec son corps, presse le mien avec sa bouche, marque ma bouche, dont les yeux s'ouvrent, les yeux les plus vivants, les plus profonds du monde, et *qui me voient*. (AM 107–108; my emphasis)
>
> Of this room, plunged into extreme darkness, I knew everything, I had entered into it, I carried it in myself, I made it live, with a life that is not life, but that is stronger than it and *that no force in the world can vanquish*. This room *does not breathe*, there is in it neither shadow nor memory, neither dream nor depth; I listen to it and no one speaks; I look at it and no one inhabits it. And yet, the greatest life is there, a life that I touch and that touches me, absolutely similar to the others, and that with its body presses mine with its mouth, marks my mouth, and whose eyes open, the most living eyes, the deepest in the world, and *they see me*.

The tomb-room, this site of solitude and writing, is cast here as a kind of congealing of space, a becoming-figure, a "life" that is other than life and that "*prend corps*," that loves—touches, kisses, even bites, *marks* with its mouth, no doubt in a *remords* that punctures and goads the compulsion it commands, through a "force" steadily growing in these last pages—and, finally, that *looks and sees him* ("*et qui me voient*"), a Galatea of writing's passion now come to life from stone, cold and darkness. The first phrase I have underscored in the passage indicates once again that this place is not of this world:

it is inhabited by a life stronger than life "that no force in the world can vanquish." To enter this room is to exit the world and to find oneself in the sphere of a death-haunted life that nothing worldly can overcome. This is one of many such locutions in Blanchot, which proliferate in the last pages of *L'arrêt de mort*, in which one term in a relation is vertiginously outstepped, but ends by being converted into something problematically *permanent*—permanent not in a new sublated presence, but precisely in its having-been-outstepped, in its disappearance and absence—an inalienable alienness. We are once again touching on the logic, and the pathos, of what I have called the *unloseable*. But this force, too, passes through the circuit of a dead gaze, which will be amplified even further—let us say vivified, figured as alive in its deathliness—in the scene that follows.

This long scene (AM 108–113) is of interest for the truly *chilling* and disorienting quality of the encounter it relates, as the narrator enters this room and senses that someone is there, that something fatal is happening, and takes it upon himself to second this unfolding but elusive relation. Despite taking place in total darkness, the scene has a vivid "visual" aspect marked by a strange haptic dimension (one might even refer to a kind of *haptic visibility*), even as it scrambles the clarity of this aspect through indirection, interruption, and rarefaction in the language.[21] The slowness of the scene, the tight weave of its terms and figures, their many undertones and overtones, would require a close and patient analysis. For my purposes, I would like simply to sketch in the images most relevant here: the hands and the gaze, abyssal elements around which the thread of an "*il faut*" is continually drawn through these pages.

Sitting on the edge of his bed, which he says is also the edge of a terrifying darkness into which he stares, the narrator waits to be lost. "*Mais se perdre*, il le faut" ("But to lose oneself, *that is necessary*"; AM 108; my emphasis). First, after speaking of the darkness, and of his fear, as of a body wandering before him, he then evokes a distantly proximate gaze, in an aside that recalls the earlier passage on a "rising" thought that looks back, intimate and extremely strange:

> Il faut beaucoup de patience pour que, repoussée au fond de l'horrible, la pensée peu à peu se lève et nous reconnaisse et nous regarde. Mais, moi, je craignais encore ce regard. Un regard est très différent de ce que l'on croit, il n'a ni lumière ni expression ni force ni mouvement, il est silencieux, mais, du sein de l'étrangeté, son silence traverse les mondes, et celui qui l'entend devient autre. (AM 109)

> It is necessary to have much patience so that, having been pushed down to the bottom of what is horrible, thought can rise little by little and recognize us and look at us. But as for me, I was still afraid of this look. A look is very different from what one believes; it has neither light nor expression, neither force nor movement; it is silent, but from the heart of strangeness, its silence traverses worlds, and the one who hears it becomes other.

Let me awkwardly paraphrase this circuitous and strangely synesthetic statement: to hear emanating from strangeness the silence of the gaze of a thought which rises from the depth and ground of the horrible, makes one become other. It is difficult to follow this strange chain of notions and figures, to be sure, but I want to focus on its opaque, central "link": *to hear the silence of a gaze of thought* . . . and to hear it coming out of a properly uncanny *strangeness*. The gaze is explicitly cast as a hinge—out of joint—between a terrifying *sight* and a transformative *hearing*. This hinge, impossible and opaque as it is, will be crucial in the passage from N.'s gaze to something like an imperative or commandment *to be heeded*—and the effacement (defacement or disfiguration) that this seems to require. After this foreboding, the gaze promptly "appears," and the strangeness becomes more *unheimlich* than ever:

> Tout à coup, la certitude que quelqu'un était là qui me cherchait fut si forte que je reculai devant elle, heurtai violemment le lit, et aussitôt, à trois ou quatre pas de moi, je la vis distinctement, *cette flamme morte et vide de ses yeux*. De toutes mes forces, *il me fallut* la fixer et elle-même me fixa, mais d'une manière très étrange, comme si j'avais été plutôt derrière moi et à l'infini en arrière. (AM 109; my emphasis)

> Suddenly, the certainty that someone was there who was looking for me was so strong that I moved backward before it, violently knocked against the bed, and immediately I saw distinctly, three or four paces from me, *that dead and empty flame of her eyes*. With all my force, *it was necessary* for me to fix her and she herself fixed me, but in a very strange way, as if I were rather behind myself, and infinitely far behind.

Here too I would like to underscore the most opaque moment of this scene by stating it as simply as possible: the narrator says that he recoiled from *a certainty* (grammatically "*elle*" = "*la certitude*") and knocked violently into the bed. As is evident by now, such concretized abstractions are the very unstable furniture of Blanchot's *récits*, and their almost seamless weaving together with physical objects provides a schema for the story's rhetoric as it continually veers toward a final "volatilization." Objects of the mind—which are also grammatically gendered object names—*are* the objects, *tout court*, that populate this tale, *thought* being only the most charged, the most intimate and abyssal, the most forceful in its attraction, so close and intimate an "object" that it *no longer is one*. This will become even clearer in a moment. For now we find ourselves staring into the dead and empty flame of a gaze that literally moves what it sees "infinitely far behind." Once again, as in the scene of J.'s living-dead gaze unto (onto) death, the narrator *sees her seeing* (noun and present participle), in an impossible and abyssal circuit, a simultaneous projection and reception of death. He sees what she sees, or we might more properly say that he sees what her seeing does, as it casts him into an infinite distance from her, and from himself, in a *recul* that both disjoins and seals their relation. These dead and empty eyes occupy a middle place, in a deathly and immobile materiality vivified by fire, between a woman's face and the death mask that will be evoked a few pages later. It is worth adding that here again the central Orphic moment of Eurydice's gaze places the narrator behind himself, and by extension behind her as well: Orpheus behind himself behind Eurydice, whose look casts *him* back into infinity. One configuration implied by the shuffling and shifting of positions would be that he "himself" also *is* Eurydice—and/or Eurydice leads the step forward.

But in terms of the plot, understood here as the dramatic scenography of this moment, it is the narrator who "advances." After sitting on the bed in the dark, "*peut-être très longtemps*" ("perhaps for a very long time"), he has the impression that no sooner has she found him than "*je la perdis*" (I lost her). When in utter darkness the gaze has been lost, what is left but to grope one's way forward, "*la main . . . un peu en avant*" ("with my hand held out before me")? Thus the hand takes over where the gaze has faded, as the narrator brushes past the strange furniture in this uncanny room, which is also a tomb, which is also the inside of a head (and so perhaps a kind of Beckettian skull), the dwelling and haunt of a thought and the spacing of a *maintenant* in which who knows whose hand is writing. I will cite this section of the scene at length partly to show the frequency of the word *main* (hand) over the course of this rhetorically complex and indeed touching moment:

> j'avançais de la manière la plus lente, j'effleurai la cheminée . . . Je voulais surtout m'approcher du fauteuil, ce fauteuil *je le voyais dans ma tête, il était là*, je le touchais. Je finis par m'agenouiller pour n'être pas trop grand, et lentement ma main passa à travers la nuit, effleura le bois du dossier, effleura un peu d'étoffe: une main plus patiente, il n'y en eut jamais, ni de plus calme, ni de plus amicale; c'est pourquoi elle ne frémit pas quand lentement *une autre main, froide, se forma* auprès d'elle, et cette main, la plus immobile et la plus froide, la laissa reposer sur elle sans frémir. Je ne bougeais pas, j'étais toujours à genoux, tout cela se passait infiniment loin, ma propre main sur ce corps froid me paraissait si éloignée de moi, je me voyais à tel point séparé d'elle, et comme repoussé par elle dans quelque chose de désespéré qui était la vie, que tout mon espoir me semblait être à l'infini, dans ce monde froid, où ma main reposait sur ce corps et l'aimait et où ce corps, dans sa nuit de pierre, accueillait, reconnaissait et aimait cette main. (AM 111; my emphasis)

> I moved forward in the slowest way, I brushed against the fireplace. . . . I wanted above all to move close to the armchair, this armchair *that I saw in my head, it was there*, I touched it. I ended by kneeling in order not to be too tall, and slowly my hand traversed the darkness, brushed against the wooden back of the chair, brushed against a bit of fabric; there was never a more patient hand, nor a calmer one, nor more friendly; that is why it did not tremble when slowly *another hand, cold, formed* next to it, and this hand, the most immobile and the coldest, let it rest on itself without shivering. I did not move, I was still on my knees, all this happened

infinitely far away, my own hand on this cold body seemed so distant from me, I saw myself separated from it/her to such a point, and as though pushed away by her into something desperate that was life, that all my hope seemed to me infinitely removed, in this cold world, where my hand rested on this body and loved it and where this body, in its night of stone, welcomed, recognized and loved this hand.

I have underscored two phrases that bring out something essential about the unreality of this scene and the strange space in which it unfolds. There is an almost perfect equivalence between the narrator's seeing the armchair in his head and its being there, his thinking it and his touching it. Likewise, the other hand his hand encounters is carefully evoked not simply as being there, being at hand (as it were), but as something that "*se forma*" (formed, formed itself)—a verbal event that one could well translate, in all its Kantian resonance, as the *sich-bilden* of a schematizing projection, the active/passive formation of a sculpturally congealed schema into a properly ghostly, and yet also bodily, presence.[22] To say this is very different from saying something like: "it's all in his head," as though the distinction between the inside and the outside of a forming-projecting imagination—in the mode of a narrator's positing nomination—still had any sense here. Fiction, here, is fictioning itself, within a space that leaves its reality radically undecidable, and this undecidability is the *point*, emerging once again as an impossible but somehow arriving encounter. That something is imagined, or rather "imaged" or "in-imaged," *eingebildet, and* that *it is happening*—this is the "secret law" that presses the fiction back into an originary moment in which the difference between image and the real is drastically shuffled. But also shuffled *off*, since this difference is the one that founds "the world" which the narrator is leaving for the sake of another, or for an *other of every world*, in a process of *dépouillement* that is moving in halting fashion toward a kind of transcendental *dépouille*: image of image as an emblem of deathly origination.[23]

At this point, then, one can speculate with a certain degree of clarity that Blanchot's fundamental gesture, carried out in the writing of this fictive but "autobiographical" *récit*—a *récit* that must tell of its own exigent origination—is to place at the heart of this originary space an animated imaging deathliness and, above all, to haunt it with a stony, icy, and impossible love, an intimately distant love that is still just barely rendered as a *scene*. In a sense, then, love is the name for the haunted exigency of its writing insofar as it remains attached to, and articulated through, the figural density of an encounter, even as this love presses writing on toward a point where it will have no end and will move beyond any possible object, where it will have stripped away, and lost, every possible figure.

In the meantime, however, the narrator of *L'arrêt de mort* appears to be there, somewhere, both before and infinitely far from a woman, a feminine figure whose hand, for now, still holds.

Unlike the uncanny gaze with its cold dead flame, the *unheimliche* maneuvers of the sculptural hand, and the *main-tenant* which they radically destabilize, do not create a circuit of looks, they only point, and grope, into the sculpted dark (cast and projected as the space of an amorous encounter). As J.'s gesture in the first part indicates ("*Maintenant, voyez donc la mort.*"), this is also a pointing toward and into death, which is the space of an uncanny touch whose complicity with writing (with the hand that writes) continues nonetheless to enter a dense bodily register, both in that room—in the bed to which he gently guides her—and in the present space of written narration.

> Je voudrais dire que le froid de ces corps est une chose très étrange: il n'est pas, en lui-même, si grand. Si je touche une main, *comme je le fais maintenant*, si ma main se couche sous cette main, celle-ci est moins glacée que la mienne mais ce peu de froid est profond, non pas le léger rayonnement d'une surface, mais pénétrant, enveloppant, *il faut le suivre* et, avec lui, entrer dans une épaisseur sans limite, dans une profondeur vide et irréelle où il n'y a pas de retour possible à un contact extérieur. (AM 112; my emphasis)

> I would like to say that the cold of these bodies is a very strange thing: in itself it is not so great. If I touch a hand, *as I am doing now*, if my hand lies beneath this hand, then that hand is less icy than mine but this little bit of cold is profound, it is not the slight radiation of a surface, but is penetrating, enveloping, *it is necessary to follow it*, and, with it, to enter into a limitless density, into an empty and unreal depth where there is no possible return to any external contact . . .

A first peculiarity: what is meant here by "*ces corps*," these bodies? Not only the cold deathly body of N., figure of darkness and stone bodied forth by and as the narrator's thought, but also the deeply cold hand holding his own *right now*. These bodies, then, are the ones that haunt the space of writing, that have haunted the time that comes to command writing. Living proof and shell of an enigma, it is a hand that leads one into what sounds a great deal like a preformulation of "literary space" ("*profondeur vide et irréelle*," etc.), from which there is no return to the world left behind. Is the hand that guides the same, ultimately, as the hand that writes? In any case, this hand here now, *maintenant*, is associated with an imperative "*il faut*" that has been taking shape and is now approaching its final articulation and affirmation. The passage continues:

> Il faut le dire, car il serait bien vain à présent de reculer, le froid d'une main, le froid d'un corps n'est rien, et même si les lèvres s'en approchent, cette amertume d'une bouche froide n'est redoutable que pour qui ne sait être ni plus amer ni plus froid, mais il y a une autre barrière qui nous sépare: celle de l'étoffe morte sur un corps silencieux, de ces vêtements qu'il faut reconnaître et qui n'habillent rien, imprégnés d'insensibilité, avec leurs plis cadavériques et leur inertie de métal. C'est cette épreuve qu'il faut vaincre. (AM 112–113)

> It must be said, for it would certainly be useless to shrink back from it now, that the cold of a hand, the cold of a body is nothing, and even if one's lips approach it, this bitterness of a cold mouth is dreadful only for someone who does not know how to be colder or more bitter, but there is another barrier that separates us: that of the dead cloth on a silent body, of those clothes that one must recognize and that clothe nothing, steeped in insensitivity, with their cadaverous folds and their metallic inertia. This is the ordeal that must be overcome.

This passage gives one of the few images of bodily love to be read in Blanchot, but in the kind of deliberately quasi-allegorical form we have already seen, here radiating with cold lips and a bitter mouth that must be outdone in coldness and bitterness by the one who receives their approach. Most peculiar of all is the bizarre evocation of the metallic cadaverous clothes that "clothe nothing," a "dead stuff" or material that sets up a barrier to such chilly goings-on in the grave-room bed. The "nothing" that these clothes would hide is like the emptiness of the schematic shells we have found strewn throughout the narrative (along with dead female bodies, trapped in "the irremediable"), not least in the hands that haunt the space of writing and that presumably would be the ones to remove these clothes, thus vanquishing the ordeal they (op)pose, unveiling the truth they conceal, and conjugating an enigmatic language incapable of rendering its core. The slippage from shells to casts to hands to cadaverous clothes to be removed, to cadavers themselves, from *dépouillements* to *dépouilles*, provides yet another chain connecting the enigma of writing's imperative with an uncanny and melancholic erotics of an otherworldly intercourse with death.[24]

THE UNLOSEABLE: SHE

Throughout all of these delicate cadaverous fumblings, a troubling question has been floating to the top of all this stuff and intrigue, or (to use another metaphor) weaving through its texture in a way that it would be easy to overlook; to ask it with a mordant flippancy meant to cut into some of the text's more mysterious atmospheric layers (and in a no-nonsense tone that is deliberately obtuse): *What happens to the girl?* Such a blunt and skeptical (and doubtless naive) question need not sound a mere simplification. Its depth also reaches into the extreme, and the essential.

What it asks is this: How is the status of the feminine figure as such being transformed in this tale of corpsely love? A first, concrete answer: even as she returns to a more recognizably human form (just after the ghostly scene I have been commenting on), she is being eaten away. Blanchot segues immediately from the above passage to the morning after, in the bedroom, and to the image of Nathalie looking at her hands and remarking with astonishment: "*Mais regardez, je fais comme les enfants, je crois que j'ai rongé mes ongles*" ("Look, I'm acting like a child, I think I've been biting my nails"; AM 113).[25] I quoted above from a passage describing the *pensée* who "rises up" for the narrator as a person who also occasionally sleeps next to him and who gnaws away at herself: "*Elle est dans ma maison . . . parfois, quoique rarement, elle dort près de moi. Et moi, insensé, je me croise les mains et je la laisse manger sa propre chair*" ("She is in my house . . . sometimes, although rarely, she sleeps next to me. And I, out of my senses, I cross my hands and let her eat her own flesh"; AM 56). Whose hands are crossing whose, it is hard to say, but that a personified thought is crossing into the body of a woman, and/or the reverse—or rather somehow both simultaneously—is beginning to accumulate its uncanny rhetorical evidence, a bitten "shell" that has taken shape around the enigma of a bizarre transubstantiation—and condensed into a pronoun: *she*. The clear presentiment is this: as the *thought* rises, the woman who embodies it must be eroded, gnawed, worn away, dissolved, effaced—or perhaps one could say "schematized." She must become a mask, a fixed and sculpted hand, a dead image of herself, and disappear into the remnants haunting a writing owing everything to "her."

An important point to note regarding this juncture of their relations is that, for the moment, the narrator resists acknowledging her transformation. He wants to remain with *a woman* named Nathalie, in a space identifiable as a city, banal and worldly still:

> Eh bien, je n'avais plus que ce désir: je voulais avec elle entrer ici, dans ce café, entrer dans l'ennui de ce cinéma, entendre en elle quelque chose rire qui ne signifiât qu'une vanité frivole; je voulais surtout *lui garder ce nom de Nathalie*, fût-ce au prix des ses ongles rongés et de son front blessé. (AM 115; my emphasis)

> Well, I had only this desire: with her I wanted to go in here, into this café, into the boredom of this movie theater, to hear in her something laugh that signified only a frivolous vanity; I wanted especially *to keep this name of Nathalie for her*, even at the price of her bitten nails and her cut forehead.

The twin movement of Nathalie's transformation into a *pensée*, beyond every name and figure (which the desire expressed here would delay), and the narrator's definitive exit from the world, both rush quickly toward a common point of suspended convergence in the book's final two pages. But as in this passage, just before this double movement is confirmed there, the narrator wants to hold on to Nathalie as a woman: "*Je lui tenais toujours la main, cette main qui vivait me donnait de l'espoir*" ("I still held her hand, this hand that was alive gave me hope"; AM 121). The narrator is still clinging to this "live" woman, resisting the fatal exit in which he is irreversibly caught up, as is she. This is the nature of the *malheur* and affliction he often refers to, as the painfully breaking attachment to a woman, a melancholic rupture whose "unfortunate" necessity will have to be totalized in the narrator's uncanny allegorical exit from world.

It is at this point of resistance, but also of ordinary time spent in "frivolity" and "chatter" that the text introduces the language of the *unloseable*. Speaking of his loquacious mood, the narrator concedes:

> Tout cela peut paraître enfantin. *Qu'importe*. Cet enfantillage fut assez puissant pour prolonger une illusion déjà perdue et contraindre à être là ce qui n'était plus là. Il

> me semble que dans ce bavardage il y avait la gravité d'une seule et unique parole, la réminiscence de ce "Viens" que je lui avais dit, et elle était venue, et *s'éloigner, elle ne le pourrait jamais plus*. (AM 117; my emphasis)

> All this might seem childish. *It doesn't matter*. This childishness was powerful enough to prolong an already lost illusion and to force to be there what was no longer there. It seems to me that in this chatter there was the gravity of a single and unique word, the remembrance of that "Come" that I had said to her, and she had come, and *she could never again go away*.

In quoting himself here, the narrator repeats the word he had said to Nathalie when he led her to the bed ("*viens*"), but he also prefigures, gravely and problematically, the well known last words of the text ("*et à elle je dis éternellement: 'Viens,' et éternellement, elle est là*"; "and to her I say: 'Come,' and eternally she is there"), giving this unique word, retrospectively and already, an almost transcendental status in the narrator's speech. What is interesting here is that the power of chatter to "prolong the illusion" of something's "being there"—the fictive and figuring operation of language par excellence—is quickly stripped down to an essential element, a center of gravity, by means of a dismissive gesture to which (as I have suggested) Blanchot has recourse at certain crucial moments shadowed by loss: *Qu'importe*. *What does it matter* if I indulged in all this childish chatter, and what does it matter if an already lost illusion had to be prolonged for a while, the essential remains, something that cannot be lost "is there" and *can never go away again*. Tendentiously, perhaps, it is this childish language that I would like to bring out in the frequent gestures made by Blanchot toward what can be called the unloseable—an irreducible "living" remnant that cannot be lost. The strange pathos of attachment one can hear in such statements should be let to resonate across the infinite separations Blanchot evokes, in affirmation and "*malheur*," as the *récit* moves toward a dimension that would seem to leave such attachments definitively behind. In that sense, the unloseable might be a "transcendental" name for a resistance, a refusal, that has its source in the figures that must be stripped away and shown in order to bear witness to what they cannot contain: empty shells as remnants and witnesses to the nothingness that must make them visible, in order to have been—a nothingness no less "of the world" than of its "other side." In another and similar register, we might say that Blanchot's female figures cannot be discarded, even in the gesture that would posit the essential beyond of all figuration. Their ghostly uncanny persistent return *is* the essential—in its "clothed" and remnant form, that of the *revenante*—compelled into fiction by the pressure of a voice striving to affirm its unconditional separation and, perhaps, its unloseable treasure. But it is very unclear what is *given*, after all, in such a return.

I pass quickly over the strange and unexpected affair of the duel in which the narrator gets involved for the sake of a *camarade*, a strife that is linked, in its insanity, with the political madness of the day, and which the narrator describes tellingly as "*la dernière grimace du monde*" ("the last grimace of the world"; AM 118). This death mask of a retreating world (a retreat and withdrawal that have a special significance in the context of 1940 France) points apotropaically toward the other side of a world into which the narrator finds himself compelled, in affliction and *malheur*, by a sorrow so great that next to it the world is reduced to "nothing":

> j'étais encore tout imprégné de la vie et du jugement du monde, c'est-à-dire . . . j'étais infidèle à une vie et à un jugement bien plus importants . . . je risquais de perdre et une vie et l'autre côté d'une vie. (AM 118–119)
>
> I was still all saturated with life and with the judgment of the world, that is to say . . . I was unfaithful to a life and a judgment that were much more important . . . I risked losing a life and the other side of a life.

This infidelity is most directly an infidelity—a disloyalty—to N., whom the narrator has neglected for the sake of this "affair." The Rilkean notion of an "other side of life," life's aspect of death that we ordinarily refuse to see (a motif taken up in *L'espace littéraire*), may be taken as a hint of both the "inner world" at stake here (the *Weltinnenraum* on which Blanchot comments at some length [EL 174–178]), and of the confluence of poetic vocation and of death that is on the verge of being fulfilled in this story. The *malheur* that Blanchot's narrator repeatedly evokes is thus the price of this *other* fidelity—a *malheur* of loss and desertion that, at this level, is openly avowed. The suspicion I have been following, however, bears rather on the specific place of the feminine in this *malheur* and its victory, its sublime (sublimely abject) overcoming, the broken and unmourned attachment that leaves its painful traces in another less visible grimace of the text.

What, then, happens to Nathalie, *insofar as* she is a woman, and a beloved, embodied woman? That is, insofar as she is not entirely coextensive with the thought that must exceed, efface, even kill and spectralize her (for surely no such absolute equivalence could be established). In Blanchot's terms: it is something that has happened long ago in the immemorial depths of fascinated childhood—J. is absurdly young, and N. is continually compared to a child (AM 123)—in the originary opening of thought and language, an opening deeply imprinted with a feminine figure herself suffused with absence and death, face of death and guiding hand of infinite inner space.[26] Put in other terms, and in reference to the equivocal process we have been following: What happens to her is that she is finally "volatilized," stripped down to a schematized and schematizing remainder—which is also the thin voice of an undying imperative.

In the final scene, everything aligns in the direction of a death mask and a pair of plaster hands. At the end of the day of the duel ("around ten o'clock," we are told, with abrupt and arbitrary precision), N. reveals that she has undertaken the "project" of having some "*moulages*" or casts made, of her hands and head, by the very same sculptor who made the casts of J.'s hands (N. has taken a card with his name—given simply as the deadly sign of X.[27]—out of the narrator's wallet, along with the key to his room, which allowed her to enter there for their incandescently cold encounter described above). This *project*, a word that during this scene is strangely and crucially "forgotten" by the interlocutors, and then recalled, as the revelatory exchange unfolds, provides the "proof" against which the narrator has struggled in his refusal to acquiesce. Indeed, it is a *projet . . . accompli*, as N. informs him, it has been accomplished—the implication being that it was carried out long ago. With a shrug of *méchanceté* ("*qui demeure quand tout s'en va*"), the narrator finally does acquiesce, in the shadow of yet another "*il faut*," this time projected into the past.

> "C'est probablement qu'*il le fallait*," murmurai-je.
> Elle saisit les mots au vol.
> "Il le fallait, n'est-ce pas?"
> Il semblait vraiment que mon acquiescement se répercutât en elle, qu'il eût été comme attendu, d'une immense attente, par une responsabilité invisible à laquelle elle ne prêtait que sa voix, et que maintenant une puissance superbe, sûre d'elle-même, heureuse non certes de mon accord qui lui était bien inutile, mais de sa victoire sur la vie, et aussi de ma compréhension fidèle, de mon abandon sans limite, prît possession de ce jeune être et le rendît d'une clairvoyance et d'une maîtrise *qui me dictaient aussi bien mes pensées que mes quelques paroles*. (AM 124; my emphasis)

> "It was probably necessary," I murmured.
> She snatched at these words.
> "It was necessary, wasn't it?"
> It really seemed that my acquiescence reverberated in her, that it was as though she expected it, with an immense expectation, in an invisible responsibility to which she lent only her voice, and that now a supreme power, sure of itself, and happy—not of course because of my agreement, which was quite useless to her, but of her victory over life, and also of my faithful understanding, my limitless abandon—took possession of this young being and gave it a clearsightedness and a mastery *that dictated to me my thoughts as well as my few words*.

Everything issues into sound and voice, call and response, echo and repercussion, accord and dictation—but first "*il le fallait*," it was necessary (probably!) to have undertaken the uncanny "project" of schematic figuration, to have allowed oneself to be haunted by the fantasmal projections that have made the story, that render it visible in its outward aspects, its only remainders in this world—a "living" proof that survives only in the shell of the voice's textual leavings. What this effectuates here, however, is the lodging of a specifically feminine figure (face) within the crux of this imperative, an emblem that can no longer be extricated from its every manifestation—as *dictated* by her.

But again, a question obtrudes: what happens to the girl? To insist on this obtuse and deeply inappropriate question may allow us to glimpse something of the absconding violence at work in the establishment, and affirmation, of a dictatorial imperative. The text has reached the precise moment when it "reveals"—when "she" has revealed—her volatile, sublime, uncanny reality to whom or to which the narrator will henceforth, in the *récit*'s last long paragraph, refer not as N. or J. (or C. or S., the initials of two women already liquidated by this point), but as *une pensée: elle*. Precipitously stripping the story of its "facts," the narrative voice lays open a core or kernel harbored beneath them after all, the story's origin, every story's origin—and from this perspective, says the narrator, all stories are the same (but as I suggested in the beginning, I don't think it is possible, or advisable, to believe in this sameness). The narrator in his final transport describes this kernel as: "*l'appel de l'affirmation toute-puissante qui est unie à moi*" ("the call of the all-powerful affirmation that is united with me"). The alliance that has been forming in his tale turns out to be a union with an all-powerful affirmation from which emanates a call, as though the relation conjugated ultimately into a kind of voice. What kind? Blanchot makes it clear that it is both indestructible and alterworldly. It begins to speak in its pure affirmation only after a final shredding or stripping away of "appearances," precipitated by N.'s "project":

> Il se pourrait que N., en me parlant de ce "projet," n'ait rien voulu de plus que déchirer, *d'une main jalouse*, les apparences dans lesquelles nous vivions. Il se peut que, lassée de me voir persévérer dans mon rôle d'homme du "monde," elle m'ait brusquement, par cette histoire, rappelé la vérité de ma condition et *montré du doigt où était ma place*. Il se peut encore qu'elle même ait obéi à un commandement mystérieux, et qui était le mien, et *qui est en moi la voix* à jamais reconnaissante, voix jalouse elle aussi, d'un *sentiment incapable de disparaître*. (AM, 126–127; my emphasis)

> It may be that in speaking to me of this "project," N. wanted nothing more than to tear apart with an ardent hand the appearances in which we were living. It could be that, tired of seeing me persist in my role as a man of the "world," with this story she abruptly recalled to me the truth of my condition and pointed with her finger to where my place was. It could also be that she herself had obeyed a mysterious commandment, which was mine too, and which in me is the forever grateful voice—it too an ardent voice—of a feeling that is incapable of disappearing.

J.'s gesture (in the first part of the *récit*) of pointing to the narrator and calling him "death," with a hand now preserved there on the writing table, a *main-tenant* severed from the moment of its index, as it were, is here transposed, through a strange reiteration of that hand pointing into the deathly central enigma of this story—that is, toward the sublime commandment that shows the narrator his place, and the truth of his "condition." The rhetoric of sublime law-giving is also proffered in terms of obedience and commandment—a commandment that mimics Kantian autonomy by being "mine" (*le mien*), a law imposed on me but also assumed by me, dictated by me and to me. But unlike Kant's universalist vision of reason, this transcendental legislation passes through, and remains (with) the singular figure of a feminine *persona*, even as the narrative is on the verge of casting off this figural occasion or "subreption" of the law's dictation. And yet this singular narration—that of a love story here reaching its extreme point in a complete *déchirement* of its appearances—nonetheless maintains the paradoxical *figure* of this feminine legislator in the very texture of that story. Like the figure of the Law in *La folie du jour*, the sublime feminine figure obtrudes into appearances, shows the mere visibility of vision, and indicates a law behind the laws of the world—the proper but vertiginous and uninhabitable "place" of another task—but in her phantomatic appearance she gives not only the law but also its displacement into a voice. It is at this level of the "exchange" that something very important happens here (or is at least projected: "*il se peut* . . ."): in a reversal by which the commandment and its dictation now originate in "me" and are obeyed by "her," there is posed in this "me" another term that is neither me nor her, a force that is a voice: "*la voix à jamais reconnaissante, voix jalouse elle aussi, d'un sentiment incapable de disparaître.*" *The voice of a feeling incapable of disappearing*: a direct transposition this time of the "jealous hand" into a commanding voice recedes back beyond all appearances, to a feeling that cannot "disappear," which means also: that cannot be lost. This feeling is the unloseable remnant of a violent experience of *déchirement* and stripping away, it is what remains when all else is lost, the important and insistent point being that it *does remain*, unconditionally. The trouble, however, is that in the economy of this remaining, in its relation to what has been left and *dépouillé*, it may at the same time be a kind of sublime compensation, a surreptitious reward, based in part on the jouissance of a female corpse.

Which leads me to ask, once more: what happens to the girl? At this point, she is indeed lost beyond telling, somewhere in the unspeakable, even as the narrator's *malheur* becomes, partly for that very reason, the excessive force driving his speech, as in the text's final passionate invocations. I cite this crucial passage in its entirety.

> Qui peut dire: ceci est arrivé, parce que les événements l'ont permis? Ceci s'est passé, parce que, à un certain moment, les faits sont devenus trompeurs et, par leur agencement étrange, ont autorisé la vérité à s'emparer d'eux? Moi-même, je n'ai pas été le messager malheureux d'une pensée plus forte que moi, ni son jouet, ni sa victime, car cette *pensée*, si elle m'a vaincu, n'a vaincu que par moi, et finalement elle a toujours été à ma mesure, je l'ai aimée et je n'ai aimé qu'elle, et tout ce qui est arrivé, je l'ai voulu, et n'ayant eu de regard que pour elle, où qu'elle ait été et où que j'aie pu être, dans l'absence, dans le malheur, dans la fatalité des choses mortes, dans la nécéssité des choses vivantes, dans la fatigue du travail, dans ces visages nés de ma curiosité, dans mes paroles fausses, dans mes serments menteurs, dans le silence et dans la nuit, je lui ai donné toute ma force et elle m'a donné toute la sienne, de sorte que cette force trop grande, incapable d'être ruinée par rien, nous voue peut-être à un malheur sans mesure, mais, si cela est, ce malheur je le prends sur moi et je

m'en réjouis sans mesure et, à elle, je dis éternellement: "Viens," et éternellement, elle est là. (AM 127; Blanchot's emphasis)

> Who can say: this happened, because events permitted it? This occurred, because, at a certain moment, the facts became deceptive and, through their strange arrangements, they authorized the truth to take hold of them? As for me, I have not been the unfortunate messenger of a thought stronger than me, nor have I been its plaything, nor its victim, for this *thought*, if it vanquished me, vanquished only through me, and in the end it has always been commensurate with me, I have loved it and have loved only it, and everything that has happened, I wanted it, and having had no regard for anything but it, wherever it has been and wherever I may have been, in absence, in misfortune, in the fatality of dead things, in the necessity of living things, in the fatigue of work, in these faces born of my curiosity, in my false words, in my lying oaths, in silence and in the night, I gave it all my force and it has given me all of its, so that this too great force, incapable of being ruined by anything, condemns us perhaps to a misfortune without measure, but, if that is so, I take this misfortune on myself and I am immeasurably glad of it, and to it [to this thought, to her] I say eternally: "Come," and eternally she is there.

The main point I would like to make about this often-cited passage can be summarized emblematically in an observation about translation: it is an unfortunate but necessary betrayal of this text to translate its feminine pronouns (*elle*, standing for *la pensée*) as "it." "She" simply does not work in English, but the pronoun that Blanchot uses necessarily also says *she*. Or perhaps, keeping in mind the "neutrality" of the "*il*" asserted by Blanchot (in essays and later writings such as *Le pas au-delà*), and counterposing, with this feminine usage, an impersonal dimension that emerges very forcefully here, we might say that there is an essential vacillation between an impersonal (neutral) grammatical femininity and a persistent and ineradicable feminine figure who cannot cease haunting, or even being, this *thought* as such. Both aspects are continually in play here, and this irreducibly double aspect is essential to the enigma the story ends by affirming: "she" *is* both a revenant and a thought, at once infinitely distant and eternally there. But the text (in its rhetoric, in the arc of its adventure, in its terminal sweeping passions) clearly inclines in this double movement rather in one direction than in the other: "thought" has the upper hand, as it were, and even in the resonant echo of the narrator's "*viens*," drawn as it is from the density of a narrated encounter, Nathalie has disappeared. At the same time, the shell of the text, and of its casts, remains precisely in and as the passage that has just been painfully traversed.

Perhaps one could amplify on the speculation given before by summarizing the *récit*'s fundamental "project" thus: To inscribe the feminine into the stripped away, volatilized sublimity of a thought that is driven into voice and speech by an eternal *feeling*, a voice that draws its law and compulsion from the particulars it passionately affirms having left—but that precisely thereby lodges these particulars in the very core (dead, empty, and blind) of that "sentimental" voice, as its intimate and *unheimlich* haunting force, indeed as the very manifestation of the law it must follow. Such is the melancholic structure behind Blanchot's complex and ambivalent liquidation of the beloved women his narrator has encountered in fascination and dread. Or rather, his narrators, for this structure is in force, in different forms and tonalities, in the other *récits* as well, but surrounded there by less circumstantial density than in the inaugural tale of *L'arrêt de mort*. We could also say that if this projects points, at least obliquely, toward the Kantian sublime, it does so by translating or inflecting it into the idiom, the idiomatics, of a *singularized* "vocation" and call ("*je l'ai aimée et je n'ai aimé qu'elle*"), in an impersonal and affective experience of thought that strives not for the universal but rather, if it strives, for a fidelity to the impossible that is henceforth (and eternally) demanded.

But there is another homology with the Kantian sublime: much as in the "Analytic of the Sublime," the imagination comes to ruin, only to reveal the true human vocation and determination, in a transcendental (supersensible) *Bestimmung* keyed to reason, that is, in an indestructible *drive* (for Kant, as we saw in the discussion of Kafka's hunger artist, reason is a drive (*Trieb*), it forces the imagination to its own ruin) leading beyond all phenomenality and beyond all world—likewise Blanchot's narrator does discover, *au fond*, an indestructible core, an unstrippable, unruinable, and unloseable force: "*cette force trop grande, incapable d'être ruinée par rien*" ("this too great force, incapable of being ruined by anything"). The close juxtaposition of this unruinable force and the "voice of a feeling incapable of disappearing" indicates that here too we have to do with something that may well be called a "vocation."[28] It is only a small and, I think, not too wrenching twist to turn this vocation and its driving force in such a way as to see it as the very ground of a writer's "call," which is here unconditionally affirmed, beyond all stories written and beyond all experiences or events leading to writing, in an affirmation that is itself even described as "all-powerful." In this tangle of forces and movements, we are no longer talking about an imperative, but something much more murky, no less a passionate compulsion than a categorical, totalizing and indestructible law. But, as suggested, we are also talking about a compensation for the sorrow and loss required to arrive at this strange "place"—especially for the loss, not to say the *casting off*, of the woman who led the way and points definitively and authoritatively to it.

Is this scandalous condition something like a transcendental fatality—according to which there would be no essential truth to be seen or sensed without a transgression, a stripping away of all phenomenality, a step out of images, figures and world and into the death-haunted abyssal ground without limit that makes them possible? Or is it the unfolding of a densely imbricated complex, the drive of a melancholic economy, crystallizing at a certain (albeit extended) historical moment of whose parameters Blanchot was clearly aware, and in which a certain *renunciation of erotic love* is cast as *the* indispensable condition for a categorical and solitary devotion to writing (carried out, moreover, in a "space" strewn with female corpses)? I believe it is important in this context to place considerable weight on the latter hypothesis, and to recall that this is in fact one of the fundamental structures of a certain philosophical/aesthetic strain of "modernism."[29] Kafka has already provided one particularly striking instance of this complex drive and dilemma (and something very similar emerges in Beckett, as we will see).

It must be said, however, that in the end Blanchot does not really conceal this complex, but rather makes it eminently readable (as the easily found "evidence" of my readings attests), even exalts it in a lyrical, not to say melodramatic, apotheosis—though we might also suspect, in what I have been calling the pathos of the unloseable, and in its signal rhetorical gesture (*Qu'importe*), an obfuscation of a certain relation to the lost objects of this melancholy: an unresolved mourning that draws the fiction's figures into an undercurrent of anxious attachment and consolation, bound into a compensatory fixation, an emphatic assertion of the inalienable and inexhaustible. *What does it matter*: all ties are broken, but I am still bound to the essential, I still and will always speak in, through, and in relation to the Thing of my severed experience, and *I cannot lose this*. The voice of a feeling, a too great force: these formulas, which proliferate in Blanchot's work, name what remains, indeed they name the final indestructible remainder, an inalienable and generous alienness, an inappropriable possession, "mine" only in dispossession, destitution and abjection.

THAT THING . . .

If in Blanchot "there is no loss," as Cixous claims, and if the *malheur* of this devastating experience—the painful passage out of the world and into the space of a "commandment" and an undying speech—has the structure of a sublime compensation driven to efface the indispensable scene of its emergence, then unlike the versions of this tale that we saw in *L'instant de ma mort* and *L'écriture du désastre*, there is in *L'arrêt de mort* a very specific and "concrete" figural remainder: the casts of a dead woman's hands and head. Let us return to them for a moment, for they have a peculiar status, as we also turn back toward the beginning of the text from the perspective of its final affirmation (and in anticipation of the next chapter, in which they will play a major role). These leftover *things* disturb, even obstruct, the process of volatilization or "sublimation" that in the end renders up the eternal presence-absence of a thought. Surely this *pensée* is still, in some sense, a woman, and as such she is not entirely effaced, at least not as a spectral and statuesque figure; she is not faceless—or handless, for that matter. Drifting about in the writer's room, she also lends him a hand, in the very act of writing. For this is clearly enough implied: hers is the hand that is writing. Indeed, as suggested earlier, he has "asked for her hand" with his fictive-genuine proposal of marriage, proffered "in her tongue" in the metro turned bomb shelter. And now he has it, has them, living severed on his table: "*je les [ai] sous les yeux et . . . elles vivent*" ("I have them before my eyes . . . and they live"; AM 21). In this sense, he has literally incorporated her. This is one aspect of the uncanny "alliance" at stake in the text, which vindicates further the prediction of the chirologist who does a reading of J.'s cast hands and proclaims: "*elle ne mourra pas*" ("she will not die"; AM 22). I would recall as well that the palms of these casts are traversed by what the narrator calls a "*profond coup de hache*" ("a deep hack"), revealing the violence of a "*chance tragique*" cutting into this life fated to live on through writing—a strange echo of the "*coup de dent à travers ma vie*" evoked in *La folie du jour* but left behind in a wake of unfinished mourning.

In bringing out the melancholic dimension of such *coups* and their attendant losses, I have stressed the effacement of figures and their conversion into a quasi-sublime affirmation; but here, as with Kafka's milk tooth, the locked box is opened and the treasure shows itself in all its banal, even kitsch, sentimentality: a set of plaster casts. It may be that somewhere along the edges of this tale's most insistent exigencies is a deliberately cultivated melancholia, engaged *for the sake of* its infinite returns as dictated in the ghostly structure of its imperative, as a writing *en revenance*. We have seen that this writing projects itself precisely by way of such an artifact, in a ghostly hand that remains strangely on display. But N. has made a cast also "of her head," which means that there must also be a mask. While the echo with the casts of J.'s hands is disturbingly uncanny, it is this cast of her "head," this death mask she has made, that suggests the most horrifying implication of the story, the narrator's "*pressentiment d'épouvante*" ("presentiment of horror"): that she is dead, is death (or that her living on belongs not to life but to "the other side of a life"), and further that this is the realm of the narrator's true love and alliance. One can also surmise that this death itself recedes back down the series of dead women who lay scattered about the text (especially J., of course), in a zone where no merely living woman will ever tread. Or receding, one could say, the way Eurydice does as she falls, with one last flash of face, back into hell. It is worth noting here, in anticipation of the next chapter and as an index of the kitschy sentiments just mentioned, that Blanchot himself reported having had a reproduction of a woman's death mask hanging on the wall of his writing space in Èze, where he wrote many of the *récits*, including *L'arrêt de mort* (this was the famous Inconnue (or Noyée) de la Seine, which appears also in Rilke's *Notebooks of Malte Laurids Brigge*, among many other places). Blanchot wrote the *récits* beneath the gaze of a woman's death mask. We may let this uncanny look serve as an emblem for the interrogation I will develop in the next chapter, concerning the death mask and the image of the corpse, as these take their place in the haunting and *hantise* of Blanchot's imperatives. This discussion will take us beyond *L'arrêt de mort* into Blanchot's analysis of the corpse-image in *L'espace littéraire*, and further into some of the philosophical considerations in a text by Jean-Luc Nancy, on the "masked imagination" that emerges in Heidegger's reading of the Kantian schematism, precisely at a point where a death mask comes onto the scene. One could say that with this conjunction of figures and concepts, in this emblem of death's feminine face as it lodges itself into the transcendental kernel of imagination, we are moving toward the central (but still empty and dead) enigma of what I am searching for in

Blanchot's passionate *relations*, the exigent pressures driving them into writing—and out of themselves, out of all relation—in and through the very possibility, and necessity, of image and voice.

This possibility is thus conditioned by an unsettling *thing* that, already in *L'arrêt de mort*, operates a figural and discursive shift into the register of the transcendental, and into the temporality of a vocalized eternity. Immediately preceding the final lyrical paragraph of *L'arrêt de mort*, the dialogue between the narrator and N. moves in a direction that threatens to reveal the enigmatic object at the center of the story's mystery. It concludes with this passionate exchange, concerning what the narrator "knows" about what N. has been up to, and about who or what she is in the end. In reference to her "project," and to the sculptor (X.) who has already been alluded to in this scene, he knows that:

> ". . . aujourd'hui vous avez été chez X. chercher . . . *cette chose?*"
> "Et après!"
> "Et que maintenant cette chose est là-bas, que vous l'avez dévoilée et, l'ayant vue, vous avez vu face à face ce qui est vivant pour l'éternité, pour la vôtre et pour la mienne! Oui, je le sais, je le sais, je l'ai toujours su." (AM 125; my emphasis)
>
> . . . today you went to X.'s to get . . . *that thing?*"
> "And then!"
> "And now this thing is over there, and you have unveiled it and, having seen it, you have seen face to face what is alive for all eternity, for yours and for mine! Yes, I know, I know, I have always known."

As mentioned, this exchange comes just before the book's long concluding paragraph (partly commented on above), in which the exactitude of these words, along with "facts" in general, are radically suspended, not to say disavowed ("*Les faits eux-mêmes, je puis rêver de les supprimer*"; "the facts themselves, I can imagine suppressing them"). What we are confronted with in this final melodramatic scene is not, in fact, an unveiling of the uncanny truth, or even of the morbid artifacts in question, but a deferral of all unveiling in the mode of indefinite reference. The scene skirts the border between thingly revelation and a more allusive suggestion of the true enigma: what exactly has been unveiled? By not saying directly, by calling it merely *cette chose*, the text leaves open a gap—the gap of symbolic or allegorical substitution—that makes it possible to wrench the entirety of the story away from these heavy-handed figurations. And yet the implication is clear and indelible: the "thing" in question is *also* the casts, especially the "face," image and gaze of an eternally living death. The feminine death mask emerges here, without directly presenting itself, as the true kernel of the work—both the enigma and the shell, or perhaps: the shell of the shell—and the gazing aspect of its cadaverous survival. As such, it locates the graphic schematism of the imperative to write.

CHAPTER 7

The Dead Look
The Death Mask, the Corpse Image, and the Haunting of Fiction

The thesis guiding this chapter can be formulated in the following terms (here stated in a condensed form that I will explicate in what follows): in Blanchot the feminine death mask is the transcendental schema of the literary-fictive work, the emblem and empty core of its most originary imperative—but as such it also marks for Blanchot the necessity, for writing, of an erotic renunciation, the sacrifice of a beloved woman.

KANT, HEIDEGGER, NANCY, AND THE SCHEMATISM

There is something extremely odd in the emphasis, toward the end of *L'arrêt de mort*, on the word *projet*, its slippery elision and anxious, dramatic (but after all, nonrevelatory) return. It is through this word, its strange forgetting and recall in the final dialogue between the narrator and N., that the casts of N.'s "head and hands" pass imperceptibly from an eventuality to something that "is no longer a project," and thus become "that thing . . . ," the sign and seal of this story's uncanny "enigma." "What was the word you said?" asks N., before both interlocutors sink into a reverie only to emerge from it (two pages later) with this word, now rendered irrelevant: "*je ne m'y intéressais plus du tout, cela concernait un autre monde, de toute manière il était trop tard*" ("I was no longer interested in that at all, it had to do with a different world, in any case it was too late"; AM 123). Thus at the very moment of its liminal dawning on him, in the transition from *pro-jet* to an *être-jeté-du-monde*, the narrator confirms a certain exit from the world, in which the temporal futurity of any "project" will have been radically transformed.

In this passage from world to its other, and from a projected scheme to one that has been "cast" and fixed into an unaccountable thing—the dead face of "*ce qui est vivant pour l'éternité*" ("what is alive for eternity"; AM 125)—the narrative teeters on the indistinct border that would separate different ways of being "thrown." The casts referred to there are a "project" first in the banal sense that, when they are first mentioned by N., having them made is something planned for and still to come, an "operation" that must be carried out but is not yet complete; but at the same time, this "project," as accomplished, twists the narrative back toward the figures of casts and hands that have long since been doing their work, beginning in the first part of the récit, where they are associated with the dying woman referred to as J. It is worth noting that the word *projet* brings with it a number of complex temporal associations that invoke a virtual relation to the future, a temporal ecstasy and a "throwing" of the sort reflected in Heidegger's lexicon—*entwerfen* (to project, to sketch), *Entwurf* (a project), *Geworfenheit* (thrownness). But the associations are also graphic and spatial, a sense all the more relevant in that we have to do with the "projection" of a set of contoured figural representations or "casts" (another word derived the semantic field of the "throw"). One could say that through the figure of the casts, the temporal ecstasies are transposed directly into spatial anxieties, making it necessary for what has been "thrown" also to be *thrown off,* but likewise revealing the impossibility of this ejection's full accomplishment. And so when N. says, propelling the final scene toward its climax: "*Ce n'est plus un projet*" ("It is no longer a project"; AM 123), she is not resolving these ambiguities so much as scrambling their very senses. In the end, this "project" is done, *and* it is still to come: is this not the temporal logic of *L'arrêt de mort*, and even of Blanchot's work as a whole? But also: this cast thing is "*là-bas,*" structuring and shuffling space in an eternal "*face à face*" without bound.

To move quickly, indeed "schematically," and to situate the death mask at the center of the concerns addressed in what follows, I would say that its displaced intrusion into *L'arrêt de mort* situates it, disjointedly, at the very juncture and origin of time and space. It is a receding figure for all figures, for the possibility of figuration and image (and thus, as mentioned in the preceding chapter, it joins the two figures of figuration privileged by Derrida, the shell/kernel and the ghost). It is as such that it can be likened to the Kantian schema, lodged at the core of the imagination, which in *L'arrêt de mort* reaches into its transcendental register—that is, into a mode of its own originary disappearance—precisely at this *crux* of vision, voice, and indelible affect (or perhaps what Kant, and Heidegger after him, calls "auto-affection"). It should also be stressed, however roughly, that for Kant the transcendental imagination is, in a sense, an apparatus of *projection*, productively anticipating the forms it can find.

It will not be possible here to give a full exposition of the complex and enigmatic notion of the transcendental schematism, nor especially of Heidegger's lengthy treatment of it, particularly in the *Kantbuch*, where it is presented as *the* crucial juncture of the first Critique.[1] I will limit myself to a mere sketch or adumbration, and this partly by way of a story—a remarkable tale about a death mask—that is also recalled in Nancy's essay, "Masked Imagination."[2] As mentioned before, Blanchot's cadaverous image-of-image, in the "Two Versions of the Imaginary," also plays an important role in these proceedings.

In a philosophy such as Kant's, a critical metaphysics constructed through a sharp division between "the empirical and the essential" (to use Blanchot's phrase)—that is, in more properly Kantian terms, between the empirical and the "pure" or "transcendental"—the moments when these two domains must come into contact are always the most problematic and *intriguing*, for they necessarily bring the transcendental into the mode of figuration, and thus, at least implicitly, of narrative.[3] This is the case with the schematism, which—analogous to the notion of "respect" in the moral philosophy, or to aesthetic judgment in the aesthetics—plays a mediating role between pure concepts and sensibility. Succinctly put, it is the projective-receptive point of contact between "the pure concepts of the understanding" and the sensible world.[4] The problem confronted by Kant is how such pure concepts can be joined with sensibility at all, in the experiential judgments that they necessarily regulate, given that "pure concepts of the understanding . . . in comparison with empirical (indeed in general sensible) intuitions, are entirely un-homogeneous, and can never be encountered in any intuition" (CPuR 271). In a sense, we have to do with a problem of *translation* between "entirely un-homogeneous" elements. In order to carry out this translation, Kant posits what he calls the "transcendental schema" (or schemata, in the plural, since each of the transcendental categories would require a schema proper to it; however, as Heidegger points out, Kant did not work these out).[5] The schematism is a "procedure of the understanding," the latter being the faculty that brings the schemata into sensibility as given phenomena in experience. The understanding does this through what Kant calls the "transcendental imagination," a productive imagination (in distinction from passive and reproductive imagination, which merely records and recombines elements of sensory experience), and the seat, as it were, of the schematism. The schema, Kant says, is to be distinguished from the image for being prior to it, as its transcendental condition, and as that which "gives the rule" for its formation. Now what is the common element that makes it possible for the pure pre-image schema to bring its formal structure into the unhomogeneous field of sensibility? That element is time, or a "transcendental time-determination," as the "formal condition of the manifold of inner sense" (CPuR 272). It is here, in the conjunction of productive imagination, schematizing image-formation, and time as "inner sense" (and therefore as the very root of sensibility), that the crux of interest to us is formed. It also makes clear the reason for Heidegger's intensive interest in Kant in the late 1920s, around the time when he wrote *Being and Time*, for at stake in these readings of Kant is an interpretation of time as the originary (or "primordial") basis of ontological understanding. Again, in order to move quickly, I would simply like to stress that the transcendental imagination is figured as something of a projection apparatus, forming and delineating images in their structural (one might say "graphic") possibility, and doing so on the basis of a transcendental temporal structure that lies at the ground of all phenomena as such. Let us read an important passage in the schematism chapter, which begins with a well-known phrase emphasizing the enigma at the core of the problem, an enigma likened to an *art*:

> This schematism of our understanding with regard to appearances and their mere form is a hidden *art in the depths of the human soul*, whose true operations we can divine from nature and lay unveiled before our eyes only with difficulty. We can say

only this much: the image is a product of the empirical faculty of productive imagination, the schema of sensible concepts (such as figures in space) is a product and *as it were a monogram* of pure a priori imagination, through which and in accordance with which the images first become possible, but which must be connected with the concept, to which they are in themselves never fully congruent, always only by means of the schema that they designate. (CPuR 273–274, my emphasis)

The schematism, then, is an art whose essential product is, "as it were" (*gleichsam*), *a monogram*. In other words, it is nothing other than an art determined as inscription, an *art of writing*, which makes experience possible in its most elementary figural delineations—through a hardly visible preinscription, an originary writing, that makes the world visible, in time.

Already the outline of the death mask is coming into view—and indeed it is Heidegger himself who allows us to make this connection in the most concrete manner possible. In the *Kantbuch*, as he elaborates the "making-sensible" (*Versinnlichung* or "sensibilization") of concepts in the schematizing production of images, Heidegger introduces a series of graphic examples meant to correspond to the temporal frames at work in various kinds of images. Building on the German word for image, *Bild*, he speaks of: *Vorbild* (preimage or model), *Abbild* (likeness), and *Nachbild* (afterimage). It is here that he evokes a death mask, in giving examples of an *Abbild*, an image made "from" (*ab-*) another image, and of a *Nachbild*, the photograph of a death mask. He also refers, necessarily, though not really substantially, to the corpse of a dead man, from whom a mask was taken (a mask of which a photograph was taken; KPM 66). The problem addressed by Heidegger in these passages is how an image is able to "offer the look" (KPM 65) of itself, *and* of the generality of the kind of thing it is (its concept), in the schematizing process, where, in a crucial ambiguity, the expression "the look" (*der Anblick*) is given both its passive and active senses. The central figure of the mask in this series of embedded images-of-images actually literalizes this play of words: the image gives the look *by looking* . . . this way or that, an ambiguity further amplified in the German term *aussehen*, which is the verb for "looking (a certain way)," in the sense of presenting an aspect or appearance, but which also implies (and literally says) "seeing (or looking) out." *Aus-sehen*: outer appearance as a gazing outward, in the two-way seeing of a single *outward look* , simultaneously "objective" and "subjective." Heidegger confirms this strange sense of how things look (back) with respect to another example—curiously *not* that of the mask but rather of a landscape, which, he says, "is called a look (image), *species*, just as if it were looking at us—*gleich als blicke sie uns an*" (KPM 65; modified). Or, in the English idiom, a *view*, in the sense of both seeing and seen. The ambiguity of these terms, their vacillation between passive/active, subjective/objective poles, would seem to indicate a deeply uncanny uncertainty and instability in the very structure of vision (yet another term marked by this ambiguity). And indeed, it is not far from here to the *spectral* gaze of death—in its central, enigmatic, and originary force—that we have been concerned with in Blanchot. The death mask thus appears to be emerging at the ghostly core of seeing, and of the seen, in general. At the same time, throughout Heidegger's analysis there is a remarkable emphasis in his language on writing, inscription, and drawing. Not only is there the writing implied in the "photograph" to which he refers (and which he describes as an *Abschreibung*, a transcription), along with the general sense that the image-formation in question is largely a kind of projective graphism by which concepts are preinscribed into the images they make possible, "sketched out" (KPM 67) in a *Vorzeichnung* or "predrawing" that gives the rule of an image's formation, but that also "distinguishes" it, marks it out (*Auszeichnen*) in its singularity—further elaborated as a "*Hineinzeichnen*," a "drawing-into" regulated by the schema's rule; there is also, in this rule-giving transcription, an imperious moment of *dictation*, when Heidegger notes that "in regulating the presentation, the rule dictates itself into [*hineindiktiert*] the presenting look" (KPM 68; modified). I bring out this small but telling point for its suggestion of a subtle *imperative force*, a strange and obscure *insistence*, at work in the graphic inscriptions of the schematism—a force and an insistence that also emanate from the impassive look of the death mask.

(In this connection, I would recall briefly that the gaze in *L'arrêt de mort* is also associated with a kind of dictation. After "acquiescing" to N.'s "project" which is no longer one, and after murmuring in resignation "*probablement il le fallait*" ("it was probably necessary"), the narrator senses "*une puissance superbe*" ("a magnificent power") which has rendered her "*d'une clairvoyance et d'une maîtrise qui* me dictaient *aussi bien* mes pensées *que mes quelques paroles*" ("a clarity of vision and a mastery that *dictated my thoughts* to me as well as my few words"; AM 124; my emphasis). Without placing too much pressure on this homology, whose instances are separated by many significant factors, I nonetheless want to suggest that this dictatorial force, and the voice it discretely implies, is at stake throughout these figural associations: specter as mask, as schema, as "inscriptive" origin *en puissance*, and as a disjointed link by which a thought is both projected by the narrator and given to him (a link by which this thought, through him, *dictates itself*, as the logic of these sentences implies within the overall context of the story). In the end, the question becomes the following: if there is a schematism of vision, is there also a schematism of speech (of the voice) and of writing, as both reception and conveyance of an impossible command? But let us leave this question aside for now.)

However, as Nancy points out, if the death mask in Heidegger gives an example of the schematizing look, it does so as a dead and blind one.[6] More surprisingly yet, the philosopher of "being-toward-death" does not make the slightest mention of the aspect of death introduced into his analysis by this example. But it is precisely this aspect that gives the example, and by extension the entire structure of the schematizing *Einbildung*, its bottomless and abyssal character. The "look" of the death mask, and of the corpse from which it was made, is in fact the *withdrawal* of the look, the occlusion of the gaze, and the infinite recession of the one who bore it. "It is," Nancy writes, "the look of the withdrawal of the look that in the end, in this text . . . [in the look] of the dead man located in the ground [*au fond*] and origin of the entire series of looks" brings out the "hidden art" of the schematism. *Au fond des images* (to use the French title of Nancy's book), in the ground, bottom, and end of images, is the blindness and deathliness that haunts and constitutes the imagination as its most productive but hollow "core."

At the same time, this obscure abyssal invisibility of the dead look reveals what Nancy calls a graphic "exigency" (GI 96) that plays across time, in particular as the singular time of a now dead life. Remarking on Heidegger's use of terms denoting writing and drawing mentioned above (*Abschreibung, Vorzeichnung, Hineinzeichnung*), Nancy states that in Heidegger's reading of the schematism, "what is at stake is a kind of design or drawing," and that "in the end we have to do with a proposition that could be called profoundly graphic or pictorial: there is a thing only through the design of the thing, and this design gives the thing the contour of a look turned toward our vision." Further, this "look" is inscribed in time in that it precedes and anticipates every given look—but not as a pregiven totality; rather, it bears the "mark of finitude," which means that "it precedes itself and therefore always succeeds itself." And here Nancy gives an example, an image, of this self-generating but finite precedence-and-succession, one that in our context cannot fail to evoke Blanchot:

> It precedes itself and succeeds itself just as the contour of a drawing anticipates itself and prolongs itself in the hand holding a pencil and moving toward the piece of paper then back away from it. In a sense, it itself sees itself and it itself illuminates itself. But it is not, for all that, a self-creating totality. It is also, in its fore-seeing, a not-seeing of its own form, which is always to come or else always already past. Thus time is the "pure image" or the "schema-image." (GI 89)

The look of the withdrawal of the look is thus likened to the drawing of the hand's withdrawal, a hand that shows ("sees" or lets see) by interrupting itself, that engages a time in which its work is invisible while being carried out, in which it disappears when the work is visible. This is a Blanchotian structure par excellence but transcribed into a different register: *noli me videre*.[7] Here it is analogized to the schema, as the look of and in(to) the mask, the look of the look offered by the dead man—or woman.

But as Nancy indicates, this withdrawal of the gaze—or "withdrawal as gaze" (GI 94)—the concealment or disappearance of "a self-showing that hides itself," which Nancy relates to the interplay of *eidos* and *aletheia* in the later Heidegger, also involves a strange demand, an exigency that, he says, Heidegger both avoids and reveals in the *Kantbuch*:

> This demand [*exigence*] states that there must also be a self-showing of the unshowable, a tracing out of effacement, a modeling of the absented gaze. In other words, there must be an *eidos* of *aletheia*, and a face of death (not only an aspect of the dead man, but through it, of that which made him die [i.e., his finitude]). (GI 96)

The logic of the schematism, as it is routed through the "look of the withdrawal of the look" in the death mask (and in the face of the dead man), implies a graphic exigency, a movement in and through contoured formation, a *demand for figuration* that inhabits the invisibility of the schema as previsible and foreseeing—that haunts it, one could say, as its rule and law. If in some sense death (finitude) occupies the transcendental origin of appearance, then death, too, must show a face, which for its part also hides this originary moment in something like a singular fold of time. For "what made the dead man die" is not only his mortality, but also his *having been* alive, his preceding passage through a singular and finite time. Nancy evokes this having-been in relation to the series photo-mask-corpse and the temporal complications it introduces into Heidegger's analysis. If the "look of the dead man" lies at the "ground and origin" of this series, and if it thus brings out the foreseeing rule of the schematism, it does so as something *past*—as a look that is no more. Indeed, it is precisely this look that has withdrawn and been effaced in what "brings it out." In his treatment of the death mask, however, Heidegger seems to collapse these "times" and to superimpose the look the dead man has now, as mask (or corpse), and the look that he *had*—presumably when he was alive.[8] Nancy claims that in a sense, Heidegger avoids the corpse, as well as the temporality of death and dying that manifestly obtrudes into the figural constellation assembled in his analyses, the implication being that Heidegger also avoids an abyssal deathliness at the heart of imagination itself, one that would propel us both in the direction of the sublime (painful limit of images), and toward "the imago of the ancestors" (GI 96), the *imagines* of the Romans, faces of death that give English its very word for image.[9]

But on the way toward this abyss, Nancy has pointed back beyond the corpse toward a singular past, the past of a looking person, as that which has been definitively withdrawn in the "look" of the mask. This withdrawal, too, involves a necessary passage through figuration and image, in that *Bilden*, as originary image formation, passes through the *Abbild* and the *Nachbild* (reproduction and copy) that offer the look of the visible: "It passes through and it escapes as a *Gesicht* of the dead man, a face, a look, a blind seeing—this *Gesicht* that bears in itself the mark of being-past" (GI 95). The dead man, whose haunting look remains, and who thus maintains a strange complicity with the very possibility of vision—this dead man, or woman, marked as *having been*. Moreover, she/he has been, for me who sees her "now," an *other*, who in dying makes appearance appear, makes "my" vision possible. The otherness of image's origin is embedded in every vision: "In the ground of every image," writes Nancy, "there is an unimaginable imagining: there is dying as a movement of self-presenting . . . and in the ground of the imagination there is the other, the look of the other" (GI 97). I believe that we can translate this by saying that every vision is haunted by the look of its constitutive other(s) whose dying/disappearance bears a double exigency, felt in the element of time, pressing as much toward figuration and image as toward oblivion, effacement, and invisibility. As Nancy writes: "The final effect of the death mask is to mask the imagination itself, even as it uncovers it as dead beneath the mask. Dead and consequently, respectively, *having been*: it will always already have begun to image (itself)" (GI 97; Nancy's emphasis).

The singularity of this haunting image-mask, this timebound movement of appearance and disappearance, is indicated further by Nancy, in a deliberate slippage from time as *le temps* to *a* time as *une fois* (once), which occurs in the following paragraph near the end of the essay.[10] Having earlier evoked the dead gaze of Oedipus's blindness, and therefore the time and image of the theater, Nancy plays on these associations:

> Entering and exiting, that is what makes the image: appearing and disappearing. Not first *representing*, but first being or making "one time, *une fois*," a first and last time, the time [*temps*] of making and taking an image, the time of time itself, which opens the eyes. The time, *la fois* (from *vix, vice*: succession in turn, the moment as access or as success-succession), that is what exits the no-time, the *sans-fois*, to return to it immediately. Scansion, eclipse, spark of inimagination.[11]

It is remarkable and instructive to see that Nancy invigorates, as it were, the analysis of death's transcendental point in the formation of images—I think we can say: in experience in general—with a discrete, complex, and nonreductive insistence on the singular time of *a life*, the animating has-beens of its always already dead figures. In this regard he also gestures toward a time of mourning (clearly implied by the figure of Oedipus), and to the persistent staging of this time in intimate connection with its inevitable occlusions and blindnesses. And surely the death mask, as a cultural artifact, is an image of mourning, one that opens a scene of mediated loss and fantasmatic recuperation (in every sense of the word: image of death also as triumph of the image?). But the image of death cannot help showing, if only by projecting and pointing toward, the withdrawal of the image into the abyssal ground of its possibility, a ground haunted, too, by a necessity dictated in the form of a singular past.

BLANCHOT'S TWO VERSIONS OF THE IMAGINARY

It is impossible in reading "Masked Imagination" not to think of Blanchot's analysis of the corpse as image in "Les deux versions de l'imaginaire," and indeed Nancy refers in passing to this connection.[12] What are the implications of this connection, and of Nancy's analysis in general, in relation to Blanchot's complex figurations of the corpse and the death mask? Let us start with the former, although it is chronologically later (Blanchot wrote about the corpse in *L'espace littéraire* after "projecting" the death mask in *L'arrêt de mort*). If Heidegger avoids the corpse, Blanchot embraces it. Without of course ever mentioning Kant or the schematism, he nonetheless situates the corpse in its transcendental function as an image preceding and grounding all images. It should be noted that the transcendental register has already been opened in the beginning pages of *L'espace littéraire*, in the chapter "La solitude essentielle," specifically in its last two sections, "L'image" and "Ecrire . . ." There Blanchot characterizes literary space as a space of images opened in solitude and fascination, a space *"en deça du monde,"* falling short of world, into which "one" wanders, driven and drawn—*"entraîné"*—by a passion of distance: *"la fascination est la passion de l'image"* ("fascination is the passion of the image"; EL 29), he writes. Such images are encountered only in a solitude rendered "essential" by being stripped of all objects, and of any subject, for that matter, of any "I" capable of acting in relation to them. Their fascinated passionate pursuit is thus also a pursuit of the origin of images, of vision itself, which reaches back away from lived experience into images that do not owe their appearance to anything that has preceded them.

> Quiconque est fasciné, on peut dire de lui qu'il n'aperçoit aucun objet réel, aucune figure réelle, car ce qu'il voit n'appartient pas au monde de la réalité, mais au milieu indéterminé de la fascination. Milieu pour ainsi dire *absolu*. (EL 29; my emphasis)
>
> One can say of someone who is fascinated that he perceives no real object, no real figure, for what he sees does not belong to the world of reality, but to the indeterminate medium of fascination. A medium that is so to speak *absolute*.

If these images are "shadows," as Blanchot often says, they are originary or originating shadows that precede any appearance in the world (absolute shadows?). And they are radically *strange*—inappropriable and yet unshakable. As we have seen, the "transcendental" in Blanchot is a trap, an oppressive but wide open enclosedness in an "outside" in which it is impossible to breathe—or to see. That is, in which possibilities approach their most intimate conditions and are thereby reversed into endless impossibility, *impossibility not to . . .* Blanchot elaborates this logic in relation to the gaze and the image in terms that are by now familiar, but no less paradoxical (though in translating them, I will inflect *le regard*, the gaze, with the double sense of *the look* discussed in the previous section). In the separation that structures fascination, Blanchot writes,

> la scission, de possibilité de voir qu'elle était, se fige, au sein même du regard, en impossibilité. Le regard trouve ainsi dans ce qui le rend possible la puissance qui le neutralise . . . La fascination est le regard de la solitude, le regard de l'incessant et de l'interminable, en qui l'aveuglement est vision encore, vision qui n'est plus possibilité de voir, mais *l'impossibilité de ne pas* voir, *l'impossibilité qui se fait voir*, qui persévère—toujours et toujours—dans une vision qui n'en finit pas: *regard mort*, regard devenu le fantôme d'une vision éternelle. (EL 29; my emphasis)
>
> separation, which before was the possibility of seeing, is frozen, in the very heart of the look, into impossibility. The look thus finds in what makes it possible the power that neutralizes it. . . . Fascination is the look of solitude, the look of the incessant and the interminable, in which blindness is still vision, a vision that is no longer the possibility of seeing, but the *impossibility of not* seeing, *impossibility that becomes*

seeing, that makes itself see, that persists—always and always—in a vision that never comes to an end: a *dead look*, a look become the ghost of an eternal vision.

Eternity, as the endlessness of an impossibility not to see, thus takes the form of a phantom that will not die, the phantom of a vision now persisting in a dead look. Vision is given over to its own impossibility of ceasing. In this respect, writing for Blanchot is a kind of endlessly obstructed seeing, and the image is what draws visibility out of itself and ever onward toward its own limit, which is precisely the limit of its capacity.

> Ecrire, c'est disposer le langage sous la fascination et, par lui, en lui, demeurer en contact avec le milieu absolu, là où la chose redevient image, où l'image, d'allusion à une figure, devient allusion à ce qui est sans figure et, de forme dessinée sur l'absence, devient l'informe présence de cette absence, *l'ouverture opaque et vide* sur ce qui est quand il n'y a plus de monde, quand il n'y a pas encore de monde. (EL 31; my emphasis)

> Writing is disposing language in fascination, and thereby remaining in contact with the absolute medium, there where the thing becomes image again, where the image, which was an allusion to a figure, becomes an allusion to what is without figure and, as what was a form traced against an absence, becomes the formless presence of this absence, the *empty and opaque opening* onto what is when there is no longer any world, when there is not yet any world.

Between a "no longer" and a "not yet" of the world—between a stripping-away that renders it as yet to be constituted—there opens an obstructing but empty space of image as a kind of transcendental mask, a figure that "alludes" in its "absolute milieu," to the figurelessness marking its limit, a figure that also, it should be noted, has the structure of a ghost: the formless presence *of* an absence. This ghosting of all images is also that of language itself. Blanchot here introduces a footnote in which he says that in literature, in literary space as he has begun to lay it out (in this first chapter of *L'espace littéraire*), language becomes an image—not a language full of more and better images, but language as an image of itself, an "imaginary" language that no one speaks, and in a chiasmic formulation he describes this language as made up of "*images de mots et mots où les choses se font images*" ("images of words and words in which things are made image") (EL 32). Blanchot wants to say that this mere image-language—like the sheer absent fascination-image—has ontological priority over anything it would be an image *of*. And it is this priority, moving "back" from image construed as "image of (derived from) the real thing" to image as unreal *precedent* to all things, that would link Blanchot's analyses to the Kantian schematism. The text begins to point in this direction precisely here, where Blanchot refers to an appendix that addresses the question "*mais qu'est-ce que l'image?*" (but what is the image?). This appendix is the essay entitled "Les deux versions de l'imaginaire."[13] The "two versions" in question correspond roughly to whether the image is thought to follow from the object, or to precede it as the ground of its possibility.

In this essay, Blanchot does not speak of the death mask (though he does cite Pascal).[14] Moving closer, it would seem, to the ground of the image series presented in Heidegger/Nancy (photo, mask, corpse . . .), everything is focused on the live corpse, so to speak, which is presented as an instance of *pure resemblance*, a kind of absolute self-resemblance. In other words, the corpse is not only an image (of the dead man, that is), but also an *image of image* as such. "*Il est le semblable, semblable à un degré absolu, bouleversant et merveilleux. Mais à quoi ressemble-t-il? A rien*" ("It is the likeness, resemblance to an absolute degree, overwhelming and marvelous. But what does it resemble? Nothing"; EL 347). In explicating this strange resemblance, Blanchot draws an analogy with the broken tool example in Heidegger's *Being and Time*, and by implication with Duchamp's ready-mades (neither of whom he mentions here, referring instead to Breton), in which the everyday object is disengaged from its absorption and invisibility in use and is opened to its own pure appearance, which can be apprehended as "aesthetic." The analogy is not meant to aestheticize the corpse, but to "imagine" it, in the sense of rendering it over to a resemblance which the person it was never had with himself (or which he had, Blanchot says, only very rarely, in strange moments of distance and absence when he is "*égaré en soi, et comme son propre revenant, n'ayant déjà plus d'autre vie que celle du retour*" ["*astray* in *himself*, and like his own revenant, no longer having any life except that of return"; EL 347, Blanchot's emphasis)]—but is this not a description of the writer whose experience and existence are in any case always central to the question at hand?). What art and the corpse have in common is that their pure resemblance *makes appearance appear*, in a resemblance pure and simple, behind which there is, as Blanchot writes in an echo of Heidegger: "*rien—que l'être*" ("nothing—but being"; EL 348).[15] That is, in making appearance appear, the corpse is nothing less than the visible cipher of being. (Nancy, in the paragraph that ends with a note referring to Blanchot, calls the Blanchotian corpse a "shifter" [GI 92].) This is no doubt the place to recall that the "ontological" discourse of *L'espace littéraire* is one that depends on a radical reduction, or what one might call a stripping away of all world, object, appearance, phenomena, on the far side of which—or *en deçà*—what appears when everything has disappeared, is the oppressive persistence of being, what both Blanchot and Levinas during this period called the *il y a*.[16] Being "manifests" when everything manifest has been stripped away, leaving nothing—but being. I use the image of stripping away partly on the basis of Blanchot's occasional use of words based on the verb *dépouiller* to describe this process—and partly to bring us directly back to the corpse, which is here emerging as the privileged site and remainder of this process, and which Blanchot refers to repeatedly in this essay as *la dépouille*. The corpse is installed, uncannily and erringly, at the very center of an ontology of the remainder, what Blanchot here calls "*le résidu inéliminable de l'être*" ("the ineliminable residue of being") (EL 342), an image-residue that is directly associated with an obsessive haunting by an image that will not let go.

This is also the place to stress, once again, the homology between Blanchot's (and Levinas') stripping away of world, this radical reduction of phenomenality in search of its essential conditions, on the one hand, and, on the other, the trajectory of the sublime as the movement toward a supersensible realm beyond all image. But here again we see that in Blanchot's version, or "translation," of this movement, the "vocation" or end, far from the treasure of a supersensible faculty, the self-grounding treasure of Reason, is rather an infinite (and infernal) alterworld of images—a subworldly (simultaneously post- and pre-worldly) space that Blanchot calls "literary," a space of wandering that never severs its ties to the forms of sensation, even as it is voided of the limited ground these would provide. The form of sensation without the presence of the senses, or of sensed things. . . . I have argued that this movement is one of loss, and indeed we are more justified than ever in seeing Blanchot's image-haunted space of literature is deeply structured as melancholy (a word Blanchot never pronounces in this essay); likewise, we have seen that this loss may not be without its surreptitious returns and compensations, to be discerned precisely in the form of residues, remains and remainders. But let us look more closely at the grounds for making the association with melancholy within the context of the "Two Versions of the Imaginary."

First of all, the very use of the word *dépouille*, together with its proximity to the persistence of a haunting image space, is here derived in part from Hamlet, melancholy figure par excellence, whom Blanchot quotes early in the essay, precisely in order to introduce something of the *il y a*. (Before giving the quotation, I should mention that there is a translation issue that I will address afterward, concerning the use of the word *dépouille*.) On the way toward the "ineliminable residue of being," one might mistakenly think that in separating oneself from the real, one is entering, on its other side, the happy realm of a transparent irreality. But Blanchot calls this "*un songe heureux*" ("a happy dream"): "*Car, dit Hamlet, échappés des liens charnels, si, dans ce sommeil du trépas, il nous vient des songes*" (very literally: "for, says Hamlet, having escaped the bonds of flesh, if, in this sleep of death, dreams come to us"; EL 342). Much like Levinas, who also cites Shakespeare (*Macbeth*) in characterizing the *il y a*, Blanchot invokes Hamlet's dreams as a "*fond*" and as a "*matérialité élémentaire*" that threaten to turn the image into an inescapable prison. Now this quotation from Hamlet comes from André Gide's translation, in which the vivid formulation of a "shuffled off . . . mortal coil" becomes the more drab "*liens charnels*" that have been rather generically "escaped." But two pages later, at the precise point where Blanchot abruptly and disconcertingly introduces "*l'étrangeté cadavérique*" as the very strangeness of the image, he reverts to a more literal translation of Hamlet's phrase, and introduces the crucial term: "*Ce qu'on appelle* dépouille mortelle *échappe aux catégories communes*" ("what one calls the *mortal remains* escapes from the common categories"; EL 344; my emphasis). In a first inversion, *this* mortal coil is less one that is escaped *from* than one that itself escapes—from the categories of language and perception that would hold it in place. Like the coil, which evokes the dead skin of a snake, the *dépouille* is something sloughed off, a residue to be left behind when the living element, the soul (in the traditional logic implied by the metaphor) makes its way into the spiritual beyond. Thus, again in the traditional logic, there are two kinds of "*demeure*," two forms of the remainder: the eternally remaining soul, and the mere thingly remnant, the inert shell that will disappear into dust. But Blanchot's *dépouille* does not stay put, nor does it remain inertly secondary to the animating force that has shuffled it off. Rather, for Blanchot, it *is* the beyond, but far from sheerly spiritual or ideal, it is a beyond of images heavily laden with a materiality they cannot quite carry—it gives the image of these images in its, in their, endless unhinged movement. Hence in a second and more profound inversion, it is the dead body that animates the prison of the soul.[17] In escaping from the common categories, the corpse becomes a thing that escapes being a thing: with the *dépouille*, "*quelque chose est là devant nous, qui n'est ni le vivant en personne, ni une réalité quelconque, ni le même que celui qui était en vie, ni un autre, ni autre chose*" ("something is there before us, which is neither the living being in person, nor any reality whatever, nor even the one who was in life, nor an other, nor anything else"; EL 344). It escapes also from its place, shuffles the very possibility of a "here," which it collapses into a "nowhere" that it brings to presence as such. It haunts, originarily.[18] But if cadaverous resemblance is a "*hantise*," Blanchot writes, it is not a visitation of the ideal, rather "*ce qui hante est l'inaccessible dont on ne peut se défaire, ce qu'on ne trouve pas et qui, à cause de cela, ne se laisse pas éviter. L'insaisissable est ce à quoi l'on n'échappe pas*" ("what haunts is the inaccessible which one cannot get rid of, which one cannot find and which, because of that, will not allow itself to be avoided. The ungraspable is that from which one cannot escape"; EL 348). The stripped away shell, become image of image, cannot be shuffled off, but rather is animated by the endless movement of which it has become a schematic haunting figure.

Now a question obtrudes: is it possible to relate this inescapability to something like a law of the image, and thus to the tragic dimension implied by the reference to Hamlet? The answer, in the context of Blanchot's essay, is no.

It is interesting to note that, whereas Levinas invokes the bad conscience of Macbeth, Blanchot, even as he draws implicitly on Hamlet's haunted anxieties, never raises the specter of guilt or bad conscience, not even residually. The *dépouille* escapes from this dimension of the haunting corpse-image as well; and yet with the corpse, Blanchot wishes to inscribe nothing less than the "last judgment" in the ground of being.

> Cet être de grand format, important et superbe, qui impressionne les vivants comme l'apparition de l'original, jusque-là ignoré, sentence du Jugement dernier inscrite au fond de l'être. (EL 346)

> This oversized being, important and magnificent, which impresses the living as the apparition of the original, unknown until now, the sentence of the last judgment inscribed in the ground of being.

If the residue has become the essential element, if the *dépouille* is not a mere inert pulp of stuff left behind by its living core, but is rather itself the deathly animating kernel of vision and judgment, then what has in fact been shuffled off is not the unspiritual body, but the very life of the person who imprisoned this body in its identity. The corpse-image takes on its essential stature by sloughing off *the person*, by becoming *impersonal*, by exceeding the living being so far that the latter recedes into invisible distances, and is thus ruptured from our space of mourning. Blanchot makes an important distinction, in referring to the corpse and its resemblance, between *le vivant* and *le défunt* (e.g., EL 345), that is, between the living person who has now entirely disappeared, and the deceased person whose *dépouille* lies there uncannily drifting among us, released into the space of pure impersonal image of itself. It is exclusively with the latter that we have to do in Blanchot's staging of the funereal scene of the corpse.

For indeed there is not much of a scene in Blanchot's descriptions, and strangely not much to see, beginning with the dead man himself. Indeed, this can even be said of the highly charged mortuary moments in Blanchot's fictions, as when Thomas confronts the corpse of Anne in *Thomas l'obscur*; there we do not see this corpse and its "look" so much as hear Thomas's murmuring discourse over it.[19] In this sense, Blanchot does not respond here to the aforementioned graphic exigency, in the singularity of its demands, (which, it must be said, opens the door to given time and loss). In "Les deux versions" Blanchot makes it clear that the corpse's self-resemblance excludes the living being whom it in fact no longer resembles, except tangentially, as it were, incidentally—or inessentially.

How could it be that the uncanny and unsettling effects of the corpse in no way depend on—to put it simply—*who she was*, the given existence that has now been rendered over to sheer image, not only in the self-resemblance of the *dépouille*, but in the singular impressions also left behind, fragile shells whose sole abode is now the scattered exteriority of memory, its returns and revenants? There is literally no place for mourning or memory in Blanchot's cadaverous scene, so impossible is it to admit that these processes, too, are not reducible to merely personal psychological phenomena. To turn the point in more Blanchotian terms, one could say that they too are part of the murmur of images. In other words, the face of the dead man or woman is singular in each case, a singularity that is indeed separated from itself, but that in *having been* the face of *someone*, haunts the "survivors" with a residue that both is and, at the same time, is not entirely and absolutely impersonal. The *persona* of the dead face remains attached, however tenuously and problematically, to the time of a life that, for its part, continues, as image (as haunting), in its very extinction. What Nancy calls a "spark of world" (GI 95) ("*un éclat de monde*"; FI 173) and a "spark of inimagination" (GI 98) ("*éclat de l'inimagination*"; FI 178), the flashing out of the image's "once" (*une fois*) in the very moment of its disappearance, is in a way snuffed out by Blanchot.[20] We might say that, where Heidegger avoided the corpse, focusing instead on its "higher level" reproductions, Blanchot pushes the ground of the image "down" to the level of the corpse, but then avoids the very ground implied by it: the no less strange spark or animate force that has been the life of the one now defunct. That *éclat* is a time structure that becomes elided in Blanchot's exclusive focus on death and worldlessness as the sole form and structure of writing (at least in *L'espace littéraire*). Blanchot does not explicitly link the corpse's errant image-of-image with writing, the movement of "*celui qui écrit*," but the implication is clear: the writer dwells, and wanders, in a worldless corpse-image of language. The decisive phrase "*l'autre de tout monde*" is even echoed in "Deux versions" in a formula meant to encapsulate the radical ambiguity of the writer's language: there we touch on "*l'autre de tout sens* . . . [*où*] *rien n'a de sens, mais tout semble avoir infiniment de sens*"[21] ("the other of all sense . . . [where] nothing has any sense, but seems to have an infinity of sense"; EL 354; Blanchot's emphasis). As before, I believe it is necessary to acknowledge what Blanchot confronts us with, and (in this case) to think through the strange way in which this *semblance* is indeed a kind of ambiguous, impersonal life—a life-death that precedes what is ordinarily called life in its "everyday" sense. Indeed, this uncanny vivification of and in death is precisely what places us in closest proximity to the haunting imperative that traverses Blanchot's writing, and we will not have exhausted the implications of this structuring element. But here is the rub: in describing the conditions of its discovery as necessarily and absolutely severing every link with, effacing every trace of, the singular residue of a leftover life, Blanchot finds himself having to liquidate a strange material obtrusion that is *also* constitutive of the ontological or transcendental dimension of the experience of the corpse—and perhaps even of literature itself. Let us call this obtrusion: the loved one lost, coming back again and again in his or her singular unmourned persistence, albeit at the risk of ponderously dragging one down. Blanchot indicates this aspect of the corpse when he describes the moment between death and the first gestures of mourning in these disorienting terms:

> Tout à l'heure, il y aura, indéplaçable, intouchable, rivé à ici par une étreinte des plus étranges et cependant dérivant avec lui, l'entraînant plus en dessous, plus en bas, par derrière non plus une chose inanimée, mais Quelqu'un, image insoutenable et figure de l'unique devenant n'importe quoi. (EL 345–346)
>
> In a moment, there will be, unmovable, untouchable, tied to here by the strangest of embraces and yet drifting with it, dragging it farther down, farther and deeper below, from behind, no longer an inanimate thing, but Someone, unbearable image and figure of the unique become just anything.

This is a strange image (if it is one), almost illegible: the corpse, or what the corpse will soon be, tightly embracing "here" and dragging it farther and farther down—the corpse, or a thing that is no longer merely a lifeless thing but that is simply Someone—Someone dragging everything down from behind, as it effaces the unique figure and becomes just whatever: *n'importe quoi*. What remains is the indifference into which the singular figure must sink so that a neutral Someone might appear. Here is a way to see this strange "image": the "figure of the unique" is sunk along with the "here," leaving the grand and neutral Someone floating on the surface, through the scrambled and collapsed space of the corpse, a space that ruins beforehand the possibility of a mourning henceforth voided of its beloved figure.

It appears that Blanchot's discourse on the corpse, and further on writing itself, is a call to suspend this in-between moment, and to let the "figure of the unique" sink into indifference, in favor of the faceless Someone emerging behind that figure, the whatever thing that is unbearable, to be sure, but whose movements still must be severed from a given past. But a corpse does not completely efface this dimension, does not become "*n'importe quoi*"—until it rots and decomposes. Is there something rotten in Blanchot's impersonal absolutes? If the only guarantor of idealism is a corpse, as Blanchot writes (EL 347), then the corpse's decomposition may be the equivocal seal of an absolute given over to its last remaining chances in literary space. But the border evoked here between the beloved's corpsely face and the implicit corruption toward which it tends may be the index of an anxiety and avoidance different from that which arises in the face of the corpse's putrefaction and bearing rather on something resembling a shattered attachment. Now my point in raising these questions is not to vindicate the perduring identity of the dead, a fading thing to be anxiously propped up by mortuary conventions, but rather to point to another anxiety that may be legible in the effacement and submersion of the corpse's singularity as it sinks into oblivion, as into the Lethe. We will turn back toward this floating corpse and its disavowed obtrusions in a moment.

RETURN TO *L'ARRÊT DE MORT*

If we return briefly to the figures in *L'arrêt de mort*, it is clear that the difficulty of effacing the graphic singularity "projected" from the kernel of the story asserts itself precisely in the narrative's haunting figural residues, including especially the cast hands and face that are folded back into the scene of the story's *writing*, watching over it and pressing it compulsively onward. There is no visible corpse in *L'arrêt de mort*. (For this we would do better to look to *Thomas l'obscur*, an earlier text that is in many ways more consonant with the analysis in "Deux versions"; but even there, as mentioned above, the corpse is less a vividly projected image than the occasion for an endless murmur of words, spoken by the male figure of the title.)[22]

Instead what we find in *L'arrêt de mort*—and after reading "Les deux versions"—is the merging or collapse of the mask and the corpse into a simultaneously living/dead figure. In the mask, Blanchot concretizes and figures the schematizing production of images as a look, a gaze out of and into death that inhabits the movement of writing as an inmost haunting force. At the same time, one could say that not only are the "living" bodies that populate *L'arrêt de mort* manifestly nothing but animated corpses, but the entire text is a kind of corpse: a dead but speaking residue, shell and mask of an animating force that, through its narrative movements, attempts to make itself visible. But this is also to say that it is a corpse that *keeps its face*, even as it is dissolved in the final defiguring "sublimation" (or "volatilization") in its last paragraph. The face, the figures, even the half-erased names all *remain*, impressed and imprinted into the body of the text. Without them, and the strange affective force that turns the narrator toward them in the first place (before being cast as "*un sentiment incapable de disparaître*" [AM 127]), the final impersonal and volatilizing declaration would be less than an empty shell; it would be the sheer emptiness of mere abstraction. Without these material and figural elements being left to *turn away*, without their scattered leavings lying strewn throughout the text that we can now look back upon after reading its final words, these words and their "all-powerful affirmation" would not register the wrenching "*malheur*" that has led there, or show the treacherous path by which they have reached this affirmation. In other words, they would not show their scars. But in doing so, they betray the melancholy attachments without which they could never have been spoken. If "she" is eternally there, if a *pensée* that names writing's most intimate haunting imperative remains unruinable, then *someone* who is not quite equivalent to a neutralized Someone remains there as well, guarding and guarded by the law of this now finished work. Blanchot's openness, after all, about this attachment and preservation belies the final passage out of this world and recalls us back from it into a singular and residual time that I cannot help calling *sentimental*, in the most banal sense possible. This is one perhaps surprising result of Blanchot's attempt to respond in *L'arrêt de mort* to the graphic or projective exigency constitutive of this story. If literary space takes one into the other of every world, at the same time it will always be the case that one will never not *have been* in the peculiarly shaped world whose obtrusive residues still demand a look.

But we should also note that the story's residue is a face, a mask, that also keeps its gender. And this gendered death mask has a history: another story that intersects with Blanchot's writing life, in one of its most sentimental aspects, a figural investment bordering on kitsch. I would now like to turn to this other story.

DEATH MASK (II): ARTIFACT

In puzzling over Heidegger's use of the example of the death mask in his analysis of the Kantian schematism, Nancy points out that there are two reasons behind its emergence (neither of which is acknowledged by Heidegger), a transcendental reason and an empirical reason. I have already discussed some aspects of the transcendental reason. The empirical reason has its place in this story as well, and provides yet another point of intersection with Blanchot's intrigues with the death mask. In 1926, around the time when Heidegger was giving a course on which the *Kantbuch* would be based, a book was published by Ernst Benkard under the title *Das ewige Antlitz*, literally "the eternal countenance" (it appeared in English as *Undying Faces*).²³ This book features 123 images of death masks (including an appendix with eleven items the editor describes as "*unechte Stücke . . . und andere zum Thema gehörende Kuriosa*" ("inauthentic pieces . . . and other odd items relevant to the theme"; 62) from the collection of the Schiller National Museum in Marbach. There is in fact a photograph of Pascal's death mask in the book (presented there as plate 11). This reference, together with the book's general success and renown, make it very plausible to claim that Heidegger had seen it and was inspired by it to choose the example he uses in the *Kantbuch*. I will also indulge in an as yet unverified conjecture that Blanchot surely knew about this book. In any case, when we turn to the last image before the appendix (plate 112), we find a reproduction of a death mask that Blanchot not only knew but of which he actually owned a copy. This is the famous mask of "L'Inconnue de la Seine," also known as "La Noyée de la Seine," the "Unknown" or "Drowned woman of the Seine." It is this mask that hung on the wall of Blanchot's writing room in Eze. Its presence there can be explained in part by the curious place it has in the art and literature of the early twentieth century. It is purportedly the mask of a young woman who drowned herself in the Seine, and whose face—so the story goes—was so beatifically serene, with its calm demeanor and its teasing hint of a smile, that it inspired an undertaker at the morgue to make a cast of it. This artifact thus entered the public sphere through legend and, perhaps more important, through commercially available reproductions. This ghostly remnant and the (entirely fictional) story behind it—with its echoes of Ophelia and Ondine, its pathos-laden lightness and beauty in death—captured the imagination of numerous artists and writers (almost all male, it should be noted), including Rilke (who refers to it in *The Notebooks of Malte Laurids Brigge*), Supervielle, Céline, Aragon, Man Ray, and many others.²⁴ I stressed earlier the projective nature of the death mask as a graphic emblem for the schematizing process of image-formation, the intimate pressing force of a haunting return; but here what becomes clear is that the death mask is itself a projection screen, an all but blank surface on which narratives and affects are projected and affixed.²⁵ The mask of la Noyée de la Seine apparently did serve as such a screen for Blanchot, who in a late text repeats the legend of the girl's death-smile—although it could be argued that this famous smile is not really much of a smile, and could even be seen as merely the effect of gravity on the dead lips of a supine corpse. (A close and less affectively preinvested look at the mask might well bear this out.) Here is what Blanchot says about it, in the opening passage of a late essay dealing precisely with questions of haunting feminine figures, mourning and melancholy:

> Quand je résidais à Èze, dans la petite chambre (agrandie par une double perspective, l'une ouverte jusqu'à la Corse, l'autre par-delà le Cap Ferrat) où je demeurais le plus souvent, il y avait (elle y est encore), pendue au mur, l'effigie de celle qu'on a nommée "l'inconnue de la Seine," une adolescente aux yeux clos, mais vivante par un sourire si délié, si fortuné, (voilé pourtant), qu'on eût pu croire qu'elle s'était

noyée dans un instant d'extrême bonheur. Si éloignée de ses œuvres, elle avait séduit Giacometti au point qu'il recherchait une jeune femme qui aurait bien voulu tenter à nouveau l'épreuve de cette félicité de la mort.[26]

When I lived in Èze, in the little room (made larger by a double perspective, one opened all the way to Corsica, the other beyond Cap Ferrat) where I most often stayed there was (it/she is still there) hanging on the wall, the effigy of the one who has been called "the unknown girl of the Seine," an adolescent with closed eyes, but alive with a smile so subtle, so full of fortune (and yet veiled), that one might have believed she had drowned in an instant of extreme happiness. So far removed from his works, she had seduced Giacometti to the point that he searched for a young woman who might have wanted to attempt once again the experience of this felicity in death.

I will return to this strange reference to Giacometti in a moment. These lines introduce an essay on Louis-René des Forêts's series *Poèmes de Samuel Wood*.[27] It is curious and striking at the outset that Blanchot would approach these poems, fraught as they are with elegiac evocations of childhood and maternal ghosts, with this uncharacteristic self-reference, a gesture he describes as "*une discrétion*" with respect to "*la hantise des poèmes*" themselves—as though this "*hantise*" were the truly revealing element here. And indeed it is clear throughout the essay that Blanchot treats these poems with a sense of extraordinary familiarity and even intimacy, no doubt seeing in them some of the essential traits of his own ghost-ridden work, certainly that part of it with which we have been concerned, and toward which this late essay turns as though in nostalgic retrospection. In other words, in approaching these poems Blanchot seems to be intensely *identified*. This image of la Noyée (as I will call her to maintain an emphasis on the aquatic element of her intrigue), called up from the very heart of Blanchot's writing practice, the feminine face of a light and ecstatic death overlooking the space of the *récits*, aligns this entire layer of Blanchot's work with the generative figures animating des Forêts's melancholic poems. For this identification hinges precisely around a feminine ghost. Blanchot cites des Forêts, who writes of a woman encountered in a dream, a *real* dream, a nighttime dream: "*Il y a aussi cette femme assise sur le rebord d'une fenêtre/Et c'est toujours la même. Qui donc est-elle? Quel signe fait-elle avec ses doigts gantés de rouge?*" ("There is also this woman, sitting on the windowsill/And she is always the same. Who is she then? What sign is she making with her fingers in red gloves?").[28] And it is here, with yet another autobiographical reference, that Blanchot tightens the knot of the intrigue in which the imperative to write has become bound to a spectral woman, who is also something like a *literary* node or residue, when he comments on the closeness this figure has for him, calling it "too real."

Figure qui me trouble parce que je l'ai rencontrée moi aussi, mais de jour, diurne et spectrale. Messagère de la Mélancolie, si semblable à l'apparition évoquée par Henry

James dans "le Tour d'écrou," immobile comme une femme fautive, légèrement détournée pour que nous échappions au souvenir de notre propre faute.

Figures trop réelles pour durer. (UV 17)

A figure that troubles me because I have encountered her too, but during the day, diurnal and spectral. A Messenger of Melancholy, so similar to the apparition evoked by Henry James in "The Turn of the Screw," motionless like a guilty woman, slightly turned away, so that we might escape from the memory of our own guilt/fault.

Figures too real to last.

The too great reality of these figures had remained with Blanchot for a very long time. Any reader of *Au moment voulu* will recognize the reference to one of them, a haunting woman who plays a very important role there, and whose melancholy figure and desolate attitude attest to her close kinship with the ghosts in Henry James' tale.

AU MOMENT VOULU AND JAMES'S GHOSTS

I would like to leave la Noyée and her mask for a moment and turn directly to *Au moment voulu* in order to follow a number of associations that will place this melancholy haunting in relation to James' ghost story. Blanchot's own comments on James, from an essay more or less contemporary with *Au moment voulu*, will further reveal some unexpected aspects of the constitutive hauntedness that he places in the very ground of narration, as its imperative force.

In *Au moment voulu* this Messenger of Melancholy shows up not as a "diurnal" specter, but rather very much as a nocturnal one. As mentioned earlier, this encounter is something like the *récit*'s "point," its animating "instant," and is there given a kind of transcendental status precisely with respect to the day—she/it (*elle*) is the nocturnal point that makes the day possible, or rather that just *makes the day*; it is "*un seul instant . . . en qui pourtant* le frisson se fait jour" ("a single instant . . . in which however *the shiver becomes day*") (AMV 144; my emphasis). The chills, shivers, and vibrations that have passed through the *récits* at various strange and feverish moments are here located at the obscure heart of an unaccountable relation, and are given an ambiguous affective dimension as the very possibility of seeing and living, while also being set against a deeply haunting and melancholy ground. Here again, but more amply presented, is the passage in which Blanchot introduces this figure.[29] Her evocation will also lead us in the direction of James's tale, from which she seems to have drifted.

> Il m'était arrivé autrefois, habitant seul dans le Sud, —et j'étais dans la vigueur de l'âge, le jour ma force était bouleversante, mais il y avait un moment dans la nuit où tout s'arrêtait, l'espoir, la possibilité, la nuit; j'ouvrais alors la porte et je regardais tranquillement vers le bas de l'escalier: c'était un mouvement tout à fait tranquille et sans intention, purement nocturne, comme on dit. En cet instant, à travers

> l'immense étendue, elle me donnait l'impression d'être assise, elle aussi, en bas de l'escalier, sur la large marche du tournant; ayant ouvert la porte, je regardais vers elle qui ne me regardait pas, et tout ce qu'il y avait de tranquillité dans ce mouvement si parfaitement silencieux avait aujourd'hui la vérité de ce corps légèrement *courbé* dans une attitude qui n'était pas celle de l'attente, ni de la résignation, mais d'une profonde et mélancolique dignité. Pour moi, je ne pouvais que regarder, par une vue qui exprimait toute la tranquille transparence d'une vue dernière, cette femme assise près du mur, la tête légèrement penchée vers ses mains . . . Jamais elle ne se tourna vers moi et jamais, après l'avoir regardée, je n'oubliai de me retirer tranquillement. (AMV 138–139; my emphasis)

> It had happened to me long ago, when I was living in the South, — and I was in the vigor of youth, during the day my strength was overwhelming, but there was a moment at night when everything stopped, hope, possibility, night itself; I would open the door and look calmly toward the bottom of the stairway: it was a movement made in utter calm and without any intention, purely nocturnal, as one says. At that instant, across the immense expanse, she gave me the impression that she too was sitting near the bottom of the stairway, on the large step where they turn; having opened the door, I looked toward her, she did not look at me, and all there was of calm in this perfectly silent movement had today the truth of this body slightly stooped in an attitude not of waiting, not of resignation, but of a profound and melancholic dignity. For me, I could only look, with a look that expressed all the peaceful transparency of a final look, at this woman sitting near the wall, her head slightly leaning toward her hands. . . . Never did she turn to me, and never, after looking at her, did I forget to withdraw in peace. (WTC 61)

As mentioned earlier, the narrator's encounter with her also gives rise to the title phrase: "*cet instant était bien le moment voulu*" ("this instant was indeed the awaited moment"; AMV 139).[30] It is a moment that shows him that "*la détresse pouvait m'apparaître avec une si extraordinaire dignité*," ("distress could appear to me with such extraordinary dignity"), for this figure is described as being in an attitude of "*profonde et mélancolique dignité*" (AMV 139) a phrase that is repeated several times, with variations, reaching back into the narrative involving Claudia and Judith as well (there it is used to describe Claudia [AMV 130] in a passage where the narrator tries to convince her to come stay with him "*dans le Sud*," in the South).[31] The references to the South are important for several reasons; the one at the beginning of the passage above introduces a distinct rupture in the narrative, leaving Paris behind, along with the two women there, and thus initiates the final section of the book, a long meditative passage that, aside from the specter that inaugurates it, essentially unhinges itself from the narrative coordinates that, however indefinitely, have situated the *récit* up to that point. At the same time, we can hear in this evocation of a solitary life in the South an allusion to the writing space in Èze mentioned by Blanchot in *Une voix venue d'ailleurs*, where hung the effigy of la Noyée de la Seine (and "she is still there" . . .). The space of writing is thus literally haunted here, and doubly so, by feminine figures uncannily keeping it company, albeit across the distance of an unbroachable relation. With a characteristic shift that we have seen repeatedly in Blanchot's narratives, a shift that renders such a reference both deeply autobiographical and radically fictional, Blanchot places his spectral visitor outside, in the night, and makes of her the very principle of writing and thought—for in *Au moment voulu* too, though in a less emphatic and elaborate way than in *L'arrêt de mort*, the truly chilling spectral presence is that of *une pensée*, a thought which at one point early in the story *opens a door* as though to enter the room (AMV 48), though she does not. Later, when a specter does appear, there on the stairway in the South, the feminine figure is explicitly a figure of melancholy; she herself appears to suffer from and also to transmit a sublime Melancholy, with an extraordinary dignity that outstrips her distress. The narrator is emphatic in insisting that if he speaks of distress and anxiety, he is also speaking of "*le frémissement de la joie*" ("the shivering of joy"; AMV 146). *Frémissement* and *frisson*: these terms bear a strange and crucial weight in the recitical reflections that traverse *Au moment voulu*; if it did not take us too far afield, I believe it could be shown that they are names for the subtle modulation of the transcendental effected by Blanchot in recitical time (he repeatedly evokes something called "*la vérité d'un frisson*" [AMV 78] or "*la vérité d'une sensation*" [AMV 93]), and as such they draw the writing of the récits away from the figural sharpness of the mask and the ghost toward something I would be tempted to call a kind of *musical* figure (a question of vibration and rhythm: a "schema" in another of its "aspects"). For now, I would like to emphasize once again the persistent spectral and figural residue that nonetheless clings to such a "pure" movement, by citing a passage that directly engages the question of the ghost as a figure. Unexpectedly, just after referring to "*le moment voulu*" and to the encounter it offers as an "image," the narrator qualifies his statements:

> Qu'on le comprenne, il ne s'agissait nullement d'une image: l'image ou la figure, si calme qu'elle fût, n'était par rapport à la dignité souveraine de l'instant qu'un reste d'inquiétude, sur l'instant l'inquiétude demeurait posée, c'est pourquoi il apparaissait. (AMV 142)

> Understand, it was in no way a matter of an image: the image or the figure, however quiet, was, in relation to the sovereign dignity of the instant, only a remnant of anxiety, the anxiety remained poised on the instant, that was why it appeared. (WTC 63)

The image, the figure, is a residue of disquiet, of an anxiety that accompanies the calm tranquility of the instant, and that thus also *appears*, in the autobiographical reference, as the "Messenger of Melancholy"—is this anxiety therefore an index of loss, despite its being merely "posed" or "poised" atop the instant, as though it could easily be cast off? Does it place the movement of appearance in an affective register that might also be characterized as a tenuous but stubborn attachment that cannot help but haunt "the pure passion of time" (AMV 144)?

A few pages later, meditating further on this nocturnal moment, Blanchot's narrator carries out the negating or rather *neutralizing* gesture beyond which the figure loses its narrative specificity, but is also radicalized in its forceful but powerless strangeness:

> La nuit, dans le Sud, quand je me lève, je sais qu'il ne s'agit ni du proche, ni du lointain, ni d'un événement m'appartenant, ni d'une vérité capable de parler, ce n'est pas une scène, ni le commencement de quelque chose. Une image, mais vaine, un instant, mais stérile, quelque'un pour qui je ne suis rien et qui ne m'est rien— sans lien, sans début, sans but—, un point, et hors de ce point, rien, dans le monde, qui ne me soit étranger. Une figure? mais privée de nom, sans biographie, que refuse la mémoire, qui ne désire pas être raconté, qui ne veut pas survivre . . . (AMV 151–152)

> At night, in the South, when I rise, I know that it isn't a question of proximity, or of distance, or of an event belonging to me, or of a truth capable of speaking, this is not a scene, or the beginning of something. An image, but an empty one, an instant, but a sterile one, someone for whom I am nothing and who is nothing to me—without bonds, without beginning, without end—a point, and outside this point, nothing, in the world, that is not foreign to me. A figure? But one deprived of a name, without a biography, one that is rejected by memory, that does not want to be recounted, that does not want to survive . . . (WTC 67)

It should be noted that nearly all of these formulations have their apparent contraries elsewhere in the narrator's reflections; but it is less a question of "contradictions" (obviously a pointless and fruitless way to approach a text such as this) than of a constitutive tension and a paradox that is here given in its most radically "purified" and neutralized aspect, which can be summarized as a kind of arrestation, a radical "nothing to be done," an empty inaccessible point that does not simply liquidate the terms of its possibility, but renders them unreachable, unproductive, "vain" and "sterile." If we are approaching an imperative here, an exigency that, by way of spectral hauntings and figural leavings, would demand something called writing, we are also confronted with what Blanchot calls (in the last paragraph of *Au moment voulu*) "*le moment absolument sombre de cette intrigue, le point où elle retourne constamment au présent*" ("the absolutely somber moment of this intrigue, the point where it constantly returns to the present"), a dark and useless point to which writing, too, has *no relation*: writing's absolute, from which writing itself is excluded. As is memory and biography. And yet despite this absolute, it is clear that writing, memory, and biography are tightly intertwined in this intrigue, a persistent fact that Blanchot signals (compounding the paradoxes) when he writes that "*le souvenir . . . est la forme pesante de ce manque de mémoire*" ("memories . . . are the ponderous form of this lack of memory"; AMV 157). Memory as "*le souvenir*"—as memory of particular memories—is precisely what gives form to a lack of memory—as power to remember—insofar as the latter is no longer linked to or filled with its "contents." But we should notice that this implies the obtrusion, after all, of the latter, if only as "form." The very schema of memory is thus the weighty and sinking form of oblivion: in these impossible formulations, are we thus turning slowly back toward the dead body, the intriguing mask of La Noyée? If so, we are doing so in a paradoxical and rupturing movement that Blanchot calls *passion*. The figural and spatial elements that link *Au moment voulu* to Blanchot's writing space "in the South," watched over by the death mask of a drowned woman, and a diurnal/nocturnal specter—immobile, impassive emblem of Melancholy—bring out a dimension of this passion that appears to be recalcitrant to the demands of pure oblivion.

Before looking further at the passion that Blanchot evokes in certain crucial moments in texts that revolve around the leavings of feminine figures, women and loved ones, we should stop for a moment on the reference to James in the preceding quotation from "Une voix venue d'ailleurs." This reference is more than a clue to the essential intrigue unfolding here; it is something of a literary confession—that is, a disclosure of an extremely intimate element of the constitution of Blanchot's literary world and practice. It thus provides an equally significant node in the triple reference to spectral melancholy animating the work of all three writers discussed in this study, Blanchot's included.

In the passage from James's "Turn of the Screw" to which the *Au moment voulu* alludes most directly, the governess-narrator relates one of her several spectral encounters in the tale:

> Looking down it [the staircase] from the top I once recognised the presence of a woman seated on one of the lower steps with her back presented to me, her body half-bowed and her head, in an attitude of woe, in her hands. I had been there but an instant, however, when she vanished without looking round at me.[32]

This is the infamous Miss Jessel, the thwarted lover who has died in mysterious circumstances and whom the narrating governess has replaced in the absent master's household.[33] In a later encounter, the ghost appears at the narrator's writing table, sitting again with her head on her hands, but then:

> She rose . . . with an indescribable grand melancholy of indifference and detachment, and, within a dozen feet of me, stood there as my vile predecessor. Dishonoured and tragic, she was all before me: but even as I fixed and, for memory, secured it, the awful image passed away. (TS 69)

I would add to these instances several other moments in Blanchot's récits, particularly *Au moment voulu* and *Celui qui ne m'accompagnait pas*, where, in no less evident evocations of James's paradigmatic specters, Blanchot's narrator describes faces spying through windows from the outside—in *Au moment voulu* he even sees himself doing so, as he lies ill in a corner of the room (AMV 92). (Indeed, there is a distinct thread in that récit that strongly indicates the narrator's own status as pure specter, pure image, a dead man returning.) These echoes, which one can rightly call translations, or even transpositions, point us in reading Blanchot's récits toward the core problem of James's story (to limit ourselves only to "Turn of the Screw"): the phantomatic nature of all narrative. That is precisely what Blanchot insists on in his 1954 essay bearing the story's title, "Le tour d'écrou," in what he calls "*le coeur malin de tout récit*," which in the context of James's story could be translated as *the malignant core of every story*. Though of course *malin* also evokes the ruse and ambiguity at the heart of all stories and storytelling, an ambiguity that, in reference to James, Blanchot locates in the fact that its protagonist is also its *narratrice*.

> Celle-ci ne se contente pas de voir les fantômes, dont sont peut-être hantés les enfants, elle est celle qui en parle, les attirant dans l'espace indécis de la narration, dans cet au-delà irréel *où tout devient fantôme*, tout se fait glissant, fugitif, présent et absent, symbole du Mal sous l'ombre duquel Graham Greene voit James écrire et qui est peut-être seulement *le coeur malin de tout récit*. (LV 178; my emphasis)

> She is not content to see ghosts, who may be haunting the children, she is the one who speaks of them, drawing them into the indefinite space of narration, in this unreal beyond *where everything becomes ghost*, everything becomes elusive, fleeting, present and absent, symbol of Evil in whose shadow Graham Greene sees James writing and that is perhaps merely *the cunning heart of every story*.

The Evil evoked here may give a clue as to the strange "*faute*" alluded to in Blanchot's encounter with his diurnal specter, that messenger of Melancholy who *turns* away so that we might escape from the memory of our own "fault." Is there an inherent link between such specters, the phantomatic space of the stories they populate and generate, and the "faulty" space of writing, itself populated by these "figures too real to last," feminine figures who all seem to embody a strange and guilty memory? Is the pressure felt by the narrator of "Turn of the Screw," in its intimate engagement with some unspeakable "vileness" (with which she is fully identified)—not to mention the melancholic force compelling these figures into view, that is, into narrative—is this also the pressure exerted on and by the writer of stories that unfold in search of their own most intimate and spectral conditions of possibility? In his essay on James, Blanchot implies that this is so, or rather he shows that James himself implies this. The latter gives the forces at work two names, which Blanchot takes up in their assonance (in French) as the very heart of what is at stake: *passion* and *pression*, the passion and pressure that animate and compel the phantomatic reality of a story *in its sheer possibility*. Blanchot's essay begins by asking about James's intense investment in his notebooks, and therefore the need for what Blanchot calls "*un schéma souvent fort grossier*" ("an often quite crude schema"), and "*la sécurité d'un canevas*" ("the security of a tableau"), in approaching a new story under construction (this in distinction from Kafka, whose every sentence, even in his notes, however preliminary, is already *"engagée dans la profondeur du récit"* ["engaged in the depths of the récit"; LV 173], is already the opening and development of a story *itself*). Blanchot explains this investment in sketches and notebooks by evoking a kind of ecstasy of the possible, when the still developing story

> est l'ivresse "bénie" de la pure possibilité, et l'on sait comment le possible—cette vie fantomatique et irréelle de ce que nous n'avons pas été, figures avec qui nous avons toujours rendez-vous—a exercé sur James une attirance dangereuse, parfois presque folle . . . (LV 181)

> is the "blessed" intoxication of pure possibility, and we know how the possible—this ghostly and unreal life of what we have not been, figures whom we are always bound to meet—exerted on James a dangerous, sometimes almost mad attraction . . .

This passion takes the form of a pressure, says Blanchot, exerted on the work, not in order to write it, but in order to maintain its indeterminacy and infinity, in order to include within it what the writing itself must hide:

> James fait l'expérience, non pas du récit qu'il doit écrire, mais de son envers, de l'autre côté de l'oeuvre, celui que cache nécessairement le mouvement d'écrire . . . ce qu'il y a derrière son oeuvre . . . (LV 182)

> James has the experience not of the récit that he must write, but of its reverse side, of the other side of the work, the one necessarily hidden by the movement of writing . . . what there is behind his work.

The double exigency cited from *L'espace littéraire* above appears here in a somewhat different guise: writing is what must interrupt this infinite expansion and inclusiveness of the *récit* as "possible," but it does so in tandem with a force pressing out from a phantom reality demanding its due. This pressure, Blanchot points out, is tellingly referred to by James at one point in his notebooks as none other than "under the pressure and the screw," which Blanchot in turn calls "*la pression de la narration elle-même*" ("the pressure of narration itself").[34] But Blanchot also relates it directly to the sordid forces at work in James's (or his narrator's) ghost story. In this sense it is something like the transcendental "subject" of that story, a story about the very conditions of storytelling:

> Or, cette pression à laquelle il soumet l'oeuvre, non pas pour la limiter, mais au contraire pour la faire parler complètement, sans réserve dans son secret pourtant réservé, cette pression ferme et douce, cette sollicitation pressante, de quel nom la désigne-t-il? Du nom même qu'il a choisi comme titre pour son histoire de fantômes: *Le Tour d'écrou*. "Que peut donner mon cas de K.B. [un roman qu'il n'achèvera pas], une fois soumis à la pression et au *tour d'écrou*?" Allusion révéla-

> trice. Elle nous confirme que James n'ignore certes pas quel est le "sujet" de son récit: cette pression que la gouvernante fait subir aux enfants pour leur arracher leur secret et qu'ils subissent peut-être aussi de la part de l'invisible, mais qui est essentiellement la pression de la narration elle-même, le mouvement merveilleux et terrible que le fait d'écrire exerce sur la vérité, tourment, torture, violence qui conduisent finalement à la mort où tout paraît se révéler, où tout cependant retombe dans le doute et le vide des ténèbres. (LV 182–183; Blanchot's interpolation and emphasis)[35]
>
> Now, this pressure to which he submits the work, not in order to limit it, but on the contrary to make it speak completely, without reserve in its secret which is nonetheless reserved, this firm and gentle pressure, this pressing movement—by what name does he designate it? With the name that he chose as the title for his ghost story: *The Turn of the Screw*. "What then do I see my K.B. case [a novel he will not finish], under the pressure and the screw, as susceptible of giving?" A revealing allusion. It confirms for us that James knows very well what the "subject" of his récit is: this pressure that the governess makes the children undergo in order to tear from them their secret and that they perhaps also undergo on the part of the invisible, but that is essentially the pressure of narration itself, the marvelous and terrible movement which the fact of writing exerts on the truth, a torment, torture, and violence that leads finally to death, in which everything seems to be revealed, but where everything falls back into the doubt and the emptiness of the shadows.

Torment, torture, violence, and death—and ultimately doubt and the void of shadows: this is the spectral domain that Blanchot identifies, through James (and to this extent in identification with him), as literary space in its phantomatic passions: the constitutive hauntedness of writing. The importance of the words *passion* and *pression* in *Au moment voulu*, in which they frequently occur (see especially 144–145), would call for closer consideration in this light, but one thing is clear: it is not untouched by something like crime, evil, and guilt as these inhabit the "malignant core of every story," particularly the haunted stories both weighted and lifted by dead and melancholy-bearing women. The "*faute*" in question surely hinges around this, but what is the crime, implicit or virtual, whose possibility inhabits Blanchot's writing? In pursuing further the powerful and destructive force of passion in Blanchot, I propose, hesitantly, to call it *murder*— and to show that along with an absolutely somber and untouchable point, the intrigue of writing, as it strives for "la pure passion du temps" (AMV 144), is conditioned by an uncanny violence that must be continually disavowed.[36]

LE GALLIENNE, GIACOMETTI, AND LA NOYÉE

It is strange to note that we have arrived at this juncture partly by way of a complex fascination with a mass produced object of kitsch sentimentality, in which Blanchot, perhaps surprisingly, did not hesitate to indulge: la Noyée de la Seine, whose peaceful quasi-smile seems far removed, despite the apparent similarity of the watery end they meet, from the sordid "vileness" of a Miss Jessel and her phantom intrigues. And yet the death mask of la Noyée harbors her own violent story, since after all, according to the legend, she was a suicide whose postmortem beauty seems to rely on the quelling of some unknown painful passion. This conjunction of beauty and destruction is part of the fascination she has exerted, and was indeed associated with her from the beginning.

I would like to refer in passing to the first writing in which she appears, a story published in 1900 by the English writer Richard le Gallienne entitled "The Worshipper of the Image," in which the mask of la Noyée plays an explicit role.[37] Taking his cues from Baudelaire, and more generally (more vaguely) from a certain melodramatic strain of decadent aestheticism, the author directly associates the beauty of the mask with Evil, in a "poetic" fetishism of beauty unto death: the poet protagonist literally falls in love with the mask, neglecting for this more perfect beauty his wife and child, both of whom die by the end, the former in a suicide that duplicates la Noyée's own demise. The wife's drowned face evokes that idealized beauty, which the stricken husband can only admire in a trance, regardless of the price, in life and corpses, paid for the spectacle. The story ends with the suggestion that the poet is definitively in thrall to the mask he has thus, finally, brought to life with his "sacrifices" which (in his hallucinatory projections) *the mask herself has demanded.* Pure image replaces living beings in the aestheticizing delirium of the transcending, beauty-worshipping poet. A close reading of this story might well reveal some disquieting similarities with Blanchot's récits, despite or perhaps because of le Gallienne's heavy-handed style, which has little in common with Blanchot's artfulness, discretion, and indirection, but which nonetheless manages to articulate more sharply (and indeed, quite possibly, in a mode so hyperbolic and literal that it verges into ironic critique) some of the less palatable impulses and consequences at stake in this fascination. The fact that in both cases we have to do with the transformation of women into a sheer (dead) image of beauty is clear enough.[38] But that in Blanchot's case it may be a question of sacrificial murder is much less apparent.

This brings us back to the strange reference, in "Une voix venue d'ailleurs," to Giacometti. To recall, Blanchot writes of la Noyée:

> Si éloignée de ses œuvres, elle avait séduit Giacometti au point qu'il recherchait une jeune femme qui aurait bien voulu tenter à nouveau l'épreuve de cette félicité de la mort.
>
> Far removed from his works, she had seduced Giacometti to the point that he searched for a young woman who might have wanted to attempt once again the experience of this felicity in death.

Giacometti is not generally associated with the sort of Baudelairean aestheticism found in le Gallienne's story, and Blanchot distances the aesthetics of the mask from Giacometti's work; but in the very same sentence, he invokes the sacrifice, and the fascinated seduction, staged in the story. I do not know if this anecdote about Giacometti has been verified. But Blanchot's reference to an artist known rather for the extreme reductions and attenuations of his disappearing figures could well, and for these very reasons, apply to Blanchot himself, suggesting through this projected sympathy that a strange undercurrent of sentimentality has survived the rigors of a later and more openly anxious figural ascesis. One might take the suggestion further and wonder whether this survival of sentimentality is not in fact constitutive of such an "ascetic" and figurally purified turn in the outward "face"—the "disfigurations"—of twentieth century art (a suggestion that will find some support in the analysis of Beckett offered in the next chapter). Aside from this allusion in "Une voix venue d'ailleurs," I know of only one other reference made by Blanchot to Giacometti, and it is strangely relevant here, in that it reinforces the artistic convergence implied by the quote above. Added as something of a non sequitur to the end of an essay on Mallarmé ("L'expérience de Mallarmé," an essay that elaborates the question of the "point" and the "exigence de l'oeuvre" that passes through it, and that also discusses suicide at length), the invocation of Giacometti's sculpture seems as forced as it is decisive. Blanchot writes:

> Quand nous regardons les sculptures de Giacometti, il y a un point d'où elles ne sont plus soumises aux fluctuations de l'apparence, ni au mouvement de la perspective. On les voit *absolument*: non plus réduites, mais soustraites à la réduction, irréductibles et, dans l'espace, maîtresses de l'espace par le pouvoir qu'elles ont d'y substituer la profondeur non maniable, *non vivante*, celle de l'imaginaire. Ce *point*, d'où nous les voyons irréductibles, *nous met nous-mêmes à l'infini*, est le point où *ici correspond avec nulle part*. Ecrire, c'est trouver ce point. Personne n'écrit, qui n'a rendu le langage propre à maintenir ou à susciter contact avec ce point. (EL 52; my emphasis)

> When we look at the sculptures of Giacometti, there is a point from which they are no longer subject to the fluctuations of appearance, or to the movement of perspective. One sees them absolutely: not reduced, but withdrawn from reduction, irreducible and, in space, mastering space by the power they have of substituting for it a depth that cannot be manipulated, that is *not alive*, the depth of the imaginary. This *point*, from which we see them as irreducible, *places us ourselves at an infinite distance*, is the point where *here corresponds with nowhere*. To write is to find this point. No one writes who has not made language able to maintain or to provoke contact with this point.

It should be noted that this is the essay in *L'espace littéraire* in which Blanchot asserts, perhaps more clearly than anywhere else, the peculiar ontological status of the work, its reduction to a "*résidue inéliminable*," which leaves only "*ce mot même*: c'est," and that constitutes the work in its most radical separation from the world, as a "pure fiction," a "*fiction absolue*" (EL 47)—and as the endless search for its own alterworldly origin (EL 46). In this sense, the concluding paragraph on Giacometti asserts nothing other than the latter's attainment in his sculpture of this Mallarméan "point," an "absolute" point of vision that makes visible the irreducible of vision as such. But now we are in a position to hear in the language of this paragraph another layer, an only slightly buried layer of death's "nonliving" habitation of the imagination: the dead gaze as the core of vision. The remainder of a reduction, a *dépouillement*, leaves precisely the *dépouille* we have already encountered: "*Ce point, d'où nous les voyons irréductibles, nous met nous-mêmes à l'infini, est le point où ici correspond avec nulle part.*" ("This *point*, from which we see them as irreducible, places us ourselves at an infinite distance, is the point where here corresponds with nowhere"). Two resonant points here: this receding into infinity is precisely the effect of N.'s dead and flaming gaze in *L'arrêt de mort*; and "*le point où ici correspond avec nulle part*" is precisely the "place" of the corpse in "Les deux versions" (where Blanchot writes: "*on ne cohabite pas avec les morts sous peine de voir ici s'effondre dans l'insondable* nulle part" ["one does not cohabit with the dead, on pain of seeing here collapse into a unfathomable *nowhere*"; EL 349; Blanchot's emphasis]; and where he also evokes (for the second time in *L'espace littéraire*) "*le résidue inéliminable de l'être*" [EL 342]). In other words, Giacometti's sculptures have the status of a death gaze, not to say a death mask, that is, they are structurally/aesthetically equivalent (if I can put it thus) to the dead gaze of Nathalie and, by extension, to the mask of la Noyée. Which means—if we can carry Blanchot's implicit logic to its somewhat jarring conclusion—that when we see these sculptures *absolutely*, we see them as the face of a dead woman. Thus when Blanchot tells us that, despite her distance from his work, la Noyée so seduced Giacometti that he wanted to reproduce her happy death in an experiment, we find ourselves lost in a dizzying play of projections: Blanchot projecting the "schematic" haunted structure of his writing into Giacometti's sensibility; Giacometti (and Blanchot) projecting a "happiness in death" onto the blank screen of a myth-inducing mask; a mask projecting a set of events (violent passion, drowning) that in principle might somehow be replayed; and finally, Giacometti projecting, or *casting*, his hidden aesthetic impulses into a bizarre reenactment that would somehow give the truth of his work (and thus we return to where we began). In any case, throughout all of these complications one thing is clear: a woman has to die. Or even: be killed. Playing off the title of Serge Leclaire's work (commented intensively by Blanchot in *L'écriture du désastre*, and itself a play on Freud's article "A Child Is Being Beaten"), one might hazard the phrase: *on tue une femme*—a woman is being killed. Could this formula indicate the hidden face, as it were, of a fantasy constitutive of Blanchot's (and not only Blanchot's) writing ethos, and of the "passion" that enlivens it? The affirmative delectation of an image's visitation, the frequenting of the ghostly shadows without which narration will never have begun, might well point in this direction.

PASSION: THREE ESSAYS

Blanchot's Hegelian-Mallarméan evocation, in "La littérature et le droit à la mort," of a murderous language that kills, that speaks the death of what it names, and his immediate association of this death with a woman—in a détournement of Mallarmé's more aesthetically banal bouquet of flowers—is well known: "*Quand je dis 'cette femme,' la mort réelle est annoncée et déjà présente dans mon langage*" ("When I say 'this woman,' real death is announced and already present in my language"; PF 313); and in a formulation that is even more telling: "*Pour que je puisse dire: cette femme, il faut que d'une manière ou d'une autre je lui retire sa réalité d'os et de chair, la rende absente et l'anéantisse*" ("For me to be able to say: this woman, it is necessary that, in one way or another, I withdraw her reality of flesh and blood from her, that I render her absent and annihilate her"; PF 312).[39] Blanchot is of course speaking in general of the conditions for all speech, a relation of suppression and making-absent, a radical *opening* of absence, that hollows the bond between word and thing; but the particular example is anything but arbitrary. Such an evocation, articulated at a crucial moment in Blanchot's argument (and, in 1948, contemporaneously with the dead-dying women in *L'arrêt de mort*), surely places us very close to the path we have been following, with the sense that something essential is indeed at stake in this particular figure of the woman who has to die, whose bodily reality must be withdrawn, so that language might speak—and, further, so that the literary voice may enter the peculiar space proper to it. In this light, these formulations present us with yet another version of the ghostly woman who watches over the vocation of the writer, the essential conditions that make the latter possible and "dictate" its form.

Now with these considerations in mind, I would also like to turn to the year 1954. Whether fortuitously or for more substantive reasons, this is the year, otherwise not extraordinarily productive, when Blanchot published almost all of the major essays that have retained our attention in these readings, as well as a number of others that resonate with similar tensions.[40] In particular, they include two essays that Blanchot's biographer aptly considers as part of a series whose central subject is "passion," but that can also be read as not very cryptic variations on the theme of *erotic renunciation*: "Orphée, Don Juan, Tristan" and "L'échec de Milena." The third essay in this "trilogy of passion" is from an earlier period (1946): "Adolphe ou le malheur des sentiments vrais" (published in *La part du feu*, along with "La littérature et le droit à la mort"). These essays all attempt to think through passion in its fundamental absence, its irreducible distance and rupture from all objects; it is on this basis that they elaborate something like a theory of desire as a passion of absence, a passionate relation founded on the impossibility of relation.

It is of great interest, then, to see how feminine figures are treated in these essays—for it is *their* absence, inaccessibility, and infinite distance that opens the space of desire, at times with unsettling consequences for the actual women who are also implicated or referred to in these essays. In this respect, these essays also bear the marks, more clearly than any of Blanchot's other writings, of a melancholic renunciation installed as the very condition of the writing vocation, the enshrinement of loss, absence, and a figure-forming (that is, ghost-making) impossibility as the very force and condition of desire. They also put into play the complex intercourse between autobiography and literature, not only in the sense that they follow this shifting border as it appears in the sentimental life of the writers Blanchot discusses (Constant, Kafka), and as it passes through their personal writings (diaries and letters) and their narratives (*Adolphe*, *The Castle*); but also in that they broach the dilemmas that traversed Blanchot's own relations with women, and with writing. Surely one of these two aspects authorizes, or incites, the other: does not Blanchot's constant reference to biographical material (in these and other essays, especially those on Kafka) indicate a powerful identification on the part of this most impersonal of writers, or at the very least a compelling acknowledgment with respect to their work that something essential *to writing* is played out in their passionate involvement with women they have known? One has every reason to believe that the same was true of Blanchot, and therefore that these essays on passion might well indicate certain contours of this dilemma as he encountered and traversed it.[41] A clearer sense of these contours may allow us to glimpse the peculiar limitations of Blanchot's writing at its most fundamentally constitutive level, limitations one could be tempted to think of as *traps*, a set of structural constraints that are intensely generative but that imprison nonetheless. It should be stressed that the point of the critical remarks that follow is not to denounce the process of literary elaboration as a merely false alibi, but, as I have attempted to do throughout, to contaminate Blanchot's thought and fiction with the intersecting relations that condition it at multiple levels, and precisely there where it would seek to touch on something like *the unconditioned of all relations*, especially insofar as *this* kind of relation is cast, essentially, as the passion of erotic distance. The central paradox of these intersecting relations is formulated early on in the essay on Constant: "*Constant est un exemple saisissant du paradoxe qu'il y a au fond de tous rapports humains, lorsque ceux-ci se donnent pour objet le manque qui les constitue*" ("Constant is a striking example of the paradox that lies in the ground of all human relations when these relations take as their object the lack that constitutes them"; PF 226). This paradox defines the crux in which human relations and writing find their common core in an emptiness and absence born from intimate distance. This early essay is full of such formulas; they read like programmatic statements anticipating the haunted narratives Blanchot would soon be publishing. In reference to Constant's passionate involvements, Blanchot writes: "*ce que telle ou telle belle apparition lui découvre, c'est l'absence non seulement d'elle à lui, mais l'absence qui fonde tous ses rapports avec les autres et qu'il tente en vain de vivre et d'approprier*" ("what this or that beautiful apparition reveals to him is the absence for him not only of this apparition, but the absence that founds all his relations with others, which he tries in vain to live and to appropriate"; PF 227). The result for Constant is a constantly vacillating double movement, a flight from solitude and a flight from relationships.

> Le principe de tous ces mouvements, c'est le sentiment de la distance qui le sépare des autres. Il sait et il sent que cette distance est à la fois la condition et l'objet de ses rapports avec le monde. Il doit être éloigné du monde s'il veut s'en rapprocher, et il ne peut communiquer avec lui que s'il devient maître de ce vide. (PF 227)

> The principle of all these movements is the feeling of distance that separates him from others. He knows and he feels that this distance is both the condition and the object of his relations with the world. He must be at a distance from the world if he wants to draw close to it, and he can communicate with the world only if he becomes master of this emptiness.

The drive to become "master of the void" provides a startling formulation of this project. Blanchot quotes Constant: "*Je n'aime qu'en absence*" ("I love only in absence"; PF 227). And in a statement that clearly expresses Blanchot's own position regarding communicative fusion (a topic of much concern to his friend Georges Bataille, to whom this essay is in part a response[42]), he summarizes the "paradox" that Constant underwent "*à l'état pur*":

> Nous n'avons pas de relations avec autrui que si nous ne sommes pas confondus avec autrui, nous ne communiquons pleinement avec quelqu'un qu'en possédant, non pas ce qu'il est, mais ce qui nous sépare de lui, son absence plutôt que sa présence et, mieux encore, le mouvement infini pour *dépasser* et *faire renaître* cette absence." (PF 229; my emphasis)

> We have no relations with another, unless we are not confused with the other; we fully communicate with someone only by possessing not what he is, but what separates us from him, his absence rather than his presence and, better still, the infinite movement of *outstripping* this absence and making it be *reborn*.

Such a statement is almost like a blueprint of *L'arrêt de mort*: to possess not presence but absence, and further to engage an endless movement that would both surpass and, as it were, resuscitate this absence (recall too that the name of the second main female character, Nathalie, evokes this rebirth). There is nothing arbitrary in this reborn absence taking the form of a *ghost*, the left-behind and re-imaged figure of a beloved; but here Blanchot associates it directly with death, "*le vide véritable de la mort . . . ce vide, plus difficile à saisir, qui est la condition de tout attachement et l'objet de tout désir*" ("The true void of death . . . this void, more difficult to grasp, that is the condition of all attachment and the object of all desire"; PF 229).

Finally, in a formulation that manages both to conflate author with fictive narrator and to pinpoint the intersection between relation-in-absence and language, Blanchot, as part of a long comparison between Constant and Proust, remarks:

> Proust, comme Adolphe, fait l'expérience du paradoxe de toute communication (paradoxe qui est aussi celui du langage), selon lequel ce qui fonde les rapports

c'est leur impossibilité, ce qui unit les êtres c'est ce qui les sépare et ce qui les rend étrangers c'est ce qui les rapproche.

Proust, like Adolphe, has the experience of the paradox of all communication (a paradox that is also that of language), according to which what founds relations is their impossibility, what unites beings is what separates them, and what makes them strangers is what brings them closer to one another.

Lest we misunderstand the nature of this rapprochement, Blanchot adds to this a final dismissal of "presence": "*Tous deux se lassent de la présence, parce qu'elle n'est qu'un contact et non pas une relation authentique*" ("Both of them grow weary of presence, because it is only a contact and not an authentic relation"; PF 231). To be sure, Blanchot is writing here in a style that we might think of, rhetorically, as a kind of identificatory paraphrase, speaking from the point of view of the author in question and presenting his experience in terms authorized and supported by quotations—often, in this case, from letters and personal writings, rather than from Constant's fiction. However, it is clear that this identification is not "merely" rhetorical, as can be inferred in part from the conflations of author and character that appear to follow from it—as when Blanchot treats Proust's novel almost as a sort of personal testimony that could serve as the basis for a description of his erotic experience (Blanchot never in fact quotes Proust's letters, referring solely to the latter's novel for his characterizations of "Proust").[43] All of this brings the essay very close to something like confessional writing. This is all the more striking in that Blanchot tends to condemn confessional writing, and in particular the diary, a form he considers to be a pathetic subterfuge of writing's more authentic task, which is to dwell in severance from measurable time, and from the beings with whom one makes mere contact there.

Now as it happens, it is none other than Constant who comes up again in a later essay (discussed earlier), published in *Le livre à venir*, on "*le journal intime*," precisely as an example of the enigmatic movement from the events of life toward something like their "shadow," true object of recitical narration. Blanchot likens this movement, and the force that effectuates it, to a magnet's powerful drawing of experience away from itself, back behind itself, into its occluded and unknown element, which is the genuine element of the *récit*'s peculiar unfolding, the shadow detached from it and from the world in which it was lived and which therefore constantly conceals it.[44] The *récit* does this, he says, "*en chassant le mouvement des heures . . . en dissipant le monde*" ("by chasing away the movement of the hours . . . by dispersing the world"; LV 254). In contrast, Blanchot calls journal writing a "trap" (one section is titled "Le piège du journal") and harshly disparages it for, among other things, clinging to calendar time, and for "turning toward the self" ("*comme s'il y avait le moindre intérêt*"; "as if there were the least interest"). In light of the present discussion, the impetus behind this condemnation takes on an intriguing aspect which appears to point more directly, albeit still quite obscurely, in the direction of the writer's erotic experience, or something like a shadowy history of love. We are still approaching this obscure space. But for now it should be remarked that in his essay on the *journal intime*, Blanchot fully affirms the profound importance and necessity of transforming the material of experience into that of the récit and its other shadow world; but again, in this *exigency of fiction* brought to bear on experience, he demands a radical transmutation that would break all ties (a demand heeded and practiced by the other two writers discussed in this study). This movement is perfectly consonant with the necessary relation to, and effacement of, feminine figures that we have traced out in Blanchot's récits, especially *L'arrêt de mort*. But in the essay's final paragraph Blanchot concedes that "a sort of necessity" continually revives the slim chances of the journal to bring into the day "the most obscure experience"—in particular the writer's attempt to chronicle the adventure of a work in a sort of "*carnet de route*"—and in doing so he brushes very close to the figural (and punctual) forms that have concerned us here:

> L'écrivain a beau savoir qu'il ne peut revenir en deça d'un certain point sans *masquer*, par son ombre, ce qu'il est venu contempler: l'attrait des sources, le besoin de saisir *en face* ce qui toujours se détourne. (LV 259; my emphasis)

> The writer may well know that he cannot return back behind a certain point without *masking*, with his shadow, what he came to contemplate: the attraction of sources, the need to grasp *face to face* that which always turns away.

Here it is the figure of the writer that casts a too real shadow on the elusive figure haunting the récit (and, like Eurydice, always turning and being cast away), as though placing a mask on it (on her). But, as we have seen, the casting of this shadow-mask, the mask of a shade, from somewhere out of the time of a life, is essential to and constitutive of that other space.

MILENA AND THE FAILURE

If stepping back from the sphere of the work to that of a life reveals the obfuscating mask *of the writer*, it might also illuminate the strange relations that hold, after all, *between* these different worlds, particularly in terms of the passion that traverses them both. Blanchot himself says as much in another essay devoted to passion in writing, this time with reference to Kafka. "L'échec de Milena" ("Milena's Failure"), written and published in the NRF in 1954, but not collected in a book until 1981, provides a startlingly candid statement on the necessity of sacrificing erotic love for the sake of writing.[45] What might not be evident, however, is the extent to which this essay, too, is something of a confession, or perhaps even a kind of unsent letter, bearing witness to Blanchot's own amorous life. Christophe Bident provides the biographical context that marks the essay's publication. Why did Blanchot wait twenty-seven years to include this article—an extraordinary and insightful essay—in a book? Like many of his critical writings from this period, it discusses a recent publication, the translation into French (in 1952) of Kafka's letters to Milena Jesenská, an event that by 1981 would have long lost its novelty. Apparently the personal subtext of the article was so evident that Blanchot waited until the death of the woman who would have recognized it as addressed to herself, namely Denise Rollin, a former companion of Georges Bataille with whom Blanchot had a passionate but infelicitous relationship beginning around 1945 (and to whom Blanchot sent inscribed copies of his books).[46] The two continued to correspond until Rollin's death, and Bident draws on this correspondence for his description of their relationship. Underscoring Blanchot's literary and personal identification with Kafka, Bident claims that Blanchot "*retrouvait . . . dans les amours de Kafka la manière tragique, incertaine et emportée de vivre les siennes*" ("recognized in the loves of Kafka the tragic, uncertain and passionate way he had of living his own").[47] But unlike in Kafka's case, it was apparently Rollin who broke off the relationship. Bident quotes her from a letter written to another correspondent in 1959: "*Cela fait maintenant 14 ans que je refuse Maurice Blanchot qui pourtant est l'être qui m'était 'destiné'*" ("For fourteen years now I have refused Maurice Blanchot, who is nonetheless the one 'destined' for me").[48] It is unclear whether this refusal was mutual, but this seems likely. In any case, the personal and publishing context provides an intriguing perspective on Blanchot's meditations on the troubled rapport between Kafka's erotic experience and his writing, and on the remarkable speculations that Blanchot permits himself there—all in the service, as we will see, of affirming the latter, and hyperbolically so, over the former.

In his reflections on Kafka's letters to Milena, Blanchot in fact stages a conflict between two passions, which by turns merge and diverge: one passion that draws Kafka into what Blanchot calls, in a troubling hypostasis, "*le monde féminin*" ("the feminine world"), and another that both exalts and threatens from below, bearing the dark forces of writing through a life that, says Kafka, must heed them when they erupt. Each of these gives rise to an intense anxiety—*Angst* is the vibratory leitmotif of the entire correspondence—but mostly for differing reasons. Blanchot quotes Kafka on the nature of the underground forces that make him write (from a letter dated September 18, 1920). I will give Blanchot's French quotation, along with some German interpolations on which I will comment. Kafka writes to Milena:

> je ne le comprends pas moi-même, je tremble seulement sous le déchaînement [*Ausbruch*: eruption], je me tourmente jusqu'à la folie, mais ce que c'est et ce qu'on veut dans le lointain, je ne le sais pas. Ce qu'on veut dans la proximité: silence, obscurité, se terrer [*Sich-Verkriechen*], cela je le sais et je *dois obéir, je ne puis autrement* [*muß folgen, kann nicht anders*]. C'est un déchaînement, il passe, il est en partie passé, mais les forces qui le font surgir continuent de trembler en moi, avant, après; oui, ma vie, mon être est fait de cette menace souterraine [*unterirdischen Drohen*]; si elle cesse, je cesse aussi. C'est ma façon de participer à la vie. (KK 167; my emphasis; German: BM, 267)

> I don't even understand it myself, I am shaking from the eruption; you can torture me [*sic*, but this is a slip in the English translation; it should read: I torture myself] to the point of insanity, but what it is and what it ultimately wants I do not know. I only know what it wants at the moment: quiet, darkness, crawling off somewhere, and I must obey, I have no other choice [more literally: I cannot do otherwise]. It is an eruption and will pass and has already passed in part, but the powers which call it forth are always trembling inside me, before and after; indeed, this subterranean threat constitutes my life, my being; if it ceases, I cease. It's how I participate in life. (LM 197)

With this quotation, Blanchot brings his commentary into one of the most emblematic points of intersection between his own writing and Kafka's, as summed up in one phrase: *Ich kann nicht anders*. Let us recall that not only did Kafka use this phrase in the hunger artist's last words, as testimony to a compulsive abjection finally avowing its banal helplessness, but Blanchot too quotes the phrase in what I have called a "translation" of Martin Luther—by which he would ironically vouchsafe the "hunched" (*courbé*) position of the writer curving down and away from the "beneficent powers," perhaps awaiting instead an upsurge of those from below.[49] Indeed, Blanchot underscores this reference by glossing the French translation in a footnote that reads: "C'est la parole de Luther: *Hier stehe ich, ich kann nicht anders*" (KK 167) ("This is the statement spoken by Luther: 'Here I stand, I cannot do otherwise'"). By the time Blanchot responded in 1985 to the question, "Why do you write?" with his version of this phrase, he had been meditating on it for quite some time.[50] In the present context, its repetition affirms above all the imperious, irresistible, and *lowly* nature of the exigency it names, which Kafka debases even further to a reptilian or (at any rate) animal "crawling away" (*Sich-Verkriechen*), as though in wounded shame. At the same time, as Blanchot emphasizes as well, Kafka has already informed Milena (in a letter dated July 18, 1920) that if she did wish to "give up the entire world" and crawl down there with him, this would in fact require—"strangely, so strangely!"—an unheard-of effort at superhuman *elevation* and upward climbing ("*über dich hinausgreifen*" [BM 123; LM 93]). As Blanchot puts it: "*il faut s'abaisser infiniment, mais aussi s'élever, s'exalter jusqu'à disparaître—'étrange, étrange*'" (KK 168) ("it is necessary to lower oneself infinitely, but also to elevate oneself, to exalt oneself to the point of disappearing—'strangely, so strangely!'"). It is in this most strange scrambling of descent and elevation that these two intersecting passions, erotic and writerly, will follow their inscrutable trajectories—to arrive, however, at a fate that has already been sealed. Milena's failure has been announced and confirmed; it is an *accompli*. But the question is exactly what relation it bears to the "side" that has succeeded—the side of writing's passion—even if at times it is exceedingly difficult to sort these out.

Indeed, if the upswelling forces of writing threaten to draw one into another world, a world that is an underworld (but also *the other of every world*), it is also the case that erotic passion is itself yet "another world," the one marked by and as the feminine:

"*Avec Milena*," writes Blanchot, paraphrasing Kafka, "*il est entré pour la première fois dans un autre monde*" (KK 162) ("With Milena, he has entered for the first time into another world"). In these letters, this *other* other world, the panic-inducing world of eroticism, strangely converges with the "dark forces" of literature, only to be refused out of an even greater *Angst*, or even a kind of disgust, as though it were much more troubling and horrific than the mere terrors of literature. In terms of Kafka's "treatment" of that world, something of this disgust and utter unbearable foreignness comes through in the "sex scene" (if one can call it that) between K. and Frieda in *The Castle*, in which the two lovers roll around in the beer-soaked garbage and muck on the floor, and K. feels he is being enticed into a place even more disorienting and "other" than the strange village world he has just entered, a place far, far out beyond the uncanny realm of the castle, an uninhabitable place where even the air is different and unbreathable (*Castle* 41; *Schloss* KA 68–69). In Kafka, this uncharacteristically lyrical scene (and it is lyrical, despite everything) speaks volumes on the relative terrors of different zones of intimate distance. For Blanchot, who of course learned a great deal from Kafka, it holds a lesson as well.

Indeed, it is precisely in relation to *The Castle* that Blanchot delivers his (auto)biographical remarks on the links and separations between these two crisscrossing passions. Kafka wrote the novel in the period following his relationship with Milena, and in its wake. Blanchot begins the final section of the essay with a reference to Max Brod's claim that in *The Castle*, "*Kafka avait traduit ses relations avec Milena*" ("Kafka had translated his relations with Milena").[51] At first Blanchot treats this claim with overt skepticism, to the point of appearing simply to dismiss it. And indeed, the form in which Brod presents it is crude enough, implying the direct transfer (or "mirroring") of real people in the novel's characters. Thus Blanchot asks, mirroring this bluntness in turn: Is Milena Frieda? Is Klamm Milena's husband? and so forth, only to conclude: It is impossible to know.

> Tout ce que l'on pressent, c'est que [l'histoire] se prolonge peut-être dans l'oeuvre, non pour s'y traduire, fût-ce au prix d'une transposition, mais pour former une autre expérience, irréductible, qui se développe selon ses exigences et pour des fins propres, expérience qui n'importe pas moins au destin de Kafka que l'histoire de sa passion malheureuse. (KK 168)

> All that one can guess is that [the story] extends perhaps into the work, not in order to be translated there, even at the price of a transposition, but in order to give form to another experience, an irreducible one, that develops according to its own exigencies and for its own ends, an experience that is no less important to Kafka's destiny than the history of his unfortunate passion.

One might be forgiven for feeling relieved at this return to the relatively familiar language of the work's radical and irreducible unfamiliarity, and to the almost reassuring mode of exigent otherness that is literary space: there is no question but that Kafka's personal experience, however pertinent and proximate, has been radically transformed. But suddenly the argument takes an unexpected turn, as Blanchot indulges in the strange exercise of decipherment or mirror-reading to which Brod has invited us: if one does "let oneself be drawn along" (*se laisse entraîner*) by such comparisons between two worlds, he says, it is astonishing and terrifying to read the letters to Milena in the reflecting light of *The Castle*. Is it possible that what Kafka experienced as admiration and "sublime passion" (as Blanchot puts it) for Milena has been rendered in the truth of the work, "*dans la vérité de l'oeuvre*," as the pitiful rapport between these two cold and lowly creatures, K. and Frieda? "*Est-ce donc là la vérité qu'il faut lire sous les belles phrases passionnées des lettres? Et cette vérité ne dit-elle pas, d'une manière plus cruelle encore que nous ne le pensions, l'échec de Milena?*" ("Is this, then, the truth that one must read beneath the fine passionate phrases of the letters? And does this truth not tell of Milena's failure in a way that is even more cruel than we thought?"). Could it be that this lover's passionate letters merely masked a more profound and cruel indifference, an experience of love that, in the crucible of the work's more radical truth (or under the pressure of its powerful magnetizing force), can only appear in its base and lowly abjection? Fearing that we have touched, quite palpably, on the private cruelty of this essay itself (having let ourselves be drawn along in turn by the correspondences reflected in it), we might well hope that Blanchot will say it is not so. But Blanchot says this: "*Il en est peut-être ainsi, en effet*" ("That is perhaps indeed how it is"; KK 169). The sublime passion of lived experience, and the shattering relation with a woman who has been loved and left behind, are diminished to lowly abjection by the work that has incorporated and transformed it. And who is to say, it may well be so. But what is striking about this statement is not so much the cruelty it imputes to Kafka, or even to the harshly sober/ecstatic operations of the literary imagination, as the fact that Blanchot, unwavering master of discretion and indirection, allows himself to make such an unjustifiable and revealing leap of judgment regarding another writer, however qualified it may be by a hedging "perhaps," which is rhetorically submerged by the more conclusive *en effet*. I submit that nowhere in all of Blanchot is a specifically confessional (and not only autobiographical) mode so clearly announced, for what else could authorize such a statement—as it encroaches with startling confidence on what is strictly unknowable in the life of another writer—besides the expression or pressure of his own experience, its peculiar form of hauntedness, which has here overtaken critical discourse, closing the distance that opens it by absorbing it unreservedly into an impassioned identification with the author in question? And, it would appear, in the desire to affirm the *failure of a woman* to overcome and draw to herself the too great force driving and "shadowing" the imperative to write.

The debasement or "degradation" apparent in this statement (the aspect of cruel admission that was surely the reason for its delayed publication) undergoes, however, a further and final reversal in the essay's last long paragraph, which almost takes on the air of an apology, not to say a kind of self-debasement, even as it echoes an all-powerful affirmation that we have seen before. In these final sentences, Blanchot speaks rather from the point of view of the work itself, as it were, not in terms of "such and such a character" projected within it, but in its entirety and "in its compact reality" (KK 169). In that perspective, the work that shares or reflects the passion of the real story is not an abjectifying transposition of individual relations, but the endless and mysterious movement of a measureless passion that can have no stopping point, a search that has always already overreached its goals, and is thus the expression of "*cette force terrible, capable de tout . . . cette force prodigieuse*" ("this terrible force, capable of everything . . . this prodigious force"), writes Blanchot, which the greatest weakness cannot extinguish, which drives K. to "*dépasser tous les buts*" ("outstrip all goals") and which likewise carried Kafka toward Milena, but was "*trop forte pour ne pas tendre infiniment au-delà*" ("too strong not to reach infinitely beyond"). But at this point, the essay ends on a downward gesture, pointing toward K.'s "cold passion," the drive leading him beyond every merely attainable goal, but, concludes Blanchot: "*à cause de cette même volonté qui est démesure, impatience, ignorance infinies, il ne peut rien atteindre, il ne peut rien*" ("because of this same will, which is infinite unmeasure, impatience, and ignorance, he can attain nothing, he can do nothing"; KK 170). The declaration of a passion that has left behind the woman who in some sense shared it, *at some point*, with the literary drive is also an ambiguous affirmation of incapacity and powerlessness, as though these fundamental conditions of literary space were also the conditions of an erotic foreclosure demanded by the endless and sterile movement of the work and its truth.

It would of course be too simplistic to say that Blanchot is, simply, speaking of himself, that he is "really" addressing a lost beloved. The layers of time and story, fact and fiction, and the dispersal of figures both real and written, are too complex, involving numerous people, places, times: Kafka, Milena, K., Frieda, Blanchot, Denise Rollin, J., Nathalie. . . . Now there is a clear justification for adding these last two, and particularly the very last name, for in these passages Blanchot is in fact quite openly quoting himself, and it is on this basis that these meditations on Kafka and Milena can be brought back to *L'arrêt de mort* and the quandaries of figural attachment and renunciation that it stages. First I would recall these sentences, which occur at a crucial moment when the narrator is desperately searching for N. before encountering her ghostly figure in his room:

> A cet instant, j'étais moi-même perdu. Ma folie ne venait plus de mon inquiétude ni de mon intérêt pour Nathalie, mais d'une impatience, chaque minute plus grande, qui *dépassait tous les buts*, et faisait de moi *un errant à la recherche de rien*. (AM 104–105; my emphasis)
>
> At that moment, I was lost myself. My madness no longer came from my disquiet, nor from my interest in Nathalie, but rather from an impatience, greater each minute, that *outstripped all goals*, and made of me *a wanderer in search of nothing*.

Blanchot's narrator describes himself in terms that Blanchot will frequently use to describe Kafka and his wandering hero K., particularly in the essay I have been discussing; and it becomes clear in this quote from *L'arrêt de mort* that the impatient passion driving him toward N. has likewise already driven him beyond any "interest" in her. But it is not entirely true that he is "in search of nothing"; nothing graspable, to be sure, nothing like an object that would terminate the searching movement, but not nothing nothing. Indeed it is this nothing that is not nothing, this nothing Thing, that Blanchot finds in both of these texts, repeating it from one to the other. In the last lines of *L'arrêt de mort* it is called "*cette force trop grande, incapable d'être ruinée par rien*" ("that too great force, incapable of being ruined by anything"; AM 127); and in the last lines of "L'échec de Milena" it is recalled: "*cette force terrible, capable de tout . . . cette force prodigieuse*" ("that terrible force, capable of everything . . . that prodigious force"), which, in this case, Blanchot explicitly conjoins with the movement of passion for a woman and that of writing, as though these had a common ground. But it is a ground that in principle—or, one might say, structurally—excludes the woman herself from the passion drawing toward her. For where, with whom, could this passion ever stop or tarry? Only an image could be equal—eternally unequal—to its *démesure*. Only something that is *left*. We saw in *L'arrêt de mort* that this image took the form not only of a ghost but also of a body that is cast and projected into the concrete remainder of a death mask (and casts of hands). This mask is the face and emblem of the too great force that has been sought, and found, somewhere "beyond" the woman who left it. In a sense, it is the shell, hollow remnant of mere facts, that now holds, without containing, the enigma of this tremendous treasure, a power incapable of being destroyed. This power, although dwelling in weakness and death, is nonetheless "all-powerful" in its affirmative *puissance*, over and against all destruction, ruin, and loss.

But let us remark that in the two *récits* that Blanchot wrote following *L'arrêt de mort*, there are no statements of this kind; there is no melodramatic insistence on omnipotent affirmation. In *Au moment voulu* (1951), which Blanchot signed over to Denise Rollin with these words: "*ce livre écrit pour vous auprès du danger*" ("this book written for you, keeping close to danger"),[52] one does have a sense of danger, from blows or ill health or from a madness seeped into the affirmative day; but there is mostly the exigency of a haunting and its dying echo, a solar eternity that engulfs or erases all figures, in the end, including that of the eternal itself. The last line of the text reads: "*Et cependant, bien que le cercle déjà m'entraîne, et même s'il me fallait l'écrire éternellement, je l'écrirais pour effacer l'éternel: Maintenant, la fin*" ("And yet, even though the circle already draws me away, and even if it were necessary for me to write it eternally, I would write it in order to efface the eternal: Now, the end"; AMV 166). The women of the story in *Au moment voulu* have not left behind any palpable residue still guarded in the present space of writing, rather they leave only a voice, a "*voix blanche*" that resounded through the apartment, and then, more enigmatically, a spectral figure who bears her melancholy openly and all the more distantly, and who does not enter the space of writing. (Indeed, it is la Noyée whose frozen look hangs there in that space, but this text does not turn to her.) *Celui qui ne m'accompagnait pas* (1953) is devoid of feminine figures, aside from the *paroles* that flurry through the house, objects of a long homage and reflection by the narrator on his "*relations avec elles*" (CQ 135), and who are at the heart of a more modest affirmation: "*l'affirmation qui persiste: j'irai de ce côté, jamais d'un autre*" ("the affirmation that persists: I will go in that direction, never in another"), an affirmation accompanied by this feeling: "*Le sentiment qui me reste: je ne céderai pas, je ne puis autrement*" ("The feeling that remains for me: I will not yield, I cannot do otherwise"; CQ 145).[53] And when we turn again to "L'échec de Milena," with its charged repetition of this phrase, *je ne puis autrement*, it is difficult not to hear something of its incapacity, its drastic reduction of "*puissance*," in the essay's final words quoted above: "*il ne peut rien atteindre, il ne peut rien*" ("he can attain nothing, he can do nothing"). The last sentence expresses very nearly the same constraint and incapacity as when one says: *il n'y peut rien*, he can't help it (*il s'en faut d'une lettre*, one might say: only a letter is lacking). As though Blanchot were saying that this too great force could not be gainsaid, while also saying that the unloseable treasure of this force is impotent, it can do nothing, it is a nothing. *Je ne puis autrement: Je ne puis rien*. The minute gap between these two incapacities is the empty treasure that Blanchot shows from out of the open shell of his somber and solar intrigues. And what remains of writing, mere shell and residue, remains, still, no less of an enigma.

PART THREE

Beckett

CHAPTER 8

Beckett's Voices and the Paradox of Expression

THE LEXICOGRAPHER'S NUDITY

The readings of Blanchot's narrative texts presented in the preceding chapters pointed to a fundamental duality structuring the literary experience: on one hand, the attempt to approach a strange and "extravagant" point that calls for the most intimate narration even as it leads into an anonymous, impersonal space severed from the (autobiographical) particularities of the path that has lead there; and, on the other hand, the persistent return of these particularities, both as compulsive figurations of the voice's inaugural moments ("primal scenes" exerting a fascination), and as the stubborn residue that haunts a narration even as it leaves behind all that is not "essential." Thus I argued for an "essentiality of the particular" in relation to the narrative voice and its most originary impulses: compelled toward a space that is other, and that is not determined as the representation of experience, the voice is also compelled *by* that which in experience has obtrusively lodged itself in the language that would coincide with life in this other space, and which thus makes the fictive voice profoundly, if problematically, autobiographical. And profoundly melancholic. For if the condition of possibility of such radical fiction is the loss of the world, the leaving behind of all familiar places and objects—and even all objects *tout court*—then the voice is driven not only by the fascination of an image (as Blanchot often puts it), but also by the indescribable charge produced by the unbridgeable distance from what has been left, a distance and a fault opened by and as language, into which every thing is irremediably cast. In other words, by the exquisite feeling of its loss, its shimmering inaccessibility.

One could say in this regard that Beckett exerted a direct influence on the previous readings of Blanchot. This is primarily because a very similar duality exists throughout Beckett's writing; and yet Beckett is much more explicit concerning the carefully cultivated melancholy, and even nostalgia, involved in this strange project. One can even say that at times, in some of the more unrestrained moments of his very style-conscious prose, he rather indulges in it. Of the three writers treated in this study, Beckett is in fact by far the most explicit with regard to the dilemma encountered (and cultivated) by one who would leave everything behind, in the hope or dread of living elsewhere. And he is perhaps the least liable to occlude a certain *sentimentality* that results, for he makes of it one of the primary drives, conditions, and even subjects of the narrative voice caught in this dilemma; but of course not without complicating it with complex strategies of irony and disavowal, some of which I will attempt to unravel here. If Kafka and Blanchot insist on the incompatibility between the world of the familiar and the worldless world of writing (put very schematically, between "home" and the homelessness of the uncanny, or between life as having been lived and life as a deathly living writing), then Beckett, in turn, shows that what lies at the extreme limit of this conflict—where the formal structures of fictive language meet the singularities of experience and of speech—is a persistent sentimentality that has no proper object (a "nostalgia" passing beyond every home), but that is nonetheless *also* driven to speech by the homely history of the particular. It is in this irreducible incompatibility, pushed to the point of paradox, that I will attempt to locate the imperative to write in Beckett.

Throughout Beckett's writing there is a strange tension between formal devices that empty the language of any expressive tone and movements of poetic transport that, despite it all, are nothing less than lyrical. As a succinct example of this strange coexistence, consider this passage from *Company*, in which the indeterminate wanderings of an unnamed figure are "placed" by an impersonal narrator:

> Nowhere in particular on the way from A to Z. Or say for verisimilitude the Ballyogan Road. That dear old back road. Somewhere on the Ballyogan Road in lieu of nowhere in particular. (C 23)

This precipitous slide from an algebraic deadpan into a sentimental sigh of remembrance would appear to be completely perfunctory, dictated by a "verisimilitude" here required for reasons as yet unclear; and it would seem that the "expression" of nostalgia—"That dear old back road"—is submerged in the flatness and indifference of the voice, as though it were merely filler for a blank variable, an affect randomly, almost comically, attached to an arbitrary signifier. Such a jarring synthesis of lyricism and abstraction is one of the most characteristic features of Beckett's texts, and as I will show (in relation to *Company* in particular), the result is often a foregrounding of linguistic formalism that puts into question the very possibility of expression, threatening to reduce every voice to the blank forms of grammar and syntax, every "character," object, or situation to the arbitrary operations of algebraic combinations, and every story to the protocols and "devices" required by fictional narration (such as the "verisimilitude" evoked above). Beckett's prose works, especially following the trio of novels *Molloy*, *Malone Meurt*, and *L'innommable*, as well as many of the late stage and television pieces, are concerned more and more with the structural conditions of fictional production and less and less with any specific narrative material; they become more and more focused on the liminality of word and image and less and less on any full fledged storytelling. Add to this a profound and ubiquitous irony, undermining nearly every impulse to express that dares to show itself as such, and one is left with a work in which any possible subject of expression is dispersed irretrievably into a radically impersonal space, where the indefinite "nowhere in particular on the way from A to Z" appears to be structurally prior to any *name* that would locate a *place* (and where time is devoid of dates and days). Such experiments leave little room for anything like "expression," and deliberately so. Beckett's remarkable statements concerning the impossibility of expression and the failure of the artist are marked, as we will see, not simply by an acceptance of a certain state of things but by an adamant *refusal* to "succeed."[1] In many of the prose works this refusal is carried out by means of an insistent foregrounding of the formal structures that undermine the singularity of the narrative voice, and that of its story. So prominent are these structural investigations in Beckett's work that there is little need to stress their importance, but it is necessary to bring out more clearly just how these structures are articulated, what specific "devices" they put into play, and exactly how these formal elements strive, and fail, to void the particularities they evoke, if only as schematic and algebraic variables; these questions will be closely addressed in what follows.

However—and to get back for a moment to the Ballyogan Road—there is a gnawing suspicion, emerging in *Company* and elsewhere, that this or that proper name, place or human figure may not be so arbitrary and disinvested as the previous quotation would suggest. After all, how is it possible to go from "nowhere in particular" to "that dear old back road" if not by way of the traces leading there, the marks and material of a prior inscription, the imprint of this or that dear old name, charged, perhaps, with an unspeakable affect? In *Company* and elsewhere, Beckett stages the torturous relation between a mute body and the words which materially impinge upon it, suggesting that the past is constructed, *ad hoc* and retroactively, by the cutting words of the present; but his texts also dramatize the precipitous *decision* required to replace a blank variable with a known quantity, suggesting a strange if unknown determinacy in these substitutions, their tenuous but insistent relation to something called "my life."[2] The fact that the Ballyogan Road has a place in Beckett's biography—and is at the very least a distinctly Irish name—is indicative of the type of prior inscription I am referring to here, and of the way in which, together with the insistence on formal operations, there is an equally insistent mode of nostalgia and lyricism punctuating Beckett's texts; no matter how radically it is ironized and at times literally deconstructed, like an exploded machine, it constantly returns, and this return is not to be dismissed as an unfortunate compromise by Beckett of his own draconian artistic credo.[3] The return of *a past*, however indefinite, distant, and unfixable, is the very tension around which revolves one of the fundamental paradoxes of these texts. If I say that Beckett's use of his own biography in the above passage (among many other places) is indicative, I am not claiming that such literal self-reference is entirely decisive. For what it indicates is not that Beckett's truly urgent concern is with the retrieval of a longed-for past that would be his own, or that the devices of fiction allow him simply to indulge in this quest in a disguised and displaced form. On the contrary, estrangement from "one's own" is the very air of Beckett's unbreathable worlds; and yet, far from disguising the nostalgia (or regret), the longing and the lyrical impulses of his texts, he works openly with these impulses, in an attempt to articulate the material and formal structures that make them possible, impossible, and inevitable. Beckett uses biographemes in such a way as to articulate the drive to speak—and the drive "to fiction"—as a drive conditioned as much by the stuff of life as by the imposing and overwhelming structures of language. The problem—the paradox—is that because this stuff itself is inseparable from language, and because "life"—certainly in Beckett—is inseparable from the possibility or the demand of its narration, it may indeed belong to no one, even as its particularities are "in each case my own" (to use Heidegger's phrase), and are, within the economy of a singular life, strangely insistent, ineliminable, "unlessenable."[4]

Obviously, Beckett's texts do not all work with this paradox in the same way. The expressiveness of Beckett's language, especially in the early trilogy, has often been commented on. Indeed, the lyrical tones of some of Molloy's and Malone's soliloquies (especially in the English versions) are unmistakable, and it is well known that Beckett deliberately struggled against the richness of his own language, partly by turning to French. At the same time, the trilogy can be seen as a progressive elimination of anything like the sort of poetic transports that are rendered poignant by the supposition of a particular subject, the "masks" (as Blanchot calls them [LV 287]) of characters named "Molloy" or "Malone," whose "experience"—though it be one of radical dispossession—is rendered in moving language. *The Unnamable*, while not entirely devoid of poetic turns and little hiccups of lyricism, is, however, unanchored by a single, fixed character to whom an expressive poetic voice could be securely attached, and in whom the experience of a subject, however artificial its construction, would be projected and unified. One of my claims, in discussing *The Unnamable*, will be that despite this deliberate and painstakingly achieved dispersal of the voice, there remains a residual expressivity which is integral to the voice's central dilemma: the impossibility of ceasing, that is, of having begun and of *having been*.[5] But it must be stressed at the outset that *The Unnamable* goes very far in the attenuation of expressivity, and that the often remarked "impasse" into which it leads—an impasse involving at its deepest level the problem of expression and fictional creation—determines the direction of Beckett's prose for the rest of his career. Unlike the trilogy, especially the first two volumes, the short prose pieces written after *The Unnamable* are known for their extreme dryness and formalism. Texts such as "All Strange Away," "Imagination Dead Imagine," "Ping," "Lessness," "The Lost Ones," and the "Fizzles" written in the 1970s, are largely concerned with the geometrical and algebraic construction of fictional spaces and their contents, rather than with the expressive or inexpressive drama of any particular, namable subject. But at the same time, these texts do not simply eliminate such a subject, which remains if only in the form of an implied fabricator; nor do they eliminate all expressive impulses and all drama.[6] Even in "Imagination Dead Imagine," whose very title indicates the tension at work here, and which is occupied with little more than determining the variables of an arbitrarily posited space (intensities and changes of light and heat, positions of bodies, dimensions of a closed space, and so on)—even here the negation of all story and drama is strangely haunted by that which it would negate, which appears in the very act of negation, compulsively elaborated in the space opened in the wake of elimination itself. Referring to the "rotunda" described in the story, and to the "bodies" said to be lying inside it, the last line of the text reads:

> No, life ends and no, there is nothing elsewhere, and no question now of ever finding again that white speck lost in whiteness, to see if they still lie still in the stress of that storm, or of a worse storm, or in the black dark for good, or the great whiteness unchanging, and if not what they are doing. (CSPr 185)

The hyperbolic terms and lyrical cadences of an "expressive" voice erupt unexpectedly into this highly formalized text, revealing the underlying impulse that sustains it to be strangely related to a "storm and stress" threatening to emerge as such, but no longer viable among the variables. It must be "expressed" *en creux*, and thus the imagination asserts its "life" all the more insistently the more its death is staged as an absorption into pure form, located nowhere in particular. A similar emergence of "drama" within the flat coordinates of the fictional space occurs at the end of *The Lost Ones*: there the "narrator," up to then concerned solely with laying out and describing, rather flatly, the enclosed fictional world in terms of its measurements and the social conventions followed by the anonymous bodies populating it, suddenly focuses on a single figure, "the last of all," whose inspection of another body, apparently lifeless, and whose own expiration are rendered with the understated pathos found in many of Beckett's stage pieces. These short post-trilogy texts, for the most part, do not fill in their blank variables with proper names or with material that would attach their nowhere spaces to any life on Earth, as does the passage from *Company* with which I began; but the possibility, or threat, of this attachment remains as a kind of unplaceable affective residue, an outlying obtrusion that, as it turns out, lies at the crux of the matter.

Now, as those few lines from *Company* already suggest, the situation is somewhat different there, and it is for this reason that this text will be so important for my purposes. *Company* is very much a divided text. On one hand, it shares with the short prose pieces an obsession with working out the fictional space as a set of arbitrary variables (measurements of space, body position, and so on); the obsessive "imagination" creating it is thus referred to as "reason-ridden" or "*entachée de raison*." What it "imagines" is an unspeaking body lying in the dark, unattached, supposedly, to any past, even as the disembodied voice it hears "tells of a past" in the second person, insisting that its stories happened to "you." Thus—on the other hand—parallel to the "timeless void" runs a set of short narratives which, at the very least, are located on earth, in a place recognizable as Ireland—and even as Beckett's childhood home—and which can be pieced together as the fragmented story of a life. In this way, *Company* foregrounds equally the two dimensions of Beckett's writing which make up the paradox I would like to discuss—formalizing abstraction and obtrusive affect, the "timeless void," with its indeterminate blanks, and the time of life on earth—and it shows how these dimensions are inextricably linked in the language issuing from a narrative voice. And Beckett's voices, despite their attenuation, are committed to being narrative voices: voices that tell stories and posit worlds in which events are said, however equivocally and indefinitely, to unfold in time. The repulsion of the subject and of a past thus draws into fictions that would be absolute, but that continually meet with the stuff of a singular time, on a scrambled border that divides "my own" from the pure forms that make it possible.

Another way to pose this problem is to point out that, regarding the apparently forced synthesis of abstraction and affect in the preceding passage, for example, it is impossible to determine which of these two terms has priority—that is, which one was forced on the other. The passage suggests, as does most of *Company*, that an impersonal language drones on in a void and "nowhere" space, blankly and indifferently, determined more by a machinelike grammar than by anything like "experience," injecting its tales with a perfunctory and artificial pathos. But the fact that this droning language drones from a voice, and that each time it speaks it has a given source in a singular instance of language, entails its own inevitable structural implications. The most important of which is perhaps this: if a voice exists, it must have *come into* existence, thus it must have an origin in time and it must have a past that has marked it in its idiomatic singularity. The unavoidable logic of this situation can be called a logic of birth, a logic of time and finite existence which necessarily saddles every voice with an at least implicit narrative of a life: an embodied existence marked by the violence of birth, and by all the dear old names. The logic of birth, however, is easily confuted by a logic implicit in the very conventions of literary, fictional narration, by which an unlocatable narrative voice is conceived as speaking anonymously from the void—or at least from the irreducible space separating the narrator from the empirical author—as positing its creatures with the sovereign speech of a god, that is, at the inevitable extreme so often evoked by Beckett, as an absolute and *creative* instance of language. Such a logic of creation *ex nihilo* opens a space in which a voice may well exist without, apparently, being burdened by the weight, the deposits or "precipitates" of a prior life, and Beckett is one of the first modern writers to radicalize the implications of this logic, revealing it both as inherent to any fictive gesture whatever, and as sharply untenable, riddled by the emptiness and vanity of a language that can in no way create what it names but that is strangely stuck with the stuff it calls forth. Now the paradox I am pointing to consists precisely in the simultaneous incommensurability and inseparability of these logics (of "birth" and of "creation"), and in the undecidable status into which this casts the question of what is real and what is artificial in a fictional text as such, what is irreducibly prior and what is a gratuitous supplement. For, referring again to the quote from *Company*, between the deadpan voice in the algebraic void and the sentimental attachment to a name and its past, which is the added artifice and which the true irreducible?

Is there an originary impersonality inherent to language that somehow produces affect (and memory) as a sheer illusion of grammar and of the protocols of "verisimilitude"? Or is there a fundamental (and painful) affective drive, intimately bound to the names and places of a particular past, that has been distanced and defused by the fiction of a placeless language without history? Is the attachment to a past merely a palliative for the horror of being at bottom nowhere and no one (and therefore of being radically, uncannily interchangeable, as Beckett's characters tend to be), or is the space of blanks and variables a desperate escape route from the places that stubbornly remain, from the painful residue, so hard to completely efface, of having been someone, of having *had* a life, out of which speech cannot help but draw its very breath—the rhythm, style, and contours of its habitus? Finally, which is more fundamental, the impossibility of expression, or the inevitability of expression?

It is well known that in his critical and polemical statements, Beckett placed much greater emphasis on the former than on the latter. But the same writer who insisted that "expression is an impossible act," also made, in another critical piece, this crucial observation: "*Avec les mots on ne fait que se raconter. Eux-mêmes les lexicographes se déboutonnent. Et jusque dans le confessional on se trahit*" ("With words one can do nothing but tell one's story. Even the lexicographers expose themselves. And we betray ourselves even in the confessional booth").[7] It is worth emphasizing that there is something vaguely obscene in this self-exposure, the French implying a kind of "coming unbuttoned." Given Beckett's emphasis on the dilemma of expression as an impossibility, I would like to bring into relief, at the same time, its *inevitability*, whereby even the lexicographers lay themselves bear, and the nameless voice in the dark gives itself away, guilty of the sin of being someone's. I want to do this in order to aggravate the dilemma constantly confronted in Beckett's writing, by sharpening both of its conflicting poles and demonstrating that neither is more fundamental than the other, that the lexicographer's nudity is as unavoidable as the self-declaiming subject's dispersal into the algebraic distances of literary language.

THE THREE DIALOGUES

Before reading passages from the fiction that will make clear what I mean when I claim that Beckett's writing is lyrical, sentimental, and at times even effusive, I would like to look closely at the text in which he lays out the uncompromising aesthetic position with which he explicitly identified himself (though here too not without a great deal of irony and rhetorical artifice). The "Three Dialogues with Georges Duthuit" from 1949 contain the extreme and often quoted statements made by Beckett concerning the impossibility of expression and the necessity of remaining faithful to a vocation of failure.[8] These statements are so radical, the destitution in which they leave the artist is so complete, that no discussion of the question of "life" or expression in Beckett could possibly disregard them. They acknowledge a point of no return and articulate a position of historical and artistic probity that cannot be mitigated in any simple way even by the counterexamples in Beckett's own work. By presenting this text first, in all its unforgiving rigor and destituted sublimity, I hope to eliminate any impression that the obtrusive or residual elements of expression and affect that I want to point out can be used simply to humanize Beckett's texts—especially in terms of the clichés concerning despair and grim negativity that used to be attached to them—or that they can be rendered familiar and manageable by replacing the image of Beckett the morbid curser of life with one of Beckett the repressed sentimentalist. Rather, let us keep to the complexity of a work at odds with itself. In that light, we will see that while expression persists in Beckett's work, despite the extreme measures called for in the "Three Dialogues," it is not so much that the artist has betrayed his principles in a moment of nostalgic weakness, as that the impossibility of expression and the "obligation to express," as Beckett famously put it, have a common origin in the dimension of language that opens at the very edge of the human.

"Three Dialogues" was first published in 1949,[9] the same year that *L'innommable* was written in French (a fact whose importance will become clear as we proceed). Although based on actual conversations and letters between Beckett and Duthuit, it was written by Beckett, who places the speaker designated as "B." very much in the piece's critical center, whereas "D." serves primarily as a puzzled, and somewhat scandalized, facilitator of the conversation.[10] Each of the dialogues treats one of three contemporary painters, Tal Coat, André Masson, and Beckett's friend Bram van Velde. The last is the only one to escape the massive act of liquidation B. performs on the entire artistic tradition falling within his cultural purview, and as such van Velde is something of an (idealized) artistic alter ego, a projected example of the radical ethos espoused by B. It is to van Velde that B. attributes the distinction of being "the first to accept a certain situation . . . to admit that to be an artist is to fail, as no other dare fail, that failure is his world and the shrink from it desertion, art and craft, good housekeeping, living. No, no, allow me to expire" (D 145). No one could accuse Beckett of inconsistency on this score; he asked for little else throughout the four decades of his career following this dialogue. "Oh all to end": this exasperated wish to expire was very nearly the last line he wrote.[11] *Its* peculiar failure, however—its failure to fail, as it were—is an eventuality that the rhetoric of the "Three Dialogues" allows B. to bracket as he pursues to its extremes an aesthetics of absolute destitution.

What does failure mean in this context? First of all, it means the refusal of what has passed for the artist's vocation throughout the modern age, that is, precisely, the impulse and the power to express, the ability to create, the mastery of the means to make. B.'s "disgust" with the "dreary road" travelled by all art hitherto, with its complacent occupation of "the plane of the feasible," is summed up in what is no doubt the most frequently quoted statement of the piece—a statement that invokes the ambiguous compulsion/imperative at the core of these declarations. In response to a question from D. regarding what he would prefer to the "puny exploits" of such a compromised art, B. intones with categorical rigor, proclaiming: "The expression that there is nothing to express, nothing with which to express, nothing from which to express, no power to express, no desire to express, together with the obligation to express" (D 139).[12] I will have more to say about this resourceless obligation in a moment. What is clear immediately and above all is that such statements are meant to mark a clean break, defiantly to stake out a territory in which would be realized, as B. puts it later, "my dream of an art unresentful of its insuperable indigence and too proud for the farce of giving and receiving" (D 141). This strange dream, in which art would no longer richly dream, removes any manifesto-like intentions from this piece: the art it proposes is so bereft, its possibilities are so meager, that any future it might have would come truly as a surprise, not as the result of a program. The "stance" that it takes makes it impossible to stand anywhere; its position nullifies every pose and posture. The odd incongruity of this text is thus that its confrontation with "a certain situation," that is, with the *present historical conditions* of artistic activity, leads to a complete detachment of art from what B. calls its "occasion." The divestment from art of its function as expression (itself a distant result, peculiar to modernity, of the liquidation of its sacred function), the fact, which up to now has not been fully recognized, that "expression is an impossible act" reveals something about art that has conditioned all of its modernist and avant-garde manifestations: its separation from every object and every world, its isolation in its own materials, its occupation of the paltry domain of its own impossible being. What distinguishes B.'s position from other experiments in modern (twentieth-century) art—in which the discovery that painting consists of nothing but paint, and the forms taken by paint on a flat surface, is often supplemented by high-flown discourses on being and spirit[13]—is that here no such supplement is provided, except perhaps the possibility of expiration mentioned above. Furthermore, the suggestion that this very dilemma, the struggle to make when there is nothing to make and nothing to make with, might become a new "occasion" for the artist only elicits one of the most scornful remarks of the entire piece, in which B. insists not merely on the indigence of art but on its "ultimate penury," as opposed to the "mere misery where destitute virtuous mothers may steal stale bread for their starving brats"; such insidious backsliding would amount to little more. No, no, says B., let the brats expire: for this art not a crumb, and no more of the miserable virtue that would justify such a subterfuge. The refusal of "living" and the failure of art to be adequate to any "occasion" whatsoever must be recognized as *absolute* in the strict sense of this word: released from all relation and condition.[14] The failure of the artist is thus the failure to relate his or her art to anything, to any object or any world, including any "self," subject, or identity that would be expressed. Thus does Beckett merge a destituted sublime with a categorical aesthetic position itself colored by a refusal of any moral ground that might rescue it from the void.

And yet it is already obvious, as I have suggested, that this notion of failure is itself bound to fail. The failure of failure is named in these dialogues with the one truly opaque term in B.'s appraisal of the possibility of expression, and the only one which he concedes as binding on the artist: obligation. Despite the annihilation of all manner and means of expression ("There is nothing to express," and so on), there remains nevertheless "the obligation to express." It is here that an occasionless art would be tied (as the word *obligation* suggests) to something other than itself, something that would preexist the resulting artwork, without which the latter would not come into being, and that would no doubt give it away as embedded in some kind of relation after all, even if this relation has also somehow removed us, sublimely and abjectly, from the realm of objects.[15] B. himself gives little away, for when asked by D. why the artist is obliged, he responds simply, "I don't know." And truly, how should he know? What sense could be made of an obligation to do something that is impossible, for which all resources are lacking and for which no object or end, no starting point or material can be presupposed as given? What would be the ground and conditions of such an empty obligation? "Who" could have dictated it and how could it ever come to be assumed as one's own? How would its binding force become manifest to the one it binds, and exactly what would it oblige one to do?

It is perhaps not surprising that in such a polemical piece as this Beckett would simply write "I don't know," and leave it at that. He is at pains to underscore the categorical nature of the position he is describing, and does not dilute this harsh injunction with any equivocations on B.'s part. The very term "obligation," with its overtones of impersonal formality, seems to tilt this minimal acknowledgment of relation into the register of a pure and materially empty injunction, whereas it brings in its train, precisely because nothing else is left by which the artist would be bound and related, echoes of compulsion and blind submission, the dimension of the body and the material world—even if it is the material world of sheer paint, or by implication of language, *and nothing else.*

B.'s steadfast and principled position in these dialogues has the steely character of an absolute. But there is much in the text as a whole to indicate that Beckett's sympathies do not lie entirely with the stone-faced dismissals of B. We should not be too quick simply to identify B. with Beckett, who joked that he didn't so much write the conversation down as "write it up," and the dramatic and rhetorical complications which he weaves into it should not be underestimated. It is most pertinent, I believe, to see the entire text as Beckett's own staging of an insoluble conflict, than to treat it simply as a dramatized opportunity to flaunt his radical opinions. It is true that in the dialogue B. overshadows D., to the point where the entire discussion becomes a matter of simply getting B. to state clearly his astonishing point of view, and to "get it over," which he tries to do in a final long-winded speech (of course failing to do so). But B. does not simply dismiss the points made by D. in their debate; the latter is an advocate for one side of the conflict: by dividing this conflict sharply into two distinct positions occupied by two interlocutors, Beckett is able thus to radicalize and to take to its logical extremes the "point of view" expressed by B.

As far as giving oneself away is concerned, the real "unbuttoning" occurs not in B.'s praise of van Velde's heroic ethos of failure (in which the painter did not necessarily recognize himself). The real rub arises in the discussion of Masson, whom D. defends and for whom B. is obviously sympathetic, despite his dismissive remarks. If van Velde serves here as Beckett's purer and, in terms of failure, more "successful" artistic alter ego, Masson is rather like a mirror giving back a negative image, in every sense: the situation is exactly the same, but everything has been strangely reversed. Not only has Masson overcome a temptation toward myth-making, but he has also begun to speak of "the void," a blankness and emptiness to which the artist must accede and which has its own troubled place in Beckett's work. D. introduces one of the great themes of Beckett's writing when he claims of Masson that he "suffers more keenly than any living painter from the need to come to rest." The problem, according to B., is that Masson "seems literally skewered on the ferocious dilemma of expression," and what's more "he continues to wriggle" (D 140). It would hardly be a stretch to describe the narrator of *The Unnamable* in exactly the same terms, although the skewer may indeed be sticking, as it were, in the opposite direction. For if Beckett, especially in the terminal text of his early trilogy, has confronted the situation he is diagnosing in these dialogues, taking for granted the impossibility of expression and the radical unavailability of objects, and "going on" from there, Masson (claims B.) has recognized the dilemma only to continue in the attempt to assert his "competence," to insist on the richness of means and ability: B. speaks of "the scars of a competence that must be most painful to him" who would paint the scarless void. Again, Beckett seems to be writing of himself in the third person, for it is difficult not to attribute such a painful competence to the author of the trilogy, in which the sheer virtuosity of those works is at odds with the search for the void that drives them. As for the scarred and skewered Masson, he is said to "move from one untenable position to another . . . seeking justification always on the same plane"—by which is meant, no doubt, the "plane of the feasible." While B. is at pains to dissociate himself from such a futile "movement," the descriptions of Masson given by both of the interlocutors present nothing so much as a negativized self-portrait of Beckett as he faces the *obligation to renounce*. D. puts it thus: "Without renouncing the objects, loathsome or delicious, that are our daily bread and wine and poison, [Masson] seeks to break through their partitions to that continuity of being which is absent from the ordinary experience of living. In this he approaches Matisse . . . and Tal Coat, but with this notable difference, that Masson has to contend with his own technical gifts, which have the richness, the precision, the density and balance of the high classical manner." Who could fail to see Beckett in this description? It applies in the most striking way not only in terms of his tendencies toward classicism (consider his great interest in Racine, his predilection for well-balanced formal symmetries, and the "classical" form of the one-act *Endgame*) but also in terms of "breaking through the partitions" of the stuff on hand. This phrase is practically a quote from the "German letter of 1937," also published in *Disjecta*, in which Beckett writes of boring holes through language "until what lurks behind it—be it something or nothing—begins to seep through" (D 172).[16]

Beckett's displaced portrait of himself, unlike the caricature of van Velde, brings out the true insolubility of the "ferocious dilemma" on which he too is skewered. The reading of *The Unnamable* I will offer here will confirm the stubbornness both of expression and of the world of objects, even when these would be utterly, sublimely renounced. If we recognize Beckett's own "competence" and his "technical gifts," if we attribute to him a richness of resources at odds with the doctrine of absolute failure but clearly reflected in his writing, then it becomes more relevant to speak simultaneously of a state of indigence *and* an active refusal, a loss and inaccessibility of objects *and* a tactical suppression and bracketing off, a stripping away of material which, for reasons as yet unclear, is better left out of the picture.

On one level—and it is in this sense that the "Three Dialogues" have political as well as aesthetic implications—this refusal is a refusal of art's redemptive pretensions. What B. is so adamantly against, what truly elicits his derision, is the desire to recuperate experience and, by means of art, to redeem "the chaos" (as he put it in an interview several years later).[17] And this desire bears directly on the virtuosity and "technical gifts" acquired through long intercourse with the cultural tradition of the West. Beckett was an extremely erudite artist; he had at his disposal a great store of cultural references, on which he draws much more overtly in his early writing than in the trilogy and after. By the time of the "Three Dialogues" he has gone a long way in renouncing the desire to saturate his writing with the meaning that would come, supposedly, with more or less explicit references to the works of earlier artists and philosophers. But later, as commentators have pointed out, these references often become nothing more than cultural detritus, barely significant relics punctuating texts caught up in the process of becoming more and more insignificant.[18] The difficulty of carrying this process to its term is summed up in an exchange in *Waiting for Godot* in which Vladimir frets that "This is becoming really insignificant," to which Estragon replies: "Not enough" (44). If the ultimate desire is in the end not to add to the "rubbish heap" of cultural artifacts (Adorno) but to accede to a space of pure meaninglessness and to the seeping stuff on the other side of language, what could be more "painful" than a "competence," based on venerable tradition and acquired with such tremendous labor, that turns out to be both a useless disappointment and forever in the way?

On another level, however—and of course these are not unrelated—this refusal to "succeed" involves a strange form of self-dismissal, an avoidance of "material" not only in terms of cultural by-products but also in relation to the powerful life of affect. It is true that the "expression" that B. pronounces impossible is not limited to the articulation of affect; as we will see in relation to *The Unnamable*, it concerns any relation whatever between a supposedly preexisting subjectivity and the language (in Beckett's case) in which it would manifest.[19] But there are very clear indications even in the desert air of the "Three Dialogues" that the "obligation to express" owes its force to the very lyrical impulses—to the "desire to express"—that are here given the status of a mirage. Indeed, it must be admitted that despite everything Beckett's work (again, especially the trilogy) displays, lavishly and passionately, a great deal of "competence" in evoking emotional intensity, and not only when it comes to bitterness, resentment and abjection. Further, among the many forms of such evocation there is an undeniable strain in Beckett's writing of a kind of glassy-eyed sentimentality that, to be sure, rarely shows itself without being deflated by sharp jabs of irony or sarcasm, but which precisely because of this uncomfortable and embattled status is very telling.[20] The link between this sentimental lyricism and the motif of separation—the definitive detachment from life on earth—will become much clearer in later works (especially *How It Is*), but even in this earlier phase Beckett gives clues, again in a negative form, that the renunciation of all objects and occasions is not *merely* a matter of scorn and derision.

In the specific context of the "Three Dialogues," one can refer to a moment that, in its effusion and "optimism," is as ironic as it is in keeping with the points I have just made. The presence of such a moment is in fact doubly ironic (and that is exactly what allows it to seep through): for this is the last place one would expect to find anything of the sort, but of course its occurrence is subjected to an immediate and merciless mockery. The moment occurs at the very end of the section on Masson. There D. attempts a final defense of Masson that both clinches the hinted-at similarities between Masson and Beckett and elicits a reaction from B. so violent, and so exaggeratedly ironic, that it is difficult not to see in it a negation, or "denegation," in the psychoanalytic sense. The passage is worth quoting at length:

> D.— Masson himself, having remarked that perspective is no more than a series of traps for the capture of objects, declares that their possession does not interest him. He congratulates Bonnard for having, in his last works, "gone beyond possessive space in every shape and form, far from surveys and bounds, to the point where all possession is dissolved." I agree that there is a long cry from Bonnard to that impoverished painting, "authentically fruitless, incapable of any image whatsoever," to which you aspire, *and towards which too, who knows, unconsciously perhaps, Masson tends*. But must we really deplore the painting that admits "the things and creatures of spring, resplendent with desire and affirmation, ephemeral no doubt, but immortally reiterant," not in order to benefit by them, not in order to enjoy them, but in order that what is tolerable and radiant in the world may continue? Are we really to deplore the painting that is a rallying, among the things of time that pass and hurry us away, toward a time that endures and gives increase?
> B.— (Exit weeping.) (D 141–142; my emphasis)

Such a precipitous exit reminds one of the refrain occurring throughout *Company* whenever the threat of encountering the dreaded "first person" arises: "Quick leave him." Is Beckett's sarcastic stage direction really nothing more than that, an impatient mockery? Or is it also—"unconsciously perhaps"—the quickest resolution of a tension rendered unbearable by a too great proximity? Is it an aloof dismissal or an urgent disavowal? Is B. crying to stop himself from laughing, or because—as the advocate of the sublime and imageless law of expressionlessness—he has had to give all that up? Taken at their letter, the measures called for by B. are sufficient to send anyone into mourning, but the weeping evoked here, however ironically, is itself a strange sign that all's not entirely lost as yet. "No future in this. Alas yes" (WH 10). Beckett's tremendous irony—which amidst the nothingness might well be considered a resource—together with the sheer extremity of B.'s draconian dismissal of "living," is enough to make one wonder why such measures are necessary. What is it about "life" that requires such a merciless "exit" and such a massive disavowal?

Here too Beckett's description of Masson shows itself to be a negative self-portrait. What could such hopes as those expressed in D.'s speech mean for the author of *The Unnamable*? From his point of view, the prospect of admitting the "immortally reiterant" and of "a time that endures and gives increase" might indeed be cause for tears. In that work, something like reiteration becomes "immortal"—or at least unable to die—only because it is a torture from which there is no escape, and in which time increases nothing but the unbearable strain of sheer endurance. What "may continue" is neither radiant nor tolerable, and we are told in the very beginning that although he is "devoid of feeling" the unnamable "know[s his] eyes are open because of the tears that pour from them unceasingly" (U 22). It is as though, having written *The Unnamable*, Beckett knows how it truly stands with such hopes as these, and in this sense his irony is razor-sharp. But the structure of irony, as described by Paul de Man with reference to Baudelaire's "De l'essence du rire," applies perfectly to Beckett's self-dispersal in the "Three Dialogues": to put it in the simplest possible terms, irony consists in the reflective act of laughing at oneself as though at an other, like the man who, capable of a philosophic "*dédoublement*," laughs at himself when he falls in the street.[21] If B.'s laughter takes the form of tears, it is in order to dramatize the redolent sentimentality of D.'s impassioned speech, but as the latter implores B. not to "deplore" such painting, one is tempted to take these terms literally and to see in them the tears and grief presentable only across such a self-duplicating distance (the Latin *plorare* meaning to cry out or wail). And if, as D. puts it in a manifestly hesitant and stuttering locution, B. strives for an imagelessness "toward which too, who knows, unconsciously perhaps, Masson tends," it may well be that for his part B. is not entirely resolute when it comes to the absolute, and destitutely sublime, renunciation of all objects and occasions, and that despite everything he "tends" toward the very sentimentality which is disavowed here.

This tendency is often made visible by the gesture of disavowal it requires, which can be seen throughout Beckett's work. To mention briefly only a few of the most obvious examples: *Krapp's Last Tape* consists of nothing but the bitter and yet nostalgic rehashing of past times and past selves, carried out every evening as Krapp records new tapes. In "Film," Buster Keaton—referred to simply as "O," the Object of the camera's gaze—looks through a stack of pictures from his life, and then rips them up, scattering the pieces in a pile on the floor; thus, apparently having obliterated all trace of his life, he finds the peace in which to sleep, only to wake horrified to the overbearing figure of himself—who has been in the position of the camera all along—stubbornly staring him down. Similarly, in "A Piece of Monologue," a sort of companion piece to "Film" (though it is much later), the speaker mentions a "blank wall" once covered with "pictures of . . . he all but said loved ones." But these have been "torn to shreds" and "swept out of the way under the bed and left. Thousand shreds under the bed with the dust and spiders."[22] And of course "Not I," whose very title gives the piece away as a self-cancelling exercise in disavowal. Here the voice is only a "Mouth" whose "vehement refusal to relinquish [the] third person" gives rise to a shrugging "gesture of helpless compassion" on the part of a mute body poised nearby (CSPl 215).

The melancholy quality of such biographically oriented texts, their staging of an unbearably painful relation to a past life as such, reinforces the sense that the irruption of sentimentality and grief in the "Three Dialogues" may not be as derisory as it seems. The exit from life and the long and slow expirations so prominent in Beckett's work must be seen as the very conditions for carrying out the harsh injunction to express, even as they prolong the agony by forever deferring the occasionless void. As Rilke wrote in the *Duino Elegies*, "It's not easy, being dead,"[23] — nor is it easy even in death to escape from something resembling a life, at least as long as the obligation to continue still drones out its "pensum" (as Beckett calls it in *The Unnamable*), the punishment with which it merges. The impulse to escape from life reveals itself to be coupled with an impulse to rehash it endlessly, and to be drawn by a strange fascination toward the desiccated remnants of what had to be "swept out of the way . . . and left."

At this point it is not possible to specify more clearly the nature of these impulses and the painful force behind the disavowals cutting through Beckett's work, but it is clear that they bear directly on the "obligation to express" in a way that belies the apparently empty formality of this obligation. There arises here in relation to Beckett the radical ambiguity concerning the imperative to write which was found in Kafka and Blanchot as well. For when Beckett writes of "the obligation to express"—after evacuating the act of expression of all possible content, detaching it from all relation to objects and the world, and even insisting on its impossibility—it would seem that this obligation could consist of nothing more than an empty and formal imperative grounded in nothing but its own contentless conditions, very much in the manner of Kant's categorical imperative. And yet, as we are already beginning to see, there is a powerful and persistent relation if not to objects and ends, at least to something like an affective drive which, we might suspect, is the true unknowable in Beckett's simple "I don't know." In this nonknowledge of grounds and reasons, obligation begins to elide with compulsion, without either of these terms fully dissolving into the other.

Are there firm grounds for taking seriously the comparison of Beckett's obligation to express and Kant's categorical imperative? The similarities are striking and more than superficial. Like the categorical imperative, the obligation to express is, indeed, categorical; independent of all "occasion," it would not be conditioned by any empirical considerations; it does not bear on consequences or on the benefits or disadvantages to persons; it is based not on values, "power," or "desire," but on a purely internal structural necessity, and, accordingly, its validity does not even depend on whether its execution is possible or not. But whereas in Kant this structural necessity would be grounded in the autonomy of reason—that is, precisely in its separation from the empirical world of ends and from the mechanism of nature—in Beckett, despite the protestations of the "Three Dialogues," the obligation to write cannot ever quite manage to free itself from the occasions which make it sensible, which make it felt.[24] However categorical and impoverished it may be, "the obligation to express" is stubbornly harassed by the profusion of sensibility and affect which is its most basic mode of manifestation. Beckett's "I don't know" is thus, at certain level, a refusal to do philosophy, at least in the sense in which philosophy has attempted to assert ethical *principles* that would be grounded in rational discourse. And yet the obligation Beckett writes of *is* a principle of sorts— it has the form of a rule and the status of a regulative limit, it is not automatically adhered to, and it requires the vigilance of an adherent—but it does not have its ground in any form of knowledge; if it is grounded at all it is in an experience of rupture, dissolution and dispossession, and is not merely an abstract principle but a mode of living in language by which the very existence of language is experienced as a material force.

Beckett uses several terms for the material and bodily force of language, terms such as "pangs," "cravings," "stirrings," "preying," "gnawing," "longing," even (in *Worstward Ho*, where several in this list appear) "secreting" and "oozing." These terms, in their very grammar, attempt to name the strange ongoing processes by which a language is both intimately connected and strangely separate from a body which, with its "remains of mind," would be their "seat and germ" (WH 9, 30) (It should be added here that there is an extreme ambiguity concerning just what craving craves, what longing longs for, what stirring stirs toward: while these terms mark the stubborn life of the mind's remains, they are invariably linked to a wish to end, a paradoxical movement toward the ceasing of movement, and are thus constituted as much by the ungraspability of death as by the insistence of life.) Few artists have gone as far as Beckett in debunking the myths of creativity and self-expression attributed to art in the modern age. But if such an uncompromising stance were enough, then that would be, literally, the end of the story, and Beckett's work would have rendered itself superfluous. It would have "succeeded" in annihilating itself, and would thus have paradoxically betrayed its vocation to fail. "No try no fail," writes Beckett in his summum of this experience, *Worstward Ho*. It is only after a long experience of "trying" that the inevitability of failure could lead to an ethos constituted by failure itself, and by the stubbornness of the effort it "obliges."

MERCIER AND CAMIER AND THE TRILOGY

Having outlined the artistic position articulated by Beckett's own critical text, which places him in a resolutely impoverished aesthetic space striving for release from all object and occasion, and which leads him to a commitment to fail "as no other dare fail," it will be useful now to turn to some of those places in Beckett's writing that belie this commitment, in order to indicate more clearly the "other side" of the tension between blankness and expressivity as it emerges in the fictional works. Despite it all, Beckett is expressive, at times even effusive. And although it will not be my purpose simply to claim that he "succeeds" at these moments, the undeniable lyricism of the passages I would like to quote will serve at least to qualify his own uncompromising statements; they may give clues as to what dangers lurk in the pang to express, and what would be avoided in its liquidation. Only then will it be possible to understand the failure which these expressive moments do not, after all, overcome, and to understand, if not to "know," something about the obligation under which Beckett places his work, about the failure to which it would remain faithful.

The demonstration for which these quotes will be used is complicated, however, by the fact that their lyricism is tuned to a resolutely minor key; if their elegiac tones express anything, it is precisely the loss and destitution about which B. is so militant in the "Three Dialogues" but that send him weeping into the wings when something like hope begins to sound. Thus these passages do not exactly "contradict" that militancy, rather they enact its consequences, but in the register precisely of the lyrical and melancholic *Stimmung* that is at stake. They put one in mind of some of the more poignant passages of Hölderlin or Trakl, and even share with these poets a taste for desolate landscapes and anonymous evening scenes. Steeped in an atmosphere of loss and renunciation, they give rise to a nostalgia with no hope of return, and point toward moments of supposed plenitude that are now so "lost" as to be nothing more than comic illusions.

A peculiar and revealing text, with regard to the question of lyrical language, is the near-abandoned *Mercier et Camier*. Written in 1946, Beckett shelved the novel for almost twenty-five years, until 1970, and it was not published in English translation until 1974. Beckett was obviously not altogether pleased with the results of his first sustained effort in French, yet he did finally publish it. It has been pointed out that, due in part to the lag of many years, Beckett's translation of this text into English is marked by an impatience with his own earlier indulgence in treating the relations of his protagonists to each other and to the world around them.[25] In addition to leaving out several pages-long passages, he omits many details that ground his characters in a world of social and material particularities (concerning money, food, etc.). One passage, in which Mercier's bracing himself on a rail while passing wind is described in exaggerated and high-flown language, is reduced in the English to a simple one-line statement: "Mercier's hand released the railing to which this attack of wind had fastened it" (MaC 77; MeC 130–131). What is curious, however, is that there are quite a number of other very poetic passages that are not undercut by such an incongruity between style and content, and with which Beckett did not seem to be at all impatient. In fact, what is remarkable about the translations of these passages is just how much of their expressivity is preserved by the older author, given the dissatisfaction just noted. While Beckett claimed that the turn to French was an attempt to write "without style," what is surprising is that, in translating a text that to some extent must have embarrassed him, he would bring out so forcefully the "expressivity" which subsisted in his supposedly flatter French. There is one passage in particular in which Beckett is at pains to convey the elegiac mood mentioned above. It occurs, significantly, just after Camier's apparently definitive departure from a now lonely and abject Mercier.

> But the least little thing halts the Merciers of this world, a murmur coming to its crest and breaking, a voice saying how strange the autumn-tide of day no matter what the season. A new beginning, but with no life in it, how could there be? More manifest in town than in the country, but in the country too, where slowly over the vast empty space the peasant seems to stray, so aimless that night must surely overtake him far from the village nowhere, the homestead nowhere to be seen. There is no time left and yet how it drags. Even the flowers seem past their time to close and a kind of panic seizes on the tired wings. The hawk stoops always too soon, the rooks rise from the fallows while it is still light and flock to their places of assembly, there to croak and squabble till nightfall. Then, too late, they agitate to set out again. Day is over long before it ends, man ready to drop long before the hour of rest. But not a word, evening is all fever, a scurrying to and fro to no avail. (MaC 76; MeC 127–128)

The passage continues in this (vaguely German expressionist) vein for several pages, and it is precisely from this section that Beckett excises the baroque bit about Mercier's "attack of wind." The result in the English is that this eruption does not undermine the mood of lamentation that is dominant here, though of course not without some playful and mocking irony ("what more can you ask? A heart in the room of the heart? Come come."). The tension out of which this mood arises is, apparently, that of the question, To be with Camier or not to be with Camier, that is, between company and solitude, and this tension is directly related to the torturous soliloquy which will become more and more central in the works following this one: "It was perhaps too great a call on his strength, this parting from Camier at so sombre an hour. Admittedly strength was needed for to stay with Camier, no less than for to stay with Mercier, but less than for the horrors of soliloquy." Fortunately, Mercier is spared the indefinite continuation of these horrors (or of the "*bataille*," as it stands in the French), but that we are approaching the space of the unnamable becomes clear in the echoes between the language used here and that of the later novel: "Yet there he is on his way again, the voice has ceased, he is over the worst . . . his being fills again with that merciful fog which is the best he knows. . . . His dim shape moves on . . . in the shadow . . . if shadow is the word for a light hardly less leaden than that of the bogland nearby." This leaden light is that which fills the "gray-black" space (as Badiou calls it) in which the voice of the unnamable refuses to cease in its solitary battle for silence. But there is articulated in this passage a relation between the "horrors of soliloquy" and the silence and stillness so fiercely sought by the unnamable which has no place in the later text. In *Mercier and Camier* this articulation occurs precisely here, where these horrors are somehow mitigated by the bodily mobility denied to the unnamable ("he is on his way again") and where this walking movement evokes a past which may well be playing itself out still in the "heart in the room of the heart." The page I have been citing continues as follows, ending the chapter with a nostalgic image from childhood:

> The collar of his coat is turned up, his right hand is in his left sleeve and vice versa, they lie jogging on his belly in senile abandon [*dans un vrai geste de vieux*], now and then he glimpses as through shifting seaweed a foot dragging on a flagstone. Heavy chains, hung between small stone pillars, festoon with their massy garlands the pavement on the street side. Once in motion they swing on and on, steadily or with serpentine writhings. Here Mercier would come to play when he was small. Running along the line of chains he set them going, one after another, with a stick, then turned back to look how the great jolts shook the pavement from end to end till it seemed they would never come to rest [*Le trottoir tressaillait, d'un bout à l'autre, de lourdes secousses, longues à s'apaiser*]. [MaC 78; MeC 132]

Regardless of whether this recounts a memory from Beckett's own past, it provides a striking image of the reverberations and echoes of a biographical remnant that may "never come to rest." These reverberations are remarked at a moment of extreme abjection and destitution, as he cuts the "senile" figure of the old wanderer that fills Beckett's narratives. Only rarely are these wanderings, and their voices and silences, related to past scenes or to a childhood that is at least in some vague and marshy way one's own. (*Company* will be a major exception to this, though not without also deepening the gulf between present and past.) But even here, there is no mention on the narrator's part that Mercier is remembering this scene, that it is returning to him from a proper past, or even that he is aware of the association at all. Beckett's characters are devoid even of this simple level of psychology. The association, and the entire temporal palimpsest evoked here, occur on the plane of an impersonal narrator's somewhat wistful relation, hovering around the character like the marine atmosphere that separates Mercier from his own body. But the image, especially in French, of "*lourdes secousses*" whose vibrations continue undiminished, and the suggestion of a sort of *correspondance* between the wavy seaweed of Mercier's present "consciousness" and the serpentine motions of the heavy chains, place this moment somewhere in the distant vicinity of a Proustian "*recherche*" stimulated by the refound objects of lost time. But of course, although he begins his writing career with Proust, Beckett does not carry out the same kind of search.[26] If Mercier stumbles across a moment from his childhood, it is without any hint of reappropriating it in any way, much less of integrating it into a work of art that would seek to purify time. The scarcity of such moments in Beckett may well have to do with a decision concerning precisely the impossibility of regaining time, once it is lost, and the preference not for the eternity of the work of art but for the silence and stillness of a long lost peace and quiet. Nevertheless the image used here suggests something extremely important concerning the temporal existence even of Beckett's disinherited wanderers: floating somewhere among the algae of present indigence, and passing through the vicissitudes of soliloquy, is the still-reverberating weight of a past that is "*long à s'apaiser.*" Long, if not endless.

Beckett's true "*recherche*" is carried out in the trilogy of novels written in the years following World War II. The object of this search is not lost time but rather the loss of time, the exit from the temporal stream, the "*apaisement*" of the voices and visions that keep it all going, a death and silence attained through the narrative voice itself. This is true of the trilogy as a whole, but especially of *The Unnamable* where it becomes explicit, and which infects the first two volumes with a kind of retroactive radicalization of their more localized goals.

Molloy: "*The spurious deeps*"

In *Molloy*, the local goal is divided in two: first there is Molloy's search for his mother, but this goal is so hilariously and brutally ironized that it is hard to take seriously on any literal level. This applies to the entire story related by Molloy, which is submerged in the latter's digressive style much as Mercier's foot is submerged in seawater. The other goal, in the second part narrated by Moran—a sort of detective employed by one Youdi—is, for some unknown reason, Molloy himself. Not surprisingly, neither of these goals is reached, except insofar as both Molloy and Moran are gradually transformed into the very image of the one they are searching for (in one case, a bed-ridden cripple, in the other, a stiff-legged vagabond hobbling around with crutches and a bicycle). As I have said, irony is the very element of this text; it is what gives it its delicious sense of artifice, despite the gritty abjection it depicts, and its wry humor. Beckett dissolves his "characters" (both of whom speak in the first person) into this element to such a degree that they are hardly characters at all; they are absorbed into their own voices in such a way as to aggravate the separation of these voices from the bodies they inhabit and from the events they recount. Both characters, it should be added, are explicit about the act of writing in which they are engaged, which ostensibly produces the text we read. Thus their narratives are mediated by a scene of writing which is itself rendered only schematically, and which is the endpoint of a long and nearly terminal experience of depersonalization, depropriation, and dispossession.[27]

In the midst of all this, however, Beckett composes passages whose lyricism is only sharpened by these devices. This time I would like to quote a passage that does not end with a "*secousse*" but rather begins with a "*bourrade dans le dos.*" It occurs after Molloy has been arrested for vagrancy and is being taken to the police station. He halts, in order to listen to "a distant music"—a strange *Stimmung* which pervades the vague landscape of this text, and which prepares the following poetic strain—but the policeman will not permit it.

> He gave me a shove. . . . While putting my best foot foremost I gave myself up to that golden moment as if I had been someone else. It was the hour of rest, the forenoon's toil ended, the afternoon's to come. The wisest perhaps, lying in the squares or sitting on their doorsteps, were savouring its languid ending, forgetful of recent cares, indifferent to those at hand. Others on the contrary were using it to hatch their plans, their heads in their hands. Was there one among them to put himself in my place, to feel how removed I was then from him I seemed to be, and in that remove what strain, as of hawsers about to snap? It's possible. Yes, I was straining toward those spurious deeps, their lying promise of gravity and peace, from all my old poisons I struggled toward them, safely bound. Under the blue sky, under the watchful gaze. Forgetful of my mother, set free from the act, merged in this alien hour, saying, Respite, respite. (MoE 26–27; MoF 29)

I have chosen this passage partly because of its similarities with the one from *Mercier and Camier*: although it takes place in the noontime heat rather than in the "autumn-tide of day," here too it is a moment of rest, a suspension of activity, through which our hero walks as a stranger. The languid sense of work having stopped, of time slowing down, prepares the tension to which Molloy abandons himself, the strain (if not the storm) and stress of a voice beside itself, as if it were another's. This tension is heightened by the use of the first person—unlike the third person relation of *Mercier et Camier*—which seems to unify the perspective even as what is expressed is nothing but a taut and unbearable "remove" from the seeming self. The nautical metaphor, in which Molloy likens himself to a ship straining its hawsers, about to plunge into the "spurious deeps," suggests that being "safely bound" by the police (and in the manner of a mad and alienated Odysseus) is somehow the condition for such tension, and that the threat of drowning "in the alien hour" ("*dans l'heure des autres*") becomes less risky (as the French makes clear: "*en sachant que je ne risquais rien*"). The deeps are "spurious" (simply "*faux*" in the French—a good example of Beckett's heightened English diction) not because they are in fact "shallow" but because they are the depths of falseness, here made alluring by the lack of real danger. This "golden moment" is thus just as much a matter of being held by force of law as of the brilliant restful day Molloy lyrically merges with here: apprehended and shoved on to the station, he is unburdened of the responsibility to act, to continue his quest for his mother, to calculate the imponderable variables of his haphazard journey. And in this calm compression he can say to himself (imploringly? thankfully?): Respite, respite. The "blue sky," image of the abyss, is punctuated only by the "watchful gaze" of the police, by which all is ordered, for the moment. But it is the "lying promise of gravity and peace" which I would like to focus on, finally, for not only does this phrase link the golden moment with the heavy chains of Mercier's childhood, "*longues à s'apaiser,*" it also points to the drive behind this lyrical outburst: the drive for a ground, for peace, for an end to the jolting waves of the surface. The falsity of this "promise," the true horrors of what lies in wait there, are suggested here, but only at a distance. For a more engulfed experience of these horrors, we will have to wait until the depths have become truly "unnamable." The question, in *Molloy*, of the relation of the mother to these depths and their false calm is an extremely complicated one, although in a way Beckett simplifies it for us. He makes it obvious that the mother simply serves a very specific narrative function, rendered comic and quasi-allegorical: as the one unquestioned goal Molloy sets himself, throughout all his divagations, she is a parody of that figure of nativity and rest, of the return to an original peace which is also an end to all.[28]

Malone Dies: *"No recovering from that"*

The "goal" toward which the hero of *Malone Dies* strains is of course indicated by the title. Malone—old, infirm, and bedridden—waits expectantly for death, and while waiting, he writes. But this straining is also a stretching and deferring, precisely in the form of writing and the extenuation of language. The first sentence comically demonstrates this (it reads best in French): "*Je serai quand même bientôt tout à fait mort enfin*" ("I shall soon be quite dead at last in spite of all"). If Molloy is happy to "stay, where he happened to be," Malone has been given this blessing, but now has to confront the dead time of waiting and an unceasing movement in stasis. That is why he writes, in his child's exercise book, with a nubby pencil he sharpens with his fingernails. We recall that this is in fact more or less the same situation Molloy is in when he writes his pages (bedridden, unable to move), but here we remain with the writer in his enclosed room (in some vaguely institutional setting; of course Malone does not know how he got there). He does not recount or reminisce in any detail about his past life (he cannot remember it), and when he tells stories, as he does to pass the time, we know that he is inventing them (how he does this without remembering his own story, or any past at all, is a question we will leave open for the moment). His life, however, is strangely present at this scene, although precisely as something completely past and gone; it is something that has failed (he complains often of never having lived), leaving him here in limbo. In fact, he has a great deal to say about his life, in this hollowed-out sense, and his speech seems compelled by nothing so much as a relation to this past life in its absence and failure. He does not recount it, however; rather, one might say that he broods on it, limiting his stories to those he invents.

This voice, therefore, which remains at every moment in the foreground, is—with respect to Malone himself—less a narrative voice than a ruminative and lyrical one, given to transports of language which he refers to derisively as "throes" ("*sursauts*"): in the "neutral and inert" present, he writes, "Throes are the only trouble, I must be on my guard against throes." As is so often the case with Beckett, the dramatic and lyrical tension of the situation, but also its abjection and destitution, are determined by an apparently complete (hellish or purgatorial) separation from life on earth, as Malone makes clear in one passage:

> In a word there seems to be the light of the outer world, of those who know the sun and moon emerge at such an hour and at such another plunge again below the surface, and who rely on this, and who know that clouds are always to be expected but sooner or later always pass away, and mine. But mine too has its alternations, I will not deny it, its dusks and dawns, but that is what I say, for I too must have lived, once, out there, and there is no recovering from that. (MD 47)

This last phrase is revealing in the French version: "*c'est une chose qu'on ne pardonne pas*" (MM 77)—having lived, once, is something *unforgivable*. It is in the element of this unrecoverable *fault* that the throes of Malone's speech continue on, somehow "after life" but before the death that would deliver him (in every sense) back into the void.

As examples of these throes, I would like to look at three passages that show very well both the stylistic movements of Beckett's prose that I have been calling lyrical and the nature of the "sentiment" in question, the relation to a life as past. Surely *Malone Dies* is one of Beckett's most lyrical works, and its lyricism hinges around nothing so much as a final decision to exit life, with many strange backward glances. As Malone says, "I was always sentimental" (MD 17; MM 31), and never more than when he is measuring the distance between the present semi-void and the life he cannot recover from. The first passage, one of Malone's most bitter but poignant monologues, is something of a "biography"—though it tells no story—leading to the present state of agitated resignation, and a summation of what life never offered. Its breathlessness and comma-spliced rhythm harks forward to *The Unnamable*. It is the longest of the three passages I will cite:

> Live and invent. I have tried. I must have tried. Invent. It is not the word. Neither is live. No matter. I have tried. While the wild beast of earnestness padded up and down, roaring, ravening, rending. I have done that. And all alone, well hidden, played the clown, all alone, hour after hour, motionless, often standing, spellbound, groaning. That's right, groan. I couldn't play. I turned till I was dizzy, clapped my hands, ran, shouted, saw myself winning, saw myself losing, rejoicing, lamenting. Then suddenly I threw myself on the playthings, if there were any, or on a child, to change his joy to howling, or I fled, to hiding. The grown-ups pursued me, the just, caught me, beat me, hounded me back into the round, the game, the jollity. For I was already in the toils of earnestness. That has been my disease. I was born grave as others syphilitic. And gravely I struggled to be grave no more, to live, to invent, I know what I mean. But at each fresh attempt I lost my head, fled to my shadows as to sanctuary, to his lap who can neither live nor suffer the sight of others living. I say living without knowing what it is. I tried to live without knowing what I was trying. Perhaps I have lived after all, without knowing. I wonder why I speak of all

this. Ah yes, to relieve the tedium. Live and cause to live. There is no use indicting words, they are no shoddier than what they peddle. After the fiasco, the solace, the repose, I began again, to try and live, cause to live, be another, in myself, in another. How false all this is. No time to explain. I began again. But little by little with a different aim, no longer in order to succeed, but in order to fail. Nuance. What I sought, when I struggled out of my hole, then aloft through the stinging air toward an inaccessible boon [*nourriture*], was the rapture [*extases*] of vertigo, the letting go, the fall, the gulf [*l'engouffrement*], the relapse to darkness, to nothingness, to earnestness, to home, to him waiting for me always, who needed me and whom I needed, who took me in his arms and told me to stay with him always, who gave me his place and watched over me, who suffered every time I left him, whom I have often made suffer and seldom contented, whom I have never seen. There I am forgetting myself again [*voilà que je commence à m'exalter*]. My concern is not with me, but with another [Saposcat, the protagonist of Malone's invented stories], far beneath me and whom I try to envy, of whose crass adventures I can now tell at last, I don't know how. Of myself I could never tell, any more than live or tell of others. How could I have, who never tried? To show myself now, on the point of vanishing, at the same time as the stranger, and by the same grace, that would be no ordinary last straw. Then live, long enough to feel, behind my closed eyes, other eyes close. What an end. (MD 18–19; MM 33–35)

There are two things I would like to point out here. The first is the movement that passes from the failure to live to a rebeginning determined by *deliberate* failure. "Nuance," as Beckett dryly puts it. This effort is one that leads precisely into "throes," into the "rapture of vertigo" and the entire language of sublimity, the abyss and nothingness that follows. The project of failure is metaphysical, in a very modern sense (a failure of experience leading to a beyond of experience). But then, most remarkable is that this language elides immediately into that of "home" and the loved one who would be there, but never has. This sentence, which evokes a love that was never had, is carried away by a veritable transport: "There I am forgetting myself again"—"*Voilà que je commence à m'exalter.*" Malone's transport makes a direct link between the metaphysics of failure, otherwise known as the sublime, and the nostalgia for a love "whom I have never seen," and thus articulates a certain failed transcendence with "homesickness." The drive toward one, "through the stinging air toward an inaccessible boon" (readable as a blessing, a "boon companion" and, in the French, a "*nourriture*" that can never be found), is the inverse side of the drive toward the other, so beautifully evoked in, and on the basis of, his absence.

The second point is contained in the last two lines. The loved one just mentioned is in some way connected to the character or "creature" Malone must "invent" in his writing (more on this in a moment), such that he may "show [him]self now, on the point of vanishing, at the same time as the stranger, and by the same grace"—in other words, the conjured creature's vanishing may be Malone's own as well, and they may both "show themselves" somehow in this common, final death/disappearance. As though Malone's very existence were located in the narrative voice with which his creature is brought into being, or as though, at least, this narration, with its terminal movement (every life must end), were a privileged path toward Malone's own long-awaited disappearance. But with a strange intervening margin, another dying after death: "Then live, long enough to feel, behind closed eyes, other eyes close. What an end." This interval, coming after the end and yet postponing the end of the end long enough "to feel" what it's like to have reached it, is an image of the trilogy's goal to which I will return.

The second passage contains another, very ironic image of this goal, together with a clear indication of the conflict that arises, when the end is near, between the void and the beauty of what has been left behind.

> I part my lips, now I have the pillow in my mouth. I have, I have. I suck. The search for myself is ended. I am buried in the world, I knew I would find my place there one day, the old world cloisters me, victorious. I am happy, I knew I would be happy one day. But I am not wise. For the wise thing now would be to let go, at this instant of happiness. And what do I do? I go back again to the light, to the fields I so longed to love, to the sky all astir with little white clouds as white and light as snowflakes, to the life I could never manage, through my own fault perhaps, through pride, or pettiness, but I don't think so. The beasts are at pasture, the sun warms the rocks and makes them glitter. Yes, I leave my happiness and go back to the race of men too, they come and go, often with burdens. Perhaps I have judged them ill, but I don't think so, I have not judged them at all. All I want now is to make a last effort to understand, to begin to understand, how such creatures are possible. No, it is not a question of understanding. Of what then? I don't know. Here I go none the less, mistakenly. Night, storm and sorrow, and the catalepsies of the soul, this time I shall see that they are good. The last word is not yet said between me and—yes, the last word is said. Perhaps I simply want to hear it again. Just once again. No, I want nothing. (MD 23; MM 40–41)

Sucking his pillow like a breast—or like Plath's "paps of darkness"[29]—Malone comes all the closer to the state of quiescence he seeks, which would also be a faultless and unbreached coincidence with "myself," an entity that is canceled by burial and darkness the moment it is found: search for self as search for the void, figured simultaneously as the womblike stasis toward which such sucking strives. Such is Malone's "happy" place in the world, at the ecstatic border of its leaving, its remainderless absorption of the thing about to sink into it. But where quiet and wisdom end, there is another ecstasy pulling fatefully in another direction, as Malone is called back "to the light" and to the things of the earth, that is, to the act of naming and invoking them in their irreversible absence, and he responds to this call with an obvious pleasure, making it clear that despite everything there is a happiness, too, in this compulsive draw of light and language to which he is subject. "Words and images run riot in my head, pursuing, flying, clashing, merging, endlessly" (MD 22; MM 40), as he writes in the same passage, and no word is ever truly the last one; it is not possible to arrive at the end of words by means of words, nor to the end of desire by the declaration that "I want nothing." (This paradox will of course be the driving force of *The Unnamable*.)

If he is being "given birth to into death," as he famously puts it, Malone is thus also in the process of discovering that this death is hardly facilitated by all his ceaseless chatter. His compulsion to chatter on nonetheless, and in particular to invent a "creature" from out of his unhinged language, is given an even clearer grounding in the following passage:

> Be born, that's the brainwave now. . . . Yes, an old foetus, that's what I am now, hoar and impotent, mother is done for, I've rotted her. . . . But why this sudden heat, has anything happened, anything changed? No, the answer is no, I shall never get born and therefore never get dead, and a good job too. And if I tell of me and of that other who is my little one [his invented creature], it is as always for want of love, well I'll be buggered, I wasn't expecting that, want of a homuncule, I can't stop [*par besoin d'amour, merde alors, je ne m'attendais pas à ça, d'homuncule, je ne peux m'arrêter*]. And yet it sometimes seems to me I did get born and had a long life and met Jackson [a hypothetical past acquaintance] and wandered in the towns, the woods and wilderness and tarried by the seas in tears before the islands and peninsulas where night lit the little brief yellow lights of man and all night the great white and colored beams shining in the caves where I was happy, crouched on the sand in the lee of the rocks with the smell of the seaweed and the wet rock and the howling of the wind and the waves whipping me with foam or sighing on the beach softly clawing the shingle, no, not happy, I was never that, but wishing night would never end and morning would never come when men wake and say, Come on, we'll soon be dead, let's make the most of it. But what matter whether I was born or not, have lived or not, am dead or merely dying, I shall go on doing as I have always done, not knowing what it is I do, nor who I am, nor where I am, nor if I am. Yes, a little creature, I shall try and make a little creature, to hold in my arms, a little creature in my image, no matter what I say. And seeing what a poor thing I have made, or how like myself, I shall eat it. Then be alone a long time, unhappy, not knowing what my prayer should be nor to whom. (MD 51–52; MM 84–85)

Being born and dying—these strangely conflated operations—are put off by the stories and the poetic invocations of life, which, it is important to note, are also invocations of past fictions: the landscape described here is one that Molloy knows well. But the true reason for telling these stories, for "creating" a creature, comes out like a slip of the tongue or an automatic confession: "for want of love." The shift from this abject but godlike gesture—necessarily an autobiographical one ("so like myself")—to a kind of ficto-cannibalism would seem to be another step toward the end, but there remains what Malone calls "my prayer," a continuation of speech with no content or addressee.[30]

This prayer is the very form of Malone's monologue. In addition to the "want of love," Malone admits in the end a "horror" which is at the basis of his verbiage, as he postpones the end that will not come of its own accord. Referring to his "themes" and fictional devices and figures, Malone writes:

> All is pretext . . . pretext for not coming to the point, the abandoning, the raising of the arms and going down, without further splash, even though it may annoy the bathers. Yes, there is no good pretending, it is hard to leave everything. The horror-worn eyes linger abject on all they have beseeched so long, in a last prayer, the true prayer at last, the one that asks for nothing. And it is then a little breath of fulfillment revives the dead longings and a murmur is born in the silent world, reproaching you affectionately for having despaired too late. The last word in the way of viaticum. (MD 107; MM 171–172)

These are the poles of Malone's experience, of Beckett's experiment: a speech in the void oscillating between nostalgic evocations and an impatient demand for a final silence and peace, for death and end. Now what is striking, and significant in terms of the question of the relation between destitution and sentiment, is that for Malone, trapped in his purgatory of writing, these two poles twist around, as it were, to intersect in the figure of a final "home" which is also the site of a perfect, uninterrupted peace: the womb,[31] the prebirth or postdeath fetus that is blocked by all this talk (whether of "life" or of an engendered "creature"), and even a delicious moment that can still be lived, for a brief instant, after all has vanished. Very near his end, Malone puts it thus:

> I am swelling. What if I should burst? The ceiling rises and falls, rises and falls, rhythmically, as when I was a foetus. . . . All is ready. Except me. I am being given, if I may venture the expression, birth to into death [*je nais dans la mort, si j'ose dire*], such is my impression. The feet are clear already, of the great cunt of existence. Favorable presentation I trust. My head will be the last to die. Haul in your hands. I can't. The render rent. My story ended I'll be living yet. Promising lag. This is the end of me. I shall say I no more. (MD 114–115; MM 183)

To be on the verge of death is identical to being on the verge of birth, for each would deliver one into a space of non-speech, where the I is not-yet or no-longer, and where the lack of language is projected as identical to a peace that can be found nowhere within language. For language, as dispersal and distance, is the ineliminable condition for any such projection, as it opens the fissures and faults, the "rendings" and railings, from which, structurally speaking, the I cannot itself be eliminated. It is merely the placeholder for the endless speech of death. Lyricism and expressivity are thus reduced to the longing and impatience, suffused into "pretexts" of speech, for a place that by definition they cannot quite reach (arrive at or return to), the nostalgia for a home that has never been inhabited; they are the not-quite of an irresistible but illusory movement toward an ultimate resting place; but also the enjoyment of evocation itself, an enjoyment arising only in the gap between language and its long lost referents. This gap constitutes the lyrical impulse in Beckett's voices, cultivated and indulged in even as it is derided.

The Unnamable

The separation of the fictional voice from the world, and from a projected end point, enters a radical and (almost) absolute phase in *The Unnamable*. In fact, the voice in *The Unnamable* attempts nothing other than to attain to a certain absolute status, both in the sense of being separated from every relation and as the point of a self-positing self-coincidence—the voice as absolute subject. The inescapable paradoxes of this project render this text almost unbearable in its suffocating atmosphere, its breathless and obsessional repetitions and impasses; but they also make of it Beckett's most comprehensive and radical experiment in the abyssal logic of the narrative voice. Not the least of these paradoxes is that between having "nothing to express" and being obliged to do so anyway, "for unknown reasons," as well as that—a corollary to the latter—between being obliged to express nothing in the void and finding that speech continually places the voice in relation rather to something of a plenum—a past, and an entire set of relations which, though bracketed, constitute the very structure of the voice, and impose on it its compulsive speculations. In discussing *The Unnamable*, I will not have much to say about lyricism, for this text is devoid of the transports and "throes" that make the first two volumes of the trilogy so strangely and incongruously beautiful. There is no sentimentality or nostalgia in *The Unnamable*; or if there is—if there is an impulse toward something like "home" and rest—it is not expressed nostalgically, but rather in the mode of a painful and impatient frustration. Unlike Malone, who still relates retrospectively to his life as a past whole (failed, and so on), the unnamable recognizes no past at all as his own. But in *The Unnamable*'s extreme sharpening of the voice's paradoxes, its elaborate cultivation of aporia and impasse, the grounding structure of the narrative voice as such is revealed, and the fundamental categories determining speech, identity and the past as a life that would be one's own are laid out exhaustively, and not merely abstractly but *en acte*, in the panicked speech of their destitution and disintegration. For this operation is carried out, and indeed made possible, by ensuring that none of these categories function, that they are in a state of constant failure, even as the voice they constitute drones on unceasingly.

How to describe what is essential about *The Unnamable*? This is difficult to do in the sense that the book's radical "accomplishment" lies just beyond the shreds of conventional and identifiable fictional form that it drags toward the terminal moment it approaches. However, it will help to map the book, however schematically, onto the progressive developments, or rather attenuations, carried out in the trilogy as a "series"

(Beckett's word) whose discreet elements are linked not in a continuity, but by multiple echoes and similarities.[32]

First there is the question of the explicit goal, mentioned above. If Moran seeks Molloy, Molloy seeks his mother, and Malone seeks death, the strangely surviving I of *The Unnamable* seeks nothing earthly whatever, not even the passage out of the earthly realm, for (one can infer) this has already been achieved, as it were, in Malone's death, or rather in his endless dying. The unnamable's goal is not a thing or person or place, nor even the end of life. Unlike Malone, he cannot wait for death, but rather, as a pure voice without life or name, he can hope for the only death possible for a voice—to go silent, to cease speaking. The problem is of course that he must do this *by* speaking. This problem generates much of the "drama" of *The Unnamable*, and it will be necessary to elaborate on the precise nature of this silence as we proceed.

Second, there is a progressive attenuation in terms of narrative structure. Molloy's and Moran's tales are told by them and about them, in the first person, and there is never any intrusion into the narrative of an explicitly authorial voice responsible for the whole. Malone, however, as an inventor of stories, is himself just such an intruding voice, immanent to the fiction but in turn creating a fictional world and interspersing his narrative with monologues and commentaries—thus introducing the decisive structural division between "creator" and "created" into the narrative voice and thematizing the figure of the narrating creator, along with many of the dilemmas that come with the job (what to say, how to continue the story, how to avoid "tedium," how to end it). Put another way, the *subject* of fictional creation is figured as such, and with this come the godlike responsibilities of fashioning a world, together with the sense that the entire game is simply a vain (and vaguely nostalgic) distraction from something more essential, in this case a "birth into death," a final end of everything. The margin between creation and ending is occupied by Malone's ruminative voice, which touches often on how things came to their present state, and the specific conditions of this vain activity. Now in *The Unnamable*, the voice is almost entirely reflective, telling only one or two "stories" and offering those not only as vain but also as ridiculous and farcical mockeries of storytelling. The "creative" gesture has been suspended, rejected as inane and revealed in its fundamental passivity, as well as its irrelevance to the goal projected out beyond all this: finally to say something absolutely true of himself, to say something *of* himself that faultlessly *coincides with* himself as speaking being, and therefore *is* himself—and thus, in closing the gap and fault of speech in speech, to make an end at last.

Third, the attenuation of space. Molloy's and Moran's stories, however bizarre, take place entirely on planet earth, and range over a considerable portion of it, through forests and fields and other vaguely Irish landscapes. Malone is rather in a kind of institutional purgatory, enclosed in a small space that appears to be continuous with some past life on earth, but that also separates him from it, placing him in an artificial space of dead sounds that may also be a Beckettian remnant-skull (MD 47). In *The Unnamable* we are finally *nowhere at all*, certainly not on earth or in the light of day, but in an indeterminate space that is both enclosed and limitless, all-encompassing and featureless.

What happens in this space? The question itself is perplexing. At first we are given a "description," such as it is, of the speaker's situation and of the things going on around him. "I have always been sitting here, at this selfsame spot, my hands on my knees, gazing before me like a great horn-owl in an aviary. The tears stream down my cheeks from my unblinking eyes" (U 6; I 11). From this position, and in a gray and leaden light, he sees none other than Beckett's own former "creations"—Murphy, Molloy, Malone, and so on—revolving around him like planets. But these revolutions hardly make for a story, and soon even these minimal conceits are dropped, or rather simply forgotten, as the speaker is absorbed entirely into the movement of speech. At one point, he asks significantly, "How, in such conditions, can I write, to consider only the manual aspect of that bitter folly? I don't know." He leaves it at that, adding only, as if to confirm the contradiction, "It is I who write, who cannot raise my hand from my knee" (U 17; I 24). Even the act of writing is not quite taking place in this strange space of writing, although this insistence on writing does establish something very important, if rather obvious: the words we read when we read *The Unnamable* are written words, and not the supposed stream of a supposed consciousness. This universe is made entirely of words, such that even these slight concessions to the logic of fiction—the positing of a world occupying space and filled by characters and events—is soon irrelevant. Even the speaker's body, of which much is made in the beginning—in terms of position and the like—is eventually dissolved into references to isolated parts whose functions are completely scrambled, such as a "mouth that hears," an "ear that sees." The only function that remains is that of the speaking voice, the only space the peculiar one opened by its speech as such.

Curiously, it is precisely here, in the rigorous refusal of fiction (as representation), that the radically fictional status of this text is located. The premise that an I inhabits an otherworldly space where he has always been and where nothing has ever changed, is extremely artificial, to say the least. But it is also here that "the real" intrudes in a way that is impossible in more conventional or "realistic" fictions. For it is this extreme artifice that allows Beckett to carry out an experiment revealing the conditions implicit in all fictional speech, if not in all speech period. The opening of an imaginary space that would be fashioned and "filled in" by a voice responsible for everything—this is the fundamental gesture of any fiction; here, however, it is presented in a state of complete suspension, an "empty" state which the speaker's weariness and equivocation prevents him from covering over with invented narratives and fictional situations (a weariness already prefigured in Malone's frequent interjections: "What tedium!" or, after beginning an episode, "No, I can't"). What is abandoned, then, is less fiction as such than *figuration*, the act of positing objects or characters that are then "naturalized" and treated, under a narrative logic, as real. What remains, therefore, is a voice whose positing gestures are self-consciously empty, "affirmations and negations invalidated as uttered, or sooner or later" (U 3; I 7–8), and yet who for some reason must still perform this gesture. The bond has been severed between the name and the figure, but the act of naming continues. That is the experimental "fiction" put into place by Beckett in *The Unnamable*, opening the voice onto the question of its own compulsion and its relation to its own source or sources.

What drives the unnamable to speak? Simply put, it is the fact *that he already speaks*. Toward the beginning he says, "The best would be not to begin. But I have to begin. That is to say I have to go on" ("*Mais je suis obligé de commencer. C'est à dire que je suis obligé de continuer*") (U 5; I 9). Beginning (here, at this arbitrary point) and continuing are the same, because the true beginning happened long ago, when, after some unimaginable prelinguistic state, speech began. "For he who has once had to listen will listen always . . . silence once broken will never be whole again" (U 110; I 132). Beckett's text relies on the notion of such a prelinguistic existence, and all its efforts are directed at "returning" to it, as it were. This lure goes under the name of "silence," a point at which speech, somehow corresponding without remainder with both the speaker and the spoken, would cease, in a final closing of the breach between language and discourse. This point, of course, remains terminally elusive, for a very simple reason: "The search for the means to put an end to things, an end to speech, is what enables the discourse to continue" (U 15; I 21). Speech cannot be silenced by speaking. And yet, for some reason, this impossible search is dictated from within language, once it has reached the degree zero I have described, where it reveals its determining limits, its originary structure.

In *The Unnamable*, this structure takes the form, first of all, of an obligation. At the end of the first paragraph the speaker says, "And at the same time I am obliged to speak. I shall never be silent. Never" (U 4; I 8). The notion of obligation comes up often, as does that of compulsion. These are not sharply differentiated, and in fact seem to be singularly merged. Already in the quote just cited it is very unclear whether the statement that "I shall never be silent" is made as a grudging resignation or as a resolute promise (the more verbal form of "being silent" in French seems to tilt toward the latter: "*Je ne me tairai jamais*"). "If only I were not obliged to manifest" (U 10; I 15). Odd obligation, to do something one cannot help doing and ceaselessly continuing to do. Beckett's text continually veers along the border between blind, pressing compulsion, on one hand, and vigilant, resolute obligation, on the other, making this one of its major paradoxes. Speech is bound to occur, and yet it is forced. What forces it?

The speaker often attributes his obligation to a "they" who somehow oversee him and are forcing him to carry out this task. At certain junctures, this "they" also appear to be responsible for introducing him into language in the first place, breaking the originary silence and inculcating him with all kinds of ridiculous ideas that continually obtrude into his speech. Many of the most sarcastic passages of the text are devoted to all the wonderful and valuable things "they" must have taught him (love, reason, God, Man, and so on). The supposition of such a "they" follows necessarily from the very open question as to where he got the language he is using and the "knowledge" and experience that this use cannot help invoking and drawing along with it, like unwelcome residues it cannot quite shed. "They" must have forced it on him, at some forgotten or unknown time, since surely he never would have taken it upon himself (and since he has never been in the world to learn about these things firsthand). "They" are therefore also the ones who, cruelly and mysteriously, require of him this impossible task.

This hypothesis, though richly used, goes the way of every other generalizable notion entertained in this text, and is recognized as sheer delusion. Or rather, to be more precise, it arises and fades away according to the shifting structure that determines it in the first place, a structure grounded in and organized by that of personal pronouns (they, but also I, he, and so on). It is impossible to overestimate the importance that pronouns have in the dizzying construction of the unnamable's monologue. Bereft of a stable name or identity, the unnamable is nevertheless supplied with every pronoun in the book, and takes full advantage of (that is, acutely suffers from) their definitive separation from the figures they would stand in for, shifting from one to another, whether strategically or accidentally, and developing his prevarications according to the logic imposed by each one. This can be illustrated with one simple example (among many possible): "They say they, speaking of them, to make me think it is I who am speaking. Or I say they, speaking of God knows what, to make me think it is not I who am speaking" (U 115; I 138). These lines capture both this text's vertiginous scrambling of speech positions and the radical paranoia that results. Who is speaking? When *I* do it is *also they* who speak (through me? to me? for me?), but their speech is indistinguishable from mine, or from *his*, this or that figure introduced into the narrative (I'll return to this) with a proper name, always replaceable by "I." True to Jakobson's characterization of pronouns,[33] the unnamable "shifts" effortlessly from one to the other according to a dizzying logic that never allows them to settle into a determined pattern of figures, *yet which constantly projects and evokes such figures by their very use*. If the use of pronouns, unmoored from all fixed referents, produces the illusion of determinate figures, it does so necessarily and inevitably, for that is the very function of pronouns—to designate "subjects" (in the grammatical sense) whose identity has already been established within the context of the present discourse. Fictional speech, of course, need not be hindered in the least by the absence of any such established identities (in the absence of a context), but in refraining from attaching pronouns to a proper name, as the unnamable does for the most part, does not eliminate the figural position opened by the pronoun; rather it invokes such a position only to leave it blank. But this blank *calls out*, as it were, to be filled in, for it necessarily brings with it the simple question: Who? Now if the pronoun in question is "I," then this question produces a very peculiar kind of illusion—not that of fictional figures or even a projected addressee (although these also follow), but the illusion of the speaking subject itself, as a fixed namable identity with a singular, determinable past. To paraphrase Kant, we might properly call this the transcendental illusion of pure (fictive) language, for it projects an originary subject where there is only a voice. But like Kant's transcendental illusions of pure reason, this illusion cannot be dissipated even if it is recognized as such, since it is structurally integral to the system that produces it. As Emile Benveniste showed in his classic articles on pronouns and subjectivity, pronouns have something of a transcendental function in language, because in indexing the "instance of discourse" in the present moment of speech, they mark the speaker's assumption of language as a whole.[34] This deictic function is supplemented, however, by a signifying function, determined by context; and this is precisely what is suspended in the speech of the unnamable. What comes to light in this situation is the simultaneous impossibility of naming the source of the voice and the imperious and insistent necessity to do so. The imperative bearing on the speaker is thus, "You must be someone," which immediately entails, according to an equally implacable temporal logic: you must *have been*. Thus the logic inherent to the structure of any speech whatever collides with its own necessary consequence, namely that "I," as such, is no one, and never has been. This collision is the form of the unnamable's torture.

Is it more correct to say that the unnamable tries and fails at this task of being/having-been someone, or rather that he refuses it in the first place? Both of these descriptions are pertinent, and while they appear to be mutually exclusive, they are also mutually reinforcing. The unnamable presents himself in a situation which seems to be imposed on him, in which he simply finds himself (a voice with no past life and an impossible task to fulfill), but it is clear that the work itself is structured by a predetermined strategy, an experimental premise of sorts, which *forbids* the voice to fully identify itself with any proper name or story, and which thus forecloses the pronominal references it cannot help mobilizing. More concretely, this formal *interdiction*, as it were, resonates in the affective register of a deeply disillusioned lassitude regarding the entire game of fictive projection, the dupery of "characters" (the "tedium" about which Malone has already complained). The unnamable voice nonetheless attempts at certain points to carry on with the farce, in ever more farcical figural reductions, through the derisory and hopeless leap by which the figures named Basil, Mahood, and finally the unimaginable Worm are invented—and at a certain level, this impossible leap is an effortless operation, a mere matter of words. But for this very reason, all of these "creatures" remain painfully artificial and contrived, as irrevocable in their being as they are "evocable," as easily dissolved from the identity foisted on them as they were subjected to it by mere speech. They do not coincide, and the series—the chain of signification and substitution, the jangling play of figures and names—comes to reveal its own unclosability, which is also that of identity itself. And so, true to the logic of a radically fictional voice, the unnamable maintains his "creative" distance from every possible proper name he might use—but here, "creative" means simply that the patent fictitiousness and arbitrariness of every name remain acutely evident and are never naturalized. And this means in turn that, since he is after all concerned with "himself," his origin and his destiny, he is faced with the quandary of being *a voice* belonging to no one, with no assignable past, and no stable unity of experience. There is nothing more insistent in this text than this particular "blank"—and all of the others proceed from this one. How could there be a voice where there is no experience, that is, no birth or infancy? How could a voice speak where there was never a passage, under particular circumstances, from infancy into speech, and thus into a singular history? The suppression or "blanking" of this linguistic-historical dimension in the voice's speech is what makes the unnamable's present so impossible, but it is also what helps to render its experiment so radical; for it reveals this dimension in a pure (precisely "blank") state as the fundamental condition of the speaking voice, its "transcendental" condition of possibility, and thus as a condition that haunts, too, every "successful" identification between a pronoun, a proper name, and a life that is someone's (mine, yours). The pronominal scattering of identification is at the basis of every "I," and of every speakable and viable identity.

That this pure or blank condition is projected in the unnamable's speech as a "silence" once lost and yet to be obtained is therefore not surprising. This silence is quite literally a kind of infancy, and Worm—the closest this condition comes to being named and figured—is indeed something like a fetus. "Worm" is the name for an impossible figure, one who is not yet one, who cannot speak and is not even sentient, and yet who would somehow be an "I." Recasting the text's major paradox in yet another form, the speaker, who longs for silence, longs therefore, during a certain stretch of his speech, to be Worm, but of course knows he cannot be both "I" and Worm. The (empty) name for a being who has not yet been disturbed by "the sound that will never stop" (U 85; I 103), Worm is incompatible with the language that is the voice's sole mode of existence, but also with even the most undifferentiated and passive reception of the world. At one point he says, "I'm worm, that is to say I am no longer he, since I hear" (U 86; I 104). Unlike Mahood (who is vaguely human), and all the other creatures of the voice (Murphy and the like), Worm is a figure of the unfigurable itself, and he is thus, somewhat surprisingly perhaps, the very name of the transcendental in this text. Worm is the unfigurable "beyond" of the voice, its structuring limit, the silence that recedes from it in both directions (past and future) and impels it on—and so also its most intimate condition of possibility. Worm is the sensate silence elusively inhabiting all speech.

It is noteworthy, of course, that this "figure" of transcendence is so *abject*. He is spoken of at times like an anti-God, for example as "all-impotent, all nescient," and is the objet of a parody of Cartesian reasoning: "Feeling nothing, knowing nothing, he exists nevertheless, but not for himself, for others, since others conceive him and say, Worm is, since we conceive him" (U 82; I 99). The logic by which an ultimate instance is arrived at through a serial ascent to greater power and perfection (and proven by the fact of being conceived as such) is turned on its head here—revealing a being with no head, no top or bottom, no front or back. But the compelling illusion persists, of a superlative ultimate instance locatable at one end or another of an irresistible movement ever onward (whether in ascent or descent it is difficult to say). Indeed, the speaker is tempted at times, by the very nature of his end-seeking project, toward a transcendental illusion which Kant explicitly diagnosed: the end of the series (of causes, origins, or grounds) as God. If, in relation to his creatures, the voice is a creator, then it follows that someone is the operator of his creation as well, and of his speech; at the end of all the "they's" there would be "the master," the absolute subject, beyond which nothing. But of this the speaker says: "The master in any case, we don't intend, listen to them hedging, we don't intend, unless absolutely driven to it, to make the mistake of inquiring into him, he'd turn out to be a mere high official, we'd end up needing God, we have lost all sense of decency admittedly, but there are still certain depths we prefer not to sink to" (U 122; I 146). Better to sink to the depths at hand, rather than straining "upwards," through some Kafka-like bureaucracy, toward the highest instance. To this illusion, the unnamable prefers the one presented by Worm, but this preference reconfigures the very notion of transcendence not as supremacy and power but as an ultimate abjection—one that is immanent to language but inassimilable to speech. The abjection of transcendence (in every sense) is stubbornly and progressively carried out by Beckett's voices as they tend to greater and greater destitution *within speech*, as they approach their most irreducible limit point in silence—their *own* silence—for which Worm is the "ultimate" paradoxical figure. As such he would be the guarantor of an autonomous structure robbed both of its ground and its "vocation" and scattered into the whirling dust of pronouns in search of stable names—that is, into radical fiction and its endless circulation.

Now, in the perspective of such a movement, what would a silence of one's "own" be? One that is somehow on the other side *of language*, in relation to language (not absolute) and yet somewhere out beyond it, or rather between it and something that can be called "sensation," but also "thought." "But how can you think and speak at the same time, without a special gift, your thoughts wander, your words too, far apart, no, that's an exaggeration, apart, between them would be the place to be, where you suffer, rejoice, at being bereft of speech, bereft of thought, and feel nothing, hear nothing, know nothing, say nothing, are nothing, that would be a blessed place to be, where you are" (U 122; I 145–146). If *The Unnamable* takes on any lyrical tones at all, it is in the evocation of this "blessed place" located *between* the suffocating terms of language (but nowhere else):

> he the famished one, and who, having nothing human, has nothing else, has nothing, is nothing. Come into the world unborn, abiding there unliving, with no hope of death, epicentre of joys, of griefs, of calm. Who seems the truest possession, because the most unchanging. The one outside life we always were in the end, all our vain life long. Who is not spared by the mad need to speak, to think, to know where one is, where one was, during the wild dream, up above, under the skies, venturing forth at night. The one ignorant of himself and silent, ignorant of his silence and silent, who could not be and gave up trying. Who crouched in their midst who see themselves in him and in their eyes stares his unchanging stare. Thanks for

these first notions. And it's not all. He who seeks his true countenance, let him be of good cheer, he'll find it, convulsed with anguish, the eyes out on stalks. He who longs to have lived, while he was alive, let him be reassured, life will tell him how. That's all very comforting. (U 82–83; I 100)

Undercut throughout by little slices of irony, this passage nevertheless expresses a certain pathos attached to the abject figures in Beckett's narratives and to the prospect of reaching a place that has always been there, and finally being "the one outside life we always were in the end." But this pathos, related directly to "life," is thus a pathos of transcendence, opening onto an outside of destitution and sensate silence far from the subject—"epicentre of joys, of griefs, of calm." This too is one of the radical revelations of *The Unnamable*, namely that transcendence is structured not only as language but as affect, as a *Stimmung* verging strangely, even here, in the direction of sentimentality; and it is in this ambiguous relation between language and affect that the compulsion to speak merges with the obligation to do so, according to an imperative determined as the proper end of the voice.

The relation to life and experience (having *had* a life, speaking out of a singular experience), which generates so much lyrical tension in *Molloy* and *Malone Dies*, is reduced in *The Unnamable* to an opaque and merely structural presupposition, a "blank," as I have called it, which insists on a content despite its radical foreclosure. This is why the last work in the trilogy is so much less "expressive" than its predecessors: it has nothing positive (no given material, no stable history) to be expressive about. Its expressivity is literally forced, by the very fact of its speech (someone must be speaking, I must be speaking, I must be someone who can say who I am, and so forth). Although, as the preceding quotations show, its language approaches a kind of lyricism when the question of a "blessed" sensate silence emerges as a beautiful prospect to be longed for in the eternal void, a strange postlinguistic "infancy" for which Worm seems to promise a figurable term. The return to this silence is linked directly with the return of the "life" that has been foreclosed, a return that disrupts the void space from the very beginning with an indefinite affectivity. In the opening pages (the "preamble" as he calls it), as the unnamable describes his situation in his unearthly and history-less abode, he intersperses several remarks of this sort: "So I have no cause for anxiety. And yet I am anxious" (U 18; I 25), or later, "So there is nothing to be afraid of. And yet I am afraid." To this latter he adds: "afraid of what my words will do to me, to my refuge, yet again" (U 20; I 27). In *The Unnamable*, fiction is once again a refuge—the more absolute the better—but one constantly besieged by the very historical and affective conditions that make speech possible, and that return to wreak havoc on the fiction of pure fiction. The unnamable presents his situation as imposed on him, but it must be admitted that it was also sought and cultivated, insofar as the fictional project for Beckett involves escape into a kind of refuge, however treacherous it is known to be, a flight into a radically other space where the voice can, to all appearances, leave behind the life so stubbornly attached to it. In the opening sentences of *The Unnamable*, the speaker wonders: "Can it be that one day . . . I simply stayed in, in where, instead of going out, in the old way, out to spend day and night as far away as possible, it wasn't far. Perhaps that's how it began" (U 3; I 7). To "stay in," where the "inside" is transformed into the place "where I have always been" and where no trace of the past remains except the voice itself: some thirty years later Beckett used these precise formulations in laying out the premise for *Company*, which shares many of the structural and temporal problems elaborated in *The Unnamable*, and which I will consider in the following chapter.

CHAPTER 9

Company, But Not Enough

In his essay "L'écriture du générique: Samuel Beckett,"[1] Alain Badiou points to a "*mutation majeure*" in Beckett's work occurring around 1960, after the trilogy and the *Textes pour rien*, and beginning especially with *Comment c'est* (1961). He claims that Beckett's experiments work their way out of the solipsistic impasses of *The Unnamable* by opening themselves to the possibility of an encounter—an unexpected event or the disruptive presence of an other (the relation of "the Two" or "the couple," as Badiou puts it). In many respects, it cannot be denied that such a "mutation" occurs in Beckett's work, and that texts such as *How It Is*, *Happy Days*, *The Lost Ones* or shorter pieces like "Enough" attest to a thinking of alterity and sociality very unlike what one finds in the monologic voices of the early trilogy. But it is an exaggeration to say that these experiments represent a massive shift from the earlier work. Badiou is indeed one of the first readers of Beckett to recognize that, as he puts it, "the stripping-down of the 'characters' . . . their poverty, their illness, their strange fixity, or else their wandering with no perceivable finality, all that has often been taken for an allegory of the endless miseries of the human condition, are only the protocols of an experiment."[2] These experiments seek, through what Badiou calls a "methodical ascesis," to articulate a "genericity" of the human, its fundamental and irreducible categories, "the treatment, by means of writing, of that which alone constitutes an essential determination."[3] But Beckett's fictions arrive at these essential determinations first of all through the functional category of the voice, which dominates all others (including those of "self" and "other"), and the problem of the fictive voice that must arbitrarily posit a world which it is entirely responsible for bringing into being—the problem of the solitary "creator"—is one that persists throughout Beckett's work. After the trilogy, it often hovers over the fictions like an unresolved question that threatens to ruin everything, if confronted directly. Beckett does not eliminate this problem in his later works, rather he suspends it, turns away from it, remains wary of its abysses, and plugs the hole it opens in the fiction with temporary stopgaps (such as in *How It Is*, where the question presses but is not pursued; in fact, it arises most persistently at the end, precisely in connection with the final dissipation of the whole). *Company* (1980), which in its last word ("Alone") would pose a major exception to Badiou's scheme, is the work in which this question returns and is treated again most explicitly.[4] In its simultaneous avoidance and posing of the question of the "creator," it is particularly appropriate for an exposition of the paradox examined in the previous chapter, which a reading of *Company* will allow us to elaborate in the starkest possible terms, and with a sharper sense of the specifically autobiographical dimension at issue.

Badiou points out that the enclosed spaces of Beckett's fictions are set up like experimental laboratories.[5] This is true of *Company* in the most literal way. Its "premise" is presented in the form of an experimental "proposition" that lays out all of the basic elements of the text and defines the parameters within which it will unfold. The short opening fragment (the entire text is divided into discrete but interrelated fragments) initiates the experiment with a statement that is both an indefinite suggestion and an absolute positing gesture: "A voice comes to one in the dark. Imagine." The next fragment begins to elaborate the scene to be imagined, summing up the basic parameters of the situation thus:

> That then is the proposition. To one on his back in the dark a voice tells of a past. With occasional allusion to a present and more rarely to a future as for example, You will end as you now are. And in another dark or in the same another devising it all for company. Quick leave him.

This situation seems relatively simple, but it is already riddled with ambiguities that the text will never fully resolve. The "proposition" seems to be made *ex nihilo*, and the existence of what it posits seems to be entirely hypothetical and virtual, a question of sheer "imagining"; but these positing gestures, and their initial elaboration (the one in the dark is "on his back," the voice tells not just anything but "of a past") are immediately cast as the mere reporting—not the imagining—of a situation already actually existing. The figure of "one in the dark" is elaborated thus:

> To one on his back in the dark. This he can tell by the pressure on his hind parts and by how the dark changes when he shuts his eyes and again when he opens them.

The pure positing gesture is replaced by another operation altogether, that of deduction based on sensory givens, and at the same time the one who imagines is displaced by the one in the dark himself as the source of (information about) the scene. What has happened to that other "devising it all for company" who is presumably the speaker of these lines and the "subject" of the imagining carried out here? Where did this body come from and how was it endowed with sentience? Is this situation being posited in the void by an as yet unlocated "deviser" (as he will be called), or does it in some sense already exist with all the material density of a "real" situation? Are the unknowns of this situation (such as the size of the space, the position of the voice, etc.) simply blank variables that can be filled in only by a quasi-divine act of fiat, or must they be discovered, or perhaps deduced, according to the protocols of reason and the force of empirical experience? Is this situation suspended in timelessness (the "timeless void" as it is called at one point), or does it have a history? Who is the one devising it all, and why must he be avoided? ("Quick leave him.") Finally, are these three figures (voice, hearer, deviser) truly separate or are they the dispersed aspects of a single figure, presented in a kind of exploded diagram?

These questions can be understood according to the distinction introduced at the beginning of the previous chapter between a logic of *ex nihilo* creation in the void and a logic of "birth," in a retrospective narration drawn out of a life and harrassed by the stubbornly resurgent residues of past time. In *Company*, these incompatible logics function side by side, and with considerable tension, as neither of them is ever completely resolved into the other, and in the end neither decisively dominates the overall fabric of the text.[6] The one in the dark is both a purely fictive creation suspended in a timeless experimental present, *and* a figure with a history who has somehow arrived at this situation as the final phase of his "life," at the endpoint of the past told of by the voice speaking there. What is remarkable, however, is the way in which Beckett's text shows that both of these aspects insistently point to an autobiographical dimension of fictional narration, whether in the form of some ultimate deviser fashioning the fiction from outside, or on the level of the figure's own narrative compulsion, which introduces stories of "a past" even into the timeless void; and both of these aspects implicate Beckett himself. *Company* is Beckett's most openly autobiographical text, not only in that he uses a number of episodes recognizable from his life,[7] but also in the sense that it demonstrates the stubborn insistence of a singular past—a past that demands to be recognized as "my own"—even in the most rarefied act of fiction. If fiction necessarily implicates a "deviser," it also implicates a devising *voice*, and with this the door is opened to the dreaded singularity of a past. The refrain that occurs when this deviser looms—"Quick leave him"—shows on the one hand that in *Company* the abysses of *The Unnamable* are guarded by the particular dread they inspire, but also, on the other, that the difficulty of having a story of one's own has become at the same time the impossibility of not having one, once a voice is instantiated and begins to operate its fictive narrations. As we will see, *Company* stages a scene in which the fictive voice's inability *not to* express itself seeps into the blank forms of fictive language (space, time and material, but also grammar and syntax), even as these forms keep life (as "mine") forever at a distance.

I have said that the two sides of this paradox are never fully resolved into one term. And yet the end of the text suggests that they do: that the hearer, the voice and the deviser are in fact a single figure who has distributed "himself" across these three terms only in the end to come back to the synthetic unity (Kant's phrase is à propos) subsisting all along. After the voice has related its stories of a past—one of which tells of having "entered dark and silence" for good (C 17), thus bridging the gap between life and the present void—it comes to an end by (apparently) tying everything together:

> But with face upturned for good [you] labor in vain at your fable. Till finally you hear how words are coming to an end. With every inane word a little nearer to the

last. And how the fable too. The fable of one with you in the dark. The fable of one fabling of one with you in the dark. And how better labour lost and silence. And you as you always were.

Alone.

This would seem to settle the question, relating everything in the end to a lone subject who has merely detoured his miserable situation into fictional devices, to no avail. But the gaps opened by these devices (between the hearer and "his" story, between the voice and the speaker's past and identity) are not so easily closed. Their disposition in the text according to the "proposition" may be artificial, but it is not sheer arbitrary artifice; rather this disposition is itself made possible by separations which are constitutive of language and which the "proposition" simply breaks down and stages in this rudimentary fashion. The deviser's "devices" which I will discuss here reveal disjunctions already operating in any narrative voice, but smoothed over by an apparently faultless functioning. In *Company*, a set of "faults" or fissures is introduced into the narrative voice such that its functioning—as an autobiographical I—is in a state of radical failure, and through these faults is revealed an originary dispersal of the subject of language that no solitude can unify—but without which no singular experience (no spoken life) would be possible.

Though they converge in the end, both sides of *Company*'s paradox remain unresolved. I will begin by focusing on the "analytic" side (the three elements of the experiment and the devices used to keep them separate) before considering the "synthetic" side (the unified "subject," the voice's stories and the continuous life they plot), in an attempt to articulate the compulsion that destructures, even as it makes possible, the speech of a voice as a relation of a past that would be its own—and that gives away a voice as necessarily having been someone's.

The most important "device" is the very reference to a deviser. It is this reference that indicates an "outside" to the space "in the dark" and establishes this space as a set of blank variables that must be spoken into determinacy. By referring to a deviser of "it all," the text places an outer frame around itself as a totality, but also implicates the one responsible for the whole, and so continually displaces the frame ("Quick leave him"). That is, the one who, like a god obliged to speak it into existence, is confronted with the blanks implied by the opening proposition, and is responsible, must *decide* how to fill them. How is such a decision possible? On what grounds can it be made? At one point in his deliberations, the deviser says: "The test is company" (C 26). It is after all "for company" that he devises "it all," and the "need" or "craving" for company is mentioned several times as his reason for devising. The problem is that, since this deviser is of course not a god but is himself merely a voice, all of his devisings are null and void, they remain mere *nominations* and not actual creations—mere "figments" as he puts it—and so are unable to provide much in the way of company. Hence the extremely equivocal procedures of the deviser, most of whose speech is taken up with proposing and retracting possible "contents" for his empty space, usually quite derisive, such as "a rat long dead" or "a fly to brush away" (he also considers various postures for the hearer, as well as possible names). After all, why multiply the emptiness? These decisions are therefore always deferred, though the blanks call out to be filled in. This "call" of a blank toward its material fulfillment is rendered literally in one instance, when the question of the hearer's abode arises. What is it made of? "Basalt is tempting" (C 33), Beckett writes in English, rendering this in French as "*le basalte appelle*" (C 44). Despite such a "vocative" temptation, this too is "left undecided," but we see emerge here something very significant: Why would basalt in particular call out so temptingly in the timeless void? What is involved in filling in this abstract variable with a specific material—in this case precisely the variable "material" with the material called "basalt"? Compelled by the logic that demands that if there is an abode, it must be made of something, the deviser is called and tempted here by nothing other than experience, singularly and unaccountably drawn by the familiarity of a specific material, or at least by its name, which in either case would have had to be acquired. Such a decision would thus singularize both the abode of the hearer and the deviser himself, who by giving in to this temptation—responding affirmatively to this call—would be giving himself away, at the very least as someone with this minute point of experience and this unjustifiable preference. (On another level, who knows what associations Beckett himself may have had with the word, or the substance.) The important point here is that this suspended passage between blank variables and determinate contents is the suspension of fiction itself, which as such brings into evidence the *demand* opened by any initial premise, however schematic. By staging the passage into the concrete (or: into the basalt) as an equivocating decision, Beckett suspends the "god-function" of the fictive voice and at the same time reveals the impulsiveness required for multiplying the emptiness through such names.

Aside from the inaugural "proposition" itself, there is only one other moment when this decision is made as a fiat-like positing gesture; the passage in which it occurs makes clear the blind impulsiveness required: "Another devising it all for company. In the same dark as his creature or in another. Quick imagine. The same" (C 33). Several pages later this addition is confirmed when it is elaborated in terms of the "crawling creator" crawling, and falling, somewhere near his creature (the hearer).[8] Of course, this inclusion of the creator within the space of his creation does not settle the question of the deviser, who remains tenaciously external to any such "figment," even one assigned his own function. But it makes clear the danger of an eventual (self) exposure lurking in the "creative" gesture, together with the threat of an infinite regress.

The problem of the deviser—the "who" responsible for "it all"—is thus particularly stubborn; he is referred to at one point as "that cankerous other," as though he were an unpleasant excrescence of the fictive situation, a sore that will not go away. His more transcendent manifestation, similar to one of *The Unnamable*'s temptations, is broached in a passage that refers explicitly to that work and preempts its pitfalls:

> For why or? Why in another dark or in the same? And whose voice asking this? Who asks, Whose voice asking this? And answers, His soever who devises it all. In the same dark as his creature or in another. For company. Who asks in the end, Who asks? And in the end answers as above? And adds long after to himself, Unless another still. Nowhere to be found. Nowhere to be sought. The unthinkable last of all. Unnamable. Last person. I. Quick leave him. (C 24)

A correlate to the question, Who decides? is an even more elementary question: Who speaks? This question, too, is left in suspension here. It cannot be answered with a proper name, and the infinite regress that results leads to a theological conclusion that Beckett parodies with his pseudobiblical language ("His soever"). And yet this passage stages a very serious and profound insight, for it shows—through a voice's question about its own origin, and thus the origin of "it all"—that this fundamental question of metaphysics and theology coincides precisely with the question of the fictive voice; and further that this question is structured at bottom *linguistically*, by the foreclosure of proper names and the emergence of an incessantly shifting pronoun: I. The first person already contains a projection of the "last person . . . of all," and is in fact the only possible "name" for it ("I am that I am"), but this name instantly points beyond itself to an ultimate instance that is "unthinkable" and "nowhere"—in other words, unfigurable and transcendental. But the transcendental status of the I, once it is located entirely within language itself, leads into language's native abyss, as it were—that of a voice definitively unmoored from names and figures, attempting to take hold of its own constitutive spacing, the gap and fault that distances *what* it says from the brute fact *that* it speaks. And this is a trap that must be forestalled lest the tortures of the unnamable begin again: "Quick leave him."

For this reason, in addition to banishing proper names, *Company* uses another device: the banishment of the I itself. The third fragment of the text, just after the statement of the "proposition," lays out the rules for pronouns to be observed in the experiment:

> Use of the second person marks the voice. That of the third that cankerous other. Could he speak to and of whom the voice speaks there would be a first. But he cannot. He shall not. You cannot. You shall not. (C 8)

The voice says "you." It addresses its stories to the hearer as though they were his own. The deviser says "he," but if he could speak to the hearer and of the hearer at the same time, there would be a first: he would say "I"; he would be both addressing himself and designating himself, as someone does who talks to himself in solitude. But for some reason "he cannot." Seen as an *incapacity*, this absence of the first person is mysterious, but at another level it is perfectly clear: it is forbidden by a commandment, "He shall not," which becomes another pseudo-biblical locution: "You shall not." By the very nature of what is being forbidden, this is a self-interdiction in every sense. It is addressed by the deviser to himself, but it also forbids that there be a self. The transcendental illusion of the I is thus placed under a ban (implicitly a ban on "graven images" and idols, on transcendental *figures*), and is displaced by the illusion that self-reference can be avoided by means of this trick. But the fact that a voice necessarily speaks of and to itself—even if through its delegates (he, you)—is acknowledged in more than one passage with statements such as this: "He speaks of himself as of another. He says speaking of himself, He speaks of himself as of another," and so forth. What all of this controlled but dangerous slippage demonstrates, finally, is the cankerous residue of self-reference adhering to the third person—as well as, conversely and simultaneously, the alterity to itself that is already inherent in the I. If the banished first person persists in the form of a detoured self-reference, it is also the case that the possibility of this banishment is already contained in the I, insofar as it necessarily has its place in relation to the other pronouns from which it is distinguished. In other words: "I," as an empty place marker, structurally implicates "you" and "he," in relation to which alone it takes on its own function. Put yet another way, there is no voice without self-designation, but also no self-designation that is not already fissured by the differential structure of pronouns.

Beckett's use of this structure as a "device" has substantive consequences for the "subject" of his narrative. As I pointed out, it also entails the banishment of the self, or rather of the subject, as such. In the timeless void of *Company*, there is no locatable subject, only subject functions: devising, speaking, hearing. By dissociating these, by exploding them as in a diagrammatic *breakdown* (in every sense), Beckett suspends their synthetic unity. This also means suspending history, and in particular the history of the hearer himself. As an unspeaking hearer with a mere minimum of mental activity, the one on his back in the dark has no history but only hears the stories of the voice ("You did this," and so forth) without recognizing them as his own. What has essentially been suspended and exploded, then, is an identification, the linkage of appropriation. The voice's stories belong to no one, neither to him nor to the voice itself, which is a pure voice function, a mere mouthpiece generating its stories as though from a combinatorial grammar machine. The deviser describes its delivery precisely in these terms:

> Another trait the flat tone. No life. Same flat tone at all times. For its affirmations. For its negations. For its interrogations. For its exclamations. For its imperations. Same flat tone. You were once. You were never. Were you ever? Oh never to have been! Be again. Same flat tone. (C 20)

Not coincidentally, the grammar machine speaks of being. Beckett's examples, reeled off like the exercises in a child's lesson book, indicate the ontological stakes of these variations. Reduced to a lifeless series of empty grammatical variables, can a voice ever express the drama of being someone? Can its stories be "my own"? Can one who uses this language (any language) ever really be? This passage, with its evocation of Hamlet, reduces the tragic theatricality of subjectivity to a residue of syntax and punctuation. And yet it is important to notice that *this residue persists*. "Oh never to have been!" Even as a subjectless statement ground out by a grammar machine, this sentence literally screams with a pathos it is not easy to eliminate. However blank and schematic, it calls for a context by which it is haunted, emptily, and projects a singular situation in which it would be enunciated, and most any reader who understands it will oblige in filling this in. In other words, it calls to be singularized in a voice attached to an experience, which is structurally implied by the very fact of being proffered in this enunciation. But Beckett's "voice" in *Company* is one that we are asked to imagine without such an experience, and the hearer as a body likewise deprived.

The gap across which the voice speaks to the hearer is a gap introduced into identification, into the assumption of an I and a past as one's own. Although besieged by the voice's stories, the hearer has no past, and yet, paradoxically, he does understand the voice and is sensitive in some way to its deadpan discharge—a fact that necessarily implies a past. "The voice is company but not enough," says the deviser, adding that "its effect on the hearer is a necessary complement" (C 9–10). The nature of this effect is obscure, to say the least, but it is clear that it is not self-recognition:

> Another trait its repetitiousness. Repeatedly with only minor variants the same bygone. As if willing him by this dint to make it his. To confess, Yes I remember. Perhaps even to have a voice. To murmur, Yes I remember. What an addition to company that would be! A voice in the first person singular. Murmuring now and then, Yes I remember. (C 16)

With the banishment of the I comes the impossibility of a voice and of memory (and the impossibility of creating company). To speak in the first person and to recognize oneself in a past is here equated with a confession. We are beginning to see that the situation at hand is one where the suspension of memory and identification would be resolved by force of speech, and thus that the voice has a purpose. Accordingly, the deviser considers a possible "optimum position" for the voice "from which to discharge with greatest effect," and wonders at what volume it might more likely achieve its object, which is:

> To have the hearer have a past and acknowledge it. You were born on an Easter Friday after long labour. Yes I remember. The sun had not long sunk behind the larches. Yes I remember. As best to erode the drop must strike unwavering. Upon the place beneath.[9] (C 34)

The scene in the dark is a scene of torture, whether as the *extraction* of a confession from an unspeaking body, or as the sheer *imposition* on it of a history that has never been its. Here too, these perspectives exist irresolvably side by side. From the point of view of the devising creator, the voice is coercing the hearer to accept a past that, along with everything else, has been conjured in the void. Its success would mean that, at the impossible moment when the body would speak and say "I remember," it would only be retrospectively assuming a history contained nowhere but in the language of the voice.

The example makes this clear: by insisting that he "remember" his own birth, and even the events of the day before, the second-person voice points up its own fraudulence and artifice. Though it is also the case that this is exactly how "memory" is transmitted collectively, by means of narration and its fantasmatic appropriation ("Yes, I remember the day you were born," and so on). This is the very model of the voice's coercions, and Beckett's joke reveals that to appropriate a language is also to be forced to accept, from another, the prehistory of a birth (the history of infancy). But what is truly in question here is not biological birth (nor living memory) but the birth of a self-referring voice as a response to an insistent address, the passage of the infant body into language and into sociality (into company).[10] Beckett makes this even clearer in another passage where the deviser, deliberating again on the voice's optimum position, brings it to rest "above the upturned face," and wonders: "Height from the ground?"

> Arm's length. Force? Low. A mother's stooping over cradle from behind. She moves aside to let the father look. In his turn he murmurs to the newborn. Flat tone unchanged. No trace of love. (C 47)

The voice's flat and repetitive stories are likened to the murmurings of parents "torturing" their infant into speech, sociality and identity. The scene staged in *Company* is nothing other than this "primal" scene lying at the origin of every I, every voice and every singular experience. But here it is staged in a state of breakdown and failure—a failure ensured by the devices that schematize the fictive void while also revealing the separations and dispersals constitutive of "successful" conjunctions of speech, material, and history, together with the compulsive forces behind their narrative syntheses.

It is here, however, in this strange scene of prenatal torture, that the paradox hinges around its ambiguous temporality and reveals its other aspect as an endless post-mortem recapitulation. For the stories imposed in the void can also be seen as the hearer's own, in a state not of eternal and absolute failure but of massive disavowal and repudiation. From this perspective, the voice is not visiting itself upon the body *ex nihilo*, it is *returning* from a life long left behind to a situation into which this body has attempted to *escape*. In this sense, the voice is harassing the hearer with memories he has spent a lifetime putting behind him; what has failed is not "having a past," but on the contrary the attempt to silence past experience by vaporizing it into the ether of algebraic formalism and "creative" abstraction. Now what is remarkable about *Company* is the way in which it links the impulse to escape—and the schematic situation into which this leads—with the very impulse to narrate a past *as it is determined within that narrated past itself*. In other words, the algebraic-grammatical operations in which the present of *Company* unfolds are pre-traced, as it were, in the narratives that appear to lead there. This can be clarified only by laying out the shape of the stories themselves, and of the trajectory traced out by these fragments taken together.

This connection (between the narrated past life and the void devised as timeless) is indicated most notably in what might be called the obsessional style of the stories—the style of their telling and that of the life they tell of. The style of the voice's narrations is no less deliberate and methodical than the deviser's imaginings, but in the story fragments the voice does not linger over undecidable particularities; in its insistence and specificity it has always already determined its variables, so to speak, filling them in without any of the deviser's hesitations. (Put another way, the schematism is fully functioning, and the preinscription of specific forms is materially available.) But they are the same variables, and details of shape, size, volume and material are often meticulously given by the voice. This style even has a name; quite strikingly, the deviser associates it with "reason," a form of thought that weighs so heavily on his devisings and imaginings that he asks at one point: "What kind of imagination is this so reason-ridden [*si entachée de raison*]? A kind of its own" (C 33). The notion that the universal and abstract forms of reason (whose "pure" form is rejected in one passage[11]) could be something of one's "own"—a singularized quality—can only be understood in terms of style, and it is precisely the *incision* and elaboration of this style (or stylus) that we see occurring in the stories themselves. Obsessional, to say the least, it leads as though compulsively to the present situation in the dark, and in this sense can be thought of as *fatal*.

The first story presented in the text is not chronologically the first—the hearer's birth is presented second, as though this first episode were somehow more decisive. Indeed, it seems to narrate the *coup d'envoi* of the entire tale, or a first incision that lays down the patterns it will follow. Combining sentiment and reason in a moment of painful rupture, it is told with a precision that leaves no room for error and bears directly on the provenance of the scene in the dark:

> A small boy you come out of Connolly's Stores holding your mother by the hand. You turn right and advance in silence southward along the highway. After some hundred paces you head inland and broach the long steep homeward. You make ground in silence hand in hand through the warm still summer air. It is late afternoon and after some hundred paces the sun appears above the crest of the rise. Looking up at the blue sky and then at your mother's face you break the silence asking her if it is not in reality much more distant than it appears. The sky that is. The blue sky. Receiving no answer you mentally reframe your question and some hundred paces later look up at her face again and ask her if it does not appear much less distant than in reality it is. For some reason you could never fathom this question must have angered her exceedingly. For she shook off your little hand and made you a cutting retort you have never forgotten. (C 10–11)

We are not told what this cutting retort is,[12] but how can we fail to relate it to the quasi-material operation the voice would carry out as it drops its words "upon the place beneath"? But rather than slow erosion, there is a sudden cut—one that opens the wound of a "never forgotten" remark strangely implicated in the impossibility of saying "Yes I remember." These are the inverse sides of the compulsively droning voice, as though this cut opened what Becket called the "oozing" of the voice itself as an ineluctable return to, and of, this moment, its "cankerous" residue. The images of cutting, torturing and wounding (in French, Beckett renders "a cutting retort" as "*une réponse blessante*") point to a dimension of affectivity that would be at the heart of this originary moment: the "never forgotten" becomes a point of compulsive speech not only because it is "unfathomable," but because *it hurts*, and somehow continues to hurt—precisely in the mode of a (flat, affectless) reason-ridden narrative speech constantly exceeding and rupturing the forms of "reason" in which it seeks a refuge. But it is precisely the violence of reason's rupture that fixes it as the dominant style of a voice hereby recounting its own origination. For what does this episode relate if not, together with an injuring mother tongue, the *aggravation* (quite literally) of reason as a means for securing the world as a measured and ordered whole, in which the disjunction of appearance and reality would be reconciled? Or rather: in which the play of mere images (sky as appearance, sky as "it is . . . in reality") would be systematically governed, and grounded, by the language that names it. But this reason, too, is a fiction—indeed, it is the very form of fiction, and the dehiscence of fiction is likewise revealed to be the essence of reason itself. The violent separation of the mother, who "shook off your little hand," does not counter but rather confirms the violence of reason, voiced already in the child's disruptive question, as it shatters the continuity of the phenomenal world. This shattering leaves its debris embedded in the "unfathomable" space opened in this scene, and by extension in the voice that has come to relate it, marked as it is by a fixation on measurement and counting and by the excessive "material" with which it cannot have done. The originary infliction staged here, in the manner of a sublime excess leaving reason itself in vacuity and ruin, thus leaves its mark as a compulsion to return which, however, is doubled by a compulsion to escape more and more into abstraction, and in this way it initiates our story.

This fatal style and its progressive flight into abstraction is developed by the voice in later episodes. The most elaborate presentation of this form of escape is given in the long section beginning "Bloom of adulthood. Imagine a whiff of that." The voice tells of the hearer waiting nervously for his lover "in the little summerhouse. A rustic hexahedron," and gives its exact dimensions. This strange mixture of irony, anxiety, geometry, and the bucolic is brought to a head when, after a flashback to father and son in the same little summerhouse—a reverie indulged in by the waiting lover—the voice goes on:

> She is late. You close your eyes and try to calculate the volume. Simple sums you find a help in times of trouble. A haven. You arrive in the end at seven cubic yards approximately. Even still in the timeless dark you find figures a comfort. You assume a certain heart rate and reckon how many thumps a day. A week. A month. A year. And assuming a certain lifetime a lifetime. Till the last thump. But for the moment with hardly more than seventy American billion behind you you sit in the little summerhouse working out the volume. (C 39–40)

In the midst of these figurings, his lover arrives. "The violet lips do not return your smile." There follows a long passage in which, as the two lovers face each other through the window, he closes his eyes and, wondering "if she has not sunk to her knees," mentally dismembers her body in order to determine whether she is sitting or kneeling outside, by comparing proportions of shins, upper legs, torsos, etc. "You leave the pieces lying there [?] and open your eyes to find her sitting before you. All dead still." In the dead still of the rustic hexahedron, he discovers that she is pregnant. "You go back into your mind. She too did you but know it has closed her eyes." As Beckett wrote in *Murphy*, "What he called his mind functioned not an instrument, but as a place," and here this is true even when the mind's functions are reduced to those of a calculator. What kind of place is it? The passage is clear: a refuge of pure abstraction in which "figures" can be manipulated effortlessly and without regard to material constraints, a "haven" from which all excess (anxiety, fecundity) has been excluded, a realm of measure and precise calculation available even when the incommensurable is "sitting before you." Life itself becomes a matter of calculating "thumps" of the heart: "Until the last thump," at which point death too could be summed up in a simple number, in a process of accounting that leaves no remainder. All that is required to enter this place is to close the eyes, and the darkness this brings is the first hint of the final darkness to come. Speaking of the hearer the voice exclaims: "How given you were both moving and at rest to the closed eye in your waking hours! By day and by night. To that perfect dark. That shadowless light. Simply to be gone" (C 41).

These tactics remain effective only up to a point. In reference to this game of "gone," in which all material and affect disappear by a kind of magical gesture, we can ask a question as naive as the boy's question about the sky, and just as disturbing: Where does it all go? As the experience of the "you" in these stories is reduced more and more to the blank spaces and abstract forms of "reason," what happens to the singular life that would be left behind in this way? And, if in fact it is left behind, what is the principle of its return? It is no doubt already clear that the voice itself is the insistent point of this return, gathering in all its flat endless repetitiveness the narrative "material" that has somehow been sliced away from the hearer's body, inflicting it on him as though out of revenge, and with more than a hint of bad conscience. The last phase of the hearer's earthly existence brings this point home.

This phase takes the process of abstraction, erasure and escape to its furthest extremes, and leads to the impossible transition from a life on earth to the otherworldly space of originary torture. It tells of a figure who is a kind of trademark of Beckett's fictions: a derelict old (or ageless) figure (in this case a man) with long white hair, wearing ancient boots, an overcoat and a worn-out block hat, all black, more or less. In *Company*, with the exception of a couple of passages where he stares immobile, this figure does nothing but walk in silence with bowed head, staring at the ground before him, counting his footsteps and stopping occasionally to add the sum—"then on from nought anew." At first his "father's shade" is with him, apparently as a figural remnant of a life long since left behind, a last residue of a heritage taken on, in part, by imitation: in the fragment relating the day of the hearer's birth, the father is a walking-escaping predecessor who leaves the house for a long hike, to avoid "the pains and general unpleasantness of labour and delivery." But in another passage we read that this shade "fell out long ago," leaving the hearer to continue with no other figures than his sums, on a path of progressive darkening, silencing and flattening of all specific singularity. "Unhearing unseeing you go your way. Day after day. The same way. As if there were no other any more. For you there is no other any more." The walks become automatic and machine-like, the exact same direction and distance every day, such that this "experience" is nothing more than a pure repetition of the same, made possible by reducing all difference (of steps, of days) to a series of marks, a serial operation whose totality or synthesis renders only a sum without remainder. The old man's "life" has become a process of "figuration" in the blankest, most restricted sense possible, as though in the end reality were nothing but a seamless, measurable continuum, and experience nothing but the registering of an uninterrupted linear progression of discrete and identical traces, and paces.

Of course, the head "finally bowed" (C 36) for good is a sufficient sign of the excessive weight that this process drags along despite itself, but the voice tells yet more explicitly what makes it hard to continue in this streamlined path of escape. Telling the hearer that, although he never used to halt "except to make your reckoning," and although there is no longer any need to do that (since every day is the same)—"save perhaps at the outermost point. To gather yourself for the return"—the voice recounts how he halts as never before, stopping inexplicably in the snow, hesitating on his heavy feet, in "a speechlessness whereof the gist, Can they go on? Or better, Shall they go on? The barest gist. Stilled when finally as always hitherto they do." This extremest point of impossible continuation opens, in the voice's narrative, onto a "vision" that occurs only later, and retrospectively:

> You lie in the dark with closed eyes and see the scene. *As you could not at the time.* The dark cope of sky. The dazzling land. You at a standstill in the midst. The quarter boots sunk to the tops. The skirts of the greatcoat resting on the snow. In the old bowed head in the old block hat speechless misgiving. Halfway across the pasture on your beeline to the gap. The unerring feet fast. *You look behind you as you could not then* and see their trail. A great swerve. Withershins. Almost as if all at once the heart too heavy. In the end too heavy. (C 38; my emphasis)

The extreme point of abstraction is also the point at which the heavy heart returns to claim its due. But this return occurs only in the time of narration, once the material deposited, as it were, in the heavy heart has been rendered into a voice, the narrative of a past. Across the divide separating him from his life, the hearer "sees" what this language alone can make visible: the "beeline to the gap" is in fact "a great swerve," in other words a turning (troping) movement which marks the path of escape as an "erring" that exceeds pure (conceptual) form, a singular trajectory that twists away from the artificial fate of sheer calculation. This divide, evoked by "the gap" toward which he rambles, is the space in which this swerving path appears for the very first time, from out of the very impulse to discard the dull heaviness that draws it out in the first place. Beckett relates this space to Hell—refuge and torment of poetic language—by means of the curious word he uses for the turn leading there: "Withershins." While evoking the feeble limbs carrying such a "heavy heart," its more precise meaning (according to *Webster's*) is "in a direction contrary to the apparent motion of the sun." This counter-sun, which is also the straying of sense and meaning given by a *contresens* (*widdersuns* or *widdersinnes*), can be associated with Dante's wandering, in the first lines of the *Inferno*, off the straight and narrow path ("*la diritta via*" [I.3], "*la verace via*" [I.12]), away from the light of day, toward a place that is found "*là dove 'l sol tace*," there where the sun keeps silent—but where the poet wanders as a witness to the tortures that his own voice will have devised.[13] Beckett makes this connection explicit in his French version (as though he realized it was not very clear in the English), where he renders "withershins" as "*dans le non-sens des aiguilles*," then adds a phrase not found in the English: "*Comme aux enfers*," like in Hell (*Compagnie*, 68). The impossible transition between life on earth and the hell of originary inscription is related by the deviser in the following way: "Slowly he entered dark and silence and lay there for so long that with what judgment remained he judged them to be final," and later by the voice in the last long section: "when you could go out no more you sat huddled in the dark," a position which gradually shifts to the permanent supine. It is in this gap, this indiscernible border between an unspeaking life and the deathlike machinery of language—but also between a life that has dwindled irresistibly toward death and a linguistic animation that is life's only remnant—that *Company* locates the impulse to speak as an insistent return, in a reemergent image that the voice alone gives to see.

UNSTILLABLE: THE FAULT OF LANGUAGE

The point of this return is encountered as an inhuman extreme within the human. This extreme has two names which seem to be opposed but in fact are not, for they have a common source in language: "reason" and "affect." I have not attempted to offer a full account of how these notions are woven through Beckett's texts, which are both "reason-ridden" and lyrical unto sentimental. But I would like to conclude by pointing out how Beckett articulates a compulsion to speak deriving from their common source and constituting also a strange poetic obligation, an imperative located at the very origin or opening of language as a singular voice.

In *Company*, reason separates language from life (as appropriated narrative). But as we have seen, language easily and already lends itself to this separation. Its forms and rules become a refuge and haven from pain and anxiety, its coldness and impersonality lead into a space determined as pure form, blank variables. But insofar as these forms are set into motion by a voice, they are also coerced toward a singular origin. On one hand, reason requires totality, it dictates an end, and thus initiates a drive, assigns the task of reaching that sublime end. In Beckett this end takes the form of an ultimate speaker, a deviser or creator responsible for the whole, an unfigurable figure who can never be located. This task fails, but does not eliminate the drive, which is already established within the voice insofar as it is constituted by the possibility, and the nagging necessity, of asking "Who speaks?" The means of coming to an endpoint must be found within language. In the meantime, however, the world and the past have disappeared, experience has been evacuated into pure form. And yet a relation to these remains even in extremest separation, a relation that is precisely one of loss. It is in the space opened by this loss, in the hell of reason's apparent counter-sensual trajectory (withershins), that the voice emerges as sentimental, nostalgic and lyrical: separated forever from life, it longs for a "home," a final resting place which is also the point of its origin, an indescribable sensate silence. Silence replaces God in Beckett's metaphysics—an ironized but dramatic metaphysics that enacts a raw subjection to language's transcendental illusions—and the drive of reason toward sublime, ultimate ends merges with an affective drive that seeks to regain the void. Or rather, it would be more accurate to say that silence replaces God as the moment of transcendence assumed (and projected) by this search, and that reason itself is inhabited by a drive determined as affect in Beckett's language: pangs, craving, need. The persistence of such a drive—presented also as a drive "for company"—in the most stripped down, isolated and minimalized space possible, is figured in this passage from *Company*:

> In another dark or in the same another devising it all for company. This at first sight seems clear. But as the eye dwells it grows obscure. Indeed the longer the eye dwells the obscurer it grows. Till the eye closes and freed from pore the mind inquires, What does this mean? What finally does this mean that at first sight seemed clear? Till it the mind too closes as it were. As the window might close of a dark empty room. The single window giving on outer dark. Then nothing more. No. Unhappily no. Pangs of faint light and stirrings still. Unformulable gropings of the mind. Unstillable.

These unstillable pangs, stirrings, and gropings are the ineliminable residual movements of "the mind" which were initiated with some first rupture of the silence, and which no amount of isolation or abstraction will bring to rest: "there's no recovering from that" (as Malone says).

The task dictated by reason thus becomes a compulsion originating in the very opening of a voice. This compulsion is one that would eat or bore its way through language until it reached the outside of language from which, supposedly, it first came. This silence is not absolute nothingness, however, but a strange margin of sensation between speech and nothingness. *The Unnamable*: "I think I'll soon be dead, I hope I find it a change. I should have liked to go silent first, there were moments I thought that would be my reward for having spoken so long and so valiantly, to enter living into the silence, so as to be able to enjoy it, no I don't know why, so as to feel myself silent, one with all this quiet air shattered unceasingly by my voice alone" (U 153; I 183). This sensate silence is the elusive and illusory moment of transcendence in Beckett's universe. At the same time, it is important to note that something of this silence takes sensible form and seems to supervene at certain moments of hiatus indicated here and there in Beckett's narratives. Most notably in *Worstward Ho*, where the voice asks: "What when words gone? None for what then. But say by way of somehow on somehow with sight to do" (WH 29). What does silence have to do with sight? Another passage tries to say: "Less. Less seen. Less seen and seeing when with words than when not" (WH, 40). The transcendence of language would take the form of pure sensation, in this case pure seeing.[14]

The possibility for such silence is perhaps least evident in *Company* than anywhere else in Beckett, but even *Company* contains an indication, at least, of what might lie beyond or behind the torturous voice:

> You are on your back at the foot of an aspen. . . . You feel on your face the fringe of her long black hair stirring in the still air. Within the tent of her hair your faces are hidden from view. She murmurs, Listen to the leaves. Eyes in each other's eyes you listen to the leaves. In their trembling shade. (C 47–48)

Here pure listening is conjoined with a sentimental memory, whose nuance of feeling and sensation manages to vibrate through the combinatorial of reason. From the voice of a mother over a cradle, to that of a mother's "cutting retort," to the voice in the dark, to this voice of a past lover, *Company* forms a chain indicating, somewhere beyond it or within its interstices, a liberation of hearing both from memory and from reason. But it is first necessary to *pass through* the traces of the past and the structures of reason and language (logos) in order to reach *its* other side, an outside proper to and made possible by this passage alone: the transcendence *of* language (in every sense) in the fugitive and unpredictable hiatus of speech.

This is why Beckett necessarily encounters, with the void fictive spaces established in so many of his works, the insistence of a prior inscription. The longing for the void necessarily collides against the obstacles already written into the language through which this longing must pass. *Company* gives a brutal image of the insistence of the past, but its return is discernible in other less torturous moments. Even the "meremost minimum" of figures in *Worstward Ho* indicates the tenacity of past life in the void of pure fiction. In trying to say or missay the vague and schematic figures in the "dim void," the voice inevitably settles on something recognizable; the voice turns "back to the bowed back alone. Nothing to show a woman's and yet a woman's. Oozed from softening soft the word woman's. The words old woman's. The words nothing to show bowed back alone a woman's and yet a woman's" (WH 35). This impossible, ungrounded decision— if we can thus characterize this product of a strange word-bearing mucosity—is unaccountably informed by an insistent figuration harking back to life on earth.[15] The other two figures in *Worstward Ho*, an old man and a child walking hand in hand, are equally unjustifiable: "Nothing to show a child and yet a child. A man and yet a man. Old and yet old. Nothing but ooze how nothing and yet" (WH 45). This "nothing and yet" is the refrain pointing out of the void to a past experience insisting and obtruding from out of *some* singularity, however indeterminate and distant. "Blanks for when words gone," writes Beckett; but on the way to the blanks is the oozing and gnawing of a singular experience, a single time, *une fois*, opened by an incision made long ago, a pre-inscription that returns in the mode of "oozing," "preying" and "gnawing."

This inscription raises the specter of an originary moment, when the silence was broken and the endless noise initiated. Among so many other instances, in a passage from *Faux départs* (an early version of "Imagination morte imaginez"), Beckett names the void toward which this breaking points, as though to something "unbroken": "*Si ça pouvait être tout sur moi enfin. Et seuls désormais l'autre vide, le silence et le noir sans* faille" (CSPr 271; my emphasis). Which can be translated: "If only that were it for me at last. And henceforth only the other void, silence, and the *faultless* dark." There is no better way to indicate the uncanny merging of compulsion and obligation in this retrojected originary moment than to remark the curious fissure introduced by this fault or "*faille*," from now on (*désormais*).

We recall that in his essay "Il faut," Philippe Lacoue-Labarthe points out that "*falloir*"—on which "*il faut*," the statement of obligation par excellence in French, is based—is related etymologically to *faillir* (to fail to . . . or to almost . . . do something) and thus to an entire constellation of words indicating failure, lack, and falling short: *défaillance* (breakdown or faltering), *faillite* (bankruptcy or collapse), *défaut* (default, defect or lack), and *faute* (fault, error or mistake).[16] And that the obligation expressed in the "*il faut*" is traversed by failure, fault and shortcoming, so that the compulsion it enjoins is also, strangely, an incapacity, or even a compulsion toward and into failure and faultiness, an "it is necessary" that simultaneously says something like: "it is faulting."

We can certainly add to this list of terms the *faille* that Beckett calls up here, along with the obtrusive remnant specter of its repair: a fault in the sense of a crack or fissure that, once opened, makes it *impossible not* to go on. The fault conjured here would be the originary opening of speech in the faultless void of in-fancy—and thus also the opening of experience and history—charged with a strange poetic responsibility, a groundless obligation pressing into painful compulsion and drawing out the stubborn residues of a life, its empty imprints and endless reverberations.

CONCLUSION

Speech Unredeemed
From the Call of Conscience to the Torture of Language

This study began with the figure, the generative topos, of a conscience that forms the writer, structures the law of writing, and even, in Kafka's case, gives scenographic shape to the fictions demanded by this law, in a process whose violence quickly comes into the foreground. This violence permeates the fictive worlds constructed from this scheme. In Kafka's search for the writer that he must become, and for the proper "space" in which to become it—cold and unlivable, or fired beyond mere living—the bite of conscience loops back onto itself in complex and paradoxical figures. But this loop forms, above all, the space of a *voice*, the resonance of a call or "invocation," as Kafka makes clear in a founding schematic projection: "And always an invocation [*Anrufung*] in my ear: were you to come, invisible court of justice" (D 31; TB 25). This invocation is *his own*, in every sense. A call that calls forth the one who calls, it is also a voice that vocalizes (in a *Stimmung* of productive anxiety) its own schema of emergence, its instance and "author." One of its first paradoxes is that if it hits its target, the one who aims is also the one aimed at, and so is immediately subjected to the very power thus assumed, in a logic that, as we have seen, requires in the end a corpse to guarantee it. The loop and bite of conscience thus seals into visibility, as in the circumscribed scenographies of Kafka's judgment narratives, the self-canceling program of its production—but not without a remainder, a survival that is precisely that of a text, or, more generally, the literary voice itself considered in its aspect of endless, unstoppable speech. We see this most clearly and brutally in Beckett (in whose unnamable voice tortured and torturer are merged), but already in Kafka the specific form of endlessness and interminability, the form of the novel, induces a shift from the explicitly juridico-legalistic schema into another more open-ended and "vocal" mode of fiction that I have designated with the term *report*. It is unclear to what extent this later narrative mode in Kafka is substantially, or one might say genealogically, continuous with the tormented and unending voice in a text such as Beckett's *Unnamable*, which is itself shot through with quasi-juridical speech structures and an unverifiable intimation of punishment (which, if it "were to come" as such—as unambiguous punishment—would constitute something of a relief). But the clear indications of such a continuity give rise to a disturbing question: Does a "call" that was long dignified as being "of conscience" find its peculiar *literary* truth in the torture of mere compulsive speech? Put another way: does *The Unnamable* voice the truth of *Being and Time* (at least insofar as the latter hinges crucially on the experience and analysis of this call)? And if this is the case, is it necessary to strip even this indefinite qualifier "of conscience" from a "vocal" phenomenon that may always have constituted the finest but sharpest kernel of literary experience, but that also, in emerging as such, pulverizes the thing thus constituted, as though reducing it to the dust of its own image? As the unnamable puts it (in a sentence quoted by Blanchot), in the pointless flurry of language, "I'm all these flakes . . . this dust of words" (U 139). This hypothesis has haunted the margins of the present study, even where conscience, guilt and their limits in compulsive speech were not directly in play. In this conclusion, I would like to look more directly at what is at stake in such a hypothesis. But I would add at the outset, playing on the figure just evoked, that even something that has been pulverized continues precisely thereby to leave a remainder and residue, and perhaps one that it is more impossible than ever to eliminate—although it may be more difficult to discern and delimit.

MOLLOY'S IMPERATIVES

There is a peculiar moment toward the end of the first section of Beckett's *Molloy* that cannot fail to draw our attention, namely when Molloy invokes what he calls his "imperatives" (MoE 117; MoF 116). Wandering in deep woods but feeling summoned to move on, Molloy grapples with this "voice" drawing him on, the neglect of which risks arousing "the painful impression of committing a fault, almost a sin" (MoE 116; MoF 116). Molloy would prefer to stay where he is, to stay in the forest, but, he says, "I could not stay, in the forest I mean, I was not free to. That is to say I could have, physically nothing could have been easier, but I was not purely physical, I lacked something . . ." (MoE 116; MoF 116). Curiously, Beckett added this last phrase, "I lacked something," to his English translation, providing a suggestive clue as to the mode of faulty excess that reaches beyond "the physical," in a way that echoes with Kafka's hunger artist and his "full to bursting" anti-being, the panther who "lacks nothing." Like the hunger artist, what Molloy lacks is not food, not something graspable and assimilable, but precisely something "beyond"—although for Molloy, and at this stage in Beckett's gradually self-stripping, self-minimizing trilogy of novels, this beyond is concretely spatial (outside the forest), and the thing it strives toward is specifically identified. Molloy refers to it as "this matter of my mother" (MoE 117; MoF 117) and his relations with her. It is in this light that Beckett parodically, but quite accurately, invokes the Kantian language that occasionally punctuates his work, in this case in one of Molloy's countless ironic asides: "Charming things, hypothetical imperatives," he muses. This odd recognition of the status of "my imperatives" as being bound to a specific task, a given and namable end, creates a crucial internal distinction between Molloy's "end" and the unnamed term toward which the trilogy is moving, approaching it much more closely in *The Unnamable*'s more categorical imperatives, and in the compulsion to move, in speech, toward no discernible end, or toward an end stripped of all qualities and all names. Already Molloy complains that his voice and its imperatives are fickle, unreliable, that they go silent and abandon him just when he has set himself in pursuit of their invocations. And indeed, it is in this silencing of every "hypothetical" call that the rest of the trilogy develops its torturous objectless speech in the direction of its own impossible transcendental, namely silence itself. I would note finally that Molloy's aside on the charm of hypothetical imperatives comes directly after the surprising remark that this imperative voice spoke to him in Latin, saying "*Nimis sero*," which could be translated loosely as "way too late." It is way too late to reach the hypothetical end projected by the imperative he cannot help following, for the mother may be long extinguished—in which case the hypothetical imperative has already merged imperceptibly into one that is de facto categorical, in that it is already deprived of any such projected ends, whose illusory avatars merely wait to be exhausted. The torture of the absolute, in the name of an unattainable end in "silence," is already nigh. This is a silence marked enigmatically by what Molloy, deep in the woods, calls a "murmur," and later hears in the incredible sound of a gong, a phenomenon he comments on with astonishment: "A horn goes well with the forest . . . But a gong!" (MoE 120–121; MoF 120). Molloy appears to announce, in a pure distant resonance that is incongruous with the nature that would frame it, the endless vibrations of an unnamable voicing that cannot cease. And this "silence" is already in league with a call that has been *dépouillé*, stripped to the point that it has become as "categorical" as it is empty, as tyrannical as it is vain. Its only commandment says: Speak. All questions of guilt and exoneration can only follow from this nonground, as they inevitably but illusorily do in *The Unnamable*, where thought itself is cleverly folded into this illusory projection, in the well chosen term that Beckett uses for this supposed punishment when he calls it a *pensum*. Even without any discernible "fault," thought, as speech, in its relation to an unreachable beyond of speech, is necessarily structured by an empty call of guilt.

HEIDEGGER AND THE CALL

It is thus not difficult to "hear" one's way "back" from *The Unnamable* to Heidegger's well-known analysis of the call of conscience in *Being and Time* formulated two decades earlier. As a phenomenological and ontological analysis, Heidegger's chapters on "the call" necessarily tend toward the emptying of any signifying content, indeed of any concrete "sounding out" (*Verlautbarung*) of the call, reducing its "discourse" to a single word: "Guilty." But this word is itself stripped of any reference to specific deeds or omission of deeds, and thus to any positive or effective judgment thereof. The call's "Guilty" is not a judgment. It is rather the "attestation" of a grounding structure of Da-sein. The German *Schuldig*, in its connotations of indebtedness and answerability (for . . .), opens for Heidegger the possibility of generalizing the structure of "guilt" beyond any given "*existentiell*" fact and thus to empty guilt, and the call that voices it, of anything other than the "nullity" (*Nichtigkeit*) that "grounds" Da-sein in its projected forerunning thrownness, as "being the (null) ground of a nullity," *das (nichtige) Grundsein einer Nichtigkeit* (SZ 285). This is the paradoxical crux from and toward which conscience "speaks," and it is in this crux, in the propulsive movement generated out of it, "vocally" and in the demand to do justice to finitude, that anything like a Heideggerian thinking of ethics would have to be based. It also formulates, in its near-tautology and its looping, suspended double negativity, the central structure of Heidegger's analysis of Da-sein, its *Ab-grund* or abyssal ground.

For our purposes, what is crucial is the resonating emptiness, the silence and "reticence" (which Heidegger insists on; SZ 296), and the objectless vector of conscience which in *Being and Time* all take the form, after all, of a *voice*, an uncanny speech that one must either heed or avoid—and a speech that is "vocalized" in the *Stimmung* of anxiety. To be sure, we do not yet quite hear the torture of *The Unnamable* in such a calling but silent voice (on the contrary), but many readers have remarked on the similarities between the indefinite but originary guilt it makes heard and the unlocatable guilt that haunts *The Trial* as a kind of ironic but constitutive transcendental limit. Here, too, we find Kafka and Heidegger strangely working over similar ground, and in the reading of *The Trial* presented earlier I attempted, in this perspective, to locate Josef K.'s exit from the regime of definite scenographic judgment, and from the "business" of his everyday life, in an indefinite anxiety that emerges explicitly here and there, but that in fact governs the entire novel (and as the affective and discursive dimension that opens the narrative to the long form). One could even formulate a certain very specific parallel: just as Heidegger criticizes Kant for reducing conscience to an image of the tribunal, and works instead to open the call, and the guilt it gives to be heard, into the indefinite field of anxiety and uncanniness, likewise does Kafka distend and distort that same image (so emphatic in his fiction up to then), to the point of withdrawing from the fictive world any direct enactment in judgment and punishment, leaving precisely nothing but anxiety and language as the actual field of the proceedings' unfolding. But as a writer of fiction, that is, as an artist who must not only analyze but execute and display the linguistic experience that follows from such a shift, Kafka shows us something that Heidegger does not: even in the space of the court's receding judgment, and in the uncanny separation from "the everyday" and from established forms of discourse, the "silence" of the call necessarily enters into its converse form in endless, anxious social speech (and, more specifically, of interpretive dialogue, a mark of the rabbinical influence in Kafka). In this space, Heidegger's distinction between "idle chatter" and authentic speech-in-reticence breaks down, and we are given over to the inessential and swarming movement of social speech as effective but uncontrollable *rumor*, as though to a phenomenon whose structure lays the ground of both law and literature.

As suggested before, one of Kafka's great insights is one that penetrates the tangled intersection of these two registers of discourse, a knot fully grasped by neither but in which each constitutes the other, in a simulacrum of speech that generates *real socially consequent effects*. Kafka's multiple, serial, and in principle endless novelistic dialogues represent a long and persuasive performance of this insight. Again, we do not quite yet hear the Beckettian torture in this speech as such—though it is certainly suggested by the flogger's beatings and the humiliating abuses of the Kaufmann Block. In this and other respects, we do find ourselves in a space that has not cleansed itself of the specter, at least, of punishment, and of the persistent, obtrusive and impossible question as to what it could be for. Thus does art draw thinking back into the inevitable singularities that philosophy would bracket (even in a philosophical discourse that foregrounds singularity, as does the early Heidegger's), and gives a face, an aspect and a texture, to the figures it invokes. Heidegger's "poetic" philosophizing, which already in *Being and Time* hovers on a strange border between conceptualization and figuration, is nonetheless spared the ordeal of its most extreme figural implications, and remains at some distance from what can be called the grain of the voice. For that we must listen to the poets themselves.

LANGUAGE SPEAKS (*DIE SPRACHE SPRICHT*)

Heidegger, however, never quite listened for anything so material and minute in scale (despite his extremely detailed readings), and he has rightly been accused of drawing only on the "gnomic" or signifying elements of the poets he comments, insofar as these both originate and countersign the ambitions of his thought. Further, one could argue that in Heidegger's general posture with respect to the tradition he addresses, and especially in his readings of the "great" German poets, there is a more or less explicit sublimity that is never quite destituted enough, despite the tonality of dearth and distress that rings throughout. Put another way, and from a different angle: Heidegger does not renounce his gods. But it could also be said that this tonality, so resonant and haunting in Heidegger's later works, and so audible in his peculiarly suggestive writing, does after all place his discourse in close contact with the extreme destitution that we have been tracing throughout this study. It is especially remarkable to note the echoes between this discourse and certain elements of the much crueler (if much funnier) world of Beckett—who in *The Unnamable* wrote (as though in answer to Heidegger), "It is easier to raise a shrine than bring the deity down to haunt it" (U 78). Once again we find our authors at work on the very same terrain as the twentieth century's great thinker of spiritual desolation, uncanniness, and poetry.

The somewhat surprising resonance between *The Unnamable* and the late Heidegger could warrant a more detailed treatment. I will limit my comments to a few observations bearing on one of the preeminent essays by Heidegger on language and poetry. Called simply "Language" ("*Die Sprache*"), the opening piece in *Unterwegs zur Sprache* was first presented as a talk in 1950. This marks it as a close contemporary of *L'innommable* (written in 1949), a fact that, I think, indicates emblematically the strange soundings these very different writings cast in much the same direction, toward the origin and essence of speech in "pain" and "silence." But they are a pain and a silence that ring, that "call," quite differently in each case—a point that can be illustrated by comparing Molloy's gong and its unsettling announcement with *das Geläut der Stille*, the "ring of stillness" or "silence" evoked by Heidegger in his talk, in a poetic space where the evening bell still seems to mean something.[1]

From *Being and Time* to "Language," this call has shifted its seat or site from conscience to poetry, in a move that confirms our sense that the call of conscience is a phenomenon that is already implicitly *literary*. Poetry, too, makes heard a call, but one that is structured less as a silent voicing of originary guilt than as a poetic naming that "primordially calls" (here Heidegger uses the verb *heissen*) "the intimacy of world and thing to come." Heidegger speaks in the same passage of an "originary calling" ("*das ursprüngliche Rufen*") and an "authentic bidding" ("*das eigentliche Heissen*"), where *heissen* indicates precisely a kind of calling that designates and names the thing called as itself.[2] My point in bringing out this shift is that it occurs across a continuity that allows us to articulate, directly if disjointedly, the earlier call of conscience with the call of poetry in Heidegger's later thought, such that the element of language and speech in the latter emerges covered, if you will, with something like the afterbirth of conscience, or at least with the genealogical markers of its descent from a mode of discourse formally structured by an originary "guilt." Schematically put: poetry (literature) is inhabited and driven by the call of an empty but pressing guilt—an incompletion or indebtedness (though it can also be called gratitude)—that forms its most intimate and indefinite imperative, an imperative *to hear and to call in turn*. This affirmation, which has marked the outer boundary of the present study, is thus discernible not only in the three authors addressed here but in Heidegger's texts as well. However, as mentioned, what one has more trouble finding in the latter's presentations is any hint of the grueling, endless, and tormenting ordeal that such an imperative gives rise to, *en acte* and in the irrecoverable absence of any determinate horizon—that is, following Heidegger, of the juncture where the divine would touch the world.

And yet the essay from 1950 is not without its aporias and abysses (not to mention a "pain" so intense and longstanding as to "petrify" the very structure of dwelling). "Language" is the first text in which Heidegger works with the non-tautological tautology in which his interrogation claims its proper beginning: "Language speaks." *Die Sprache spricht*. It is in this little phrase that the abyss of language opens, and Heidegger does not hesitate to draw our attention to it.[3] But let us watch what he does in the face of this abyss, for it is rather the opposite of what the authors discussed in this study have done in the face of their intractable and bottomless tasks, namely he *goes upward to the heights*:

Language is: language, speech. Language speaks. If we let ourselves fall into the abyss denoted by this sentence, we do not go tumbling into emptiness. We fall upward, to a height. Its loftiness opens up a depth. The two span a realm in which we would like to become at home, so as to find a sojourn for the life of man. (*Poetry, Language, Thought*, 191–192)

Die Sprache ist: Sprache. Die Sprache spricht. Wenn wir uns in den Abgrund, den dieser Satz nennt, fallen lassen, stürzen wir nicht ins Leere weg. Wir fallen in die Höhe. Deren Hoheit öffnet eine Tiefe. Beide durchmessen eine Ortschaft, in der wir heimisch werden möchten, um den Aufenthalt für das Wesen des Menschen zu finden. (*Unterwegs zur Sprache*, 13)

But what happens if the "depth" of the abyss is no longer "spanned," bounded, or (literally) "measured across" (*durchmessen*) the lofty heights gained by this attitude, as it casts its gaze over a landscape of dearth in search of a homely (*heimisch*) locale where man might properly sojourn in thingly inwardness?[4] Surely there is no better place to search for an answer to this question, precisely in the years 1949/1950, than in the prose of Samuel Beckett. For it is there that we see a manifestation of this experience, that *language speaks*, in its irreducibly brutal, naked and compulsive form. But we will do so by way of one of its most incisive contemporary readers, the Blanchot of *Le livre à venir*.

NOTHING ADMIRABLE

The prose in *The Unnamable* is indeed one that goes "tumbling into emptiness," with a peculiar and paradoxical *resoluteness* that calls into question Heidegger's occasionally heroizing elaboration of that concept, along with the entire structure of being-toward-death as the movement toward an end that *can come*, that is able to happen. Here, too, fiction presses thought, and the thought of death in particular (so central to twentieth century philosophy), into zones of experience made possible only by the collapse of what Adorno liked to call "aesthetic distance"—a distance that has defined philosophy since Plato.[5] Put simply, the literary voice has long known that it necessarily outlives itself, outlives life, and carries on its most essential operations in a space where no end can ever reach it. It is impossible for a philosophy such as Heidegger's to withstand such a neutralization of ends without revealing the nostalgia underlying its invocations of wholeness and retrieval. In *Being and Time*, death is the guarantor of this residual wholeness. In the later Heidegger, it is projected into "the fourfold" and the uncertain return of the gods. But if we accept that the limit experience traced out by the catastrophes of the twentieth century is one in which what looms is something like: nothing is coming, nothing is happening any more, *rien n'arrive*, then we find ourselves in the necessity of another mode of thinking. Blanchot called this *the impossible* (as did Bataille), and, as noted earlier, this was precisely the most radical level of Blanchot's critique, both explicit and oblique, of Heidegger's discourse on death as "potentiality-of-being"

(*Seinkönnen*), as *possible*. Blanchot rather attempted to think death as that which can never arrive, and so as that which can never *resolve*—or (a fortiori) be the basis of any resoluteness. For Blanchot, precisely also in the late 1940s and '50s, literature and the "call" of a literary voice bring language into the essential dimension of an endless and empty exigency, drawing it on into a mode of speech that only with difficulty can be called *literature*. This is no doubt one reason for the shift from the *roman* to the *récit* in Blanchot's narrative works of that period, a move that signals much more than a change of generic labeling. One can think of this shift in a sense as a demotion of, or even from, Literature, but also an opening of form, strangely suffocating, that would do justice to the endless wandering—the "homelessness"—of speech *in its purely vocal aspect*, stripped as far as possible of its supports in the traditional resources of literary fiction.

Now it is precisely for such a radical stripping away, and for its painful movement from literary forms to naked and obsessive speech, that in a 1953 essay Blanchot praises the third volume of Beckett's trilogy. "Où maintenant? Qui maintenant?"—a title that takes up the point where Beckett begins the endless end—shows us a Blanchot who has discovered a writer and a text so close to his own thinking and experience that he is led to offer what can only be called an unmitigated endorsement. In this essay Blanchot makes of Beckett, and of *L'innommable* in particular, a fully realized exemplar of his own extreme conception of literature, the very one he is working out during this period, in both narrative and critical works, under the title of "literary space." Much could be said about this striking convergence between texts (*The Unnamable*, and Blanchot's récits from the 1950s) which are superficially so different, but whose kinship Blanchot attests by mobilizing, with a lack of reservation that is quite unusual, virtually all of the key terms and phrases that define this conception, as any cursory reading of the essay makes clear.

I would simply like to make one observation which is vehiculated by this evident identification on Blanchot's part, namely that the essay brings out in Beckett's text elements of this "experience" (as he calls it; LV 289) which he displays in his own narratives only in oblique, muffled, or highly allusive and attenuated forms. I am referring especially to the aspect of acutely painful torment taken on by the narrative voice itself, as well as the fall or "descent" (LV 294) into sheer compulsive speech that renders derisory any talk of talent, success, accomplishment, or cultural value—or, certainly, of anything resembling the sublime structure that would secure a compensation to be had in reaching past the extremes, the unlikely treasure to be found by hitting bottom, arriving *au fond*. For in *The Unnamable*—and in the literary space that this book "makes sensible in the most abrupt manner" (LV 294)—there is no bottom, there is only this profusion of floating words, in a pulverization and scattering of the one who ought to be speaking them.

This native emergence of Beckett's empty obsessive speech within "literary space" *in general* is clarified when Blanchot speaks of the non-figure of "l'Innommable" (written strangely with a capital) as "*un être sans être qui ne peut ni vivre ni mourir, ni cesser ni commencer, le lieu vide où parle le désoeuvrement d'une parole vide et que recouvre tant bien que mal un Je poreux et agonisant*" ("a being without being that can neither live nor die, neither cease nor begin, the empty place in which what speaks is the idleness of an empty speech and which is barely covered over by a porous and agonizing I"; LV 290). To the suspension in a neither-nor of *désoeuvrement* and empty speech, recurrent moments in Blanchot's discourse on literary space, is added a panic and urgency much less emphasized in that discourse but deeply characteristic of the overtly suffering voice of the unnamable. Does Beckett's disarming exposure of a voice in the grip of such a panic somehow allow Blanchot to foreground this suffering and dissolution in a way that the tone and movement—one might say the reserve and nobility—of his own works do not? Indeed, I wonder if ultimately Blanchot did not work too hard to maintain his noble manners—and if Beckett's bawdiness and vulgarity did not allow for a more radical shedding, and thus a more palpably painful scattering of remains.

In the same passage, Blanchot also calls this empty speech "*une survivance parlante, le reste obscur qui ne veut pas céder*" ("a speaking survival, the obscure remainder that refuses to yield"; LV 290), and thus evokes the very remainder we have been concerned with throughout this study, the obtrusive and excessive thing that is left when the world has been left, has been stripped away, *dépouillé*, but not dissolved to nothing, returning rather as its own evacuated fantasm—referred to here (partly with Sartre in mind) as "*l'imaginaire.*" The work, writes Blanchot, does not return the living writer to the world, but rather "*prive ce vivant de monde en lui donnant pour séjour l'espace de l'imaginaire; et c'est en partie, en effet, le malaise d'un homme tombé hors du monde et, dans cet écart, flottant éternellement . . . traversé de fantômes, ses créatures, auxquels il ne croit pas . . . qu'évoque pour nous* L'innommable" ("deprives this living being of world by giving him as a dwelling place the space of the imaginary; and indeed, what is evoked for us in *The Unnamable* is in part the anxiety of a man who has fallen out of the world and, in this distance, eternally floating . . . traversed by phantoms, are his creatures, in whom he does not believe"; LV 294). This quotation gestures at two important things: first the floating, haunted and unlivable nature of the "*séjour*," the dwelling or *Aufenthalt* granted to one who seeks to inhabit this abyssal crack in the world designated in the simple phrase and fact that *language speaks*, period. Second, Blanchot is here extending a critique of "sublimation" and literary redemption, a critique which dispenses with the notion that the work can help make the writer's peace with the world from which it must initially separate. This is a critique that has already been elaborated in the essay (LV 291–293) with reference to Freud and to Sartre's book on Genet, the latter being the name of another transgressive voice engaged in working over the substance of the waste products that have generated it. These critical remarks, whose ground is prepared by Beckett's "porous and agonizing I," constitute a vindication on Blanchot's part of the writer's radically unredeemable and downward-sloping position, insofar as he or she moves bare and unsheltered through this treacherous space called literary. The limit cases of torment, madness and suicide wrought by the unredeeming rigors of art are invoked here in the names of Michelangelo, Goya, Nerval, and Hölderlin (LV 293). But here too, as elsewhere in Blanchot's writing, one has the sense that the "experiences" signaled by these names are called up from across a distance that remains "aesthetic," a distance that may protect Blanchot's work from its own most unforgiving insights, and keeps at bay the messy baseness of the position into which the conditions they reveal implacably drag the writer, with no regard for his more angelic eternities.[6]

To be sure, at one level Blanchot is very clear: the work does not redeem the writer but rather demands his "sacrifice," his transformation into "*personne, le lieu vide et animé où retentit l'appel de l'oeuvre*" ("no one, the empty and animated place in which resounds the call of the work"; LV 293). This call, whose kinship with Heidegger's should be apparent even across the distance it plots, does not project any resolute habitation of the world, does not open any "sojourn" or dwelling other than the one that Blanchot calls *literary*—though he does so with less and less justification, with more and more risk of mitigating his own radical claims with the security of a traditional category.[7] And yet Blanchot himself is emphatic regarding the irrelevance of conventional aesthetic or cultural perspectives on what is "accomplished" in *The Unnamable*, and of any admiration one might be inclined to have for what has been performed there. He evokes this irrelevance in unequivocal terms, in a passage I will cite at some length, for it is here that Blanchot articulates more clearly than anywhere else, I believe, the sort of destitution of aesthetic grandeur and redemption, the "putdown" of any claim to our admiration, that has been a guiding thread of this book.

> Il faudrait peut-être admirer un livre privé délibérément de toutes ressources, qui accepte de commencer à ce point où il n'y a plus de suite possible, s'y tient obstinément, sans tricherie, sans subterfuge et fait entendre pendant trois cents pages le même mouvement heurté, le piétinement de ce qui n'avance jamais. Mais cela, c'est encore le point de vue du lecteur étranger, lequel considère tranquillement ce qui lui semble être un tour de force. Il n'y a *rien d'admirable* dans une épreuve à laquelle on ne peut se soustraire, rien qui appelle l'admiration dans le fait d'être enfermé et de tourner en rond dans un espace d'où l'on ne peut sortir même par la mort, car, pour y tomber, il a fallu précisément déjà tomber hors de la vie. *Les sentiments esthétiques ne sont plus de mise ici*. Peut-être ne sommes-nous pas en présence d'un livre, mais peut-être s'agit-il bien plus que d'un livre: de l'approche pure du mouvement d'où viennent tous les livres, de ce point originel où sans doute l'oeuvre se perd . . . (LV 291; my emphasis)

> Perhaps we ought to admire a book deliberately deprived of all resources, which accepts to begin at that point where no continuation is possible, stubbornly stays at this point, without trickery, without subterfuge, and for three hundred pages gives us to hear the same colliding movement, a trampling along that never moves forward. But this is still the point of view of the reader who remains foreign to the work, who calmly considers what appears to be a tour de force. There is *nothing ad-*

mirable in an ordeal from which one is incapable of removing oneself, nothing that calls for admiration in the fact of being imprisoned and of turning in circles in a space from which one cannot exit even by death, since in order to fall into it, it was necessary precisely to fall out of life. *Aesthetic sentiments are no longer relevant here.* Perhaps we are in the presence of a book, but perhaps it is a question of something much more than a book: the pure approach of the movement from which all books come, toward the originary point where no doubt the work is lost . . .

This stark acknowledgment of the torture, compulsion, and lack of freedom, the downright abjection, that natively constitute the literary voice at its most "originary point" is congruent, I would argue, with the sort of "confession" voiced in "A Hunger Artist." "I always wanted you to admire me," says the dying artist, just before definitively withdrawing any legitimate grounds for this demand. "But you shouldn't admire me . . . *I can't help it.*" There as here, in this passage by Blanchot on Beckett, "aesthetic feelings no longer have any place," including of course the feeling of or for the sublime—whose genealogy in the moral law and its categorical imperative, and in a call of conscience resounding even into the deep anxieties of late modernity, thus finds itself shorn of any remnants of nobility and dignity and reduced to an unredeemable movement of vocal torment. And if aesthetic feelings are neutralized, then so, no doubt, is the socio-aesthetic category of literature. As Beckett reminds us, "*Quand on s'écoute vraiment, ce n'est pas de la littérature qu'on entend*" ("when one really listens to oneself, it's not literature that one hears"). If Blanchot wants to make the writing of this strange and unruly remnant voice something other than, and even "perhaps much more" than a book, this is by virtue of a strange turn belied by the starkness of his own analyses, or at least that of their object.

MY SOLE OCCUPATION IS TORTURE AND BEING TORTURED

What does it mean that the limit-image of the literary vocation in late modernity is one of torture, abjection, and the compulsion of enforced speech, or that the limit-thought of metaphysics in its waning is one in which the being of language unfolds in an infernal endlessness of imaginary speech? In lieu of an answer to such an enormous question, which must be treated elsewhere, I will conclude with a final glance at Kafka, as he places himself, once again, in the uneasy position in which it is played out.

A strange motif runs through Kafka's correspondence with Milena Jesenská, where the author of "In the Penal Colony" invokes several times the conjunction of bad conscience and torture. Consider this passage, which occurs in the same letter that Blanchot quotes in "L'échec de Milena," thus placing it in close connection with writing's compulsions, with the havoc it wreaks on his life—which it also fully constitutes—and even with the disastrous past "engagements and similar things." Here Kafka evokes a "punishment for all one's debauchery" that would consist in having one's head placed in a vise and having "the screws . . . slowly tightened." Apparently Milena has accused him of resorting to old maneuvers in the difficult conflict of love vs. writing.

> You're also right [he says] to place what I've now done in the same category as the old things; after all, I can only go on being the same person and go on living the same life. The sole difference is that I already have experience; I don't wait with my screaming until they tighten the screws to force the confession—I start screaming the minute something starts to move in the distance, so over-alert has my conscience become—no, not over-alert, not nearly alert enough. (LM 198)

In the best known of these passages, Kafka even reproduces a note already quoted (in Chapter 3), on the beaten animal, the whip and its knots, and links torture more directly with language and speech.

> Yes, torture is extremely important to me—my sole occupation is torturing and being tortured. Why? For much the same reason as Perkins and, just as thoughtlessly, mechanically, and in line with tradition; namely, to get the damned word out of the damned mouth. I once expressed the stupidity in this as follows (it doesn't help at all to recognize the stupidity): "The animal wrests the whip from the master and flails itself in order to become the master, unaware that this is only a fantasy created by a new knot in the master's whip." (LM 214–215)

Finally, in a letter from a few months earlier, writing itself is the explicit domain of an infernal torture of conscience, presented with an inflection that speaks directly to the question as to what is admirable or worthy in all this. Milena has sent him a request to answer some queries about "The Stoker," which she is currently translating.

> I am happy to be able to make a small offering with the few notes you requested on "The Stoker"; this will serve as a foretaste to that torment of hell which consists in having to review one's entire life with the knowledge that comes of hindsight, where the worst thing is not the confrontation with obvious misdeeds but with deeds one once considered worthy. (LM 12)

These letters were written in 1920. If, as I have argued, Kafka has by this point in his work turned away from the tribunal as a fictive schema, he is still very much preoccupied (at least in this charged correspondence with a lover) with the violence, sadism and haunting bad conscience that underlies it, and his later work is not devoid of this dimension of aggressive or transgressive masochism. The hunger artist attests to this, as a figure who draws down a posture that had been presented so insistently as "worthy." But I have also argued that this downward movement itself, in all its critical irony and lucid emptiness, points away from the punishing hell invoked here—the voice as a hell of punishment—toward another mode of literary space, and another form of the imperative, that courts a freedom not to be found in these traps. Literary space may necessarily remain a kind of hell, a purgatory of sheer images and endless wandering (and speaking) (as in *The Castle*), and it may inevitably lead into suffocating underground spaces dug and mapped by paranoia, and inhabited by uncanniness itself (as in "The Burrow"). But insofar as it makes even a minute opening in and with the stuff of time (as in the tiny hole of the ape's past in "A Report to an Academy"), drawing speech through it toward what is unaccountable in its having to take place, it may also find a slim margin of freedom to maintain. In this light we might recall that four years after writing the letters to Milena, in the face of a looming death, Kafka writes "Josefine the Singer," in which the artist can do little more than manifest the compelling nothingness of her own voice, only in the end to rise unredeemed, "like all her brothers," into the remnants of a speech that tells, in all fault and failure, of her enigma.

NOTES

Introduction: "Why Do You Write?"—The Fault of Writing

1. Kafka, LFr 10.
2. From the flyleaf at the beginning of *L'espace littéraire*; this "author's biography" was no doubt written by Blanchot himself.
3. From *Rockaby* (CSPl 282).
4. Lacoue-Labarthe, *Heidegger and the Politics of Poetry*, 38. The comment is made partly in reference to Blanchot.
5. J.-F. Fogel and D. Rondeau, eds., *Pourquoi écrivez-vous? 400 écrivains répondent*, 188. Kevin Hart cites this text and comments on Blanchot's statement in *The Dark Gaze: Maurice Blanchot and the Sacred*, 204–205.
6. In the well-known letter to Max Brod (July 5, 1922) in which Kafka claims that "writing . . . is the reward for serving the devil" and an unleashing of the "evil powers." LFr 332–335.
7. See Hölderlin's "Remarks on Antigone," in *Essays and Letters on Theory*, 113 (my emphasis); *Sämtliche Werke und Briefe*, 2:395–396. Lacoue-Labarthe comments on this "singular theology" of Hölderlin's in *Heidegger and the Politics of Poetry*, 39.
8. Blanchot marks the trajectory or "itinerary" in question very explicitly in his essay "L'itinéraire de Hölderlin," in EL 363–374. For Blanchot's reading of Romanticism see also "L'Athenaeum," in EI, 515–527.
9. Arthur Rimbaud, *A Season in Hell*, 86–87.
10. The discussion here and elsewhere in this study of the ethical ambivalence of the imperative, the insistent and intimate force it exerts on thought and language, owes a great deal to Jean-Luc Nancy, especially "Le Katègorein de l'excès" in *L'impératif catégorique*. The imperative, says Nancy, is what haunts and obsesses, it is a *hantise* that inhabits us in the register of the uncanny: "*La proximité de l'impératif pourrait bien être l'*Un-heimlichkeit *qui hante notre pensée . . . qui n'inquiète que parce qu'elle est si proche dans son étrangement . . . L'enjeu n'est pas un autre que celui de l'éthique—non cependant au titre d'une science ou d'une discipline, et pas non plus au titre d'un sens ou d'un sentiment moral, mais au titre, précisément, d'une hantise . . . Dans le temps de la hantise, il ne peut et il*

ne doit y avoir qu'une pensée et qu'une éthique—si c'en est une—de la hantise (11) (The proximity of the imperative might well be the *Un-heimlichkeit* that haunts our thinking . . . What is at stake is none other than ethics—not however as a form of knowledge or a discipline, nor as a sense or a moral sentiment, but precisely as a haunting obsession. . . . In the time of hauntedness, there can and must be an ethics—if it is one—only of hauntedness)." The imperative in question is thus one that demands what Avital Ronell has called "haunted writing"; see *Dictations: On Haunted Writing*.

11. This is one aspect of Jacques Derrida's reading of Kafka in "*Préjugés: Devant la loi*," in *La faculté de juger*.

12. *Pourquoi écrivez-vous*, 232.

13. I am referring to the well-known line in Hölderlin's elegy "Brot und Wein" ("Bread and Wine"): "*wozu Dichter in dürftiger Zeit?*" What are poets for—what good are poets—in a time of distress?

14. For an interesting and pertinent discussion of the intersections between the sublime and the abject, see Claire Lozier, *De l'abject et du sublime: Georges Bataille, Jean Genet, Samuel Beckett*.

15. "Quand on s'écoute, ce n'est pas de la littérature qu'on entend." Charles Juliet, *Rencontre avec Samuel Beckett*, 13.

16. The question of art's poverty and its resistance to redemptive temptations is treated with perspicacity in Leo Bersani and Ulysse Dutoit, *Arts of Impoverishment: Beckett, Rothko, Resnais*.

17. Such a turning away, as a mode of critical dissatisfaction with the world as factually "given" and with its implicit imperatives of affirmation and consumption, receives a broad and nuanced philosophical treatment in the analyses of Rei Terada, *Looking Away: Phenomenality and Dissatisfaction, Kant to Adorno*.

18. Philippe Lacoue-Labarthe has linked Blanchot's near-death narrative in *L'instant de ma mort* to the mythic schema of the *nekuia*, by way of an autobiographical tradition of "autothanatography" passing through Rousseau, Montaigne and Augustine, among others. See "The Contestation of Death," trans. Philip Anderson, in Kevin Hart and Geoffrey H. Hartman, eds., *The Power of Contestation: Perspectives on Maurice Blanchot*, 141–155, esp. 147.

19. The question of the incentive or *Triebfeder* of the moral law, which Kant identifies as "respect," will be taken up below in chapter 1. See especially *Critique of Practical Reason*, Chapter III, "On the incentives of Pure Practical Reason," in *Practical Philosophy*, 198–211.

20. The compulsive forms of reason become explicit in Beckett's obsessional voices, as in *Company*, where they weigh on an "imagination . . . so reason-ridden" (C 33). This text also asks, in one of many futile attempts to comprehend the conditions its own origination, the very Kantian question: "Pure reason?" and responds in equally Kantian fashion: "Beyond experience" (C 52). On madness in, or the madness of, Kant's pure reason, see Monique David-Ménard, *La folie dans la raison pure: Kant lecteur de Swedenbourg*. In a similar register, and precisely in reference to Swedenborg, Jacques Derrida touches on the madness and hallucination implicit in any poetic voice, in any "hearing oneself"

(*s'entendre*)—and thus in close proximity to Beckett's "listening to oneself" (*s'écouter*) quoted above—in "Qual Quelle: Les sources de Valéry," in *Marges de la philosophie*, 353–356.

21. Kant, *Critique of the Power of Judgment*, sect. 29, 153.

22. Ibid., sect. 27, 141.

23. Kant does mention melancholy in certain early texts, as he does briefly in *Observations on the Feeling of the Beautiful and the Sublime*, section one, 47–48. It is quite significant that the melancholic aspect of the sublime would emerge in this heavily empirical work, focused on "feeling," from Kant's "pre-critical" period. At one level, the present study seeks to restore such sensible elements to an experience that nonetheless retains a certain "transcendental" and "critical" structure.

The long footnote that Kant appends to that passage in the *Observations* (48–49) provides an extraordinary dramatization of the leaving behind of all worlds that is likewise at stake in the literary space navigated by the writers discussed here. Kant quotes at length a story from *Bremen Magazine* ("Carazan's Dream") in which a reformed miser recounts the dream that saved him, and taught him love for his kind. In this dream, he dies and is condemned for his sins to total solitude. He finds himself flying through the cosmos, eventually leaving behind every last world and star and all of creation itself, doomed forever to "the shadow of the boundless void sink[ing] down into the abyss before me. A fearful kingdom of eternal silence, loneliness and darkness! Unutterable horror overtook me at this sight . . . just as every moment increased my distance from the last inhabited world." This is nothing less than a parable of a certain literary space (only mitigated by its moralizing frame), and thus also precisely a picture of the horror from which Kant's later version of the sublime sought to redeem the cold and ultimate realm of reason, by nothing more than its own means—a version that would thus be free of all compromise with sentiment and sensibility.

24. One equivocal heir to romanticism in this respect is Flaubert, whose extreme skepticism and disdain for his age did not prevent him from having an exalted sense of writing's vocation, the sort of devotion it required, the torture this entailed, and the ecstasy it promised—and occasionally delivered.

25. On "the hyperbologic," see Philippe Lacoue-Labarthe, "The Caesura of the Speculative," in *Typography: Mimesis, Philosophy, Politics*, 231; and *Heidegger and the Politics of Poetry*, 45. For a commentary on this concept, in connection with "presentation" and the sublime, see John Martis, *Philippe Lacoue-Labarthe: Representation and the Loss of the Subject*.

Lacoue-Labarthe has also referred to a "sublime of destitution" in reference to Celan (*Poetry as Experience*, 89). While I am thus clearly indebted to Lacoue-Labarthe when I speak of a "destitution of the sublime," I would like to stress the inversion of terms: with this formula I do not wish to attribute anything sublime to destitution; rather, in its double ambiguity, the phrase is meant to indicate, on the one hand, the destitution that has always been operated by the sublime experience (even in Kant, who nonetheless rewards and "restitutes" it, in the end, with Reason), and on the other hand, an extreme impoverishment irreversibly undergone by whatever it is that once could be considered sublime, which would thus be rendered into to a mere leftover of itself, its only remaining possibility.

26. "A Piece of Monologue" (CSPl 265).

27. The "assumption" of language as a whole, by way of the pronoun "I," is laid out in Emile Benveniste's classic essay "The Nature of Pronouns," an analysis that will inform my reading of Beckett. This connection has been made by other readers of Beckett as well; for example, see Daniel Katz, *Saying I No More*.

28. Abrupt, but also gradual to the point of never-ending. "*Aussitôt quoique peu à peu*" ("all at once yet little by little") (LV 26), as Blanchot liked to put it.

29. One could say that chapter 7 thus arrives at something of a theoretical "ground" or "core" for the present study, if its purpose were not to show precisely the abyssal and empty structures of seeing involved in such figures. The texts I am referring to are Jean-Luc Nancy, "Masked Imagination," in *The Ground of the Image*, 80–99, and Martin Heidegger, *Kant and the Problem of Metaphysics*, sects. 20 and 21, 65–71.

30. In the solitude of literary space, writes Blanchot, everything has disappeared, but this disappearance is itself a kind of appearance: "'tout a disparu' apparaît. Ce qu'on appelle apparition est cela même: est le 'tout a disparu' devenu à son tour apparence" (EL, 340) ("'everything has disappeared' appears. What one calls apparition is precisely this: it is the 'everything has disappeared' that has in turn become appearance").

31. Lacoue-Labarthe, "Il faut," in *Heidegger and the Politics of Poetry*, 38–59.

32. This is from the well-known letter to Georges Izambard dated May 13, 1871: "*Les souffrances sont énormes, mais il faut être fort, être né poète, et je me suis reconnu poète. Ce n'est pas du tout ma faute*" (my emphasis).

Chapter 1: Kafka's Teeth: The Literary Gewissensbiss

1. LFr 10; Br 21: "So ist es mit mir: Gott will nicht, dass ich schreibe, ich aber, ich muss."

2. See Clayton Koelb's commentary in *Kafka's Rhetoric*, 236. Koelb mentions that this passage comes after remarks by Kafka not on writing but on what he has been reading—a point that will take on greater importance below when we look further at the correspondence with Pollak.

3. I stress this "in part" because I do not mean to suggest that this is the entire set of conditions out of which Kafka wrote what he wrote. I am delineating here the discursive configurations through which the necessity of writing is genetically linked with a field of figures and movements that come to form the obsessive features of his first mature fiction, beginning with "The Judgment."

4. Much later, in the period following the composition of "The Judgment" and in the midst of his correspondence with Felice, Kafka will draw out for the latter an image that projects, in almost comical fashion, a very similar movement of release within captivity. In response to Felice's naive statement that she would like to sit next to Kafka when he writes, he informs her that this would ruin the possibility of writing, since for that one can never be alone enough. To illustrate the point, he elaborates the following fantasy, which combines imprisonment, monastic isolation, and Poe-like entombment:

I have often thought that the best mode of life for me would be to sit in the innermost room of a spacious locked cellar with my writing things and a lamp. Food would be brought and always put down far away from my room, outside the cellar's outermost door. The walk to my food, in my dressing gown, through the vaulted cellars, would be my only exercise. I would then return to my table, eat slowly and with deliberation, then start writing again at once. And how I would write! *From what depths I would drag it up*! Without effort! For extreme concentration knows no effort. (LFe 156; BF 250; January 14–15, 1913; my emphasis)

It is worth noting how this remarkable sketch inverts the architecture of "Before the Law," while also locking the door leading into *this* law's interior—in which, as Kafka goes on to stress, failure and madness are no doubt inevitable.

5. So Kafka writes in a letter to Max Brod (July 5, 1922), in which he claims that "writing is the reward for serving the devil," and involves a descent to the "lower regions" and a release of the "dark powers" (LFr 333; BFr 384).

6. August 24, 1902: "I sat at my fine desk . . . it's a respectably minded desk which is meant to educate. Where the writer's knees usually are, it has two horrible wooden spikes. . . . If you sit down quietly, cautiously at it, and write something respectable, all is well. But if you become excited, look out—if your body quivers ever so little, you inescapably feel the spikes in your knees, and how it hurts. I could show you the black-and-blue marks." This image is a harbinger of the many invocations of physical torture, in conjunction with "excitement" and quivering pleasure, that one finds in Kafka's diaries, but also of course in "In the Penal Colony," as well as in the *Letters to Milena*. Kafka's strong association between writing and torture was formed very early on, in the shadow of a disciplinary process of training, self-formation, and the dangerous courtship of ecstatic states.

7. The novel both does and does not fit within this characterization in ways that will be explicated below. As the terminal moment of the judgment narratives, *The Trial* also brings about a dissolution of the juridical scheme, a decisive loosening of its grip, partly by way of an expanded form.

8. See Reiner Stach, *Kafka: The Decisive Years*, which covers this period in Kafka's writing life.

9. Georg Bendemann, Gregor Samsa, the penal colony officer, and Josef K. are all done away with in the end. Only "The Stoker" presents a less murderous outcome, but if Karl Rossmann survives the end of the story (to become the eponymous protagonist of a novel Kafka called *Der Verschollene*), the title character of this opening chapter is no less summarily eliminated, not killed but reduced to abject subhumanity. The culmination of Kafka's murder stories comes in "A Fratricide," after which the death or disappearance of central characters is much more rare, and when it does occur, as with "A Hunger Artist" or "Josefine the Singer," it is rid of its legalistic burden.

10. This comment is made in reference to an attempt to "write about Paris," following Kafka and Brod's visit there the previous summer.

11. Kafka indicates his awareness of this immediate and pervasive literariness in a diary entry for February 19, 1911, where he ascribes "perfection" even to the most banal of

sentences: "He looked out of the window" (D 38). This elated investment in such a flat and minimal narrative sentence is not the mere delusion of a good mood. Rather, it bears witness to a kind of love. Kafka did not regard his stories as offspring and "sons" for nothing. It is also an ecstasy of potentiality experienced as partially realized by *any* sentence, even when not carried to term, as it were, in a work.

12. Walter Benjamin, "Franz Kafka on the Tenth Anniversary of his Death."

13. On Kafka, food, and the body, see Mark Anderson, *Kafka's Clothes*, especially chapter 3, "Body Culture," 74–97.

14. I am referring to stories such as "Investigations of a Dog" and "Josefine the Singer," among others. This point is made, for example, in Martin Greenberg, *Kafka: The Terror of Art*, and in Stanley Corngold, *Lambent Traces*. Greenberg makes an apt distinction between "dream narratives" and "thought-stories" (13–14).

15. As Martin Greenberg has suggested (*Kafka*, 14), *The Castle* can be seen as combining these different narrative modes (visual/scenographic and vocal/discursive). This is true in the specific sense that the novel integrates long stretches of first person speech into its otherwise highly visual narrative. At the same time, *The Castle* displaces the effective power of judgment, law and guilt into the domain of dialogic speech, rumor and social ostracism— for example, in Olga's tale of her sister Amalia, who refuses the advances of a castle official and thus brings social ruin on the family, a condemnation that has nothing to do with legal proceedings or a discreet act of judgment. It is precisely here that the more radical vision articulated in *The Castle* is evident in relation to its legalistic predecessor, *The Trial*.

16. In this perspective, it could be very revealing to juxtapose certain elements of Kafka's work with those aspects of Heidegger's thought that resonate with it. Despite the obvious and enormous differences that separate these near contemporaries (Kafka was only six years older), they nonetheless converge on a similar terrain, namely (to mention only one of the most readily apparent) that of the uncanniness and anxiety pervading the rapid modernization of the early part of the twentieth century. To my mind, such an encounter, if it were to take place, would likely fall under the anachronistic rubric "Kafka, critic of Heidegger."

17. Freud, *Jokes and their Relation to the Unconscious*, chapter 7, "Jokes and the Species of the Comic," esp. pp 200ff. (In German: Fischer Studienausgabe, Band IV, *Psychologische Schriften* [1970], 186ff.).

18. The editors of the English translation of the *Letters* identify her thus (condensing Max Brod's longer note in his edition): "Selma Kohn Robitschek, daughter of the chief postmaster of Roztok (Roztoky), on the left bank of the Moldau, 7 1/2 miles north of Prague. For one summer the Kafkas lived in their house, and Franz and Selma spent much time in the forest, where he would read Nietzsche aloud" (LFr 425).

19. I am referring to a letter including the famous statement that likens reading a book to suffering an "axe on the frozen sea inside us." It is rarely remarked that this is a farewell letter to a friend; it stands out as the culmination of the judgment/punishment structure Kafka is developing in these letters. I will return to the passage at the end of this section.

20. Kafka's father was the owner/manager of a shop that sold fashionable accessories. See Anderson, *Kafka's Clothes*, especially the "Introduction" and Chapter 1, "The Traffic of Clothes." Anderson in turn recognizes a debt to Klaus Wagenbach's *Franz Kafka* for knowledge of the "young Kafka," and to Gerhard Kurz, ed., *Der junge Kafka*.

21. On Kafka and *Der Kunstwart*, see Anderson, *Kafka's Clothes*, 59–62.

22. Anderson provides an illuminating discussion of the women's fashion reform movement, in which Kafka took some interest. See ibid., 62–66.

23. Anderson also quotes this sentence (*Kafka's Clothes*, 34) as a crucial statement for understanding the young Kafka's desire to fuse art and life, to merge language, as ornament, and the writerly self.

24. This life-long attempt to escape the father's all-embracing realm of influence is of course the leitmotif of the *Letter to His Father*, written in 1919.

25. Mark Anderson sees the "stripping away" carried out by Kafka in his writing as not only a flight from the self but more specifically as "the repression of his own aestheticist origins, his negative relation to fin-de-siècle ornament" (*Kafka's Clothes*, 7). However, this negative relation need not be understood as repression, nor even as simply negative. I prefer to regard it as the complex movement of a long and deliberate liberation from, and surpassing of, aestheticism, and thus a liberation of literature itself from the metaphysical regime of the aesthetic—but one that necessarily leaves a residue of its contexts and occasions.

26. See Corngold, *Lambent Traces*, 43, for one example. Corngold is one of the few readers of Kafka to point out in this connection the importance of celestial bodies, fire, and combustion in the projection and figuration of this process, aspects that will be important here as well.

27. Anderson, *Kafka's Clothes*, 57.

28. This phrase is from a diary entry Kafka wrote in 1917 after completing "A Country Doctor" (D 387; TB 389). In that story, the breach and its residue take the form of a festering worm-eaten wound, an image that seems to belie Kafka's ecstatic celebration of a pure and immutable transcendence.

I should add that the remarks in this and the following paragraph are also meant as an acknowledgment, but also a critique of the limits, of Stanley Corngold's emphasis on Kafka as "an ecstatic." ("My Kafka is an ecstatic," he writes [*Lambent Traces*, xiii]). There are many compelling reasons for seeing Kafka in this light, and the consequences of doing so are very important. But it is equally important to insist on the extent to which his canniness and *sobriety* determine the peculiar concreteness of his art. To my mind, this sobriety makes Kafka not only an ecstatic but also a *critical artist*, in every sense. Regarding Kafka's vacillations between art and religion, and his sobriety, in the end, on this question, see Blanchot's incisive commentary in *L'espace littéraire*, 101.

29. Corngold quotes this passage (*Lambent Traces*, 203), as does Anderson (*Kafka's Clothes*, 4), each with very different intentions. Neither, however, comments on the fragment's self-cancelling rhetoric.

30. Deleuze and Guattari, *Kafka*, 96 n16. They are referring to the same aphorisms in the Blue Octavo Notebooks from which the above quote is taken.

31. As when Beckett attempts, in the concluding gesture of *Ill Seen Ill Said*, to "devour all": "Not another crumb of carrion left. Lick chops and basta" (ISIS 59). It is worth noting that Kafka had already provided in his first publication (*Betrachtung*) an even more succinct version of the remainderless stripping away enacted in the *Allerheiligste* aphorism, one that foregrounds the specifically fictive sphere in which this process takes place, when he wrote the single sentence fragment that makes up the text "The Wish to Become an Indian":

> If one were only an Indian, immediately mounted and off on the speeding horse, leaning sharply into the wind, and were jerkily quivering again and again over the quivering ground, until one shed [*liess*] one's spurs, for there were no spurs, until one threw off [*wegwarf*] the reins, for there were no reins, and barely saw the land ahead as a smoothly shorn heath, horse's neck and head already gone. (CS 390; E 34–35)

These leavings and castings-off make it clear that the true irreducible substrate of fictive projection (*if only*) is the "sheer" spatial topos or schematic "ground" required for its elaboration, but likewise that the self-dissipating fiction necessarily does leave a remainder, in the textual fragment that bears witness to its disappearance *and* to the very figures that are shed, in all their fantasmatic density. In other words, the imaginary movement of abstraction into pure space reveals the obtrusive singularity of speech in time. Another late text of Beckett, "Imagination Dead Imagine," concisely charts a similar movement.

32. Brod, *Franz Kafka*, 58. Brod also recalls Pollak "as a young man who passed severe judgments" (56).

33. Stanley Corngold has commented on these astronomical images in *Lambent Traces: Franz Kafka*, 22–24, and, with Benno Wagner, in *Franz Kafka: The Ghosts in the Machine*, 45.

34. On Kafka's desire for reading as submission and being engulfed in the text, see Clayton Koelb, *Kafka's Rhetoric*, 88. Koelb quotes Gustav Janouch's *Conversations with Kafka*—in which Kafka speaks of books as "a sea in which one can easily drown"—and remarks (with reference to Harold Bloom's *The Anxiety of Influence*): "The 'good' reader is submissive to the authority of the author and wants nothing more than to be flooded by that author's discourse . . . to drown in the text of authority."

35. See especially *Critique of Practical Reason*, Chapter III, "On the incentives of Pure Practical Reason," in *Practical Philosophy*, 198–211.

36. Freud, *Jokes and Their Relation to the Unconscious*, 200. Freud also speaks, in a chapter on "The Purpose of Jokes," of another voice that speaks compulsively *against* the moral law, remarking how it is "impossible to stifle the voice within us that rebels against the demands of morality" (*Jokes*, 110).

37. On the instantiation of the critical agency or "instantiation" (in German, *die kritische Instanz*) of the superego and its grounding in the narcissistic, devouring (oral), and aggressive drives of the id, see Freud, "Mourning and Melancholia," 249–250, and *The Ego and the Id*, especially chapter III, "The Ego and the Super-Ego (Ego-Ideal)." This knotted thread of bad conscience passes directly through Nietzsche as well, especially *On the Genealogy of Morals*, and onward to the Foucault of *Discipline and Punish*.

38. Goethe is not mentioned in this letter, and yet it is as though he too delivers this blow of a "*Faust*" that strangely resonates in its diabolical literary violence.

39. It could be argued that Kant's obliviousness to the tragic consequences of his own thought is what made it possible in its radicality—insofar as the havoc that it wrought was, in his view, fully compensated by the supersensible treasures of thought (reason) that it secured. Things were not so clear, or balanced, for Hölderlin. The phrase "wandering under the unthinkable" occurs in his "Remarks on Antigone." See Hölderlin, *Essays and Letters on Theory*, 110. On Hölderlin's reading of tragedy and his refiguring of Greek "grandeur" in its paradoxical inimitability, see Philippe Lacoue-Labarthe, "The Caesura of the Speculative" and "Hölderlin and the Greeks" in *Typography: Mimesis, Philosophy, Politics*.

40. For a remarkable reading of sublimity as wound and assumed castration (and blindness) on the part of male poets seeking to inscribe themselves in the lyric tradition, see Catherine Maxwell, *The Female Sublime: From Milton to Swinburne*. Although it deals with a different canon, genre, and set of topoi, Maxwell's analysis touches on a number of points of concern in the present study, not least the "inner vision" that, in his own way, Kafka dramatically asserted in relation to the sort of violence I underscore here. Likewise, in anticipation of the discussion below of Blanchot's feminizing of the sublime, we can note Maxwell's assertion in her introduction: "I see feminisation for male poets . . . as . . . implicit to the poetic tradition which dates from Milton's construction of himself as inspired bard. In my view, male poets' adoption of feminine identities and images is less a matter of *appropriation* than of *compulsion* as they are *driven* towards feminisation in order to attain vision." *Female Sublime*, 2 (author's emphasis).

41. Despite their enormous differences, one might link this "vocation" and call to the "call of conscience" in Heidegger's *Being and Time*. See the Conclusion below for a discussion of this vocal and, I will argue, essentially literary phenomenon.

42. We are touching here on the very structure of sublime transmission, that is, of tradition itself insofar as it is sublime, "monumental" (in Nietzsche's sense), and structured as immeasurable debt. It is striking to note how this is played out in one of the founding critical documents of this tradition, the treatise "On the Sublime" attributed to Longinus, in ways that seem indeed to have been transmitted directly to Kafka. In chapter 14 of this treatise, the function of literary precursors as projected and idealized judges, and as contestants in a grueling *agôn*, is dramatically explicit. The author even exhorts any writer who would strive for "sublimity of thought and expression" to imagine a *courtroom* full of such judges, first by asking: "How perchance would Homer have said this, how would Plato or Demosthenes have made it sublime?" and then by staging a scene, in which one finds, in what is surely not a coincidence, a combination of astronomical and juridical figures. "Emulation," writes the author,

> will bring those great characters before our eyes, and like guiding stars they will lead our thoughts to the ideal standards of perfection. Still more will this be so, if we give our minds the further hint, "How would Homer or Demosthenes, had either of them been present, have listened to this passage of mine? How would it have affected them?" Great

indeed is the ordeal [*agonisma*], if we propose such a *jury and audience* as this to listen to our own utterances and make believe that we are *submitting our work* to the scrutiny of such superhuman witnesses and judges. (*On the Sublime*, xiv.2–3; my emphasis)

The text continues with another question which would lead the writer, if somewhat deliriously, into something resembling "the invisible court" that Kafka will evoke in his diaries (as we will see in a moment): "If I write this how would all posterity receive it?" or more literally: How will it be heard in all time to come? Kafka's own legalistic and literary delirium will do nothing other than bring to extreme explicitness, in the terms of his own historical situation, the constitutive fantasies of the tradition that he is striving to inherit. But this extremity may also provide the conditions for an exit from this program.

43. See Freud, *Civilization and Its Discontents*, especially chapters 7 and 8.

44. On Kafka's method of writing and his predilection for first drafts, see Malcolm Pasley, "The Act of Writing and the Text: The Genesis of Kafka's Manuscripts," in Anderson, *Reading Kafka*.

45. In the first chapter of *Lambent Traces* ("In the Circle of 'The Judgment'"), Stanley Corngold comments on a number of the same quotations and images that I will address here, particularly this "combustion" (15) of the straw-heap bachelor writer and the celestial comet that will enter our telescopic horizon in a moment. Focusing on "the relation of diary writing to the ecstatic writing of fiction," Corngold also wishes to gauge the strange passage into literary writing from something more "autobiographical" that will have preceded it. In language that is very close to my own formulations, he writes that "Kafka's diary entries exist to produce a draught of transformation in which their own beginnings can be blown away" (18). My argument differs from these remarks, however, by insisting that the stubborn fallout from this transformative draft—especially in the more explosive implications of this "being blown away"—forever clings to the absolute textual objects it would engender. In that sense, this residue is the mark of their constant betrayal by the singular conditions that produced them.

46. One could no doubt link this *Bildung* (formation) as *Einbildungskraft* (imagination), image formation as imaginative faculty, to the schematism that haunts and structures it in Kant. I will return to this suggestion below.

47. Kafka's interest in "body culture" in general, and in the body's relation to writing in particular, is well known. See Anderson, *Kafka's Clothes*, 74–98.

48. See CPuR, 392–393. Kant also speaks of this as a "need of reason," a *Bedürfnis*, and thus as a kind of drive.

49. This discussion obviously draws on Heidegger's analysis of the "call of conscience" in *Sein und Zeit*, where we read that "Der Ruf kommt *aus* mir und doch *über* mich": the call comes *from* me and yet *over* me (BT 254; SZ 275); Heidegger's emphasis). That analysis also relies on figures of sound and voice to characterize the "silence" of the "discourse" of conscience, while pointing beyond any legalistic understanding of conscience, for which Heidegger criticizes Kant, who renders it in the "mere image" of a court of justice (BT 251; SZ 271). These questions are discussed further in the Conclusion.

50. The not so innocent nature of this innocence will become clear as we proceed, especially with reference to a much later letter with which Kafka concluded another relationship, breaking off his second engagement to Felice Bauer. (See Chapter 3, "The Human Tribunal?")

51. In "The Judgment" it is a letter, which is never presented, for it is merely a metonymy of Georg's "devilish . . . being." In "The Metamorphosis," it is Gregor Samsa himself. In *The Trial* there is a scene in which this object is, in fact, a piece of paper, deliberately and absurdly held aloft by Josef K., as if to solicit a final judgment in his case. But one of the two other men present abruptly dismisses the gesture: "Thanks, I already know all that" (T 130; KA P 174). This scene occurs in K.'s office, where he has already received a visit from a very judgmental uncle ("K.'s Uncle Karl"!) (T 88; KA P 118). I will return to this scene in Chapter 3.

52. One might also include here the writer's as yet unrealized "people" evoked by Deleuze, in terms of the very minor "health" that was of great concern to Kafka: "Health as literature, as writing, consists in inventing a people who are missing." *Essays Critical and Clinical*, 4.

Chapter 2: The Ecstasy of Judgment

1. *The Trial* is more complicated in this regard, since unlike in the other judgment stories, no judgment scene is ever staged. I will comment on this difference in Chapter 3.

2. "The animal wrests the whip from its master and whips itself in order to become master, not knowing that this is only a fantasy produced by a new knot in the master's whiplash" (BON 24). We will have more than one occasion to return to this whip in what follows.

3. The emphasis on freedom can be heard particularly in the emphatic appearance of the word in the final sentence of "Investigations of a Dog." The ape in "Report to an Academy" chews over the notion of freedom as well. We will return briefly to the question of rumor and gossip below, in relation to "The Metamorphosis" and, especially, *The Trial*.

4. There are many possibilities, but I will pose as a rhetorical question one that is particularly intriguing: To what kind of friend would one not want to confess that one is engaged to a woman, because it would forever ruin a "peculiar relationship" between bachelors? Kafka's work still awaits a subtle, nonreductive reading that would draw out the many homoerotic aspects of his writings, while maintaining the essential ambiguity of this question.

5. Max Brod, *Franz Kafka: A Biography*, 129; cited by Anderson in his "Introduction" to *The Sons*, xv.

6. Commentators and biographers have often pointed out that Kafka wrote "The Judgment" only days after initiating his correspondence with Felice Bauer (she had not yet replied), with whom he later associated several details in the story (see the diary entry dated February 11, 1913), and to whom he dedicated it upon publication. Without developing this connection further here, one can nonetheless point to the obvious parallelism,

in which letter writing is caught up in an ambivalent economy of persuasion, seduction and increasing potency.

7. Regarding the trap: At a decisive moment just before the judgment is pronounced, Georg screams: "So you've been lying in wait for me!" The father responds "with pity" that this remark is no longer relevant—because now Georg knows, or at least palpably feels, that the trap was fashioned from out of his own fantasmatic elaborations.

Regarding this *strife*: The word *devil*, like its German equivalent *Teufel*, derives from the Greek *diaballein*, meaning literally to "throw across," but also to introduce division through accusation and slander. The importance of slander in Kafka's work, most pointedly in the first sentence of *The Trial*, is well known ("Someone must have slandered Josef K . . ."). I would propose that slander *and* actual guilt are the twin founding assumptions of Kafka's judgment stories, a paradox that necessarily requires fictional treatment—or indeed that schematizes the performative generation of fictive realities in their juridico-legal aspect, and in their staging of sublime speech.

8. One notes as well that the friend in Russia is described at one point as an "altes Kind," an old child, an image that in fact materializes in the father. Thus all three of these figures are linked in a strange virtual childhood, forming an imaginary vector that points beyond them to an unlocatable engenderer, the instance that has authored them all.

9. *Nippen* is also the verb used for the hunger artist's occasional sips from a glass of water, his only intake as he sits in his cage (CS 268; E 191).

10. See Politzer, *Franz Kafka: Parable and Paradox*, 61n.

11. For some reason this sentence is omitted from Brod's edition of the *Tagebücher*.

12. On the ambiguity of such falls and deflations that would not merely prolong the sublime in another flatter or "lower" topology, see Anne-Lise François, *Open Secrets: The Literature of Uncounted Experience*. This study approaches the problem of the sublime from a very different angle than the one taken here, but as a critique of literary modes of sublimity and redemption, it inevitably intersects at many points with the problems in which Kafka—uneasy heir to expressive romanticism—is absorbed throughout the stories of concern to us here, and as he winds his way out of magnitude and toward a less dramatic mode of "making nothing happen."

13. Maurice Blanchot, commenting on the sister's gesture of standing and stretching her "young body" in the story's final sentence, writes: "*le geste de la jeune soeur, son mouvement d'éveil à la vie, d'appel à la volupté sur lequel le récit s'achève, est le comble de l'horrible, il n'y a rien de plus effrayant dans tout ce conte*" (PF 18; "the young sister's gesture, her movement of awakening to life and of calling up pleasure and desire with which the story concludes, is the height of horror, there is nothing more terrifying in the entire tale").

14. There are other striking echoes of "The Judgment" in the first "judgment scene" of "The Metamorphosis." Worth particular mention is the way Kafka relocates specific items and gestures in describing how the Prokurist grabs hold of the "*Geländer*," the rail of the staircase, as he begins his descent; Gregor glimpses him "clinging [*festhielt*] ridiculously with both hands to the railing on the landing [*Geländer des Vorplatzes*]." Further, when

Gregor finally lunges at the Prokurist, who in a bizarre gesture I find it hard to picture, had "his chin on the banister [*Geländer*]" and "was taking one last backward look," the narrator relates that he "leaped [*machte einen Sprung*] down several steps at once and vanished. 'Aieee!' he yelled; it was the last sound heard from him, and it echoed through the whole stairwell" (Sons 69; E 71). Like Georg zooming down an inclined plane, the Prokurist springs out of the house under an energizing compulsion.

15. The justice system of "In the Penal Colony" equates accusation with guilt, thus elevating slander to the status of legally binding condemnation. Likewise, the officer says that while the accused does not know his sentence (his "*Urteil*"), when it is inscribed into his flesh, "he will learn it on his body" ["*er erfährt es ja auf seinem Leib*"] (CS 145; E 155). I will return to these and similar statements later in a discussion of *The Trial*, a text which notoriously begins with a presumption of slander. The peculiar gesture of "The Metamorphosis" is to give stark graphic form to such bodily "conversions" of the symbolic action of the law, but also to locate that law in the sphere of public speech.

16. There is, of course, a well-known tradition in modern German thought, passing especially through Schopenhauer and Nietzsche, that gives music a privileged metaphysical status. Kafka was certainly aware of this tradition. I would say, much too quickly, that the major difference between Kafka's treatment of music and its investment by the metaphysical (or antimetaphysical) tradition is that in Kafka, while music clearly does have a privileged status at certain moments, this privilege has less to do with the "will" or "spirit" evoked by philosophy and more to do with the unaccountable, the "enigma" that will be central, for example, to the influence felt in Josefine's paradoxical *powerlessness*. I will be able to deal with the question of music in Kafka only in a very oblique manner, but we will return to this paradox.

17. One cannot help recalling as well the moment early in *The Trial* when Josef K. finds himself alone with Fräulein Bürstner in her room, and wildly kisses her "like a thirsty animal lapping greedily at a spring it has found at last. Then he kissed her on the neck, right at her throat, and left his lips there for a long time" (T 33; KA P 48). Gregor's vindication of his animal form, in relation to the fantasmatic sister-object imprisoned in his room, turns this aspect of the story toward the thirsty dog–like shame that ends *The Trial*, precisely at the moment of Josef K.'s execution by stabbing. In this sense it is important to differentiate among Kafka's animals: while all of them can be seen as vehicles of flight (as Deleuze and Guattari stressed), those born from the pressurized economies of Law and punishment bear the mark of their human subordination to the point of carrying it into death. On the other hand, a figure like Josefine, for example, the eternally insubordinate, merely disappears—or so we are told.

18. "*Es ist schon in Ordnung.*" Although with many obvious differences, this phrase is precisely analogous to the one Kafka uses to dispense with another starving character. After the hunger artist dies, sinking into the straw of his cage, the overseer of the circus shouts, "*Nun macht aber Ordnung!*" (E 200). In both cases, the moment of a corpse's cleanup marks a new "order," a change of regime whose promise would be built on the disposal of an incompatible remnant that has no place. And both give way to images of

delicious edible meat, whether provided to a healthy panther or carried up the stairs by a butcher's boy.

19. One thinks again of the famous first sentence of *The Trial*. But as was pointed out earlier, such slander is one mode of a general strategy employed by Kafka at a very deep level of his fictional worlds, whether in the form of gossip, hearsay, or legend.

20. The translation reads: "in a voice as hard as an anvil." This smoothes out the strangeness of the phrase with a simile that introduces a metaphorical object (the anvil) not present in the German, in which a hammer strikes rather the hardness of the voice itself.

21. The stoker's violent fist flailing, which appears as a reflexive substitute for articulate speech, recalls in the most striking manner a text that Kafka may well have read (though I have no evidence for this), Melville's *Billy Budd*. There, too, justice is trumped by discipline, after the main character has failed to speak, using his fist instead. The two stories intersect in a number of ways, but it is especially the marine setting on board a ship, and the question of justice versus discipline, along with a "confrontation" of innocence and evil and the conjoined motif of fist-in-lieu-of-speech, that recall *Billy Budd*.

22. This image places the abject stoker in some proximity to the odd nonhuman figure of Odradek in "The Cares of a Family Man," whose laugh can be produced only by someone "without lungs" and makes a sound "like the rustling of fallen leaves" (E 130).

23. Here, too, we are reminded very vividly of *Billy Budd*; the uncle's words are practically a paraphrase of that tale. But whereas in Melville's story the captain is haunted by the death of the innocent sailor, there is no sign of any such bad conscience on the part of the men in power in "The Stoker."

24. It is not difficult to see in all this hand holding and kissing, distraught renunciation, and warnings to remain within accepted boundaries to maintain a socially sanctioned "position," a very suggestive evocation of forbidden eroticism. The generalized taboo nature of the "treasure" is reinforced by the impersonal grammar Kafka uses ("one must renounce") which I will comment on in a moment.

25. To be precise: this is partly a question of focalization. As the stoker looks around, the perspective is entirely focused on him, but from nowhere in particular, certainly not from any precise point of view in the room, and his gaze does not encounter any of these people either. In this private moment *à deux*, the stoker sees only the bliss that is coming to meet him [*widerfahre*]. All of this produces a strange and artificial halo around this moment, withdrawing it from the otherwise well-defined staging of the scene.

Chapter 3: Embodied Violence and the Leap from the Law: "In the Penal Colony" and The Trial

1. For this reason too they should be distinguished from the undead or undying figures such as Odradek and the Hunter Gracchus. Could it be that the radical homelessness and indissoluble melancholy of these latter somehow protect them from the violent extinction inevitably administered by the Law?

2. It is worth recalling the radiance of the father in "The Judgment" ("He radiated insight"), which, as a manifestation of a "higher" power, is perfectly continuous with the justice that shines at the decisive moment from the tortured face of the penal colony victim, an image to which we will return in a moment.

3. See Friedrich Nietzsche, *On the Genealogy of Morals*, second essay, section 6 (Kaufmann translation, p. 67; Nietzsche's emphasis); and Michel Foucault, *Discipline and Punish: The Birth of the Prison*.

4. The noun *die Beize* is a remarkably apt and suggestive condensation of the set of associations I am trying to bring out: as a substance used in etching, called *mordant* in English, it conjoins inscription with the biting remorse and wit at issue here; as a liquid with acidic properties, it is also a *marinade* or pickling sauce that pungently bites into whatever it is applied to. In the context of the story, it suggests that the body installed in the machine is a surface both etched and eaten, an incised material and a kind of tidbit, simultaneously chewed and seasoned—while of course also making clear the sadistic element of the procedure.

5. This suggestion is made by Robert Buch in *The Pathos of the Real: On the Aesthetics of Violence in the Twentieth Century*, 42.

6. In that sense, this moment could be juxtaposed with Blanchot's evocation of a death mask in *L'arrêt de mort* (discussed in Chapter 7), and with his meditations on the image in *L'espace littéraire*, especially the sentence I have quoted above: "Idealism has, in the end, no other guarantee than a corpse" (EL 347). In that sense, the death mask would be the very face of idealism.

7. For an insightful discussion of conscience in terms of binding performative speech acts, see Karen S. Feldman, *Binding Words: Conscience and Rhetoric in Hobbes, Hegel and Heidegger*.

8. It is surely not a coincidence that Kafka returns to this image of puckered lips at such an analogous juncture, when the refusal of food and the deterritorialization of the mouth cross in the imminence of death. In the later story, the hunger artist purses his lips "as though for a kiss," not to hearken to transcendence, but, on the contrary, to deliver the punch line of the joke he has become.

9. The phrase "by force of speech" may be heard as a displaced (but directly obverse) echo of Dina Al-Kassim's insightful study *On Pain of Speech: Fantasies of the First Order and the Literary Rant*, which deals with similarly compulsive speech situations in relation to power and subjection, albeit in quite different contexts. See especially the chapter devoted to another writer deeply concerned with appearances and with the "seduction of the public," and who also had some trouble with the courts: "On Being Stubborn: Oscar Wilde and the Modern Type" (61–118).

10. The law that the machine is initially set to inscribe on the prisoner's body reads "Honor your superiors!" This commandment dictates the form of a relationship to hierarchically defined *figures*. "Be just!" rather enjoins a way of being that would be determined by a *concept* (justice) functioning as a regulative idea. But both of these have their source in the old commandant's law book, closely guarded by the officer, and neither of them

extricates judgment from the violence that founds it, and that ravages a body in the name of the new regime.

11. It is worth saying a word about this crank, which is more deeply embedded in Kafka's technological imagination than might first appear. First, the Muirs' rendering of *Kurbel* as "lever" is somewhat inaccurate (and, as is often the case, it fails to preserve the oddness of Kafka's language and image), for the German word indicates rather a mechanical crank that one must turn over and over, not a lever that displaces or turns something on with a single movement (Corngold's translation corrects this inaccuracy; see *Selected Stories*, 56). It is the sort of thing used to open shutters, or the top of an old-fashioned desk . . . Indeed, Kafka uses the same term in describing the bizarre "*Schreibtisch*" that so fascinates Karl Rossmann during his brief stay with his New York uncle, with its hundred compartments that can be shifted into countless unexpected permutations by turning a "*Kurbel*," also called there "*ein Regulator*" (A 39). The penal colony machine, which combines sewing machine, typewriter, and primitive word processor (and even, as suggested earlier, a kind of baster), is a not too distant relative of this desk. If we recall the torturous writer's desk equipped with spikes that Kafka evokes in a letter to Oskar Pollak, the genealogy of the present torture machine becomes even clearer.

12. This sentience even rises to the level of a complex awareness, specifically in connection with the disposal of the corpse: "The harrow tried [*wollte*] to move back to its former position, but as if it had itself noticed [*als merke sie selbst*] that it was not yet freed of its burden, it remained instead over the pit" (CS 165–166; E 175).

13. As mentioned above, the image of the death mask anticipates certain aspects of the analysis presented below in Part II on Blanchot (especially Chapter 7). There the death mask is linked to writing's haunted visions of a feminine figure of the law, in terms of a complex "transcendental" schematism derived from Kant and passing through Heidegger (and Nancy). While there is not space to develop these motifs here, one might well approach "In the Penal Colony" in terms of haunting and the schematism, particularly by way of the old commandant's writings/drawings, originary *Schriften* that are also *Zeichnungen* (both the machine's mechanism of inscription and the old commandant himself are referred to with the term *Zeichner*, a designer/drawer/draughtsman). The topos of a haunting return is introduced most explicitly in the story's coda, with the hidden gravestone of the old commandant and its promise of a coming "resurrection"; but the old commandant represents a spectral and haunting element throughout the story. Likewise, the link with the officer's living-dead face, as a mask-like remnant of that old spectral order, could also be developed. One major difference between the specific schematic configurations traceable in Kafka and in Blanchot is no doubt indicated by this difference in gender.

14. See Corngold, *Franz Kafka: The Necessity of Form*, 232; Corngold cites Hartmut Binder, *Kafka-Kommentar*, 218–261; see also Mark Anderson, *Kafka's Clothes*, p. 188.

15. John Zilcosky brings out the significant aspects of travel evident even within the relatively limited geographical scope of *The Trial*. See *Kafka's Travels*, chapter 3, "Traveling at Home: *The Trial* and the Exotic *Heimat*," 71–102.

16. In the chapter entitled "The Flogger," to which we will return.

17. John Zilcosky has remarked on the suggestive connotations of this traveler's outfit in *Kafka's Travels*, 75. A more literal translation of the phrase would read: "similar to *those* travelers' outfits with various folds. . . ." With this plural demonstrative ("those . . ."), Kafka twists this unusual clothing item into a very uncanny sense of familiarity, as though the narrator were referring to outfits we have all seen before. In another register, it is intriguing to note that the term *Anzug* can denote the first move in a chess game, for the guard is clearly a pawn whose movement initiates this game, and he will soon be captured—showing up later as the object of the flogger's blows.

18. Deleuze and Guattari rightly emphasize the novel's interminability (see *Kafka*, 44). The execution itself occurs abruptly, without judgment. Josef K. never encounters the invested authority who would judge or condemn him. Moreover, at the beginning of that final chapter, he is not in motion; he sits and waits for it.

19. Deleuze and Guattari also argue against the placement of the execution scene at the end of the novel ("The idea of ending with K.'s execution is contradicted by the whole direction of the novel and by the quality of 'unlimited postponement' that regulates *The Trial*" [*Kafka*, 44]). They argue as well for repositioning the chapter "In the Cathedral," citing Herman Uyttersprot, *Eine neue Ordnung der Werke Kafkas?* The question is in a way neutralized by the Stroemfeld/Roter Stern facsimile edition of *Der Process*, a boxed edition in which each chapter occupies a separate booklet, making it possible for the reader to experiment with various orderings. Regarding the execution scene, one possibility seems highly plausible: having written the scene early on, Kafka then proceeded to write a novel that turned out to be quite incongruous to the logic and substance of that scene. A similar point could be made regarding the "deathbed scene" that Brod claims Kafka described to him as the end of *The Castle*; but in that case, this scene was fortunately never written (or has not survived).

20. Ritchie Robertson cites a study by Eric Marson, *Kafka's Trial: The Case Against Josef K.* (St. Lucia, Queensland, 1975), that divides the novel into three "phases" according to K.'s relations with the court; the second phase of non-contact with the court begins after the "Flogger" chapter, which is placed just after the scene I am referring to; both scenes serve to sequester the court's doings, for the rest of the novel, within a sealed off space to which K. will not return. See Robertson, *Kafka: Judaism, Politics, Literature*, 105.

21. "Seasickness on dry land" is an often-quoted phrase from the early story "Description of a Struggle." It characterizes from the beginning the very nature of literary space for Kafka. See in particular Walter Benjamin, "Franz Kafka: On the Tenth Anniversary of his Death," in *Illuminations*, 130; Charles Bernheimer, *Flaubert and Kafka*, 146; and Walter Sokel (cited by Bernheimer), "Language and Truth in the Two Worlds of Franz Kafka" (1979), reprinted in *The Myth of Power and the Self: Essays on Franz Kafka*, 82.

22. I am referring to Kafka's parable "The Silence of the Sirens," written in 1917.

23. It is worth noting that this term is used to describe the penal colony prisoner's understanding of what has happened when the officer places himself in the machine, his sense of "some great reversal [*irgendeines grossen Umschwungs*]." [E 173] But his notion of that turnaround is defined entirely by revenge.

24. This is clearly the case, for example, in Blanchot's novel *Aminadab*, an overtly Kafka-inspired work in which the main character Thomas enters a strange boarding house where he will wander as though in an alternate and endless space, and from which he never exits. His entry itself is staged as a passage into a space governed by socially effective but deeply arbitrary fictions (on this point, see my "Translator's Introduction" to the American edition). While similar in structure, this scenario obviously differs from that in *The Trial* (see note 26).

25. The visit to Titorelli sums up very well the simultaneous contiguity and eccentricity of K.'s subsequent dealings with the court: the painter is only marginally attached to the court, and K.'s interview with him seems to take him far afield from the direct channels that, one might think, would be more effective. But it is Titorelli who gives him more concrete information than anyone in the novel, and it turns out that his garret studio is in yet another attic occupied by law court offices. K. responds to the unsavory news of this unintentional return—revealed only at the very end of the long conversation—by fleeing yet again, pressing a handkerchief on his face to ward off the stench.

26. It is true that one can imagine a scenario in which K. would become accustomed to the unappetizing air of the law court and its offices, but without melting into the inert servility of the other petitioners. He could then embark on a purely "internal" adventure, encounter Titorelli not obliquely but "from the inside" (along with other such figures, such as a nurse in the infirmary, to begin with), and thus follow an erring path deeper and deeper into the realm that, in the actual novel, he so acutely dreads. But the novel I am describing here would quickly exceed the restricted legalistic framework of *The Trial*, and would rather come to resemble a novel like . . . *The Castle*. Or, even more closely, like Blanchot's *Aminadab*.

27. He had entertained such a wish many times before. Consider this statement from the *Diaries* (December 16, 1911): "The moment I were set free from the office I would yield at once to my desire to write an autobiography." He goes on to imagine that "the writing of the autobiography would be a great joy because it would move along as easily as the writing down of dreams, yet it would have an entirely different effect, a great one . . ." (D 140).

28. "Let the last trump sound when it will, I shall come forward with this work in my hand, to present myself before my Sovereign Judge, and proclaim aloud: 'Here is what I have done . . .'" Rousseau, *Confessions*, 19.

29. If we recall that this *Gericht* founded on *Gerücht* (rumor) has a terrible smell (*Geruch*)—along with the strange link connecting it to the deathly world of justice's highest demand (as found in "In the Penal Colony"), *Sei Gerecht*! (Be just!)—and moreover that *Gerücht* has an etymological connection with *Geschrei* (scream) and *Ruf* (call), then we might begin to wonder whether Kafka's thinking about justice, punishment, the writing vocation, and literary space was not significantly inflected by the suggestive properties of a certain chain or cluster of signifiers.

30. This is the name that Alfred Hitchcock used for the mystery, the desired object or goal, that drives a plot without ever actually needing to be attained—indeed without needing to exist—for the substance of the story lies elsewhere. In reference to *The Castle*,

this is not to say that K.'s supposed profession of land surveyor is completely arbitrary and meaningless; on the contrary, it carries a great deal of symbolic freight that demands to be read. But in its concrete specificity it remains completely indeterminate (and nondetermining) with respect to K.'s actual adventure. Like the interior of the castle itself, it functions as a projected end that structures his movement as a quest, even as the true mystery emerges, rather, in his encounters and in the texture of the novel's dialogues.

31. In early 1917 Kafka wrote two extremely dreamlike narratives that deal with violence, culpability, and punishment: "A Fratricide" and "A Country Doctor." These are indeed the last stories of this type that Kafka wrote. The latter of the two, however, already shifts the terms of the judgment in question: while the doctor is implicated in the violation of the maid, Rosa, whose victimization is reflected in the rose red wound of the patient he cannot cure, he is not judged guilty by a "court" but rather stripped by his community of his sacred status (an implicit status that the story brings out in order to explicitly disinvest it: "It's only a doctor, it's only a doctor"), and of his clothes. This downgrade of the sacred exception is a concern that will lead directly to later stories like "A Hunger Artist" and "Josefine the Singer."

32. The episode has been much commented, but see especially Elias Canetti, *Der Andere Prozess: Kafkas Briefe an Felice*, and Stach, *Kafka: The Decisive Years*, 433–443.

33. Canetti, *Der andere Prozess*, 125.

34. "For secretly I don't believe this illness to be tuberculosis, at least not primarily tuberculosis, but rather a sign of my general bankruptcy" (LFe 545; BFe 756).

Chapter 4: Degradation of the Sublime: "A Hunger Artist"

1. That there are other hunger artists within the world of the story is indicated primarily by the title itself: "*A* Hunger Artist." As with the titles of many of Kafka's later stories ("*A* Country Doctor," "*A* Report to an Academy," "*A* Little Woman," etc.)—all of which stand in distinct contrast to the judgment stories ("*The* Judgment," "*The* Metamorphosis," etc.)—the indefinite singular marks the central figure with an implied if shadowy multiplicity, while also marking the voice itself as one among many, and so as only part of the overall "rumor" of discourse. The implications of Kafka's use of such titles would be worth examining more closely.

2. See the fascinating historical study by Breon Mitchell, "Kafka and the Hunger Artists," 236–255.

3. See especially Margot Norris, "Sadism and Masochism in Two Kafka Stories," 430–447. Mark Anderson, citing the connections made by Norris, stresses that the penal colony machine is already engaged in aesthetic production, as indicated by the many "embellishments" to which the machine devotes most of the twelve-hour execution. See *Kafka's Clothes*, 174–175. The word *Umschwung* occurs at significant moments in both stories to describe the shift from an old to a new regime; in "A Hunger Artist" (CS 273; E 196) it involves a decline in popularity, a shift from one regime of spectacle (or entertainment) to another (the Muirs circumlocute the word as a "change in public interest").

4. Freud, *Jokes*, 200. Freud cites Alexander Bain, *The Emotions and the Will* (London, 1865).

5. It is worth nothing that the narrator of "A Little Woman" (one of Kafka's last stories) uses precisely these terms, when he refers to "*das Gericht der Öffentlichkeit*," literally "the court of publicness," whose judging "gaze" the bitter little woman would like to direct at him ("*ihren vollen Blick auf mich richtet*") (CS 319; E 185; my emphasis).

6. This movement shows up elsewhere in Kafka, and in more ambiguous forms that call the metaphysical destination itself into question. In his essay "Kafka et Brod," Blanchot speaks of this transgressive movement in relation to K. in *The Castle*, and to his "volonté altérée et insatisfaite qui dépasse toujours le but et tend toujours au-delà" (KK, 149) ("thirsting and unsatisfied will that always surpasses the goal and tends always beyond"). Likewise, in "L'échec de Milena" ("Milena's Failure"), Blanchot evokes this movement "qui dépasse infiniment l'expérience commune" ("which infinitely surpasses common experience") and (again in reference to K.'s endless movement in *The Castle*) that could "d'une manière tout autre qu'humaine dépasser tous les buts" ("surpass all the goals in a way that is quite other than human"); but he adds, underscoring the failure at issue with the hunger artist as well: "mais, à cause de cette même volonté qui est démesure, impatience, ignorance infinies, il ne peut rien atteindre, il ne peut rien" (KK, 170) ("because of this same will, which is infinite unmeasure, impatience, and ignorance, he can attain nothing, he can do nothing"). See Chapter 7 for further discussion of this passage.

7. Kant, *Critique of the Power of Judgment* (Sections 25–27), 131–143.

8. Never does Kafka imply any overt condemnation of such a "worldly" attitude. On the contrary, one of the central dilemmas of certain of his late texts involves granting this attitude its rights, even when it is contravened by a different order of movement and activity, often associated with artistic or spiritual claims. This dilemma, and the careful due given to both "sides," can be read very clearly in a text like "On Parables"—where a similar clash between the pragmatic and the paradoxical is staged ("When the wise man says, 'Go over' . . .")—or especially in "Josefine the Singer."

9. These remarks refer both to Beckett and, of course, to Blanchot's "literary space," a notion derived in large part from a reading of Kafka. It is in this light as well that Blanchot comments on the extreme worldless destitution and compulsion in Beckett's trilogy. See "Où maintenant? Qui maintenant" in *Le livre à venir*, 286–295 (discussed in the Conclusion).

10. In the long letter to Max Brod of 5 July 1922, where he explains his realization that writing is the "reward for serving the devil [*Lohn für Teufelsdienst*]" (LFr 333; Br 384).

11. Freud, *Jokes and Their Relation to the Unconscious*, chapter 7, "Jokes and the Species of the Comic," esp. pp 200ff. (In German: Fischer Studienausgabe, Band IV, *Psychologische Schriften* (1970), 186ff.) Freud distinguishes between the joke (*der Witz*) and the comic (*das Komische*), but says that some comic stories can simultaneously have the status of jokes and vice-versa (203).

12. It is quite strange to note that in a much earlier and more explicit treatment of "unmasking" ("Unmasking a Confidence Trickster"), Kafka unexpectedly introduces the incongruous detail of *snapping teeth*. Just before the unmasking in question, the narrator

remarks: "I heard a sound in his mouth that was like the snapping of teeth [*Aneinanderschlagen der Zähne*]" (CS 395; E 24)—as though this were the sound one hears before being "taken in" by a trickster. We recall a similar warning sounded at the beginning of the stoker's trial scene, as well as in "The Metamorphosis," just when Gregor's starvation encounters its limit in a sound of a different order, in music.

13. Just as "On Parables" shows that, in the dialectic between literalism (or common sense) and allegorical speech, by settling on the former you may win in reality, but "in parable you have lost"—likewise the hunger artist "wins" in parable by dislodging his own literalism from the apparent obviousness with which he proffers it.

Chapter 5: Pointed Instants: Blanchot's Exigencies

1. This sentence presents itself as a simplifying restatement of a much more complex formulation: "*l'on n'écrit que si l'on atteint cet instant vers lequel l'on ne peut toutefois se porter que dans l'espace ouvert par le mouvement d'écrire. Pour écrire, il faut déjà écrire*" ("one writes only if one reaches that instant toward which one can move, however, only in the space opened by the movement of writing. To write, one must already be writing.") These sentences are in the last paragraph of "Le regard d'Orphée" (EL 232). Their paradox structures the terrain, and the twisted time, essentially in question here.

2. Rarely will any recourse be made here to biographical information, though I will have occasion to cite the helpful biography by Christophe Bident, *Maurice Blanchot: Partenaire Invisible*.

3. I borrow this phrase from Richard Stamelman, *Lost Beyond Telling: Representations of Death and Absence in Modern French Poetry*; Stamelman himself borrowed the phrase from John Ashbery. I would also like to cite here a work that has informed my reading of Blanchot's ghostly frequentation of dead and dying women: Elisabeth Bronfen, *Over Her Dead Body: Death, Femininity and the Aesthetic*.

4. In *L'arrêt de mort*, Blanchot's narrator describes a remnant "proof" of the events he wants to approach as the mere "shell of an enigma" ("*l'écorce d'une énigme*" [AM, 9]), a phrase we will return to. This shell is also the work itself.

5. Blanchot wrote a great many letters over the course of his long life. It has been said that in his personal correspondence, at least in the later years, he would customarily end a letter with a request that it be destroyed (a very Kafka-like gesture that one can only assume was, Brod-like, largely disregarded). It is difficult to know whether or how many of these documents will eventually be published. Aside from scattered letters published in various places, largely of a more or less public nature to begin with, there are three small books devoted to Blanchot's correspondence. *Lettres à Vadim Kozovoï (1976–1998)*. Jean-Luc Nancy has prefaced a letter by Blanchot on his political experience: Maurice Blanchot, *Passion politique: Lettre-récit de 1984, suivi d'une lettre de Dionys Mascolo*. Most recently, Pierre Madaule has published five decades of letters between himself and Blanchot, in Blanchot and Madaule, *Correspondance, 1953–2002*. I am unaware of what Blanchot may have left behind in terms of papers, drafts, and notebooks.

6. In referring to the "*récits*" I mean, in a loosely "technical" or pseudo-generic sense, the short narrative works written between 1948 and 1962, namely: *L'arrêt de mort* (1948), *La folie du jour* (1948), *Au moment voulu* (1951), *Celui qui ne m'accompagnait pas* (1953), *Le dernier homme* (1957), and, more marginally, *L'attente l'oubli* (1962). In my view these texts constitute the "kernel" of Blanchot's work and are the center of gravity of the present readings—especially *L'arrêt de mort*, in which, however, the work's status as a mere "shell" or leftover is brought vividly into relief. My attention will focus largely on this initial *récit*, though the other *récits* will be touched on below (at the end of this chapter) in terms of the Blanchotian "point" of narration.

7. The phrase "*jeté hors du monde*" first appears in "Kafka et l'exigence de l'oeuvre" (EL 82; it is repeated in the same essay on page 88). In the context of that essay, Blanchot is drawing on the well known passages occurring late in Kafka's diaries where the latter reflects upon exile from the world and on literature as "another world" that, perhaps, he now inhabits (see Kafka's diary entries dated January 28 and 29, 1922). Similar expressions can be found elsewhere in *L'espace littéraire* and in *Le livre à venir*. Blanchot writes of being rejected or thrown out of life (EL 58), of being pushed and falling out of the world (EL 244; LV 294) or being deprived of world (EL 81–82; LV 294), of the writer being "*jeté hors de ce qu'il peut*" ("cast out of what he can do") (EL 318 and 322). This last formulation bears the mark of Blanchot's wrangling with Heidegger over the question of "possibility" and *pouvoir*, a fundamental motif in *L'espace littéraire*.

8. I am referring here and below to the developments in *Being and Time* on mood (*Stimmung*), anxiety, uncanniness, the "call of conscience," and guilt, especially sections 29, 40, 54, and 58.

9. The question of the call of conscience is taken up again in the Conclusion.

10. Aside from certain indications internal to Blanchot's work, I will also relate this notion of a "treasure" to an incisive remark by Hélène Cixous: "Nothing moves Blanchot except a desire to keep his treasure." Cixous is referring to the short autobiographical text from *L'écriture du désastre* entitled "Une scène primitive?" to which we will turn below. See the chapter entitled Maurice Blanchot, "The Madness of the Day: A Text of Evasion" in Cixous, *Readings: The Poetics of Blanchot, Joyce, Kafka, Kleist, Lispector and Tsetayeva*, 95–109, esp. 100.

11. Numerous moments in the analyses of *L'espace littéraire* bear this out. For a particularly dense and complex version of this conflation, see "La solitude essentielle et la solitude dans le monde" (EL 337–340), which on its first page refers explicitly to Heidegger, but speaks without transition of "*cette négation qui est le travail, et qui est le temps*" and continues in a distinctly Hegelian mode. One might well find that during this period Blanchot's discourse on death, insofar as it too is a critique of Heidegger, also problematically Hegelianizes the latter. This is a question that will have to be taken up elsewhere.

12. For Heidegger's analysis of boredom as a privileged affect, a *Grundstimmung* or fundamental mood and "attunement," see *Fundamental Concepts of Metaphysics: World, Finitude, Solitude*.

13. Along these lines, Blanchot's rejection of "reality" as material for fiction becomes explicit in a number of essays written during the war. See especially "Le roman pur" and "Mallarmé et l'art du roman" (both published in *Journal des Débats* in 1943).

14. Blanchot also writes of "la perte de l'être," the loss of being: what appears in the time of the absence of time, he says, is "the fact that nothing appears, the being that is in the ground [*au fond*] of the absence of being, which is when there is nothing, which is no longer when when there is something: as if there were beings only through the loss of being, when being is lacking" (EL 26).

15. For an analysis of Blanchot's relation to the sublime, and in particular the "temporality of the sublime" in *L'instant de ma mort*, see Yves Gilonne, *La rhétorique du sublime dans l'oeuvre de Maurice Blanchot*, 191–214; see also 31–73. This well-informed and detailed study gives very little attention to Blanchot's fiction and virtually none at all to the *récits*.

16. See especially "La rencontre de l'imaginaire," in *Le livre à venir*, 9–18.

17. With this phrase I am quoting the title of Nancy's collection of essays, *The Ground of the Image*. Nancy himself chose this English phrase to translate the title of his book, *Au fond des images*.

18. I am referring to the *second* flyleaf of *L'espace littéraire*, where Blanchot speaks of the mobile and shifting "center" toward which a book, even a fragmentary book of elucidations, is imperiously drawn, as though toward its most secret, intimate "point." In *L'espace littéraire*, he says, that point lies in the direction of the essay "Le regard d'Orphée."

19. Nancy's essay is found in *The Ground of the Image*. In it, he comments on Heidegger, *Kant and the Problem of Metaphysics* (where the "schematism" from the *Critique of Pure Reason* is given tremendous importance) and its odd evocation of a death mask.

20. The quoted phrase is from Blanchot's essay on Henry James ("Le tour d'écrou" in *Le livre à venir*, 173), where he contrasts the latter's penchant for preparatory notebooks with the narrative fragments in Kafka's diaries; unlike James's second order sketches, Blanchot writes, even Kafka's abandoned sentences are "*engagée[s] dans la profondeur du récit.*" A literary essay, while certainly different from a preparatory sketch, nonetheless shares something of this reflective second order distance from the space and "depth" in question.

21. It is jarring, and in some respects even inappropriate, to use the language of gender equity in a direct paraphrase of Blanchot, who was never concerned with this question and whose language, both in its singular idiom and as a reflection of French usage, remains squarely within the masculine norms of discourse in referring to the writer "himself" (with everything that accompanies and follows from this). Blanchot did, if rarely, write on women writers (Woolf, Duras, Weil), but it is clear from countless indices (and paradigmatic figures, especially Orpheus), that for him this adventure is gendered as masculine. My purpose in broaching the question of femininity in Blanchot will be not so much to directly remedy this preponderance (much less to level accusations at Blanchot) as to show how certain related linguistic, figural and fantasmatic structures are implicated or embedded in the work, and, at the same time, to bring into relief the masculinist malaise that haunts it. The use of more inclusive language, however internally incongruous it

may be, only reflects a historical reality that, in turn, ought to be brought to bear on our reading of this work—while also acknowledging that Blanchot *does* articulate something fundamental about writing—regardless of who writes—which the critical aspects of the analysis presented here could not simply dissolve.

22. What I have attempted to reduce to a brief description has been carefully and eloquently detailed in a much longer commentary, in Anne-Lise Schulte Nordholt, *Maurice Blanchot: L'écriture comme expérience du dehors*.

23. The essay I am quoting from, "Il ne saurait être question de bien finir," from *Le livre à venir*, 41–49, was first published under the title "Quand la morale se tait," *Nouvelle Revue Française* 13 (January 1954): 492–501.

24. It is worth noting that, in addition to Rilke, Blanchot in this same passage also quotes Kafka, who evokes a similarly resounding "mandate" (LV 44–45).

25. This phrase ("other solitude") evokes Blanchot's earlier essays, published in *L'espace littéraire*, "La solitude essentielle" and its addendum in the appendix, "La solitude essentielle et la solitude dans le monde." I would add that the passage I am paraphrasing is one of the very few in which Blanchot explicitly evokes a "bad conscience," along with a "fault" that separates the writer from the world—here presented as a burden imposed by "our time" (LV 47) but one that does not touch on what is essential in writing's exigencies.

26. It is here that one can see a deep kinship that Blanchot recognized between himself and Beckett, in this reduction of literary speech to nothing but an incalcitrant voice, in an exigency that Blanchot attributes to the writer of *L'innommable*, calling it "*l'exigence qui l'a entraîné hors de soi, l'a dépossédé et dessaisi*" ("the exigency that drew him out of himself, dispossessed him and ungrasped him"; LV 290). In this respect, the exigency is one that demands the very movement of reduction and stripping away that leaves the "inelim-inable residue" of essential concern in my readings of Blanchot, the voice as "*le reste obscur qui ne veut pas céder*" ("the obscure remainder that will not yield") as Blanchot puts it in the same essay (LV 290). To amplify comments made above regarding the corpse and the death mask in Blanchot, and the process of "*dépouillement*" that renders them up, it is interesting to note that in this essay Blanchot refers to the characters in Beckett's trilogy, such as Molloy, as "masks" (LV 287), in order to figure them as inessential compromises, as signs that this errant speech has not yet been stripped or reduced enough. . . . But Blanchot's own masks, these shells of irreducible enigmas, will problematize this relegation of the figure.

27. This is the title of an essay from *L'entretien infini*: "Le rapport du troisième genre (l'homme sans horizon)" in EI, 94–105 (*The Infinite Conversation*, "The Relation of the Third Kind (man without horizon)," 66–74).

28. This slightly apologetic attitude for broaching the theme of literature, formerly an almost exclusive preoccupation, can be read in an essay title such as "La littérature encore une fois," in EI, 583–595.

29. The opening section of *Le livre à venir* containing these two chapters is called "Le chant des sirènes," thus explicitly including Proust within the sphere of this emblematic song, as one of its privileged figures.

30. Derrida's critique of Husserlian phenomenology surely owes a great deal to Blanchot's reflections on the spacing of time in literary experience (which themselves take up elements of Heidegger's thinking on time, as we have seen). A closer examination of the various points of convergence in their language would be revealing, and might indicate something of the "literariness"—by way of language's search for its temporal and spatial grounds—at work in this originary spacing, which Derrida called "différance." Such an analysis might also provide a different inflection of the deconstructed "voice." See especially *La voix et le phénomène*; and "La différance," in *Marges de la philosophie*.

31. Regarding the fictional status of Proust's tales of involuntary memory, we need only refer to the rather banal piece of toast in the opening passages of *Contre Sainte-Beuve*, a taste sensation that only later became a madeleine. Blanchot most likely did not know of this early version until after writing these essays (*Contre Sainte-Beuve* was not published until late 1954, the year Blanchot's essays appeared in the NRF). But it is clear that he did not consider these experiences as biographical transcriptions, a notion he dismisses in a later section on *Jean Santeuil*, another early text in which, he says, some readers wanted to find "*le prototype de l'événement tel qu'il fut réellement vécu*" ("the prototype of the event as it was really lived"), a naiveté that provokes a kind of sententious sigh: "*tant est grand le besoin de situer l'insituable*" ("so great is the need to situate the unsituatable") (LV 29).

32. The entire question of homosexuality in Proust's life and work reveals this fungibility in the clearest fashion possible. Blanchot, for his part, makes the awkward gesture in an earlier essay of referring to "*Proust [qui] n'aime Albertine que lorsqu'elle commence à s'en aller . . .*" (PF, 230) ("Proust [who] loves Albertine only when she begins to leave . . .").

33. Blanchot critiques these images (the seed, the ripening fruit, the hard rich resistant kernel) in a long contemporary essay on another modern master of deep interiority: see "Rilke et l'exigence de la mort" in *L'espace littéraire*, 158 (and elsewhere). See also the opening page of the book (EL 13), where such an image is explicitly demoted to the status of the inessential.

34. This reading of *L'instant de ma mort* has been informed by Derrida's book length commentary on Blanchot's short text: *Demeure: Maurice Blanchot*. Derrida stresses the relation between testimony, fiction and the singularity of death, and, in his title, he makes a connection between the notion of a "demeure," a dwelling or remaining (Blanchot uses this word, or forms of it, several times in *L'instant de ma mort*), and the "*mourir*" inscribed in the title, by way of the archaic French word *demourance*, a state of waiting, lagging behind, dwelling indefinitely that invokes also the "last resting place" (*Demeure*, 101–102). As a confirmation of the autobiographical dimension of the story, Derrida quotes a letter he received from Blanchot, dated July 20, 1994, that begins: "*Il y a cinquante ans je connus le bonheur d'être presque fusillé*" ("Fifty years ago, I had the good fortune of almost being shot to death").

35. Vlassov was a Russian general who, having been captured and threatened with the systematic starvation and destruction of his soldiers, went over to the side of the Germans. (See Derrida, *Demeure*, 97.)

36. See Bident, *Maurice Blanchot*, 229–230 and 582–583.

37. Regarding the resonance of dates in Blanchot, I cannot help mentioning also that Kafka's famous night of writing "The Judgment" occurred on the evening of Blanchot's fifth birthday, on September 22, 1912. Finally, allow me to add that September 22 is also the birth date, many years later, of my own late brother, to whom I here pay discrete homage (as I always did when these dates came up in my reading about or in Blanchot, including EL 66).

38. Blanchot can be very strident regarding the nullity of the factual past. I let the following from *L'arrêt de mort* stand in for a more developed comment on this aspect of Blanchot's rhetoric (of course it is a fictional narrator who speaks, but the tenor of the passage converges with many points articulated elsewhere and otherwise):

> Je voudrais, maintenant, noter autre chose. Je parle de faits qui semblent infimes et je laisse de côté les événements publics [it is 1938, the Munich accords, etc.]. Ces événements ont été très grands et ils m'ont occupé tous les jours. Mais, aujourd'hui, ils pourrissent, leur histoire est morte et mortes aussi ces heures et cette vie qui alors ont été les miennes. Ce qui parle, c'est la minute présente et celle qui va la suivre. A tous ceux qu'elle abrite, l'ombre du monde d'hier plaît encore, mais elle sera effacée. Et le monde qui vient tombe déjà en avalanche sur le souvenir d'autrefois. (AM 76)

39. Proust, *Le temps retrouvé*, in *A la recherche du temps perdu*, 3:890.

40. One might well hear in this *instance*, evoked within a context saturated by guilt and implicit judgment, the *kritische Instanz* that for Freud constitutes the superego, that self-judging agency that, in the wake of its constitutive losses, splits itself off from the ego and sets itself up as the administrator and enforcer of unattainable ideals. In Freud's schema, the formation of this *instance* is grounded in melancholy, and thus also in the "precipitate of abandoned object-cathexes" (that is, the accumulated residue of lost love), that forms the layered geology of the ego, insofar as it "contains the history of those object choices"—a geology that Proust elaborated in recognizably similar terms. See Freud, *The Ego and the Id*, SE vol. 19, 29; and "Mourning and Melancholia."

41. See Heidegger on the call of conscience and guilt, *Being and Time*, sections 54–58.

42. Hélène Cixous, "Maurice Blanchot, The Madness of the Day: A Text of Evasion," in *Readings*, 95–109. The texts collected in this book were transcribed from Cixous's seminars and have not to my knowledge been published in French; I will therefore quote them only in English.

43. Appearing on the first page of *Première livraison*, 4, 1976, the text bore the title "Une scène primitive."

44. Speaking to his "companion," he says: "*Je viens de tirer les rideaux des grandes baies, et je regarde*," and he continues: "*Je retrouvai là, joyeusement* préservé, *le petit jardin—à peine un jardin, quelques pas de terre enfermé entre des murs—, qui s'étendait juste devant moi, un peu au delà des vitres, au delà mais à ma portée, de sorte qu'en regardant au dehors, j'avais aussi le sentiment de toucher le fond d'un souvenir . . .*" (CQ 84; my emphasis). The passage continues in an overtly nostalgic vein.

45. Close not to the "wild heart" of Joyce, echoed by Lispector and commented by Cixous, but to a dead one. Though this dead heart too may indeed be "wild," in its way—dead, and yet living on, if only in the language that ineluctably "supposes" it.

46. I underscore this word, *project*, in order to emphasize its charged scenic, graphic and sculptural resonances. In these respects, it will be significant, as a noun, in the discussion of *L'arrêt de mort* in Chapter 7.

47. One might bring this implicit question into proximity with Adorno's explicit version, which he proposes as the last "negative" survival of "metaphysical experience," arrived at through the question, "Is that all?" See Adorno, *Metaphysics: Concept and Problems*, 143. It should be noted how different this question is from Heidegger's rendering of philosophical astonishment as: "Why is there something rather than nothing?" Heidegger does relate this astonishment also to a discovery of nothingness, but he does not say, as Blanchot does, that "nothing is what there is." Finally, one should note that Blanchot's scene recounts a rupture that occurs within childhood and its delimited boundaries, and that the nothing revealed is also the destruction of childhood, a leaving of it—its *dépouillement*, and thus something like its remnant and cadaver.

48. Kant, *Critique of Practical Reason*, in *Practical Philosophy*, 269. As mentioned before, Cixous gives some insightful attention to this aspect of Blanchot's text, in close relation to Kafka's "Before the Law"; see *Readings*, 23–27.

49. To be fair, the statement can be read to mean that "he will weep no more" *about this*, that nothing is what there is. . . . But that is not what Blanchot writes, choosing instead a categorical rhetoric that is central to the melancholic economy interrogated here.

50. The question of humor and comedy in Blanchot, while not the moot point it might at first seem to be, is a subtle and complex one. I will attempt to bring out some hints of *Witz* and humor at various points in the discussion.

51. Gerald Prince asked a similar question in his article "The Point of Narrative: Blanchot's *Au moment voulu*," *SubStance* 5, no. 14 (1976): 92–98.

52. Compare *Le Dernier homme*: "*A peine l'eus-je effleurée qu'elle se dressa d'un bond en criant des mots indistincts . . .*" (DH 80) ("I had only barely touched her when she leaped up, crying out indistinct words . . .").

53. I will comment further in Chapter 7 on this very Jamesian figure of spectral melancholy taken up by Blanchot in *Au moment voulu*.

54. This scene occurs when Judith sits up in bed, screams (in Latin), then collapses, peering out of "avid eyes."

Chapter 6: The Shell and the Mask: L'arrêt de mort

1. See Christopher Fynsk, *Language and Relation*, 245–271. Fynsk's chapter is one of the most complex, nuanced and thoughtful readings of *L'arrêt de mort* that I have seen; its interrogations and reflections are very close to those I will present here. But like many discussions of *L'arrêt de mort*, it is marked by a crucial omission or evasion, namely of a certain aspect of the manifest content of the *récit*, in which the sacrifice demanded of the

narrator is the sacrifice of erotic love, and of a woman. I will discuss Fynsk's reading in more detail in what follows. In addition to Derrida's reading of *L'arrêt de mort* in *Parages* (on which Fynsk draws as well), see Leslie Hill's discussion of the text in *Blanchot: Extreme Contemporary*, 144–157, which touches on many of the motifs I will address in what follows.

2. Beckett's works often include a moment in which this problem is explicitly thematized as part of the arbitrary positing gesture of fiction: how to scatter or dissolve what has been conjured, as when the voice in *Company* confronts the "problem" of its figments and wonders "how [to] dispel them" (C 31).

3. For an interesting discussion of this figural inevitability, particularly as it relates to the uncanny, see Adam Bresnick, "Prosopoetic Compulsion: Reading the Uncanny in Freud and Hoffmann." Similarly, for a reading of Blanchot's death mask in terms of prosopopoeia, see J. Hillis Miller, *Versions of Pygmalion*, 179–210.

4. Fynsk, *Language and Relation*, 269.

5. In *Specters of Marx*.

6. Derrida, "Moi—la psychanalyse (1979)," 152.

7. Derrida, *Spectres de Marx*, 194; *Specters of Marx*, 120.

8. This play on words is suggested by a passage in Blanchot's essay on Proust in *Le livre à venir*, "L'expérience de Proust." In a reflection on Proust's first unpublished novel, *Jean Santeuil*, Blanchot considers, with visible disapproval, Proust's penchant for "scenes": "*Proust a un certain goût pour les scènes classiques auxquelles il ne renonce pas toujours. Même la grandiose scène finale a un relief excessif qui ne répond guère à la dissolution du temps dont elle cherche à nous persuader. Mais précisément, ce que nous apprend Jean Santeuil, ainsi que les différentes versions que nous ont conservées les Carnets, c'est l'extraordinaire travail de transformation qu'il n'a cessé de poursuivre pour user les arêtes trop vives de ses tableaux et pour rendre au devenir les scènes qui peu à peu, au lieu d'être des vues fixées et figées, s'étirent dans le temps, s'enfoncent et se fondent dans l'ensemble . . .*" (LV 35–36; my emphasis). Here, rather than volatility, the figure is one of erosion. But these "*arêtes . . . vives*" are of the essence in Proust, however pulverized or distended their sharp corners may be; and in a passage such as this Blanchot somewhat embarrassingly figures Proust as a writer . . . *almost* just like himself. Indeed, if the extreme attenuation of Blanchot's *récits* consists, after all, in such an erosion or filing away of life's sharp contours, there is no question but that the debris of this operation has fallen into their faultlines and crevices, more or less legibly, more or less hidden from view.

9. On *L'arrêt de mort* as a trap for readers, see Pierre Madaule, *Une tâche sérieuse*.

10. It is curious that two of the women in *L'arrêt de mort* bear the names of figures from the sphere of Bataille's work: Simone is the name of one of the main characters in *L'histoire de l'oeil*; and Colette cannot fail to evoke Colette Peignot, aka Laure, whose death in 1938 has often been associated with the death of J. in *L'arrêt de mort*. For an intriguing commentary on this constellation of figures, see Milo Sweedler, *The Dismembered Community*.

11. Indeed, even the invocations of calendar time early in the text are disjointed from real historical time, as has often been pointed out: the one very precise date evoked,

Wednesday, October 13, 1938, the one date of which the narrator says he is sure (AM 11), in fact did not exist on any calendar. Such is the rigidity of the "pitilessly precise dates" Blanchot refers to: an objective and, to that extent, irrefutable break from the world. As we saw, Blanchot exploits such minute but irremediable fractures in his other historically embedded narrative, *L'instant de ma mort*.

12. Like the "coup de dent" from *La folie du jour*, this "coup de hache" echoes, but even more literally, with Kafka's sublimely painful ax-blow of reading. Indeed, the chirological context makes this very much a question of reading, of deciphering a law that has been scrambled in the scars left behind by an unaccountable violence. In this case, however, it is the hand itself, by way of the feminine figure who has left it behind and from whose life it continues to "live," that the law in question will be given its minimal delineation—that of a compulsive drive to write.

13. There is an entire subgenre of tales involving a severed and reanimated hand. To refer only to two writers Blanchot surely knew: Maupassant wrote not one but two severed hand stories ("La main" and "La main écorchée"); and there is Nerval's "La main enchantée." See the article by Susan Hiner, which makes a connection (extremely suggestive in the present context) between the figure of the severed hand, the French Revolution (the Terror), and a newfound liberation from verisimilitude in the fantastic: "Hand Writing: Dismembering and Re-Membering in Nodier, Nerval and Maupassant." Hiner also analyzes a text by Nodier and pertinently mentions Breton's *Nadja* (an important precursor for Blanchot, and for *L'arrêt de mort* in particular), specifically Nadja's vision of a flaming hand over the Seine. The lineage back from Blanchot to one of the main sources of the thinking of the uncanny thus follows a direct path, passing through Nadja, to Nerval, and to Hofmann.

As is evident in the quoted passage, in *L'arrêt de mort* Blanchot appropriates the topoi of fantastic literature while strangely divesting them of their shock value, to the point of making them almost unnoticeable. One could say that this is his general treatment of the fantastic modes of the uncanny: "*rien d'extraordinaire*," which suggests that the uncanny is all the more unsettling without the shivery macabre effects that give many of Poe's tales (for example) their melodramatic tone. However, the image of the shivers, a chill that is both a sign of sickness and a site of truth, is not unimportant for Blanchot, who gives *le frisson* a deeply enigmatic significance, especially in *Au moment voulu*. We are also touching here on a Jamesian "chill" which Blanchot brings into the peculiar atmosphere of sensation and thought in which the *récits* unfold.

14. I am referring to the section bearing this title ("La préhension persécutrice") in the first essay of *L'espace littéraire*, "La solitude essentielle" (EL 18–20).

15. J. too is described as having entered the narrator's room one night by mistake (that is, because of a misunderstanding), thus initiating their relationship (AM 16–17). This is one of numerous such chance encounters in Blanchot's narratives. This element of chance brings in another related literary association, this time with surrealism, on which Blanchot wrote appreciatively on several occasions, emphasizing the importance of "*le hasard*." (See, for example, "Le demain joueur," in *L'entretien infini*.) The numerous echoes between

Breton's *Nadja* and Blanchot's chance recitical encounters with women has been fruitfully explored, especially by Michael Holland, "Rencontres piégées: 'Nadja' dans *L'Arrêt de mort*," in *Violence, théorie, surréalisme*, 117–138. Blanchot returns again and again to such accidental encounters with feminine figures who happen to inhabit a room close by, who haunt the spaces inhabited by his narrators, somewhere just beyond the curve of a hallway, the turn of a stair, and who gesture or even enter for unknown reasons, and who remain.

16. It is remarkable to note that although Fynsk cites this passage, in a spirit not foreign to my own interest in it (that is, with the question of the *récit*'s originary imperative in mind), in commenting on the quote he nonetheless elides the very blatant and literal presence of a ghost, a spectral woman, evoked here, and even dismisses its "present reality" (preferring to emphasize, more equivocally, the scene's Derridean *pas* and the figure's status as a "thought"; see *Language and Relation*, 258–259). But in the logic of the narrative, the ghost is real, and she is a woman—and to that very extent she is not quite or not only the *thought* that will be evoked later; and besides, does she even precede by steps (*pas*), or rather does she not glide along in classic spectral fashion? Might such a possibility cause a certain trouble for Derrida's own reading? In any case, as an out and out ghost, she introduces into the narrative a properly figural twist, a knot that the narrator's "ruses" cannot so easily undo. To recognize all this in unequivocal terms is only to acknowledge the very literal fantasmatic moment in Blanchot's narrations, and in his very thinking of literature. The more troubling elision, which I am tracking here, bears on the feminine aspect of this apparition—an elision that both Derrida and Fynsk carry out systematically, despite their attention to this aspect on a more general level.

17. I would like to interject here a question based on what might at first seem like a far-fetched association: Could Blanchot be playing on the Snow White *Märchen*? The Grimms' tale is a story that begins with blood, and includes melancholy loss, malignant maternal powers, exile, wandering, death by poison, and a kind of embalmed preservation—all themes present in *L'arrêt de mort* (recall that J. even calls her mother "*la reine mère*," the queen mother; AM 12) and elsewhere in Blanchot; most decisively, it culminates in the resurrection of a female character from an arrested death in a glass coffin, thanks to a man who has fallen in love with an image, a convergence of motifs that would reflect quite strangely on the tale at hand. More tendentiously, one could say that, like the narrator of *L'arrêt de mort*, the Prince is also a man who has found, *in the image of a dead woman as such*, a treasure that must not be taken away from him. A closer examination of these similarities might be fruitful, if only to amplify the ways in which Blanchot's story draws on a tradition of dead-woman aesthetics. For more on the place of the Grimms' *Märchen* in this tradition, see Bronfen, *Over Her Dead Body*, 99–107. Bronfen actually mentions Blanchot in this connection, but in reference to the analysis of corpsely resemblance in "Les deux versions de l'imaginaire" in *L'espace littéraire*, not to *L'arrêt de mort* (see Bronfen, 104).

18. See the discussion in chapter 7 of Nancy, *Au fond des images*, translated as *The Ground of the Image*.

19. Fynsk also speaks of "the gaze of fascination, a blind seeing that is *contact* with the outside." See *Language and Relation*, "Crossing the Threshold," 239 (Fynsk's emphasis).

20. This alliance is one of Derrida's major preoccupations in "Survivre."

21. Christopher Fynsk aptly emphasizes the aspect of touching in *L'arrêt de mort*. *Language and Relation*, 265–266.

22. Here too I am anticipating a more detailed analysis in the next chapter, based on Nancy's discussion of the dead gaze—the "look" of the image—in relation to the Kantian schematism, in his essay "Masked Imagination."

23. Here again, allow me to refer to the analysis below of Blanchot's reflections on the corpsely image in "Deux versions de l'imaginaire."

24. For a fine discussion of the relation between death and the feminine that touches on many of the motifs discussed here (the death mask in particular), as well as on Lévinas's "response" to Blanchot's elaborations of these motifs, see Andreas Gelhard, *Das Denken des Ünmöglichen*, 213–235, and "Antworten, II (Lévinas)," 236–252.

25. This quotation, together with Blanchot's frequent insistence on the extreme and startling youth of his most highly charged feminine figures, provides some justification for formulating my obtuse question as one about a "girl" with and to whom "something is happening" here. A certain "girlishness" is inscribed directly into her most fleshly, embodied gestures, precisely when she begins to be "gnawed" away.

26. Fynsk also speaks of the youth and "in-fans" of J. and the "dead child" she evokes ("On Death Sentence," *Language and Relation*, 250), in relation to Blanchot's reflections on the necessary killing of the child in *L'écriture du désastre* (based on Serge Leclaire, *On tue un enfant*); but in doing so he turns away from the feminine aspect of the woman who must, in fact, be killed. She too, the woman as such, is a figure for this immemorial relation to language's opening, and her death is the explicit drama of *L'arrêt de mort*. I will return to this ambiguous killing in the next chapter. For some unusual remarks on childhood fascination and the feminine figure of the mother, see Blanchot's "La solitude essentielle" (EL 30).

27. Derrida relates this X to the doctor's remark concerning the narrator's imminent and already overdue death—"*il faut mettre une croix dessus*"—and to the chiasmic movement operated by the sculptural artifacts: from death to death, from sculpture to writing. *Parages*, "Survivre," 208–209 (bottom segment of the page).

28. It is interesting to note Blanchot's use of the word *vouer* in this sentence ("*Cette force trop grande . . . nous* voue *peut-être à un malheur sans mesure . . .*"), which will be echoed in the profession of exclusive devotion to the literary vocation in the liminal note to *L'espace littéraire* ("*Sa vie est entièrement* vouée *à la littérature . . .*"). The too great force is, after all, the fundamental drive behind the writer's vocation. And, of course, these uses of *vouer* also invoke a kind of condemnation, the doom of an unfortunate destiny, and of a great misfortune—the "*malheur*" that Christopher Fynsk is right to emphasize. Marking a destiny and a destination, it bespeaks a *Bestimmung*, a vow, the voicing of a strange self-affirming fate: *amor fati*.

29. A similar observation is made with great insight, and in ways that are highly relevant to the present discussion, in Kaja Silverman, *Flesh of My Flesh*; see especially chapter 2, "Orpheus Rex," which addresses the Orphic myth that is constitutive of Blanchot's literary schema.

Chapter 7: The Dead Look: The Death Mask, the Corpse Image, and the Haunting of Fiction

1. Martin Heidegger, *Kant and the Problem of Metaphysics* (hereafter KPM); Heidegger also discusses the schematism in *Logic: The Question of Truth*.

2. Jean-Luc Nancy, *The Ground of the Image*.

3. On the inevitability of narrative in Kant's transcendental thought, with particular attention to the questions of exemplarity and "respect," see J. Hillis Miller, *The Ethics of Reading*, especially chapter 2, "Reading Telling: Kant," 13–39.

4. The title of the chapter in question in *The Critique of Pure Reason* is: "On the Schematism of the Pure Concepts of the Understanding."

5. With the exception of one "example" he gives: "number" as the "the pure schema of magnitude" (CPuR 274). KPM 75.

6. Nancy, "Masked Imagination" in *The Ground of the Image*. It is to this essay that I owe the impetus of this reading of Blanchot in relation to the schematism. — Regarding the discursive and fantasmatic use of the death mask, it will be necessary to bring out the way in which it also becomes a projection *surface*, giving back the images and affects attributed to it. To anticipate: the difference with Blanchot is that he goes so far as to animate and spectralize it—and to gender it feminine. Heidegger, for his part, refers to the death mask of Pascal.

7. For Blanchot's comments on the work's refusal to be read, its "*noli me legere*," see "La solitude essentielle" (EL 17–18).

8. There is some ambiguity on this point. As Nancy presents it, the collapse or superimposition occurs by way of a singular expression, *beziehungsweise* (meaning: respectively, with respect to the variables involved), used by Heidegger at a crucial moment, when he writes that "the death mask . . . gives the 'image' of the dead person, shows how the dead person appears, or respectively [*beziehungsweise*], appeared . . ." (KPM 66; modified). In "the image of the dead person," Nancy seems to be placing the stress on *person*, where both the corpse and the death mask show an image of *that person* whose disappearance has left the remainder of a blind/invisible look, rather than on the corpse itself (the look that it had when the death mask was made, for example). Here I would like to amplify this ambiguity, and point further toward that effaced/revealed pastness.

9. See *The Ground of the Image*, 152 n. 18.

10. It should also be recalled that the schematism is an operator of unity and unification (in the "synthesis of the sensory manifold," as Kant says), of "the one" (in the minor mode of multiplicity), and therefore of singularity.

11. I cite this paragraph also for its evocation of the theater, and in anticipation of Beckett, whose attention to these questions, to the movement of time and appearance in their singularities, is legible in the very titles of some of his plays and short prose pieces, which resonate here and elsewhere in Nancy's essay: *That Time* (*Cette fois*), *Come and Go*, *Imagination Dead Imagine*.

12. *Ground of the Image* 152 n. 18.

13. For a detailed and faithful commentary on this appendix, including its engagement with both Sartre's and Levinas's contemporaneous reflections on the image and the imaginary, see Anne-Lise Schulte Nordholt, *Maurice Blanchot: L'écriture comme expérience du dehors*, especially chapter 8, "L'écriture, expérience de l'imaginaire."

14. *L'espace littéraire*, 341.

15. This phrase and other similar ones occur several times in *L'espace littéraire*; it restages Heidegger's refrain in "What Is Metaphysics?" (which itself stages a discourse that would deny "the nothing," an invocation of "beings themselves—and nothing else").

16. See Emmanuel Levinas, *De l'existence à l'existant*.

17. This phrase alludes to the well-known formula of Michel Foucault, in *Discipline and Punish*, 30.

18. In this respect, it demands to be read in terms of the "hauntology" evoked by Derrida, precisely in close proximity to Hamlet. I cannot pursue this thread here, but will return to it elsewhere. See Derrida, *Specters of Marx*.

19. One apparent exception to this is the body of J. in *L'arrêt de mort*, described in disorienting detail as she dies. But this is precisely not a dead body "lying in state," but rather a resurrecting body. When J. "really" dies, the text of the first part ends, and like her heartbeat, her image too "*s'éparpilla comme du sable*" ("scattered like sand"; AM 53).

20. In evoking the flashing appearance of the "one" of the image, Nancy refers as well to the singularity of birth (GI 96). We could no doubt also liken this *éclat* to Beckett's "birth astride of a grave," when "the light gleams an instant then it's night once more" (*Waiting for Godot*, 57). Even Beckett's serial repetitions and porous, merging identities do not manage to completely efface the allure (at least) of singularity that in part structures them.

21. This is the "third level" of ambiguity, as laid out in the chapter's final paragraph. The first two "levels" are "*le niveau du monde*," and then that of the two versions. This third level is something like the radical synthesis of the two versions, their simultaneous indistinction.

22. These similarities resound even in the earlier novel's use of language, which anticipates that of *L'espace littéraire*, sometimes with exact phrases; e.g. both describe the corpse as "cet être de grand format" (*Thomas l'obscur*, 101).

23. Ernst Benkard, *Das ewige Antlitz: Eine Sammlung von Totenmasken mit einem Geleitwort von Georg Kolbe*. The English translation, by Margaret M. Green, was "published by Leonard and Virginia Woolf at the Hogarth Press," as we read on the title page, in 1929. Heidegger's course was given in fall and winter 1925–1926. See *Logic: The Question of Truth*, 297.

24. Information on the history of l'Inconnue de la Seine and the fascination with the story behind the mask can be found in Hélène Pinet, "L'eau, la femme, la mort: Le mythe de l'Inconnue de la Seine," in *Le dernier portrait*, catalogue of an exhibit at the Musée d'Orsay in Paris, March 5–May 26, 2002 (this book is cited by Nancy in "L'imagination masquée"). See also Anja Zeidler, "Influence and Authenticity of l'Inconnue de la Seine," part of a website entitled "A Reader's Guide to William Gaddis's Recognitions," www.williamgaddis.org/recognitions/inconnue/index.shtml.

25. And yet if anything is revealed in the ambiguity of the passive-active "look" discussed above, it is that these two aspects have an essential point of homogeneity: the argument is precisely that in looking at the death mask one sees its (withdrawn) looking-back-at-us (*gleich als blicke sie uns an*) as the generative image of the very conditions of seeing (it) . . . the seeing-seen of vision.

26. Blanchot, *Une voix venue d'ailleurs*, 16.

27. Louis-René des Forêts, *Poèmes de Samuel Wood* (Montpellier, France: Fata Morgana, 1988). For a fine commentary on this and other works by des Forêts, see Ann Smock, *What Is There to Say?*

28. Louis-René des Forêts, *Poèmes de Samuel Wood*, 10.

29. A part of this passage was previously cited in the last section of Chapter 5.

30. The entire sentence reads: "*Jamais cet instant ne fut troublé, ni prolongé, ni différé, et peut-être m'ignorait-elle, et peut-être était-elle ignorée de moi, mais il n'importait, car pour l'un et pour l'autre cet instant était bien le moment voulu*" ("Never was this instant troubled, or prolonged, or deferred, and perhaps she ignored me, and perhaps she was ignored by me, but it didn't matter, since for one and the other this instant was indeed the awaited moment"; AMV 139, my emphasis). Here the narrator describes a relation with a feminine figure that is no relation, while also subtly evoking the time of death in this citation of the well known Nietzschean injunction: "*Stirb zur rechten Zeit*" ("Die at the right time") from *Thus Spoke Zarathustra* (book I, section 21).

31. We find an intriguing precedent to this in *The Castle*, when Frieda argues that she and K. must go south: "If you want to hold on to me, we must leave and go somewhere else, to the south of France, or to Spain." To which K. replies: "I cannot go abroad. . . . I came here in order to stay here. I will stay here." The narrator continues: "And in a contradiction he didn't bother to explain, he added as if speaking to himself: 'Now what could have attracted me to this desolate land other than the desire to stay?'" (*The Castle*, Harmon trans., 136). This statement resonates richly with Blanchot's penetrating remarks on Kafka and literary space (indeed, the very notion of literary space for Blanchot appears to be derived in significant ways from *The Castle*). It is interesting to note that just after this exchange, Frieda remarks: "Better to have this *pretty mask torn off* . . . so that I can live with you in peace" (my emphasis). Finally, I would note too that in a later scene in the Herrenhof, after K. is abandoned by Frieda, who now lives with one of the assistants, K. spies her at a very Blanchotian "bend in the hallway" (*Castle*, 245). Such bends and turns, present also in abundance in James's tale, enigmatically mark the geometry of desire and spectral encounter in Blanchot's récits, including *Au moment voulu* (as will be evident in what follows here).

32. James, *The Turn of the Screw*, 41–42.

33. The text does not specify the manner of her death, but I cannot help seeing her appearances by the lake, "the Sea of Azof," as a suggestion that she met her end as a Noyée... Joyce Carol Oates makes a similar assumption in her story "Accursed Inhabitants of the House of Bly," where in the opening paragraph she describes Miss Jessel as "condemned to the eternal motions of washing the mud-muck of the Sea of Azof off her body, in particular the private parts of her marmoreal body." See Oates, *Haunted: Tales of the Grotesque*.

34. The phrase is found in *The Complete Notebooks of Henry James*, 259; the passage is reprinted in the Norton Critical Edition of *The Turn of the Screw*, 108.

35. Here Blanchot concludes his essay with the writer's dying words in James's story, "The Middle Years": "We work in the dark—we do what we can—we give what we have. Our doubt is our passion and our passion is our task. The rest is the madness of art."

36. The unsettling relation between speech and murder in Blanchot (see for example EI 271–280) is thoughtfully explored, by way of Melville, in Ann Smock, *What Is There to Say?*, chapter 2, "Speak or Kill: Blanchot, Melville." Smock also cites Christopher Fynsk, "On Death Sentence" (170 n. 3).

37. The story is cited in Pinet, "L'eau, la femme, la mort: Le mythe de l'Inconnue de la Seine," in *Le dernier portrait*.

38. No literary account of Blanchot's tropic mobilization of dead women in the space of fiction could overlook the multiple and significant ways in which he draws not only on James, but also on Poe, for whom poetry and fiction find their most profound animating force in the passionate entombment—not to say encryption—of the melancholy beauty of lost and dead beloved women. In "Ligeia" one finds striking similarities with *L'arrêt de mort*. And of course it was Poe who famously declared that "the death of a beautiful woman is unquestionably the most poetical topic in the world." Poe continues with a sentence that is less often quoted: "and equally is it beyond doubt that the lips best suited for such a topic are those of a bereaved lover" ("Philosophy of Composition"; see also Bronfen, *Over Her Dead Body*, chapter 4, "The 'most' poetic topic").

39. This détournement was discussed, at a time when very little had been written on the question of women in Blanchot, by Larysa Mykyta in "Blanchot's *Au moment voulu*: Woman as the Eternally Recurring Figure of Writing," *boundary 2* 10, no. 2 (Winter 1982): 77–95. Mykyta's PhD dissertation, "Vanishing Point: The Question of Woman in the Works of Maurice Blanchot" (SUNY, 1980) is cited by Lynne Huffer in "Blanchot's Mother," *Yale French Studies* 93 (1998): 175–195, as is Jane Gallop's "Friends/Corpses/Turds/Whores: Blanchot on Sade," in *Intersections: A Reading of Sade with Bataille, Blanchot and Klossowski* (Lincoln: University of Nebraska Press, 1981), 35–66. Derrida's "La loi du genre" was also published around this time (in 1980). More recently, the question of feminine figures in Blanchot was taken up in the collection of essays titled *L'oeuvre du féminin dans l'écriture de Maurice Blanchot*, ed. Eric Hoppenot (Grignan: Les Editions Complicités, 2004).

40. I am referring especially to several essays collected in *Le livre à venir*: those grouped under the title "Le Chant des sirènes" ("La rencontre de l'imaginaire," and "L'expérience de Proust"); the essay on James, "Le tour d'écrou"; and "Il ne saurait être question de bien finir" (first published as "Quand la morale se tait"). In these concluding sections, I will discuss "L'échec de Milena," also written in 1954, but not collected in a book until 1981 (more on this below); and "Orphée, Don Juan, Tristan," it, too, from 1954 and later collected in *L'entretien infini*.

41. This discussion owes much to Blanchot's biographer, Christophe Bident, who provides some illuminating information on Blanchot's relationships with women. See Bident, *Partenaire invisible*, 103–109 and 272–278.

42. On Bataille, Blanchot and the question of "communication" and sacred fusion, particularly as it relates to erotic experience and, even more pointedly, to the expulsion of a woman from the sphere of thought and text, see Milo Sweedler, *The Dismembered Community: Bataille, Blanchot, Leiris and the Remains of Laure*.

43. The jarring effect of this conflation of Proust and his narrator was pointed out above; it is in this essay that Blanchot refers to Proust who "loves Albertine only when she begins to leave" (PF 230). It should be noted that what Blanchot thus says here about "Proust" is presented, according to the rhetorical structure of the essay, as homologous with what he says about Constant, based significantly on the latter's personal writings, and on *Adolphe*.

44. "Le journal intime et le récit" (written in 1955) in *Le livre à venir*, 254.

45. "L'échec de Milena" was eventually collected in *De Kafka à Kafka*, a small paperback bringing together all of Blanchot's writing on Kafka, along with "La littérature et le droit à la mort."

46. Bident devotes a brief chapter to Denise Rollin and her relationship to Blanchot in *Partenaire Invisible*, 272–278.

47. Ibid., 278 n. 2.

48. Ibid., 275.

49. See the Introduction and *Pourquoi écrivez-vous?* 188.

50. Blanchot had also used this phrase in *Celui qui ne m'accompagnait pas* (published in 1953): "*Le sentiment qui me reste: je ne céderai pas, je ne puis autrement*" ("The feeling that remains for me: I will not yield, I cannot do otherwise"; CQ 145).

51. Brod writes: "In *The Castle* we may find Kafka's relationship to Milena mirrored with peculiar skepticism and bitterness." *Franz Kafka: A Biography*, 219–220.

52. Bident, *Partenaire invisible*, 313. The expression *auprès de* is difficult to translate here; it implies staying side by side with someone or something, or in some cases keeping watch next to the bed of someone who is ill or dying.

53. The last two texts that can be considered *récits*, *Le dernier homme* (1957) and *L'attente l'oubli* (1962), do revolve once again around feminine figures, but they are not "literal" ghosts.

Chapter 8: Beckett's Voices and the Paradox of Expression

1. In "Three Dialogues with Georges Duthuit" in *Disjecta*, to be discussed later. In a letter from the period of the "Three Dialogues," Beckett speaks admiringly (referring to Dante's "neutrals") of "*il gran rifiuto*," the great refusal. *Letters: 1941–1956*, 136 and 142 n. 3.

2. This phrase occurs in many of Beckett's texts, in the often retrospective *Malone Dies*, for example, and throughout *How It Is*. By emphasizing decision here, I do not mean to evoke a masterful self-governing subject; instead, I am merely distinguishing this process from one carried out by something like an algebraic grammar machine or, for example, a computer. The narrative material exceeds the blank forms of a formal process, and must have come from elsewhere. For an interesting discussion of Beckett and computers, see J. M. Coetzee, "Samuel Beckett's *Lessness*: An Exercise in Decomposition." After a computer-aided analysis of the word units used in "Lessness" (by which it is discovered that the second half of the text is an exact but recombined repetition of the first), Coetzee concludes: "The residue of the fiction is then not the final disposition of the fragments but the motions of the consciousness that disposes them according to the rules we have traced, and no doubt others we have failed to trace"—rules which, it must be added, can in no way account for the original selection. This residue of a "motion" is also the sticky stuff attaching the voice to its imponderables, and to its past.

3. As expressed in "Three Dialogues"; more on this later.

4. As he writes in *Worstward Ho*. It is in such a movement toward an "unlessenable" remainder that Beckett's voices converge with what in Blanchot is described as the "irreducible, ineliminable residue" of an uncanny being in language (EL 47 and 342). As with Blanchot, the question here is what that residue consists of, and what peculiar shapes it compulsively and repeatedly gives to see.

5. Along with the "*gran rifiuto*," Beckett also refers in his letters from this period to the phrase voiced by Dante's characters, whose "*cri commun*" (as he calls it) is: "*Io fui*," I was (*Letters 1941–1956*, 90). This is the refrain of the hell of having been.

6. See note 2.

7. From the "Three Dialogues" and "La peinture des van Velde, ou le monde et le pantalon," in *Disjecta*, 143 and 119, respectively.

8. *Disjecta*, 138–145.

9. The following discussion of the "Three Dialogues" owes much to the section on it in Bersani and Dutoit's essay in *Arts of Impoverishment: Beckett, Rothko, Resnais*, especially 11–27.

10. With the publication of Beckett's letters from this period, we can see how the "Three Dialogues," as a piece of writing, evolved out of this correspondence. One of the main differences between the two, however, consists in the "staging" that Beckett adds to the exchange in the published dialogue, along with the pungent irony this staging helps to introduce. In the letters, Beckett is for the most part quite earnest, as he anguishes over the difficulty of what he is trying to say, and struggles with the sense that he is forcing his

own views and dilemmas onto van Velde's painting. In one revealing signoff, following the longest of his disquisitions on painting, and in a statement that clearly announces the "Three Dialogues," Beckett writes: "I am no longer capable of writing *about*. So, if you are not altogether sick of me, you are going to have to ask me questions. I shall try to answer. But bear in mind that I who hardly ever talk about myself talk about little else" (*Letters 1941–1956*, 141). This remark also echoes the logic of the self-exposing lexicographers mentioned earlier.

11. "Stirrings Still" (from 1989), CSPr 265.

12. D.'s reaction to this statement, together with B.'s resolute refusal to qualify it, is worth quoting here in the dramatic form that Beckett gives it:

> B.—[. . .] together with the obligation to express.
> D.—But that is a violently extreme and personal point of view, of no help to us in the matter of Tal Coat.
> B.—
> D.—Perhaps that is enough for today.

B.'s silence here, as though in recognition of its stubborn indefensibility, marks the categorical register of his position, together with its universal extension, regardless of how irrational, "violent," and "personal" this may be. As such it is also something of a "cannot do otherwise," but one that patently has no justifying grounds or guarantor. The blank space marks out that emptiness as well.

13. Such as those offered by Mondrian or Kandinsky, at whom Beckett takes a jab in this piece, referring to "the every man his own wife experiments of the spiritual Kandinsky" (D 144). On Mondrian (among others) and the ontology of "the grid" see Rosalind Krauss, "Grids," in *The Originality of the Avant-Garde and Other Modernist Myths*, especially page 10: "But if it is materialism that the grid would make us talk about . . . that is not the way that artists have ever discussed it. If we open any tract . . . we will find that Mondrian and Malevich are not discussing canvas or pigment or graphite or any other form of matter. They are talking about being or mind or spirit. From their point of view, the grid is a staircase to the Universal, and they are not interested in what happens below in the Concrete." In another essay in the same collection ("LeWitt in Progress"), Krauss links Beckett's work directly with that of Sol LeWitt, whose apparently transcendent and rational series of fragmented cubes are, she claims, as mad and arbitrary as Molloy's obsession with sucking stones. It is interesting to note, as Krauss does, that in 1969 LeWitt did a drawing that accompanied the text of Beckett's play "Come and Go" as published in *Harper's Bazaar*.

14. It should be noted that Beckett's statements are of course quite different from an aestheticist "art for art's sake" position, where the latter envisions an autonomous artistic sphere in which aesthetic pleasure would compensate for the exclusion of all that would inhibit, repress or block this pleasure. The lack of relation espoused by Beckett here would not open an autonomous space of aesthetic pleasure, but the beleaguered and indeed fragile space of an indigence that must be closely guarded, so strong are the temptations of

expression (or the "temptations of style," as J. M. Coetzee has put it; see "Samuel Beckett and the Temptations of Style").

15. Bersani and Dutoit take as their starting point Beckett's failure to fail, in order to demonstrate that his insistence on nonrelation leads to "the representation of the *genesis of relations*" (*Arts of Impoverishment*, 26; authors' emphasis). This interesting point will be taken up in the reading of *Company* presented below.

16. In yet another act of self-dismissal, Beckett later referred to this letter as "German bilge." In any case, the bilge, and the threat or promise of its seeping into this dialogue, are to be distinguished from the spiritualizing discourses on painting mentioned above; the insidious materiality of the image renders it incompatible with an abstract transcendence. For Beckett transcendence is not abstract; its radical ambiguity is made clear in the hesitation between "something or nothing," and again when, later in the 1937 letter, he mentions "the latest work of Joyce" (i.e., *Finnegans Wake*): "There it seems to be rather [than a "mocking attitude toward the word"] an apotheosis of the word. Unless perhaps Ascension to Heaven and Descent to Hell are somehow one and the same. How beautiful it would be to believe that that indeed was the case" (D 172). Any ascent would thus also be a mocking parody of ascent, its destination no less infernal than sublime.

17. See Tom Driver, "Beckett by the Madeleine." Beckett also speaks of "the confusion" and "the mess." About which he says: "It is all around us and our only chance is to let it in. The only chance of renovation is to open our eyes and see the mess. It is not a mess you can make sense of . . . To find a form that accommodates the mess, that is the task of the artist now."

18. See Adorno's essay on Beckett, "Trying to Understand Endgame." See also Bersani and Dutoit, *Arts of Impoverishment*, 19.

19. As the unnamable says, "If only I were not obliged to manifest" (U 10).

20. Alain Badiou is one of the first readers of Beckett to point out the importance of this sentimental side of his work. See "L'Écriture du générique: Samuel Beckett," in *Conditions*.

21. See "The Rhetoric of Temporality" in *Blindness and Insight*.

22. Beckett, *The Collected Shorter Plays*, 266.

23. Compare this phrase to Malone's (quoted below): "Yes, it is no good pretending, it is hard to leave everything" (MD 107).

24. We recall that this also applies to Kant's moral philosophy, which must call on a feeling that is not a feeling, a "respect" that is not "pathological," in order to secure an incentive, a *Triebfeder* that is somehow uncompromised by sensibility. It is interesting to note that Beckett appears to have had more than a passing acquaintance with Kant, indicating in a letter that he possessed the philosopher's complete works. See *The Letters of Samuel Beckett: 1929–1940*, 581, 622.

25. Steven Connor, "'Traduttore, traditore': Samuel Beckett's Translation of 'Mercier et Camier.'"

26. Beckett's first published prose work was an essay on Proust, written in 1931, and later published as *Proust* (Grove Press, n.d.).

27. For an insightful discussion of these aspects of the trilogy, and one of the first to rigorously place them in relation to deconstructive modes of textuality, see Thomas Trezise, *Into the Breach: Samuel Beckett and the Ends of Literature*.

28. Molloy's mother is, ironically, or not so ironically, in a position analogous to the fatherland Ithaca and Penelope in the *Odyssey*, whose journey's are evoked at several points in the narrative, especially in the long episode with Lousse. There Molloy mentions, unexpectedly and rather dreamily, "the black boat of Ulysses," likening himself to one of the latter's slaves watching from the poop "the proud and futile wake" (MoE, 68). Molloy stays with Lousse "a year perhaps" (MoE, 68) the same amount of time Odysseus stays with Circe, who is also invoked when Molloy accuses Lousse of "having drugged my food and drink with noxious powders and potions" (MoE, 71). He even refers to her "miserable molys" (MoE, 72), the strangely Molloy-like name of a "pharmakon" given to Odysseus by Hermes as protection *against* Circe's sorcery (*Odyssey* 10:287–306). Such scrambling of references, and the offhand manner in which Molloy/Beckett makes them, renders these searches for sources somewhat inconsequential, in the end; in no way does this or any other classic text provide the kind of "key" which is hidden in Joyce's novel, for example. Molloy's invocation of earlier narratives does not provide Beckett's text with an underpinning or inject it with mythological meanings, but it does suggest that Molloy's journey resembles that of Odysseus, or at least of one of his slaves, with this radical difference: "it bears me from no fatherland away, bears me onward to no shipwreck" (MoE, 68). The terms, and terminus, of the epic are withdrawn, and yet the movement toward an unquestioned goal insists on its own parodic figuration.

29. "Drunk as a foetus / I suck at the paps of darkness." This very apt Beckettian image is found in Sylvia Plath's "The Stones" in her "Poem for a Birthday" series.

30. Compare this devouring and deferral, as well as the closing of the eyes behind closed eyes, to the less "unhappy" version of this post-annihilation moment in *Ill Seen Ill Said*. Attempting to dispel and end his fiction, the narrator says: "Farewell to farewell. Then in that perfect dark foreknell darling sound pip for end begun. First last moment. Grant only enough remain to devour all. Moment by glutton moment. Sky earth the whole kit and boodle. Not another crumb of carrion left. Lick chops and basta. No. One moment more. One last. Grace to breathe that void. Know happiness" (*Ill Seen Ill Said*, 59). The "nourishment" provided in this late text is no longer so frustratingly inaccessible as it is throughout the early trilogy. Though it is clear that this rotting word leftover has less to do with food than with reaching one free breath just beyond it.

31. James Knowlson reports a conversation with Beckett in which the latter claimed to have "intrauterine memories." He told the biographer of his experience in psychoanalysis in the early 1930s:

> I used to lie down on the couch and try to go back in my past. . . . I certainly came up with some extraordinary memories of being in the womb. Intrauterine memories. I remember feeling trapped, of being imprisoned and unable to escape, of crying to be let out but no one could hear, no one was listening. I remember being in pain but being unable to do anything about it.

It is tempting to see in this an encapsulation of the Trilogy as a whole, an image for the origin that is also an illusory endpoint. See Knowlson, *Damned to Fame: The Life of Samuel Beckett*, 171.

32. Indeed, Beckett himself refers to all of his fictions, beginning with Murphy, as a "series," a structure which becomes explicit in the *Unnamable*'s own references to earlier works. See *Letters 1941–1956*, 55.

33. Roman Jakobson, "Shifters and Verbal Categories," in *On Language*.

34. Benveniste, "*La nature des pronoms*" and "*La subjectivité dans le langage*," in *Problèmes de linguistique générale*, 1:251–257 and 1:258–266, respectively. Daniel Katz has pointed out the striking relevance of Benveniste's treatment of pronouns for an understanding of pronominal operations in Beckett. See *Saying I No More: Subjectivity and Consciousness in the Prose of Samuel Beckett*, esp. 20–24.

Chapter 9: Company, *But Not Enough*

1. In *Conditions*, 329–366.
2. This quotation is taken from the short book Badiou published on Beckett, based on the earlier essay: *Beckett, L'increvable désir*, 19.
3. Badiou, *Conditions*, 330–331.
4. The entire "late trilogy" (*Company, Ill Seen Ill Said*, and *Worstward Ho*) is devoted to an exploration of solitude—the solitary fictive gesture—and introduces the question of sociality or "company" largely by way of this gesture.
5. Badiou, *Beckett*, 48.
6. Paul Shields articulates this paradox in a highly pertinent way when he writes that Beckett "wants to invert *creatio ex nihilo* in his fiction, to conjure nothing from the imitative something that already is." At the same time, it is important to acknowledge that there is a positive, if compulsive, force that impels the positing of *something*. See Shields, "Beckett's Labour Lost: *Company* and the Paradox of Creation."
7. This is confirmed by his biographers. See Knowlson, *Damned to Fame*, 574–575.
8. Is it not clear that this decision is motivated in the end by a certain assonance? Consider this passage: "Can the crawling creator crawling in the same create dark as his creature create while crawling? One of the questions he put to himself as between two crawls he lay" (C 52).
9. The last phrase of the passage is from the well-known lines spoken by Portia in *The Merchant of Venice* (IV, i, 186). "The quality of mercy is not strain'd, / It droppeth as the gentle rain from heaven / Upon the place beneath." These words are meant to forestall a torturous punishment. The implication in Beckett's use of the phrase for a torture scene already underway is, surprisingly, that *this* form of torture (the past imposed, drop by drop, as language) is itself a kind of mercy—or conversely, that "the quality of mercy," while perhaps unstrained, is nonetheless a kind of torture.
10. This point is made persuasively in Bersani and Dutoit's discussion of *Company* in "Beckett: Inhibited Reading," *Arts of Impoverishment*, 65–77.

11. At one point, when the deviser wonders if the hearer might somehow be aware of his creator (crawling nearby), he asks, "Might the crawling creator be reasonably imagined to smell? . . . How much more companionable could his creator but smell. Could he but smell his creator. Some sixth sense? Inexplicable premonition of impending ill? Yes or no? No. Pure reason? Beyond experience. God is love. Yes or no. No" (C 51–52). So much for spirituality, metaphysics, and religion. In any case, this passage makes explicit the ongoing reference *Company* as a whole makes to Kant's thought.

12. In *Malone Dies*, Beckett had related a version of this story, in a style that is recognizably different: "One day we were walking along the road, up a hill of extraordinary steepness, near home I imagine, my memory is full of steep hills, I get them confused. I said, The sky is further away than you think, is it not, mama? It was without malice, I was simply thinking of all the leagues that separated me from it. She replied, to me her son, It is precisely as far away as it appears to be. She was right. But at the time I was aghast" (MD, 98). Enoch Brater details this and many other allusions found in *Company*, whether autobiographical, auto-textual (references to Beckett's own texts), or more broadly literary. See Brater, "The Company Beckett Keeps: The Shape of Memory and One Fabulist's Decay of Lying."

13. Dante writes, "I cannot rightly say how I entered it, I was so full of sleep at the moment I left the true way" (*Inferno* I.10–12).

14. On this point, see Gilles Deleuze's essay on Beckett, "L'Épuisé."

15. Arguably, and residually, even to Beckett's mother: the old woman who, like the ones in *Ill Seen Ill Said* and *Worstward Ho*, was a figure of endless mourning, wearing black for years after the death of Beckett's father.

16. Philippe Lacoue-Labarthe, "Il faut," in *Heidegger and the Politics of Poetry*.

Conclusion: Speech Unredeemed: From the Call of Conscience to the Torture of Language

1. The German *das Geläut* could be rendered more neutrally as "sound," but it carries a distinct connotation of bells or chimes. In the context of Heidegger's reading of Trakl's poem "Ein Winterabend," it echoes the latter's phrase "*die Abendglocke läutet*" (the evening bell, or vespers, rings). Hofstadter translates the phrase as "the peal of stillness." Heidegger, *Poetry, Language, Thought*, 207.

2. Ibid., 206; Heidegger, *Unterwegs zur Sprache*, 28.

3. He does so by quoting a letter to Herder from Hamann, in which the latter speaks of an "abyss" opened in reason by language. *Poetry, Language, Thought*, 191; *Unterwegs zur Sprache*, 13.

4. I do not wish to caricature Heidegger's discourse in late essays such as "Language," which is marked by extreme tensions and paradoxes, and a deep acknowledgment on the part of its author of the harsh conditions confronted by his epoch, for which he does not seek any facile solutions. It is also an intensely "poetic" discourse, not in its tropes and messages, but in its tone and *Stimmung*, and in that sense Heidegger does perform and convey the substance of his questions. However, he also preserves his thinking from the

very corrosive elements it continually attempts to treat, and appears to wish at some level to reinstitute the losses so extensively surveyed, and even to insist despite his own insights on the possibility of a unified grandeur. In the light of Heidegger's own compromises, followed by a highly scandalous "reticence" during and long after the period when this essay was written, it is difficult not to respond to these equivocations with impatience and sarcasm. Beckett himself is a powerful ally in this regard (as Adorno well knew).

5. And that is fully maintained even in Descartes's very narrative *Meditations*, which vividly stage madness, delusion and regressive infinity, but only as hypotheses, not as risky conditions menacingly undergone in the very speech that evokes them. The narrowness and erosion of this buffer is what will fascinate Beckett in his important philosophical precursor.

6. This is a question that would require a closer look at the récits written after *L'arrêt de mort*, texts that are certainly not without a certain calm but threatening madness.

7. Indeed, one must admit that the invocations, at the end of the essay, of a language that no longer speaks but *is*, of "art" and "literature" in their "essential researches" (all recurring themes in *L'espace littéraire*) ring rather hollow in the wake of this otherwise lucid commentary on a work that appears to have irreparably corroded them from the inside.

BIBLIOGRAPHY

Adorno, Theodor. *Metaphysics: Concept and Problems*. Edited by Rolf Tiedemann, translated by Edmond Jephcott. Stanford, Calif.: Stanford University Press, 2000.
———. "Notes on Kafka." In *Prisms*. Translated by Samuel Weber and Shierry Nicholson Weber. Cambridge, Mass.: MIT Press, 1983.
———. "Trying to Understand Endgame." In *Notes to Literature I*. Edited by Rolf Tiedemann, translated by Shierry Weber Nicholson. New York: Columbia University Press, 1991.
Agamben, Giorgio. *Nudities*. Translated by David Kishik and Stefan Pedatella. Stanford, Calif.: Stanford University Press, 2010.
Al-Kassim, Dina. *On Pain of Speech: Fantasies of the First Order and the Literary Rant*. Berkeley: University of California Press, 2010.
Anderson, Mark. *Kafka's Clothes: Ornament and Aestheticism in the Habsburg Fin de Siècle*. Oxford: Oxford University Press, 1992.
Badiou, Alain. *Conditions*. Paris: Editions du Seuil, 1992.
———. *Beckett: l'increvable désir*. Paris: Hachette, 1995.
Beckett, Samuel. *The Collected Shorter Plays*. New York: Grove Press, 1984.
———. *Compagnie*. Paris: Minuit, 1985.
———. *Company*. New York: Grove Press, 1980.
———. *The Complete Short Prose*. Edited by S. E. Gontarski. New York: Grove Press, 1995.
———. *Disjecta*. New York: Grove Press, 1984.
———. *Endgame*. New York: Grove Press, 1958.
———. *Fin de partie*. Paris: Minuit, 1957.
———. *How It Is*. New York: Grove Press, 1964.
———. *Ill Seen Ill Said*. New York: Grove Press, 1981.
———. *L'innommable*. Paris: Minuit, 1953.
———. *Malone Dies*. New York: Grove Press, 1956.
———. *Malone meurt*. Paris: Minuit, 1951.
———. *Mercier and Camier*. New York: Grove Press, 1974.
———. *Mercier et Camier*. Paris: Minuit, 1970.

———. *Molloy*. Translated by Patrick Bowles and Samuel Beckett. New York: Grove Press, 1955.
———. *Molloy*. Paris: Minuit, 1951.
———. *The Unnamable*. New York: Grove Press, 1958.
———. *Waiting for Godot*. New York: Grove Press, 1954.
———. *Worstward Ho*. New York: Grove Press, 1983.
Benjamin, Walter. "Franz Kafka: On the Tenth Anniversary of his Death." Translated by Harry Zohn. In *Illuminations: Essays and Reflections*, edited by Hannah Arendt, 111–140. New York: Schocken, 1969.
Benkard, Ernst. *Das ewige Antlitz: Eine Sammlung von Totenmasken mit einem Geleitwort von Georg Kolbe*. Berlin: Frankfurter Verlags-Anstalt, 1926.
Benveniste, Emile. *Problèmes de linguistique générale*. Paris: Gallimard, 1966.
Bersani, Leo, and Ulysse Dutoit. *Arts of Impoverishment: Beckett, Rothko, Resnais*. Cambridge, Mass.: Harvard University Press, 1993.
Bident, Christophe. *Maurice Blanchot: Partenaire Invisible*. Seyssel: Champ Vallon, 1998.
Binder, Hartmut. *Kafka-Kommentar*. Munich: Winkler, 1975.
Blanchot, Maurice. *Aminadab*. Paris: Gallimard, 1942.
———. *Aminadab*. Translated by Jeff Fort. Lincoln: University of Nebraska Press, 2002.
———. *Au moment voulu*. Paris: Gallimard, 1951.
———. *Celui qui ne m'accompagnait pas*. Paris: Gallimard, 1953.
———. *De Kafka à Kafka*. Paris: Gallimard, 1981.
———. *Infinite Conversation*. Translated by Susan Hanson. Minneapolis: University of Minnesota Press, 1993.
———. *La folie du jour*. Montpellier: Fata Morgana, 1973.
———. *La part du feu*. Paris: Gallimard, 1949.
———. *Le livre à venir*. Paris: Gallimard, 1959.
———. *L'entretien infini*. Paris: Gallimard, 1969.
———. *L'espace littéraire*. Paris: Gallimard, 1955.
———. *L'arrêt de mort*. Paris: Gallimard, 1948.
———. *The Last Man*. Translated by Lydia Davis. New York: Columbia University Press, 1987.
———. *Lettres à Vadim Kozovoï (1976–1998)*. Paris: Manucius: 2008.
———. *L'instant de ma mort*. Montpellier: Fata Morgana, 1994.
———. *The Madness of the Day*. Translated by Lydia Davis. Barrytown: Station Hill Press, 1981.
———. *Passion politique: Lettre-récit de 1984, suivi d'une lettre de Dionys Mascolo*. Paris: Galilée, 2011.
———. *Une voix venue d'ailleurs*. Paris: Gallimard, 2002.
———. *When the Time Comes*. Translated by Lydia Davis. Barrytown, N.Y.: Station Hill Press, 1995.
Blanchot, Maurice, and Pierre Madaule. *Correspondance, 1953–2002*. Paris: Gallimard, 2012.

Brater, Enoch. "The Company Beckett Keeps: The Shape of Memory and One Fablist's Decay of Lying." In *Samuel Beckett: Humanistic Perspectives*, edited by Morris Beja, S. E. Gontarski, and Pierre Astier, 157–171. Columbus: Ohio State University, 1983.

Bresnick, Adam. "Prosopoetic Compulsion: Reading the Uncanny in Freud and Hoffmann." *The Germanic Review* 71, no. 2 (Spring 1996): 114–132.

Brod, Max. *Franz Kafka: A Biography*. New York: Schocken, 1963.

Bronfen, Elisabeth. *Over Her Dead Body: Death, Femininity and the Aesthetic*. Manchester: Manchester University Press, 1992.

Buch, Robert. *The Pathos of the Real: On the Aesthetics of Violence in the Twentieth Century*. Baltimore: Johns Hopkins University Press, 2010.

Butler, Judith. *Excitable Speech: A Politics of the Performative*. London and New York: Routledge, 1997.

———. *The Psychic Life of Power: Theories in Subjection*. Stanford, Calif.: Stanford University Press, 1997.

Canetti, Elias. *Der Andere Prozess: Kafkas Briefe an Felice*. Munich: Hanser, 1969.

Cixous, Hélène. *Readings: The Poetics of Blanchot, Joyce, Kafka, Kleist, Lispector and Tsetayeva*. Minneapolis: University of Minnesota Press, 1991.

Coetzee, J.M. "Samuel Beckett's *Lessness*: An Exercise in Decomposition." *Computers and the Humanities* 7, no. 4 (March 1973): 195–198.

———. "Samuel Beckett and the Temptations of Style." In *Doubling the Point: Essays and Interviews*, edited by David Attwell. Cambridge: Harvard University Press, 1992.

Connor, Steven. "'Traduttore, traditore': Samuel Beckett's Translation of 'Mercier et Camier." *Journal of Beckett Studies* 11 and 12 (1989): 27–46.

Corngold, Stanley. *Franz Kafka: The Necessity of Form*. Princeton: Princeton University Press, 1990.

———. *Lambent Traces: Franz Kafka*. Princeton: Princeton University Press, 2004.

Corngold, Stanley, and Benno Wagner. *Franz Kafka: The Ghosts in the Machine*. Evanston, Ill.: Northwestern University Press, 2011.

David-Ménard, Monique. *La folie dans la raison pure: Kant lecteur de Swedenbourg*. Paris: Vrin, 1990.

Deleuze, Gilles. *Critique et clinique*. Paris: Editions de Minuit, 1993.

———. *Essays Critical and Clinical*. Translated by Daniel W. Smith and Michael A. Greco. Minneapolis: University of Minnesota Press, 1997.

———. "L'épuisé." In Samuel Beckett, *Quad et autre pièces pour la télévision*. Paris: Editions de Minuit, 1992.

Deleuze, Gilles, and Félix Guattari. *Kafka: Toward a Minor Literature*. Minneapolis: University of Minnesota Press, 1986.

De Man, Paul. "The Rhetoric of Temporality." In *Blindness and Insight*. Minneapolis: University of Minnesota Press, 1983.

Derrida, Jacques. *Demeure: Maurice Blanchot*. Paris: Editions Galilée, 1998.

———. *La voix et le phénomène*. Paris: Presses Universitaires de France, 1968.

———. *Marges de la philosophie*. Paris: Minuit, 1968.

———. "Moi—la psychanalyse (1979)." In *Psyché: Inventions de l'autre*, 145–158. Paris: Galilée, 1987.

———. "Préjugés: Devant la loi." In *La faculté de juger*. Paris: Minuit, 1985.

———. *Specters of Marx*. Translated by Peggy Kamuf. New York: Routledge, 1994.

des Forêts, Louis-René. *Poèmes de Samuel Wood*. Montpellier: Fata Morgana, 1988.

Driver, Tom. "Beckett by the Madeleine." *Columbia University Forum*, Summer 1961, 21–25.

Feldman, Karen S. *Binding Words: Conscience and Rhetoric in Hobbes, Hegel and Heidegger*. Evanston, Ill.: Northwestern University Press, 2006.

Fogel, J.-F., and D. Rondeau, eds. *Pourquoi écrivez-vous? 400 écrivains répondent*. Paris: Libération, 1985.

Foucault, Michel. *Discipline and Punish: The Birth of the Prison*. Translated by Alan Sheridan. New York: Vintage, 1977.

François, Anne-Lise. *Open Secrets: The Literature of Uncounted Experience*. Stanford, Calif.: Stanford University Press, 2008.

Freud, Sigmund. *The Standard Edition of the Complete Psychological Works of Sigmund Freud*. Edited by James Strachey. London: Hogarth Press, 1960.

Fynsk, Christopher. *Language and Relation: . . . that there is language*. Stanford, Calif.: Stanford University Press, 1996.

Gallop, Jane. "Friends/Corpses/Turds/Whores: Blanchot on Sade." In *Intersections: A Reading of Sade with Bataille, Blanchot and Klossowski*, 35–66. Lincoln: University of Nebraska Press, 1981.

Gelhard, Andreas. *Das Denken des Unmöglichen: Sprache, Tod und Inspiration in den Schriften Maurice Blanchots*. Munich: Wilhelm Fink Verlag, 2005.

Gilonne, Yves. *La rhétorique du sublime dans l'oeuvre de Maurice Blanchot*. Paris: L'Harmattan, 2008.

Greenberg, Martin. *Kafka: The Terror of Art*. New York: Horizon Press, 1968.

Hart, Kevin. *The Dark Gaze: Maurice Blanchot and the Sacred*. Chicago: University of Chicago Press, 2004.

Hart, Kevin, and Geoffrey H. Hartman, eds. *The Power of Contestation: Perspectives on Maurice Blanchot*. Baltimore: Johns Hopkins University Press, 2004.

Heidegger, Martin. *Fundamental Concepts of Metaphysics: World, Finitude, Solitude*. Translated by William McNeill and Nicholas Walker. Bloomington: Indiana University Press, 2001.

———. *Kant and the Problem of Metaphysics*. Translated by Richard Taft. Bloomington: Indiana University Press, 1990.

———. *Logic: The Question of Truth*. Translated by Thomas Sheehan. Bloomington: Indiana University Press, 2010.

———. *Poetry, Language, Thought*. Translated by Albert Hofstadter. New York: Harper and Row, 1971.

———. *Unterwegs zur Sprache*. Stuttgart: Günther Neske, 1993.

Hill, Leslie. *Blanchot: Extreme Contemporary*. London and New York: Routledge, 1997.

Hiner, Susan. "Hand Writing: Dismembering and Re-Membering in Nodier, Nerval and Maupassant." *Nineteenth Century French Studies* 30, nos. 3 and 4 (Spring–Summer 2002): 301–315.

Hölderlin, Friedrich. *Essays and Letters on Theory*. Edited by T. Pfau. Albany: State University of New York Press, 1988.

———. *Sämtliche Werke und Briefe*. Munich: Carl Hanser Verlag, 1970.

Holland, Michael. "Rencontres piégées: 'Nadja' dans *L'Arrêt de mort*." In *Violence, théorie, surrealism*, edited by Jacqueline Chénieux-Gendron and Timothy Matthews, 117–138. Paris: Lacanthal & Ritter, 1994.

Hoppenot, Eric, ed. *L'oeuvre du féminin dans l'écriture de Maurice Blanchot*. Grignan: Les Editions Complicités, 2004.

Huffer, Lynne. "Blanchot's Mother." *Yale French Studies* 93 (1998): 175-95

Jakobson, Roman. "Shifters and Verbal Categories." In *On Language*, 386–392. Cambridge, Mass.: Harvard University Press, 1995.

James, Henry. *The Complete Notebooks of Henry James*. Edited by Leon Edel and Lyall H. Powers. New York: Oxford University Press, 1987.

———. *The Turn of the Screw*. Edited by Deborah Esch and Jonathan Warren. New York: Norton, 1999.

Juliet, Charles. *Rencontre avec Samuel Beckett*. Montpellier: Fata Morgana, 1986.

Kafka, Franz. *Blue Octavo Notebooks*. Translated by Ernst Kaiser and Eithne Wilkins. Cambridge: Exact Change, 1991.

———. *Briefe an Felice und andere Korrespondenz aus der Verlobungszeit*. Edited by Erich Heller and Jürgen Born. Frankfurt: Fischer, 1967.

———. *Briefe an Milena*. Edited by Jürgen Born and Michael Müller. Frankfurt: Fischer, 1986.

———. *The Castle*. Translated by Mark Harman. New York: Schocken, 1998.

———. *Complete Stories*. Edited by Nahum N. Glatzer. New York: Schocken, 1971.

———. *Diaries*. Edited by Max Brod. New York: Schocken, 1976.

———. *Gesammelte Werke in acht Bänden*. Edited by Max Brod. Frankfurt: Fischer, 1983.

———. *Kafka's Selected Stories*. Edited by Stanley Corngold. New York: Norton Critical Edition, 2007.

———. *Kritische Ausgabe in 15 Bänden: Schriften und Tagebücher*. Edited by Jürgen Born, Gerhard Neumann, Malcolm Pasley, and Jost Schillemeit. Frankfurt: Fischer, 2002.

———. *Letters to Felice*. Edited by Erich Heller and Jürgen Born. New York: Schocken, 1973.

———. *Letters to Friends, Family and Editors*. Translated by Richard and Clara Winston. New York: Schocken, 1977.

———. *Letters to Milena*. Translated by Philip Boehm. New York: Schocken, 1990.

———. *The Sons: The Metamorphosis, The Judgment, The Stoker and Letter to His Father*. Edited by Mark Anderson. New York: Schocken, 1989.

———. *The Trial*. Translated by Breon Mitchell. New York: Schocken, 1998.

Kant, Immanuel. *Critique of the Power of Judgment*. Edited by Paul Guyer. Cambridge: Cambridge University Press, 2000.

———. *Critique of Pure Reason*. Edited by Paul Guyer and Allen W. Wood. Cambridge: Cambridge University Press, 1998.

———. *Observations on the Feeling of the Beautiful and the Sublime*. Translated by John T. Goldthwait. Berkeley: University of California Press, 1960.

———. *Practical Philosophy*. Edited by Mary J. Gregor. Cambridge: Cambridge University Press, 1996.

Katz, Daniel. *Saying I No More: Subjectivity and Consciousness in the Prose of Samuel Beckett*. Evanston, Ill.: Northwestern University Press, 1999.

Knowlson, James. *Damned to Fame: The Life of Samuel Beckett*. New York: Simon & Schuster, 1996.

Koelb, Clayton. *Kafka's Rhetoric: The Passion of Reading*. Ithaca, N.Y.: Cornell University Press, 1989.

Krauss, Rosalind. *The Originality of the Avant-Garde and Other Modernist Myths*. Cambridge, Mass.: MIT Press, 1985.

Kurz, Gerhard, ed. *Der junge Kafka*. Frankfurt: Suhrkamp, 1984.

Lacoue-Labarthe, Philippe. "The Contestation of Death." In *The Power of Contestation: Perspectives on Maurice Blanchot*. Edited by Kevin Hart and Geoffrey H. Hartman. Baltimore: Johns Hopkins University Press, 2004.

———. *Heidegger and the Politics of Poetry*. Translated by Jeff Fort. Champaign-Urbana: University of Illinois Press, 2007.

———. *Poetry as Experience*. Translated by Andrea Tarnowski. Stanford: Stanford University Press, 1999.

———. *Typography: Mimesis, Philosophy, Politics*. Edited by Christopher Fynsk. Stanford, Calif.: Stanford University Press, 1998.

Laplanche, Jean, and Jean-Bertrand Pontalis. *Vocabulaire de la psychanalyse*. Paris: PUF, 1967.

Levinas, Emmanuel. *De l'existence à l'existant*. Paris: Vrin, 2002.

Longinus. *On the Sublime*. Translated by W. Hamilton Fyfe. In *Aristotle Poetics, "Longinus" On the Sublime, Demetrius On Style*, 119–254. Cambridge, Mass.: Harvard University Press, 1973.

Lozier, Claire. *De l'abject et du sublime: Georges Bataille, Jean Genet, Samuel Beckett*. Oxford: Peter Lang, 2012.

Madaule, Pierre. *Une tâche sérieuse*. Paris: Gallimard, 1973.

Martis, John. *Philippe Lacoue-Labarthe: Representation and the Loss of the Subject*. New York: Fordham University Press, 2005.

Maxwell, Catherine. *The Female Sublime: From Milton to Swinburne*. Manchester: Manchester University Press, 2001.

Miller, J. Hillis. *The Ethics of Reading: Kant, De Man, Eliot, Trollope, James, and Benjamin*. New York: Columbia University Press, 1989.

———. *Versions of Pygmalion*. Cambridge, Mass.: Harvard University Press, 1990.

Mitchell, Breon. "Kafka and the Hunger Artists." In *Kafka and the Contemporary Critical Performance*, edited by Alan Udoff, 236–255. Bloomington: Indiana University Press, 1987.

Mykyta, Larysa. "Blanchot's *Au moment voulu*: Woman as the Eternally Recurring Figure of Writing." *boundary 2* 10, no. 2 (Winter 1982): 77–95.

Nancy, Jean-Luc. *Au fond des images*. Paris: Galilée, 2003.

———. *The Ground of the Image*. Translated by Jeff Fort. New York: Fordham University Press, 2005.

———. *L'impératif catégorique*. Paris: Galilée, 1983.

Nietzsche, Friedrich. *On the Genealogy of Morals*. Edited and translated by Walter Kaufmann. New York: Vintage, 1967.

Nordholt, Anne-Lise Schulte. *Maurice Blanchot: L'écriture comme expérience du dehors*. Geneva: Droz, 1995.

Norris, Margot. "Sadism and Masochism in Two Kafka Stories." *MLN* 93, no. 3 (1978): 430–447.

Oates, Joyce Carol. *Haunted: Tales of the Grotesque*. New York: Dutton, 1994.

Pasley, Malcolm. "The Act of Writing and the Text: The Genesis of Kafka's Manuscripts." In *Reading Kafka: Prague, Politics, and the Fin de Siècle*, edited by Mark Anderson, 201–214. New York: Schocken, 1989.

Politzer, Heinz. *Franz Kafka: Parable and Paradox*. Ithaca, N.Y.: Cornell University Press, 1966.

Presa, Elisabeth. "White Work." In *After Blanchot: Literature, Criticism, Philosophy*, edited by Leslie Hill, Brian Nelson, and Dimitris Vardoulakis, 257–269. Newark: University of Delaware Press, 2005.

Prince, Gerald. "The Point of Narrative: Blanchot's *Au moment voulu*." *SubStance* 5, no. 14 (1976): 92–98.

Proust, Marcel. *A la recherche du temps perdu*. Edited by Pierre Clarac and André Ferré. Paris: Gallimard, 1954.

Rimbaud, Arthur. *A Season in Hell*. Bilingual edition, translated by Louise Varèse. New York: New Directions, 1961.

Robertson, Ritchie. *Kafka: Judaism, Politics, Literature*. Oxford: Oxford University Press, 1985.

Rolleston, James. *Kafka's Narrative Theater*. University Park: Pennsylvania State University Press, 1974.

Ronell, Avital. *Dictations: On Haunted Writing*. Lincoln: University of Nebraska Press, 1986.

Sabin, Margery. "Signs of Life and Death in Beckett's Trilogy." In *The Dialect of the Tribe: Speech and Community in Modern Fiction*, 241–291. Oxford: Oxford University Press, 1987.

Shields, Paul. "Beckett's Labour Lost: *Company* and the Paradox of Creation." In *Samuel Beckett Today/Aujourd'hui* 11 (2001): 478–485.

Silverman, Kaja. *Flesh of My Flesh*. Stanford, Calif.: Stanford University Press, 2009.

Smock, Ann. *What Is There to Say?* Lincoln: University of Nebraska Press, 2003.

Stach, Reiner. *Kafka: The Decisive Years*. Translated by Shelley Frisch. Orlando, Fla.: Harcourt, 2005.

Stamelman, Richard. *Lost Beyond Telling: Representations of Death and Absence in Modern French Poetry*. Ithaca, N.Y.: Cornell University Press, 1990.

Sweedler, Milo. *The Dismembered Community: Bataille, Blanchot, Leiris and the Remains of Laure*. Newark: University of Delaware Press, 2009.

Terada, Rei. *Looking Away: Phenomenality and Dissatisfaction, Kant to Adorno*. Cambridge, Mass.: Harvard University Press, 2009.

Trezise, Thomas. *Into the Breach: Samuel Beckett and the Ends of Literature*. Princeton: Princeton University Press, 1990.

Wagenbach, Klaus. *Kafka*. Translated by Ewald Osers. Cambridge, Mass: Harvard University Press, 2003.

Zilcosky, John. *Kafka's Travels: Exoticism, Colonialism, and the Traffic of Writing*. New York: Palgrave Macmillan, 2003.

INDEX

abjection, 5, 13, 26, 44, 62, 64, 67, 73, 76, 78, 82, 84, 88, 101, 124, 117, 151–52, 160, 207–8, 286–87, 305, 310–12, 318–19; abject bodies, 62, 89, 92, 94, 98, 124; and compulsion, 284, 357; and destitution, 152, 245, 311, 314; and ideal, 89, 97; in "The Stoker," 89–92, 94, 96–100; and sublime, 46, 239, 302; in *The Unnamable*, 326–28, 362*n*14, 365*n*9, 374*n*22. *See also* destitution

abstraction, 105, 224, 232, 264, 294, 298, 368*n*31, 399*n*16; in *Company*, 338–42, 344

Adorno, Theodor, 304, 353, 387*n*47, 399*n*18, 403*n*4

aestheticism, 28–29, 275, 398*n*14; in Kafka, 28–29, 367*n*25, 398*n*14

aesthetics, 250, 258; aesthetic distance, 353, 355; aesthetic sentiments, 357; and dead women, 390*n*17; and the law, 121; of the sublime, 7, 45, 150–51. *See also* Beckett, Samuel: aesthetic positions

Alighieri, Dante, 8, 343, 397*nn*1,5, 402*n*13

Al-Kassim, Dina (*On Pain of Speech*), 375*n*9

Anderson, Mark, 28, 32, 366*n*13, 367*nn*20–23,25,27; 370*nn*44,47; 376*n*14, 379*n*3

anxiety, 18, 19, 26, 119, 122–23, 167, 169, 263, 269, 283, 328, 340, 347, 350, 355, 366*n*16, 382*n*8

appearance, 29, 30, 32, 34, 49, 60, 68, 71, 75, 90; before an audience, 75; before a judge, 48, 53; and corpse, 258; deceptive/false, 142–43; as diabolical, 29, 77, 90, 143;
fictive, 95; of figure, 254, 269; 145, 147, 340; and image, 256; of the law, 139; and mask, 255; mere appearance, 29, 30, 32, 141–42; outward/external, 21, 28, 29, 251; as performance, 49, 56, 75; of Gregor Samsa, 77–82, 87; and schematism, 250–51; as *Schein*, 106; social, 30, 59, 80; and speech, 90, 93–94; of the stoker, 89; stripped away, 241–42; sublime, 101; of transcendence (ideal), 105–6; of the writer/of writing, 48–51, 53, 58, 74–75, 77. *See also* disappearance; ghost; image; phantom; specter

art, 5, 7, 33, 265, 276, 300–4, 308, 312, 355; as appearance, 77, 99, 258; for art's sake, 398*n*14, 403*n*7; exigency of, 176; in "A Hunger Artist," 122, 146–48, 153–54; in "Josefine the Singer," 160; and law, 177; and life, 22, 29–30, 165, 168, 367*n*23; and philosophy, 351; presentative task of, 145; and religion, 367*n*28; as remnant, 32–33; schematism as art, 217, 250–51, 253; and self, 30; and sublime, 25

autobiography, 10, 195; autobiographical tradition, 362*n*18; and fiction, 180, 184, 191, 269, 279, 318; and writing, 10–11, 20, 38, 140, 293, 370*n*45. *See also* compulsion; exigency; fiction; haunting; voice

automatism: bodily, 70, 78–79, 93, 153; in "A Hunger Artist," 157–58; mechanical, 108, 114–15, 124; psychical, 157; and writing, 221. *See also* compulsion

autothanatography, 362*n*18

413

Badiou, Alain: on Beckett, 311, 330–31, 399*n*20, 401*n*2
Bataille, Georges, 280, 283, 353, 388*n*10, 396*n*42
Baudelaire, Charles, 199, 275, 306
Bauer, Felice, 17, 47, 124, 140–43, 364*n*4, 371*n*50, 371*n*6
Beckett, Samuel, ix, xi, 1, 3–5, 8, 9, 11, 12–14, 33, 34, 47, 148, 166, 233, 245, 276, 293; aesthetic positions, 8, 299–304; "All Strange Away," 296; autobiographical dimension, 318, 331–33, 402*n*12; *Company*, 11, 12, 294–95, 297–98, 305, 311, 330–45, 362*n*20, 388*n*2, 399*n*15, 401*nn*4,6,10, 402*nn*11,12; *Endgame*, 303; "Fizzles," 296; *How It Is*, 305, 330, 397*n*2; *Ill Seen Ill Said*, 368*n*31, 400*n*30, 401*n*4, 402*n*15; "Imagination Dead Imagine," 296; "Lessness," 296; *Letters*, 397*nn*1,5,10, 399*n*24, 401*n*32; "The Lost Ones," 296; *Malone Dies/Malone meurt*, 294, 296, 314–22, 325, 328, 344, 397*n*2, 399*n*23, 402*n*12; *Mercier et Camier*, 309–14, 399*n*25; *Molloy*, 294, 296, 312–14, 318, 321–22, 328, 348–49, 352, 384*n*26, 398*n*13, 400*n*28; *Murphy*, 322, 326, 341, 401*n*32; "Ping," 296; and sentimentality, 294, 298–300, 305–7, 315, 320, 328, 343–45; "Three Dialogues with Georges Duthuit," 8, 299–309, 397*nn*1,3,7,9,10; *Unnamable/Innommable*, 1, 5, 12, 294, 296, 300, 303–4, 306–7, 310–12, 314–15, 318, 320–29, 330, 332, 334–35, 344, 347–56, 384*n*26, 399*n*19, 401*n*32; *Worstward Ho*, 14, 308, 345–46, 397*n*4, 401*n*4, 402*n*15
Benjamin, Walter, 22, 377*n*21
Benkard, Ernst (*Das ewige Antlitz*), 264–65, 393*n*23
Benveniste, Emile, 325, 364*n*27, 401*n*34
Bersani, Leo and Ulysse Dutoit, 362*n*16, 397*n*9, 399*nn*15,18; 401*n*10
Bident, Christophe, 190, 282–83, 381*n*2, 396*nn*41,46,52
Blanchot, Maurice, ix, 1–5, 6, 8, 9, 10, 12–13, 21, 33, 38, 49, 120, 163, 293, 294, 296, 307, 348, 353–57, 361*nn*4,5,8, 369*n*40, 376*n*13, 381*nn*3,5, 382*n*10, 383*n*13, 383–84*n*21, 385*n*30, 387*nn*47–50, 388*n*3, 390*n*16, 391*nn*24,25,28, 392*n*29, 392*n*6, 393*n*13, 395*nn*35,36,38,39, 396*n*42; "all-powerful affirmation," 6, 8, 241, 264, 287, 288; *Aminadab*, 191, 378*nn*24,26; *L'arrêt de mort/Death Sentence*, 8, 9, 12, 13, 164, 170–72, 186, 188–90, 193, 194, 197, 203, 206, 209, 212, 213–47, 248–49, 252, 255, 263–64, 269, 277, 278, 280, 282, 287–88, 375*n*6, 381*n*4, 382*n*6, 386*n*38, 387*n*46, 387–88*n*1, 388*nn*9,10, 389*nn*11,13,15, 390*nn*15,17, 391*nn*21,26, 393*n*19, 395*n*38, 403*n*6; *Au moment voulu*, 203, 204–7, 213, 267–72, 274, 288, 382*n*6, 387*nn*51,53,54, 389*n*13, 394*nn*30,31, 395*n*39; autobiographical compulsion, 200; autobiographical narratives, 173–75, 187, 191, 195, 197, 199–201, 203, 208, 219, 234; autobiographical references, 193, 266, 269, 279, 286, 385*n*34; *Celui qui ne m'accompagnait pas*, 197, 200, 271, 289, 382*n*6, 386*n*44, 396*n*50; confessional mode, 219, 271, 281, 282, 286; *dépouille/dépouillement*, 171–72, 186, 214–16, 219, 234, 236, 242, 258–61, 277, 349, 355, 384*n*26, 387*n*47; *Le dernier homme*, 207–8, 214, 382*n*6, 387*n*52, 396*n*53; "Deux versions de l'imaginaire," 62, 171, 216, 255, 257–63, 277, 375*n*6, 390*n*17, 393*n*21; "L'échec de Milena," 278, 282–89, 357, 380*n*6, 396*nn*40,45; *L'entretien infini*, 178, 361*n*8, 384*n*27–28, 389*n*15, 395*n*36, 396*n*40; erotic attachment/relationships in, 170, 178–79, 226, 236, 396*nn*41,46; *L'espace littéraire*, 21, 163–64, 167–69, 171, 174–75, 216, 229, 239, 246, 255, 257–58, 262, 273, 276–77, 361*n*2, 367*n*28, 375*n*6, 382*nn*7,11, 383*n*18, 384*n*25, 385*n*33, 389*n*14, 390*n*17, 391*n*28, 393*nn*14,15,22, 403*n*7; "L'expérience de Proust," 179, 183–86, 192–93, 202, 219, 364*n*28, 385*n*31, 388*n*8, 396*n*40; *La folie du jour/Madness of the Day*, 170, 177, 203–4, 208–12, 215, 242, 246, 382*n*6, 389*n*12; and Heidegger, 167–69, 180, 198, 255, 258, 261–62, 353, 356, 382*nn*7,11, 392*n*6; on

idealism and the corpse, 62, 263, 375*n*6;
L'instant de ma mort, 170, 175, 187–95, 196,
197–99, 202, 206–9, 211, 219, 245, 272–74,
281–82, 296, 354–56, 362*n*18, 383*n*15,
385*n*34, 389*n*11; on the *journal intime*,
165–66, 396*n*44; *De Kafka à Kafka*, 283–87,
380*n*6, 396*n*45; *Le livre à venir*, 165, 166,
168, 174–86, 192–93, 281, 353–56, 364*n*28,
380*n*9, 382*n*7, 383*nn*16,20, 384*nn*23–26,29,
385*n*31, 388*n*8, 396*nn*40,44; love in, 169,
172–73, 179, 189, 209, 212, 219; *La part du
feu*, 49, 278–81, 372*n*13, 385*n*32, 396*n*43;
"La rencontre de l'imaginaire," 174–76,
179–83, 383*n*16, 396*n*40; "Où maintenant?
Qui maintenant," 296, 354–56, 380*n*9,
382*n*7, 384*n*26; and Snow White, 390*n*17;
"Le tour d'écrou," 272–74, 383*n*20,
396*n*40; "(Une scène primitive?)," 10, 170,
175, 187, 195, 197–203, 207, 211, 382*n*10,
386*n*43; "Une voix venue d'ailleurs," 179,
267, 268, 271, 275, 276, 394*n*26; women in
récits, 12, 13, 164, 169, 172–73, 179, 186, 204,
206–7, 214, 217–28, 233, 237, 239, 246, 248,
249, 267–68, 271, 277. *See also* compulsion;
literary space; mask; murder; passion
Brod, Max, 35–36, 66, 143, 285–86, 361*n*6,
365*nn*5,10, 366*n*18, 368*n*32, 372*n*11, 377*n*19,
380*n*10, 396*n*51
Bronfen, Elisabeth (*Over Her Dead Body*),
381*n*3, 390*n*17, 395*n*38
Buch, Robert (*Pathos of the Real*), 375*n*5

Canetti, Elias, 142
child/childhood/childishness, 38, 62, 67,
69–73, 135, 105–6, 187, 192, 196, 199–202,
211, 236, 238, 239, 266, 272, 277, 297, 311,
314–15, 340, 346, 372*n*8, 387*n*47, 391*n*26
Cixous, Hélène, 196, 202, 212, 245, 382*n*10,
386*n*42, 387*nn*45,48
Coetzee, J. M., 397*n*2, 399*n*14
compulsion, ix, x, 1, 2, 4, 5, 7, 10, 11, 13, 24,
30, 37, 42, 44, 47, 60, 64, 71, 72, 74, 77–81,
84, 97, 100, 116, 127, 132, 137, 145, 155–58,
160, 173, 176, 195, 206, 223, 230, 243–44,
284, 300, 307, 323, 333, 338, 340, 346, 357,

369*n*40, 380*n*9; compulsive narration, 202,
332; compulsive speech, 139, 318, 323, 340,
343, 348–49, 353–54, 375*n*9; compulsive
writing, 221, 263, 357, 389*n*12; figural, 10,
11, 200, 293; prosopoetic, 388*n*3; of reason,
362*n*20; of voice, 215, 339, 344, 368*n*36,
384*n*26, 397*n*4
conscience, 31, 42, 45, 51, 72, 117, 358, 375*n*7;
bad, x, 4, 10, 14, 44–47, 59, 61, 64, 67, 71,
72, 73, 78, 94, 103, 114, 119, 125, 133, 134–35,
147–49, 170, 177, 194, 260, 341, 357–58,
368*n*37, 374*n*23, 384*n*25; bite of (*Gewissensbiss*), 41–42, 45, 62, 72, 84, 115, 117, 133,
149, 159, 210, 347; call of, 47, 52, 167, 194,
347–50, 351, 357, 369*n*41, 370*n*49, 382*nn*8,9,
386*n*41; and discipline, 51; as *kritische
Instanz*, 48, 170, 210, 368*n*37, 386*n*40;
literary, 41, 44, 46, 51–52, 57; and sublime,
47–48; and torture, 358; voice of, 47, 52,
167, 210; as wound, 39, 41, 58, 83, 152. *See
also* guilt; haunting
Constant, Benjamin, 279–81, 396*n*43
Corngold, Stanley, 30, 120, 366*n*14,
367*nn*26,28,29, 368*n*33, 370*n*45, 376*nn*11,14
corpse/cadaver, 60, 62–63, 72–73, 75, 77, 97,
98, 100, 101, 104–5, 108–9, 117–18, 120,
122, 128, 150, 155, 158, 186, 254, 277, 347,
343*n*18, 375*n*6, 376*n*12, 387*n*47; and death
mask, 247, 251–52, 254, 384*n*26, 392*n*8; as
dépouille, 172, 214–16, 234, 236, 258–61,
277; and glass coffin, 216, 227; as image, 12,
62, 169, 171–72, 216, 246, 249, 255, 258–65,
393*n*22; of women, 214, 217, 220, 242, 244.
See also haunting

degradation, 61, 64, 68, 83, 157–58, 286;
as translation of *Herabsetzung*, 26, 145,
156–57. *See also* sublime
de Man, Paul, 306
Deleuze, Gilles, 58, 371*n*52, 402*n*14
Deleuze, Gilles and Félix Guattari, 33, 80, 88,
367*n*30, 373*n*17, 377*nn*18,19
Derrida, Jacques, 101, 216–17, 226–27, 249,
362*n*11, 362*n*20, 385*nn*30,34,35; 388*nn*1,6,7;
390*n*16, 391*nn*20,27; 393*n*18, 395*n*39

des Forêts, Louis-René, 266
destitution, xi, 8, 13, 26, 31, 46–47, 62, 75, 106, 109, 117, 147, 154, 157–58, 173, 245, 309, 311, 314, 319, 320, 327, 328, 351, 356; of art/artist, 8, 26, 160, 299–301; and compulsion, 160, 380n9; and melancholy, 169–70. *See also* sublime

diabolism, 67–73, 77; diabolical innocence, 141–42; diabolical trickery, 14; and dissimulation, 59; and Goethe, 369n38; and slander, 90; and speech, 60, 89, 94; of writing, 153. *See also* appearance

disappearance, 4, 31–33, 88, 100, 158, 231, 249; appearance of, 13, 28, 29, 364n30; and dying, 254–55, 317, 392n8; of figures, 178, 368n31; and gaze, 253; of image, 261; of women, 13, 214, 228

enigma, xi, 9, 26, 88, 89, 100, 115, 146, 159, 160, 165, 172, 177, 183, 195, 200, 201, 203, 214, 215, 218, 220–21, 235, 236, 241, 243, 246, 247–50, 288, 289, 359, 373n16, 381n4, 389n13

erotics, 236; and writing, 281–85, 287. *See also* renunciation

escape, 11, 30–31; into abstraction, 340–41; into art, 30; of corpse (*dépouille*), 259–60; from death, 189–90, 208; and fiction, 328; from the law/the court, 129, 131–32, 142; from life/past, 299, 307, 338; from memory, 267, 272; from self, x, 30, 367n25; from time, 163, 195; and walking, 342

exigency, 64, 76, 175–79, 187, 195, 203, 210, 253, 288, 354; and autobiography, 132, 133; of court/trial, 132, 135; of fiction, 282; of figuration, 168, 254; graphic, 253–54, 261, 264; of super-ego, 170; of the work, 276; and writing, 13, 29, 53, 91, 119, 173, 183, 192, 221, 234, 247, 270, 273, 284–85, 384nn25,26. *See also* imperative

exile (banishment), 46–48, 55–56, 58–59, 64, 65, 68, 77, 89, 124, 154, 169, 382n7, 390n17; of "I"/self, 335–37

experience, 6, 129, 199–201, 293, 298, 325, 363n23; and art, 304, 356; creative, 166, 282; and death, 187–92; depersonalized, 22, 312; erotic, 281, 283, 396n42; of failure, 308; failure of, 316; of judgment/the law on body, 121; limit, 353; linguistic, 39, 308, 350; literary, 143, 169, 172–75, 178–86, 214, 285–86, 293, 348, 354, 385; and literary space, 130–32; lived, 22, 54, 165, 256, 286; metaphysical, 387n47; and narration, 214; as past, 8, 197, 328, 338, 346; reduction to abstraction, 341–44; singular, 294, 328, 333–34, 338, 346; of the sublime, 7, 46, 150–52, 159, 363n45; transformed by writing, 53, 163–64, 168, 186, 281–82, 285–86; violent, 242; and voice, 326, 337; and writing, 75, 163–66, 244, 273. *See also* uncanny

expulsion, 12, 46, 56, 78, 79, 87, 89, 96, 127, 130, 396n42; of bodies/corpses, 62, 101; of food, 111; of inner contents (expression), 74, 116

failure, ix, 13, 18, 80, 85, 178, 188, 359, 365n4, 380n6; of art/artist (in Beckett), 26, 295, 299–301, 303–4, 308–9, 314, 316, 399n15; of idea/ideal, 61, 93, 95, 104; and "*il faut*," 13–14, 346; and language, 75, 320; Milena's, 282, 284, 286; to present, 59–61, 70; as remnant/residue, 33–34; of speech (defense), 21, 61, 63, 69, 89, 94, 113–15, 153; spiritual, 33; in/of sublime, 4, 7, 144; of transcendence, 61, 104, 115, 316; of (narrative) voice, 320, 333, 338; of writing, 34, 93, 128, 220

fantastic, 217, 221, 223, 389n13

fault, xi, 1, 9, 13, 17, 19, 43–44, 49, 58, 59, 101, 110, 138, 177, 267, 272, 315, 317; and default, 4, 5, 11, 13, 40, 48, 52, 88, 97, 159, 346; as fissure/gap/separation, x, 1, 104, 159, 132, 163, 164, 167, 168, 171, 181, 319, 333, 346, 384n25, 388n8; and "*il faut*," 13–14, 47, 181, 346; and imperative, 53, 348; of language, xi, 163, 167, 293, 319, 335, 343; as opening (rupture)/as originary, xi, 10, 11, 17, 30, 47, 104, 132, 159, 171, 195, 293, 319, 333, 346; of speech/voice, 321, 333, 349, 359; of writing, x, 2, 14, 164, 168

faultlessness, 43–45, 58, 104, 158, 202, 317, 321, 333, 346
Felman, Karen S. (*Binding Words*), 375n7
fiction, x, 8, 9, 11; absolute, 171, 276, 298; and autobiography, 10–11, 13, 20, 22, 38, 54–56, 74, 165, 174, 182–84, 197, 199–200, 269, 287, 296, 385n31; and court/tribunal, 53, 56; and "creator"/creative gesture, 321–22, 325, 330, 334, 388n2, 401n6; as false speech, x, 90; and figuration, 10, 20, 170, 178, 276, 322; formal structure/devices of, 294–95, 297, 319, 320, 322, 331–33; haunted, 164, 178, 245; and ideal, 63, 102; and imperative, 20, 114, 167, 192, 282, 347; and judgment, 18, 21, 48, 53; and loss/melancholy, 170, 245, 293; as mode of reality, 22, 179, 183, 234; as other world/space, 6, 71–72, 92, 98, 129–31, 152, 168, 180, 186, 191, 322, 328, 345, 378n24; as performative, 68; radical, 8, 9, 10, 38, 70, 138, 269, 293, 327; and reason, 340; as remnant/remainder/residue, 34, 368, 397n2, 400n30; and self-defense/accusation, 63, 73, 153; and slander, 372n7, 374n19; and social reality, 63, 68; and thought, 350, 353; and voice, 320, 321, 330, 347, 354
Foucault, Michel, 104, 368n37, 375n3, 393n17
François, Anne-Lise (*Open Secrets*), 372n12
freedom (liberation), 14, 20–21, 22, 25, 55, 62, 71, 96, 100, 102, 103, 116–17, 119, 123, 127–29, 141, 157–59, 176, 177, 186, 191–93, 348, 357, 358, 359, 367n25, 371n3, 376n12, 378n27, 389n13, 400n30; bodily, 71, 158; Freedom Goddess (*Freiheitsgöttin*), 92; psychical, 157
Freud, Sigmund, 26, 42, 45, 48, 61, 68, 103, 145, 156–57, 170, 202, 277, 355, 366n17, 368nn36,37, 370n43, 380nn4,11, 386n40, 388n3. *See also* melancholy/melancholia; super-ego
Fynsk, Christopher, 214–15, 228, 387–88n1, 388n4, 390n16, 391nn19,21,26,28, 395n36

ghost, 12, 169–72, 206, 207, 216–19, 223–24, 227, 234, 238, 246, 249, 252, 257, 266, 267–74, 279, 280, 288, 390n16. *See also* Derrida, Jacques; haunting; phantom; specter
Giacometti, Alberto, 266, 275–77
Gide, André, 259
Goethe, Johann Wolfgang von, 24, 28, 31–32, 46, 51–52, 54, 57, 59, 369n38
gossip, 62, 81–82, 121, 134, 138, 371n3, 374n19. *See also* rumor
Greenberg, Martin, 366nn14,15
guilt, x, 4, 18–22, 24, 26, 48–52, 63–66, 71–73, 77–79, 88–89, 101, 106, 118, 120–23, 125, 131–32, 140–41, 188, 193–95, 260, 266–67, 272, 274, 299, 348, 372n7, 373n15, 379n31, 386nn40,41; and anxiety, 122, 131; and the call, 167, 349–50, 352, 382n8; and death, 61, 73, 77, 120; and gossip/rumor, 82, 366n15; and speech, 61, 69, 71, 98–99, 102–3, 104; and writing, 49, 59, 64–66, 132, 134–35, 177. *See also* conscience; judgment; punishment

Hamlet, 259–60, 336, 393n18
Hart, Kevin (*The Dark Gaze*), 361n5
haunting, 108, 147, 159, 160, 169–73, 191, 206–7, 221–23, 233–37, 240, 243–44, 246, 253–55, 258–65, 267, 274, 286, 288, 326, 351, 355, 361–62n10, 374n23, 376n13, 383n21; and autobiography, 10–11; and conscience, 73, 358; and corpse, 87, 102; and figuration, 178; *hantise*, 202, 246, 260, 266, 361–62n10; hauntology/*hantologie*, 216, 393n18; and ideal, 60–61; and image, 179; and imperative, 8, 62, 114, 167, 262, 264, 270, 361–62n10; and music, 119; and narration, 215, 219, 267, 272; by the past, 184; as remnant/residue, 194, 200–2, 293; and women/feminine figures, 206–7, 213, 217, 265, 267, 269–70, 376n13, 390n15; and writing, 164–65, 263, 274, 277. *See also* uncanny; voice
Hebbel, Friedrich, 28, 41, 74; as figure of sublimity, 46, 50, 58–59
Hegel, Georg Wilhelm Friedrich, 105, 168–69, 190, 278, 382n11

INDEX

Heidegger, Martin, 10, 167, 296; avoidance of corpse, 254, 255, 261; *Being and Time/Sein und Zeit*, 250, 258, 348–53, 369*n*41, 370*n*49, 382*n*8, 386*n*41; and Blanchot, 167–69, 382*n*7; boredom and transcendence, 169, 382*n*12; broken tool as image, 258; and call of conscience/guilt, 167, 349–50, 356, 369*n*41, 370*n*49, 386*n*41; and death mask, 12, 228, 252, 258, 264–65, 383*n*19, 393*n*23; and destitution, 351; and Kafka, 366*n*16; on Kant/schematism, 172, 200, 246, 249–54, 364*n*29, 376*n*13, 392*nn*1,6,8; "Language"/"Die Sprache," 351–53, 402*nn*1–4; on nothing/nothingness, 198, 387*n*47, 393*n*15; temporal ecstasies, 180, 249; and throw/project, 249; uncanniness (*Unheimlichkeit*), 167; and wholeness, 353; and world, 168–69

hell (infernal afterworld), 7, 8, 12, 127, 206, 212, 246, 259, 343–44, 357, 358, 397*n*5, 399*n*16; and reason, 344. *See also* literary space; world

Hill, Leslie (*Blanchot, Extreme Contemporary*), 388*n*1

Hiner, Susan, 389*n*13

Hölderlin, Friedrich, 3–4, 14, 46, 309, 356, 361*nn*7,8, 362*n*13, 369*n*39

humor, 145, 155, 202, 312, 387*n*50

hyperbologic, 10, 38, 363*n*25

ideal, ix, 7, 33, 42, 47, 51–53, 58–63, 88–89, 91–93, 95–98, 105, 109, 142, 148, 386*n*40; ideality, ix, 59, 92–93; idealization, 28, 31, 40–41, 44, 52, 152, 170, 275, 369*n*42; literary, 42, 58, 69, 102; of writing, 34, 48–49, 74, 120

idealism, 62, 93, 263, 375*n*6

il faut, x, 13–14, 47, 163, 176–77, 181, 218, 223, 225, 229, 231, 235, 240, 278, 284, 286, 346, 364*n*31, 381*n*1, 402*n*16

il y a (Blanchot, Levinas), 258–59

image, 3, 7, 69, 171, 200–2, 255, 375*n*6; Gregor Samsa as, 80, 84; of image, 216, 234, 249, 251, 258, 260, 262; of language, 8, 21, 175, 257; and literary space, 168–69, 175, 179–82, 186, 256–59, 359; and look, 251, 394*n*25; as pure circulation, 59, 71, 74, 318; and schema/schematism, 172, 250–54, 263, 265, 370*n*46, 391*n*22; and the sublime, 45–47, 48, 118, 195, 306; terror image (*Schreckbild*), 66, 68, 75. *See also* appearance; corpse; mask

imagination, 192, 234, 253–54, 331, 370*n*46; and reason, 7, 297, 339, 362*n*20; ruination/destruction of, 7, 152, 195; and the sublime, 150, 244; transcendental, 172, 200, 246, 249–50

imperative, xi, 2, 6, 8–11, 13–14, 25–26, 30, 34, 45, 47, 49, 54, 76, 78, 88, 95, 97, 114, 141, 155, 176, 177, 195, 207, 218–19, 228, 229, 232, 235, 240, 244, 246, 248, 262, 264, 270, 300, 325, 328, 343, 352, 358, 361–62*n*10, 390*n*16; categorical, 1, 2, 8, 45, 172, 307–8, 349, 357; hypothetical, 348–49; to speak, 59; to write, 17–18, 20, 22, 24, 25, 48, 53, 57, 59, 62, 64, 66, 101, 104, 117, 119, 130, 132, 138, 139, 145, 150, 151, 164, 167, 172, 175, 192, 197, 217, 236, 239, 247, 266, 286, 294, 307. *See also* exigency; *il faut*

Inconnue de la Seine, 246, 265–67, 269, 271, 275, 277, 289, 394*n*24, 395*nn*33,37

interiority/internal object, 11, 21, 26–27, 28–29, 31–32, 36, 40, 42, 47, 58, 62, 67–70, 77, 80, 94, 96–98, 107, 116, 120, 122, 145, 146–48, 153, 157, 159, 173, 385*n*33; inward/inwardness, 35–36, 72, 74, 96, 97, 105, 117, 146, 173, 353

Jakobson, Roman, 324, 401*n*33

James, Henry, 267, 271–74, 383*n*20, 387*n*53, 389*n*13, 394*n*31, 395*nn*32,34,35,38, 396*n*40

Jesenská, Milena, 278, 282–89, 357–59, 396*n*51

jokes, 5, 31–32, 41, 45, 145–46, 155–59, 211, 366*n*17, 368*n*36, 375*n*8, 380*n*11; as comic *Herabsetzung* (degradation, putdown), 26, 45, 68, 156; compared to the comic, 380*n*11. *See also* humor

judgment, 9, 20, 41, 55, 58, 59, 75, 95–96, 100, 102, 104, 115, 120, 194, 250, 366*n*15; and court/tribunal, 50–53; dreamlike, 88, 117; last, 260; paternal, 64, 66, 68, 71; of public, 154; scene, 21, 22, 24, 32, 54–57, 59,

66, 69–71, 77–78, 82, 89, 90, 108, 112, 118, 136, 372n14, 386n40; scenography of, 11, 26, 48, 73, 130, 165, 347, 350; self-, 48; and speech, 71, 121; stories/narratives, 11, 21–22, 24–26, 40, 47, 49, 54, 56, 60–62, 72, 75, 76, 83, 86, 88–91, 101, 103, 112, 113, 118, 119, 120–22, 125, 126, 128, 132–33, 139, 140, 144, 145, 153, 160, 178, 347, 365n7, 371n1, 372n7, 379n1; of writing, 53, 66–67, 114, 136

Kafka, Franz, ix, 1, 3, 4, 5, 6, 8, 9, 11, 12; aestheticism, 28–29; autobiographical element of writing, 21–22, 26, 30, 54, 59, 74, 101, 102, 104, 165; autobiographical writing in *The Trial*, 132–35, 138; "Before the Law," 138, 365n4, 387n48; "The Burrow," 25, 35, 88, 359; *The Castle*, 8, 25, 40, 81, 138, 139, 168, 279, 285–86, 359 366n15, 377n19, 378n26, 378–79n30, 380n6, 394n31, 396n51; "A Country Doctor," 33, 367n28, 379n31, 379n1; desire to write autobiography, 378n27; *Diaries/Tagebücher*, 6, 21–23, 34, 40, 48–59, 63, 74–76, 94, 128, 131, 137, 140, 143, 152–53, 165, 166, 347, 365–66n11, 367n28, 372n11, 378n27, 382n7, 383n20; disciplinary instruments, 125–28; disciplinary regime, 83, 90, 99–100; disciplinary subjection, 97, 109–10, 126; discipline and body, 99, 145–47, 152; discipline and justice, 91, 95–96, 104 374n21; discipline and language, 97; discipline and punishment, 86, 117, 139; discipline and violence, 100, 117–18; discipline and writing, 19–20, 23, 34, 44, 45, 48–50, 71, 101, 365n6; "A Fratricide," 97, 365n9, 379n31; homoeroticism, 371n4, 374n24; "A Hunger Artist," 4, 5, 6, 25, 26, 37–39, 45, 88, 104, 111, 122, 144–60, 284, 348, 357, 358, 365n9, 372n9, 373–74n18, 375n8, 379n31, 379nn1–3, 380n6, 381n13; hunger/food/nourishment, 4, 5, 6, 23, 24, 38–39, 45, 62–63, 70, 72, 75, 83–86, 88, 102, 108–11, 115–16, 145, 148–51, 155–59, 365n4, 366n13, 375n8; "In the Penal Colony," 5, 11, 21, 47–48, 56, 60, 61, 62, 81, 101–28, 140, 141, 145, 148, 357, 365n6, 373n15, 375n2, 376n13, 377n23, 378n29, 379n3; "Investigations of a Dog," 25, 366n14, 371n3; "Josefine the Singer," 25–26, 96, 100, 144, 160, 359, 365n9, 366n14, 373nn16,17, 379n31, 380n8; "The Judgment," 11, 18, 21, 24, 29, 34, 40, 48, 49, 53, 57, 58, 60, 63–80, 83, 87, 102, 113, 127, 140, 364nn3,4, 371n51, 371n6, 372n14, 375n2, 379n1, 386n37; *Letters to Felice*, 17, 47, 124, 140–43, 364–65n4, 371n50, 371n6, 379n34; letters to Oskar Pollak, 18–20, 21 27, 28–32, 34–42, 45–47, 50, 58, 59, 66, 72, 74, 75, 83, 136, 145, 152, 364n2; "The Metamorphosis," 11, 21, 60, 77–88, 111, 121, 122, 127, 371n51, 371n3, 372–73n14, 373n15, 379n1, 381n12; military discipline, 88, 93; rabbinical influence in, 350; "Report to an Academy," 25, 126, 139, 140, 144, 359, 371n3, 379n1; slander, 71, 81–82, 90–91, 138, 372n7, 373n15, 374n19; "The Stoker," 11, 21, 60, 61, 62, 88–100, 107, 112, 113, 117, 127, 358, 365n9, 374nn21,23,25, 381n12; teeth/toothlessness/bite, xi, 9, 32, 34, 35, 36–38, 41–42, 45, 47, 58, 59, 62, 72–73, 78, 83–85, 91, 109, 111, 116–17, 149, 156, 158–160, 210, 246, 347, 375n4, 380–81n12; traffic/circulation, 28–30, 39, 59, 64, 66, 69–71, 74, 76–77, 79, 87, 89, 92, 93, 96, 98, 120, 126, 367n20; *The Trial*, 11, 12, 21, 23, 47, 62, 81, 92, 97, 101–2, 118–25, 126, 128–41, 350, 365n7, 366n15, 371n51, 371nn1,3, 372n7, 373nn15,17, 374n19, 376n15, 377n19, 378nn24,26. *See also* conscience; judgment; murder; power; rumor; speech; torture

Kant, Immanuel, 3, 6–7, 42–47, 52, 105, 150–52, 170, 172, 195–96, 200–1, 216, 217, 228, 234, 241, 244, 246, 248–51, 255, 257, 264, 307, 308, 324, 327, 332, 348, 350, 362nn19,20, 363nn21–23,25, 369n39, 370nn46,48,49, 376n13, 392nn3–5, 399n24, 402n11. *See also* aesthetics; imagination; law: moral; reason; sublime; subreption; transcendence; vocation: of reason (*Bestimmung*)

Katz, Daniel (*Saying I No More*), 364n27, 401n34

Knowlson, James, 400–1n31, 401n7

Koelb, Clayton (*Kafka's Rhetoric*), 364*n*2, 368*n*34
Krauss, Rosalind, 398*n*13

Lacoue-Labarthe, Philippe, 2, 10, 13–14, 346, 361*nn*4,7, 362*n*18, 363*n*25, 364*n*31, 369*n*39, 402*n*16
law, x, 3, 4, 6, 8, 12, 18, 19, 25–26, 47, 69, 75, 81, 86, 88, 96, 104, 106, 109, 111, 115–16, 139, 196, 228, 244, 313, 365*n*4, 375*n*10; and body/affect, 45, 79, 82, 99, 103, 110, 117, 120–24, 129–31, 243, 373*n*15; as feminine, 170, 172, 173, 210, 242, 376*n*13; and gossip/rumor, 81; and image/appearance, 81, 118, 139; instantiation/representatives of, 42, 58, 61, 100, 102, 118, 119, 144; and literature, 61, 350; moral, 7, 42–45, 151–52, 195, 201, 357, 362*n*19, 368*n*36; and speech, 4, 61, 62, 63, 76, 97, 99, 101–2, 154; and the sublime, 8, 20, 25 46, 125, 169–70, 241, 306; and violence, 102, 116–17, 125, 374*n*1; and writing, 17, 19–20, 59, 114, 128, 139, 177, 217, 347, 389*n*12. *See also* imperative; sublime/sublimity
Le Gallienne, Richard ("Worshipper of the Image"), 275
Levinas, Emmanuel, 258, 259–60, 391*n*24, 393*nn*13,16
lies, 66, 133, 138, 142, 224
life, 41–42, 148, 157–58, 173, 180, 199, 205, 212, 217, 219, 220, 240, 255, 294, 296–97, 299, 300, 314, 320, 321, 327–28, 336, 341, 372*n*13; abstracted, 338–42; art and, 22, 29–30, 165, 168, 367*n*23; and death, 230–31, 239, 246, 253, 260–62, 343; disavowal of, 306, 338; disrupted/ruptured, 131–32, 164, 169, 174–75, 183, 187, 191–96, 200, 207, 210, 226, 246; exit/escape from, 306–7, 315, 338, 341–42, 343, 350, 357, 382*n*7; and fiction, 273; "Fuck life" (Beckett), 2; inner, 23–24, 58, 88, 153; and language, x, 10, 54, 163, 293, 343; as narration, 296–98, 332–33, 339; past, 183, 185, 307, 314–15, 317–18, 320–21, 325–26, 328, 336, 338; as remnant/residue, 11–13, 38, 179, 185, 221, 262, 296, 299, 308, 314–15, 341, 343, 345; and return, 8, 10, 169, 227, 258, 328, 338, 345, 346; urban, 29; and voice, 344, 353; in the world/on earth, ix–x, 213, 219, 229, 239, 297–98, 305, 315, 321, 341, 343; and writing, x–xi, 1–2, 5, 13–14, 17, 21–24, 40, 54, 58, 94, 124, 132, 133–35, 140–41, 153, 163–67, 174, 179, 182–85, 187, 197, 202, 230–31, 264, 281–84, 294, 357
literary space, 7, 8, 11, 13, 126, 130–32, 152, 163–65, 167, 169, 171, 173, 174, 179, 184, 187, 212, 223, 235, 256–57, 263–64, 274, 286–87, 354–55, 358, 363*n*23, 364*n*30, 377*n*21, 378*n*29, 380*n*9, 394*n*31
literature, ix–x, 1, 2, 4, 5, 17, 22, 28–30, 37, 39, 49, 57, 61, 143, 159, 164, 172, 178–79, 257, 262, 285, 350, 352, 354, 357, 367*n*25, 371*n*52, 384*n*28, 390*n*16, 403*n*7; fantastic, 221, 389*n*13; the nonliterary, 5
Longinus (*On the Sublime*), 369–70*n*42
loss, 9, 12, 38, 47, 90, 93, 98, 155, 156, 169, 170, 184, 190, 192–96, 201–2, 209, 211–12, 213, 239, 245–46, 255, 259, 269, 279, 288, 309, 344, 403*n*4; of being, 383*n*14; disavowed, 170, 196, 201, 238; and literary space, 131, 167–70, 173–74, 244; of loss, 102; and melancholy, 9, 47, 90, 386*n*40, 390*n*17; of power, 78; of speech, 71; and the sublime, 7–8, 152, 169–70, 195, 201–2; totalizing, 12, 46–47, 93, 152, 170, 201–2; of woman, 214, 226; of world, 7, 152, 167, 169, 172, 195, 201, 284, 293
Luther, Martin, 2–4, 6, 7, 284
lyricism, 8–9, 13, 172, 245, 247, 285, 294–97, 299, 305, 309, 312–15, 319–20, 327, 328, 343, 344, 369*n*40

Macbeth, 259–60
mask, 106, 108, 171, 228, 282, 296, 384*n*26, 394*n*31; death mask, xi, 106, 117, 157, 172, 214, 216, 228, 248, 249, 271, 376*n*13, 388*n*3, 391*n*24, 392*n*6, 394*n*25; death mask in *L'arrêt de mort*, 12, 164, 219, 226, 228, 229, 233, 237, 238, 239, 246, 247, 255, 263–64, 288, 375*n*6; death mask in Derrida, 227; death mask in Heidegger, 12, 246,

249, 251–54, 264, 383*n*19, 392*nn*6,8; and Giacometti, 275–77; "Masked Imagination" (Nancy), 172, 228, 246, 249, 254–55, 364*n*29, 391*n*22, 392*n*6; as transcendental emblem, 248, 257, 265; unmasking (in Kafka), 156–57, 380*n*12. See also *Inconnue de la Seine*
masochism, 52, 61, 125, 358
Masson, André, 300, 303, 305–6
Maxwell, Catherine (*The Female Sublime*), 369*n*40
melancholy/melancholia, 7, 9, 12, 13, 45–47, 61, 62, 90, 93, 96, 130–31, 145, 151–55, 157, 158, 169–70, 172–73, 179, 194–96, 202, 206, 207, 215, 217, 236, 237, 244–46, 259, 264–69, 271–72, 274, 279, 288, 293, 307, 309, 363*n*23, 374*n*1, 386*n*40, 387*nn*49,53, 390*n*17, 395*n*38
Melville, Herman, 174, 182, 183, 374*nn*21,23, 395*n*36
Miller, J. Hillis, 388*n*3, 392*n*3
modernism, 173, 245
mourning, 46, 62, 100, 201–2, 213, 217, 226, 239, 245–46, 255, 261–63, 265, 306, 386*n*40, 402*n*15
murder, x, 48, 62, 97, 101, 102, 103, 114, 115, 118, 125, 128, 217, 274–75, 278, 365*n*9, 395*n*36
music, 62, 84, 85, 86–87, 88, 104, 111, 124, 148, 153, 160, 180–81, 269, 313, 373*n*16, 381*n*12
Mykyta, Larysa, 395*n*39

Nancy, Jean-Luc, 12, 172, 228, 246, 249, 252–55, 258, 261, 264, 361–62*n*10, 364*n*29, 376*n*13, 381*n*5, 383*nn*17,19, 390*n*18, 391*n*22, 392*nn*2,6,8, 393*nn*11,20, 394*n*24
Nietzsche, Friedrich, 32, 45, 84, 91, 104, 147, 366*n*18, 368*n*37, 369*n*42, 373*n*16, 375*n*3, 394*n*30
Nordholt, Anne-Lise Schulte (*Maurice Blanchot*), 393*n*13
nostalgia, 12, 103, 145, 179, 266, 293–96, 306, 309, 311, 316, 319–21, 344, 353, 386*n*44
Noyée de la Seine. See *Inconnue de la Seine*

obsessional style, 338, 339, 398*n*13
obsessional voices, 262, 362*n*20

passion, 8–9, 12, 28–30, 38, 96, 106–8, 151, 158; in Blanchot, 170, 172, 173, 177–79, 197, 215, 230, 242–44, 247, 256, 270, 271–75, 277, 278–79, 282–88, 395*nn*35,38
performance, 36, 75; bodily, 23, 70–71, 147, 151, 159, 351; and death, 71–72, 75; and fiction, 59; and speech, 68, 76, 92, 94–95, 107–8; and writing, 49, 56, 63, 75. See also theater/theatricality
performative: and death/killing, 63, 70–72, 75, 118; dogmatism (authoritarian), 106; effects, 56; and fiction, 56, 372*n*7; gesture, 95, 98, 99, 322; and judgment, 56–57, 59; mastery, 70–71; and power, 103, 178; speech, 59–60, 68, 71, 75, 91, 98, 103, 113, 375*n*7; sublime, 114
phantom, 257, 355; phantomatic nature of narrative, 242, 272–74. See also ghost; specter
Pollak, Oskar, 18, 29, 31–32, 36, 40, 42, 368*n*32. See also Kafka, Franz: letters to Oskar Pollak
power, 57, 68, 82, 83, 87, 98, 104, 116, 125, 159–60, 240, 252; of appearance/image, 78–80, 84; and authority, 89–92, 114; to express, 300, 301; higher, 73, 124, 375*n*2; indestructible, 288; linguistic, 65, 68, 75, 106; of moral law, 7, 42, 151–52; paternal, 67–69, 73, 75, 78, 87, 107; performative, 114; of reason, 150, 151–52; of the *récit*, 180–81; relations of, 64, 76; of song, 160; in speech, 57, 59–61, 63, 67, 69, 71, 95, 103, 113–14; sublime, 21, 25, 26, 42–44, 52–53, 58, 73, 86, 93, 103, 113, 114; will to, 147; and writing, x, xi, 19, 63
powerlessness, 53, 67, 76, 208, 287, 373*n*16; of speech, 176–78
pronouns: and narrative structure, 324–27, 335–36, 364*n*27, 401*n*34; she/*elle*, 237, 243
Proust, Marcel, 33, 179, 182–86, 192, 202, 219, 280–81, 311, 384*n*29, 385*nn*31,32, 386*nn*39,40, 388*n*8, 396*n*43, 399*n*26

punishment, xi, 18, 20, 21, 24, 26, 44–46, 48–49, 56, 66, 70, 77, 82–84, 86, 104, 109, 112, 115–19, 123–26, 128, 152, 153, 154, 307, 347, 349–51, 357–58, 366n19, 373n17, 378n29, 379n31, 401n9; sublime, 46, 103. See also torture

reason, 151–52, 308, 323; and affect, 343–44; combinatorial, 345; as compulsion, 344, 362n20; drive/demand/need of reason, 7, 150–51, 244, 344, 370n48; excess and violence of, 340; as fiction, 340; and hell, 344; and imagination (in Beckett), 297, 339; and obsession, 297; practical reason, 43–44; pure reason, 6, 7, 47, 62, 324, 362n20, 402n11; and sensibility, 151; as treasure/reward, 151, 152, 195, 259, 363n45, 369n39; and uncanny, 201; voice of, 43, 45, 52, 152. See also melancholy/melancholia

renunciation, 48, 62, 90, 94, 96–97, 150–51, 168, 173, 287, 303–5, 306, 309, 351; erotic, 214, 244, 248, 278–79, 374n24; of love, 13, 387–88n1; of world, 284

revenance, 10, 213; en revenance, 200, 246; revenants/revenantes, 169, 199, 221, 238, 243, 258, 261

Rilke, Rainer Maria, 177, 219, 239, 246, 265, 307, 384n24, 385n33

Rimbaud, Arthur ("A Season in Hell"), 3, 14, 361n9

Rollin, Denise, 283, 287–88, 396n46

romanticism, 3, 7, 34, 361n8, 363n24, 372n12

Ronell, Avital (*Dictations*), 362n10

ruination/ruins, 4, 7, 32, 33, 47, 61–62, 76, 90, 92, 97, 117, 152, 164, 173, 195, 199–201, 244, 263, 264, 288, 330, 340

rumor, 18, 35, 40, 62, 81, 90, 119, 122, 133, 138–39, 144, 154, 350, 366n15, 371n3, 373n29, 379n1; as hearsay, 94, 138, 374n19. See also gossip

sadism, 41, 45, 52, 61, 69, 124, 125, 368, 375n4

schematism, 131, 172, 216, 246, 247, 248–55, 257, 264, 339, 370n46, 376n13, 383n19,

391n22, 392nn1,4,6,10; schematization, 53, 234, 237, 239, 263, 265, 338, 372n7

Smock, Ann (*What Is There to Say*), 394n27, 395n36

specter, 169, 199, 217, 223, 252, 267–72; feminine, 171. See also Derrida, Jacques; ghost; haunting; phantom

speech, x, 5, 10, 11, 25–26, 47, 66, 76, 88, 93, 102, 139, 160, 191, 294, 299, 315, 322–28, 333, 346, 349–351, 355, 359; and the body, 80–81, 91, 92, 121–22; and death, 63, 75, 102, 192, 278; diabolical, 68–69, 72, 89–90, 94; endless, 319, 321, 323, 347; and fiction, x, 57, 73, 92, 130, 133, 322, 324, 351; first person, 366n15; and ideal, 93, 95; literary, ix, xi, 8, 61, 164, 182, 354, 384; loss of, 71, 77–78, 93–95, 96, 327; narrative, 180–81, 216, 340; as performance, 68, 94, 107; productive of reality, 68–70, 91; self-actualizing, 73, 125, 130, 298; self-defense, 59, 60–61, 71, 79–80, 107, 112, 119, 121, 132–33; and silence, 326–27, 345, 350, 352; and social existence, 94, 95, 98, 338; sublime, 69, 125, 154, 245, 372n7; and violence, 118. See also compulsion; failure; guilt; law; murder; performative; power; rumor; torture; voice

speechlessness, 88, 89, 342

Stimme (voice), 24, 26, 91, 113–14

Stimmung (mood, tonality, vocalization), 24, 43, 46, 47, 119, 125, 144, 167, 173, 198, 202, 309, 313, 328, 347, 350, 382nn8,12, 402n4. See also vocation: of reason (*Bestimmung*)

sublime/sublimity, 2, 4, 6–9, 13, 19, 20, 21, 25, 26–28, 31, 39–48, 50–53, 58–62, 68–69, 73–74, 75, 76, 83, 86–87, 92–93, 102–4, 111, 113–14, 116–17, 118, 124, 125, 136–39, 143, 146, 149–55, 157, 173, 189, 196, 201–2, 210, 214, 217, 223, 239, 241–42, 243–45, 246, 254, 259, 269, 286, 304, 306, 316, 340, 344, 351, 354, 357, 363nn23,25, 369n40, 369–70n42, 372nn7,12; degradation of the (in Freud), 26, 145, 156, 202; destitution of/and, 7–10, 13, 19, 25–26, 69, 102, 144–45,

152, 158–59, 169–70, 186, 195, 300–2, 306, 363–64*n*45, 399*n*16
subreption, 7, 9, 48, 52, 73, 75, 128, 149, 151, 159, 189, 195, 242, 259
super-ego, 45, 48, 52, 135, 170, 368*n*37
Sweedler, Milo, 388*n*10, 396*n*42

Terada, Rei (*Looking Away*), 362*n*17
theater/theatricality, 12, 21, 59–61, 63, 67, 70, 76–78, 86, 88, 90–91, 93–96, 99, 101, 112, 116, 123, 127, 136, 152, 154, 225–27, 255, 336, 393*n*11
torture, x, 5, 12, 20, 31, 32, 48, 104, 110–11, 117, 123–24, 138, 274, 284, 295, 306, 310, 325, 335, 337–38, 340–41, 343, 345, 347–51, 357–58, 363*n*24, 365*n*6, 375*n*2, 376*n*11, 401*n*9
Trakl, Georg, 309, 402*n*1
transcendence/transcendental, ix, 6, 7, 12, 17, 39, 44, 60–62, 72, 80, 89, 93, 96, 104–6, 109, 111, 115–16, 122, 124, 145, 148, 154, 157, 159, 188, 192, 195, 200, 214, 215, 216, 238, 241, 244, 247, 264, 267, 269, 273, 275, 324–28, 334; and abjection, 326–27; and death (finitude), 254–55; death mask/corpse as transcendental, 216, 234, 246–49, 255, 262; failed/ruined, 61, 104, 115, 316; in Heidegger, 169, 198; in Kant, 6, 172, 244, 249–50, 363*n*23, 392*n*3; literary, 18; materiality of, 399*n*16; and pronouns, 325, 335; and sensibility, 32–33; and silence, 345; transcendental illusion (projection), 52, 101, 105, 139, 324, 326–27, 344; transcendental residue, 60, 202, 217, 234; and violence, 215; and vision/the image, 255–57; and voice, 326. *See also* imagination; schematism
translation, 3, 4, 5, 6, 7, 9, 85, 91, 150, 156, 167, 191–92, 194–95, 200, 234, 243, 250, 259, 272, 283, 284, 285, 309–10, 348, 376*n*11, 377*n*17, 402*n*1
Trezise, Thomas (*Into the Breach*), 400*n*27

uncanny, 2, 10, 22–23, 135, 201, 218, 221, 225, 230, 232–38, 246–47, 251, 258, 261, 294, 361*n*10, 388*n*3, 389*n*13; uncanniness, 167, 169, 350–51, 359, 366*n*16, 382*n*8
Unheimlich/Unheimlichkeit, 167, 172, 201, 232, 235, 244

van Velde, Bram, 300, 303–4, 398*n*10
violence, x, 14, 26, 35, 43–47, 56, 60, 61, 76, 82, 88–89, 93, 98, 100, 101–4, 109, 112, 117–18, 124–26, 164, 174, 187, 192, 194, 200, 203–10, 215, 240, 242, 246, 274, 340, 347, 358, 369*n*38, 376*n*10, 379*n*31, 389*n*12; and the sublime, 6, 43, 49, 104, 116, 125, 369*n*40
vocation: literary, 1, 4, 5, 7, 14, 17, 18, 29, 33, 44, 47, 48, 51, 54, 56, 84, 103, 114, 125, 153, 160, 170, 173, 175, 177–78, 180, 182, 184–85, 186, 187, 192–93, 195, 197, 200–2, 239, 244, 259, 278–79, 299–300, 308, 357, 363*n*24, 378*n*29, 391*n*28; of reason (*Bestimmung*), 7, 43, 62, 150, 151, 195, 201, 244, 391*n*28; sublime, 19, 45, 52, 144, 155, 202, 244
voice, x, xi, 8, 10, 18, 19, 24–26, 47, 50, 52–53, 62, 76, 90, 91–94, 96, 113, 125, 159, 160, 177–78, 195, 201, 202–3, 213, 218, 238–49 *passim*, 252, 288, 293–99, 310–14, 320–45, 347–51, 353–55, 357–59, 368*n*36, 379*n*1, 384*n*26; animal, 78; as autobiographical, 219, 293, 333; and body, 82; deconstructed, 385*n*30; and fiction, 54, 320, 388*n*2; first-person, 22, 25, 54, 144, 188–89, 305, 312, 321, 335–37; hallucinatory, 362*n*20; haunted, 215, 219; marked by past, 12, 397*n*2; narrative, 12, 139–40, 144, 159, 167, 181, 193, 203, 217, 219, 241, 293, 294, 317; and rumor, 139; vocalization, 47, 125. *See also* compulsion; conscience; reason; *Stimme* (voice); *Stimmung* (mood, tonality, vocalization)

world, ix, x, 7, 177, 216, 352, 356; attachment to, 12; of eroticism, 285–86; everyday/familiar/ordinary, 56, 68, 130–31, 135, 163, 167, 175, 198, 210, 294; exit from/leaving of, ix, x, 3, 7, 12, 30, 152, 167–71, 172, 214–15, 217, 226, 229, 231, 234, 237, 244–45, 248, 264, 293, 317, 355, 363*n*23, 382*n*7; external,

world (*continued*)
39, 315; feminine, 283, fictional/fictive, 6, 9, 18, 51, 53, 92, 133, 152, 164, 277, 297, 321, 347, 350, 374*n*19; higher, 94, 106; hole in, 149, 159; inner, 23–25, 59, 77, 153, 239; and language/naming, x, 21, 57, 163, 278, 355; making of (world formation), ix, 91–92, 131, 136, 172, 251, 321; other, 3, 6, 8, 10, 21, 30, 54–57, 74, 127, 129, 131–32, 137, 167–68, 214, 223, 230, 234, 236, 241, 282, 284–85, 296, 322, 341, 355, 382*n*7; positing of, 298, 322, 330; return to, 167, 189, 192, 235; of the senses/phenomenal, 29, 151 53, 155, 250, 340; separation from, 135, 137, 226, 276, 280, 281, 301, 307, 320, 324, 355, 384*n*25, 389*n*11; social, 17, 24, 97, 130, 309; as totality, 7, 151, 169, 195; underworld, 13, 259, 284; unworldliness, 172, 175, 189, 192; worldliness, 151, 167, 188, 189, 214, 238, 241, 380*n*8; writing's relation to, 8, 17, 21, 256–57, 258–59, 262. *See also* life; loss

Zilcosky, John (*Kafka's Travels*), 376*n*15, 377*n*17